On Air

Also by Mike Carlton

Cruiser: The Life and Loss of HMAS Perth *and Her Crew*
First Victory 1914: HMAS Sydney*'s Hunt for the German Raider* Emden
Flagship: The Cruiser HMAS Australia II *and the Pacific War on Japan*

MIKE
CARLTON

On Air

EBURY
PRESS

EBURY PRESS

UK | USA | Canada | Ireland | Australia
India | New Zealand | South Africa | China

Ebury Press is part of the Penguin Random House group of companies whose addresses can be found at global.penguinrandomhouse.com.

Penguin Random House Australia

First published by William Heinemann Australia in 2018
This paperback edition published by Ebury, 2019

Cover photography by Tim Bauer, Photo Pty Ltd
Cover design by Alex Ross © Penguin Random House Australia Pty Ltd
Typeset in 12/15 pt Bembo by Midland Typesetters, Australia

Printed and bound in Australia by Griffin Press, part of Ovato, an accredited ISO AS/NZS 14001 Environmental Management Systems printer

NATIONAL LIBRARY OF AUSTRALIA
A catalogue record for this book is available from the National Library of Australia

ISBN 978 0 85798 781 5

penguin.com.au

FSC www.fsc.org
MIX
Paper from responsible sources
FSC® C009448

Contents

To my parents and brother, Peter, in gratitude,
and to my children, Alexandra, James and Lachlan, with love

‘We know the truth not only by reason, but also by the heart.’

Blaise Pascal

‘In all life one should comfort the afflicted, but verily, also, one should afflict the comfortable, and especially when they are comfortably, contentedly, even happily wrong.’

John Kenneth Galbraith

‘Drive away and try to keep smiling. Get a little rock and roll on the radio and go toward all the life there is with all the courage you can find and all the belief you can muster. Be true, be brave, stand.’

Stephen King

PART 1

1

In the name of the Father

'PRODDY DOG, SHITTING ON a log, eating maggots from a frog . . .' The taunt echoes down the decades in the reaches of my mind. I heard it first when I was perhaps nine years old and waiting for a train on Sydney's lower North Shore, conspicuously alone in the blue cap, grey woollen shorts and red-and-blue tie of Barker College, an Anglican private school. A scrum of older kids in the uniform of a nearby Catholic school surrounded me, jeering and spitting, their faces twisted in mockery and loathing.

I stood there quaking in fear, unaware that the crushing weight of the English Reformation was being loaded upon my schoolboy shoulders: Henry VIII and Clement VII, the sacking of the monasteries, wretched Anne Boleyn and saintly Thomas More on the scaffold, the Statute of Praemunire, Cromwell's rape of Ireland, King Billy at the Boyne. All my fault. One of the kids snatched my cap and hurled it onto the tracks.

I could have told them I had been christened *Michaelus Iacobus* – Michael James – in the Latin rite, blessed with holy water by a Roman Catholic priest at the font of no less than St Patrick's Cathedral in Melbourne. *In nomine Patris, et Filii, et Spiritus Sancti* . . . But I didn't know that then. So I burst into tears. Exultant, the Spanish Inquisition melted away and caught the train in the opposite direction.

Sometimes the knife cut the other way. Fast-forward ten years. 'You're a fucking mick,' said an ABC executive, one of my bosses, as the two of us stood at a pub urinal, swaying unsteadily after a long afternoon at the bar. 'You're a left-footer.' We had been arguing about something. 'You talk the sort of shit I'd expect to hear from the son of a Catholic priest,' he sneered.

No tears this time: I was strong and up for it. The Irish rose within me and I shoved him headlong into the trough, where he lay struggling on his back, his suit drenched in the foaming urine. 'Outside if you want to finish it,' I said.

He declined the offer. It was not my smartest career move, but he avoided my eyes the next day and never spoke of it again.

The sectarian insult is rare now, although it occasionally flickers back to life. The cut no longer draws blood. Sometimes it's even amusing. I long ago learned to live with it.

✧

A few years before senile dementia tormented my mother to a miserable death, she wrote an account of her love affair with the Roman Catholic priest she married and who fathered her two sons. I had never quite believed she would do it, for she was an intensely private woman who held her secrets close. But she had promised it to us and she kept her word – page after page, neatly typed and carefully corrected.

She left the document with my younger brother, Peter, to be opened only after her death. 'You must not show it to Michael,' she told him.

She was proud that I was a journalist but she didn't trust the species – including me – and I think she feared that if I got my hands on it she would read it the next day, luridly embellished and splashed across page one of the *Sydney Morning Herald*. She and my father had been headlines before, when news of their marriage leaked to the newspapers in the late 1940s, adding fuel to the fires of religious hatred that still fiercely burned in Anglo-Irish Australia. The bigots capering around the flames had painted her as the Protestant whore who lured my father from his priestly vocation, or him as the papist rapist who seduced the young virgin in the evil surrounds of the monastery. There was not a sliver of truth to such caricatures, but they had hurt nonetheless. The slur would occasionally intrude into my life, too, over the years.

My mother was born in 1922, christened Enid Alison, the younger daughter of Robert and Winifred Symington, who scratched away at an existence of middle-class respectability in a cramped Federation cottage at Chatswood, on Sydney's North Shore. Bob, my maternal grandfather, had a family tree rooted in the Ulster Protestant ascendancy. Win, an energetic snob, liked to bask in the glow of a distant blood connection to the Scottish Clan Arbuthnott, also Protestant, a minor noble house which had produced a long and stolidly undistinguished line of viscounts and baronets, and scattered their offspring around the colonies.

So far as I can gather, the Arbuthnotts have done little of interest since 1420, when one Hugh Arbuthnott joined a posse of fellow lairds in Kincardineshire to do away with a turbulent local notable, Sir John Melville of Glenbervie, Sheriff of the Mearns. The wretched Melville, an officious bully, had aroused the ire of King James I of Scotland, who, in a fit of royal temper, snapped to his gathered courtiers: 'Sorrow gin that sheriff were soddin and supped in broo.'[1] Taking the king at his word – not always a wise move – Arbuthnott and his co-conspirators loyally hacked the man to pieces in a hunting forest, stuffed him into a cauldron and boiled him, whereupon they indeed 'supped of ye broo' before reporting the good news back to the throne. James, who had not expected things to go quite that far, cast around for a punishment for the killers but was snookered when Hugh sent in the lawyers:

> The Laird of Arbuthnott claimed and obtained the benefit of the Law of Clan MacDuff which, in case of homicide, allowed a pardon to anyone within the ninth degree of kindred to MacDuff, Thane of Fife, who should flee to his cross, which then stood between Lindores, on the march between Fife and Strathearn, and pay a fine. The pardon is still extant at Arbuthnott House.[2]

Win – I called her Nana – outclassed Dame Edna Everage in her reverence for proper behaviour in public, and was probably unaware of this distasteful stain on the escutcheon. The Clan Arbuthnott crest – 'a peacock's head, couped at the neck, proper' – hung in a frame above the fireplace in her bedroom. It's good to have Hugh lurking in my distant background. What a wonderful Murdoch executive he would have made.

Bob had qualified as a barrister but never practised, choosing instead to serve the citizens of New South Wales as the Supervising Horticultural Inspector of the Department of Agriculture. By night he pored over his stamp collection, books and books of it. Demonstrating the bottomless financial incompetence which remains a hallmark of my family, he knocked back the opportunity to snap up large tracts of land in Chatswood at a bargain price, on the grounds that the place was too distant from the city ever to become anything. A giant Westfield shopping mall now sits on the acreage he was offered. Sorrowing for the inherited riches that might have been, I give a strangled little sob whenever I enter its gleaming portals.

Win, the eldest of seven children, was short and shrewish, and made her husband's life a misery for reasons I can only guess at. It might have been because, born in the late Victorian era and schooled by a mother notoriously prone to retiring to her bed with the vapours, she regarded sex as a disgusting perversion that men insisted upon and which women were forced to endure – although only for procreation, and never again after that. Bob apparently got by as best he could. 'Don't let me catch you abusing yourself like your grandfather does,' Nana barked at me one day when I was eight or nine. I hadn't a clue what she was talking about.

The family escaped the ravages of the Great Depression, Bob Symington clinging to his job in the public service while legions of other men were thrown out onto the streets. As a teenager, Enid travelled by train each day to Hornsby Girls High School at the northern terminus of the North Shore railway line, where, in another well-established family tradition, she scraped by, doing as little work as she could get away with.

Religion glimmered, or perhaps glowered, in the background, more as a polite social convention than a matter of Christian conviction. Nice people went to church, but not ostentatiously; an exception was my mother's elder sister, Auntie Dorothy, who flaunted her piety by snubbing the doggedly low-church Anglicans at St Paul's, Chatswood, to worship with the Anglo-Catholic congregation of Christ Church St Laurence at Railway Square in central Sydney, a pile of sandstone Gothic Revival and soaring stained glass notorious for its bells and smells and high camp priests frocked in gorgeous raiment. In 1935, at the age of fifteen, Enid was, at Dorothy's insistence, sent there to prepare for her confirmation. She loathed it. The odour of sanctity repelled her, and she decided she was finished with religion for life. But religion had not finished with her.

✧

My mother came to womanhood as Australia went to war. Slender, with long and wavy brunette hair, she was at once touchingly naive and quietly determined to have her own way. She left school in 1939, was told that no, it was not possible for her to become a motor mechanic, as she had hoped, and glumly went off to a secretarial college in the city, where well-bred young ladies were taught typing and the mysterious hieroglyphics of Pitman shorthand. In January 1943 she enlisted in the Women's Auxiliary Australian Air Force, the WAAAF, more in the hope of throwing off the yoke of her mother than from any burning desire to beat Tojo. A posting to a frontline Spitfire squadron would have been nice, she thought, but to her dismay she ended up as a uniformed typist working at an RAAF office in Sydney's George Street, and still living at home at 53 Orchard Road, Chatswood.

Wartime Sydney, though, throbbed with an almost manic gaiety that masked the horrors of the ever-lengthening casualty lists in the newspapers and the anxieties of families pulled apart. For an attractive young woman in her twenties, there were parties and dances galore, where dashing boys in uniform competed for your arm in a foxtrot or a fling at the latest American craze, the jitterbug. A few faded photographs in a family album show Enid's slight figure in her blue WAAAF uniform, slender-waisted, with neatly waved brunette hair tumbling to her shoulders.

She was a virgin, and determinedly so. Her mother had warned that if a girl did IT before marriage (Enid typed the capitals in her memoir), it showed on your face, a shameful stigma. But she happily flirted with men, once scoring a fully fledged, gold-braided commander of the Royal Navy, who bought her a fluffy white teddy bear at Romano's nightclub and played Noël Coward's amusing ditties on the piano. Invited home to Chatswood, he entranced my grandmother, who, believing an Englishman with a *Horse & Hound* accent to be God's highest creation, would have married her daughter off to him in a heartbeat. Sadly, it turned out the cad was already hitched.

All the while, though, Enid had been writing to a young American sailor, a correspondence they had begun some years earlier, as teenage penpals. Donald Francis Littmann, a boy from San Francisco, was two years older than her and, as she described him to me much later, tall and darkly handsome. Complete with a crew cut, he was the epitome of the all-American male.

They met in the flesh for the first time when he suddenly and unexpectedly turned up in Sydney in 1942, after the bombing of Pearl Harbor, in the crew of the cruiser USS *Chicago*. Their friendship flowered to romance. He gave her a gold lapel pin with the letters USN picked out in tiny pearls. She would always refer to him as a naval officer, but he was actually a junior enlisted sailor, a Radioman 3rd Class. That's Sydney's North Shore for you.

When his letters stopped for a few weeks, Enid feared he had been killed. Unerringly, she went straight to the top. With the unlikely blend of unworldly naivety and shrewd calculation she displayed all her life, she wrote directly to no less than the Commander-in-Chief of the United States Pacific Fleet, the legendary Admiral Chester W. Nimitz, to ask if he could kindly give her any news of her boyfriend.

Indeed he could. And did. From his headquarters in Hawaii, no doubt welcoming a break from his tedious day job of rebuilding the smoking ruins of his command and prosecuting the war against Japan, the admiral replied on CINCPACFLEET stationery with a personally signed note. Young Donald had been away at sea on active service, but was alive and well and had been contacted and told to write, he said.

I admire Nimitz for this beyond words. Less so my mother, who, with airy nonchalance infuriating to the journalist in me, noted that 'I received a reply which I no longer have'.

Eventually it came to marriage. In the winter of 1944 Don proposed by letter and she accepted, although insisting that he must slip the engagement ring on her finger in person. Plans were laid in a whirl of excitement. America! It was as far from Chatswood as the moon itself, almost impossibly exotic, glamorous, dazzling. And most of all California, which meant Hollywood and the films, Clark Gable and the Andrews Sisters, enormous automobiles smothered in chrome, San Francisco and the Golden Gate Bridge. Enid asked at the US consulate about travelling to the States as a war bride. There were entire boatloads of them going, apparently. Don's mother sent a welcoming letter and some money for her trousseau. There was only one hitch: the Littmanns were staunch Catholics. Enid would have to convert.

This concerned her not at all. If that was what her husband wanted, so be it. To the horror of the Symingtons, who regarded Catholicism as a papist confidence trick played on Italians and the working-class descendants of scrofulous Irish convicts, she agreed to take instruction in the faith. An RAAF doctor she had been seeing recommended a certain Father Jim Carlton, a priest of a French order, the Missionaries of the Sacred Heart. She telephoned to make an appointment to see him in the week after Christmas 1944, at the monastery where he lived in the Sydney suburb of Kensington. Only as she stepped from the tram was she struck by the enormity of what she was about do. She described the moment in that typed account she left before her death:

> I was absolutely petrified about going there as I really didn't know what I was getting myself into. I arrived at 1 Roma Avenue, Kensington, and there was the huge monastery perched on a hill with a long path leading up to the big, heavy front door. There were no trees or gardens and no signs of life at all, just rows of blank windows.
>
> I went up to the front door and pushed the button, which set a deep bell ringing miles away inside. A brother came to the door and ushered me into the parlour – I can see it now – very bare and stark, a large room with a high ceiling, stiff, high-backed chairs

> ranged around the walls, and a huge heavy wooden table with some religious magazines and, of course, some religious pictures on the walls. I sat there for a few minutes, waiting in fear and trepidation, then heard footsteps approaching on the tiled floor of the hall. The door opened.
>
> I find it very hard to write the next bit because it doesn't make sense. It is quite illogical, I can't begin to explain it or even understand it – I can only say it happened. When Father Carlton came into that room and smiled at me I immediately – and I mean instantly – knew two things: that I would never marry Don and that this was the man I would love. Love at first sight, if ever there was any such thing. His smile was so intimate and so overwhelmingly welcoming. Here was a dedicated priest, who had been in the church for 14 years, ordained for seven, dressed in his long black soutane, clerical collar, brown leather belt with crucifix, black shoes: a complete missionary priest, and I knew I wanted only him.[3]

✧

Jimmy Carlton could run. Like the wind, people said, like greased lightning. From childhood he loved the sport of athletics, and he would eventually soar all the way to the Olympic Games, sprinting for Australia at Amsterdam in 1928 with high hopes of a world record. Then, when he was on the brink of international success and fame, the pinnacle in sight, he turned his back on the glittering prizes and a worldly life to join the priesthood.

The Carltons were Irish Catholics to their boot heels. The founding father of the Australian line, another James Carlton, was born in 1820 in the village of Kesh, near the banks of Lower Lough Erne in County Fermanagh, in what is now Northern Ireland. His father, Anthony, had been a farmer, but the young James, a tall and strapping lad, saw no future for himself toiling away on the land in mainly Protestant Ulster. In January 1841, aged twenty-one, he married a local dairymaid, nineteen-year-old Ellen Ryan.

Their timing was good. With the transportation of convicts to Australia coming to an end, the colonial government of New South Wales was offering a handsome bounty to attract free settlers:

'£38 towards defraying the expense of a married man and his wife, not more than 40 years of age, etc.'[4] The Sydney-based migration firm of Gilchrist and Alexander had agents actively recruiting in Scotland and Ireland, and James signed on with them. Four months later, with Ellen already pregnant, the Carltons sailed from the Scottish port of Greenock, on the River Clyde, in the migrant ship *Percy*, on a fast passage which deposited them on the shores of Botany Bay that August.

Alone in this strange land, they found their way to the gentle green slopes and vales of Dungog, in the upper Hunter Valley, north of Newcastle, kindly farming country which, on a misted winter's morning, might not have looked too different to Fermanagh's fields. There, working hard over the decades, and apparently with a canny head for business, James amassed a substantial fortune, becoming an important local landowner, a Justice of the Peace and a magistrate, building a handsome, two-storey sandstone house they christened 'Pine Brush'. Ellen dutifully bore him thirteen children, two of them dying in infancy.

A late photograph of James shows an unsmiling Victorian patriarch, spade-bearded and clad in fustian black, holding what might well be a Bible on his knee. This was my great-great-grandfather, a bush magnate both wealthy and pious enough to donate money and some acres to build a Catholic church near his home. Every Sunday, with his brood about him, he rode there in his carriage to Mass.

James died in 1892, 'after a long illness which was born with Christian fortitude', the local paper noted.[5] The final paragraph of his will declared that 'it is my earnest wish that each of my said children shall continue to be a strict Roman Catholic and approach Holy Communion at least once a year and shall neither taste, touch, or handle intoxicating liquors outside his or her home'. Ellen outlasted him by eleven years. The two of them lie in the East Maitland cemetery, beneath a towering monument admiringly described by the local newspaper as:

> a massive marble pillar set in a substantial freestone basis, the whole being topped by a cross; but by the exercise of skill and ingenuity

> the height of the monument has been increased by an exquisitely sculptured figure of Resignation . . . The treatment of the robes, head, and face of the figure is truly artistic.[6]

Not bad for bog Irish. My father, James Andrew, was a great-grandson, born in 1909 to Vincent Leslie Carlton and his wife, Catherine, whose family name of Brennan wound back to Fenian convicts. Vincent, a butcher from the northern New South Wales town of Lismore, sailed for the Great War in 1916 with 'Newcastle's Own' 35th Infantry Battalion to fight in the trenches and survive the slaughter of Messines and Passchendaele, Villers-Bretonneux and Amiens. Luck was with him. At disastrous, senseless Passchendaele in 1917, 508 men of the 35th went over the top in sheeting rain and stinking mud; only ninety remained unwounded by the end of the day, my grandfather among them.

After the war Vincent moved his family to Sydney, perhaps to seek a city education for Jimmy and his younger siblings, Mary and Michael. The first mention of Jimmy shows up in February 1920, the month of his eleventh birthday, when he won a certificate for coming 'First in Order of Merit' in fifth class at the Marist Brothers' High School, a Federation pile of laced verandahs in inner-city Darlinghurst.[7]

Keen to match their people against the Protestant Establishment which largely ruled Sydney and Australia to its own satisfaction, the Catholics kept an eye out for youthful talent both sporting and scholastic, seeking young men who could be thrust forward as champions of the faith. In 1923, as Jimmy turned fourteen, the Marist Brothers moved him on and up to their educational crowning glory, St Joseph's College at Hunters Hill, one of the city's Great Public Schools, and known as Joeys. It was a mighty leap for the son of a country butcher, entry to a privileged world of splendour and promise. The Marists are a French order, and St Joseph's rose magnificently above the Lane Cove River, a grand stone palace that might well have housed some prince of the church atop a hillside in the Auvergne. On Sundays and feast days the old chapel, with its painted altar, gold and silver pillars and adoring angels, would ring with schoolboy voices piping that defiant Catholic hymn:

Faith of our Fathers, living still,
In spite of dungeon, fire, and sword;
Oh, how our hearts beat high with joy
Whene'er we hear that glorious Word!
Faith of our Fathers, Holy Faith!
We will be true to thee till death!

The school's motto is *In Meliora Contende* – 'Strive for Better Things'. If Joeys was not, perhaps, so academically inclined as its nearby Jesuit rival, St Ignatius College, it was then – and remains – one of Australia's great sporting nurseries in the tradition of muscular Christianity.

Jimmy set about striving. Sport gave him wings. Broad-shouldered, his long-legged body both slender and muscular, with a well-chiselled face topped by a shock of brown hair, the young man swept all before him. He sent Joeys' records toppling, on the running track and the rugby field. At the GPS athletics carnival in 1924 he won both the under-sixteen 100-yard and 220-yard races in record times; the next year, when he was barely sixteen, he was dashing about on the left wing for the First XV, a position he would make his own for three years.

The college's legendary rugby coach Francis Xavier Gaffney – a nuggetty Welshman better known and revered as Brother Henry, 'The Wizard of Hunters Hill' – took Jimmy under his wing. 'Possession, position, pace!' Henry would shout as he dived into a practice ruck or hurled himself along a back line, soutane flying.[8]

Over two years, 1926 and 1927, Jimmy scored at least one try in every GPS rugby game he played, a feat unequalled at Joeys to this day. And between 1925 and 1927, against all comers, he won the GPS athletics treble of the 100-yard, 220-yard and 440-yard sprints. There was simply no one to touch him.

These days every known sport from downhill skiing to darts is available to any lounge-room couch potato at the flick of a TV remote, all of it drenched in marketing and megabucks. A century ago, the amateur ideal was held high. Upper-class schoolboy sport drew eager crowds, particularly football, rowing and athletics, which were enthusiastically covered by the newspapers and the cinema newsreels. Thousands would turn out for the excitement, and my father built a public following as a sprinter with a suburban athletics club, the Botany Harriers, which recruited talent from Joeys. The *Sunday Sun* newspaper gushingly reported on Jimmy Carlton's performance in a club competition at the old Sydney Sports Ground in 1927:

> This 18-year-old schoolboy has caught the public imagination as no athlete before him has done.
>
> In soaking rain they lined up for the 220 yards final. Five men dashed off over a sweep of sodden grass that was enough to make even Nurmi despondent.[9] Before those flying legs had moved 50 yards a roar rose from the crowded stand – 'Jim!' 'Jim!'
>
> A compact figure in blue trunks with cerise trimmings leapt forward. 'Carlton! Carlton!' the crowd shouted in a fervent chant. Jim swept to the front, a rhythmic human engine of speed. Those long legs shot forward with an easy precision. His arms did not beat the air wildly. But how he sped over the grass!
>
> 'Jimmy's won!' 'Carlton's won!' they yelled. Of course he had won, and in seconds equal to the record despite the slippery foothold.
>
> Carlton did not wear the white smock like garb of the mighty runners of Olympus, but you felt that had the St. Joseph's College boy leapt off against those dark-skinned young gentlemen in the smocks he would not have been far behind when the myrtles were being handed out.
>
> Jim Carlton has been selected to represent N.S.W. at the Australasian championship meeting to be held at the end of the month in Wellington, N.Z.
>
> St. Joseph's College Old Boys have handed to the N.S.W. Athletic Association a cheque to pay the expenses of Jim Carlton's trip.[10]

The money was not wasted. Smockless, Jimmy claimed his two favourite events, the 100-yard and 220-yard sprints, to become the new Australasian champion. In a story headlined 'Carlton's Amazing 100 Yards', Sydney's *Referee* magazine recorded that he'd won the 100 in 10.2 seconds, a full two yards in front of the rest of the field, and against a buffeting Wellington wind. There was 'warm applause for wins by the visitors, and Carlton, the wonder-boy, in particular'.[11]

The new year, 1928, began with promise. Jim's results in his final school exams, the NSW Leaving Certificate, had won him an Exhibition – a scholarship to study Law at Sydney University, and a place in the colonial Gothic halls of St John's, the university's Catholic residential college. The dazzling victories kept coming on the athletics track, and in the autumn – to the acclaim of the newspapers – he was the first athlete named in the Australian team for the Olympic Games in Amsterdam.

This was not the gaudy, drug-infested Olympic circus of our time, with its legions of pampered adolescent superstars fretting about their magazine profiles and their sponsorships, trailed by a *chef de mission* and a baggage train of lawyers, agents, coaches, preening sports scientists, psychologists and physiotherapists, cooks and bottle washers, all cresting a wave of corporate gold and dancing to the honking patriotism of a fawning television rights holder. In 1928 they were strictly amateurs, in every possible way.

The P&O mail steamer *Naldera* sailed from Woolloomooloo on 1 May with a team of just eighteen young Australian Olympians, herded by their manager, a Mr Les Duff, who grew ever more choleric and despondent as the enterprise fell apart around him in comic disarray. Everyone porked up during the seven-week voyage; despite Les's best efforts 'to have their supplies of potatoes and fatty substances cut off from the galley . . . you can imagine my dismay when, on the last day of the voyage, I discovered that they had found ways and means whereby their prohibited foodstuffs had been obtained,' he reported.[12] He was also outraged to find that Australia's first female Olympic sprinter, Edie Robinson, was being massaged by a man, and insisted that a chaperone be present.

The team's hotel turned out to be a fleapit some 36 kilometres from the Olympic stadium, and the driver of the wheezing old bus assigned to take them back and forth kept getting lost. Sometimes they did not get back to their digs until after nine at night, only to find the kitchen closed. Les reported angrily that cups of tea were not included in their lunches or dinners; the grabby Dutch charged extra. The swimmers, including the celebrated Andrew 'Boy' Charlton, had nowhere to train but a greasy Amsterdam canal, and someone had forgotten to pack a starting pistol for race practice. One by one, everyone came down with various ailments, from bee stings to sprains to gastroenteritis. The sole Australian gold medal went to the Sydney rower Bobby Pearce. Charlton, who should have won one, was among the walking wounded.

My father, laid low by some mystery bug and a sore leg, ran well below his best times and failed to make the final of either the 100-yard or the 220-yard events. And yet he loved it, exulting in the magic of it all. Foreign travel for Australians was a privilege for the rich. It was true that his father, Vince, had been to London and Paris, but only on a brief leave from the killing fields of Flanders. At nineteen, Jim had seen the world during the dizzy, deluded peace of the 1920s. Stopping over in London – proud, imperial London – he ran for an invitation Empire team against a team from the US. At a reception at Australia House he sipped cocktails and chatted with that gilded darling of the age, His Royal Highness Edward, Prince of Wales. Jimmy Carlton treasured his green-and-gold Olympic blazer all his life and wore it on special occasions, as you did then. His competitors' medal, given to every Amsterdam athlete, sits framed in my study as I write.

At his homecoming, the newspapers wrote of Jim's 'plucky Olympic struggles', but more disappointment fell upon him. The grandees of the Sydney University Law School declared themselves unamused by the young man postponing his studies for this passing Olympic frivolity. His sporting prowess cut no ice and, at a stroke of a pen, they cancelled his scholarship. There were mutterings about underhand anti-Catholic bigotry, and there was probably some truth to them, but to no avail. That was that and he was sent down. Forced to leave St John's and support himself, the butcher's son found a job as a clerk with the MLC insurance company.

In the Depression years, Australians clung to sport as a balm for their miseries. Don Bradman, just a few months older than Jim, began his rise to greatness at this time, knocking up his famous 452 not out for New South Wales in a Sheffield Shield game against Queensland at the Sydney Cricket Ground in January 1930. Bill Woodfull's cricketers regained the Ashes in England that year, and Phar Lap won his Melbourne Cup on November's first Tuesday.

Jimmy played rugby for Randwick in Sydney – the storied Galloping Greens – and a couple of games on the wing for New South Wales, against Victoria and a visiting England team, but running remained his true love. Fully grown now, 182 centimetres tall and weighing a lean 76 kilograms, he kept getting faster. A delighted crowd at the Melbourne Cricket Ground on 25 January 1930 saw him equal the world record time for the 100 yards – 9.6 seconds – only to have the feat disallowed by the judges, who said he had been helped by a slight following breeze.

This was a blow, much to the disgust of the spectators and the sportswriters, but Jim took it with a becoming calm. 'I do not want to challenge the decision of the referee in any way,' he told Melbourne's *Sporting Globe* newspaper. 'It would show bad sportsmanship on my part. We must bow to the verdict of those in charge – men with experience and who are fair-minded.'[13]

Everything I read of my father in those days says that he was a popular young man, not shy but not forward either, admired in his humble Christian piety and well liked for a genuine, sunny modesty. These are not qualities that my loving family and closest friends would rush to ascribe to me. Occasionally sports editors invited Jim to try his hand at journalism. In December 1931 Sydney's *Sunday Sun* ran a long feature 'special' he had written under the headline 'How to Train for Sprint Racing', adorned by half a dozen pictures of the author in action, arms powering, legs pumping.

'Go to bed early when you are in racing trim and eschew dancing and all such exercises that put strain on the muscles . . . Have a hot bath at least once a week and take things easy on the track the next day,' he advised his readers. 'As for food, I don't diet to any extent. I might cut out highly starchy foods, but any food, plain home-cooked meals, with plenty of green vegetables, are suitable to the athlete in training.'[14]

✧

Sporting officialdom clobbered Jim Carlton again in 1932, with a capricious ruling that rocketed the athletics world into uproar. Controversy flamed in big black headlines and furious letters to editors.

The Depression was at its cruellest that summer. Across the nation, long lines of beaten men, many of them veterans of the Great War, shuffled into soup kitchens for their sole meal of the day, a thin gruel and a crust of bread. The unemployment rate had hit 30 per cent nationally, with some 40,000 men said to be homeless and sleeping rough beneath piles of old newspapers in streets and parks.

Jim was fortunate to keep his job at MLC, and he kept running. Sport was the anaesthetic to dull the pain, and there was a feast of it on offer in Sydney on the weekend of Saturday, 16 January 1932. 'It is doubtful whether sporting enthusiasts have ever been presented with such a bill of fare as is available this afternoon,' said that day's *Sydney Morning Herald*. 'Champion athletes, lawn tennis players and swimmers will all be seen in competitions.'[15]

Thousands took themselves to the SCG for the Australian Track and Field Championships on the Saturday, and again the next Monday. There was high excitement and eager anticipation. Australia's best would be competing for selection in the Olympic team for Los Angeles later in the year. Strapped for cash in these desperate times, the Olympic officials thought they might be able to send a squad of just ten, with a manager and a trainer. Jim Carlton was the name on everyone's lips. They had come to see him, and he did not disappoint. On the Saturday he won the 100 yards in 9.8 seconds, within a whisker of the world record. On the Monday, with the crowd on its feet and roaring, he ran his greatest race yet, the 220 yards. From a rocketing start he powered home in 20.6 seconds to equal the world record, a thrilling feat that had the stands and the famous old Hill in raptures. An Australian was up with the world's best.

Then the blow fell. The official referee, a Mr Laurie Drake, ruled that the run had been wind-assisted. A breeze across the ground, at 8 miles per hour from the south-south-east, had pushed the runners along. The time could not stand.

This provoked a furious row among the officials on the field, and a bellow of dismay from the crowd when the decision was announced on the loudspeakers. Jimmy, though, took the shock with his customary calm, manfully concealing his disappointment at a decision that was palpable nonsense. The 220-yard race was run around a circular track, an arc. A following breeze might assist on a straight track, as in a 100-yard race, but there could be no question of a helping wind on a curve. Drake was an experienced official and a former athlete, but he had been a walker who had never actually *run* a race. His ruling was howled down in the newspapers for the next few days.

The athletics writer for the Sydney *Sun* argued that:

> The flags flying on the stand poles were flapping, not stretched out. The wind was not felt on the ground because the hills and the stands made a break. Not a paper was blown from the press table on a level with the runners. Mr. Drake's sense of fairness was overdone! Carlton should not have had his great achievement taken from him on the judgment of one man, who after all, is not a human wind gauge.[16]

Others piled on. Mr Tas Ferguson, the honorary secretary of the South Sydney Amateur Athletic Club, wrote to the *Sun* a week later:

> That J. Carlton was assisted by an eight to ten miles an hour wind when he won the 220 yards Australian championship in world's record time, as stated by Referee L. J. Drake, is all bunk.
>
> I was appointed an Inspector on the afternoon of the second day when Carlton ran his furlong, and, in my opinion, there was not sufficient wind during the run to straighten out the flags on top of the stands at the Sydney Cricket Ground. Therefore, there was practically no wind on the oval during the record-breaking effort . . .
>
> In my opinion, I consider that the governing body should overrule Referee Drake's findings, and grant Carlton his record.

The governing body did not. It stuck with Drake. Jim Carlton's friends and admirers would have to comfort themselves with the thought that, no matter, he was still off to Los Angeles to win the Olympic glory which had eluded him in Amsterdam. The *Referee* magazine nailed his colours to its mast:

> Australia's Greatest Athlete
>
> ---
>
> CARLTON PUTS HIMSELF IN WORLD SPRINT CLASS
>
> ---
>
> EQUALS WORLD'S BEST IN AMAZING FURLONG SPRINT
> Australia now looks to Jim Carlton to bring a world's sprint title to Australia. For the Australian championships at the Sydney Cricket Ground on Saturday showed definitely that he is the greatest Australian amateur runner of all time.[17]

Everyone agreed that Los Angeles gold awaited. There was nothing more certain. On 20 January the *Sun*'s sports editor, Claude Corbett, wrote: 'When you watch the twinkling feet of Jim Carlton carrying him on to amazing victory in times alongside the best ever accomplished . . . there is a feeling of elation that "Australia will be there."'

Yet Corbett had missed the big story of the moment. That same day, a rival newspaper, *The World*, hit the streets with the scoop that Jim Carlton had run his last race. It was over. He was retiring from athletics just a few weeks before his twenty-third birthday. He had decided to become a Roman Catholic priest.

The news blasted onto the nation's other front pages the next day, the headlines coming thick and fast: 'Jimmy Carlton Will Not Go to Olympic Games', 'Sacrificed Triumphs for His Religion', 'Loss a Shock', 'Great Hopes Vanish', 'Carlton to Take Vow of Poverty in New Career'. On and on it went. The *Bulletin* called it 'the most staggering experience that has struck NSW since Lang won the election'.[18]

At Sydney's State Theatrette, the Cinesound Newsreel had film of Jim farewelling his trainer, George O'Hanlon, and then speaking directly to the camera: 'As you all know, I have run my last race and I will now be saying goodbye to the athletic track for good. I desire to wish those who are going to the Olympic Games the very best of luck, and I hope that my successor in the running world will have an excellent spin.'

This was no sudden fit of pique at having his world record time rejected. The Joeys boy had been contemplating a priestly vocation for the past two years, keeping the secret even from his family until the last minute. And he would not be a workaday parish priest, he hoped, but a missionary of the Order of the Sacred Heart, a rather more demanding affair. In December 1931, even as he was training for the championships, he had written to the Provincial of the Order, Father Arthur Perkins, at the Sacred Heart monastery in Kensington, asking to be admitted as a novice. His parish priest at Maroubra provided an enthusiastic reference:

> Unspoiled by success, modesty is one of the strongest traits of his character, and now with the world's achievements at his feet, he spurns them and devotes his life to training for the Sacred Ministry. Coming from a thorough Catholic home, he is imbued with the highest ideals of the priesthood and has imbibed the true spirit of Catholicity.[19]

Understandably keen to recruit a celebrity to its ranks, the church snapped him up. Jimmy was overjoyed. From his parents' small cottage in suburban Kingsford, he replied to Perkins with a letter of thanks in the neat, precise handwriting the Marists had drummed into him:

> To weigh the advantages of a glamorous few years of athletic or temporal success against the priceless gift of a vocation would indeed be futile, to say the least of it.
>
> The position as I see it, Father, is a very simple one. I have been given certain gifts by God through no merit of my own, and to allow such gifts to stand in the way of my vocation would be a misuse of those gifts.
>
> I think it therefore no sacrifice to part with the glamour of a few athletic achievements to enrol in the army of the Sacred Heart.
>
> I have no fear, Father, of effectively effacing myself in the life that I have chosen, because prayer will be my means and that indeed should be my staff . . .
>
> I ask your prayers, Father.
>
> Yours sincerely, Jim Carlton

The public reaction to his decision was extraordinary, a moving outpouring of respect from all quarters, typified by Jack Allison, the Honorary Secretary of the NSW Olympic Council:

> It was the action of a great, clean-living man who, in the world of sport purely for the love of sport, was prepared on the eve of his greatest triumph to renounce all things worldly.
>
> Few men, I think, would have been big enough to do as Jimmy Carlton has done. His loss to Australian sport is immeasurable, but he has decided on the greatest step a man can take, and apparently he is well content.[20]

So he was. Jim Carlton's last public appearance was on Saturday, 23 January at the Sacred Heart seminary, a crenellated stone villa named St Mary's Towers, built in 1842 by Sir Thomas Mitchell, the colonial surveyor-general and explorer, set in idyllic farmland at Douglas Park south of Sydney. The newspaper photographers were there to snap a smiling, if slightly self-conscious, young man in a three-piece suit as he strolled along a colonnade and across a sunny lawn with a brace of black-frocked priests.

'It is a change from chalk to gold,' he told the reporters. 'Please thank everyone for their kindness and help. It hurts to part with old friends, and it is a wrench to cut running right out of my life. I loved it, and enjoyed it for many years. But I have no regrets. I am sacrificing nothing. I am content.'

Then the church gathered him to its breast, to bring him to the eternal mysteries of the faith.

2

God, how we loved each other

When the gates of the Sacred Heart seminary closed behind Jim on that Saturday back in 1932, it was the beginning of seven years of study for the priesthood. Seven grinding, testing years – first in the novitiate, then in the Apostolic School and the seminary proper, as Brother Carlton set himself to master an eye-watering curriculum of Philosophy, Sacred Scripture, Apologetics, History, Greek, Hebrew, Moral and Pastoral Theology, Canon Law, Dogmatic Theory, Sociology and – last but not least – Homiletics, the art of writing or preaching sermons. Latin he was spared; he had already done that at Joeys. The regime was austere, demanding long periods of prayer and meditation and, above all, obedience.

Jim did well, often brilliantly. He got high marks, dropping below 80 per cent just once, in Hebrew. Through those years the reports of his Prefect, or tutor, invariably spoke warmly of application and high achievement. 'A stalwart member of the Scholasticate. Has worked excellently,' wrote a Father Morris in 1935. 'Liable to force himself too much, but this term has gained more serenity and patience . . .'[21]

By 1939 his superiors judged him ready to be a priest. That autumn, his final report recommended Brother James Carlton for ordination 'without hesitation'. His piety was solid, he was faithful to prayer and eager to work for the Sacred Heart at any post, it said. The section labelled 'Chastity' noted: 'There is no external sign of anything amiss. He is above suspicion.'[22]

My grandfather did not live to see the day. Vincent, the old soldier, had died suddenly that March, aged just fifty-five. Jim's mother and his devoted sister, Mary, took the train to Melbourne for his ordination on Sunday, 23 July. Beneath the needle spire of St Patrick's Cathedral, in the lustre of massed candles, the air heavy with smoky incense and ancient Latin liturgy, Jim and his fellow ordinands prostrated themselves at the feet of that turbulent Irish priest Archbishop Daniel Mannix, then stood to receive his apostolic kiss of peace.

'Today is the happiest moment of my life, the realisation of my boyhood dream to become a Catholic priest,' he told a writer for the *Sporting Globe* after the deed was done.[23] That afternoon he flew to Sydney, and the next morning celebrated his first Mass at Kensington, a solemn figure in lace vestments and the spectacles he now wore for reading. The church played the publicity for all it was worth. Two renowned Catholic cricketers were there to take communion, Bill 'Tiger' O'Reilly and – a special pleasure – Stan McCabe, an old schoolmate from Joeys. Jim's fame had not diminished; the newspapers covered it all very kindly.

As a missionary priest, Father Carlton was not assigned to a suburban parish in the normal way. If the war had not intervened, he might have found himself preaching the Word of God at some sun-bleached, clapboard chapel in the Pacific Islands or beyond. As it was, he remained mostly at Kensington, relieving at a suburban church occasionally and firing off applications to become a chaplain to one of the fighting services, all of which were knocked back by his Sacred Heart superiors for reasons never explained.

✧

If my father felt the same rush of instant love that struck my mother when they first met, he did not show it. Through January 1945 they saw each other twice a week in the monastery parlour as priest and pupil, he explaining Catholic doctrine, she at least outwardly demure in her WAAAF uniform. Father Carlton and Corporal Symington.

Jim crossed his private Rubicon on his birthday, 10 February. He was thirty-six. Enid had a small gift for him, three linen handkerchiefs she had embroidered with his initials. There, in the quiet of his only home and in the sight of his God, he burned his boats. Surprised and moved, he leaned over and gently kissed her. 'That was the start of something big!!' Enid wrote in her memoir:

> From that moment on we knew our relationship had changed and become completely personal. Jim tried very hard to control it but neither he nor I could help our feelings. You can't really conduct a personal relationship in a monastery parlour, so we made other arrangements. There was a phone box near where I got off the tram and I would ring him from there. He would then leave the monastery and walk over to the Australian Golf Club which was almost next door. We would meet there and walk together in the deserted scrub which edged the grounds. Jim would leave his clerical collar etc under a bush and just have a sports shirt on and ordinary trousers.
>
> God how we loved each other . . .[24]

By March 1945, just a few weeks after that fateful kiss, Jim came to realise that he ached to marry Enid. He left no diary or memoir, but his few surviving letters show a man capable of deep introspection, entirely equipped to examine his beliefs and his motives and his emotions. I imagine the workings of his mind must have been excruciating, that dark night of the soul evoked in the poem by the sixteenth-century Spanish Friar and Catholic mystic St John of the Cross, of whom Jim would have been well aware:

> In an obscure night
> Fevered with love's anxiety
> (O hapless, happy plight!)
> I went, none seeing me
> Forth from my house, where all things quiet be . . .

The saint, though, was journeying towards God. Jim was heading the other way. To surrender his vocation would be dashing that boyhood dream, breaking the hearts of his devout mother and family, disloyally abandoning every solemn promise to his superiors, betraying every sacred vow he had made before God at risk of the eternal damnation of his soul. All for a woman. The sin of carnal lust, perhaps. I am not certain, but I am fairly sure from my mother's guarded hints in later life that my father was still a virgin. Alone in the monastery he confronted his conscience, desperate to reconcile it with the sexual and emotional urges of a virile young man.

And if the crisis of the spirit was not enough, there were practical obstacles to surmount: he had no money and no job, no home to go to, no wartime food or clothing coupons, no way of supporting a new wife, let alone the child he so eagerly wanted. Every hand would be turned against him. Against them. Putting aside all this, he made his decision. He would leave the priesthood – jump the wall, as they called it – and marry this Protestant girl, come what may.

Enid and Jim kept courting. 'We loved each other desperately, but sex didn't come into it,' my mother wrote firmly.[25] Amused by the irony, they went secretly to the movies to see *Going My Way*, in which Bing Crosby played a feisty young Catholic priest overturning stodgy tradition in a conservative New York parish. Enid took her seat first. Jim waited until the lights went down to slip in beside her and sit holding her hand in the dark. Once, she took him home to meet her mother, who, canny as ever, recognised that her dizzy younger child was infatuated with this older man. And a Catholic at that – and, incredibly, a priest! The horror! All Chatswood would be scandalised. It must be stopped. Not realising that he was head over heels as well, Win telephoned Jim at the monastery the next day and suggested that he had best bow out and leave the instruction of her daughter to the nuns of a nearby convent.

Nothing came of that. Undaunted, they made their plans. The tenth of the month had been a lucky date for them, they decided – the day of the first kiss. So they would marry on 10 April, a Tuesday, just three and a half months after they had met. Enid had £40 in a savings account, which would tide them over.[26] She wrote to Don, the American sailor, and ended their engagement, returning the money his mother had sent. She arranged leave from the WAAAF.

She went secretly to see the Reverend Fred Dillon, the rector at Chatswood's Anglican church, St Paul's, who agreed to perform the service. She bought Jim a brown sports jacket, a delightful thrill for her. He was due to relieve the regular priest in a Catholic parish near Kensington, which would give him an excuse to slip away without arousing suspicion. On Thursday, 5 April, packing a few belongings in a cheap suitcase, Jim left the monastery and the Missionaries of the Sacred Heart for the last time, moving into a cheap rented room in Surry Hills, in inner Sydney. Later that day he rang his superiors to tell them only that he needed a break and had gone away to think things over, without any mention of marriage.

Enid was all for doing the deed and telling her mother and father afterwards, but friends persuaded her not to. That same Thursday evening she had dinner with them in the cottage at Chatswood – a beef casserole and bread fritters with apricot jam, she recalled – and when her father went out after the meal she dropped the bombshell on her mother.

> To say she was stunned would put it mildly, but there was nothing she could do about it. She immediately rang my sister who lived a few streets away and she came round to Orchard Rd. They didn't try to dissuade me, it was too late for that. However, it was arranged that Jim would come to the house on the Friday – I would be at work – and they would talk to him and thrash it out.[27]

From that moment, events began to gather speed. Jim did go to Chatswood, where he was savaged by Dorothy, who was a blunt and quarrelsome woman. But it was agreed that he would stay there until the wedding day, sleeping on a couch. That night, in drenching rain, he and Enid walked to St Paul's for a pre-marital talk with Mr Dillon – 'a task Jim found terribly difficult', Enid wrote.[28] Sheltering briefly from the rain under a shop awning, he begged her to ask Dillon to marry them that very night, to get it over with. She said no.

At the rectory they filled out the required forms, giving his occupation as 'teacher' and his address as 'Roma Avenue, Kensington'.

> That weekend remains a complete blur. I can't recall a single moment of it. I know Jim stayed on at Orchard Rd. On the Monday, the 9th, Jim and I went into town and bought my wedding ring at Angus & Cootes – a thin yellow gold ring engraved with orange blossom. I bought a fawn wool skirt to take away with us. I already had the dress I would wear for my wedding . . . one of the few ready made dresses I ever had. It was pale blue satin-backed crepe with short sleeves, and the breast pocket and collar were trimmed with crystal beading. I'd bought a navy felt hat with a rather poke bonnet-shaped brim and a scooped out hole in the back of the crown, all edged with navy grosgrain ribbon. I had navy court shoes. Jim wore a grey double-breasted suit – I don't remember how or when he got that. I rather vaguely think my mother lent him the money to buy it.[29]

So far, so good. A car was hired to take Enid and her bridesmaid – a trusted friend from the WAAAF – the couple of kilometres to the church. There was a wedding cake with tiny cream-coloured organdie flowers on it, for a small celebration at home afterwards. None of Jim's family would be there; they knew nothing. On Enid's side there would be only her parents, her sister and a favourite aunt, and another friend from school. On a superstitious whim, Enid asked Jim to spend the wedding eve at the friend's flat, so he would not see her until she walked down the aisle the next day.

Then it began to unravel. Not long after Jim left, the phone rang at Chatswood. The caller gave his name as Eric Miller, identified himself as a barrister and said that Father Carlton had provided the Chatswood phone number as a contact. He now needed to talk to Jim most urgently.

Someone had evidently smelt a rat, as Enid put it. Gripped by fear, she took the man's phone number and passed on the message. Reluctantly, Jim agreed to see him in the city early the next morning. The wedding was scheduled for ten o'clock.

Miller was indeed a barrister, and a King's Counsel to boot: a young man with a dazzling legal career, of a type usually described in the newspapers as a 'leading Catholic layman'. He had been at Joeys a few years ahead of Jim, and they knew each other slightly. As barristers like to do, he rolled out the heavy artillery. When my father arrived at his chambers[30] at the legal rookery of Sydney's Phillip Street, he found waiting for him not only Miller but the Father Superior from the monastery and 'various other members of the Catholic hierarchy', in my mother's words. There were a couple of other laymen as well. Jim was surrounded and outgunned.

What was said there I do not know. Perhaps they bullied and threatened him, perhaps they pleaded and cajoled. Quite likely both. Now, in the twenty-first century, it is a commonplace for priests to leave the church, a parting generally handled with tact and understanding, and not raising an eyebrow. In the mid-twentieth century it was shocking, even wicked, an apostasy to be stopped at all costs.

In the crudest terms, the church was desperate not to lose one of its favourite sons, with all the negative publicity that it knew would follow. To be fair, it is also likely that at least some of those present genuinely believed they were saving headstrong young Father Carlton from the perils of sin. Jim gave them no hint that he was to be married in just a few hours, although they almost certainly feared something in that direction. Miller extracted a promise that Jim would not do anything irrevocable. One of the laymen there offered the use of a cottage in Wentworth Falls, a few hours west of Sydney in the Blue Mountains, where Jim could go to think things over in solitude.

Jim rang Enid at Chatswood to tell her this at around eight o'clock, two hours before the wedding was to happen, but said he would come to see her. Convinced that he was backing out, she fled to her bedroom, sobbing. Her lover-in-waiting had abandoned her virtually at the altar.

> For the first, and only time in my life, I had hysterics after I put the phone down . . . I wouldn't let them console me and just lay on my bed crying, until Jim came in view, walking down from the station.
>
> I knew Jim would be going through torment in the first few weeks away from the church and that the hierarchy would never leave him alone – he was too valuable a member and too well

> known to have it made public that he had left the church. I knew I had to be with him through his ordeal and that, if I wasn't there, he'd never go through with it.
>
> I had all this mentally prepared to tell him, but he didn't need it. He came in to me, took me in his arms, and said we were going on with our marriage then and there. He felt his promises and commitment to me outweighed those he had made that morning at the meeting.

An hour later they were at St Paul's for that terrible, pregnant moment in the old Anglican rite: 'If any man can show just cause, why they may not lawfully be joined together, let him now speak, or else hereafter for ever hold his peace . . .'

Silence.

Then: 'I require and charge you both, as you will answer at the dreadful day of judgment when the secrets of all hearts shall be disclosed, that if either of you know any impediment, why you may not be lawfully joined together in Matrimony, you do now confess it. For be you well assured, that if any persons are joined together otherwise than as God's Word doth allow, their marriage is not lawful.'[31]

Another silence.

What went through my father's mind at that point? All his life he had believed that this God, Dillon's *Anglican* God, was a figment of the Protestant imagination, formed in schism and heresy. And now . . .

The moment passed and they were married, 'in the name of the Father, and of the Son, and of the Holy Ghost. Amen.'

Mr and Mrs Carlton began their honeymoon in the borrowed cottage at Wentworth Falls that night, after a slow train journey from Sydney and a trek squelching across some paddocks in pitch blackness and icy rain, during which the young bride frightened herself by crashing headlong into the back of a cow. Her description of that first evening together is so vivid, so poignant, that I cannot better it:

> The house had a long hall from front to back with every room opening on to it, and every single door was locked. At last we found a room with a big, old-fashioned double bed and single bed in it.

> There were old, floppy kapok mattresses rolled up on the beds, but no sign of blankets. We'd brought sheets with us. We couldn't find blankets anywhere so we took the thin kapok mattresses of beds in other rooms to cover us.
>
> I was absolutely exhausted, emotionally and physically and dreaded coping with my wedding night. After all, I hardly knew this man I was now married to – I'd never yet called him 'Jim', only 'Father!' It probably sounds ridiculous, but that's how it was. I simply couldn't bring myself to get undressed in front of him. I got as far as my petticoat, but I didn't have to say anything, and Jim just went out of the room and stayed out until I was safely in my exquisite white wedding nightgown, in the huge old bed, under a kapok mattress. Then Jim discovered he had forgotten to bring pyjamas and he appeared in his singlet and underpants.
>
> I think we probably made Michael that night . . .

✧

Honeymoon over, and anxious to escape the stress of Sydney, where Jim was still a familiar face, the newly weds moved to Melbourne after a month or so. He found a humdrum job as an accounts clerk with the Felt and Textiles Company, work he hated but which paid enough for them to rent part of a small cottage in Black Rock, on the bay south-east of the city. My mother was indeed pregnant with me, and due to give birth in January 1946.

This time away from Sydney was an idyll for them. They made good friends, a few with young children, some of whom would stick for life. At weekends they splashed around in Half Moon Bay, opposite the rusting hulk of the old Victorian warship *Cerberus*, and in May Jim took Enid into town for the VE Day celebrations.

A few passing clouds darkened those sunlit days. To everyone's dismay, not long after the wedding Don Littmann turned up unannounced at the house in Chatswood, smart in a uniform newly tailored for his promotion to Petty Officer 1st Class, and eager to be reunited with his fiancée. He had fought throughout the Pacific War, north and south, east and west, most of it in an ancient destroyer-minesweeper. Of all the letters he and Enid exchanged, the only one that never arrived was the one she sent to call the marriage off. 'The hardest letter I ever wrote,' she said. And he had never received it.

Appalled and embarrassed, my grandmother invited him to stay the night, which he did, but in the morning when she awoke he was gone, forever.[32]

Another, darker cloud bore down in August 1945. The newspapers finally got wind of Jim and Enid's marriage. The news broke on Friday, 17 August in Sydney's *Daily Telegraph* and *Sydney Morning Herald*. It was somewhat overshadowed by the marginally more important surrender of Japan and the end of World War II, but big enough nonetheless. 'Athlete Retires From Priesthood, Marries,' said the *Telegraph* headline, with a library picture of my father in his vestments, celebrating mass.[33] Other papers did much the same, many of them quoting my grandfather: 'The bride's father (Mr R. B. Symington) said last night that Carlton found he had taken the wrong step in entering the priesthood . . .'[34] My mother never forgave him for that. It was a gratuitous slur, entirely false and none of his business anyway, but Bob Symington was a self-important bore who loved parading in whatever limelight might come his way, and she suspected he had leaked the story for that reason. He might well have done. He and my father never got on. We shall return to him later.

The coverage was accurate and restrained, and entirely fair. With a few exceptions, the days of vindictive tabloid sleaze had yet to arrive in Australia. Nonetheless, the cat was out of the bag, to the delight of the bigots on all sides. They seized it and began flailing about. My parents began to get mail from strangers, a lot of it an outpouring of sectarian filth; most came from bigoted Protestants, my mother remembered. A rabidly anti-Catholic newspaper, *The Rock*, harried them from time to time. Others, less vicious, prayed for their salvation, and a man in Cairns regularly sent them religious tracts and books.

The Catholic Church itself said nothing publicly, refusing even to acknowledge that Father Carlton was off and away, but internally there was consternation. It hit hardest on the community of the Sacred Heart, where he still had many friends. In a report written by the Father Provincial, the Very Reverend Father J. M. Kerrins, on 20 August, wounded pride, indignation and affronted piety positively smoke off the page. It begins with an account of the meeting in the chambers of Miller KC:

> After some conversation, Father Carlton admitted he had become involved with a person of the opposite sex. After being exhorted to break this liason [*sic*] and return to the monastery, and after being promised every assistance, including secrecy, regarding what he had done (the members of the community at this time new [*sic*] nothing of it) he agreed to return and said he would telephone Father Superior later in the day regarding the hour and manner of his return . . .
>
> In any case he did telephone during the afternoon but only to announce he was not returning, as he had 'closed the door behind him' and was going away from Sydney. It transpired later that he had gone through a form of marriage in the Church of England that afternoon.
>
> He did leave Sydney that afternoon, '*cum muliere*,' and later left for Melbourne with her and is still living with her.[35]

The Latin lands with a thud: *cum muliere* means 'with a woman'. The writer can't bear to put the vile thought in English. Concluding there had been 'a form of marriage', the report goes on that:

> The fact of his marriage is admitted by himself, his own mother and sister and the parents of the other party as well as the officiating clergyman, and despite the fact that the news has been published everywhere, it has never been denied.
>
> There is no doubt that he has incurred dismissal according to Code 646 of the Code of Canon Law, and the declaration of this fact was issued by the Provincial Council in its session of August 10th 1945.[36]

That was it – Father Carlton was no more. The rumour went around that he had been excommunicated, cast out of the church by Pius XII, but this was false. Catholic Canon Law carefully lists the sins or crimes for which excommunication is the penalty, and leaving the priesthood is not one of them. But at St Joseph's College there was anger and anguish. He had been their golden-haired boy; now he had shamed and betrayed them. Like Stalin purging a failed Soviet field marshal, every trace of young Jimmy Carlton was erased from the halls and playing fields. Photographs of his sporting teams were taken from walls, while the record books were rewritten to omit his name and his feats. He became a pariah, an outcast, an Orwellian unperson. To speak his name at Joeys would be heresy. To all intents and purposes, he had never existed. This exile would last for some forty years.

Eventually the public nastiness slowed to a trickle and Enid could concentrate on the business of carrying me. Yet that, too, became snared in religious fear and loathing. They had booked for the birth at the Mercy Hospital in Heidelberg, then and now a great Catholic hospital for women. A couple of months before the due date, Fred Dillon, the Anglican priest who had married them at Chatswood, turned up at Orchard Road in a lather, bursting to speak to my grandmother. There was dreadful news, he frothed. He had heard – he knew for a fact, actually – that the staff at the Mercy would never let a priest's baby live. He feared the child would either be allowed to die – or, worse, be murdered. Everyone knew that was the sort of thing that Catholics did. He beseeched Win to get my parents to go somewhere else.

Even now I have goosebumps as I write this. Strangled with the umbilical cord? Left on a snowy hillside to die, perhaps? However preposterous, it is still a chilling thought. Not that the Catholics *would* have done it; I don't believe that for a moment. It's that someone *thought* they would that's so macabre.

And it was for Jim and Enid, too. At Win's insistence, they found a small private hospital in Armadale, a few suburbs away from Black Rock. From my mother's description, the place was a den of Dickensian squalor, staffed by brutes and harridans, where expectant women and new mothers were made to shell the peas and fold the nappies, and were ordered to lie in bed at attention when Matron came to inspect them. She spent a lot of her long labour parked in a hard wooden chair, with the midwife absent for most of it, returning only to bark orders. Fathers were never present in those days. The obstetrician, a bully whom she loathed, never turned up.

In the midst of a stinking Melbourne heatwave, with my mother alone, in severe pain and believing she was dying, I entered the world on the morning of Thursday, 31 January 1946. There was a modicum of payback a few days later. To Enid's singular delight, when the obstetrician came to circumcise me I peed all over him. My lifelong suspicion of authority was grounded in that brief moment, I think.

A few weeks later I was christened at St Patrick's Roman Catholic Cathedral. *Michaelus Iacobus.*

✧

My father's job had been getting him down, and in May 1947 my parents took me back to Sydney by air, a flight on which I howled blue murder all the way, and pissed on the hostess, as they were called then. This was becoming a habit. Not really expecting much, Jim applied for an advertised teaching position at an Anglican private school for boys, Barker College. The school cautiously asked if he had 'severed his Catholic associations'. The Anglicans of the North Shore wanted no papist Fifth Columnist in their midst. To surprise and delight all round, he got the job. The headmaster of the day, Bill Leslie, was an innovative educator with the vision to build one of Australia's great private schools, and he snapped up Jim for his sporting talents, as bait for the wealthy parents he was keen to attract. Mr Carlton would teach in the primary school and coach the athletics team and the First XV rugby side. The two men hit it off from the word go.

Founded in 1890 and named for an Anglican bishop, Barker is some 30 kilometres north of Sydney in suburban Hornsby, its green and tree-studded campus sloping down the western side of the ridge which carries the Pacific Highway along the spine of the North Shore. It was then a day and boarding school, boys only, under the control of the Sydney Anglican diocese. My parents were offered a two-bedroom flat in a small block owned by the school on the other side of the highway – the first home they could reasonably call their own, and mine too. They loved everything about the place.

Barker had none of the ecclesiastical grandeur of Joeys – perish the papist thought! – but its core buildings of warm brown brick, red-tiled roofs and colonnades of plain, cream-painted Tuscan columns are no less pleasing. Low and long, the place looked like the sort of regimental barracks that the British Army threw up during the Raj. The masters' common room was a collegiate retreat of pipe-smoking, chalk-dusted colleagues. Further down the slope of the ridge, the big Number One Oval, the locus of sporting life, did duty for cricket in summer, athletics in autumn and rugby in winter, and all could be viewed from a handsome war memorial pavilion.

Jim had spent most of his life in institutions ruled by a firm but benevolent hierarchy, and Barker was another. He was on familiar ground. Enid unashamedly enjoyed the status that came with being a master's wife at a private school, and consort of the coach of the First XV, mingling with wealthy parents who were several notches up the totem pole from Orchard Road, Chatswood. Afternoon tea with the headmaster's wife called for best hats and handbags. The school kitchen was renowned for its scones, dolloped with strawberry jam and cream. Contentment piled upon the two of them.

The only problem was Jim's family. The breach had been painful and profound. I do not know how or when he told his widowed mother, Catherine, that he had left the priesthood and married, but it must have been excruciating for both of them. Everything she had dreamed for him had been smashed. And now there he was with a son, who, according to Catholic doctrine, was illegitimate, a bastard; worse still, he was ensnared in the Protestant lair. Catherine had no choice but to accept this ghastly fait accompli, but she did so with ill grace.

Enid dreaded Catherine's occasional Sunday visits to the flat. A small, stringy woman clad in widow's black, she would inspect the place for order and cleanliness, marching about with a menacing glare like some sergeant major. Jim's sister, Mary, was colder still. She had adored her elder brother once, but after the schism they barely spoke. Hoping to smooth things over, and without telling my father, Enid took me one day to call on Mary at her home in Mosman. We were turned away at the door.

I have fragments of memory of the Hornsby years, like a shifting kaleidoscope with some of the pieces missing. My father would hoist me onto his shoulders so I could ring the big brass school bell to call the boarders to prep or dinner; one time I was allowed to bang the bass drum of the school cadet band. After my afternoon nap I would stand in my cot at the window, waiting to watch him cross the highway on his way home. I have visions of barracking crowds at school football games; of him and some men friends drinking beer from pewter mugs; of Enid clad in a golden ball gown for a school dance; of picking wild blackberries down by the railway line which ran below the flats, when the shrill whistle of a steam locomotive frightened me out of my wits.

My father and I were blokes together. Once, with my mother in a bad mood for some reason, he took me off for an afternoon to see the dinosaur bones at the Australian Museum in the city. We returned with a peace offering of a Violet Crumble bar, an Enid favourite. Another time, when Jim was ordered by her to whack me for some infant outrage, he took me into my bedroom and told me to yelp when he thumped the pillow, a betrayal of maternal authority I told her about only years later, as a teenager. My playing companions then were two girls of about my age, the daughters of the school chaplain, the Reverend Hubert Dixon, who lived in the same block.

In 1949, at the age of three, I was enrolled in the Peter Rabbit Kindergarten – which august establishment, I am pleased to record, thrives to this day in the grounds of St Paul's Anglican Church at Wahroonga, near where we lived. The memory darkens. Early at this beginning of my scholastic career I saw a teacher smack a child. Distressed and scared, I fled. Somehow I crossed the Pacific Highway by myself, through the traffic, and even more surprisingly caught a bus home, turning up at the flat unannounced to stun and amaze poor Enid, who burst into tears.

Barker took me in the next year, when I was four. My first teacher, Miss Stewart, had magic powers and could make fairies dance on the classroom ceiling. She also gave us cake to eat. I was devoted to her. Less benign was the school swimming coach, a beefy former championship wrestler named Alf Vockler, who, operating on the

Darwinian principles of natural selection, chucked you into the pea-green and almost certainly toxic depths of the school's pool to see who sank and who swam. I sank, in terror, only to be fished out by my outraged father.

Jim and Enid were a gregarious couple who made friends easily, and their life together bloomed. Returning to his boyhood love of athletics, Jim was appointed a selector and coach for the New South Wales Amateur Athletic Association. When the *Sunday Herald* newspaper started up in 1949, they asked him to write an athletics column, which he jumped at, not least for the handsome extra whack to his teacher's pay. This was the first Carlton connection with the Fairfax empire. At Barker, Jim's football teams revered him, something I know for a fact, for I met many of his players much later in life, men who would invariably tell me just that, without being asked. The boarders would come across to the flat on Friday nights to plot the strategy for the Saturday game, and then again for a post-mortem; Enid would feed them homemade chocolate cake.

In the Barker community they were close to the Dixon family, but their most intimate confidant was the school doctor, Niels Pedersen, a burly Danish-born GP with a practice he ran from his big Federation home not far away in Hornsby. A bachelor at the time, Niels would often be at the flat to brave my mother's haphazard attempts at cooking. At Christmas he would join us for a fortnight's holiday on the beach at Ettalong, on the lower Central Coast, staying in a ramshackle cottage lent to us by the parents of one of the Barker footballers.

Ettalong was intensely thrilling. Unsewered, the place had an outside toilet reached by thrashing your way through an overgrown backyard as menacing as an Amazon jungle. Inside this creaking temple was a big, black cylindrical pan emptied each week by the dunny man, a fearsome ogre. When you perched on the cracked wooden seat to do poo, you faced the perils of falling into the stinking excrement or of being attacked by the platoons of redback spiders whose home it was. To the grief of their parents, hundreds of children died this way all the time, I thought, either spirited away in the bottom of the pan by the ogre who took them home to eat them, or carted off to hospital with spiders munching their flesh. Many of them in Ettalong itself.

A lot of stuff spooked me at that age. I cannot see a crocodile today without an atavistic chill of fear, aroused by a memory of the beast with the ticking clock in its belly in J. M. Barrie's *Peter Pan.*

✧

The Sydney winter of 1949 was unusually bleak and wet, punishing days and nights made more bitter still by a wave of strikes in the New South Wales coalmines. Power blackouts, often very long ones, plunged homes and schools, shops and factories into sudden, dark silence. The gas went off too.

The times were miserable. The miners of the Hunter Valley and the Illawarra had entirely legitimate grievances about their pay and working conditions, which were appalling, but at bottom the strikes were a fight for the soul and control of the Labor Party. More than that. At the zenith of its power, the Australian Communist Party was struggling to foment a workers' uprising, dreaming of the Leninist revolution of the proletariat that would bring down capitalism itself. Violence flickered in a uniquely Australian way, like this punch-up in a park:

> *Soldiers' Wild Fight With Communists*
> In a wild, bare-knuckle fight in Marrickville Park yesterday afternoon, soldiers knocked down several Communists, giving them black eyes and bleeding noses.
>
> There were about eight on each side in the melee, in which men grappled and rolled on the ground amid a big, surging crowd.
>
> The Communists and soldiers fought after A.L.P. speakers had conducted a public meeting in opposition to the coal strike.
>
> The meeting, by nearly 400 votes to 14, denounced the strike as a political conspiracy.[37]

The strike began with more than 23,000 miners walking out on 27 June. Determined to 'teach the Reds a lesson', Ben Chifley's federal Labor government rushed through laws confiscating the funds of the Miners' Federation, and a few weeks later eight leaders of the union were jailed under emergency legislation.[38] Desperate to end the strike in what was a federal election year, Chifley sent in the army. On 1 August some 2500 soldiers began working the open-cut mines in the Hunter. Two weeks later, beaten into submission, the miners went back. The conservatives crowed from the rooftops, with none other than Warwick Fairfax hitting the typewriter in his harbourside mansion in Sydney to write a turgid, by-lined commentary for the newspaper he owned:

> This strike was one of many caused by wreckers seeking to discredit and destroy all parties and institutions through which reforms could be brought about. Why do Communists do this?
>
> Because Communism has become nothing but a tool to forge the sword of tyranny and dictatorship; a sword that is meant to cut its way through living flesh for the onward march of Russian imperialism . . .[39]

I dimly remember the blackouts: dinner of bread and butter, and bed by the light of candles stuck in bottles. I did not know that my father had fallen ill that winter, stricken by a cold and then bronchitis brought on, they thought, by chilly outdoor afternoons and evenings coaching the Barker rugby team in what seemed like unending rain. Then, at home in the flat, there was often no relieving warmth of a decent shower or a hot dinner. Gradually but inexorably, this illness morphed into asthma, bringing on ever more frequent fits of coughing and wheezing, of gasping for air. To add to the misery, my mother miscarried at this time, losing a baby she so desperately hoped would be a girl. She had bought pink baby clothes and picked a name: Penny.

There was better news that Christmas, when she conceived again. But Jim's asthma kept getting worse, the attacks more frequent. Niels Pedersen prescribed a regime of injections, which brought some relief, and he taught Enid how to administer them by getting her to practise with the hypodermic syringe on an orange. They saw various specialist doctors and even a herbalist, but nothing seemed to have any lasting effect. The invention of the pocket-sized adrenaline inhaler for asthmatics was still six years away. My father took to sleeping on a bed placed out on the small, open balcony of the flat, partly in the hope of getting some fresh air at night, partly to allow his wife to get some sleep without being disturbed by his barking cough. It must have been misery.

All through 1950 he grew weaker, succumbing to coughing fits in the classroom and playground. Sometimes Enid would be called over to the school to give him an injection that would get him home. He bore it stoically, even cheerfully, but there was no escaping that the fine young Olympic athlete had become a dependent cripple.

My brother was born in September 1950 in the Sanatorium, invariably called the San, a hospital in Wahroonga run by the Seventh-Day Adventists, and a far cry from my squalid beginnings. Furious that he was not a girl, my mother in a postpartum delirium ordered the obstetrician to take him away or give him away.

I was little happier. Promised for months that he would be someone to play with, I felt grievously betrayed when he turned out to be a wrinkled and largely immobile pink object wrapped in a long white shawl. For this crime I inflicted occasional punishment upon him for the next sixteen years or so. My father, though, was delighted. 'We boys', he would call the three of us, to my mother's silent chagrin. They christened him Peter, with the second name Niels. An Anglican baptism, not Catholic.

✧

The early months of 1951 saw Jim go downhill again, and he spent time in the nearby Hornsby Hospital. On the day he was due to come home, Enid went over to the school to pick roses from the manicured gardens there – flowers to welcome him. A friend, the school matron, Sister Ella Halley, stopped her in her tracks. I loved Ella Halley, who spoke with the rich brogue of her native Scottish highlands, who smelt of flowers and talcum powder, and who was always good for a cuddle and a chunk of her homemade shortbread to nibble. She was also fey, in the old Scots sense of the word, meaning one possessed of clairvoyance, a second sight. Disturbed, she saw that my mother had picked red and white roses, and urged her not to arrange them in the same vase. In Highland folklore, she said, red and white flowers together were blood and tears, meaning a death in the family within a year. Laughing, my mother thought no more of it and plonked the flowers together.

That April, Niels Pedersen had worse news. This big, gentle man – I loved him too – came to my mother one night and said she must face the fact that Jim would eventually be stricken completely, and unable to work. She would have to become the breadwinner. There was no choice, no hope for better. It was a devastating blow. Jim was forty-two years old; she was twenty-eight. They had been married for not quite six years, in exultant happiness. Now this was to be snatched away.

A couple of days later, a family friend came to visit. Rob Solomon had been one of my father's favourite pupils at Barker, a dashing inside back in the First XV and a handy sprinter, good enough for Jim to recommend him for a Rhodes Scholarship, which he won.[40] It was Wednesday, 4 April. Seeing Jim prostrate and distressed in bed, Rob chatted briefly and left. My mother's memoir carries the story:

> Later on, about 10pm, Michael suddenly woke and cried – a thing he never did. He thought there was a moth in his room and he was frightened of it. When I'd settled him down the baby [Peter] suddenly woke screaming – again this was unusual. I remember thinking 'what a night this is going to be.'
>
> I got into bed, but Jim called me out to him on the balcony and I found him absolutely struggling to breathe. I prepared the injection and gave it to him. He was breathing terribly loudly, fighting for every breath. But suddenly there was complete silence and he fell back in my arms on the bed.
>
> That sudden silence was frightening, but I realised he had died.[41]

3

Chatswood, mon amour

I HAVE NO MEMORY of my father's death, none at all, save that I was sent to stay for a while with my mother's cousin, Auntie Billie. Like Miss Stewart, she had magic powers and could make your glass of milk turn pink by uttering a spell, so long as you turned your back while it happened. But if I felt any sense of loss or grief, my mind has erased it completely. I had just turned five. My father was there. Then he wasn't. That was it.

That night my mother called for help from the neighbours. They summoned more help. Her mother and sister came up from Chatswood. Niels Pedersen arrived and, at Enid's specific request, the Barker chaplain, Hubert Dixon, drove to the local Catholic church and returned with the parish priest, Father Michael Farrell, who administered the last rites, the Sacrament of Extreme Unction and the Apostolic Pardon:

> *Per sacrosancta humanae reparationis mysteria remittat tibi omnipotens Deus omnes praesentis et futurae vitae poenas, Paradisi portas aperiat, et ad gaudia sempiterna perducat.*

> By the Sacred mysteries of man's redemption may almighty God remit to you all penalties of the present life and of the life to come: may He open to you the gates of paradise and lead you to joys everlasting.[42]

Then the undertakers took James Andrew Carlton away in a long wicker casket, a sight Enid could not watch.

Over the next two days the little flat filled with flowers and gifts of food. There was open weeping when the death was announced at a school assembly, and the story was on page one of most of the big newspapers. The funeral was on Friday, 6 April, four days short of what would have been their sixth wedding anniversary. The entire Barker student body lined the Pacific Highway as the hearse was driven away from the school to the Northern Suburbs Cemetery, where Father Farrell conducted the burial service by the graveside in the Catholic section. Again, my mother could not bear to be there. She stayed away to mind 'we boys'. Uncle Niels stood in for her. But she was grateful for the Catholic funeral, and for the generous decision of the Missionaries of the Sacred Heart to pay the undertakers' bill and the cost of placing a red granite headstone on the grave. She would always say she had taken Jim from the Catholic Church and then given him back, which was true enough.

Then began the competition for my soul. First, Barker offered to educate me for free, for the next twelve years. My mother politely declined, explaining that it would be unfair to have the older boy at a private school and (eventually) the younger one at a state school. So Bill Leslie, the headmaster and my father's friend, asked the school council to take on the two of us, and it did. An anonymous parent offered to pay for our textbooks, and he or she did. We both won academic scholarships a few years down the track, but these were acts of extraordinary generosity for which Peter and I are grateful to this day.

Hardly was that organised, though, when my Catholic godfather, one of my father's oldest friends, fronted at the flat with a priest and offered to give me any Catholic education my mother might choose. Joeys would be glad to take me on. But they were not at all interested in Peter, who had been baptised an Anglican. Again my mother declined; the godfather left, never to be seen again.

The church gave it one last try. Two nuns appeared out of the blue at the flat one day, knocked at the door and said they could take both boys off Enid's hands and bring us up in a nearby Catholic orphanage. My grandmother sent them packing.

The widow now contemplated a cheerless future. She would have to leave the flat, with Peter six months old and barely weaned. She had hardly any savings and no job. Jim had taken out a small insurance policy, and his sporting friends rallied around with a public appeal for a memorial fund, which was handsomely answered and which helped a lot, but it could never be enough to put a roof over our heads. There was nothing for it: there was only one place she could go. With the heaviest of hearts, she took us to live with her mother and father in Chatswood.

✧

Enid must have hated it. She had never got along with her father, nor he with her. Fat and wheezing, Bob Symington carried the burden of a disappointed life like an anvil around his neck, but not in quiet desperation. Just the opposite. For whatever reason he threw tantrums of volcanic force at least once a week, and sometimes more. Birds fell from the trees. Cats fled howling. The neighbours slammed their windows closed. My grandmother shouted back. I have a clear memory of him prostrate on his stomach in the backyard by the orange tree, his face an aubergine purple, the Supervising Inspector of Horticulture hammering the lawn with his fists and feet, bellowing like Hitler learning that Rudolf Hess had flown to Scotland. My mother and Nana – we'll call her that from now on – tried to shelter me from these explosions, but it was impossible. The house was too small. For a long while this strange adult behaviour worried and frightened me, although it would blow over. Until the next time.

Fifty-three Orchard Road was one of those ubiquitous brick cottages thrown up in their thousands across Sydney by the property developers of the Federation era. Fenced from the road by a clipped privet hedge, it stood across from a small park and Chatswood Oval, where local boy and cricket immortal Victor Trumper had learned to play. The Gordon Rugby Union club played there too. At the front of the house there was a little terrazzo-tiled verandah on one side and an attempt at a bay window on the other, beneath a red-tiled roof. The front door opened to a central hall, with a bedroom and a lounge room to the left and two more bedrooms to the right. The kitchen was just big enough to take a small table and chairs, where we ate. Four of us did, anyway; bellowing Bob often found himself exiled to the nearby sunroom, known grandly but inexplicably as the breakfast room. There he dined alone, farting audibly.

Food was cooked on a gas stove made by the Australian Metters company, an upright blue-and-cream contraption which had a picture of a kookaburra with a worm in its beak on the enamelled oven door. These sold in their hundreds of thousands – a marketing triumph – as the Early Kooka. Ba boom. On reflection, 'cooked' is the wrong word. 'Heated' might cover it. 'Burned' is better still. No matter who was preparing the meal, Nana or Enid, it was invariably overdone to buggery. Lamb chops, sausages and the occasional bit of Sunday roast beef were supercharged to the consistency of old boots. Vegetables, no matter what they were, emerged from their saucepans a uniform shade of khaki and with the consistency of toothpaste, all the vitamins discarded in the green boiled water. It's a wonder we didn't get scurvy. I still have nightmare visions of a regular family staple, tinned spaghetti on toast. Pudding, as we called it, was almost always tinned peaches and homemade custard, which actually wasn't too bad. None of the adults drank alcohol, although not from any particular religious conviction. 'It makes me feel all funny,' my mother used to say. But a bottle of sweet sherry and another of a fruity white wine known as Barossa Pearl was kept on standby for visitors. I once tasted Barossa Pearl, an oily glurp that might have done for brake fluid.

When we first moved in, there was only a cold water tap in the kitchen and an ice chest, not a refrigerator. Eventually a hot water service appeared, and with it a gas refrigerator, to much excitement. Luxury! The bathroom, hardly larger than the bath itself, had a gas hot water heater which had to be kick-started by taps and dials and switches, then lit by matches which blew out at just the wrong moment. It would have detonated like a bomb if you got it wrong. The laundry beyond the kitchen had no washing machine, only a giant gas copper which took hours to heat. On washdays it was a geothermal wonder, like the Rotorua geysers. You could have taken a sauna.

The backyard boasted two citrus trees, lemon and orange, and a gnarled old camphor laurel which did splendid service as a fort, castle, wigwam, pirate galleon, battleship and space rocket. Most of all, it was a refuge from my brawling grandparents. In summer, the camphor laurel was a home for squadrons of cicadas: Greengrocers, Yellow Mondays, Black Princes, Cherry Noses and Piss-whackers, quite literally the world's noisiest insects. Black Princes were especially prized. You could pull off their wings and sell them to the local chemist, who made medicines out of them.

The wooden palings of the back fence slumped beneath the weight of the choko vine – obligatory in every Australian suburban garden – which ran riot, like a triffid. My brother and I were force-fed its revolting fruit, boiled to a mush and smothered in a glug that looked and tasted like wallpaper glue. I cannot see a choko today without feeling an urge to vomit.

Nana slept in state in the bedroom with the bay window, her wretched husband in the smaller room behind that, known as his study. My mother, brother and I were jammed into the third bedroom, Peter in a cot at first. Later there were bunks for the two of us. This accommodation problem was at least partly solved when Bob went barking mad. One day he flooded the bathroom and emerged stark-naked, dripping wet and cavorting like a satyr. The cops were called to bundle him away; he died in the Callan Park psychiatric hospital a few weeks later, entirely unlamented. As far as I know, he had no other relatives. Nobody ever spoke of him again. Peter and I were moved into his room.

All in all, I was not having much luck with grandparents. After my father's death, his side of the family cut us off completely. We might never have existed. Or they might never have existed. Catherine had always blamed Enid for luring him from the priesthood, something she had not dared say while he was alive but which she made clear afterwards. Mary thought the same. I saw Catherine only twice again, each time by accident. Once, my mother and I ran into her in the street at

Chatswood. I had to be told who she was. They exchanged a few terse words before Catherine caught a tram. The last time was when I was in primary school, coming home on the train in my Barker uniform. A skinny, wizened woman dressed in black took the seat next to me and, after a short silence, asked if I was Michael Carlton.

'Yes,' I said, puzzled.

'I'm your grandmother,' she said.

I think there might have been a few more perfunctory questions and she left the train a couple of stops later. That was that. I have no idea when she died or where she is buried, and I don't intend to find out.

Nana, on the other hand, was full on. It would be nice to report that she was the granny from Central Casting, an apple-cheeked, lavender-scented old dear, all kisses and cuddles and a dab hand at sponge cakes. But she wasn't. Cuddles were certainly off the menu. I don't think I ever got one from her, perhaps because she spent most of her waking hours encased in an enormous whalebone corset, which she called her step-ins, and which lent her the rigidity of a petrol drum. She was bigoted, opinionated and bossy; there were times in my later adolescence when I could quite cheerfully have strangled her.

Eventually I realised that Enid felt the same way. Marriage had been her escape route from Chatswood and her coldly dysfunctional parents, but Jim's death had cruelly ended all that. She felt bound to her mother, hand and foot, seemingly forever. I would hear muffled arguments and a few times I found her sobbing softly in her bedroom. She would never explain why she was crying but would hold me as tightly as if her life depended on it. Perhaps it did. 'You're the man of the family,' she would sometimes tell me. I took this very seriously, a duty laid upon me.

In time I understood that many of the arguments were about parenting. Nana had Edwardian notions of children being seen and not heard, and insisted that her daughter apply them. Michael was rude, lazy and ill-disciplined, she nagged. It was a generation gap beyond bridging. Nana laid down the law.

'Michael, I want you to go to the dagoes to get the fruit and veg,' she would say. The dagoes were an Italian family, the Tesorieros, who owned the greengrocer's shop in Victoria Avenue, a welcoming cave of wonderful and mysterious cooking aromas – or, in Nana-speak, 'filthy foreign muck'. 'Shopping at the dagoes' with Nana was a cringe-making ordeal. She ordered them around like Catherine the Great. *Basta!* In that pushy way that migrants still have, the Tesoriero *bambini* all grew up to be lawyers, doctors and engineers – and one a journalist.

Lesser still were the chows, or sometimes the chinks, who ran Chatswood's only Chinese restaurant. 'Always wash your hands after touching money,' Nana would say. 'You never know if a Chinaman's had it.'

Sometimes, on birthdays or special occasions, I would be sent to the chows with two of our kitchen saucepans, one to be filled with sweet-and-sour pork and the other with a glutinous concoction called chop suey, whatever that was. Mostly cabbage, from memory. We never ordered chicken, though. As everyone knew, the chicken in Chinese restaurants was actually cat, domestic pussies kidnapped by fiendish Orientals prowling around the neighbourhood in the dead of night.

A Chinese boy of about my age lived up the road. If I was hanging over the front gate when he and his parents passed by, they would smile and say hello. When Nana caught them at it, the cheeky sods, I was ordered there and then to come inside and never to talk to them again. 'They're different to us,' she barked. 'They smell.' She would be speechless and much affronted if she could see Chatswood today – one of the biggest Chinese communities in Australia, block after block of what were once Federation shops and cottages replaced by soaring home unit towers of remarkable ugliness. The place looks like Hong Kong.

Nana's political opinions came from pretty much the same box. Devoid of any particular ideology or underpinning philosophy, her views were driven largely by the iron rules of good manners and middle-class respectability, two of her unswerving preoccupations. That meant the Liberal Party. Every so often, frocked up in her best hat and gloves, she would sortie into town on a mission known as Helping Menzies. Robert Gordon Menzies, who became prime minister for the second time when I was three and wouldn't quit until

I was twenty, was her *beau idéal* of the true gentleman, the bunyip aristocrat and Empire statesman of towering stature and infinite wisdom who spoke properly (a high commendation) and could be relied upon never to embarrass us in front of the Queen. For many years I believed Nana was a powerful figure in the great policy councils of the Liberal Party. I discovered only very much later that Helping Menzies operated at a lower level altogether: it consisted of serving sandwiches and lamingtons and pouring cups of tea at the Liberals' talkfests. The Great Man had actually spoken to Nana on one of these occasions, however, thanking her for a proffered scone.

Only common and ignorant people voted Labor. Soon-to-be Labor leader Arthur Calwell – always referred to by his surname only, and spoken with a snarl – was vulgar himself, certainly a Catholic and quite possibly a commo. You could tell all this from his voice, which, unlike that of Mr Menzies, had the timbre of a chainsaw in a bucket of gravel. I wasn't sure what a commo was, but it was clearly a low and detestable form of life; you wouldn't let one within a mile of the monarch. I would encounter both Menzies and Calwell years later.

My mother, bless her, never sought to shove religion down my throat. I imagine she'd had more than enough of it herself, and was content to leave it to the school to do what it thought it should in that direction. I was not packed off to the local parish Sunday School to colour schmaltzy pictures of biblical parables, like so many of my friends. At Barker we had weekly scripture classes – known rather oddly as Divinity – but it was all very low-key in a genteel, Anglican sort of way. The miracle of the loaves and fishes and so on. Those were the days before the Sydney Anglican Diocese went all madly evangelical and in-yer-face.

Nana, though, had other ideas. In 1959, when the hot-gospelling American evangelist Billy Graham turned up in Sydney, she seized the opportunity to shove me headlong in the direction of God. Tanned and toothy, oozing piety, ostentatious virtue and folksy Southern Baptist charm from every orifice, Graham took Australia by storm and then some. The show was known as the Billy Graham Crusade, probably not a term they would use now. But you had to be there. All around the country the crowds were extraordinary, in the hundreds of thousands. And that was without the local Catholics, who were banned from any contact with his contaminating Protestant heresies. In Sydney alone, over a week or so in May, nearly a million people went to be swept up in the soaring Graham oratory. His final performance filled both the Sydney Cricket Ground and the adjoining Showground to overflowing, with an astounding 150,000 bums on seats; thousands more remained outside, clamouring to get in but having to content themselves with hearing it on the loudspeakers. Country people around the nation got it on radio or, if they were especially fortunate, grainy black-and-white television.

Nana dragged me along for the show. Graham's shtick was uncomplicated: *Gimme that old-time religion.* At about a million decibels he shouted first and at length about the Snares of Satan, the Day of Judgement, the Wages of Sin and the Torments of Hell that awaited the wicked, the Eternal Damnation of the Fiery Pit. An enormous choir sang hymns. Billy returned to the stage and got off another rant about Salvation, which could be rock-solid-guaranteed by acknowledging the Lord Jesus Christ as your One True Saviour and Allowing Him into Your Life. You did it with the power of prayer – or *the pah of pray-ah*, as Graham pronounced it. More from the choir: 'What a Friend We Have in Jesus', which, of course, was the favourite hymn of 'mah good fraynd and a true Christian gennelman, President Eisenhower'.

As it so happened, you could save yourself right there and then by coming forward. 'Come forward, my friends, come forward! Repent! Gain the Gift of Eternal Life!' Yes, brothers and sisters, all you had to do was leave your seat, move towards the stage and Give Yourself to God, via Billy himself or one of his hundreds of specially trained counsellors, who were waiting to lay their well-scrubbed hands upon you. An ecstatic horde lunged to the front; this was not the meek inheriting the earth so much as the wild-eyed and hysterical grabbing it by the balls before it got away. The halt, the weak and the blind were trampled in the rush.

'Up you get,' hissed Nana. 'Off you go.'

I twitched and hesitated, but she had the better of me – I was only thirteen – and she hoisted me out of my seat by an ear and propelled me towards the stage. In short order I found myself kneeling in the midst of the wailing, hollering mass of The Forgiven. People were tearing their hair and rending their garments, bawling and sobbing. Billy beamed down upon us, all sweat and dentistry.

At home that night I gave it a fair try. Truly, I did. I knelt in *pray-ah* at the end of my bed, reminding the Lord that I had given myself to Him that afternoon, and asking for some acknowledgement that He was now In My Life. I was not sure what to expect. A trio of angels out in Orchard Road or just a clap of thunder would have done the job. But there was nothing. Not one damn thing. Silence. The Lord was not *thay-ah*; he was obviously busy *elsewhay-ah*. Presumably He would get back to me when He was free.

Patiently, I tried this for a week or so, always in the correct posture, kneeling in supplication with the palms of my hands together. Nothing – no result at all. Clearly God was not interested. Well, bugger Him. Feeling badly let down, I resumed my life of sin.

✧

It is received wisdom that the 1950s were stodge and boredom, a decade of stultifying cultural inertia. All wrong; far from it. Confident and optimistic after the war, the United States seized economic and social leadership of the planet, an exploding creativity emphatically flaunted in the iconic automobiles rolling off the production lines in Detroit. Each new model was bigger and faster than the last, smothered in lumps of chrome and headlights, with ever more extravagant tailfins, like some sculpted sci-fi rocket ship. Hollywood was entering a golden age. Marilyn Monroe, Humphrey Bogart, Audrey Hepburn, Marlon Brando, Doris Day, John Wayne, Katharine Hepburn, James Dean, Elizabeth Taylor, Gary Cooper, Grace Kelly, James Stewart and Sophia Loren were all on screen, to pick just a handful. The studios were making movies like *Singin' in the Rain*, *Ben-Hur*, *Some Like It Hot*, *On the Waterfront*, *Blackboard Jungle*, *High Noon*, *The Ten Commandments* and *The African Queen*, directed by, oh, John Huston, Alfred Hitchcock, Stanley Kubrick, Elia Kazan and the fabulously named Cecil B. DeMille. 'Bigger than *Ben-Hur*' and 'Ready when you are, Mr DeMille' entered the language. Disney alone produced the classics *Peter Pan*, *Alice in Wonderland*, *Cinderella* and *Lady and the Tramp*. In music, Frank Sinatra and Ella Fitzgerald were shooting skywards, Chuck Berry was writing his rock'n'roll classics, and Elvis Presley, Bill Haley and Buddy Holly began dragging what the record industry called 'race music' into the white mainstream. Broadway was on fire with *My Fair Lady*, *Paint Your Wagon*, *Guys and Dolls* and *Can Can*. All in the 1950s.

The purpose of that long but far from complete list is to emphasise that I missed most of it. America was transcendent but Australia was still at peak colonial cringe in the direction of Britain, the Mother Country. For the Queen's coronation in 1953 I was given an enormous cardboard diorama of Buckingham Palace and The Mall, which I could embellish with golden coaches and the household cavalry. When Elizabeth and Philip visited the next year, the nation went stark raving mad. Huge crowds flocked to adore them. Our school exercise books had their pictures on the front cover. At the official banquet in Sydney – held at the top-floor restaurant in the David Jones department store, the only place big enough – the jewel-encrusted society matrons of the Eastern Suburbs stood on their chairs and clambered atop the tables to see their demure sovereign, who must have thought she'd arrived among savages. At my eighth birthday party, sponsored by Uncle Niels, the cake was made in the shape of the liner SS *Gothic*, which had carried her to Australia.

My cultural upbringing was almost exclusively Anglo. As an infant I had been read May Gibbs' *Gumnut Babies* and *Tales of Snugglepot and Cuddlepie*, and been terrified by the evil Banksia Men. At the Christmas concert in second class I myself made a particularly fetching gumnut baby, decked out in a green knitted tea cosy, underpants and a crepe-paper fig leaf, a performance even more admired than that of the year before, when I had been a shepherd watching flocks by night. But that was where the canon of Australian writing stopped – for me, anyway. To this day I have never done Norman Lindsay's *The Magic Pudding*, for example, nor Ethel Turner's *Seven Little Australians*. When I began to read to myself, I plunged into English children's literature, devouring the works of Enid Blyton and Arthur Ransome. Upper-middle-class children called Julian and George, Peggy and Nancy, dashed about the English countryside, helpfully solving crimes and mysteries which had proved impenetrable to the police, or sailing in the Lake District and on the Norfolk Broads. Good work, Famous Five! Jolly fine show, Swallows and Amazons! A measure of the innocence of the age was that one of the Swallows was nicknamed Titty. In Blyton's *Faraway Tree* series there were two playmates called Fanny and Dick, later changed to Frannie and Rick.

From there I graduated to the stirring *Biggles* books of Captain W. E. Johns. Squadron Leader James Bigglesworth DFC RAF (his rank changed from book to book) led a truly heroic flying career across two world wars, smiting first the beastly Hun – there was a particularly nasty Prussian brute named Von Stalhein – and then the Yellow Peril. 'Biggles smiled thinly as he got the Jap in the Hurricane's gun sights!' The books had titles like *Biggles Defies the Swastika*, *Biggles Delivers the Goods* and *Biggles Pulls It Off*. (Okay, yes, I made up that last one, but you get the picture. He never married.) In these escapades he was loyally assisted by his cousin The Honourable Algernon Lacey and chums Ginger Hebblethwaite and the monocle-wearing Lord Bertie Lissie. All four of them were served by the very much lower-class but loyally dependable Flight Sergeant Smyth.

I had no idea then, but the books were appallingly Anglo-supremacist, class-ridden and racist. *Biggles in Australia* portrayed Indigenous people as virtually sub-human savages. But I loved the stories, and for quite a while I was Biggles myself, the camphor laurel tree in the backyard doing sterling service as a Battle of Britain Spitfire. *Bandits twelve o'clock high, Red Leader. Take that, Von Stalhein! A stream of tracer bullets flew towards the diving Messerschmitt . . .*

Biggles' fictional stories were eventually replaced for me by the slew of factual war memoirs that began to hit the bookstores in the mid-1950s, mostly published in paperback by Pan Books. The shelves in the local library and therefore in my bedroom were stacked with *The Dam Busters*, *Reach for the Sky*, *Boldness Be My Friend*, *Ill Met by Moonlight*, *Enemy Coast Ahead*, *The Naked Island*, *Escape – or Die* and *The Colditz Story*. The last two were escape narratives, a hot favourite, tales of upper-class officer prisoners of war, public schoolboys all, defying their captors in Stalag this or that with implacable sang froid, thus:

> '*Englischer* squadron leader, for you ze war is now over. *Bald wird der Führer im Buckingham Palast leben!*'[43]
> 'Not while I'm alive, you Jerry swine!'
> '*Achtung!* To ze Cooler!'

But it was a novel that became one of the great cultural signposts of my life. In the lounge room at Chatswood I found a copy of *The Cruel Sea*, Nicholas Monsarrat's spellbinding story of the Royal Navy in the Battle of the Atlantic. I was eleven. My mother said it was too old for me but I read it anyway, devouring it by torchlight under the bed covers after lights out. Winston Churchill wrote in his memoirs that the only thing that ever truly frightened him during the war was the U-boat peril. Monsarrat himself had been an officer of the Royal Navy Volunteer Reserve at sea in the Atlantic convoys, and he got the peril absolutely right in language of moving power. The chief protagonists, a Lieutenant Commander Ericson and a Lieutenant Lockhart, embodied the spirit of the age.

I have never found a book that gripped me more, and I have read it again and again, to the point where I can quote whole slabs of it. I still have that original copy, the pages now brown and mottled. *The Cruel Sea* pointed me towards what would become a lifelong passion for naval literature, both historical and fictional. The camphor laurel tree now morphed into the corvette HMS *Compass Rose*. From her icy, storm-swept bridge Commander Carlton sank U-boats in the backyard at every point of the compass, a weary but heroic figure in gold-braided peaked cap and salt-encrusted duffle coat.

✧

From that backyard we could see something very exciting happening not far away in Willoughby. Sir Frank Packer, the media mogul, was building the transmission mast for Australia's first television station, TCN-9. Its orange and white steel tracery rose steadily above the rooftops, an Eiffel Tower down under. Sometimes after school I would ride my bike – a second-hand but refurbished blue and white Speedwell – to see the work go on.

Television arrived in Australia for the Melbourne Olympic Games in 1956, but it took a long while after that to get to 53 Orchard

Road. This was most likely because a TV set, as it was called, cost a lot of money. Nana's public explanation to enquiring neighbours was that there was nothing she would want to watch, the programs were often vulgar, and, anyway, the whole thing was almost certainly a passing fad. The first television I ever saw was in the window at Cassidy's, an electrical retailer in Victoria Avenue. Some families used to take stools and chairs along to sit on the footpath in the evening to watch a flickering grey-and-white screen not much bigger than a cornflakes packet. There was no sound, but no one seemed to mind. Sometimes Auntie Sheila, an honorary neighbourhood aunt, would invite my brother and me up the road in the afternoons to watch the TV at her place. How fabulous, how glamorous it was. I fell deeply in love with Annette Funicello, the raven-haired, startlingly talented beauty of *The Mickey Mouse Club*.

It was radio that ruled the roost at home. The wireless, as everyone called it. We had two sets, one in a big brown wooden cabinet about the size of a modern dishwasher, which stood in a corner of the lounge room, and a second and smaller plastic mantel radio in my mother's bedroom. The grown-ups enjoyed serials and quiz shows, especially those hosted by the New Zealand–born Jack Davey, one of the biggest stars Australian radio ever produced; he was famous for his opening line, 'Hi ho, everybody!' A talented and cheerful ad-libber with a lightning wit, he was also a notorious gambler whose debts frequently had to be paid by his radio employers before various well-muscled and persuasive gentlemen came around to collect them. Taken a bit in drink one evening, and live on air, Davey got into terrible trouble by varying his standard opening words with the memorable line: 'When roses are red, they're ready to pluck; when girls are sixteen, they're ready to . . . [pause] . . . Hi ho, everybody!' When he died of cancer in 1959, 150,000 people went to his funeral in Sydney.

His rival on air was the American-born Bob Dyer, who had come to Australia playing a banjo in a Tennessee hillbilly vaudeville act and eventually cracked the radio big time. Renowned for his *Pick a Box* quiz show, he was, in Nana's firm view, common and vulgar.

Best of all my grandmother loved *Blue Hills*, an ABC radio serial about life in the bush which ran for twenty-seven years, in fifteen-minute episodes, until 1976. There was also *The Quiz Kids*, in which stratospherically intelligent adolescent wunderkinder explained the Theory of Relativity, quoted Søren Kierkegaard or critiqued the novels of the Brontë sisters in fifteen seconds flat. Many of them grew up to be High Court judges or alcoholics or both. We did not, though, listen to *Dad and Dave*, a turgid tale of rural idiots living in Snake Gully, or the larrikin comic Roy Rene's character Mo. They were both vulgar.

There was kids' radio, too. From the age of seven, as soon as I was eligible to join, I became an Argonaut. Almost everybody did. *The Argonauts Club* was part of the afternoon ABC *Children's Session*, a show largely devised by two extraordinarily talented women, Nina Murdoch and Ida Elizabeth Jenkins. The bouncy opening theme is stuck in my head:

> Come, Old Mother Hubbard, and Jack and Jill
> And Tom the Piper's son,
> Leave your cupboard, forget your spill –
> We're going to have some fun.
> The wireless says to hurry and run
> To leave your games and toys;
> The wireless says the time has come
> For all the girls and boys.
> So come with a hop, a skip and a run,
> it's time for the Session, it's time for the fun.

It was terrifically aspirational, based very, very loosely on the Argonauts of Greek mythology, high culture for kids of the most elevating sort. You joined up to enter competitions and win points for poems, paintings, drawings or songs that you sent in. There were lectures on art and music, theatre and dance. When you were accepted for membership you were given a classic-sounding ship name and number – I can't remember mine, but I was something like Tinea 21 or Preposterous 32 – and they sent you a handsome badge of an Argonaut galley and a pledge which read:

> Before the sun and night and the blue sea, I vow
> To stand faithfully by all that is brave and beautiful,

> To seek adventure and, having discovered aught of wonder, or delight, of merriment or loveliness,
> To share it freely with my comrades, the Band of Happy Rowers.

You get the drift. The front man was a Scottish-born actor named Atholl Fleming, a moustachioed ex-military chap who had been gassed and bayoneted on the Somme. He had an avuncular port'n' Stilton voice, it being holy writ at the ABC in those days that only posh British accents could strike the approved tone on the wireless. Australian accents were vulgar and common.

As Jason, captain of the good ship *Argo*, Fleming exhorted us happy listeners to ever greater artistic triumphs. If they liked your poem or your painting it got a mention on air, a point or two, a certificate and a compliment: 'Well rowed, Arthritis 43!' Super-talented Argonauts received the Order of the Dragons Tooth for gaining 150 points, and the Order of the Golden Fleece for 400 points. Real suckholes could win the highest award, the Golden Fleece and Bar, for 600 points. Fleming, who was also known as Uncle Mac, had the gig on *The Children's Session* for some thirty-one years until the ABC finally axed the show in 1972. Only baby boomers would remember him now, but in his day he was a much-loved national figure.

The song that closed the show is echoing around my brain as I write this:

> A jolly good night to you and you, and you, and you, and you.
> The time has come to finish and the session now is through.
> The thought is old, is old, is old but the wish tonight is new –
> A jolly good night to everyone . . .

Down market, the commercial stations also ran children's serials, which I devoured as well. Some were American, like *The Air Adventures of Hop Harrigan*, who was a feisty, crime-solving aviator, a sort of Yank Biggles. There was another Australian one called *I Hate Crime*, featuring Larry Kent, a former newspaperman from New York City who, improbably, migrated to Australia and set up shop as a private detective. It had lines in it like: 'She was blonde. She was beautiful.

And she had a gun. It was pointing at me.' On second thoughts, perhaps that one was not a kids' show.

I think my favourite was probably *Tarzan*, also made in Australia, and brought to you by Pepsodent toothpaste ('You'll wonder where the yellow went, when you brush your teeth with Pep-so-dent'). Tarzan was played by the actor Rod Taylor, and each show began with the King of the Apes bellowing his famous war cry of Ah-Ooooh-Aaaaaaah-Ooooooh-AAAH-AAAAAAAAAAAH. Cue jungle drums and lots of ooga-ooga music. Tarzan had been born Lord Greystoke, the child of aristocratic British parents murdered in darkest Africa by a tribe of apes, who then kindly nurtured the young toff to manhood. He swung through the jungle in a loincloth, invariably to rescue his wife, Jane, from some hideous predicament.

For a while there the camphor laurel tree became the African jungle. I would climb into its branches in my loincloth – white Y-fronts – bawling the war cry to attract the attention of Claudia Collis, a girl of about my age who lived next door. I desperately wanted her to see me in my jocks. Even more desperately, I wanted to see her in her undies. It turned out the urge was mutual. Eventually, by negotiation, we achieved a joint showing in the narrow, overgrown, spider-infested passage between our house and the side fence. Happy days.

The wireless eventually came calling. A former comedy writer named Keith Smith, who billed himself as the Pied Piper, had a knack for doing radio chats with kids, never the easiest gig in the world. At the height of his not inconsiderable fame in the 1950s he had two shows going, a fifteen-minuter on the ABC called *A Word from Children*, and a half-hour called *The Pied Piper*, which was recorded before a live audience by Sydney's 2GB. Out of the blue one day he turned up at my school and I was one of the precocious brats chosen to talk to him for the ABC show. I can't remember what on earth he asked, or my responses, but Smith's routine was largely to bowl up leading questions that would get kids to blurt out funny or embarrassing things about their families. 'What does mummy say when she gets cross with daddy?' Yuk, yuk. My, how we gathered around the big radio in the lounge room a few days later to hear it. This, my very first radio outing, was such a howling success that a few weeks later I was invited to go on Smith's other show, *The Pied Piper.*

Scrubbed by my mother to a gleaming pink, brushed, combed, polished and primped in my Barker uniform, I was taken to the famous Macquarie Auditorium, a theatre in Phillip Street (now long gone) done up as a radio studio for the big quiz shows and live dramas that were the big advertising earners before TV killed them off. Jack Davey himself had trod that very stage.

Again, I haven't a clue what Smith's questions were or what I said, although I recall you had to finish off by asking a riddle. What stayed with me was the spellbinding excitement of it all. Men and women bustled about with clipboards and headphones. To one side, behind a clear glass window, there was a darkened cave full of winking lights, a fairy diamond mine, where important-looking people silently opened and closed their mouths like goldfish. Cables and wires were everywhere, snaking away from shiny, chrome-plated microphones the size of pineapples. Mysterious people said things like 'Standby . . . quiet please . . . five, four, three . . . rolling . . . cue Keith!' and suddenly there were boxes on the walls flashing their red and white On Air signs. 'Applause, please.' An audience, dimly seen beyond the stage lights, chortled and clapped at every witty sally.

I loved it. I was entranced. For a week I was dancing on air, dizzily waiting for the show to be broadcast. Again we assembled around the enormous wireless set at the appointed time. 'This is Radio 2GB Sydney, key station of the Macquarie Broadcasting Network!' said a plummy voice. Up came the theme music. Then Smith was into his spiel.

We listened and listened, waiting and waiting, only to find that almost my entire performance had been edited out. Other kids, who were quite obviously not nearly as funny or clever as me – some of them even vulgar and common, actually – had made the cut. I only got to ask my riddle at the end, which would have taken all of ten seconds. The shame, the humiliation. This was my first bleak disappointment in radio. It would not be the last.

In bed that night I sobbed myself to sleep with hot, salty tears, vowing that I would show 'em. One day I would be famous.

✧

When my brother started at Barker at the age of five, my mother at last felt able to get into full-time work. Before that she had been earning a little extra money teaching migrants English by correspondence, which she found both useful and enjoyable. Sometimes these 'New Australians' would come around to our place with little gifts of thanks. When a grateful Greek brought us a box of homemade dolmades, Nana inspected them as if we'd been given some dog turds.

After casting around, my mother scored a job as secretary to a doctor, an ophthalmic surgeon with a practice in Chatswood that was an easy walk away. It made a big difference to our lives. She was no longer reliant on the widows' pension or the charity of her mother. We still had no car in the family, but we could now afford outings by bus or tram, sometimes to Balmoral Beach on Sydney's Middle Harbour, or to Taronga Park Zoo in Mosman. Enid would put together a packed lunch for the three of us, and after a swim or a romp we would sprawl on the sand, chomping into what was mutually agreed to be our favourite food: a bread roll with butter, a circular slice of a bland luncheon meat known as Devon sausage, and a dollop of tomato sauce. Bliss.

At around the same time I became a Wolf Cub. I enlisted in the 1st Lindfield Cub Pack, which operated a couple of suburbs up the North Shore line, headquartered in a black-painted wooden shack on the edge of a chunk of National Park bushland. Frugal as ever, my mother found me a second-hand uniform from a friend. It was a pair of shorts and a shirt, both of navy-blue wool, and the 1st Lindfield blue and grey scarf, which was rolled in a triangle and held together by a little ring of plaited leather called a woggle.

(The things you learn: I discovered on writing this that the woggle was actually invented in 1923 by a Tasmanian Boy Scout named Bill Shankley, thus becoming – along with the stump-jump plough, the Holden ute, the Hills Hoist and Kylie Minogue – one of Australia's indelible contributions to civilisation. Woggles, I believe, are still worn today, worldwide, although very likely made in China, I suppose.)

This striking ensemble was completed by a small green woollen peaked cap with yellow piping; a wolf's head was stuck on the front when you won your Tenderfoot badge. No sillier uniform has ever been inflicted upon Australian youth. In yet another round of the cultural cringe, it was a perfect facsimile of the outfit for British cubs. No doubt it was ideally suited for wintry days in London or Birmingham, but it was a prickly, sweaty straitjacket on an Australian Saturday afternoon in January.

Our leader was Akela, the name borrowed from Rudyard Kipling's *Jungle Book*. From Monday to Friday, Akela was a slender brunette named Nola Beatty, bank clerk. At weekends she transformed into Wolf Cub Heroine, a human whirlwind in a khaki skirt and brown felt, lemon-squeezer Scout hat, capable of felling whole gum trees with a blow of her hand, of leaping up rocky crags like a gazelle, of wrestling bears, of swimming swollen torrents while fighting off crocodiles. She was also good with grazed knees. We cubs worshipped her. The Saturday meeting would begin with us arrayed in a circle before her, squatting on our haunches. 'Dyb, dyb, dyb, dyb!' she would cry, the Scouts' acronym for Do Your Best. 'Ah-kay-la! We'll dob, dob, dob, dob,' we piped back – Do Our Best. Then we would leap into the air, uttering a ferocious wolf cub howl.

I took all this very seriously. You could win proficiency badges for things like tying knots, lighting fires, boiling eggs, civic good works and being generally helpful. Obedient to orders, I was ever alert to help old ladies across roads or direct people to the nearest police station or post office. I learned to tie knots strong enough to rope a rodeo steer or haul a howitzer from a bog, skills I retain to this day. Trained to the peak of ruthless efficiency, fit to every tingling nerve, I collected badges to be sewn on my shirt sleeve until it looked like a patchwork quilt. I also scored two silver stars to wear on my cap.

Akela eventually bestowed upon me the ultimate reward for all this dob-dob-dobbing, a promotion in the field to the high rank of Sixer of the Brown Six, which meant I got to wear two yellow stripes on my badged sleeve, and to issue orders to my squad of younger and lesser Cubs. The burden of command lay heavily upon my shoulders. I bore it nobly.

4

A scout is clean in thought, word and deed

TELEVISION EVENTUALLY CAME TO Orchard Road in 1960. An HMV 21-inch set in a brown wooden cabinet replaced the big old wireless in the corner of the lounge room, to much disgruntled muttering from Nana, who saw it as the descent of the Visigoths upon us. Within weeks she was its greatest devotee, a worshipper at the altar of the cathode ray tube.

Sound and vision were plucked from the ether by a set-top aerial that looked a bit like a giant corkscrew and which had to be constantly fiddled with to get a picture that wasn't a polar blizzard. The first thing we ever watched when it was plugged in was a movie, *The Lives of a Bengal Lancer*, a 1935 Hollywood epic improbably starring Gary Cooper as a British army officer in the Raj, battling it out with the unruly natives.[44] We gaped at it open-mouthed, thrilled to bits, although for all the good the dodgy aerial was doing it could have been shot in midwinter on the Yorkshire moors. As a respectable North Shore family, we watched the ABC's seven o'clock news every evening – and only the ABC, never the commercial muck. It was read by the likes of James Dibble, John Chance and Martin Royal. Nana was a stern editorial critic. 'I don't like his tie,' she would snap. Or, 'He needs a haircut.' At times it was hard to tell what these men were wearing: some gizmo called the horizontal hold would cark it, producing a picture of zebra stripes, or the vertical hold would set the image tumbling over itself: you got twenty-four or more James Dibbles, disappearing to infinity. There were knobs to adjust all this, but they worked only fitfully.

Videotape had barely been invented, so, apart from movies, pretty well everything was broadcast live. Two particular family favourites were *Hal Lashwood's Alabama Jubilee* and *Cafe Continental*, which the ABC alternated week by week. Time's kindly erosion of memory has largely erased the Alabama thing from my mind, although I can dimly recall banjo-wielding minstrels cavorting in blackface, white gloves, top hats and striped pants. *Cafe Continental* was a much more sophisticated affair, with a compere who smarmed around in a dinner jacket dripping a cosmopolitan glamour rarely seen in Chatswood. His name was Hal Wayne, which was almost certainly not how they had known him at his birthplace in faraway Czechoslovakia. Extras lolled at little cafe tables, brandishing coffee cups, ostentatiously lighting each other's cigarettes, laughing uproariously and applauding the passing parade of accordion players, operatic sopranos, jugglers, conjurers, Cossack dancers and performing dog acts. The scripts were excruciating, as I recall, along these lines:

> HAL: Vell! Look, efferyone! Look who has choined us here in ze cafe! It is my old friend Andrzej, ze vorld-famous Gypsy violinist! Ha ha! Vot are you doing here, eh?
>
> ANDRZEJ: Hal! I voss chust passing and tort I vould drop in to giff some musick to you . . .

Cue furious clapping from the tables. We clapped at home, too, to demonstrate how worldly we were. We knew sophistication when we saw it.

Meanwhile, over at Willoughby a bespectacled young Brian Henderson was reading the news for the Packers' Channel Nine and fronting *Bandstand*, a dance and Top 40 music show for teenagers with, yes, a format pinched from American television. If I had been very good I was occasionally given access to this vulgarity. Col Joye and the

Joy Boys, Judy Stone, Noeleen Batley, Digger Revell and the Denver Men, Little Pattie, Lonnie Lee, Johnny Devlin, Peter Allen, the Dell-tones, Olivia Newton-John and a zillion others strutted their stuff, all members of the *Bandstand* family. Most were acts from Sydney. The males all wore very tight suits, three buttons done up, with skinny neckties. Col Joye was known as the Gentleman of Rock 'n' Roll. The girls were dressed in . . . well, I'm not sure, but it was unquestionably decorous, with no plunging necklines or skimpy skirts. Whatever he got up to in private – and the stories were many and lurid – Sir Frank Packer was a public prude. His television station would be respectable.

Without doubt, the show blazed a trail. It was thought that three gangly kids from Queensland might go far, although the Bee Gees was a pretty silly name that would have to be changed. The *Bandstand* studio audience – girls in rope-stiffened skirts, boys in tight-cuffed pants and duckbill haircuts – jived along. Starstruck, I would ride my bike to the studio gates after school, hoping to catch a glimpse of somebody recognisably famous. Such a happy day it was when Hendo gave me a wave as he zoomed past in a green and white Studebaker coupé. Little did I imagine . . .

Eventually, I made it on to *Bandstand* as one of the dancing teeny-boppers. In secret, in case my family found out. Cruelly, Brian would always say he had no recollection of my stellar performance, even though I had been right up the front and hogging the camera like Bronwyn Bishop.

In fact, my first TV appearance came earlier, as a Channel Ninepin on Desmond Tester's *Cabbage Quiz*. Old Desmond was a small expatriate Pom, relentlessly cheerful, with a face like an affable kipfler potato. From a showbiz beginning as an actor in pre-war British movies, he had found his way to the Packer fun factory, first as on-air talent and later as a production executive. The idea of the *Cabbage Quiz* was cheap and simple. There was a prize if you got an answer right – a pen or a book or something. But get it wrong and a chortling Desmond would load you up with a cabbage, which you had to clutch in ignominy and despair while the world watched.

I ended up with enough cabbage to feed a platoon of Prussians. But that was not the point. I had been in a television studio, a magic place even more exciting and exotic than the Macquarie Auditorium. I had spoken to Desmond, and he to me. They put make-up on you, which set like brown cement. Blokes in jeans and T-shirts walked around with long poles, clanking away at the hot lights overhead, obedient to the commands of a disembodied voice from somewhere high above. The sets and backdrops, which looked so opulent on screen, were actually flimsy, grey-painted plywood. Big cameras with four fat lenses glided silently and suddenly on rubber wheels. Soundless gnomes nipped about behind them, making sure the cables didn't get tangled. There was an overhead microphone that wound out on a telescopic boom like a giant fishing rod. Red lights winked. The floor manager did his countdown: 'Here we go. Quiet. Ten seconds . . . five . . .' Better than this, even, was that people knew you had done it. 'Saw you on TV last week,' they'd say. It was intoxicating, mesmerising. I wanted it.

✧

There was, however, the matter of my education. When we moved to Chatswood I first had to catch a bus to and from Barker by myself – at the age of five, something probably unthinkable today. There was no choice. My mother entrusted me to the care of a regular driver from the bus station at Chatswood and we would grind up the Pacific Highway to Hornsby for 15 kilometres in the morning and down again in the evening. With stops and starts it took about an hour each way. Somehow it worked. I was never molested, never lost. After a few years I was deemed old enough to catch the train without hurling myself out the manually operated doors or sticking my head out the window and smashing it on a steel railway stanchion.

Barker's primary school – the Junior School, they called it – was set up in a rambling Federation house called Rosewood, at the bottom of the campus. There were lawns to romp on, and big earthen banks where you could make roads and play with model cars called Dinky Toys. Down one fence there was a rabbit warren of scrub and tangled blackberry bushes where your gang could hide, to sally forth to do battle with another gang. A lot of alpha male fighting went on. A bloody nose was the red badge of courage. John Brice, a fellow alumnus of the Peter Rabbit Kindergarten, once stabbed me with a pencil. I still have the battle scar. Every morning, at break, we were ordered to drink a small bottle of milk, collected from a crate in the playground. This was just drinkable in winter. In summer, after cooking for hours in the sun, the milk had turned into stinking globs of pure penicillin. It was revolting.

Academically, I cruised along without making too much effort, generally at or near the top of my classes. In English I dashed off spirited compositions, as we called them, about What I Did In My Holidays. In the beginning we wrote with slender wooden pens tipped by removable steel nibs, which were dipped in little ceramic inkwells sunk into our desks. These, too, were a useful stabbing weapon. Copperplate writing was the go, heavy on the downstroke. Get it wrong and you could be smacked across the knuckles with the teacher's ruler. Later we were allowed to switch to fountain pens, but never to the new fangled ballpoints, which were an abomination, we were told.

In other fields of study I knew a Plantagenet from a Tudor or a Stuart, and I could parrot the names of all the coastal rivers of New South Wales from the Tweed to the Shoalhaven, for what it was worth. Learning by rote was the accepted method. History was the mindless tedium of memorising dates: 1770, Captain Cook. 1788 Captain Arthur Phillip. 1813, Blaxland, Lawson and Wentworth crossed the Blue Mountains. Poor Cook, the great navigator and explorer, copped a terrible beating in a popular verse of the day:

Captain Cook
Did a poop
Behind the dunny door.
The cat came in
And licked it up
And so he did some more.

Always good for a laugh, that.

In mathematics we chanted our multiplication tables every morning, up to twelve times twelve. We swallowed other vital facts: in a right-angled triangle the square of the length of the hypotenuse equals the sum of the squares of the lengths of the other two sides. I'm still not entirely sure what that means or why I needed to know it. Maths was my only true stumbling block, a failing that began to make itself apparent around Year 6. Soon enough it was grimly clear that I was a complete dunce at the subject. Like a great many journalists, I still am. If I were to chop off even one finger in some accident, decimals would be lost to me.

Mr Morris, my class teacher that year, told me not to worry about this. I had learned all the maths I would ever need to know, he assured me. I could add up and subtract, divide and multiply, so long as there was a sheet of paper on which to scratch the calculations. That was enough. My forte was English, he said. At worst I would be a journalist, at best a great dramatist, like the amusingly named William Shakespeare, a well-known English playwright. My mother hit the roof when I gleefully reported this back to her, but Mr Morris was entirely correct about the maths and pretty much everything else. He was the best teacher I ever had.

John Morris rejoiced in the nickname 'Beaky', bestowed in tribute to his enormous nose. It was roughly the shape of a ship's rudder, an organ so vast that it appeared around corners well before the rest of him. In a headwind he would have had to tack down the street like a yacht. This fazed him not at all. In fact I think he enjoyed the singularity of it, and nobody ever got into trouble if he overheard you calling him Beaky. Born in the working-class London borough of Hackney, he had emigrated from Britain after the war as a Ten Pound Pom, fed up with the class system, he told me much later. Australia seemed a better bet and for him it was; so, too, for the legions of kids who passed through his hands, first at Barker and later at Sydney Grammar. He had the gift of making every subject he taught pregnant with possibilities, sparkling with the excitement of discovery. He transmitted his enthusiasm to you and, in turn, you wanted to do anything to please him. His classroom rang with laughter. My brother says that Beaky once turned up at our home clad in a chimpanzee suit. It was he who urged me to listen to *The Goon Show*, that seminal BBC radio program (relayed on the ABC) which exploded all the conventions of broadcast comedy and set an entirely new course for British humour.

Beaky had known my father, and I think he took a special interest in me. More likely he took a special interest in everybody. I am sure it was he who turned me on to the beauties of the English language. He wrote poetry himself and was always dashing off acerbic letters to newspaper editors. He devoured encyclopaedias by the truckload, soaked up a vast general knowledge, and blitzed the field when he appeared as a quiz contestant on *Pick a Box* and another television smash, Tony Barber's *Great Temptation*, which won him a fair bit of money. Politically, he was a bomb-throwing leftie, I suppose. He had been disciplined in the RAF during the war for circulating communist pamphlets; long after my year with him, which was 1957, he became a gritty opponent of Australia's involvement in Vietnam.

Best of all, he despised meaningless and officious authority, and did his best to upset it, which cannot have sat easily with his job in an Anglican private school. Spurning the usual nativity tableau and worthy carolling at the end-of-year Christmas concerts, he wrote his own comedy and satirical sketches for his classes to perform. One of these nearly brought him undone. In my year with him there was a well-known TV commercial for Viscount cigarettes, with a catchy jingle. The closing lines went: 'Day time or night time, it's always the right time, to light up a Viscount, the best of them all.' Beaky decided to take a shot at it. He asked me and a couple of other kids to draw and paint a larger-than-life head-and-shoulders portrait of Field Marshal Viscount Montgomery, the victor of Alamein. This we did, copied from a photograph, and rather a good one it was, as I remember. In his black Tank Corps beret with its two badges, old Monty was instantly recognisable. Beaky despised him, for some unexplained reason. 'Weah heah to kill Jairmans,' he kept muttering to us in a Monty voice.

On the night of the concert, the portrait was placed on an easel on stage in the school assembly hall, shrouded by a sheet. A line of angelic kiddies, me included, stood in front of it, warbling the cigarette jingle. We were the closing act. At the climactic moment the sheet was whipped away and Beaky himself bounded on stage, that great nose to the fore like a Dreadnought battleship preparing to ram. He was brandishing a cigarette lighter. Cackling maniacally, he set fire to the picture, which had been sprinkled with kerosene. *Whooomp!* Up it went in tongues of flame and choking black smoke.

There was uproar. Half the parents were grossly offended by this gratuitous insult to the Great Man. When they got over their shock, they booed and hissed, probably the first and only time this has ever happened at a school concert anywhere in all history. Other parents, entirely reasonably, feared that the conflagration might burn down the hall and perhaps the entire school. A few dived for the exits with shouts and screams. Someone rushed on stage with a fire extinguisher, smothering with foam everything in sight, including us, and the stage curtains jerked closed on the chaos. It was, truly, one of the Great Moments. It nearly cost Beaky his job, I think, but for me it was a first heady taste of the thrill of both shocking and amusing an audience with outrageous behaviour. Subvert the dominant paradigm!

Beaky was delighted when I became a journalist, and he did me the honour of following my career, occasionally firing off a note of congratulations or perhaps a reproof for some sin of grammar or syntax. He died in late 2014, genuinely mourned by all who knew him, leaving his body to science.

✧

'Are you going to be as good as your dad?'

People kept asking me this at school athletics carnivals or pretty much any time I walked onto a football field. They meant it kindly, as encouragement, but I came to dread it. I had my father's physique and I was a fast enough runner, winning things ever since an early triumph in a kindergarten egg-and-spoon race, which passed into family legend. Nobody had explained to me that you weren't allowed to hold the egg in place with your thumb. But I shrank from shouldering the burden of their expectations. Why should I be as good as my father? And what if I wasn't? Sensibly, my mother understood this and made it plain: I did not have to compete with him. I should not even try. But the thought was enough to turn me off athletics for a few years. James Andrew Carlton hovered in my outer consciousness, though, a distant presence. I had no sense of bereavement, but my mother's words – 'You're the man of the family' – stayed with me. On special occasions, such as school speech nights or a rare outing to a cheap restaurant, I was allowed the enormous privilege of wearing my father's wristwatch.

Barker was keen on cricket. I hated it. It was obvious from day one that I was never going to be any good. Couldn't bat, couldn't bowl, couldn't field. In fact, then and now, I could not hit the side of a barn with a bucket of ping-pong balls. We were made to play it, though – good for character, team spirit – and I usually ended up in a fielding position best described as 'Sir, do we *have* to have Carlton on our team again?' Banished to the outfield, whenever a ball came my way I would be daydreaming about the Battle of the Atlantic or admiring an aircraft passing overhead. Four!

I tried tennis for a bit, but that was no better. I had the hand–eye coordination of a duck. After a while it became crushingly obvious that I was lousy at any game that required hitting a moving object with a stick, bat, racquet, cue or club, thus ruling out everything from ice hockey to badminton. I can enjoy watching cricket now, and I relish the ethos of the game at Test level, but that's it. Golf and I will remain forever strangers.

Swimming got me in. After my first terrifying encounter with Alf Vockler I came to love it, the sensuous silkiness of water on the body, the sheer delight of moving easily through liquid. Barker had a 25-metre outdoor pool, powered by a snorting, wheezing pump and an ancient filter system that never got the contents any clearer than a solid khaki. The daily addition of litres of schoolboy urine probably didn't help. The occasional turd floated by. We did not care. There was an hour of swimming class every Wednesday, and you could stay back after school to use the pool on specified days as well. We splashed and bombed in our regulation navy-blue speedos, first the old-fashioned, clingy cotton ones that had a skirt at the front to mask your pointy bits and weighed about a kilo wringing wet. When a new and briefer design arrived, unskirted, in a fabric called Terylene – as worn by Olympic champions – we seized it. The greasy Barker pool was my introduction to a lifelong love of water and the beach, a fundamental part of the Australian birthright.

Then there was rugby. Union, please, not League, which was common and vulgar. Soccer, of course, was a game played only by wogs and dagoes. It's true that, like almost every former football player I know, the older I get, the better I was. My shape and speed inevitably had me out on the wing, my father's position. For those who don't know rugby, that's pretty much the show-off slot on the field where you get to display your dash and flair, as opposed to the muddied oafs grinding their brutish, anonymous faces into each other's arses in the forward pack.

I ponced up and down like a cut-price Adonis, turning on a dazzling burst of speed and the occasional three-point try on those rare occasions that the ball ever made it out that far along the backline. In those days the wingers also got to throw the ball into the lineout, which I did with balletic skill. My only failing – and it was pretty fundamental – was that I was a lousy tackler. I missed almost every time, tackles that Nana herself could probably have made. Not so much because I was frightened of the violent body contact, although there might have been a bit of that; it was more the hand–eye coordination thing again. There would be some pint-sized kid from Knox Grammar or St Aloysius, ball held tight, head down, legs pumping, steaming towards the tryline with only me in his way. I was the last line of defence, the last hope. The moment was mine, and all eyes upon me. Carefully choosing exactly the worst moment, without fail I would make a heroic lunge in the wrong direction. The opposing midget would deftly dodge my flailing arms and skip over the line for another easy three points. The shame was mortifying.

No doubt pleased to be rid of me, the school accepted a proposal from my mother that I be excused the compulsory Saturday cricket games so I could concentrate on my soaring career in the Cubs. At the age of eleven, laden with all the laurels and honours a Cub could command, I had to put it all behind me and move on and up, to become a Scout.

It was back to square one again. In the 1st Lindfield Scout Troop I was now the lowest form of life, surrounded by boisterous adolescents whose voices were breaking as they plunged into puberty. Some of them were as old as fourteen. Their khaki shirts were decorated, badged and bemedalled like a North Korean general's. My own shirt, second-hand again, bore all the marks of the previous owner's achievements, which my mother had laboriously unpicked. The woggle remained the same and so did the ridiculous blue, knee-length woollen shorts, but the green Cubs' cap gave way to the marginally more sensible brown felt Scouts' hat, like Akela's. You were supposed to steam and iron the brim to a steely flat rigidity, but the grizzled teenage veterans at 1st Lindfield liked to wear theirs floppy, as if they'd just returned from fighting the Japanese on the Kokoda Track.

I was assigned to a group of six or eight boys of varying ages, known as a patrol. We were commanded by a patrol leader, whose rank was denoted by two vertical white stripes sewn to his left chest pocket. The days of dybbing and dobbing were over. I was to be inducted into the arcane mysteries of Scout lore, as laid down by the movement's founder, the storied Lieutenant General Robert Stephenson Smyth Baden-Powell, 1st Baron Baden-Powell of Gilwell, OM GCMG GCVO KCB DL.

B-P, as he was reverently known, was long dead by the time I got there. But he had served two monarchs, Victoria and Edward VII, as a soldier and builder of Empire. A product of Charterhouse, a posh British public school, in an army career of three decades he had fought the Ashanti, the Zulu, the Ndebele, the Shona and the Boer. In the Second Boer War, when still a colonel, he had commanded the beleaguered garrison at the Siege of Mafeking, boldly holding out against a far larger force of marauding Afrikaners for 217 days. When Mafeking was relieved in May 1900, there was near-hysterical rejoicing throughout the Empire and Baden-Powell was acclaimed a hero, an inspiration. He returned home in triumph, like Caesar. It was Edward himself who urged B-P to put his knowledge of scouting and bushcraft, his tenets of discipline and loyalty, to the great service of bracing the physical and moral fibre of the boys of the Empire. Or the white ones, anyway.

His Lordship set it out in a manual called *Scouting for Boys*, first published in 1908.[45] In it was all of life as he saw it. It opened with The Promise:

> On my honour I promise that I will do my best. 1) To do my duty to God and the Queen. 2) To help other people at all times. 3) To obey the Scout Law.

As with the biblical Commandments, there were actually ten Scout Laws, exhorting Scouts to be honourable, useful, friendly, courteous, obedient and thrifty, and to smile and whistle under all difficulties. Law Number 10, always the most invoked, proclaimed: 'A Scout is clean in thought, word and deed.' There were detailed chapters on such topics as Scoutcraft, Woodcraft, Camp Life, Patriotism and Chivalry of the Knights. B-P offered useful advice on how to track a giraffe or a wildebeest across the Serengeti; on closely observing your fellow bus passengers in case one of them might be a criminal; on what to do if you encountered a corpse; and on how to avoid disease (breathe through your nose and keep your blood in good order). In the chapter titled Endurance there was a stern caution against drinking and smoking, and an entire section warning of a practice B-P could bring himself to refer to only as 'beastliness': 'a secret vice which gets hold of so many fellows'.

It was pretty opaque, but apparently beastliness could be brought on by the reading of trashy books or from looking at lewd pictures. Also by indigestion, constipation, bad dreams or sleeping on your back. But if you had any manliness in you, temptation could be spurned by bathing at once in cold water and by exercising the upper body.

Swot that I was, I sucked all this in, voraciously. Within months I was ready for the 1st Lindfield annual camp, highlight of the year. Canvas tents, ridge poles and stout timber uprights, wooden staves, miles of rope and other camping paraphernalia, kitchen pots and pans, billies and kettles, and provisions for a week were loaded aboard an open truck. In what today would be regarded as criminally negligent folly, we perched with our hiking packs atop that great heap of cargo, open to the elements, utterly unprotected, clinging to whatever we could and singing lustily as this juggernaut lurched up the Pacific Highway towards the Colo River. It was a miracle no one was killed.

My patrol leader, Chris, was all Baden-Powell could have hoped for. Fourteen years old, a star student and athlete at Shore – the Sydney Church of England Grammar School – scion of a wealthy family, long of limb and chiselled of chin, his eyes a piercing blue, he had the bearing of a junior Greek god. He was the Scout Law sculpted in bone and muscle. If there was a sudden call for a criminal to be laid by the heels or a wildebeest to be tracked, Chris was your man. Under his crisp command, in no time our tent was erected as taut as a drum, its square lashings and frapping turns rock-solid, each rolling hitch a thing of beauty. Up went the kitchen and the bracken-covered bush larder. Our scoutmaster, known as Skipper or Skip, was loud in his praises. That night we made merry around the campfire with yarns and songs. There was one song called 'Ging Gang Goolie', which I won't inflict on readers in its entirety. You'll get the drift when I tell you its closing lines: 'Shally wally, shally wally, shally wally, shally wally / Oompah, oompah, stick it up your joompah.' Tired but happy, we retired for the night.

I was almost asleep when I heard a panting and grunting noise from the other end of the tent. Puzzled, I looked over. In the moonlight, I could see Chris's sleeping bag pulsating and leaping as if there was a ferret inside that was trying to claw its way out. Other boys began to notice too. The grunting grew louder, the ferret more vigorous; Chris's face, oblivious to his audience, was contorted in what looked like pain. What on earth could be happening? Was he having a fit?

'Should we call Skip?' I asked the boy next to me, a seasoned campaigner of twelve.

'Nah,' he said. 'He's got a stiffy. He's just giving it a rub.'

Stiffies I knew. This unpredictable phenomenon had been creeping up on me with increasing frequency for some time, often at hideously embarrassing moments. The sight of Claudia Collis splashing under the hose next door was a common accelerant, as were those gentlemen's picture magazines you read at the barber while waiting for a haircut: 'Our photographer caught busty Belinda trying out her new bikini at Sydney's Bondi Beach . . .' There'd be Belinda bazooming out of a cossie that these days wouldn't alarm a closed order of nuns, but which then was the very height of *phwoar*. Up I would go. And a stiffy was a feature of my mornings as regular as the sunrise, although I had no idea why. At that stage, my mother's attempts at sex education had been limited to: 'Don't touch yourself down there, Michael, it's dirty.' Never in all her life did I hear her utter the word 'penis'.

'Giving it a rub?' I asked. 'What for?'

'He's pulling himself off. Wants to spunk.'

Spunk? Pretty much at that moment Chris gave a final exultant gasp and the leaping ferret subsided. After a short pause for heavy breathing, he sat up and surveyed the admiring audience. 'There ya go,' he said with a wide grin. He subsided contentedly onto his pillow, a rolled towel.

I pondered this for quite a while. Could this be beastliness, perhaps? Surely not.

✧

The coming of television in 1956 sent radio heading for the rocks. The audience voted with its feet for the new medium and the big-money sponsors followed. A few of the top radio stars made a successful change to the small, grey screen, among them Bob Dyer with *Pick a Box* and a pop-eyed radio comic in Melbourne, Graham Kennedy. Others, like Jack Davey, tried but never quite made it. Radio, both as entertainment and as business model, was in deep trouble.

Three things came together to save it, a junction at the perfect moment. The Americans had invented the transistor in 1947, but it was the Japanese ten years later who showered the waiting world with cheap, small, mass-produced transistor radios. If you wanted to listen to something, you were no longer anchored to the big brown wireless in the corner of the lounge room. You could move your battery-powered tranny around the house, from the bedroom to the laundry to the garden, or take it to the beach or the races or wherever. Cars began to appear with transistor radios as a standard feature.

The second saviour was the Top 40 format. Radio hit parades of pop music had been around for a while, a list of ten or twelve songs played rather decorously over an hour in ascending order, usually on a Saturday night. 'And now our Number One tune is . . .' Top 40 blew that apart, with a playlist of 40 songs (often more) played on high rotation throughout the day and night. That in turn gave birth to the disc jockey as radio star.

The third of the trinity was rock'n'roll itself. When Bill Haley and the Comets blasted onto the airwaves and the charts with 'Rock Around the Clock' in 1954, the genie was out of the bottle. This was something new, thrilling and even sexy for the disc jockeys to play: then Chuck Berry did 'Sweet Little Sixteen', Jerry Lee Lewis made 'Great Balls of Fire' and Elvis Presley had a brace of hits including 'Hard Headed Woman', 'Don't' and 'Wear My Ring Around Your Neck'.

Slowly, Australians also got in on the act. Johnny O'Keefe, a son of the Mayor of Waverley in Sydney, had met Haley when he toured Australia in 1957 and been starstruck. Short and tending to podgy, O'Keefe was an unlikely candidate for rock'n'roll fame. As a singer he was dead ordinary, missing notes left, right and centre. But he had a knockabout larrikin charm, an inborn showmanship and a manic determination to succeed, and in 1958 he and his band, the Dee Jays, released a string of hits, including 'So Tough' and his signature song, 'Wild One'. With his outrageous suits of gold lamé and fire-engine red, JOK was on the way.

Sydney's oldest commercial station, 2UE, on air in 1925, was the first to pick the trend. Like so much in Australian commercial radio, the Top 40 format was pinched from the US, the supposed font of all radio creativity and wisdom. If it was Yank, it had to be good.

A Scottish-born businessman, John Lamb, a former tailor in Newcastle and radio buff, had bought 2UE from the John Fairfax newspaper company in 1954 for the bargain basement price of £165,000 (about $5.5 million nowadays). Two years later that decision was looking like a shocker; the shower of gold was rapidly drying up. Lamb, wealthy and astute, sent program executives to camp in American hotel rooms, where they listened to the most successful radio stations there. The Top 40 is what they came back with. Best of all for the penny-counting Lamb family, the format was cheap to run. No more costly drama productions or live quiz shows. All you needed was a pile of records and half a dozen announcers, who, in the early days at least, came pretty cheaply too.

Salvation! In March 1958 2UE released its first Top 40 list of songs, a cheaply printed single sheet of paper to be given away free as a promotional gimmick in record stores and electrical shops. Ostensibly it was compiled from retail sales figures of pop music, but in fact it was usually fiddled by the program directors to push the songs and hits they liked or that would appeal to their target audience. Or, in some cases later on, songs the record companies had bribed them to push. Pat Boone's 'April Love' was the first Top 40 number one.

At which point cue the disc jockey, another American creation faithfully copied here. The music and the advertising had to be glued together with snappy chat, rapid-fire patter studded with the latest American slang. 'Hey there, hep cats, now let's dig this!' Bob Rogers, a bespectacled farmer's boy from country Victoria, was arguably Australia's first true DJ, beginning his radio life as a junior dogsbody at Melbourne's 3XY in 1942, then working his way on air at stations around the country, as you had to do then.[46] In 1957 he was the first to play Slim Dusty's iconic 'Pub With No Beer' and turn it into a hit. It made his career. A year later Bob launched the first Top 40 shows for the Lamb family and 2UE. His opening theme was (and still is) Bunny Berigan's 'I Can't Get Started', a smoky old trumpet piece. It would fade down after a couple of bars and then on he'd come, all razzle and dazzle: 'Hidey-hodey, every-bodey! You're with me, Robert B. On 2UE . . .'

Top 40 took off like a rocket. The audience surged back to daytime radio. In Sydney, 2UE had it all. Gary O'Callaghan, built like an Irish jockey but big-voiced, did the *Breakfast Show*, rabbiting on about the weather and the traffic and, at eight-fifteen every morning, introducing Sammy the Sparrow for the kiddies. Gary did the sparrow voice as well, talking to himself in a falsetto squawk. 'Eeeeee, hello, boys and girls, hello, Uncle Gary!' Sponsors queued to get back on board. Pretty soon Sammy was eating Anderson's famous pork sausages for breakfast and saving his money with the Bank of New South Wales. Talking fauna were big on breakfast radio back then. At rival 2UW, breakfast presenter Russ Walkington had Gerald the Grasshopper.

And then there was John Laws, born in New Guinea, tall and lanky, a two-time survivor of polio. Like Bob Rogers, John had learned the trade by flogging his way around small-time country radio stations where you had to do everything. The apprenticeship was a hard grind, but invaluable. First, you learned to operate a radio panel with all its meters and knobs and dials and faders and turntables, and how to cue a record so that the song started exactly when you wanted it to. You watched the studio clock like a hawk, timing your music to end right on the pips before the news. God help you if you crossed late to Randwick in Sydney or Flemington in Melbourne and missed the start of the next race, networked by one of the big-city stations.

With that mastered, you began to discover what a microphone could do with your voice. How to read a commercial and make it sound as if you meant it. How to announce the funeral notices in a suitably Gothic tone. Often on the smaller stations you had to sell the advertising time to local businesses. On pain of death, you had to play or read the commercials in the right order at the right time. And, as they said, when you finished your shift on air you shoved a broom up your arse and swept the studio floor on the way out. If you got all that right, then perhaps – just perhaps – you might be snapped up by one of the big-city stations for stardom. Not many were.

Even in the early 2UE days, the John Laws voice had an almost hypnotic quality to it. A deeper, more resonant baritone than the Rogers tenor, it loved the microphone and the microphone loved it. He had the patter, too, made familiar by repetition. Buddy Holly, one of the biggest rock stars of the day, he invariably introduced as 'the twenty-one-year-old, bespectacled Texan boy'. And so on. It was Laws who thought of getting friendly Qantas stewards to bring him the latest hit records from the States so he could play them before the record companies released them in Australia. That was the beginning of his rivalry with Bob Rogers, a clash that became radio's angriest and longest-lasting feud.

A wealthy uncle gave my mother one of these new radios, a model about the size and weight of a hardback novel, made by National Panasonic. It came in a brown leather case, with a telescopic aerial about a metre long. Its reception was way better than that of the big box in the corner, which tended to whistle and fart in unsettled weather. We thought it was Christmas. I would race home from school, snatch the radio from my mother's bedroom, fling myself on my own bed and listen to Laws or another jock, Tony Withers, until the thing was prised from my grasp and I was ordered to do my homework. Most of my school friends did the same. It was enthralling, engrossing, exciting.

On Tuesdays, when 2UE published its Top 40 list, I ran down to Cassidy's store to collect it. Tens of thousands of other people were reading it too. Would Elvis the Pelvis knock the Everly Brothers from the top spot? Oh, look, Ricky Nelson is on the way out at number thirty. And who was the Big Bopper? We compared notes at school the next day, gravely offering our own predictions for the coming week.

Once Bob Rogers turned up at Chatswood High School to broadcast his show live there, splendid in a black bomber jacket with 'Robert B' embroidered on the back in purple. Nana would have deemed it common and vulgar, but I went along and was in awe. Magic! I watched, spellbound, as he cued the discs on turntables as big as car tyres. He wore headphones. 'Hello, Mr Rogers,' I said.

'Hidey-hodey,' he replied.

How wonderful it was! Sneakily, when no one was home, I practised cueing discs on my mother's little HMV record player. You lowered the stylus onto the record, then squawked it back and forth until it was in exactly the right spot for an instant start. Sadly, it actually didn't work on domestic players. Radio studio turntables were different. My mother never discovered why her treasured albums of Rodgers & Hammerstein musicals were scored and scratched at the start of the first track.

I can't pretend I decided then that I wanted to be in radio. There was no thunderclap moment when the clouds parted to reveal a future in broadcasting shimmering before me. But the seed Keith Smith had planted with *A Word from Children* had begun to grow. I was only dimly aware of it at the time, though, if at all. I still wanted to command a destroyer.

✧

A lot happened in 1958. Charles de Gaulle was elected President of the French Fifth Republic. After a hard-fought battle in the College of Cardinals, Angelo Giuseppe Roncalli became Pope John XXIII. Nikita Khrushchev bested his rivals in the Kremlin to seize the Soviet premiership, and Fidel Castro started his revolution in Cuba. In the US, the junior Senator for Massachusetts, the Democrat John F. Kennedy, won a second term in Washington and began his campaign for the presidency in the election due two years later. In a typhoon of publicity, Elvis Presley was drafted into the US Army.

At the age of twenty, Australia's Herb Elliott became the youngest man to run a mile in under four minutes, and kept grinding down the times until in August, in Dublin, he stunned the crowd with a world-beating 3:54.5. The artist Albert Namatjira, the first Indigenous person to be granted Australian citizenship, was sentenced to six months' jail for the crime of supplying alcohol to an Aboriginal ward of the state. Robert Gordon Menzies, with Nana's invaluable help, won his fifth election against a Labor Party still shattered by its infamous 1950s split. Holden released its FC model with a stonking 2.2-litre engine and a three-speed manual gearbox; the truly rich could buy it with a two-tone paint job. St George beat the Western Suburbs Magpies 20–9 to win the New South Wales Rugby League premiership, while Collingwood beat Melbourne in the Victorian Football League decider. The Antarctic explorer Sir Douglas Mawson died.

And Michael Carlton went to high school.

5

Kiss me goodnight, sergeant major

THE JOURNEY UP THE hill from the Barker Junior School to the Senior School was a leap in time and space. Suddenly you were at the bottom of the heap again, surrounded by boys of great experience and seniority. It was like being a rookie on the astronaut program. The compensation was that at last you got to wear long pants instead of knee-length shorts, and white shirts instead of grey ones, a rite of passage. The uniform was a suit of jacket and trousers, in wool of battleship grey, made by the Stamina company, complete with grey socks, black shoes and a red-and-blue-striped Barker tie.

The rich kids, or even the moderately comfortably-off kids – I was beginning to notice the social layers – bought their uniforms from David Jones or from Peapes, an upmarket, now defunct menswear store in the city. My stuff came from the school clothing pool, second-hand. Not once in five years of secondary education did I have a jacket that matched the pants, a sartorial burden I bore with increasing despair as I got older and more clothes-conscious, but which nobody else ever seemed to notice. Still, long pants were long pants, and for the first few weeks I preened in public with what I believed was an elegant nonchalance, certain the admiring eyes of the world were upon me.

We also wore boaters. If the Wolf Cub cap was silly, the straw boater was downright ludicrous, another imperial cultural cringe. Chaps wore them at Eton and Harrow and, indeed, at the famous Henley Regatta on the Thames. They were, therefore, more than good enough for Barker and most of Sydney's male private schools. The only other known wearers were American barbershop quartets and the ageing French *chansonnier* Maurice Chevalier. With a straw brim about five centimetres wide, they were useless for keeping the sun off your face, and in drenching Australian rain they tended to melt into a sodden lump of gluey straw.

There were some advantages, though. When it was properly coated in clear varnish, as you were supposed to do, the brim had the tensile strength of cold-rolled carbon steel, making a useful weapon which you could either bring down on your opponent's nose with the force of a guillotine blade or hurl horizontally like a lethal frisbee. Glen Mace, the most rebellious kid in our class, turned up the brim of his boater at each side so he looked like Hopalong Cassidy, a great crime. The nerds plonked theirs flat on their heads. The rest of us, effortlessly cool, wore ours *à la mode* Chevalier, tipped forward at a gravity-defying angle that permitted vision from one eye only.

Books and anything else were carried in a brown Globite suitcase, an Australian invention that in its day ranked as a cultural icon alongside Vegemite and the Early Kooka stove. I had vaguely understood that Globite was a rare mineral, probably mined in a remote part of the Northern Territory, but it was actually a brand name for bags made from a mysterious compressed fibre of some sort. They were useful for sitting on while you waited for a train and, in an emergency, could also be deployed as a shield from flying boaters.

The train to school was a forty-minute journey to Waitara, nine stations up the North Shore line. Again, cool came into it. The carriages were known as Red Rattlers. Some were made of vintage wood from the 1920s. None had automatic doors. Cool was to stand as close to the open doors as possible while the train thundered along, swaying effortlessly like a sailor on a rolling deck. I suppose hundreds of kids died this way each year, falling from the doorways, the railway lines strewn with their corpses, the authorities covering up the statistics. Almost as perilous was the way you alighted from the carriage, which had to be done at speed. As the train clattered into the station you jumped out, boater in one hand, Globite in the other, and skidded to a halt in an upright position. Occasionally you might misjudge the leap and skid to a halt against a file of waiting passengers, mowing them down like ninepins. Get it wrong entirely, which a few kids did, and you could plough a furrow along the station platform with your face, leaving a trail of flesh and blood.

It was on the train home from school that I was molested by a paedophile. I would have been about fourteen. A small, hunchbacked man squeezed into the seat beside me, holding a raincoat over his lap to conceal the grope he was making for my groin. Bewildered and frightened, I jumped from the carriage at the next station. The memory of the creep of his caterpillar fingers has never left me.

Enid and I now had to decide what subjects I would study. Classes then were allocated by academic ability, the supposedly smart kids in the A class, the dopes in the C. I was in the A class more by accident than design, which meant that there were some subjects I had to do and some I could not. We were shunted into Latin. The C class boys did woodwork instead, a division I have forever regretted. Even though it was largely concerned with the manufacture of trays, chopping boards and the occasional small bookcase, woodwork would have been far more useful to me. To this day I cannot hammer a nail without splitting the timber or crushing a thumb. I have a reverent respect for carpenters and cabinetmakers.

Meanwhile, I hated Latin. With the arrogance of youth, I could see no point in learning a dead language that nobody spoke anymore, and our Latin teacher Jack Saint, a ponderous drone, was incapable of awakening us to its magic. People said it was useful if you wanted to become a doctor because parts of the body were named in Latin, but that wasn't a big drawcard. Period after period after tedious period we parroted the verbs – *Amo, amas, amat, amamus, amatis, amant* – or trudged through the bogs and thickets of Julius Caesar's account of his Gallic Wars. In three years I never got much beyond his first sentence: *Gallia est omnis divisa in partes tres blah blah blah.* In my final Latin exam, for the Year 9 Intermediate Certificate, I scored an imposing nine marks out of 100. Three were for neatness and spelling my name correctly at the top of the paper, I was acidly informed.

French was better. Eventually you could speak to French people. In France, even. And you had to pay attention in the classes because our first French teacher, a *boulevardier* named Spike Jones, had 360-degree vision, over-the-horizon radar and a throwing arm which could project a piece of chalk to hit your nose with the accuracy and velocity of a fly-by-wire missile. Spike was eventually replaced by Mr Schloss, a genuine Frenchman from Alsace, for whom I still feel deep pangs of guilt.

Mr Schloss – inevitably nicknamed Slosh – had reputedly been in the Resistance and tortured by the Gestapo, but even that could not have prepared him for the hell we put him through. We were merciless. Short and dumpy, he was shaped like a brioche, with the face of one of those particularly doleful Russian clowns and an accent in English which we mocked as endlessly comical. How we laughed. Discipline was beyond him and, alert to any perceived weakness in a teacher, we seized upon it like timber wolves at a deer. Slosh's classes were never conducted at any level below uproar. We rarely bothered to do any homework or hand it in for marking, and we swapped identities regularly, so that the poor man was never sure if he was talking to Carlton, Rigney, Mace or Sheppard. Again we learned by rote: *La plume de ma tante est sur le bureau de mon oncle. Le papier de mon oncle est sur le bureau de ma tante.* Someone discovered the line *Voulez-vous couchez avec moi ce soir, chérie?* With an air of puzzled innocence, one of us would ask him to translate it on an almost daily basis. Doggedly, he did. He gave his all in the service of *la patrie* and *la culture française*. If I am wrong and there is a God, I hope he has assigned Mr Schloss a place of honour in a celestial *Académie française*, to savour a Lafite Rothschild and enjoy a romping *déjeuner sur l'herbe* in some sun-dappled forest glade with the very willing Mesdames de Montespan and de Pompadour. He earned it.

Despite all that, I did manage to learn a bit of French. But as Beaky had correctly divined in sixth class, mathematics and the sciences were a dead loss. Algebra, logarithms and trigonometry were utterly beyond me. Chemistry was taught by a grizzled bear named 'Loco'

Latham, who inhabited a dark and stinky cave of a laboratory in the bowels of the school, where no daylight penetrated. It was smelly because Loco, against all the rules, chain-smoked his way through his classes. Only the swots sitting in the front row could see him through the choking fug, and then but dimly. For everyone else it was like trying to find Colonel Kurtz in *Apocalypse Now*.

Nor could he see most of us, and his incoherent mumble did not help the teaching process. 'Mmmahummerherm hydrogen peroxide,' he would mutter. 'Ummmerum sulphuric acid hermemmeah.' This would be followed by a rasping cough. Sometimes in the gloom you could detect a sudden bright flash or an extra cloud of smoke, or perhaps some purple liquid fizzing in a test tube, but to what purpose it was impossible to say.

Most of us just did whatever took our fancy. Garry Weatherspoon, a serial masturbator and much admired for it, sharpened up his technique beneath the bench in the back row. Graham Lawson devised a trick of extinguishing all the Bunsen burners by blowing sharply into a rubber tube. I bent my best efforts to drawing warships in my experiment book. In forty minutes I could turn out a battleship *Bismarck* or a Tribal Class destroyer accurate to every halliard and gun turret.

There were other weird and wacky teachers. Stacey Hunt, the economics teacher, was a likeable man and good at his stuff, but he came to grief over the iron laws of supply and demand when the police arrested him for shoplifting at Woolworths. A search of his room at school found a trove of treasure he had nicked from the boarders: watches, transistor radios and the like. Mr Sillitoe, a relief geography teacher, bald as a ping-pong ball, lasted a term after he assured us that the world was in fact flat. In the olden days, ships had fallen off the edge. Another man, whose name I have forgotten, vanished overnight after he was caught in the boarders' showers ordering the lads to bend over and touch their toes while he inspected their bums for cleanliness.

Yet these were the exceptions, not the rule. The teachers weren't all nuts – by no means – and we didn't beat them all. Far from it. My maths teacher, Gordon 'Grim' Miller, ran a tight ship. 'I will explain this again for Carlton,' he once said with a heavy sigh, eyeballs rolling.

'Not because Carlton is bad at maths. But because Carlton is abominably, appallingly bad at maths.' It was a fair comment.

The man who truly ran the show, though, a fearsome disciplinarian who cowed us all, was Bob Finlay, the deputy headmaster and senior English teacher. I can't recall ever seeing him smile, perhaps because he bore the sorrow of a daughter accidentally burned to death in a fire at the Barker flats where we had lived. But he had been a friend of my father, and I know now that he took an extra interest in my welfare. It was hard to see it at the time. Short and stout, with a clipped moustache and a gimlet gaze behind heavy spectacles, he was known as the Little King, after a popular newspaper cartoon strip. He glided silently along the corridors and around the playgrounds as if he rolled on rubber tyres, a pile of books and a box of chalk held out in front like a rocket launcher, academic gown swishing behind. He smoked a foul-smelling pipe which emitted a cloud of sulphurous fumes that must have drilled holes in the ozone layer. It was like a gas attack on the Western Front. If you were downwind, the stink gave you some warning he was about and you could take cover. Upwind, you were lost.

Mr Finlay could descend like sudden death on the bold and the bad, with the frightening command to 'see me in my study after three o'clock'. That almost always meant a beating, ferocious whacks on the backside with a thin rattan cane about a metre long. The number of strokes you got depended on the enormity of the crime. Six was the most ever given, always known as 'six of the best'. And Bob Finlay was a master of the art. You kept your pants and jocks on, but he still left thin red lines across your buttocks, as neatly placed as tram tracks. It hurt. You had to clench your teeth and bear it. To cry was to show weakness. At lunchtime you went to the toilets to drop your daks and display the wounds to a knowledgeable and admiring crowd. It sounds barbaric, but that's the way it was. A couple of teachers were clearly sadists and enjoyed it. Others shrank from it, preferring to keep you back after school, endlessly writing lines. 'I must not pick my nose in class, I must not pick my nose in class . . .' Most of us preferred the cane. It was quicker.

For all this, Bob Finlay was a good and caring teacher. Probably a great one. He was passionate about the English language and he transmitted that passion to me and many others with force and dedication. Anything I write today – the career I followed, the money I earned, the life I lead – is built on the foundations he laid. He taught us grammar and syntax, parsing and analysis, the lot: subject, verb and object, tenses, active and passive voice, nouns, pronouns singular and plural, gerunds, prepositions, conjunctions, past and perfect participles (and the evil of the dangling participle), subjunctives and superlatives, adjectival phrases, adverbial clauses, split infinitives, the correct placement of apostrophes and commas. He showed us what Winston Churchill called that noble thing, 'the essential structure of the ordinary British sentence'. For that I am ever grateful. And saddened that this treasury of knowledge is all but lost in an era when everything – a Shakespearean sonnet or a Tweet – is just another 'text'.

There was one more lesson he left us, or me anyway. It was a lesson of character. There was an old bloke named Tom, a taciturn and simple man who spent his days and years endlessly raking fallen leaves in the school grounds, mumbling to himself. One day Bob Finlay caught a clutch of boys tormenting him, stealing his rake and his hat, scattering the piles of leaves he had gathered. The Little King went critical mass. The tormentors each got six of the best, delivered, I imagine, with extra ferocity. The next day he ordered the entire school to an assembly, and there, arcing up in a crescendo of anger, he flayed us as the insensitive, arrogant, conceited little sons of wealth and privilege that many of us undoubtedly were. It went for about half an hour. It was unforgettable. One phrase stuck with me, indelibly: 'the dignity of labour'.

✧

Life away from school began to hum. I did jobs for pocket money, riding my bike to deliver orders for a chemist, and polishing the brass nameplates of the doctors in the building where my mother worked. My first big break in the news business came when I got a job selling newspapers for Kenny at Chatswood Station, before and after school.

Kenny – I never discovered his surname – was a little bloke who wore a cloth cap and hobbled with a stick. Everyone knew him. He had a green-painted wooden stand of newspapers and magazines, which he trundled into position on one side of the station. I covered the other side with a bunch of papers held in a leather strap slung over one shoulder and a leather moneybag around my waist. Kindly and amiable, Kenny taught me the skills of the trade. There was the paper-seller's cry: '*Paaaaaaaaaaayyyy-erp. Teleherald. Sun-a-Mirraaaaaah. Last race!*' There was the art of extracting the correct paper from your bundle, folding it in half at lightning speed and slipping it into the buyer's hand while taking the money and juggling the change with the other. You lingered a bit over the change, though, in the hope of a tip. I think I could still do it. Kenny got a bit cross when I ventured to lift the marketing strategy by shouting out the front-page headlines from the afternoon tabloids – 'Harbour Ferry Crash!' He thought it a bit excessive. 'Something the Yanks do, but not us,' he cautioned.

At fifteen I moved into retailing. Grace Bros, a national chain of department stores, opened up in Chatswood, smack-bang on the land my grandfather had rejected as too far from town. They wanted kids who would work on busy Saturday mornings until midday, when everything shut down, and over the Christmas rush. It was glamorous, exciting, very grown-up. You got real pay: £1.0.10 for three hours on Saturday – worth about $30 today. I was assigned to the menswear department, first selling socks and undies – hard to go wrong there – and then the more tricky business of men's casual, which meant shorts, shirts and swimwear. The Head of Menswear, Mr Stanhope, took me in hand, demonstrating how to work a cash register, how to take a lay-by. He fed me the lines. 'Yes, sir, suits you very well,' I would say with lofty assurance to customers three times my age. 'And it practically irons itself . . .'

The affable Mr Stanhope was pleased with my progress, so much so that over the Christmas holiday period, when I was working a full day, he would invite me to share his morning tea break or sometimes even lunch in the staff canteen, a signal honour for one so junior. Occasionally he would slip me a free pair of undies or swimmers. 'A little reward,' he would say with a conspiratorial wink. 'Pop into the changing room and try them on. I'll see if they fit.' I was flattered by his helpful concern.

One day, to much excitement, the Menswear Buyer – an exalted figure senior even to Mr Stanhope – announced that there would be a fashion parade of men's casual wear on the Saturday before Christmas. The Grace Bros display department laid out a catwalk and lighting, rows of chairs and a PA system. The storeroom out the back was jammed with racks of clothing, mirrors, make-up persons, hairdressers and assorted hangers-on. Three male models tossed their heads, flexed their biceps and snorted and pranced like racehorses.

Mr Stanhope grabbed me by the arm, in high fluster. 'One of the models hasn't turned up,' he hissed. 'We need four! You'll have to go on.'

'Me?'

'Yes, you. It's easy. Someone will hand you the clothes. You're the right size. Put 'em on. Watch what the others do. You walk out when your name's called. Smile. Stroll around, turn this way and that, come back in for the next lot. *You can do it!*'

Never had I been offered such a fabulous opportunity to show off. I *could* do it. I *would* do it. I was daubed with make-up. My hair was sprayed. It felt a bit uncomfortable at first, stripping stark-naked behind a curtain in the storeroom and whipping into a new lot of this and that, but I went to it with a will. Mr Stanhope looked on approvingly. Lining up with the three thoroughbreds – who either ignored the intruder or glared as if I had just farted – I sauntered in and out along the catwalk in tailored shorts, beach shorts, beach shirts, beach pyjamas. The woman at the microphone – whose mission in life was evidently to coat, spray, soak and paint herself in anything ever made by Elizabeth Arden, Max Factor and Helena Rubinstein – gave a running commentary. 'Now here's Michael. And, ladies, he's wearing the new Casben drip-dry swim shorts in a lovely high fashion shade of teal and coral . . .'

I was loving it. What a hoot. The world was watching. I was a star. There was even the odd spattering of applause. And I was getting paid extra, too. I started to prance like the racehorses, seeing a modelling career ahead, or at least a rewarding sideline. My last bit of gear was a pair of speedos, fire engine red. I slipped into them behind the curtain. It was all too much for Mr Stanhope. Wild-eyed, grinning like a cat, he plunged a hand inside them and began to rearrange my penis. 'Just want to make sure everything's sitting right,' he snorted heavily, fumbling away.

God – he was a poof! I snatched his hand out but, against all my will, against every desire of my being, I could feel my groin starting to stir. Nothing could stop it. I lurched out of his grasp. Waiting at the entrance to the catwalk for my turn, I suddenly saw that the sister of a schoolmate had joined the crowd. She was right at the front with her mother. I'd had the hots for her for a while. Kim Slater: blonde, gorgeous, an Abbotsleigh girl. Infinitely desirable. It was too much, way too much.

Kent or Clint Racehorse finished his speedo walk and I was back on. 'Now here's Michael again,' smarmed microphone lady. 'And Michael's wearing —'

She stopped with a little gasp as I stepped into the light. Rampant. What Michael was wearing was the Empire State Building down his sluggos. It could not have been more obvious if King Kong had been clutching it with one hand and Fay Wray with the other. There was no escaping it – not for me, not for anyone within a hundred metres. Kim Slater stared open-mouthed.

After a strangled gulp, the compere carried on bravely, although her make-up had cracked like a dry billabong. 'These, er, red racing speedos . . . um . . . a must for the active young man at the beach or pool . . .'

Every eye in Grace Bros was on me – at least, that's how it felt. There were sniggers, chortles, titters. Kim Slater giggled. Terrified that his thrusting member might escape entirely, mouth contorted in a ghastly rictus, the active young man raced around the catwalk as if it were on fire and plunged back into the safety of the storeroom.

'You were fabulous,' said Mr Stanhope, dewy-eyed. 'Lunch?'

✧

Big Tobacco got us early. I guess I was about thirteen when I smoked my first cigarette, coughing and gagging. An older kid gave it to me at Scouts, a token of acceptance into the higher councils of the tribe. We had a smoke or two before the meeting on a Friday night, hiding away under the Scout Hut, occasionally enhancing the pleasures of tobacco with a simultaneous wank. My subconscious dredges up a cringe-making image of four or five of us seated in a circle in the darkness, shorts around our knees, solemnly waving a cigarette in one hand and jacking off with the other.

Stuyvos were the preferred brand. The commercial for Peter Stuyvesant cigarettes on television was high glamour, and the extended version for the cinema – about two minutes long, in Technicolor and CinemaScope – was a work of art. Jet airliners left the runway to a stirring brass fanfare. There were shots of yachts, sports cars, ski slopes, the Eiffel Tower. Suntanned models in outsized sunglasses lounged about in Monte Carlo or on the Piazza Navona, puffing away and laughing uproariously. 'Paris, Rome, London, New York. Wherever life is young, gay, exciting – there you'll find Peter Stuyvesant,' said the voiceover. 'The international passport to smoking pleasure!' We took this very literally, and we were hooked. Stuyvos were reckoned to be far superior to the Marlboro brand, with its hokey cowboy image. A packet of twenty cost about 1/6, or 15 cents.

Gradually I ascended the Scouting totem pole until, at fourteen, I attained the honour of commanding the Kookaburra Patrol. Skip had a day job as a bank clerk, but he was also an officer in the army reserve and he drilled us like the Brigade of Guards. We sprang to attention. We snapped off salutes. We barked commands. We marched in step. Baden-Powell would have been cheering from the grave. Then, gradually, it began to pall, until it was no longer fun. I had loved Scouts but by fifteen I had grown out of it. Saturday sport was becoming more important. More urgent still, sex was beginning to rear its beautiful head. With girls, that is.

Here I was pretty much flying blind. My mother's second and final attempt at sex education had lumbered to a halt with the Delphic pronouncement that 'it' was something very beautiful that happened between men and women when they married, for the purpose of having children. Full stop. Before I hit puberty I had pieced together the basics with the usual exchange of information and misinformation in the playground, but the details were hazy at best. For quite a while we believed that sperm had superhuman powers. One drop of semen could seep through your underwear and pants, and fight its wiggling way towards and into the nearest vagina, where it would cause an immediate pregnancy. Everyone knew this for a fact. There were also women called nymphomaniacs who did it all the time with anyone, although they were mostly Catholic. This was also a fact. Nervously, I entered the arena.

The train to and from school was the starting place. There were two boys' private schools on the upper North Shore line, Barker and Knox Grammar, and three girls' schools: Ravenswood, Pymble Ladies' College and Abbotsleigh. All of them solidly and politely Protestant. The trains were crammed with their students by the hundreds, morning and afternoon, rattling juggernauts of hormones. The eternal mysteries of the human mating process sorted it all out, more or less successfully. We moved in small packs: boys with boaters hung over their foreheads desperately attempting to look cool, girls equally cool and elaborately pretending not to see us. Then the two would mingle and meld, meeting and parting.

Miss Kaye's Dancing Class was held every Friday at a council hall near Killara Station, then pretty much the epicentre of North Shore niceness. It was a compulsory rite of passage where, our parents hoped, we would meet the opposite sex in a respectable, supervised gathering while acquiring the necessary social graces. Unfortunately, they were right: it was indeed respectable and supervised. The class began with some forty or fifty boys from the private schools lining one wall; girls from the private schools lined the opposite one. We wore sports coats, shirts and ties, pants of polished cotton and a litre or so of Old Spice aftershave. On our feet we had suede desert boots with soles like tractor tyres; these were universally if puzzlingly known as 'brothel-creepers'. The girls did Barbie Doll circa 1960, with swirling frocks held up and out by petticoats stiffened with circles of rope. They had beehive hairdos fixed like fibreglass with a hairspray called Gossamer, which could have doubled as an anti-fouling paint for yachts. Miss Kaye, who was built like a rake and about as friendly, would give the command: 'Take your partners.' The boys would rush towards the waiting girls, who were all named Jan, Kim or Michelle. The girls got no say in it. They had to dance with whoever grabbed them, acne or not.

'Tonight we will practise the foxtrot!' Miss Kaye announced. She would start up the gramophone and grab the nearest boy, who, tomato-red with embarrassment, would be pushed around the hall in a wrestler's stranglehold while she shouted out the time-two-three-four, one-two-three-four, back-two-three-four. In this way we were also introduced to the waltz, the barn dance, the tango and – in a moment of utter madness – the cha-cha. Ham-fisted and tangle-footed, I plodded around the floor, never learning a step. I tripped, I fell over, I stamped on girls' feet. There was only one dance we actually wanted to do: the twist, a craze inspired by the American singer Chubby Checker, in which you tried to corkscrew yourself into the floor. The Stomp, an Australian creation, came later.

The magic thing was that you actually got to touch girls. Hold them in your arms. Feel their bodies against yours, pliant or not as the case might be. Smell their breath, their perfume. Occasionally, if you were lucky, you might be permitted to gently brush a breast with the palm of your hand, or to allow your other hand to wander down below the waist to rest lightly on an upper buttock. Sometimes, just sometimes, there might be a nanosecond or two when your groin came together with hers. It was erotic, intoxicating. And that was about as far as it went. The dance hall was next door to a small and shrubby park, but there was no getting off there. Aware of the perils, the girls' fathers were patrolling outside like the SAS, waiting to drive them home.

Private parties kicked the action along rather better. They were mostly someone's birthday party, held at home, and there was one pretty much every weekend, so long as you were on the uber-cool list. With the host parents confined to the kitchen, there was a chance for some serious snogging – and maybe, in one of the bigger houses, an opportunity to disappear into a bedroom or the darker corners of the garden. The boys ran a scoring system to tally their sexual success. A Number 2 was a kiss, or a pash. A Number 4 meant you got to grope a breast, but only a clothed one. Number 6 signified getting your hand inside a bra – or, if you were dead lucky, removing the bra altogether; you learned to undo a bra strap with a quick flick of one hand. And so it went on, up the scale. I think an actual penetrative bonk was notched at 18 or 20, but I can't be certain of that because I don't think any of us actually achieved one during our school years.

I definitely didn't. It was the blokey boasting of a Monday morning that mattered most: 'Scored a Number 8 on Saturday, mate. Phwoar.'

For all our bravado, in fact we were scared to bits at the thought of getting a girl up the duff, as we delicately put it. Australian society then wallowed in a perpetual moral panic that teenagers were 'heavy petting' or 'going too far', and there were frequent stern if opaque lectures about the dangers of such wickedness. We carried condoms in our wallets, though, in case one of the helpful Catholic nymphomaniacs turned up, but these were more for show, really. Buying a condom – known as a franger – was itself an act of raw courage. You couldn't do it in school uniform, and you couldn't do it if the chemist knew your parents. Worse, you couldn't buy it from a female shop assistant, who would think you were a sex maniac. If there was a girl serving behind the counter you had to spend half an hour or so insouciantly inspecting the shelves of toothpaste and aspirin, in the hope that a male might take her place. We greeted the arrival of the contraceptive pill for women in 1961 like the Liberation of Paris, but the delirium evaporated when we discovered that family doctors were not exactly rushing to prescribe it for their patients' teenage daughters.

More prosaically, as I was embarking on the sexual adventure, most girls, even the slender ones, were still wearing what they called girdles. God knows why. A girdle was actually a corset of some elasticised stuff – useful, I suppose, for holding up your nylon stockings with suspenders. But it was also a de facto chastity belt: it set up an almost impenetrable barrier to a wandering hand, or a wandering anything else. The true sexual revolution began with the arrival of pantyhose, and not a moment too soon.

✧

Other revolutions were stirring. In my last two years of high school, beginning in 1961, the known world shifted on its axis in profound and often frightening ways. At first there was optimism. The charismatic John F. Kennedy, aged just forty-three, was inaugurated as the youngest man ever elected President of the United States that January, pledging that America would 'pay any price, bear any burden, meet any hardship, support any friend, oppose any foe to assure the survival and the success of liberty'. Kennedy's apparent vigour and soaring oratory were inspiring. More than a match for the Cold War thugs in the Kremlin, everyone said. The American culture magnet had already drawn me in. I knew nothing of international politics, but Kennedy, with his Harvard drawl, was every bit as glamorous and enticing as *Leave It to Beaver* and *I Love Lucy* on television. I wanted to *be* an American, a longing only inflamed by the dreadful news in April that the Soviet Union had rocketed Yuri Gagarin into space, the first man there. A week later Kennedy was entangled in the Bay of Pigs attack on Fidel Castro's Cuba. The Cold War iced up. That August the East Germans began to build the Berlin Wall. In Australia, after a landslide against him, Prime Minister Robert Menzies scraped home at the federal election with a working majority of just one seat. Television saw the first *Four Corners* program on the ABC. On the vulgar commercial stations, a Melbourne schoolteacher, Barry Jones, blitzed the field on Bob Dyer's *Pick a Box* to win more than £14,000.

Australians had worries close to home. To the north, Indonesia's volatile President Sukarno had staked a claim to the Netherlands East Indies territory of West Irian, or West Papua, securing substantial military aid in ships and aircraft from the Soviet Union to add muscle to his bombast. 'The war machine in Indonesia is taking shape,' warned the *Canberra Times*.[47] Still clinging to the White Australia policy, backing the wrong horse on the wrong side of history, the Menzies government publicly supported the Dutch and privately pleaded with Washington to do something, anything, to hose down the crisis. West Irian was eventually shoved onto the backburner, with a United Nations compromise providing for a plebiscite down the track. Still, it had been a diplomatic defeat for the Dutch and a victory for Sukarno, whetting his appetite for foreign adventuring.

If 1961 had been dodgy, the next year was worse, and not only because Marilyn Monroe was found dead in her bed that August, or because Nelson Mandela was jailed for five years in November. Marilyn I knew from her swimsuit photographs. Nelson, who didn't have swimsuit shots, was less prominent at the time. The Americans began the year well, getting the astronaut John Glenn into orbit in

February, but it was downhill after that. Monolithic communism was on the march, near and far. On 24 May the Menzies government announced it would send up to thirty army advisers to South Vietnam to help train local forces fighting the Viet Cong insurgency. It was 'in response to a request from the Vietnam government', said the defence minister, Athol Townley, tossing up the first of what would become a torrent of lies about Australia's involvement in Indochina. In fact it was the Americans who put the arm on us.[48]

I cannot say now which, or how much, of these happenings entered my teenage world then. If you had asked me to find Jakarta or Saigon on a map I couldn't have done it. The smattering of political geography we got at school was confined to those bits of the globe still pleasingly coloured British imperial pink. For all we knew, the Queen still ruled greater India and always would.

It was the Cuban Missile Crisis of October 1962 that alerted me and my peers to the dangerous possibilities of the world. For thirteen desperate days there seemed every chance that the US and the Soviet Union would plunge themselves and the planet into nuclear war. The origins of the crisis were complex – there was fault and folly on both sides – but in essence the Soviets were provoked by the stationing of US nuclear missiles in Turkey and Italy. The Kremlin retaliated by deploying missiles to Cuba. An American U2 spy plane found and photographed the first Cuban missile sites on 14 October. In meeting after meeting, the Kennedy administration considered its possible responses, which included a full-scale military invasion of Cuba, but eventually settled for a blockade. Soviet ships carrying missiles to the island would be stopped in international waters and turned back – or, if necessary, sunk.

At about that point the crisis became public, its tensions playing out in Washington and Moscow, at the United Nations in New York, and in the world's media. Grainy television pictures showed the Americans' reconnaissance photographs; charts recorded the progress of the missile ships towards the island and the US Navy's movements to intercept them. Kennedy and Khrushchev stood eyeball to eyeball. The fear worldwide was palpable, pervasive. Transfixed, our parents and teachers talked of little else. Stanley Kramer's haunting

1959 film *On the Beach* had portrayed the end of a nuclear world in Melbourne, and now it seemed possible we were heading for just that. We kids were swept up. I followed it on television, on the radio, in the newspapers.

Khrushchev had betted that Kennedy would crack, but in the event it was he who blinked. On 26 October he sent a long and rambling letter by teleprinter to the State Department in Washington: he would remove his missiles from Cuba if Kennedy promised there would be no invasion. The crisis had effectively ended. The world breathed again. It was the first time I had closely followed a news story in the media. That month I applied for a job as a cadet journalist at the ABC.

Discipline at Barker had pretty much collapsed by my final year, 1962. When the long-serving Bill Leslie died in 1957, the school council had buckled to the cultural cringe and hired a master from England's Rugby School named John Dewes, who was also a former England Test cricketer. The job should have gone to Bob Finlay, but his wife – a blunt and quarrelsome woman – was not thought to be sufficiently *grande dame* for a headmaster's consort.

Dewes was a disaster. Accustomed to British deference, he never got the measure of Australian schoolboys. Or their parents, for that matter. He struggled to maintain order, a losing battle not helped by the ill-concealed contempt of most of his teaching staff. I became one of the class clowns, a rebel, a show-off entertainer ready with a smartarse one-liner that could crack up a classroom at a teacher's expense. This got me caned a good few times, but the notoriety was worth it. 'He behaves like a lout,' wrote Dewes in one of my end-of-year reports.

Yet, paradoxically, I wanted authority of my own. I loved the school cadet corps – probably a hangover from all the marching and saluting in the Scouts. From the age of fourteen it was compulsory to be in the cadets. We wore slouch hats and, in winter, the same khaki uniform of long woollen tunic and trousers that had seen the Australian Imperial Force off to war in 1914. Some of the smaller kids were barely bigger than the First War vintage .303 Lee Enfield rifles we carted around on parade. I took to the drill like a native-born Prussian. My boots gleamed. My belt brass shone. My summer uniform of khaki cotton shirt and pants was so heavily starched and ironed that it gave off static electricity. By the end of my first year I could dismantle and reassemble a Bren light machine gun at warp speed, and in my second year they made me a sergeant in the Signal Platoon. Once a year we went into camp at an army base in Singleton, in the Hunter Valley, where we got to fire live ammunition and eat revolting food cooked by drunks rounded up from the local pubs. In my third and final year they wanted me to become a cadet under officer, but I knocked that back. It would have meant going to a training camp in the school holidays, and abandoning my retail career at Grace Bros. So they promoted me to warrant officer first class and made me the school's regimental sergeant major. In that exalted rank, you switched from the slouch hat to an officer's peaked cap, which I carefully bent and pummelled and wore at an angle like Field Marshal Rommel. At our final parade I got to bark all the orders and to wear a sword slung off a polished leather Sam Browne belt. There's not been much call for it since, but I could still do the drill for saluting with a sword. Or strip a Bren gun, if needed.

To everyone's surprise, my own not the least, Barker also made me a school prefect. I assume this was on the principle of having me inside the tent pissing out, rather than the opposite, and for a while it worked. I more or less behaved myself until the final day of school before our Leaving Certificate examinations, when about twenty of us ran riot. That night we did wheelies on the main school oval in Alan Macfarlane's father's car; hanged from the flagpole an effigy of 'Stiffy' Steanes, the much-loathed physics teacher; and drenched the boarders' dormitories in flour and water. And we would have got away with it if I hadn't left a list of the participants in my desk. Someone ratted on me, Dewes got hold of the list the next morning and we were all formally suspended from the school.

My mother, fretting that she had raised a delinquent, set about pushing me in the direction of a job. I was still only sixteen. An arts degree at university was a possibility, but only if I won a scholarship; there was no way we could afford the fees. At my insistence, we enquired about me becoming a naval cadet midshipman, but it was quickly obvious that my maths simply weren't up to the job. Bang went my dream of commanding a destroyer – much to the relief of my mother, who had been reliably informed that life in the Navy was wet, dangerous and badly paid.

Almost as an afterthought I tossed around the idea of becoming a journalist. I was good at English. I could spell and write. I could even type, a rare skill then for a male; my mother had taught me on her portable Olivetti at home. One of the main characters in *The Cruel Sea* had been a journalist in civilian life, which I took as a good omen. On television we religiously watched a British TV drama called *Deadline Midnight*, in which hard-drinking, chain-smoking, wisecracking but generally likeable Fleet Street newspaper reporters regularly stormed into the editor's office shouting, 'Hold the front page!' All the signs were right. It was not as glamorous as the Navy, but it had a certain zing to it, I thought. My mother feared that journalists were a bit raffish – even bohemian and loose-living – but she helped me compose a letter offering my many talents to the four Sydney morning and afternoon newspapers.

The editors of the *Sydney Morning Herald*, the *Sun* and the *Daily Mirror* didn't bother to reply. The editor of the *Daily Telegraph*, then owned by Sir Frank Packer, wrote back to say that they would be hiring copyboys in the new year, and suggested that I have a crack at that. That didn't sound much fun. The copyboys in *Deadline Midnight* just scurried about fetching coffee and cigarettes for the hard-bitten but kindly reporters, a task rather beneath me, I thought. And, as Nana acidly assured me, the *Telegraph* was read only by common and vulgar people.

Then someone suggested the Australian Broadcasting Commission. This struck me as odd. It hadn't occurred to me, or my mother, that the ABC would employ journalists. We had vaguely assumed that the news was composed by the man who read it. James Dibble, or whoever, popped into the studio an hour or so before the bulletin, skimmed the newspapers, noted down the interesting bits and then served them up on air. With many misgivings and not much hope, we reworked our letter and sent it off.

A reply came a week later. The ABC News Department was planning to employ a cadet journalist in its Sydney newsroom. Mr Michael Carlton should, at his convenience, telephone the office of the Controller of News, Mr W. S. Hamilton, to make an appointment for an interview. It was October 1962.

PART 2

6

Now take out all the adjectives

THE ABC'S SYDNEY NEWSROOM lurked like an old hooker in Kellett Street, a grimy back lane in Kings Cross. It was above a Woolworths store. You walked past the bouncers and cockatoos for a couple of brothels and illegal gambling joints, squeezed around a row of Woolworths' smelly rubbish bins, and presented yourself at a narrow doorway guarded by an ABC commissionaire in a grey uniform. With the approval of this ancient worthy you caught a rackety lift to the second floor and stepped straight into the reporters' room.

I arrived there on Monday, 7 January 1963. To this day I haven't a clue how or why I scored the job. The small but formidable W. S. 'Wally' Hamilton and his Director of TV News, a beefy and wheezing former Queensland copper named Keith Fraser, had interviewed me at the Gore Hill television studios even before I sat my Leaving Certificate exams. I have no memory of anything they asked or anything I said. A week later a letter came to Chatswood informing me that J. Stanton, Director of Administrative Services, was pleased to offer me an engagement as a Cadet Journalist, Sydney, at a salary of £11.18.6 per week (about $330 in today's money).

Riches! It was even better than Grace Bros. I bought a cheap navy-blue suit and a couple of white shirts. Attired in this finery, I presented myself as instructed to the newsroom chief of staff. Pleasingly, the place looked just like *Deadline Midnight*, only grottier. In the reporters' room and the sub-editors' room next door, any oxygen molecules had been driven out by a fug of cigarette smoke, the fumes of greasy fried food and the strangely sweet and sour smell of carbon paper and photocopying gunk. Naked fluorescent struggled against the gloom. Old newspapers lay in heaps on the floor.

The reporters' room had about six battle-scarred wooden desks, on which sat overflowing ashtrays and some of the first typewriters ever made, clunky black Remingtons and Underwoods invariably missing a key or two, and usually tipped on their backs when they weren't in use. In one corner was a bank of radio receivers that were tuned to the police, fire brigade and ambulance frequencies; they squawked and farted, monitored by a reporter known as the Emergency Roundsman. In their room, the four or five sub-editors sat around a U-shaped table, with women who would type the bulletins from the copy scrawled with corrections and markings. There was another, even smaller room in which the teleprinters sent and received news from interstate and overseas. The little studio where the news bulletin was read sat in another corner, behind double wooden doors. On the floor below there was a rehearsal room for the Sydney Symphony Orchestra, then owned by the ABC. Every so often, without warning, the entire building would be rocked by tweets, plunks and bangs as they tuned up for Beethoven's Fifth. It was heaven. All I had imagined and more. I had passed the Leaving Certificate with honours in English and economics, but to hell with university. Here was life!

There were a few formalities. Bizarrely, I was required to sign an oath of allegiance declaring that I would faithfully serve Her Sovereign Majesty Queen Elizabeth II. I suppose that's still on file somewhere. I was issued with a ballpoint pen, a reporter's notebook and a style guide, which laid down, in pedantic detail, the language that could and could not be used in ABC news bulletins. There would be lessons in Pitman shorthand at Miss Hale's Secretarial College in the city. I should also join the union, the Australian Journalists' Association. To begin to learn the trade I would accompany the senior men – they were all men – on reporting jobs, to see how they did it and how they wrote their stories afterwards. I was photographed for a police press pass. After four years as a cadet, I would be a fully fledged journalist.

Gradually I found my feet, sorting out who was what. A young man I had taken to be a journalist of vast seniority and experience turned out to have been the junior cadet, bottom of the ladder, until I came along. Debonair, and with an impressive mane of long blond hair, Stuart Littlemore radiated self-confidence. He had won a lustrous fame in the newsroom after an encounter with Wally Hamilton as he was reading the enormous *Oxford English Dictionary*, which was kept on a shelf by the lift.

The Controller of News enjoyed employing waspish sarcasm at the expense of his troops. 'Don't tell me there's a word in the English language you don't understand, Mr Littlemore,' he hissed.

'Not anymore,' said Stuart, shutting the book with a bang.

I had been in the place only three weeks when I first tasted the adrenaline rush of a fast-breaking news story. It was 29 January, two days before my seventeenth birthday, a sleepy summer Tuesday afternoon. The senior cadet, John Lawler, a seasoned veteran of twenty-four, and I were the only available bodies in the newsroom. The police and ambulance radios crackled into life: a shark attack in the harbour, possibly fatal. The chief of staff burst from his office. 'Get going, Lawler, take Carlton with you!'

Johnny Lawler, bless him, owned a Triumph TR3 sports car, shiny in British racing green. With the top down, he gunned it out of the Cross like Juan Manuel Fangio, and we vroomed across the Harbour Bridge towards Middle Harbour, me navigating with a street directory. I have not had a more exciting ride, ever. God, was journalism always like this? The cops and various witnesses and bystanders were still milling around at Sugarloaf Bay as we skidded to a halt.

Wide-eyed, I watched as Lawler got the details. Marcia Hathaway, a thirty-two-year-old actress, was on a boating picnic with friends, and had been splashing in the shallows when the shark attacked. Her fiancé had wrestled with the beast in water crimson with her blood. The ambulance taking her to hospital had broken down on the steep hill out of the bay, and another had to be called.

We ran back to the TR3 and raced to the Mater Hospital in North Sydney. 'Wait here and keep an eye out in case anything happens. I'm going to file,' Johnny said. He disappeared in search of a telephone.

Fear gripped me. In case *what* happened? I hadn't a clue.

A knot of reporters were slouching around outside the casualty entrance, men far older than sixteen-year-old me, waiting to find out if the actress was alive or dead.[49] One of them eyed me off. He was a tall, pockmarked man, in his forties perhaps, sporting the sort of snappy fedora hat that police detectives wore. 'You new?'

'Er, yes.'

'ABC?'

'Yes.'

'Okay. Hang around, son. I'll let you know if anything's up.'

I could have kissed him. He turned out to be Ced Culbert, legendary police reporter for the *Daily Telegraph*, a maestro of the trade who could easily have ground me into the dust beneath his heels. He never did. I ran into him a lot over the next few years, here and there, and his courtesy and kindness to a whippersnapper never abated. They were a special breed, those old-time police roundsmen: Ced, the grizzled Bill Jenkings of the *Daily Mirror*, tubby Basil Sweeney of the *Sydney Morning Herald*. They would have killed their grandmothers to scoop each other, but there was also a collegiate decency to them and they could enjoy a drink together after their papers had gone to bed. They knew all the cops, they knew all the crims, and they danced a fine line between the two.

More often than not the cops were the crims. Sydney then was on track for peak police and political corruption. One day in a lift at the Sydney CIB, the old Criminal Investigation Bureau in Central Lane, Ced introduced me to Detective Sergeant Ray 'Gunner' Kelly, a celebrated hero of the tabloid headlines who was always ready with a quotable quote. In a smartly tailored suit, his hair slickly Brylcreemed and parted in the centre, and with a gaze like an electric drill, Kelly was a crack detective who had solved some famous murder cases. He was also as crook as Rookwood. He shook my hand, unsmiling. 'Get in my way and I'll fucking shoot you,' he growled.

'He means it,' said Ced as the lift doors closed behind him.

I didn't doubt it. Kelly and a contemporary, Detective Sergeant Fred 'Froggy' Krahe, were both multiple murderers, widely feared, and skimmed a lucrative take from the Sydney underbelly of illegal gambling clubs, abortion rackets, brothels, SP bookmakers, car theft gangs and drug dealers. In effect, they franchised crime to the likes of the Kings Cross stripclub and brothel king Abe 'Mr Sin' Saffron, the brutal murderer, gangster and police informer Lenny 'Mr Big' McPherson, the gambling czar Perce Galea, and the standover man, rapist and assassin-for-hire Arthur 'Neddy' Smith.

I had heard some of this as gossip, but it never occurred to me that here was a story worth reporting. Nor would I have had a clue about how to go digging for it. The roundsmen never wrote it either; at the very least, no copper would ever talk to them again. Their careers would be dead and they might well be too, on a one-way trip outside the Sydney Heads with a hessian bag for a shroud and a concrete gravestone. Fred Krahe was quietly eased out of the New South Wales police force in 1972, supposedly on health grounds, although the word was he'd murdered his ex-girlfriend, a prostitute named Shirley Brifman. To its great discredit, the *Sydney Morning Herald* hired him as a 'crime consultant'.

The CIB offices and cells were a Dickensian dystopia. They smelt of crime and fear, of blood and piss and shit. It was certainly an eye-opener for a well-bred Barker boy. At nine o'clock every morning there was a press conference held by the CIB boss, Detective Chief Superintendent Ron Waldron, who would lean back in his office chair and flick through the blotter for a chortling rundown on the previous night's villainy. 'Marrickville: man up dog,' he would say. 'Coogee: pair of poofs in a dunny. Don't s'pose you'll wanna run that. Darlinghurst: prozzie bashed with a cricket bat . . .'

The ABC at that time was not big on crime stories, but Waldron's revelations were fabulous grist to my social mill up on the North Shore, where nothing ever happened.

✧

The first job I covered by myself, and the first written words of mine ever broadcast, were about a Girl Guides' afternoon tea. A new chief

Guide had been installed in office. I gave it all I had, as if it were the Queen opening parliament.

'Not bad,' said the chief sub-editor, Sid Mounsey. 'Now go back and take out all the adjectives.' Sid looked like a cheerful goblin who'd been dragged through a bush backwards, but he was a brilliant journalist, a maestro. With minutes to go before the flagship seven pm bulletin – white-knuckle time – he could dictate the lead story off the top of his head, in flawless sentences with all the facts in place, while one of the typists banged it out. I could do it myself eventually, but it was a skill that took years to perfect. Sid cared for the cadets, too, polishing our work with infinite patience. A stickler for accuracy, he drummed into us the ABC's holy writ of impartiality and balance.

For me that first year was a steep learning curve. When the Queen turned up for her second Australian tour, I was sent to cover the rehearsal for her arrival. 'All is ready for the Queen's visit to Sydney tomorrow,' I wrote stuffily. 'A dress rehearsal at Circular Quay this morning went smoothly.' This duly went out on the lunchtime news bulletins. An hour later I was suddenly summoned to the subs' room to find Sid and a semicircle of heavies glaring at me. Silently, he pushed the afternoon newspaper first editions across the table. 'Royal Chaos,' said one front page. 'Royal Shambles,' said the other.

It was true. The show had gone like a Charlie Chaplin movie. A ferry acting as the royal yacht had crashed into the wharf. The stand-in for Prince Philip had fallen into the water and had to be fished out. An awning had collapsed, the red carpet had been in the wrong place and the PA system hadn't worked. I had naively assumed that the ABC – the national broadcaster! – would not wish to embarrass Her Majesty by reporting these calamities, any more than her loyal subjects, our listeners, would want to hear them. So I had ignored them. This explanation was not well received.

Still, I was gaining skills and confidence. A lot of time was spent tagging along with older journalists as they reported the routine drudgery of minor court cases, traffic accidents and local council meetings, interspersed with the occasional lecture on the hazards of the trade: the rules on contempt of court, on stories that were *sub judice*, on libel and defamation, on reporting parliament. Miss Hale's shorthand classes were a crashing bore. They taught you antiquated business phrases like 'With reference to your esteemed communication of the 3rd Inst'. Littlemore and I used the class as an excuse to nick off to the pub. Neither of us ever got anywhere near the required shorthand speed of 120 words per minute, but no one seemed to mind.

Other jobs were sheer delight. My favourite was the Shipping Round, a relic of colonial days when the world's news arrived in Sydney by sea. In the early 1960s the big shipping companies – P&O and Shaw Savill from Britain, Lloyd Triestino from Italy, and the American Matson Line – were still running regular passenger services to and from Australia. Their public relations people would pump out a list of supposedly interesting passengers on board, and lay on a launch to get reporters out to the ship to interview them as they steamed through the Heads. I loved it. The British ships arrived at dawn. You had to jump from a small, tossing launch onto a rope Jacob's ladder slung over the liner's side, and haul yourself up hand over hand, sometimes in pitch dark. The Matson liners from San Francisco, *Monterey* and *Mariposa*, came in mid-morning, before lunch. None of the passengers was ever all that fascinating: retired politicians, retired orchestral conductors, retired novelists, retired baseball players, retired Hollywood actors. But the cultural cringe was still hot and strong, and we were eager for their opinions on just about anything. 'Why have you come to Australia?' we would ask them solemnly, incredulous that people of their stature would deign to grace our insignificant little country with their presence. 'What do you think of rock'n'roll music?'

The perk was the nosh afterwards. P&O would always invite us to a pig-out English country house breakfast in the first-class restaurant, which is how I first tasted kippers, kedgeree and devilled kidneys, scarfing it all down as we steamed slowly up the harbour. Matson did a lavish buffet lunch on deck, where I discovered the delights of a well-made mai tai, Virginia ham quiche, coleslaw and American cheesecake. (Quiche for comment.) Stuffed to the gills, I would stagger back to Kellett Street and bang out some anodyne load of guff: 'A former British Foreign Secretary, Lord Tosspot, said today Australia had an important role to play in world affairs. Arriving in Sydney on the liner *Himalaya*, Lord Tosspot said *blah blah blah* . . .'

It was hardly news, but it was good training. And Sydney has always loved ships. When P&O brought the sleek white liner *Canberra* into service in the early 1960s, she was greeted like royalty with a week of celebrations.

✧

Life was looking up. I was still living at home, paying my mother a token amount of board, and had enough money left over for a few beers or to take a girl to the movies. Most of my mates from Barker were playing Saturday football in the blue-and-white-striped shirt of the Lindfield Rugby Club – all very rah-rah private school. I played as often as I could – my tackling had improved – but I was frequently rostered to work at weekends, which stuffed things. The football actually took second place to the club's primary activity, which was getting pissed at the upmarket Greengate Hotel in Killara on Friday and Saturday nights, despite the fact that, at seventeen, we were still under the legal drinking age. Mad as cut snakes after a couple of schooners, we would finish the night with a rousing rendition of the club song:

> We are the boys from Old Lindfield Club
> We're never happy till we're in the pub
> Hey there, ho there, bring in the gin
> We never let a sober man in . . .

You get the picture. I imagine we were obnoxious. An alternative to the Greengate was Peyton's Place, a small coffee shop on the Pacific Highway at Roseville, provocatively named for the notorious American novel *Peyton Place*, a raunchy tale of sex and lust in a small New England town. To much controversy, the novel had been banned in Australia by the grandly titled Department of Trade and Customs Literature Censorship Board, joining a list that included such corrupting filth as Vladimir Nabokov's *Lolita*, James Baldwin's *Another Country* and Aldous Huxley's *Brave New World*. Customs officers at airports and seaports rifled through passengers' bags to see if this trash was being smuggled in. If they'd known what went on at the coffee shop they might have banned that too.

There was a large room out the back, completely blacked out, with throbbing music, where partly clothed teenage bodies writhed and groped and grunted in sweaty, ostentatious ecstasy. Young men could only enter this steamy sanctum if we had a girl with us. Change was afoot. In winter, we were now wearing duffle jackets and corduroy pants. The girls had switched out of rope petticoats and beehive hair in favour of tight Black Watch tartan skirts, black pantyhose, their fathers' outsized sweaters and, bizarrely, white lipstick. We thought we looked like soulful, caring aesthetes.

Sex was still my chief preoccupation. For all the feeling and fumbling, I had yet to do *it*. Other guys had; at seventeen, I was in serious danger of being left behind. The problem was solved after I persuaded my mother to go halves with me in a car. We scraped together a deposit and became the proud owners of a brand-new, sky-blue Morris 850, the famous Mini Minor. It was the first car our family had ever had. No matter that it was hardly bigger than a supermarket trolley, or that it barely had enough power to pull the leaves off a wet lettuce. It transformed our lives. No longer reliant on trains and buses, Enid could visit friends or go to my brother's school sporting events. I had it most nights and weekends, for parties or trips to the beach – and, eventually, for sexual triumph.

For a few weeks I had been dating Narelle Gibson, a couple of years older than me, and a reporter on the Packer magazine, the *Australian Women's Weekly*. We had done a bit of heavy fumbling at Peyton's but that was it. As I was driving her home one Saturday afternoon after the football, she suddenly plunged first a hand into my groin, then her head. A nymphomaniac! At last! I nearly drove under a semi-trailer. Thinking quickly, breathing heavily and trembling mightily, I realised we were near the Lane Cove River, and very close to a spot in the bush where some of us, wagging school, used to have a smoke and go skinny-dipping. I hurled the Mini down the rough dirt track like it was an armoured personnel carrier, and we crunched to a halt beneath a tree.

Bonking in a Morris 850 is not easy. I'm sure it has been done, but not by me. We tried, but the gear lever and the handbrake kept getting in the way. Grabbing a towel from the back seat, we tumbled out of the car onto a nearby rock, and tore off each other's clothes. Bush flies, insects and ants looked on in awe. 'Condom!' she breathed. I had one. In my wallet. Frantically, I ripped it out of its packet and then realised, like a blow to the head, that I hadn't a clue how to put it on. I had never worn one. Did you unroll it first. Or blow it up like a balloon?

Happily, Narelle knew the drill. She slipped the thing on and we got down to *it*. My recollection is not so much of the orgasm as of a feeling of exultant triumph, a delicious wave of rampant masculinity fulfilled. At last I was a man. I gave a Tarzan sort of yell. Birds fled screeching.

'That was quick,' said Narelle.

✧

The culture was changing at accelerating speed. On commercial radio, the disc jockeys had begun to play the music of an English pop group from Liverpool, four blokes with outlandish, pudding-basin haircuts and sharp, skintight suits. The Beatles seemed an odd sort of name, but they had two smash hits that year, 'I Want to Hold Your Hand' and 'She Loves You'.

My go was more the surfing sound. The beach had captured me, body and soul. Before we could drive, we usually hitchhiked to the beach and back. At weekends, Mona Vale Road, the main artery from the North Shore to the northern beaches, was lined with boys and girls thumbing a ride. And you always got one, although we all knew not to go with a certain middle-aged blond man in a red sports car, who would try to grope you.

To start with, Newport was our preferred beach. It was cool – speedos for guys and ever-briefer bikinis for girls. Blithely unaware of the dangers of skin cancer, we sprawled for hours on the sand, transistor radios blaring, all of us drenched in a greasy oil called Skol, which was the colour of cognac and about as useful for preventing sunburn. I had tried riding friends' surfboards, with mixed success, but I preferred bodysurfing, the matchless thrill of zooming down a crystal wave and crunching face-first into a sand bank.

Surfing music had begun to arrive in Australia from California: rock instrumentals in the beginning, with a lot of tremolo picking on

Fender Stratocaster guitars, and a fast *dunka-dunka-dunka* electric bass. An Australian group from Sydney's southern beaches, The Atlantics, shot up the Top 40 chart with their own composition, 'Bombora', which began with a pounding tom-tom riff and became a huge international hit.

Come the hour, come the man, who in this case was a new addition to the disc jockey ranks in Sydney commercial radio: the blond and baby-faced Ward Austin. Ward was probably half-mad, if not more. He believed himself to be the reincarnation of some Confederate general of the American Civil War, he only ever wore white jeans and T-shirt topped by a white Stetson, and he tooled around town in an enormous white Ford Fairlane convertible with the red, white and blue Dixie flag painted on the boot, below his name in curly letters. His real surname was Gargan, although everyone knew him as 'Pally', because that's how he started his show on air. 'Any time you're ready, Pally!' he would bellow. Then there'd be a rebel yell to Warwick, his panel operator, and a hollered incantation he'd invented as a signature: 'A rickapoodie and a fandooglie!' The phrase entered the local language for a while, along with another of his favourite lines: 'Too much for the human unit!'

Pally was actually very good at it. He rated his head off, becoming compulsory listening for every teenager in Sydney, although he kept getting sacked by radio stations for unspecified atrocities. Another would hire him immediately. Scandalously, deliciously, he married his second wife, Irene, when she was just seventeen, half his age at the time. He specialised in surf music and the whole surf craze. On his explicit command we switched our loyalties from Newport Beach to the next one north up the coast, Bilgola. I came to know Ward much later and liked him, although with his glory days long gone he was an alcoholic wreck, his boyish good looks destroyed. There was an Elvis impersonator at his funeral in 1998. Radio can spit you out.

I'm pretty sure it was Ward who first played the Beach Boys in Sydney. By 1964 their hits were coming like waves themselves. 'Surfin' USA', 'Surfer Girl', 'Little Deuce Coupe', 'Fun Fun Fun', 'Be True to Your School', 'Don't Worry Baby', 'I Get Around' and more all appeared that year, as singles or on albums, all of them classics. The

California Sound and the culture it embraced – surf, sun, sand, girls, cars – fitted in perfectly down under across the Pacific. More than ever I wanted to become an American, and I investigated ways of blonding my hair. It was said you could do it with a bucket or two of Ajax, the household cleaner, but it never worked for me. Brian Wilson and the Beach Boys recorded the soundtrack to my life. I know every word, every harmony.

Dimly, through all the beachgoing and partying, another thought was creeping up on me: there was an awful lot I did not know. When I had started the ABC job, I'd begun buying *Time* and *Newsweek* magazines, largely as a fashion accessory to demonstrate my exotic new status to anyone who might be looking. They were then at the height of their reach and influence. When I began to actually read them, a lot of the time I had only the haziest idea of what they were on about. Who were Mao Tse-tung, Chiang Kai-shek, Ho Chi Minh, Jomo Kenyatta, Sukarno, Jawaharlal Nehru? The collapse of empires after World War II and the surging nationalism of colonised peoples had entirely passed us by at school. History had stopped in 1945, and even then it had been full of holes as big as the Grand Canyon. We got the Nazis, but not socialism or communism. Neither the Industrial Revolution nor the Soviet Revolution ever merited a mention. British history was largely a stately procession of kings and queens, not the abolition of slavery or the great reform bills of the nineteenth century. Worse, Australian history had pretty much ended with Governor Macquarie. We were taught nothing about the Eureka Stockade, the struggle towards Federation or the Great Depression of the 1930s. Indigenous Australians, so far as they existed, were merely another sort of fauna. American history was non-existent.

This was not the fault of Barker College or its teachers. They had to push the New South Wales school syllabus, which was handed down from on high. With a very few exceptions – Hitler, Churchill – that syllabus could not have been updated since around 1914. It would have been familiar to Edwardian schoolboys, and British ones at that.

And if the teaching of history was a shambles, the syllabus for English literature was almost criminally negligent; absurd and pernicious. The only Australian writing we ever encountered was a couple of Henry Lawson short stories and 'The Man from Snowy River'. American literature, like American history, had never happened. The only true literature was English, and that, too, had pretty much screeched to a halt before World War I. For my English honours exam in my final year we got Shakespeare's *Julius Caesar*, George Bernard Shaw's *Pygmalion* (first performed in 1913) and a chocolate box assortment of Chaucer, Milton, Keats, Tennyson and Wordsworth. From the great sweep of centuries of the English novel, the examiners had chosen arguably one of the dullest ever written, George Eliot's *Silas Marner*, published in 1861. Here is one of the questions from my final exam paper:

> Give your considered opinion of the criticism that George Eliot's characters in *Silas Marner* are interesting only when she lets them *talk*. (You may limit your answer to a discussion of two characters if you wish.)

Gawd. Silas Marner would not have been interesting if he'd arrived naked, riding a unicorn with a stripper, a squad of Nubian slaves and a jazz band, bawling the 'Hallelujah Chorus'. Shakespeare and the romantic poets stuck with me because I loved the language and the imagery – 'The splendour falls on castle walls, and snowy summits old in story' – but that was about it. Music and art were not taught at all unless you wanted to pay extra for lessons after school hours. From memory, Barker had two pianos, each stuck in a room the size of a bus shelter, and no art room at all.

We – that is, the first of the baby boomers – were appallingly badly educated. This unwelcome truth, a nagging doubt at first, began to creep up on me as I listened to some senior journalists talking books in a pub one day. Who on earth was George Orwell, and why had he written something about 1984, which was still twenty years away? Science fiction, perhaps? I resolved to find out.

I did, and that got me going. Taking off from Airstrip One, I began with gathering speed what would eventually amount to my own private arts degree. I read and read and read. Books, books, books. With hindsight, I should have asked for advice and guidance, but

I simply went at it. 'Eclectic' covers it; 'haphazard' would probably be better. I plunged into Charles Dickens, Graham Greene, Agatha Christie, Jane Austen, Evelyn Waugh and more Shakespeare. I had a whack at Patrick White. Proust beat me, but I managed Tolstoy and Joyce. Lunging across to America, I devoured Mailer, Hemingway, Steinbeck, Thurber, Fitzgerald and Sinclair Lewis, and was utterly captivated by J. D. Salinger's *Catcher in the Rye*. For a while there I *was* Holden Caulfield. Somewhere in the middle of all that lot I went factual and philosophical, buzzing like a fly at a barbecue from William L. Shirer's *Rise and Fall of the Third Reich* to John Stuart Mill's *On Liberty* to Bertrand Russell's autobiography to J. K. Galbraith's *The Affluent Society*. It took years, but it began in 1963.

✧

Rupert Beaumont, God love him, was the ABC's state political reporter in Macquarie Street. He was a small and knobbly man with a wry sense of humour, bustling here and there like a busy hobgoblin, sporting the RAAF moustache he'd grown during the war. He regarded the politicians whose words and deeds he covered with something between amused contempt and grim resignation. 'Dopey pack of bastards,' he would say with a shrug and a sigh.

We cadets were sent to him to be instructed in the mysteries of politics, of parliament, of cabinet government, and of the arcane rituals and practices of the Press Gallery. It was a gentler, much slower time then, a far cry from the frenetic gyrations of social media and the 24/7 news cycle of blogs and Twitter. This was a good thing, because Rupert did take a cooling drink against the heat of the afternoon; he was generally half-pissed, and often more, by around four o'clock.

It was easy enough to do. The gallery then enjoyed many of the same rorts and privileges as the MPs themselves, meaning you could whistle up a liveried waiter from the parliamentary dining room to deliver lunch, dinner or a late-night snack to your office in the gallery's rabbit warren, complete with beer or wine, and all heavily subsidised by the unknowing New South Wales taxpayer. (They did a particularly fine Welsh rarebit, I recall, splendid on white bone china beneath a silver cloche emblazoned with the state's coat of arms and motto, *Orta Recens Quam Pura Nites* – 'Newly risen, how brightly you shine'.)

Rupert would have a post-lunch cold one or three as he gathered his thoughts for that night's seven pm story. Then there would be a short snooze. In exchange for his friendship and his knowledge, we would type up and correct his stuff for him; if he was too sodden to actually speak, we could dictate it down the phone to a copytaker back at the newsroom, explaining that he had been suddenly called away. Everyone liked him.

Rupert's great strength was to break stories. He got scoops, much to the approval of his superiors and the baffled chagrin of his competitors. He knew what was going on before anybody else did, and he wrote it: 'The ABC's state parliamentary reporter understands that the government is about to introduce . . .'

The reason was a simple but well-guarded secret. It was a journalist's dream. Late one evening, when the house was in session, Rupert had wandered into the office of the Speaker – the Labor MP for Wyong, the Honourable Raphael Septimus 'Ray' Maher MLA – looking for a chat. As you do. What he got was the Speaker with his pants around his knees, newly risen and brightly shining, fucking a young woman typist on his office couch. As you might. Rupert made his excuses and left. As you would.

Bright and early the next morning, Maher, a pillar of the Labor Party, a devout Catholic and happily married husband and father, came to him with an urgent offer too good to refuse. If his old mate Rupert – a good bloke if ever there was – could see his way clear to staying shtum about his unfortunate discovery, the Speaker would be able to provide him with all sorts of inside information from the bowels of parliament and government. The secrets of the caucus room. The deal ran to the satisfaction of both parties for several years until another woman secretary accused Maher of flashing her in a corridor. Despite his entirely reasonable explanation that he had absent-mindedly forgotten to zip up his fly after taking a leak, there were threats of criminal charges, and good ol' Ray was forced to quit the speakership. The scandal helped Labor lose the 1965 election after twenty-four years in government – a remarkable eight terms. The leader of the new Coalition government was the Liberals' Robin 'Bob' Askin.

A genial, hail-fellow-well-met figure, Askin as opposition leader had been an almost permanent fixture in the Press Gallery offices. He was always loitering there for a beer, a chat, to swap gossip and racing tips into the night. Ah, the jokes, the laughter. He even deigned to recognise a nobody like me, affable as all get-out. 'Give us a call if you need anything, young fella,' he would say. 'Always ready to talk to the ABC.'

Askin was one of the first politicians I encountered close-up. Much flattered by the attention, I thought he was a terrific bloke. Rupert, however, did not. 'Fucking lying prick,' he would say. 'Wouldn't trust the bastard as far as I could spit.' I thought this harsh, but Rupert was right. Askin had been an SP bookie in the army during the war. As premier, he turned out to be a criminal racketeer who was hand-in-glove with two equally crooked police commissioners.

✧

World news arrived in the newsroom on two chattering teleprinters, clunky black machines that looked like big typewriters. One banged out the service from AAP, the Australian Associated Press, which itself was a mix of stories from Reuters, the Associated Press of America and Agence France-Presse. The other carried the American wire service, United Press International. This never-ending flow of news, day and night, was augmented by reports from the ABC's own foreign correspondents in Asia, Britain and the US.

The foreign editor was Anne Ringwood, one of a handful of women working in the Sydney newsroom. Female journalists notionally had equal pay with men, but they rarely had equal jobs. On newspapers they were largely confined to writing about fashion, cooking and social gossip. Anne had a formidable talent and a formidable personality which did not suffer fools gladly, no matter what rank they held. She could be a bossy pedant and we cadets shrank from working for her, although if you stuck around long enough you could detect a kind heart beneath her armoured exterior. She had to be tougher than tough to survive in that world of alpha males, and she was. But I learned a lot from her.

The news from overseas in 1963 drifted in like a gathering storm, culminating towards the end of the year in an almighty thunderclap that shook the heavens. Australians felt they were living in an ever more dangerous world, beset by threats from near and far, happenings over which we had little influence and no control.

It was the British who shocked us first, with their ongoing push to join what was then the European Economic Community of Belgium, France, Italy, Luxembourg, the Netherlands and West Germany. Many Australians, especially those making their living on the land, regarded this as rank treachery, a betrayal of the ties of kinship and Commonwealth. Our agricultural exports to Britain would collapse, they feared. There were gales of relief when the President of France, Charles de Gaulle, vetoed the British application with the splendidly Gallic retort that '*l'Angleterre, ce n'est plus grand chose*' – 'England is not much anymore'.

Closer to home, the war in Indochina was waxing hotter, with much solemn pontificating about the Domino Theory, which held that if Vietnam fell to communism, the rest of South-East Asia would inevitably succumb as well. There were disturbing television pictures of Buddhist monks burning themselves alive in Saigon in protest at the brutal regime of Vietnam's Roman Catholic president, Ngo Dinh Diem. That November, Diem was murdered in the first of what would be a rolling series of military coups either tacitly backed or actively fomented by the US.

The Indonesians, too, were getting antsy again. The formation of the independent state of Malaysia in August 1963 enraged the Sukarno government in Jakarta, which viewed it as *Nekolim* – neo-colonialism – a devious trick by the wicked British to keep their blood-stained fingers in the local pie. The foreign minister, the truculent and belligerent Dr Subandrio, announced a policy of *Konfrontasi* – confrontation – and Indonesian commandos began to mount cross-border raids into Malaysian Borneo, where they were met and invariably bested by British Gurkhas. Giant posters went up all over Jakarta and the rest of Indonesia, exhorting the nation to *Ganyang Malaysia* – crush Malaysia. The Australian Army had fought in the Malayan Emergency of the 1950s to put down a communist insurgency there. Now it was looking as if we might have to take on the Indonesians. Much alarmed, the Menzies government rushed to order twenty-four American F-111 strike bombers for the RAAF, an aircraft still on the drawing board but which would be capable of bombing Jakarta from Australia and returning without refuelling.[50]

Then came the thunderclap, later in November. It is now a baby-boomer cliché that we remember where we were when we heard that John F. Kennedy had been assassinated in Dallas. I was at home at Chatswood. It was twelve-thirty pm on Friday, 22 November in Texas when the shots were fired, but just before dawn on Saturday in Sydney. I had the day off and was planning to go to the beach when a mate rang with the news. Not long after that, the office called me in to work. It was all hands on deck, even the most junior.

I spent that day juggling the teleprinter copy for Anne Ringwood. Story after story spewed from the machines, printed on long, billowing streamers of paper about the size of a modern roll of kitchen towel. Each story and update had to be sorted, numbered, compiled and paperclipped in the right order, tens upon tens of thousands of words for Ringwood to distil into the stories for the news bulletins. It doesn't sound like much but it was exacting work, even if I never wrote a word myself.

Only the next day did I begin to comprehend the enormity of the crime. News from overseas was so much more interesting. In time, I thought, I might have a shot myself at becoming a foreign correspondent.

7

What do you think of Australia?

TELEVISION WAS THE NEXT hill to climb. As a second-year cadet, no longer at the bottom of the totem pole, I was sent off to learn the trade in the TV newsroom at the ABC's Gore Hill studios, on Sydney's lower North Shore. Gore Hill was glamorous, fabulous. Australian television was not yet ten years old. The ABC was making all its own programs, and the place was a teeming anthill of actors, screenwriters, directors, producers, script assistants, make-up and wardrobe people, set designers and builders, graphic artists, journalists, presenters, studio technicians, film cameramen and film editors. Very different to what the TV hacks sneered at as 'steam radio'.

The newsroom itself was in the bowels of the building, with the usual clutch of battered desks and typewriters and a cluster of film editing suites. Not that viewers saw much film in the news bulletins of those early days. The ABC board, in its wisdom, had decreed that pictures should be kept to a minimum, lest any mindless visual frivolity distract from the gravitas of the news itself. This changed over time and by stealth, but it took years.

It was still a great training ground. We were taught the different sorts of film in use, what cameras could and could not do, how to work with a film crew, how to do a stand-up reporter's piece to camera, how to script to a film story and, later, how to put a news bulletin to air as a studio director in a control room. A lot of it stuck: a 400-foot magazine of 16-millimetre magnetic stripe film turns through a BL Arriflex camera in eleven minutes . . .

Most of the cameramen were gnarly old-timers who'd worked on the Movietone and Cinesound cinema newsreels before the arrival of television, and they imposed an iron protocol. Woe betide the whippersnapper journalist who dared touch a camera or, worse, peer through the eyepiece to look at the shot without asking permission. They had film assistants, trainees my own age, who did the donkey work: carting the heavy wooden tripods and aluminium boxes of gear about, reloading the magazines, positioning the lights. Some of those assistants went on to be giants in Hollywood, feted by the great movie directors: feature-film cinematographers Don McAlpine, Geoff Burton, Dean Semler and John Seale all cut their teeth at the ABC, shooting traffic accidents, cats trapped in drains, and celebrities arriving at airports.

Back in radio, other cadets were being hired. The newsroom was expanding, with more reporters and sub-editors, and it moved from shabby Kellett Street to a large and alarmingly well-lit building a few hundred metres down from the Cross on William Street, at the corner of Forbes Street. My place at the bottom of the cadetship ladder was taken by Bob Connolly, another private-school boy, who would go on to be an award-winning film director with a fascination for Papua New Guinea. He was followed by Jeff McMullen, a Parramatta kid who soared to be an ABC Washington correspondent and a star reporter on *Four Corners* and then Nine's *60 Minutes*. Roger Allebone, a teenage giant with the build of a triathlete, came after McMullen.

Jeff, Roger and I morphed into a tri-headed social beast, surfing at Whale Beach, behaving atrociously at the same parties and playing for the newsroom's rugby league team in the journalists' competition. Game for anything and bold as brass, Roger radiated the sort of manic energy that would have taken a couple of Turkish trenches single-handed in 1915. He was honoured in the office for having once ridden his motorbike up to the newsroom in the lift, and then thundering around and around the subs' table in a cloud of exhaust smoke. Women adored him. Once, he lent me his bedroom for a tryst with a girlfriend, promising that he would be away for the weekend, only to turn up at around midnight and clamber into bed with us. 'I lied,' he grinned.

Flinging caution to the winds, Wally Hamilton hired the ABC's second female cadet, Diane Willman, a tall and imperious figure. Told that a woman could never become an ABC foreign correspondent, she quit in disgust and courageously took herself to Beirut to report the Lebanese civil war that erupted in 1975. The first woman cadet, Glennys Bell, was now a graded journalist in her mid-twenties and a very good one, making it through the all-male ruck after enduring the countless atrocities heaped upon her. I saw her one morning in the Gore Hill office, a slight figure lying across a desk with her dress above her knees, spreadeagled where the burly male chief of staff and office bully had physically hoisted her. Half a dozen chortling men stood there in a semicircle. 'Hurr hurr, haw haw. Show us your knickers,' they bawled. 'Go on, be a sport!' I was appalled by it then and I am again as I write this now, but I did not have the courage – or the seniority – to do or say anything. I have regretted this ever since. Glennys took it with a glazed smile and an outward bravado that was born, I suppose, of bitter experience. After more taunts and sniggers she was released. Women had to play the boys' games to get ahead, to cop whatever humiliation was dealt out by the alpha males of the herd. At the same time they had to know their place. It was rare for a woman to be invited to the long boozing sessions across the road at the Gladstone pub in William Street, the blokey hangout of choice.

One Monday morning we discovered another new body in the reporters' room, a scrawny man in his mid-twenties sitting silently at a desk and staring about with the mournful air of a disappointed cocker spaniel. Lank hair fell down his domed skull to his shoulders. Naturally, we ignored him until the chief of staff emerged from his office. 'This is our new cadet,' he said. 'Bob Ellis. He used to edit *Honi Soit*. You've probably heard of him.'

No, we hadn't. *Honi Soit* was the Sydney University student newspaper, we knew, but none of us moved in those circles, nor did we want to. Editor? Piss off. We were far too hard-bitten and street-smart to mingle with undergraduate dilettantes. The only climbers higher than us on journalism's Kosciusko were the cadets at the *Sydney Morning Herald*, Granny herself, who made it plain that they viewed us electronic upstarts as circus jugglers, clowns and sword-swallowers.

'Umble mumble,' said Ellis.

We inspected him from a distance. People who knew the late, great *littérateur* in full bloom, when he was almost spherical, will be surprised to learn that back then he was built like a small garden rake. Or so it appeared. It was hard to be certain because he was encased from head to toe in a greatcoat that would have done handsome service for a marshal of the Soviet Red Army, a garment so voluminous that he had to take two or three steps before it began to move. He might have had shoes on, then again he might not.

'Look after him, someone,' said the chief of staff, disappearing whence he had come.

'Ahem harrumph,' said Ellis.

Someone remembered that the newcomer did have a claim to fame. At the height of the Cuban Missile Crisis, and fearing annihilation, Ellis had fled with a girlfriend to the Blue Mountains, west of Sydney, there to indulge in an end-of-days orgy of sexual abandon while awaiting the nuclear winter. This might not have mattered much in the scheme of things except that the girl was the daughter of David McNicoll, the grandee editor-in-chief of the *Daily Telegraph* and *consigliere* to its owner, Sir Frank Packer. Moreover, Ellis had borrowed McNicoll's Jaguar for the journey. All hell had broken loose, with the cops called in and dire threats of criminal charges for car theft and kidnapping. The uproar died down eventually. We looked upon Ellis with new respect.

My favourite encounter happened when I was subbing. Ellis had been assigned to cover one of the early anti–Vietnam War demonstrations outside the US Consulate in Sydney. With the bulletin deadline closing in and no sign of his story, the chief sub sent me to find out what was happening. Ellis was still in the reporters' room, sucking a pen and typing furiously. He had been so inspired by the fervour of the demonstrators and the rightness of their cause that his words had taken wing. Looking over his shoulder, I saw that he'd written a poem in rhyming couplets. 'What do you think?' he beamed.

The chief sub looked at me aghast when I handed him the blacks. 'Christ,' he said. 'You've got five minutes to put it into prose.'

Ellis was a puckish goblin in the newsroom. He leavened the solemnity no end, but he did not last long. He had greater things to do, as a writer, director, political speechwriter and polemicist, and he went off and did them. At times I thought he was plumb crazy, and at other times a genius. At his best he wrote like a corrupt, impious angel; at his worst it was ranting rubbish. We were not close but we stayed friendly thoughout.

In our last encounter not long before he died in 2016, he bombarded me with fiery emails and phone calls beseeching me to lead a quixotic campaign to proclaim the innocence of the corrupt former Labor MP and union official Craig Thomson.

Only much later did I learn that Ellis had bedded the two daughters of fellow-travelling Sydney bohemian, playwright Dorothy Hewett. Now in their fifties, both women wrote of living with their exotic, erotic mother in what one of them called 'a brothel without payment', where visitors, including Ellis, laid the girls – then aged around fourteen or fifteen – as part of the entertainment. Seventies notions of free love cannot conceal the dark conclusions about Ellis.

✧

Much like the Shipping Round was important, airport arrivals were big news. A pack of about a dozen reporters with attendant newspaper photographers and TV camera crews lurked at the ramshackle Sydney international terminal from dawn each morning, waiting for the first flights to arrive. There weren't many: a couple of Qantas and BOAC jets from London or Hong Kong, a daily Pan Am aircraft from Los Angeles, and a handful of flights across the Tasman from Auckland. The Mascot terminal building dated from well before World War II. Infested by rats and cockroaches, it was divided up with plywood partitions that wobbled like a cheap theatre set if you slammed a door.

I did the Airport Round for almost a year, in some style. At vast expense to the taxpayer and much to the envy of the pack, I was picked up from home each morning by a uniformed driver in a Commonwealth car, a sleek grey Humber Super Snipe. When my morning's work was done and my stories filed, I glided back to the office the same way. The ABC was like that then.

If they wanted the publicity, the famous, not-so-famous and once-famous at the airport were ushered into a cramped and stuffy interview room, where they were bombarded with questions of mind-blowing banality. 'What do you think of Australia?' was standard fare for a while, although that lost its oomph after the actress Vivien Leigh replied: 'I don't know, young man, you're standing in the way.' The Mascot Press Corps, as we grandly styled ourselves, was notorious worldwide for its arrogance and ignorance. The distinguished British conductor Sir Malcolm Sargent was questioned at length on the music of the newly emergent Rolling Stones, a subject on which he had little to say. Someone asked Ray Charles what it was like to be blind. I asked the dancer Ginger Rogers if she suffered from varicose veins. Celebrities who cooperated – which meant not keeping the pack waiting, and providing the answers we demanded – were treated with sycophantic deference. Others copped the opposite. I was not there for it, but when Frank Sinatra arrived in Sydney for the first time, jetlagged, he turned up an hour late for his news conference and grunted monosyllabic answers. Much offended by this insolence, the pack exacted condign retribution. Sinatra was asked to spell his surname and to explain what he did for a living, and was dubbed 'Cranky Frankie' by the afternoon tabloids.

I ran foul of no less than the prime minister. Understandably, I suppose, Robert Menzies regarded the Mascot pack with weary contempt. When returning from one of his junkets to Britain or the US, he would deliver a short statement for the cameras, take no questions and march from the room. When he came back from Washington in 1964, I was ordered by the chief of staff, on pain of death, to ask him a question written for me.

'Ladies and gentlemen,' the PM began when he arrived, 'I have had important talks with our great friend President Johnson at the White House. I have had a long and tiring flight home, and have nothing more to add at this time. I shall make a full report to parliament in Canberra next week.' Then, as usual, he turned from the bank of microphones and moved for the door.

Quaking in my boots, my voice an octave or two higher than normal, I stepped forward. 'Mike Carlton, ABC Television,' I squeaked. 'Prime Minister, what did you discuss with the President?'

There was a silence as deep as the grave. It went on for about a year. The entire airport screeched to a halt. Aircraft on finals aborted and went around again. Open-mouthed, Menzies' praetorian guard and my colleagues in the press pack stared at me in horror and amazement. Ming himself stopped mid-stride and swung back, his famous eyebrows knitted together like copulating caterpillars.

His eyes drilled into mine. 'I've not seen *you* before,' he boomed. 'And I have no wish to see you again.'

Turning on his heel, he sailed for the exit. If only I'd had the wit to explain that I was the grandson of Win Symington, the Liberal Party scone-maker. When I told Nana about it that night, she was scornfully dismissive. 'Well, of course Menzies wouldn't have time for someone as unimportant as you,' she snapped.

The Beatles arrived in the midst of a typhoon, or near enough to it. The wind screeched. Rain blasted across the tarmac in horizontal sheets. It was breakfast time on Thursday, 11 June 1964. In that more gentle era, the welcoming crowds were allowed onto the tarmac, and some 2000 people turned out to scream their heads off as the Fab Four stepped down from their plane. Or the Fab Three plus one: Ringo Starr had been left behind in Britain with tonsillitis, and they had brought a stand-in drummer, Jimmie Nicol. Australia was in a fit of national hysterics as never before or since, gripped by Beatlemania. People wore plastic Beatle wigs and queued to buy Beatle bracelets, scarves, boots, suits, pencil cases, wine glasses, make-up compacts, dolls, posters and hairbrushes. The commercial radio stations and Channel Nine turned on live outside broadcasts from dawn that morning, a stunning technical feat for television then: amazingly, the pictures were carried all the way to Melbourne on the brand new coaxial cable. Even the staid old ABC joined in, flinging up its skirts with a half-hour special called *B-Day* narrated by Kit Denton (father of Andrew). John Lennon spoke on ABC Radio's *Guest of Honour*, a flagship talk show usually reserved for visiting Nobel Prize winners and others of the great and good.

At the airport the group trundled slowly around the tarmac on the back of a flatbed truck, drenched in the downpour but still doggedly waving at the fans. One mother of a disabled child broke from the throng and thrust the wee mite into the arms of Paul McCartney, apparently hoping for a cure. I was corralled with the rest of the reptiles, jotting in a sodden notebook. Perhaps 20,000 people had jammed into Macleay Street at Potts Point to camp outside the Beatles' hotel, and they stayed there for two days, many longer.

That afternoon there was a news conference with drinks and canapés laid on, and the Beatles mingled with the hacks for an astonishing three hours, without complaint. The grandest names in Sydney journalism turned up to gawk, so they could tell their daughters they'd been there. I scored a longish chat with Lennon and McCartney – about what I now haven't a clue, but I imagine I grovelled – and I got the autographs of all four of them, which, naturally, I have since lost. Their first Sydney concert was a week later, 18 June, at the old stadium at Rushcutters Bay, a tumbledown slum with a tin roof that made the average shearing shed seem luxurious. You could hardly hear a note for all the teenyboppers screaming in orgasmic ecstasy and the thud of their fainting bodies collapsing to the wooden floor. 'Thousands of girls under sixteen who occupied the most expensive seats seem to be in a state of delirium, laddering stockings and losing their shoes,' the *Sun-Herald* reported. 'Many were hurried off to the first aid room, too excited to stand anymore.'[51]

It was wonderful. Other superstars came and went, but there was nothing on that scale again. The Rolling Stones toured six months later, on a joint ticket with Roy Orbison, and they did the bog-standard airport news conference. A hack from the *Sun* collected their empty Coke cans and sold them, for a pound each, to the fans outside. 'Yeah, Mick drank from that one . . .' I've run into Jagger several times since, in Sydney and London. He is invariably amiable but laconic, giving the impression that, inwardly, he is stifling the boredom by enjoying some hilarious private joke. The Big O, when he fronted, got a grilling about his very obviously tinted jet-black hair.

The famously taciturn Marlon Brando surprised us by agreeing to be interviewed when we discovered him hiding behind dark sunglasses in an airline lounge, on the way to see his then girlfriend in Tahiti, but he just mumbled. Poor Ray Charles sprawled before us on the couch, scratching and lurching and flinging his limbs about in a convulsion, barely able to speak.

'What was all that about?' I asked someone in all innocence.

'Heroin,' was the reply. 'He's had to go cold turkey for the tour and it's killing him.'

Nobody wrote that story.

✧

The Airport Round had been enjoyable, having a tissue-thin glamour to it. When drinking with my mates at the Greengate or trying to impress girls, I didn't so much drop the names of the celebrities I met as hurl them into the ring with a resounding crash. But the frivolity palled after a while, and I asked to go back to general reporting. Much of what I did then has faded in the fog of time, although I powerfully recall the first *Voyager* Royal Commission in 1964.

The aircraft carrier HMAS *Melbourne* had collided with the much smaller destroyer HMAS *Voyager* during exercises off Jervis Bay, south of Sydney, on the evening of Monday, 10 February 1964. Of *Voyager*'s 314 officers and sailors, eighty-two were killed, including the captain, Duncan Stevens. It was the Royal Australian Navy's darkest hour in peacetime. I remember seeing *Melbourne* limp into Sydney Harbour with a great hole carved out of her bow.

The commission was led by a senior judge, Sir John Spicer, who had once been a Liberal senator for Victoria, and attorney-general in the first postwar Menzies government. There was huge public interest, whipped along by the newspapers and politicians, and largely focused – as these things always are – on who was to blame. As a cadet, I was assigned to be a gofer for the experienced reporter covering the hearing, Tony Ferguson.

Melbourne's commanding officer, Captain John Robertson, endured an age in the witness box. He was a tall man, dignified in civvies – a grey double-breasted suit – and grew ever more hesitant as counsel assisting the commission, Jack Smyth QC, tore him to shreds with evident venom. Robertson was a fine naval officer but he was a fish out of water in a courtroom, and Smyth was vicious. The captain became flustered, confused. The collision was, in fact, the fault of *Voyager* and her captain, a sick man unfit for command and known to his sailors as 'Drunken Duncan'. But his father, Major General Sir Jack Stevens, had friends in high places and it was settled that Robertson should be the scapegoat. The fix was in.

Spicer's report, a deceitful farrago, pointed the finger at Captain Robertson, and his naval career was ruined. A second Royal Commission in 1967 absolved him of blame but it was too late. It was shameful. To this day his family has not received the apology the Navy owes.

✧

Every so often we cadets would be despatched to the bush or interstate to relieve journalists who were taking leave at the ABC's country radio stations. I did time at Albury, Wollongong, Grafton and Orange in New South Wales, and a couple of months in Hobart as well. It was easy enough if you were at a two-man country newsroom, working with another journalist who knew the territory and the people, but much harder if you were flying solo.

At my first gig in Albury I was alone with two local, seven-minute news bulletins to fill each day, and only the vaguest idea of how to do it. I didn't know the name of the mayor, let alone anyone else. Somehow I scraped by, helped by a raging bushfire which broke out nearby and provided more than enough news to go around. Country journalism is unforgiving. Get the name of the president of the local RSL or bowls club wrong, or forget to run the scores of last Saturday's football match between Woop Woop and Funnel Web Gully and there'll be thirty phone calls to set you right.

In the spring of 1964 the ABC sent me to Darwin, for what became three of the longest months of my life. It was the old town as it was before Cyclone Tracy wrought lethal havoc ten years later, a drowsy, blousy colonial outpost of nondescript office buildings, tin sheds, pubs, stinking-hot fibro houses hoisted on stilts, and red dust roads. In the dry season the heat was almost a physical assault. I was put up in a Commonwealth hostel for junior public servants, a long bus ride out of town. It was all blokes, and everyone dressed for work in 'Territory rig': a short-sleeved, open-necked shirt, 'tailored walk shorts' and knee-high socks. There weren't any women in Darwin unless they were somebody's long-suffering wife or one of the gaggle of broken whores up from the south to ply their trade one last time. I didn't have sex in all the time I was there. Blokes, blokes, blokes.

The hostel had rows of huts like *Stalag Luft III*. All that was missing were the machine gun towers and a *Luftwaffe Feldwebel* to do the shouting; that was provided by the drunks who staggered home at three in the morning. I got a shabby room to myself, a cell with a ceiling fan that moved the air and the flies around but had no cooling function. There were mouldy communal showers and a greasy dining room which dished out tepid evening meals of incinerated buffalo and congealed cabbage, endless cabbage. It was as near to being in jail as I have ever come.

The ABC office was in the centre of town, insofar as the place actually had a centre. I was the sidekick to the Regional Journalist, Darwin, as he was officially designated, a man named Bud Eastley, who eventually became the national chief sub in Sydney. We had three bulletins to fill each day – morning, noon and evening – which was not always easy, because not much news happened. Self-government for the Northern Territory was still fourteen years away. The place was run by an administrator appointed from Canberra, usually some retired political drone from down south, advised by a Legislative Council of public service chieftains. The administrator would make the occasional pronouncement about something or other, and we'd pad out the rest of the bulletin with car accidents and minor crime. Occasionally a crocodile would eat someone.

I couldn't see any point to Darwin. There probably was one but I never discovered it. In 1942 it had made a useful target for the Japanese, but there'd been nothing very interesting since. The population seemed to be mostly junior pen-pushers like my fellow inmates at the hostel, sent up from Canberra to serve the needs of other junior pen-pushers sent up from Canberra, and around and around they went. Take out the public service and there wouldn't have been much left. If you saw Aboriginal people, it was a terrible fact that they were usually dead-drunk in a park or on the beach.

The main industry was drinking. There was nothing else to do. It was Darwin's proud boast that the male population alone drank more beer each year than Belgium. Bud introduced me to the Victoria Hotel on Smith Street, always known as the Vic, and owned by a third-generation Chinese-Australian family, the Fong-Lims. Built partly of an ochre-coloured local stone and partly of corrugated iron, with a beer garden of sorts tacked on one side, it was a rough old joint dating back to the nineteenth-century colonial days when Darwin was known as Palmerston. Two of the Fong-Lim brothers, Richard and Alec, ran the bar with a rod of iron for a shifting clientele of more public servants, crocodile hunters, miners, stockmen, blow-ins from 'down the track', and the journalists and printers from Darwin's only newspaper, the *Northern Territory News*. Richard would break up the fights and throw the combatants out onto the street, sometimes barring a serious offender for a month or so.

And the Vic was one of Darwin's posher pubs. You took your life in your hands if you went to drink at the Don Hotel, a couple of blocks away, where blood flowed in the gutters. All the pubs were whites only. Aboriginal men and women were still not allowed to drink (and had been given the vote only two years before).[52]

I spent a lot of time at the Vic – most nights, in fact, anything to avoid the heat, boredom and filthy food of the hostel. The legal drinking age in the Territory was twenty-one, but nobody – certainly not the Fong-Lims – cared that I was only eighteen. The beer was good and cold, a suitable accompaniment for the Vic's signature dish of beef curry and rice, which could blow your head off.

My drinking mates were two blokes a little older than me, an acne-scarred printer from the paper named Mick, and a scruffy, red-haired plumber unsurprisingly known as Bluey. They were cheerful, easy-going. We knocked around, watching the local footy on Saturdays or going for a swim in one of the (hopefully) crocodile-free waterholes out of town. Every so often Mick and Bluey would take themselves off to one of the knock shops to ease the tension, but, North Shore boy that I was, I could never bring myself to accompany them. One night I got so pissed I couldn't type the next morning's news bulletin. Mick did it for me, a kindness marred by Bluey spilling his Bacardi and Coke all over its pages. The newsreader had to pull the soggy sheets apart to read them.

More often than not we were joined at the Vic by one of the truly vivid characters of the Top End, and one of the most extraordinary figures I have encountered in journalism, the editor of the *NT News*, Jim Bowditch. He was a little bloke in his late forties or early fifties, as lean and wiry as a dingo, with a beaky nose, big dark eyes and a striking head of wavy silver hair. During the war, Bowditch – he was always called by his surname – had been a sergeant in that storied commando force, Z Special Unit, in which he was awarded his parachute wings, the Distinguished Conduct Medal and a slate of reprimands and punishments for assorted military crimes, misdemeanours and insubordinations. In June 1944 he was one of five commandos who slipped out of Darwin in a Dutch submarine and were put ashore on a jungle island off the tip of West Papua, where they were to keep watch and make radio reports on a Japanese air and naval base in nearby Sorong Harbour. One dark night Bowditch paddled alone into the harbour to plant limpet mines on shipping there, making a successful getaway before they exploded. For three months the team dodged the searching Japanese, until an American PT boat pulled them out in September.

I learned of this much later; Bowditch never spoke of it. Z Unit commandos had been sworn to secrecy after the war, a gag not lifted until 1980. All we knew was that the editor of the *News* had been in the army and liked a fight. Sober, he was a genial raconteur, everyone's mate. Drunk, he was a lunatic. And with his small frame, it didn't take much to get him there; two beers were enough to push him over the cliff. At which point he would leap from his chair, turn his empty glass upside down in the traditional challenge, put up his fists and quite literally offer to take on the bar. 'Who wants it?' he would shout as he lurched and tottered on his skinny legs, arms flailing. 'Come on, ya bastards! I'll fight the lot of ya!'

Most times there were no takers. His chief sub-editor and sportswriter, Peter Blake, would get him in a headlock and forcibly sit him down, or Richard Fong-Lim would grab him by the collar and fling him into the street. 'There goes Bowditch again,' we'd say, turning back to our drinks. On rare occasions a newcomer might take up the offer and the brawl would ricochet around the beer garden, overturning tables, pot plants and jugs of beer, and causing mayhem until Richard called the cops.

'Yer coming with us, Mr Bowditch.'

'Piss off, you cunts. I'm not going anywhere.'

'Yes, you are.'

Bowditch would then take a swing at one of the officers, who would dodge it with practised ease. With a heavy sigh the biggest cop would tuck him under an arm and march out, the editor hollering, 'Police brutality! Assault!' as they threw him, still flailing, into the back of the truck. Sometimes they just drove him home, an address they knew through weary experience. If his wife refused to let him in, which was often, or if he had actually managed to biff a copper, they would charge him, which meant a night in the cells and an appearance in the magistrates' court the next morning.

This presented no great problem: the chief magistrate was Bowditch's golfing partner. The editor would fess up, all contrition. There would be a stiff lecture from the bench – 'a man of your position in the community . . .' – then a slap on the wrist and the two would adjourn to lunch.

Best of all, Bowditch would insist that his newspaper report the whole thing on its front page: 'The editor of the *Northern Territory News* was fined £100 yesterday after pleading guilty . . .' Inside the paper there would be a stern editorial exhorting the police to do their proper job of catching real criminals instead of loitering outside pubs to harass innocent drinkers enjoying a night out.

For all the colour and movement of his chaotic life, Jim Bowditch was actually a bravura editor in the old-fashioned way. He put out a good paper. His politics were on the left, and he cared passionately about fairness and social justice, often to the displeasure of his absentee proprietor, Rupert Murdoch, who had bought the *News* in 1960. Bowditch reported fairly and at times courageously on Indigenous issues when that was hardly a popular thing to do. One of his mates, Brian Manning, was a leader of the local branch of the Communist Party. Together they knocked a big dent in the White Australia policy with a stirring and successful campaign to prevent the Menzies government from deporting three ethnically Malay divers who had lost their jobs in the pearling industry.

Towards the end of my stay in Darwin, Bowditch offered me a job. I could be the *NT News*' senior reporter, he said. It was flattering and the role came with a pay rise; I even thought about taking it for a bit. But all that boozing at the Vic had made me fat and sluggish, bursting out of my shirt and shorts. I liked Bowditch and he liked me, but I was homesick, and had no wish to become just another beer-gutted, alcohol-pickled Territory drifter. I was back in Sydney on Christmas Eve.

James Bowditch DCM died of pneumonia in 1996, and was given the military funeral he merited. His daughter Sharon married the legendary Murdoch editor Col Allan.

✧

The Shrimp changed everything. In October 1965 Jean Shrimpton, the first of the supermodels, was paid a stonking £2000 to fly from Britain to add international glam to the Spring Racing Carnival in Melbourne. She blew them away. The little white sleeveless dress she wore on Derby Day, with its hemline a shocking 10 centimetres above her knees, shook Melbourne to the core. More scandalous still, she hadn't bothered to wear hat, gloves or stockings.

The matrons of Toorak were outraged. 'If Miss Shrimpton wants to wear skirts four inches above the knee in London, that's her business, but it's not done here. I feel we do know so much better than Miss Shrimpton,' hissed Lady Nathan, a former lady mayoress. 'We all dress correctly here.'[53]

Fleet Street hit back. 'Surrounded by sober draped silks and floral nylons, ghastly tulle hats and fur stoles, she was like a petunia in an onion patch,' said the *Evening News*.[54]

The Shrimp and her dress had proclaimed the arrival in Australia of Swinging London. We raced to get on board. The music of the Beatles, the Stones, the Kinks and the Who blasted from our trannies. Carnaby Street told us what to wear: Mary Quant's ever-shorter miniskirts for the girls, skin-tight shirts and jackets for the boys. The craze for James Bond books and movies took off. Shaken, not stirred, London was the epicentre of our pop-cultural ambitions and pretensions.

I saw my first ever E-Type Jaguar at Sandringham Beach in Melbourne – a stunning 3.8-litre convertible in a pale, opalescent grey – and promised myself that one day I would have one. Ceding the Morris Mini to my mother, I bought a second-hand MG sports car, an MGA 1600 Mark II roadster in a glorious cherry red, for an eye-watering £815.[55] An MG was the car of choice for us North Shore blades. The Westies were hotting up and lowering their FJ Holdens, but outside the Greengate on a Saturday night there were MGs stretching to the horizon, from rattly old TCs to the new MGB, with the occasional Triumph TR3, Sunbeam Alpine or little Austin-Healey Sprite to leaven the mix. When the pub closed at ten o'clock it was like the start at Le Mans as we raced to get to the party of the night, blithely unconcerned that we were already half-pissed. Random breath-testing was still seventeen years away. As long as you didn't weave along the road too obviously or hit something, you were okay. Some of us even affected string-backed driving gloves and long scarves, and we ardently followed the Formula 1 Grand Prix careers of the British drivers Graham Hill, John Surtees and Jim Clark, and Australia's own Jack Brabham.

During the week, if I was rostered off for two days and there was no one else around, I'd fang the MG down to Bilgola for a surf, crash on the beach to read my way through more of my private arts degree, then sink a couple of late-afternoon schooners in the beer garden at the Newport Arms hotel. On summer weekends the Arms was a teeming mob of half-naked, sunburned teenage bodies, thousands of us, patrolled by the pub bouncer, a local surf lifesaver, footballer, standover man and small-time criminal named Tim Bristow. He was much feared. Look at Bristow the wrong way and he would rearrange your teeth and face, and then throw you out onto the footpath. Great was the day when Bristow incautiously decided to take on Tony Madigan, the Australian Olympic boxer who had twice gone the distance with Muhammad Ali. Madigan beat Bristow to a pulp, to a standing ovation.

✧

Back at work in Sydney, I spent a few months grinding away at the subs' desk, cutting or rewriting reporters' copy under the mordant eye of Sid Mounsey. It was drudgery, but useful practice in the arts of brevity, speed and accuracy. Sid was the first of many senior journalists who would take time to teach me the ropes, mentoring me in my career. They did it not because I was any good but because they were. They cared about journalism in general and about public broadcasting in particular, and they saw it as both an obligation and a rewarding pleasure to pass on what they knew.

Towards the end of that spell of subbing I was pushed up the totem pole to become late-evening chief sub: I was still a teenager, but was now in charge of all the bulletins that went to air from nine o'clock at night. For a few weeks I had three former newspaper editors working for me on the desk, men much older than me but whose careers had somehow gone off the rails. It was tricky. They could have screwed me over no end, or been condescending, but instead they treated me kindly while gently correcting some clunking error I had made.

With the seven pm bulletin put to bed, we would repair for an hour to the Gladstone, where the saloon bar was always full of ABC people and their ilk: journalists, producers, announcers, actors. Norman 'Nugget' May, the star sports commentator, was a regular. So was the actor Bill Hunter, perched on a stool and cracking jokes. My first stirrings of political awakening probably began at the Gladdie, listening to journalists far more experienced than me sounding off about the iniquities of politicians and governments. Then as now, the politics of a majority of journalists fell to the left of centre, in varying degree; this was startling at first to a North Shore private-school boy, scout patrol leader and MG driver.

It troubled the Menzies government, too. At one stage, with the evident agreement of ABC management, ASIO sent in a spook to masquerade as a newsroom journalist and report our conversations. The poor dear could barely type, let alone compose a news story, but she hung around like a bad smell, trying to ingratiate herself. It was obvious who she was and what she was up to, so we helpfully invented lurid gossip to please her masters.

There was no Pauline epiphany on the road to Damascus for me; it was more a slowly dawning realisation that the adulation of Robert Menzies at 53 Orchard Road Chatswood was by no means universal.

It turned out there were even people who despised him and all his works. I kept listening and reading, listening and reading.

A stretch in the Press Gallery in Canberra took me further down that track. Old Parliament House, that low white wedding cake squatting up from the lake, was a universe apart from the soulless sterility of the present building. Quaintly, it smelt of wax floor polish, with a patina of warm timber and shiny brass. The offices of the newspapers and broadcasters were jammed together upstairs, cheek by jowl, and became ever more cramped as ever more journalists were shoehorned in. The place reeked of cigarette smoke, and was alive with ringing telephones and the chatter of typewriters. Politicians and their advisers were thrown together with the hacks, like it or not. If you loitered long enough in King's Hall, the wide, pillared foyer which separated the chambers of the Senate and the House of Representatives, you would encounter anybody and everybody who mattered in the affairs of the nation: a passing parade of government, opposition and public service. It was political theatre on an intimate stage, tragedy and comedy and farce.

MPs had their private bar and dining room, forbidden to the public and reptiles of the press, but the crucible was the Non-Members Bar, where anyone who worked in Parliament House could go for a drink and a light meal. Gossip flew, lies were told, truths were dug up. Scandals erupted and died. Reputations were made and destroyed. Dangerous liaisons, sexual and otherwise, were knotted and unravelled. Ministers and frontbenchers would send their offsiders to the Non-Members' to take soundings, or to spread rumours and leaks. Sometimes they appeared themselves. The great beasts of the Press Gallery held court, giants such as the *Sydney Morning Herald*'s chief political correspondent, Ian Fitchett, a celebrated grandee who had famously bested Menzies in a spirited exchange. Angry at some coverage he was getting from the *Herald*, Menzies had snapped at him, 'I'll make you eat crow!' Unruffled, Fitchett shot back: 'I will be happy to eat crow, Prime Minister, provided it is garnished with the sauce of your embarrassment.'[56]

Another of the gallery bestiary was Alan Reid, the chain-smoking chief correspondent for the Packer *Daily Telegraph* and Channel Nine.

Wily and scheming, Reid was nicknamed 'the Red Fox'. It was he who whipped up the devastating scare about Labor's 'Faceless Men' during the 1963 election, with his front-page story and its accompanying pictures of Labor's parliamentary leader, Arthur Calwell, and his deputy, Gough Whitlam, standing under a street light outside a meeting of the ALP Federal Conference, waiting to be told what policy had been decided within. Reid was gruff but generous with his time and knowledge to us tyros, and I learned a lot from him then and later when I worked at Nine. Less valuable was the ABC bureau chief, Jack Commins, a pompous grandee who had been in the gallery since 1945, but – as everybody said – without ever breaking a story.

✧

I was graded in November 1965. Still nineteen, I was no longer a cadet but a fully fledged D-grade journalist, on a fabulous £25.16.0 per week.[57] It had taken me three years to get there, fewer than the specified four, although this was no great coup. Only a few plodders ever did the full stretch.

The horizon looked bright, although there was a low rumble of thunder from beyond the hills. In November 1964 the government had introduced a National Service Scheme, as it was soothingly called. Conscription for the army. Continuing *Konfrontasi* with Indonesia and the ever deteriorating war in Vietnam had spooked the Menzies cabinet. Young men turning twenty were compelled to register with the Department of Labour and National Service to take part in what we would eventually call 'the lottery of death'. The days of the year were inscribed on marbles in a barrel. If the marble with your birthday was drawn out, you were in. Pass the medical exam and you were conscripted for two years' full-time service in uniform, followed by another three years part-time in the Army Reserve.

The thunder grew closer, louder. On a quiet autumn afternoon in Canberra – it was Thursday, 29 April 1965 – Menzies plunged the nation into war. Without warning or notice – either to his backbench or to the opposition – he rose in a half-empty House of Representatives to make an announcement:

> The Australian government is now in receipt of a request from the government of South Vietnam for further military assistance. We have decided – and this has been in close consultation with the government of the United States – to provide an infantry battalion for service in Vietnam . . .
>
> The takeover of South Vietnam would be a direct military threat to Australia and all the countries of South-East Asia. It must be seen as part of a thrust by Communist China between the Indian and Pacific Oceans.[58]

The lie had begun. Menzies, ever the silver-tongued conjuror, who had himself evaded service and conscription during World War I, set out deliberately to deceive the Australian parliament and people. The regime in Saigon was in fact deeply reluctant to have another foreign flag flying on its soil and more foreign boots on the ground. The Americans were enough. The 'request' from South Vietnam was a confection. It had been extracted only after constant diplomatic badgering, pleading and pushing from an Australian conservative government that was desperate to get into the war, burning to demonstrate to the US that we were an ardent, loyal ally. Compounding the lie was the folly of the 'thrust by Communist China', which the prime minister himself might perhaps have believed, but which history has unmasked as a strategic and geopolitical delusion. The treacherous duplicity of Menzies and his Minister for External Affairs, Paul Hasluck, would cost 521 Australian lives.

The next month, May, an advance detachment of the army's 1st Battalion sailed for Vietnam in the troop carrier HMAS *Sydney*, soon to be nicknamed the *Vung Tau Ferry*. And the government upped the ante again to make conscripts liable for military service overseas.

My marble would be in the barrel for the first ballot of 1966. If it was drawn out, I might have to fight in Vietnam. This was not what I had planned.

8

Good evening, Vietnam

My mother and Peter came to Mascot to see me off, but not to Vietnam. Boys my age and younger, in slouch hats and jungle greens, were flying from Sydney to the sprawling US base at Bien Hoa, north of Saigon. I was boarding a Qantas 707 to Singapore to become an ABC foreign correspondent.

I turned twenty in January 1966. For the first three months of that year I sweated blood, waiting to see if my ballot marble would turn up. If it did, there were only two ways out. University students or apprentices could get a deferment, but that didn't cover me. I could fail the medical exam somehow, or become a conscientious objector. Neither seemed a goer. Like most Australians at that time, I had fallen for Menzies' deceit. I took it as read that communism had to be stopped, and I had no genuine belief in pacifism. Most of the newspapers, chiefly the Fairfax press, were shouting their support for the war. Only Rupert Murdoch's new national daily, the *Australian*, dared raise a voice against the ferocious rattle of sabres and the printers' ink patriots, branding our involvement as reckless and wrong. 'It could be that our historians will recall this day with tears,' wrote the columnist Douglas Brass.[59]

My marble was not picked out. On 16 March 1966 the National Service Department posted me a small printed card advising that 'you have been granted indefinite deferment of your liability to render national service, and consequently, under present arrangements, you will not be called up'. I was rostered off work the day I got it. I remember gusts of relief and the triumphal joy of belting the MG down Mona Vale Road to dive into the embracing surf at Bilgola.

Now, six months later, I was off to South-East Asia anyway, still not quite believing it.

In September Wally Hamilton called me to his office to ask if I would be willing to relieve some of the regular correspondents who were taking home leave. It would be for about six months, and he would jump me from D-grade to B-grade journalist to do it.

Christ! I was flabbergasted. B-grade! Overseas! A foreign correspondent! I sold the MG, got deliriously drunk at some farewell parties, and bought new socks and underwear. D-day was Wednesday, 2 November.

My mother left in her papers a small black-and-white photograph she took at the airport. 'Qantas plane on which Michael left for Singapore,' she wrote on the back. She tried to suppress her tears as I disappeared through the doors of the departure area, tears of pride for the firstborn son soaring, tears of sadness for the chick flying the nest. She had done her best to rear me, supervising my schooling and fretting about my manners and my sex education, insisting above all that I should become her idea of a gentleman who could make his way in the world. It had not been easy. Money had always been tight and there had been no husband and father to help bear the burden or to be the male role model. But she was confident she had succeeded. I would be a credit to her and the memory of my father. Enid Carlton never remarried. She carried a candle for Jim for the rest of her days, and still spoke of him to me as 'Daddy' even when I had given her grandchildren. I was the man in her life to whom she could confide at least some of her hopes and fears, and who could stand up to Nana, her ever more querulous mother. Now I was leaving and she would have only Peter, who had just turned sixteen. He might have been glad to see me go. Like many younger brothers, Peter had been forced into the backyard supporting role. Never the goodie, always the baddie; the Indian, never the cowboy; the beastly

Hun, not the dashing Spitfire pilot. At last he could get out from under the domineering elder brother. I tried to make amends for this later by stumping up the money to buy him a brand new school uniform suit from David Jones, the first our family had ever owned.

I flew first class, up the pointy end, as prescribed for overseas travel in the industrial award for ABC journalists. God knows how the union ever got that through. I sank back in the seat as James Bond-ishly as I could manage. I could have been in the Peter Stuyvesant commercial. 'More champagne, Mr Carlton? Will you have the smoked salmon or the caviar?' The steward flourished the silver servers, spooning out a splodge of beluga onto the fine bone china with little mounds of chopped onion, tissue-thin slices of lemon, crumbled hard-boiled egg, a delicate sprig of parsley. I had never imagined such luxury, such elegance. 'The captain would like to invite you to the flight deck . . .'

✧

Singapore was an assault on all the senses. It was like diving headlong into a curry. Tony Ferguson met me at the old Paya Lebar airport. He drove us into the city on streets steaming from the monsoon rain at twilight, weaving through a teeming, farting, honking tangle of cars, motorbikes, buses and taxis, past the Chinese shop houses ablaze with lurid neon signs and food stalls lit by bright white pressure lamps, along dark, curving avenues fringed with palms. The night air was hot and sweet and sour, cloying and clinging. Intoxicating aromas floated on the breeze: the perfumes of mysterious fruits and spices and of meats cooked on charcoals, blended with the sharp whiff of two-stroke exhaust and tropical decay. It was ambrosia.

My room at the Cathay Hotel was about the size of the house at Chatswood. You could have floated a yacht in the bath. A year ago I had been sweating in my cell in the Darwin hostel. Now this! Sikh porters in turbans flung open doors. Chinese waiters beamed and bowed. The butter at breakfast came in little curls, garnished with a purple Singapore orchid. The Cathay had been the first air-conditioned building in Singapore before the war, then the Japanese propaganda ministry for the Greater East Asia Co-Prosperity Sphere, then the post-war headquarters of Lord Louis Mountbatten. From my balcony I could see the colonial pillars and gables of the Chinese YMCA, which had housed the *Kempeitai*, the Japanese secret police. Beyond that was the green hill of Fort Canning, where Lieutenant General Arthur Percival had realised the game was up in 1942.

Newly independent, Singapore was throwing off its colonial bonds. There were still British Army officers in the streets and young squaddies from Manchester and Glasgow trying their luck by night with the transvestites of raunchy Bugis Street; you could get a blow job beneath your table while you drank. Rather more toney, the Tanglin Club had yet to admit its first Chinese member. Europeans at the top of the tree lived in elegant villas, each with a houseboy, a cook, an *amah* for the kiddies, gardeners and a *syce*, or driver.

Lee Kuan Yew, the island's charismatic prime minister since 1959, was laying the first building blocks for an economic and financial powerhouse. I filmed a television interview with him in his office, uneasily aware that I was in the presence of an intellect far more powerful than mine. He was courteous but aloof, with a coldness to him. Harry Lee – as his undergraduate contemporaries at Cambridge knew him – maintained the forms of parliamentary democracy while ruthlessly jailing or bankrupting his opponents, but his vision for Singapore was unswerving and ultimately triumphant.

Life was good. The ABC office at 15 Peck Hay Road was the headquarters for a network of correspondents in Jakarta, Kuala Lumpur, Saigon and Tokyo. It also managed the Asian operations of Visnews, the international television news film agency. The senior journalist who ran the show, J. A. Hollinshead – always known as Peter – was one of the best bosses I ever worked for, brilliant and gregarious and funny, and fiercely protective of his troops. He had the clout to fend off meddling editors back in Sydney and Melbourne and haughty Australian diplomats abroad, many of whom could never get it into their gilded heads that the ABC and its overseas shortwave broadcasting service, Radio Australia, were not theirs to command.

I knocked around with some of the local staff my own age, an Indian journalist, Bernard Joseph, and a Malay film editor, Yahya bin Aman, who invited me into their social group of dances and parties. Chinese girls would dance with a Westerner happily enough but not much more, understandably fearing they'd be labelled molls or gold-diggers.

In October, Peter Hollinshead took me to lunch at the posh and fiercely air-conditioned Gordon Grill in the Goodwood Park Hotel. Over an enormous Australian steak and icy Tiger beer, surreally surrounded by Scottish tartans and Monarch of the Glen antlers hanging off the baronial panelled walls, he asked me to go to Thailand to cover a visit by President Lyndon Johnson. And then after that, would I go to Vietnam? It would only be for a few months, to relieve the correspondent there, Don Simmons. I did not have to go. I could say no. He would understand.

Jesus. Vietnam. The war. I had escaped conscription. Now they wanted me to go anyway. And over Christmas, too. But it was the hottest story in the world and getting hotter, and no young journalist would have backed out.

'No heroics, then,' said Peter. 'A dead reporter is no bloody use to anyone.'

✧

Bangkok was an eye-opener, kicking off with some lurid offers from the taxi driver bringing me from the airport. 'You like nice girl, mister?'

'No, thank you.'

'Very clean – she my sister.'

'No, thank you.'

Pause. Then: 'You want nice boy? I get you him tonight.'

'No, thank you.'

Longer pause. Then: 'Maybe you like dog. Or donkey. Also can do.'

The Johnson visit was a run-of-the-mill reporting job, mostly to do with pumping out statements from the White House spokesman: 'Today the President met with . . .' It was the first time I had laid eyes on an American president and his travelling circus, but most notable was the egregious self-importance of the White House press corps members who tagged along with him, a gaggle of fops and prima donnas if ever there was. Some were not entirely sure what country they were in. For some reason, there were three of us from the ABC on the job: Tony Ferguson, me and Tim Bowden, a witty and irrepressible Tasmanian who worked not for the News Department but for what was then called 'Radio Talks'.

It was Tim who insisted that we should see a live sex act. After a well-oiled dinner, and by arrangement with one of Bangkok's ever-helpful taxi drivers, we found ourselves at a grubby shack in a shanty town alongside a *klong*, one of the city's greasy canals. On stage, a naked Thai male made a perfunctory show of screwing an equally listless Thai woman. There were some unusual positions, which I memorised for future use, but in fact the whole performance was dismally unerotic.

Rather more in tune with the zeitgeist, an American reporter for UPI introduced me to the throbbing, robbing bars and strip joints of Patpong Road, the city's sleazy red-light district for tourists. He took me to a high-class whorehouse where he had friends. It was the first time I had ever paid for sex, and I got my money's worth. I had a look at Wat Traimit, the Temple of the Golden Buddha, where I heard a lady from Texas complain that it was not air-conditioned. Then I flew to Saigon.

✧

The Air Vietnam jet landed as if it was making a dive-bombing run, plunging from on high, nose angled hard down at speed, a dodge to minimise the chance of getting hit by a surface-to-air missile on the way in. It was mid-evening at Tan Son Nhut Air Base, already dark, but there were enormous lights blazing over the runways and tarmac. The air stank of jet fuel, hot and acrid. Military aircraft came and went within seconds of each other, apparently at random. A fat-bellied Hercules C-130 transport trundled into the air, followed by a brace of CH-47 Chinook helicopters, then the earth-trembling roar of an F-4 Phantom jet fighter with white-hot spears of flame shooting from its twin afterburners.

Don Simmons was supposed to meet me but he didn't, so I caught a taxi to downtown Saigon and the Continental Hotel, where I had a booking. Except that they didn't have the booking and they didn't have a room. I could try the Caravelle Hotel across the square. The

Caravelle did not have a room either. Perhaps monsieur could take a taxi down Tu Do Street towards the river, where the Majestic Hotel might be of help.

The Majestic was not of help. It was full too, and by now I was getting seriously spooked. The streets were emptying for the eleven pm curfew, which was just fifteen minutes away, and I had nowhere to go. The neon was switching off. I was alone in a strange city at war with, for all I knew, a Viet Cong battalion poised to attack along the next block. Away across the river, smoky white parachute flares were floating in the sky. I could hear the distant thump of heavy artillery.

The taxi was one of those ancient 4CV Renaults designed not long after the fall of Napoleon III, the size, shape and speed of a large tortoise. The driver, who was built like a small tortoise, spoke no English and only slightly more French than me. *Je voudrais un hotel, tout de suite!* Seeing us outside the Majestic, a young Vietnamese squeezed into the back seat beside me, yacked back and forth with the driver, then said in English that he would help. We set off. I could have kissed him – and it turned out that was what he'd been hoping for. With a winsome smile and fluttering eyelashes, the youth thrust an exploratory hand between my thighs.

'Stop the taxi. Stop the fucking taxi!' I threw the groper out, pulled fifty US dollars out of my wallet and waved the bill at the driver, shouting, 'Hotel!' as forcefully as I could.

This produced the desired effect. The streets were deserted by now – eerily so, having been splashed by a warm rain – but after another couple of blocks and several twists and turns the Renault spluttered to a halt outside a small, evil-looking building bearing a flickering hotel sign. I lugged my suitcase into the lobby, determined to stay the night there, come hell or high water. The sour-faced woman on the desk looked at me in astonishment: no room.

Nearly weeping, I pulled out another fifty-dollar bill. It was illegal to use American currency in Saigon but I didn't care, and again it worked. The hag pocketed the money, shoved a key across the desk and sullenly pointed to the elevator. I found the room and crashed on the unmade bed fully clothed. All night I was kept awake by opening and slamming doors, the creaking and hammering of bed springs, and cries of orgasmic pleasure. I had fetched up in a brothel.

✧

Don Simmons and I found each other the next day. He was in US Army combat fatigues, complete with an enormous Browning .45 pistol in a holster slung on his hip, which I found a trifle disconcerting. Journalists were supposed to be non-combatants, unarmed. But Simmo liked guns.

We whipped around downtown Saigon sorting out my accreditation, first with the South Vietnamese Government Press Office, then with MACV – pronounced Mac-Vee – the US Military Assistance Command, Vietnam. The American one was impressive – a card with my photograph on it which gave me the travel, accommodation and messing privileges of a US Army major. All you had to do was flash it and you could go anywhere in the country, any time, and all for free, courtesy of the American taxpayer.

Then it was off to the Bank of India to exchange a fistful of dollars for wads of the local piastre. The Bank of India was actually two furtive, nervous gentlemen from Bombay secretly holed up in a hotel room running a black-market currency racket, an illegal enterprise which could have got them shot. Presumably they were bribing the right people. Everybody used them. They paid the going market rate for US dollars, not the absurdly low official rate, which was universally ignored.

That afternoon, in a grubby auditorium on Tu Do Street, I got my first taste of the Five O'Clock Follies, the media briefing held by the Americans each day to spin the war. A crew-cut colonel – sometimes Army, sometimes Air Force, sometimes Marines – would take the stage in a uniform so sharply starched and creased it could have cut cheese. He would rattle off a blizzard of statistics in the jargon and acronyms so dear to the Pentagon and its far-flung legions. There were body counts for skirmishes and battles, and lists of prisoners, bases and weapons captured, and of targets supposedly taken out in the theatrically named but ultimately unsuccessful Operation Rolling Thunder, which was the sustained bombing of North

Vietnam. There were numbers for the Viet Cong cadres who, seeing the light of democracy and freedom, 'rallied' to the government side in the Chieu Hoi or Open Arms program to encourage defectors. In the early years of the war these outpourings were accepted as graven truth. Later they were widely regarded as fiction, and there would be jeers and laughter from the hacks as the briefer rocketed into some wild flight of fancy. The phrase 'credibility gap' entered the language.

Simmo left the next day. I scammed a room at the Caravelle and began to get my bearings. Saigon at war was a harlot of a city, living on the edge. She must have been beautiful once, a French flower of *l'Extrême-Orient*, a voluptuous *fille de joie* with her Belle Époque opera house, the twin spires of the Cathédrale Notre-Dame de Saïgon, the Rue des Fleurs leading to the flamboyant tower and white colonnades of the Hotel de Ville. Now the bigger buildings downtown were barricaded by huge drums filled with concrete, walls of sandbags, coils of barbed wire and guard posts manned sometimes by American soldiers, or perhaps a couple of White Mice, the derisive nickname for the timid local cops.

The open squares, boulevards and side streets, smoky and dirty, were jammed with snarling Japanese motorbikes, those ancient Renault taxis, and US military trucks, buses and cars. Every so often there would be the screech and whoop of sirens as an EOD jeep – Emergency Ordnance Demolition – punched its way through the traffic to some new bomb scare. Beggars and hookers, touts and rent boys trawled for trade on the footpath outside the open terrace of the Continental, where Graham Greene had supposedly written *The Quiet American*. Occasionally you would get a tantalising glimpse of a young woman gliding by, slender as the stem of a rice plant in her *áo dài*, the exquisite Vietnamese national dress of a long silk tunic and flowing trousers.

By night the bars and restaurants pounded to American music, which consisted entirely of a single song, both maudlin and slurpy-patriotic, 'The Ballad of the Green Berets', sung by one Staff Sergeant Barry Sadler. If there were Green Berets – Special Forces soldiers – in the joint when they played it, they would jump onto the tables and salute, with tears in their drunken eyes. The bar girls would sit on your lap, for a price, automatically assuming you were an American. 'Hey, where you bin all my life, GI? You werry hansum. You buy me one Saigon tea.' They twittered to each other like sparrows. 'Saigon tea' was generally flat Coca-Cola, which cost the equivalent of a couple of bucks. Round-eyes, as the girls called us, drank beer, either the villainous local 33 brand, or Tiger from Singapore and San Miguel from the Philippines. There was no sex in the bars, but you could negotiate an after-hours encounter. 'You wan' fuck me? Short time, long time?' It was not hard to smuggle them back to the hotel.

My guide to this and much more was Neil Davis, a Tasmanian-born film cameraman for Visnews, who, over the years, became almost a romantic figure of the war. In 1966, at the age of thirty-two, his bravery and skill under fire had already made him a name. Tall and handsome, with wavy blond hair and sleepy blue eyes, he also radiated a magnetic attraction for women such as I have never seen in any other man, before or since. He didn't have to lift a finger and they threw themselves at him in waves, leaping in and out of his bed in astonishing numbers. 'What can you do?' he would shrug helplessly, with a lop-sided grin.

In my first few weeks in Vietnam I was nervy and out of my depth, and Neil showed me the ropes. There were little things, like learning to sit facing the door of a bar or restaurant, your back to the wall, so you'd be the first to see if someone chucked a grenade in. (It never happened to me, but I still sit that way in a restaurant today.) And there were the big things: the tricks of getting around the country, of dealing with the American military, of deciding whether a story was actually worth covering or just another piece of trumped-up propaganda.

I think Neil was addicted to the adrenaline rush of danger, although he never swaggered, unlike some of the more idiotically gung-ho American correspondents, who stomped about the place living out their John Wayne fantasies. He was laconic, urbane and funny, but above all modest.

More than once, using his carefully built network of contacts, Neil was able to film the war from the Viet Cong side, as no other cameraman could. On Wednesday, 30 April 1975 he was there, camera rolling, when tank number 843 of the Peoples' Army of Vietnam burst through the gates of the Presidential Palace in Saigon to bring the southern regime crashing down and the US to the humiliation of defeat. It was a matchless world scoop.

✧

The man going up in the elevator in the Caravelle had tired, rheumy eyes, a trimmed grey moustache and beard beneath a nose like a pickled gherkin, and an air of moody melancholy. I recognised him immediately.

'Mr Steinbeck!' I gushed, thrusting out a hand to shake. 'I've read all your books!'

John Steinbeck, giant of American letters, winner of the 1962 Nobel Prize for Literature, had come to Vietnam to report on the war for *Newsday*, a prestigious New York newspaper. We had all heard that he was In Country. I babbled at him like a schoolgirl meeting Elvis. He took it well. I had, in fact, read *Of Mice and Men* and his masterwork, *The Grapes of Wrath*. Picking my Australian accent, he asked what I was doing in the country and then, to my astonishment, suggested we have breakfast together.

So we did. He talked, I listened. He was upbeat about the war, in no doubt of an ultimate US victory. Much of the American media reporting had been biased and pessimistic, he thought. He held the prevailing view that it might take time, but the might of American military technology could not be beaten by an army of black-pyjama'd peasants in sandals made from car tyres. Naturally, I agreed.

The American Left had already begun to criticise the war, and Steinbeck's sometimes vitriolic attacks on anti-war protestors in his *Newsday* pieces would be seen by many of his friends and admirers as a betrayal. Like many before him and since, the great author had succumbed to the schmoozing showered upon him by his friend Lyndon Johnson, and by the MACV commander, General William C. Westmoreland. Breakfast, though, was good.

✧

Saigon sorted, it was time for a look at the war. The Australian Task Force was based at Nui Dat in Phuoc Tuy province, about

90 kilometres to the south-east. Spiffy in a newly tailored safari suit of dark green – now a fashion joke, but useful then for its capacious pockets and easy care – I hitched a ride there on an RAAF Caribou transport aircraft. We flew low over the villages, farms and stretches of rubber and jungle.

'The Dat' was still new, set on a low hill in a cleared rubber plantation, a sprawl of canvas tents, dugouts, and roads bulldozed in the red dirt. It was a bastard of a place, a dustbowl in the dry and a quagmire in the monsoon wet. The 5th and 6th Infantry Battalions of the Royal Australian Regiment – known as 5RAR and 6RAR – had dug themselves in, the diggers living in small tents they called hoochies. There were gunners there too, with the big 105-millimetre howitzer artillery pieces, and cavalrymen riding their boxy, thin-skinned armoured personnel carriers.

I was not welcome. The Task Force Commander, Brigadier David Jackson, had fought in World War II and Korea with distinction. Like most officers of his vintage, he viewed journalists as troublemakers, an unnecessary evil only marginally less verminous than the Viet Cong. My request to go out on an operation or a patrol with one of the battalions was firmly knocked back. I would get in the way and be a danger to everybody.

This was a crushing blow to the former Regimental Sergeant Major of the Barker College Cadets, and I took it with ill grace, while privately conceding that there probably wasn't much call for a sword drill in Vietnam. And the Bren gun was no more either. I protested, but got nowhere.

The army decided it would show me the wonderful good works it was doing in its Civic Action Program to win the hearts and minds of the local people. For days they bounced me around on the back of a dusty Land Rover so I could inspect some renovated school classrooms here or a newly dug well there – all worthy stuff, but hardly news. In the villages the people would stare back, silent and sullen, or ignore us – except for the kids, who would run after us for the lollies we threw to them. The Australians called the Vietnamese 'noggies', which I think was a corruption of the common family name of Nguyen.

Trying to speak to individual diggers was useless. Many didn't want to talk at all, and those who did have something to say quickly found that a sergeant or an officer was hovering within earshot, so they clammed up too. It was infuriating, although with hindsight I'm a little more understanding. I'd turned up only a few months after the bloody Battle of Long Tan, in which eighteen Australians had been killed. It was a fight they had very nearly lost.

On the late afternoon of Thursday, 18 August, about 8 kilometres to the east of Nui Dat, just over 100 Australians of D Company, 6RAR, ran at full tilt into the local D445 Viet Cong battalion, a force of around 2500 men. In a tropical downpour, the diggers were pinned down in the rubber under withering fire, facing annihilation. They were saved by their training and courage, and the inspired leadership of their company commander, Major Harry Smith; by the valour of the RAAF helicopter crews who resupplied their ammunition; by the men of B Company, who fought through to join them; and, finally, by the armoured personnel carriers, which – as the cavalry always must – arrived at the eleventh hour with the firepower to turn the battle. They found the bodies of 245 Viet Cong soldiers the next day. But it had been a close-run thing.

Sometimes the Australian wall of silence did crumble a bit. The war became a little clearer for me one night in the officers' mess at the Task Force headquarters, drinking late with a young lieutenant and a captain. We were knocking back beers beneath the wildly incongruous William Dargie portrait of the Queen in her yellow 'wattle dress'. Her Majesty was at war with Ho Chi Minh, courtesy of her Australian and New Zealand dominions, but not any of the others. Lips loosened, the two officers laid it out for me. Or at least some of it. Two villages had been bulldozed to make way for the Nui Dat base, the people forcibly uprooted from their homes and ancestral graves without compensation.

'Of course they hate us,' said the captain. 'Why wouldn't they? Don't give *me* that fucking "hearts and minds" bullshit. We're trained killers.'

There was more, much more, about the difficulty of telling friend from foe: the farmer in the conical hat placidly hoeing his rice field by day would very likely be 'Charlie', a Viet Cong guerrilla with an AK-47 rifle by night. The local officials representing the Saigon government were incompetent or corrupt. Much of what the Australian Army put out in its official press releases and announcements was more bullshit. And so on.

I took it all in but I could not report it. Rule number one: what's said in the mess stays in the mess, and I had been told all this in confidence. But it moved me a long way up the learning curve. That night awakened my first doubts about the course of the war. But defeat was still unthinkable.

Back at home, others were also having doubts. In early 1966 the first stirrings of anti-war feeling focused on conscription, not so much on the war itself. Laden with the imperial baubles and honours he so coveted, Menzies had retired from his long prime ministership that January, turning the Lodge over to his deputy, Harold Holt. In June, Holt flew to Washington, where he made that infamous declaration to Lyndon Johnson that 'you have an admiring friend, a staunch friend, that will be all the way with LBJ'. That spectacular grovel galvanised the protest movement.

When Johnson returned the visit in October – becoming the first serving US president to come to Australia – he was met by enthusiastic crowds, particularly in Melbourne, where they estimated that 750,000 people turned out to welcome him. Holt, like one of Johnson's family pet beagles, rolled over to have his tummy tickled by the master seducer. But there were substantial public protests, too. In Sydney, demonstrators lay down in front of the presidential motorcade, prompting the fawning premier, Bob Askin, to order his driver to 'run over the bastards'. In Melbourne they threw paint bombs at Johnson's limousine, chanting, 'Hey, hey, LBJ, how many kids did you kill today?' The ABC, disgracefully toadying to a request from the government, decreed that news and current affairs programs must not refer to 'conscripts' but to 'national servicemen'.

In the political arena, opposition to the war was carried by Labor leader, Arthur Calwell, in parliament and at public meeting after public meeting. Calwell had got it right as early as 1965, in a speech crafted for him by Labor's master wordsmith, Graham Freudenberg:

> Our men will be fighting the largely indigenous Vietcong in their own home territory. They will be fighting in the midst of a largely indifferent, if not resentful, and frightened population. They will be fighting at the request of, and in support, and presumably, under the direction of an unstable, inefficient, partially corrupt military regime which lacks even the semblance of being, or becoming, democratically based . . .
>
> We have committed ourselves to the propositions that Communism can be defeated by military means alone and that it is the function of European troops to impose the will of the West upon Asia. These are dangerous, delusive and disastrous propositions.[60]

Politics turned ugly. In June 1966, after he left a meeting at suburban Mosman in Sydney, Calwell was shot at by a would-be assassin, Peter Kocan. The bullet was deflected by his car window and he received only minor cuts from broken glass, but it was a sign of the furies aroused in Australia by the war. Most people, though, were still all for it. In the federal election of 26 November, a poll that was largely a referendum on Vietnam, Holt rode the wave of Johnson's visit to score a slashing win, better than any of Menzies' victories. Labor lost ten seats, retaining just forty-one against the Coalition government's eighty-two. It was the beginning of the end for Calwell. Gough Whitlam was hovering in the Labor wings.

That Christmas, my editors in Sydney ordered me to record messages from diggers to their families, to be broadcast in a national ABC Radio special. Again, it was hardly news-gathering. But at least the army was willing to cooperate, and I taped what felt like endless hours of blokes saying, 'Cheerio and Happy Christmas to Mum, Dad, big sister and little brother, me girlfriend and me mates in the footy team back in Echuca (or Ipswich or Bunbury), and see you all soon.'

One of them, though, blew me away. I found a young Australian soldier about my own age in the big American military hospital at Tan Son Nhut, lying in a room by himself, heavily bandaged. His bed-covers were heaped high over him, with plastic tubes looping from every part of his body. He was grey and groggy from the painkillers, but he brightened when he heard my Australian accent and, after a few false starts, I managed to record his message. He was from country Victoria, and he made a special point of telling his fiancée not to worry – he was getting better all the time and would be back home in a month or so. He managed a brave, wan smile, and reached for my hand to shake.

I smiled back but I could have wept. He was the first combat casualty I had seen. I made some encouraging noises and left. There but for the grace of God . . . When I was out of his hearing, I asked the American nurse what had happened to him.

She was matter-of-fact. 'His balls were blown off by a landmine,' she said. 'But he doesn't know it yet.'

✧

I spent Christmas Day at Nui Dat as homesick as everybody else. Long past midnight we sank cold stubbies in the soldiers' bar known as the Diggers' Boozer. Charlie could have taken the Dat without firing a shot. On Boxing Day I woke in a weapons pit with a hangover that would have killed a black dog. I had not heard from my family, nor they from me. There was just no way to do it. It was the most miserable Christmas of my life.

My last trip to the Task Force offered a little more theatre. South Vietnam's prime minister, Air Vice Marshal Nguyen Cao Ky, went to inspect the place before a visit to Australia. Much excitement. A former commander of the VNAF, the South Vietnam Air Force, Ky was a swaggering little spiv. With his oily black hair slicked down and his moustache clipped to perfection, he was renowned for his flamboyant uniform of jet-black flying suits with a purple scarf at the throat. Often he sported a pearl-handled .45 revolver on each hip. Decent Vietnamese called him a cowboy. The Americans despaired but had to deal with him. He had emerged from the country's revolving-door shambles of coup and counter-coup, and had seized power by the simple stratagem of threatening to use his air force to bomb his Saigon rivals off the planet. They thought he was just mad enough to do it, and he was. He ran the show with sufficient ruthlessness to provoke a series of army mutinies and a Buddhist revolt.

On 12 January 1967, a sunny Thursday, Ky and his entourage were shown around the base by the Australian brass. I was trailing along in the media pack to report this inspiring scene. The procession stopped at the 5RAR area, where a couple of diggers were waiting to display an 81-millimetre mortar to the guest.

Would the prime minister like to fire the mortar at the enemy? Indeed he would. Much sycophantic laughter. Cameras clicked and rolled. Ky was handed a mortar bomb, which he plopped down the tube as instructed, and we stood back for it to rocket away high into the sky and off to the distant foe.

It did not. With a bang and a hiss and a thump, it wobbled out of the tube and plopped onto the dirt about ten metres away, where it lay rocking slightly.

There was a nanosecond of frozen silence and then all hell broke loose. Ky's bodyguards, four of the biggest Vietnamese the world has ever seen, flung him to the ground and piled on top of him. Everyone else headed for whatever cover they could find, which was not much. I plunged into a nearby sandbagged weapons pit, landed on top of my tape recorder and smashed it. We waited. And waited. And sweated. If the bomb exploded it would wipe out a great many people, Ky included. After an eternity, some munitions experts arrived and gingerly removed the thing. We breathed again.

At the end of the visit, the media pack of Vietnamese reporters and photographers and a few Americans and Australians were summoned into the presence of a colonel. 'We require that you don't report that unfortunate incident with the mortar,' said Blimp sternly. 'Security reasons.'

There were puzzled looks and scornful laughter from the reptiles, something the colonel was clearly not accustomed to. 'Well, you won't be using our facilities here to send your reports,' he snapped. We were dismissed.

I took the first plane back to Saigon that evening, writing the story as we flew, and I got it away to Sydney from the Reuters office as soon as I hit town.

✧

Incoming! A rocket lands with a clang. It is not the boom or the whoomp you get in the movies, more the sound of a giant with a sledgehammer hitting an empty cast-iron water tank, magnified about a million times. It echoes, reverberates.

Four rockets hit as I arrived at Dong Ha, a US Marine Combat Base about 10 kilometres south of the Demilitarised Zone, the DMZ, which drew the line between North and South Vietnam.[61] It was dusk, the sun already below the hills. I sprinted from the runway, where I had jumped down from a big Chinook transport helicopter, following the bodies hurtling into a sandbagged underground shelter. It was the first time I had been under fire, however marginally.

Oddly, I wasn't scared but incredulous. Why were they rocketing *me*? Michael Carlton of 53 Orchard Road, Chatswood, had done them no harm; what possible reason could they have for trying to kill me? Ridiculous as it sounds, I took it very personally. I was annoyed, even resentful. Surely there was some mistake.

After about five minutes I was rescued by a marine first lieutenant assigned to mind me. 'Happens all the time,' he said cheerfully. 'The gooks sneak up in the boonies, fire off two or three, then they're gone. They never do much damage, but it keeps you awake.' He complimented me on my English.

I explained.

'Oh,' he said. 'I thought you were from Austria.'

After the taciturn and suspicious Australian military, the Americans were a joy to deal with. You could talk to anyone, ask them anything, entirely without supervision or clumsy attempts at censorship. From bird colonel on down to the lowest E-2, they would reply candidly and at length. And invariably politely.[62]

'Where are you from, man?'

'Phoenix, Arizona, sir.'

'And how's your war?'

'Shit, sir. All fucked up. The gooks whipped our ass last week . . .'

More extraordinary still was the awesome scale of the American military presence, which you could only begin to appreciate by getting out of Saigon. The logistics effort was almost magical. In the morning the Yanks could seize a flat, empty patch of dirt in the highlands or a swamp on the coast. With unstoppable American can-do, by the afternoon it would be a fully functioning base with an airstrip, communications, accommodation for an infantry battalion, half a dozen heavy artillery pieces ringed around the perimeter, a field hospital and probably a PX – a Post Exchange, or canteen – serving soda, pizza and burgers.

A Marine major in an operations hut filled me in with a map and pointer, again unheard of with the Australian Army. 'We're here. The enemy is there . . . and there . . . and there. Most of them main force NVA.' That meant not Viet Cong guerrillas, but fully trained regular troops of the North Vietnam Army, a serious proposition. 'Do you wanna go on a patrol?'

I did indeed want to, but was gently told I couldn't possibly do it in my safari suit and suede desert boots. In thirty seconds flat they had me kitted out in Marine combat fatigues of green-and-brown-patterned jungle camouflage, with matching helmet and tough boots of canvas, leather and rubber. 'Would you like a sidearm, sir? Colt or Smith & Wesson?' I declined the gun, which they thought was odd. But there was an optimistic notion at the time that if a journalist was captured without a weapon, he could wave his press card and, as a non-combatant, be set free. This would prove to be very wrong.

That night, throbbing with excitement and naked fear, I boarded another Chinook with a squad of about two dozen marines assigned to an ambush patrol, commanded by a lieutenant. After around ten minutes the chopper set us down in a jungle clearing, from which we trudged deeper into the scrub for about an hour. It was dark, clouds hiding the stars. The idea was to set an ambush, lying quietly in wait for the enemy to stumble upon us. Which we did, sliding and slumping into the undergrowth. Two possibilities occurred to me. One, that the enemy, having no doubt heard and observed the helicopter, would therefore give the area a wide berth. Two, and more likely, the enemy would seize the chance to come straight at us in strength.

The first happened, or didn't happen. We lay there all night, not sleeping, talking in whispers if at all. The People's Army of Vietnam declined to appear. As dawn broke, the marines shot off a few rounds from their M16s for the fun of it, pulled cigarettes from their pockets and lit them with the ubiquitous Zippo lighters. The Chinook had us back at Dong Ha for breakfast, which seemed to consist entirely of ice-cream. My overwhelming emotion was relief that I hadn't been under fire – and that I was alive and safe. At least I could now say I had gone in harm's way. The lieutenant told me I could keep the uniform. 'A souvenir of the Third Marines,' he said. 'Nice to have you with us.'

From the vast air base on the coast at Da Nang, I flew eastwards to the US Navy's Yankee Station, in the Gulf of Tonkin at the top of the North China Sea. Here were the big, prowling aircraft carriers of the 7th Fleet, launching bombing strikes on North Vietnam. The Royal Australian Navy was about to enter the war at the sharp end, sending the guided missile destroyer HMAS *Hobart* to join the fleet on the Gun Line, the ships bombarding the Vietnam coast. I wanted to see how it worked, and what the Australians could expect to get into.

For the boy who had read *The Cruel Sea* at the age of eleven, who had so longed to join the navy, the 7th Fleet was seventh heaven. They flew me out in a Grumman Tracker – a stubby, fixed-wing, propeller-driven aircraft – for a landing on the carrier *Coral Sea*. At first sight, the carrier was a speck in an endless ocean. Within minutes we touched down on the flight deck, with a tremendous roar of engines and an almighty, neck-snapping jerk as the arrestor wire pulled the Tracker to a stop. I was exploding with excitement, and there was more to come. A US Navy Huey helicopter was waiting to carry me to the USS *Hoel*, a Charles F. Adams class DDG, meaning a destroyer sister-ship of the *Hobart*.

I had assumed the chopper would land somewhere on the destroyer's deck, and I would step lightly on board. 'No, sir,' I was told. 'We're dropping you by wire.' My God. I had never imagined this.

They clipped me into a harness, attached that to a steel cable running from a winch, and told me to sit in the chopper's open doorway with my legs over the side. Whipped by the wind, buffeted by the noise of the engine and the whoppa-whoppa of the rotor blades, I was too exhilarated to be scared, pumping adrenaline to my eyeballs. The *Hoel* was pitching and rolling in a moderate sea, with whitecaps on the wave crests. As they spun me down on the wire, like a spider on the end of a line of web, the destroyer's after deck would come up to meet me, then fall away into a trough between the waves to be metres below. 'Pick your moment,' I'd been told. As my feet touched the deck my knees buckled, the wire slackened, strong hands grabbed me and unclipped the harness, and I was on board.

It turned out the *Hoel* wasn't on the Gun Line, as I had hoped. There would be no bombardment. She was acting as plane guard for the *Coral Sea*, which meant hanging about with the carrier during flying operations, ready to race to the rescue of any pilot who got it wrong and landed in the drink. But the experience was still valuable, and worth reporting. And the American welcome was as warm as ever, the more so when I produced a bottle of Scotch I had brought along as a token of our trans-Pacific friendship. The US Navy is dry – no alcohol. I passed a pleasant evening on the bridge with the Officer of the Deck and the half-dozen sailors of the watch sipping happily at the Johnnie Walker as they kept station on the carrier. Two days later I was back on the *Coral Sea*. The catapult launch from the carrier was another neck-snapping, orgasmic thrill.

So ended my Vietnam, for the time being. I had no idea I would return in a few years, when the war was all but lost. It felt good to leave, the strain draining out of me as I sank back into the seat of the Pan Am 707 – the 'Freedom Bird' – that lifted me out of Tan Son Nhut.

Back in Singapore, there was a new assignment waiting for me: Indonesia.

9

Three years of living wonderfully

SUKARNO, GREAT LEADER OF the Revolution, President for Life of the Republic of Indonesia, sat at his ease on a gilded sofa in the Merdeka Palace in Jakarta.[63] Fleshy and jocular, splendid in the sort of crisp, white uniform last seen on Hermann Göring, he looked like the man in charge. Medal ribbons cascaded down his tunic. On his head was his trademark *pitji*, the plain black oval cap worn by many Indonesian Muslim men. Alternately chuckling and growling, he bantered with a throng of local and foreign journalists and photographers in Indonesian, English and Dutch – and, once or twice, in French or German.

It was March 1967. I had not seen him before. It was mesmerising. A hero to tens of millions of Indonesians, an ogre to many Australians, Sukarno radiated charisma. The hacks chortled at his jokes or shrank from his scowl. But in fact he was no longer the man in charge, and we all knew it. So did he. This was his last media conference – his last hurrah. Like most revolutionaries, he had been a patriotic visionary and a spellbinding orator, but also a reckless adventurer and womanising narcissist who was incapable of nurturing the independence he had done so much to win. Now his power had gone.

For years Sukarno had juggled the three rival strands of Indonesian politics in a balancing act he called *Nasakom*, an acronym for nationalism, religion and communism.[64] It couldn't hold forever and it didn't. On the night of Thursday, 30 September 1965, the Indonesian Communist Party, the PKI, attempted a coup. Six of the army's most senior generals were kidnapped and hacked to death, their bodies stuffed down a rural well known as the Crocodile Hole. Carelessly, the plotters left off the list the man best placed to hit back: Major General Suharto, another hero of the revolution and the commander of *Kostrad*, the army's strategic reserve, which had troops in the capital. Suharto launched a counter-coup and began to round up the PKI leaders.

This touched off one of the most violent convulsions of the twentieth century. In the year that followed, hundreds of thousands of Indonesians were slaughtered in a nationwide purge fomented by the army. Most were communists or their sympathisers. Others were simply the payback victims of village rivalries or enmity. Nobody knows how many died, but some rural rivers in Java and Bali quite literally ran with blood. Well after it was over, the foreign minister, the wily but likeable Adam Malik, privately admitted to me that at least 600,000 had been killed, but some studies have put the toll as high as 3 million. To this day few Indonesians will speak or write of it.

Suharto and the army, on the right of Indonesian politics, began to point the finger at Sukarno as the architect of the coup, charging that he had wanted to drag the country into the communist orbit. They whipped up fierce and often violent street demonstrations by howling mobs of students in Jakarta, day after day, and began the long and intricate process of easing him out of the palace. On 12 March 1967 the Indonesian parliament formally gave Suharto the job and title of Acting President. Sukarno was placed under house arrest at Bogor, in the West Java countryside.

I had arrived in Jakarta just weeks before, in late January. The ABC bureau chief, Philip Koch, had covered the coup and the tumult that followed brilliantly, often at great personal risk. But he was moving on and I was replacing him. This meant I was up a notch as well, from B-grade to A-grade journalist. I was thunderstruck when they told me. Sydney had sent me to Asia to relieve for a few months. Now I was confirmed as a full-time foreign correspondent, with a bureau of my own to run, following a story almost as important for Australia as the Vietnam War. I turned twenty-one that same month. On my birthday, Koch and Neil Davis bought me champagne in the plush red Ramayana Bar of the Hotel Indonesia, the only Western hotel in town. It all felt very grown-up.

✧

Jakarta today is one of Asia's tiger cities, a sprawling metropolis of crystal skyscrapers and the world's worst traffic jams. In 1967 it was a rotting slum, ruined by Sukarno's disastrous economic policies. Inflation had been running at an eye-watering 600 per cent a year. The central downtown boulevard, Jalan Thamrin, was lined with the rusting skeletons of unfinished buildings. There was exactly one traffic light in the entire city. A lurid billboard three storeys high and a block long was still exhorting the masses to *Konfrontasi* with Malaysia, although Suharto had already abandoned that fight. The few vehicles on the streets were ancient Russian-built trucks and buses lurching along in clouds of smoke, or the smart new Toyota jeeps of corrupt army generals. They honked their way through milling hordes of *becaks*, the trishaws pedalled by brawny drivers who lived rough; they both bathed and shat in the city's network of filthy brown storm-water canals. There was barely an Indonesian middle class at all, just a small, rich and corrupt elite, and millions in poverty. Towering over all this was the *Monumen Nasional*, an extravagant phallus of Italian marble soaring to the sky in a stony clearing opposite the palace. Topped with a flame clad in pure gold, it was known as 'Sukarno's last erection'. Families huddled in tin shanties and makeshift tents in its mocking shadow.

I loved Indonesia from day one. Philip stayed for a few weeks to settle me in. I moved into the old Dutch bungalow the ABC rented in Kebayoran Baru, a leafy suburb in south Jakarta. It was primitive but deliciously exotic. Without hot water or even a shower in the bathroom, you sluiced yourself down from a freshly filled tank of cold water. But there were cool tiled floors and airy ceiling fans, and the tropic evenings were fragrant with the heady perfume of *kretek* – clove cigarettes – and the spice island aromas of the food sellers pushing their carts. The calls of the hawkers and the mellow tonk-tonk of the *becak* bells drifted in through the windows. Little gecko lizards made their *tjitjak* chirps in the eaves and ceilings.

To minister to my needs I had a Javanese houseboy, a cook, a wash girl, a driver for the ABC office's Holden, and a gardener and night-watchman. If I dropped a sweaty shirt on the floor at lunchtime it would be washed and ironed and ready to wear again that evening. Tumiyo, the houseboy, made a mean gin and tonic with fresh-cut limes. Papaya and mangoes and the sweet little hairy red fruit known as *rambutan* arrived for breakfast, washed down with freshly made *Kopi Tubruk*, a coffee brew thick enough to grease an axle. Sometimes there would be that Indonesian breakfast staple, *nasi goreng*. Dinner would be buffalo, chicken or goat *saté* in a homemade peanut sauce, or a rich curry. This cost me a few dollars a month and a car boot load of bags of rice.

The office staff were also paid with some cash and a lot of rice, a 20-kilogram sack of it for a family each month, and 10 kilos for a single. It was the one reliable hedge against the still crazy inflation, and the surplus could be sold or bartered. I changed my US dollars into rupiah at the Bank of China, a black-market operation not unlike Saigon's Bank of India. A Chinese woman in the upmarket suburb of Menteng did the deal in her lounge room.

The ABC office itself was another slum, a single room on the top floor of a three-storey building of crumbling concrete, peeling paint and disgusting smells from the drains, with a boxy air conditioner coughing away in the corner. The sole telephone rarely worked; the Jakarta network had pretty much collapsed years before. On the plus side, the office at 40 Jalan Kebon Sirih was only a shortish walk from the presidential palace, most of the major government buildings and many of the foreign embassies.

The people were wonderful. Jafar the office boy – he and everyone else were actually older than me – spoke not a word of English but shyly made the coffee and opened the bags of letters that arrived each day from Indonesian listeners to the ABC's shortwave service, Radio Australia. This was no small deal. The audience was huge. In a nation of islands pretty much starved of their own radio and television services, hundreds of thousands – probably millions – of Indonesians got their news and entertainment from Radio Australia, broadcast from Melbourne. It was quite common to meet some army general, cabinet minister or newspaper editor who would tell you, gratefully, that he had learned to speak English by listening to RA's language classes. Largely forgotten now, Radio Australia then was a stunningly successful projection of Australian soft power and culture. For a while, in the office I had another Australian, Alan Morris, to handle the RA business.

My young secretary, Anna Fernandez, a Christian of Timorese background, spoke Indonesian, English and Dutch. The office driver, Victor Laurens, also a Christian in his twenties, had mixed Dutch heritage. Jokey and streetwise, he was learning from Neil Davis how to shoot news film and would go on, much later, to become Suharto's personal cameraman. I'm pretty sure Vic also saved my life. Last, at the top of the office heap was a local journalist, Hidayat Djajamihardja. In his mid-twenties and newly married, he was the reporter who did most of the legwork. Hidayat was a Muslim from what was once the Sundanese kingdom of West Java, and was entitled to call himself *Raden*, which meant he had aristocratic blood, although he never used the handle. Far smarter than me, and also speaking three languages, he had studied for a while at Columbia University in New York. Loyal and energetic, handsome and dashing, he had sources and contacts right to the top of the Jakarta tree. He and his wife, Lily, are valued friends to this day. I couldn't have done the job and survived in Indonesia without them.

Not that the work was all that hard. Modern foreign correspondents are driven frantic by the 24/7 news cycle, the exploding technology of the internet and social media, and by the incessant demands of their often ignorant editors back home. My bosses couldn't even reach me. Indonesia's international telecommunications had barely moved on from 1901. I would write one story a day, which had to be typed and carried by hand, first to be cleared by the government censors, and then on to the nearby *Telekom* office, for transmission to Sydney by an operator dit-dah-ditting with Morse code. For an urgent story, you could bribe the operator to put your copy at the top of the pile. If I tape-recorded some feature piece for radio, or if there was TV news film to send, the quickest way get it off was to go to the airport, find a passenger on a flight to Singapore and ask them to carry it for you in their hand luggage. They would be met at the other end. We called it pigeoning. It's unthinkable today – but it never failed.

Hidayat worked the local angles: the press conferences, ministerial briefings, the parliament, the Foreign Ministry and the military. Sometimes I would accompany him, or we would both hit the streets for yet another student demonstration. These could get dangerous, and even turn fatal without warning. Every so often the capital would be convulsed by anti-Chinese riots, generally in Glodok, the Chinese quarter. Businesses and houses would be torched, and Chinese people bashed or worse. At one riot outside the massive red-ochre ramparts of the Chinese Embassy, I watched a howling mob turn on a Chinese boy who had tried to slip past. They opened his throat with a broken bottle and he died in a pool of his own blood, metres from where I was standing.

I was transfixed. It was the first cold-blooded murder I had seen.

Vic the driver grabbed me by the arm. 'We need to get out here fast, boss. They'll kill any foreigner next.' I was the only European in sight. The thugs were already starting to mutter at me and glare with menace, their blood up.

We raced for the trusty Holden and escaped in a screech of smoking tyres as the ringleaders pounded towards us, throwing rocks.

It was not always so exciting. The entire Jakarta population, Indonesian and foreign, crashed for a siesta in the heat of the afternoon. In the cool of the evening, after a monsoon downpour had settled the dust, I would hit the slightly less lethal diplomatic drinks and dinner circuit to trade information and gossip. 'The Defense Attaché of the United States of America requests the pleasure . . .' 'Her Britannic Majesty's Chargé d'Affaires will be At Home . . .' 'The Ambassador of the Federal Republic of Germany has the honour . . .'

At first, the only foreigners in Jakarta were diplomats and journalists, with a few desolate airline managers. The usual carpetbaggers – Texan oil racketeers, British finance swindlers, Japanese property sharks and car salesmen – took about a year to decide that Indonesia was safe enough for them to turn up and plunder the place in shonky deals with well-placed and ever-eager army generals. In the meantime, Sukarno's flirtation with communism had attracted a massive contingent of diplomats and correspondents from the Soviet bloc, all of whom were now sadly out of favour in Suharto's New Order, and wondering what on earth to do with themselves. There were only three or four journalists from Britain, the US and Australia, plus a disciplined squad of Japanese. It was a hoot to drink in the upstairs bar at the Hotel Indonesia with moustachioed, pink-cheeked Russians from *Pravda*, *Izvestia* and the *Tass* newsagency, with beefy Germans from Radio East Berlin, and with Czechs, Poles, Hungarians and Yugoslavs. If the Russians were allowed out of their embassy compound it was odds-on they were KGB; we would therefore address them solemnly as Colonel, which they took with chortling good humour.

One Russian couple, Andrei and Olga, took a particular interest in me, with invitations to their bungalow for vodka and *pirozhki*; every so often they even offered all-expenses-paid VIP holidays to Moscow and Leningrad. They were very nice. Olga had been a university gymnast and would strip naked and turn into a pretzel between courses at dinner, her shaven pudenda vibrating a metre from my face. My, how we laughed. More *Moskovskaya*, Comrade! *Na Zdorovie*! Andrei made it hospitably clear that I was free to whip her off to the bedroom, but I resisted the temptation until one evening she threw herself across a coffee table and pulled me down upon her shapely loins. What else could I do? Happy days.

I haven't the foggiest idea what the KGB wanted from me, but I discovered Olga had also made a play for a British journalist. 'Volga Olga', we called her. Once Andrei came to me with a puzzled air. 'Thiss new record by the Baytles,' he said. '*Back in the USSR* – what exaykly do et minn? Could ay perhaps borrow et?' I lent it to him gladly but could not clear up the mystery.

The Russians did love a party. In 1967 they threw the mother of all diplomatic receptions to commemorate the fiftieth anniversary of the Great October Socialist Revolution, filling the grand ballroom of the Hotel Indonesia with everybody who was anybody. Beneath an enormous picture of Lenin and a forest of scarlet hammer-and-sickle banners were long tables laden with Russian delicacies and tubs of vodka and *Sovetskoye Shampanskoye*, Crimean fizz. At the centre of each table was a block of ice topped with a bowl the size of a car tyre, heaped with Black Sea caviar. There were kilos and kilos of the stuff. You plopped it onto your plate with a soup spoon and hunks of bread, and swilled it down with shots of vodka so cold it felt like gargling razor blades.

The foreign correspondents – Western, Japanese and Eastern bloc – milled in a corner and took turns to propose toasts, which went swimmingly until one lunkhead Russian raised his glass and invited us to drink to the glorious victory of the Vietnamese people over US and Western imperialism. A visiting writer from *Time* magazine took a drunken swing at him and the brawl was on, lurching into the groaning table. It didn't last long. Muscular goons from the embassy frogmarched us from the room and flung us out to the hotel driveway, along with the unfortunate and volubly protesting French ambassador, who had been an amused but innocent bystander.

✧

I began to teach myself Bahasa Indonesia with the help of the people at the office, the servants at home and the bartenders at the hotel. It is an easy enough language to learn. Unlike English, the verbs conjugate with simple logic, and when you've grasped that, all you need to do is build your vocabulary. Setting a target of five new words each day, I was speaking it reasonably fluently after about six months, albeit a low-class, slangy patois. In a receiving line at the Merdeka Palace one time I chatted briefly in Indonesian with Suharto himself, who, pleasingly, told me with some amusement that I had a rough Jakarta accent.

My mother was endlessly impressed. When I had a few weeks off I brought her first to Singapore and then to Jakarta and Bali for a holiday, the first time she had been abroad. She was entranced, enraptured, not least because the Indonesians she met gave her a gracious welcome. Only one thing troubled her. Towards the end of her visit, she very hesitantly put some questions to me. 'Are you . . . *sleeping* with Indonesian girls, Michael?'

I admitted that I had, once or twice.

Long pause. Then: 'You wouldn't *marry* one of them, would you?'

'No plans to,' I said, 'but why not?'

This produced a very much longer pause, until: 'Darling, they're *natives*.'

✧

Then along came the band. At a private party one Saturday there was a group of four Indonesians – three guitars and drums – playing Beatles and Rolling Stones covers, with a splash of the Bee Gees thrown in. They were good, very good, although their amplifiers and speakers were sadly old and underpowered. The Rhadows, they called themselves. Towards the end of the night, they allowed me and a mate, Ed Blanche, the correspondent for the Associated Press of America, to do a few songs with them. Okay, we pushed ourselves on them. But it went off like a rocket – one of those jams that just worked. Ed, a red-bearded Englishman my own age, was a serious guitar player. I could do a passable Mick Jagger impression and bash a bit on drums. We blew them away, and vice versa. Afterwards, the lead guitarist, a lanky Ambonese named Bram Titaley, offered us a friendly joint and asked if we would like to do regular gigs with them. Would we what? We jumped at it. Rock'n'roll had only recently returned to Indonesia. Sukarno had banned it as *Nekolim* decadence, but now rock was roaring back.

Bram, also in his twenties, was a sublimely talented guitarist whose sliding tremolo riffs were magic. He could play anything after one listen, and so could Johan the bass player and Rudi on rhythm. Iwan the drummer had atomic wrists. If they'd been born in Los Angeles they'd have been the Doors or the Eagles. Meanwhile, Ed and I had money. We beefed up the amps and speakers, bought a couple of new Yamaha guitars, renamed the band Escape, and imported a load of the latest rock albums from a store I knew in Singapore. Bram could make his Yamaha sound like a Fender Strat. We were off.

Unable to train my curly hair into a John Lennon cut, I grew an enormous Jimi Hendrix afro. Ed went for the long-haired, bearded Jesus look. We got the guys out of their tight-buttoned Beatle suits and into some glam-rock flared pants, psychedelic shirts and boots the size of small cars. On some songs Bram would sing and we'd do the backing vocals; on others we'd go the reverse.

Within a couple of months we were the hottest act in Jakarta. Chiefly because there wasn't much competition, and Indonesians got a kick out of seeing two Europeans go ape on stage. It was surreal. By day I was the diligent ABC bureau chief. By night I was a rock star. The groupies began to flock around us, Javanese and Sundanese girls bathing in the glamour of it all. Abandoning Islamic maidenly decorum, they screamed at every Jagger-style pelvic thrust and hung around for us after the show, which was nice. Perhaps Sukarno had a point.

Bram was married with kids, but the other guys were single, on the make and grateful for the attention. They liked it even more when the European girls from the embassies made a play for them. We all became good friends, and expanded the repertoire to include some Creedence Clearwater Revival covers and the Beach Boys, with a bit of Chuck Berry thrown in. The Hotel Indonesia gave us a regular Friday and Saturday night gig in their upstairs nightclub, which we played in a purple haze of cannabis fumes to sell-out audiences of Westerners and wealthy locals. Pot, or *ganja*, was illegal in Indonesia even then, but the equivalent of a few bucks could buy you an envelope of the local weed from street stalls all over town. Of excellent quality, it was openly smoked by the locals and foreigners without trouble.

We played the diplomatic parties as well. Our most exotic gig was a lavish dance thrown at the mansion of an army general to celebrate the Islamic circumcision of his youngest son, a grand festive occasion. If it sounds frivolous, it was – but foreign journalists did not get to meet the ruling elite at home all that often. We picked up some valuable contacts. Playing in Escape gave Ed and me a direct pipeline into Jakarta society that few blow-ins could achieve. And above all it was fun.

There was one crater on my superhighway to rock god heaven. At around peak afro, I was told that the ABC's general manager, the starchy, pipe-smoking Talbot Duckmanton, would be paying a state visit to Indonesia. There would have to be meetings, a cocktail reception, a select dinner for VIPs, posh as all get-out. I chickened and got my hair trimmed way back.

On the night of the party, every inch the Singapore-tailored foreign correspondent in crisp white linen, I introduced the boss to the guests as they arrived: the Minister for Information, the Director General of the Foreign Office, the head of TVRI, Brigadier-General Sumitro, the editor of *Kompas* . . .

One after the other, they expressed their amazement at my sudden hair loss. In English. 'Where is your afro, Michael?' they cried. 'What have you done with your hair? Are you no longer in your band?'

Duckmanton's smile grew ever more gritty until he could take it no more. 'What *is* all this about?' he hissed.

Weakly, I confessed everything. Or almost everything. I didn't think he'd want to know about the groupies or the *ganja*. All things considered, he took it rather well.

✧

There was also work to do. The story boiled along and I stayed across it, running to keep up. Few things in Indonesia are ever simple, least of all its political processes, which are shaped with all the complex nuance of the ancient Javanese *Wayang Kulit* puppet theatre, familiar in every village. Acting President Suharto faced a delicate task. He had to ease Sukarno out of power without alienating the tens of millions of Indonesians who still idolised him as the revolutionary hero and father of the nation. *Bung Karno*, they called him – Brother 'Karno.

Suharto went at it with infinite subtlety. Within a year he had manipulated Indonesia's temporary, unelected parliament to the point where it bestowed the full presidency upon him. While it was taken for granted that Suharto would become president – there was no one else – there was infinite haggling over his term of office and the authority he would have. Working the lobbies and corridors, it was Hidayat who broke the story that he would be granted five years in power. I wrote it, bribed the Morse code operators with a month's pay to send it immediately, and the ABC ran it as a world scoop.

The *Orde Baru*, the New Order government, moved to extend its reach across every aspect of Indonesian life, trumpeting a strident anti-communism – to the great relief of the Western embassies. It was a military dictatorship in everything but name, based on a concept the army had invented for itself: *Dwifungsi*, or Two Functions, which gave Suharto and his loyalist generals both military and civilian authority. The new president's smartest move, though, was to understand that he could remain in power only if he wrenched the country's economy back on track, and held out the hope of rising standards of living for the masses.

There were two killer indices for ordinary Indonesians: the cost of rice and the cost of cooking fuel, usually kerosene. Politically, it was imperative for Suharto to get them under control. Indonesia's universities and bureaucracy were stuffed to the rafters with economists boasting degrees from the best American, British and Dutch universities. Most had been sidelined under Sukarno and were now busting to get into the game. Suharto did not have a clue about economics and never pretended that he did. It was said that his eyes would glaze over when the subject came up in cabinet meetings, chiefly because the technocrats liked to hold their discussions in the English they had learned at Harvard, Berkeley or Oxford, which was beyond him. But he had the instinctive good sense to let them get their hands on the levers. It must have been like trying to raise the *Titanic*, but – ever so slowly at first – things began to move. Inflation was subsiding. That, too, was a story worth reporting.

Suharto came down hard on his critics and rivals, sometimes brutally, and he, his family and his cronies began to accumulate vast wealth. A law was passed making it a serious offence to 'disrespect' the president, which silenced much of the opposition. Indonesians would eventually whisper the acronym KKN, for *korupsi, kolusi, nepotisme* – corruption, collusion, nepotism – which became hallmarks of the regime. It was common knowledge that the Suharto family was corrupt, but we did not imagine the spectacular extent of it. They got away with billions.

The big story for Australians was the so-called Act of Free Choice in 1969, which cemented what had once been Netherlands New

Guinea into the Indonesian Republic. After a long diplomatic conflict, and sometimes armed conflict too, the United Nations handed that western half of the island of New Guinea to Indonesia in 1963 on one condition: there should be some sort of plebiscite – an 'Act of Free Choice' – which would give the people a vote on whether they wanted to be Indonesians or to have their own independent state. This was to take place in 1969. Conservatives in Australia, including successive federal governments, regarded the Indonesian push with deep suspicion. With their customary paranoia, they saw it as a territorial thrust into our part of the world, and fretted about how they could stop it or blunt it. The hope was that the Americans would do something, anything, to make Indonesia back off.

My challenge was to get to West Irian so I could see what was happening. There were reports of an independence movement, of sometimes violent unrest and savage repression by the army, but the place was closed to foreign journalists. In 1968 the United Nations sent a Special Representative to get the Act of Free Choice underway, and I figured we had a chance to take a look too.[65]

Hidayat had cultivated a relationship with the Indonesian military commander in West Irian, Brigadier General Sarwo Edhie Wibowo, a pivotal figure with much blood on his hands. It was Sarwo Edhie, on Suharto's instructions, who had orchestrated the massacre of the communists after the PKI coup in 1965.[66] Nominally a Muslim, he was a profound believer in ancient Javanese mysticism, as was Suharto. He was also a well-trained soldier, with Western sympathies. He had done the US Army's Infantry Officer Advanced Course at Fort Benning in 1958, and as a colonel he had studied at the Australian Army Staff College at Queenscliff, in Victoria. We heard he kept a photo of the Sydney Harbour Bridge on his desk. He was worth a try. In August 1968 Hidayat and I tracked him down at Jakarta airport as he was about to fly back to Irian. Would he give us permission to get in?

To my astonishment, he did. He snapped open a shiny briefcase – I gaped at the .45 Magnum inside – and pulled out the official letterhead of his *Tjenderawasih* army division and a fountain pen.[67] There and then, he wrote a personal letter to Suharto's right-hand man, the second most powerful figure in Indonesia, Brigadier-General

Ali Murtopo, explaining that he had invited two ABC journalists to go into West Irian.

All doors opened. I would be the first Western journalist there, an exciting scoop. A couple of days later I stepped from a Garuda plane at Biak, an island off the western tip of Irian, with an Indonesian cameraman, Yusuf Anwar. Suddenly I was in Melanesia. The locals had coal-black skin and fuzzy hair. They had not seen a European in years and they looked at me in amazement. An old man stumbled across the tarmac towards me, hands outstretched in welcome, crying, 'Oom, Oom,' the Dutch word for 'uncle', which is how he would have addressed his former colonial masters. Two Indonesian soldiers grabbed him and dragged him away.

That night, in the Biak Hotel, a waiter whispered to me in halting English that he hoped the Dutch would return. When I woke the next morning I found a note pushed under my door, also in crude English, to tell me that a Free Papua Movement would fight for independence. Please report this to the world, it urged me.

Sarwo Edhie's letter allowed me to go anywhere I wanted, and I did, although I was closely followed by Indonesian security spooks. There was no way I could meet the freedom fighters. They were in hiding. But as I travelled around, first to some coastal towns and then to a Dutch Christian mission deep in the highlands, there were constant discreet whispers and a couple more handwritten notes. It was obvious that the independence struggle was alive, although in what strength I could not tell. There was no way of contacting anyone.

The mission, though, was extraordinary, peopled by near-naked women and tribesmen wearing nothing but long, pointed penis gourds tied to their waists. They stank of the rancid pig fat they smeared on their bodies. Milling around me, they fingered my hair and my white skin in wonder, grinning broadly. When I tape-recorded their voices and played it back to them, there was a stunned silence. Some stood catatonic with shock. A few ran off in evident terror. It took the missionaries a while to explain to them that I had not kidnapped their spirits.

I flew out again after a week, in a clapped-out Garuda DC3. As the plane took off from Biak, one engine coughed and spluttered to a halt. The pilot nursed it back to the runway on the other engine and we sat there in the baking heat wondering what to do next. There was not another flight for a week. Eventually, two Indonesians appeared with a ladder, a length of timber and a hammer. I watched, wide-eyed, as they thumped the dead engine with the piece of wood. That done, the pilot fired it up again with an almighty bang and a cloud of blue smoke and we were off once more, back to Bali, me whimpering in terror all the way. I have never been so glad to get off a flight.

The stories I wrote for the ABC played it straight. I reported what I had seen and heard, including the whispers and the notes. Radio Australia broadcast it back, which I thought would bring the Indonesian authorities down upon me like the wrath of God, but to my surprise nothing like that happened. They played it cool. It was the Western diplomats in Jakarta who got their knickers knotted, not least at the Australian Embassy, which went into an almighty tizz.

The problem was that the fix was in. In Washington, Richard Nixon and his National Security svengali Henry Kissinger had decided that Suharto, resolutely anti-communist, had their seal of approval and would be supported. They wanted the Free Choice thing to be over and done with as quickly and quietly as possible, with the Indonesians staying firmly in the saddle, and bugger freedom for the Papuans of West Irian. Canberra, which had initially balked at the Indonesian takeover, quietly changed tack and, as ever, meekly went along with the Americans. Nobody needed interfering journalists writing about freedom fighters and independence movements, which would only chuck a spanner in the works.

The Americans and the Indonesians got their way. There was no plebiscite. Sarwo Edhie, cunning as ever, had stitched up a charade to give a vote to 1025 carefully selected, supposedly representative Papuans. And there was no secret ballot, only a show of hands under the general's beady eye. The chosen few knew what was good for them – and their families – and they voted yes. The United Nations turned a blind eye to this travesty. Nixon, when he visited Jakarta in 1969, privately gave Suharto the green light. The Act of Free Choice was an Act of No Choice.

West Papua now forms two provinces of the Republic of Indonesia. The Free Papua Movement – the OPM, or *Organisasi Papua Merdeka* – struggles on, but the sad truth is that it's a lost cause. Indonesia would no more relinquish its ownership of West Papua than Australia would abandon Tasmania. And there is no international pressure for it to do so, none at all.

✧

My relationship with the Australian Embassy in Jakarta wobbled from cool to fraught. The senior diplomats there and back in Canberra believed that the ABC in general, and Radio Australia in particular, should obediently parrot the foreign policy line as it was handed down. Nor was it just Jakarta. The Saigon Embassy, notoriously a nest of exquisite social and sexual butterflies, was equally known for trying to force its world view down journalists' throats. All in Australia's national interest, of course. The diplomats could never understand that the ABC was independent of government and would broadcast the news as it happened, whether they liked it or not.

The ambassador in Jakarta for most of my time, Gordon Jockel, was a career diplomat with a towering reputation. A sophisticated policy analyst of high intellect, a foreign affairs professional to his fingertips, he went on to become head of the Joint Intelligence Organisation in Canberra, the government's top spook. He retired laden with laurels and the thanks of a grateful nation.

Jockel also gave good hauteur, and we did not get on. He wanted to run me; I was not going to be run. After my West Irian reports he invited me to his office for a dressing-down. Frostily, he told me that I had not been 'helpful'. My stories had been 'unfortunate'. I must understand that it was in no one's interests to stir up trouble in the province. He would be very pleased if I did not do it again, and I could always come to the embassy to find out what was actually happening. Equally politely, I explained that I was not there to be helpful. Nor was I seeking the embassy's advice on how to do my job. I was there to gather news, to report it as accurately as I could, and would continue to do so. He thought I was an impertinent upstart. I thought he was an officious bully.

I had experienced this sort of diplomatic kicking before. A year earlier, the US Ambassador, Marshall Green, had summoned me and tried exactly the same thing after we had reported on the anti-Chinese riots. Unhelpful, regrettable, etc. I had explained to him, too, that I was not an instrument of Australian or American foreign policy.[68] Nor was the ABC a propaganda arm of government like the Voice of America, I said, a hit he took rather badly.

But now it was my own people taking shots. Junior diplomats I knew told me quietly that Jockel had decided that I had to go, and was urging the then External Affairs Department in Canberra to lean on the ABC to remove me. I found out, very much later, that this was true.

Things came to a head in May 1969, when Hidayat reported that the Indonesian Air Force had bombed and strafed rebellious tribespeople in a town in Irian. This was entirely accurate, as Jockel conceded, but again it was 'not helpful'. He doubled down on his efforts to have me fired. Cables flew back and forth between Jakarta and Canberra. The ABC office 'thought of itself very much as a news gathering body on the same basis as the other external news agencies in Jakarta, and shared the same attitude to stories and scoops', Jockel huffed, as if this were some wicked aberration. Worse, 'the office had had no contact with the embassy before filing these stories and conducting its interviews'.[69]

Canberra replied that the ambassador should 'consider what opportunity may be open to you in Jakarta to talk discreetly and privately to Radio Australia/ABC correspondent there about the implications for Australian/Indonesian relations of reports he sends'.[70] In other words: try again to jerk Carlton into line. But we had gone too far down the track for that.

While I was on leave for a couple of months, Jockel had yet another bite in a letter to the Foreign Affairs department in Canberra:

> I wonder if the Minister and/or the Department are sinking their teeth into the ABC over the adventures of their youngsters in Jakarta or trying to define the relationship between the government and Radio Australia. If it is 'all too difficult', I wonder if the

> Department could go for more mature representation by the ABC in Jakarta. This year there have been three relief persons in charge of the ABC/Radio Australia office, and our best guess is that the present youth is to be relieved in July by Michael Carlton, who is about 24 years old and, when here previously, did not think it was part of his job to consult seriously with the embassy.[71]

Warming to the theme, he fired off a more formal cable a few days later:

> I should like the Department to think about working on Duckmanton to get the ABC staff position in Jakarta stabilised . . . a mature and experienced person is very much needed in the interests of both the government and the ABC itself. The foreign correspondents here are a volatile group with a strong Australian element, and there is a natural tendency for the youthful ABC staff to be over influenced by them. This being so I intend to proceed cautiously about taking the ABC staff into my confidence for discreet and private talks.[72]

The External Affairs mandarins in Canberra did indeed try to browbeat the ABC. Again as I learned later, both Talbot Duckmanton and the Controller of News, Wally Hamilton, were 'informally' approached and invited to knock me off. To their credit, they declined. They saw, correctly, that there was more at stake than the future of Michael Carlton. It had happened before: the diplomats were mounting a full-frontal assault on the independence of the ABC. If they were allowed to succeed, the thin end of the wedge would be in and they would shove it deeper.

Not once did I get word from Sydney, or from my immediate boss in Singapore, Peter Hollinshead, that my reporting was not up to scratch, that I should lift my game, that I should 'consult' with the embassy. They let me get on with it. I saw out my full three-year term in Jakarta, apparently without leaving Australia–Indonesia relations in ruins.

✧

The end came with a rush. Time was up, too quickly. I realised I had fallen in love with Indonesia, with the ravishing beauty of her islands and the character of her people. The sweet, terraced green of the *padi* rice fields was engraved on my memory. I had marvelled at the ancient grey stones of the Hindu temple of Borobodur; swum in the limpid waters of the Kepulauan Seribu – Jakarta's Thousand Islands; peered in awe into the sulphurous, bubbling crater of Tangkuban Perahu, a live volcano in West Java. I had bargained for the intricate filigreed silverware of the craftsmen near the Sultan's palace in Yogyakarta, and feasted on pork at a Balinese wedding. When I first went to Bali, as a reporter at the many-splendoured funeral of a prince, there was only a handful of Europeans on the whole island, mostly artists hidden away in the hills. The island that the Indian prime minister Jawaharlal Nehru had proclaimed to be 'the morning of the world' was pure, pristine. The Invasion of the Bogans was decades away.

After three years I could think in Bahasa Indonesia as well as speak it. I had eventually become accustomed to the polite but sometimes maddening Javanese custom of never giving no for an answer, of always telling you what you wanted to hear, whether it was fact or not. I had almost begun to do it myself. Less happily, I would not miss the punishing layers of pointless bureaucracy, which drive even the locals nuts.

There were also expatriate vignettes to pack away, some good, some not so. Blanche d'Alpuget – the future wife of Bob Hawke – was in Jakarta then with her first husband, a diplomat at the embassy. I have no real memory of it, but when we meet now she invariably reminds me of a rollicking party when I climbed naked up a flagpole in her front garden. On a slow week night some of us correspondents, topped up with Bintang beer, would offer the *becak* drivers a month's pay to let us race their machines in the circle around the Welcome Monument outside the Hotel Indonesia. Ed Blanche and I once dined at home with one of Sukarno's mistresses, a Javanese of porcelain beauty in her twenties, who received us reclining on a stuffed Sumatran tiger in her drawing room. At one party, the UPI correspondent, an amiable Texan named Joe Galloway, introduced me to his friend the photo-journalist Sean Flynn, the impossibly handsome son of the legendary Australian actor Errol Flynn. It was Sean who gave me my first (and only) LSD tab. He would be captured by the Viet Cong and murdered in 1971.

Saying goodbye to the people in the office was hard. Hidayat had gone to Melbourne to write and broadcast for Radio Australia, but the others had been loyal friends and workmates for all my time in Jakarta. They had supported me to the end, and I felt the parting keenly. I flatter myself that they did, too.

The servants at home were another tough farewell. In retrospect, even having domestic servants sounds appallingly imperialist and paternalistic, but it wasn't then. In Indonesia's chaotic economy, I was their meal ticket, literally. I paid well over the going rate, picked up their doctors' bills and paid for them to travel back to their villages on holidays. They, in turn, helped teach me Indonesian and many of the customs of the country, and always with a sense of fun. In 1969 I told them the news that Neil Armstrong had landed on the moon, pointing up to the night sky. They looked at me in disbelief and burst out laughing. '*Aduh!*' said Tumiyo the houseboy. '*Saya pikir Tuan telah memiliki terlalu banyak minum*' – 'I think Sir has had too much to drink.' I had paid for the birth in hospital of his two children. We hugged each other in tears when we said goodbye.

And then there was the band: the musicians, the roadies, and some of the girls. We played one last almighty concert which I can only dimly remember, for all the obvious reasons. I woke the next morning in a bed at Bram's house with his wife feeding me coffee. There were tears then, too, as they saw me off at the airport a few days later. We would meet again down the track, but there was no way of knowing that then.

Indonesia remains one of the sunniest memories of my life. In January 1970, I was back at the ABC office in Singapore, where they gave me my next assignment: Vietnam again.

10

Ho Chi Minh: my part in his downfall

There was no point anymore to covering the Australian war, although I did try. In early January 1970, not long after I arrived back in Saigon, I flew down to the Task Force base at Nui Dat to see what was doing. It was impossible to find out. By this stage of the war the army had clamped an iron-clad censorship on everything media. The brass in Canberra had decreed that no reporter could speak to any Australian soldier without the approval of an army public relations officer, who had to be present. If you tried to buck the system, your accreditation would be cancelled and you would be thrown off the base.

This meant being escorted everywhere by the PR hack on the ground, Major Ernest Ross Smith, who had been – for a nanosecond – a junior journalist on the *Daily Telegraph* in Sydney. Ernie was a pain in the arse. Smug and officious, a service revolver slung on his hip, he paraded around the Dat like Field Marshal Blamey. People called him Ernie because he disliked it. I suppose he was only doing his job, but his smarmy presence, hovering over your shoulder, ensured that no soldier ever said anything of any interest whatsoever. Ask some corporal the time of day and Ernie would glare at you both with flinty suspicion. Even officers senior to him were not permitted to speak without his say-so. 'I don't think we should talk about that, Colonel,' he would interrupt. Journalists were expected to confine themselves to reheating official communiqués remarkable only for their bland evasions: 'Australian casualties were reported to be light . . .' I could have done this just as easily from Sydney.

American and British correspondents had long ago given up trying to pierce the jungle-green wall, and never bothered to report the Australians. It wasn't worth the trouble. And the Australian Task Force was not doing a lot anyway. Phuoc Tuy province had been largely 'pacified', with Charlie keeping his head down. Exasperated, after a couple of days I chucked it in and went back to Saigon, hoping never to return. Which was exactly what the army wanted. Censorship of the media allowed it to deceive the Australian public about the course of the war, revealing only what was favourable, concealing its failures and blunders, painting itself in the best possible light. The Vietnam moratorium movement in Australia was catching alight, and the government and defence chiefs were terrified of anything that might add fuel to the fire. The veteran Melbourne correspondent Denis Warner, who had covered his first war from 1941, described this gag as 'the most blatant attempt to impose censorship at source that I have encountered in any Army in any war at any time'.[73]

Worse, though, was that in keeping journalists away, the army betrayed its own soldiers. When the diggers came back to Australia to a cool and sometimes hostile reception, it was partly because no one at home knew what they had endured. They never had the chance to tell their story on the ground in the way the American soldiers did. The Australian people were fed official news of battles won and heroism aplenty, but almost nothing of the grinding boredom, the longing for home and family, the mateship, and the real fear that is the day-to-day lot of every soldier at war. The army never let its soldiers in Vietnam display a human face. It was a shameful denial of their democratic rights, for which they paid dearly.

The good news was that this time around I had a flat to live in. It was spartan: a bedroom, lounge room, tiny kitchenette and bathroom above a hairdressing salon. But 23 Han Thuyen Street was dead central, on the wide, leafy boulevard that swept from the cathedral to the

Presidential Palace (and down which the North Vietnamese tanks would roll in 1975). It was also a stone's throw from the Reuters office where I filed my copy, and a pleasant walk to the centre of town for the hotels, bars and restaurants, and the Five O'Clock Follies. A pilot for Air America, the CIA's secretive private airline, lived in a flat across the hall. As I came and went, there would be a warm greeting from the smiling proprietor of the hair salon. Only after the war did I learn she had been a Viet Cong colonel, and commander of the local district.

Even better news: the ABC now had a full-time cameraman spending most of his time in Vietnam. Derek McKendry was from the Waikato, on New Zealand's north island, blond and pink-cheeked with that dairy-fed look about him that a lot of Kiwis have, and about five years older than me. We got off to a rocky start when I carelessly introduced him to someone as 'my cameraman'. He was not amused.

'Listen, Digger,' he snapped. (He called all Australians 'Digger'.) 'I'm not *your* fucking cameraman. I am *a* cameraman, or *the* cameraman, or even *the ABC's* cameraman, but I am not *yours*.'

I made an abject apology. We would become close mates in shared danger.

Saigon had changed since my first visit in 1966, and not for the better. War corrodes all it touches. The old whore was nastier, dirtier, more corrupt. The traffic was snarlier than ever, choked by the purple fumes of the motor scooters, motorcycles, trucks and old taxis. By night the bars were more garish than I remembered, the neon brighter, the rock music louder, the drinks more expensive, the bar girls more shrill and predatory. 'You no buy me one more Saigon tea, you Number Twelve. Aussie Cheap Charlie.' There were more maimed beggars on the pavements, pathetic figures in tattered remnants of their South Vietnam Army (or ARVN) uniforms, in grim contrast to the snake-hipped rent boys and nightclub hustlers who had the money to bribe their way out of conscription for the army.

Yet it was also exhilarating. Perhaps because I had grown up. I was now twenty-four, with three years in South-East Asia under my belt. Each morning, if I was in town, I would stroll down Tu Do for breakfast at the art-deco Café Givral opposite the Continental, where – just as they had done for Alden Pyle, Graham Greene's *Quiet American* – they served big bowls of *café au lait*, buttery croissants and brioche, and creamy *oeufs brouillés*. Lunch could be at any one of a couple of dozen Vietnamese restaurants scattered around Hai Ba Trung or Nguyen Hue, places where I first tasted pho. In the evenings I went for drinks on the terrace at the Continental; if I'd had enough of the American military and wanted to avoid them, I'd go to the Royale, where the elderly *patron*, morose and moustachioed, displayed the crests of the old French Air Force *escadrilles* on his walls. Dinner might be in Cholon, the Chinese quarter, or more French at Ramuntcho's on Le Loi Street, around from the Givral, or at La Cave down by the river, where you were waited on by the proprietor's daughter, a Eurasian girl of exquisite but untouchable beauty. Late-night drinks at the Angel Bar on Tu Do and then home to bed, either alone or with company.

Saigon could be dangerous at times, even for non-combatant journalists. Four correspondents, three of them Australian, were killed during the Viet Cong Tet Offensive of 1968 when their jeep rounded a corner and drove into a roadblock manned by the Viet Cong in Cholon.[74] My own brush with danger, rather less dramatic and definitely less creditable, was my own stupid fault. Drinking late in a nightclub in Cholon with some friends from Reuters, I foolishly went up to the empty stage and started to bang away at the drums.

The joint was almost empty, but a South Vietnamese Air Force captain, in uniform, left his seat and swayed slowly towards me. He was even drunker than I was. He pulled a gun, the biggest .45 I have ever seen, and pointed it straight at me. The black hole of the muzzle was quivering slightly, about two metres from my face. He shouted at me in English – 'You fuck off!' – and waved the gun.

I put my hands in the air and froze.

He approached and put the gun to my temple. I could feel the steel. He shouted again: 'You fuck off quick!'

I unfroze and ran for the door, expecting the bullet. It didn't come. The Reuters journalists joined me outside, where I was leaning limply against a wall, breathless and shaking. 'We had to pay your bill,' said one primly. 'You should have told the little chap you were British.'

✧

Derek and I were not in Saigon very often. There was no news to be had there beyond the ever more creative evasions, exaggerations and outright lies of the crew-cut colonels at the Five O'Clock Follies. The war had destroyed Lyndon Johnson's presidency. Richard Nixon and Henry Kissinger were casting around for ways to end it that could be sold as an honourable victory. All the action was now to the west of Saigon, towards the Cambodian border, where the North Vietnamese braved terrifying attacks by waves of the big B-52 bombers to roll truck convoys of weapons, ammunition and fresh soldiers down the Ho Chi Minh Trail by night.

We went to have a look, flying on an American C-130 to the big base at Cu Chi, north-west of Saigon about halfway to Cambodia, and the headquarters of the US Army's 25th Infantry Division. From there we took a Huey chopper further north-west to a small American fort, as they called it, about 3 kilometres from the border. 'Fort' was too big a word. Patrol Base Kotrc was a forlorn circle of red dirt about 200 metres in diameter, barricaded by sandbags, concertina razor wire and Claymore anti-personnel mines, the lot dominated by a lopsided timber lookout and communications tower flying the Stars and Stripes.[75] There were straggled rows of tents, foxholes and weapons pits, also sandbagged, between lines of pierced steel planking. Three of the big American 105-millimetre howitzer field guns stood ready, their olive-green barrels aimed at the horizon.

'Welcome to the Wolfhounds.' A young captain shook our hands, said he was pleased to have Australians visit with him, and led us to his command tent. The Wolfhounds were the US Army's 27th Infantry Regiment – motto *Nec Aspera Terrent*, 'They Fear No Difficulties' – and the captain had an infantry company under his command on the base, about 250 men all up, including the gunners. Most were kids younger even than me, boys from Maine and Minnesota, Wisconsin and Tennessee, California and the Carolinas, from sea to shining sea, suntanned and shirtless. They chewed a lot of gum. Many of them wore the three-starred peace symbol along with the dog tags around their necks. The black guys seemed to stick together. The captain, skinny and bespectacled, looked like a teenage Woody Allen. He told us, very proudly, that he was a Reserve Officer Training Corps graduate from Ohio University who had majored in speech and drama. 'Jesus, Digger,' said Derek later. 'He's not John Wayne. What've we got ourselves into here?'

But we had the run of the place, and once again the Americans talked. About how they hated the war, how fucked up it was, how they despised Nixon, how they longed to go home. There was no Ernie Ross Smith to silence them. Some were curious about Sydney, thinking it could be a good place for R and R, although few of them seemed to have any clue where it was: 'Is it a long ways from here?' We were offered a joint in exchange for more information on Australia. 'Do people there speak English?' The welcome whiff of cannabis fumes hung heavy in the night air. The entire patrol base was getting high.

We had a scratch dinner with the captain, who was not high. When it got dark he gave us night-vision scopes to look through, which revealed the headlights of the North Vietnamese convoys moving south down the trail in streams of eerie, fluorescent green light. We were kept awake most of the night by the brain-splitting crash of the howitzers just metres away, shooting 'H and I' – Harassment and Interdiction fire – which basically meant firing shells at random to keep the enemy down. For about twenty minutes around midnight the earth trembled like the very crack of doom itself as the B-52s unloaded their cargo into Cambodia a few clicks away. It was scary at our distance; it must have been terrifying to the VC hidden in their tunnels directly beneath those tumbling bombs.

The next morning, with Derek filming on the BL Arriflex camera, we moved out of Kotrc on a RIF, a Reconnaissance in Force patrol. The idea was to poke around in the boonies to see what, if anything, turned up. There were about thirty or forty of us in a platoon led by a baby-faced lieutenant, who was backed up by an older sergeant. I remember being simultaneously apprehensive and curious, but not scared. Widely spaced, we trudged first along a nearby muddy stream or canal, then into a marsh or swamp, and then through low scrub for kilometre upon monotonous kilometre, heading further west towards Cambodia. The grunts were wearing steel helmets. I was not. Some of them were smoking Camels or Lucky Strikes, which seemed a bit informal. The sun was on our backs and it was humid, not a breath of breeze. We were stinking hot and sweaty, with strange insects coming at us.

So were the Viet Cong. After a couple of hours we saw a small clearing some distance ahead. As the platoon approached it, there was the sudden, shocking bark and splatter of automatic weapons fire from the scrub on the other side. Happily, I was towards the back of the platoon.

My recollection of what happened next is jumbled and fragmented, like some lethal kaleidoscope. I hit the dirt, scrabbling for cover. There was nothing but a few spindly bushes. The soldiers around me were shooting back and shouting. 'Motherfuckers! Fucking gooks! Goddam motherfuckers!' Their M16s barked. There were hollow bangs from a Dooper, the grunts' nickname for the M79 grenade launcher.

Through the corner of one eye I could see Derek sprawled on his side, filming still. War cameramen have it tougher than the journalist. They have to get the picture while the reporter can cower in fear, which I was doing. Yet at the same time I felt ethereally detached, as if this were some dramatic performance with me as an impartial but interested spectator. The noise of combat is almost a physical assault on body and mind. It is not like the movies. The very air splits in shock. A couple of times there was a zingy, buzzy, zippy sound as bullets flew perhaps a couple of metres above my head.

After about three years of this – actually about five minutes, I suppose – the shooting faded and stopped, to be replaced by an echoing silence. No one had been hit. I lay there, still shaking, but at the same time curiously, stupidly proud that I had been under fire and lived. The lieutenant had called in Cobra helicopter gunships which putter-puttered overhead after about ten minutes and laid down rocket and machine-gun fire where the concealed enemy had been. The rest was anticlimax. By late afternoon we were back at Kotrc for a swim and splash in the muddy pool just outside the wire.

There was an ARVN patrol base just a short walk away, a very similar outfit manned by an infantry company, and it seemed like a good idea to go and talk to them. The captain spoke passable English.

He was surprised to see us, and even more surprised to learn that we were Australians, and with elaborate courtesy he insisted we stay for dinner. It was simple but delicious – a pho, from memory. The conversation was stilted but friendly. Had the Americans been over to eat with him, I asked, or had he dined with them?

He looked bemused, as if he had not understood what I said, but then smiled wryly. No, it had never happened. He shrugged, with the air of a man shunned by foreigners in his own country and unable to do anything about it.

I have often wondered since what happened to him. Was he killed? Did he surrender and get hauled off for 're-education'? I hope things went well for him.

That evening Woody Allen told us there would be a night AP, or ambush patrol, and we would be welcome to accompany it. He was keen to make sure we got everything we wanted, he said. Derek and I declined on the grounds that we couldn't film at night, but more because we'd had enough excitement that day. We wandered off to talk with more of the grunts and smoke another joint before turning in.

Then a bizarre thing happened. As we were getting ready to hit the sack – the slang was infectious – a red-haired boy lunged into our tent, shaking and sobbing. 'I don't wanna go,' he blubbered. 'I don't wanna go. You're newsmen. Tell 'em not to make me go.' He threw himself at Derek, imploring and begging, clutching and clinging. 'I can't fucking go,' he bawled. His pupils were small pinpricks in wild eyes – the boy was zonked on heroin. He had been assigned the AP. The commotion attracted a sergeant, who burst into the tent and dragged him out by the scruff of the neck, swearing at him and apologising profusely to us.

We slept like babies that night and woke late to find the base locked in a ghastly silence. There was no morning bustle, none of the usual blare of rock music from AFVN, the US Armed Forces' radio network in Vietnam. We found Woody Allen in his tent, dishevelled and pallid, his eyes evidently red from weeping. He had killed some of his own soldiers. The AP had been attacked. He had ordered artillery fire down on the attackers but he got the map coordinates wrong. The shells had landed on the patrol. Three soldiers were dead and two wounded.

Other boys were crying too, for their lost buddies. There was an air of muttering menace, as if they wanted to attack their officer. It would be far from the first time that had happened. The senior enlisted men were moving among them, hosing things down.

Derek and I looked at each other. We could have been on that AP. I remember murmuring to the captain some inane remark about the fortunes of war. 'Please don't put it in your news,' he implored. I felt a wave of pity for him and a wave of revulsion for the war itself. The speech and drama graduate from the American Midwest, utterly out of his depth in this alien land, seemed a sad metaphor for the whole hideous mess. Time to leave.

We caught the first chopper back to Cu Chi. A colonel joined us for a lunch of excellent steak and salads with those greasy American dressings that look and taste like someone else has eaten them first. 'You want Ranch, Thousand Island or Roquefort?' He wanted to hear about the friendly fire deaths. 'Too bad,' he said. He also wanted to ask about R and R in Sydney. They all did. Deep beneath us, in the vast warren of the Cu Chi tunnels, the VC were also having lunch. The Yanks had no idea they were there.

✧

Billy McMahon, the Australian foreign minister, came to visit in April 1970. Reluctantly, we followed him down to the Dat to film him posing with the diggers, always a favourite activity for politicians of any colour. Ernie Ross Smith buzzed about him like a blowfly at a barbecue.[76] Billy gave what he imagined was a rousing speech, absurd bombast in his curious, quacking delivery. I guffawed aloud, thinking of Napoleon at the pyramids: 'Soldiers! Four thousand years of history look down upon you!' Billy was no Bonaparte. Ernie shooshed me. That night they put on a movie, *The Battle of Britain*. It was surreal. Sitting in the rubber trees and the dust of Phuoc Tuy province, the diggers cheered as Michael Caine and Edward Fox clawed Messerschmitts out of blue Kentish skies.

There were still some 7000 Australians in Vietnam, including two infantry battalions. The Americans had around 335,000 troops, down from the peak of more than half a million under Johnson in early

1969. The new buzzword from the White House and MACV was 'Vietnamization': code for the Americans handing over the war to the South Vietnamese (whether they were ready or not), declaring victory and getting the hell out as soon as possible, if not sooner. McMahon got the full spiel from the US Ambassador in Saigon, Ellsworth Bunker, and the MACV commander, General Creighton Abrams, and he duly parroted it to me when we filmed an interview with him back in Saigon.

We were at the residence of the Australian ambassador, and it was late in the evening. The war was going very well, McMahon assured us. It was taking longer than originally expected, perhaps, but there was no doubt that communism would be defeated. The South Vietnamese would soon be ready to step up. Vietnamization was already proving to be a success, a *great* success. Blah, blah.

Interview over, he shook hands, told us he was off to bed and disappeared. We were still packing the camera gear when there was a strangled scream from down the hall, followed by cries for help.

'Perhaps Charlie's got him,' said Derek hopefully.

'Let's give them some time,' I said.

With McMahon still bawling, the minder from the embassy rushed to the bedroom and we listened, thrilled, to the sounds of thumps and bangs.

After about five minutes he returned. 'He was frightened by a gecko that fell on his head,' he grinned. 'I had to kill it.'

✧

Derek and I covered as much territory as we could in Vietnam, always with the Americans. Regrettably, looking back, we spent barely any time with the ARVN forces, a grave omission. It was their war, their future, and we should have been across it. But few of us bothered, apart from Neil Davis. With hindsight, there was a racist bias to it, if an unconscious one. Covering the Americans was so much easier and, to be honest, much safer. You could understand what was going on, especially if things turned ugly.

Which occasionally they did. At Pleiku, in the Central Highlands, we arrived at an American airfield in the midst of a rocket attack, and had to run for our lives. In nearby Kontum, we were leaving on one of the big Chinook transport helicopters when a fragment of shrapnel smashed into the engine of the front rotor and sent the aircraft crashing to the ground. Happily, we were only a couple of metres off the dirt, meaning we got no more than a severe jolt.

'Most inconvenient,' sniffed Donald Wise, the veteran correspondent for London's *Daily Mail*, who was with us. 'Who knows when the next one will be along?'

Urbane and languid, tall and skinny as a beanpole, impeccably dressed and boasting a cavalry moustache, Wise was much loved. He had fought as a lieutenant in the British Army in Singapore in World War II, and spent three years as a prisoner of war of the Japanese, much of it on the Burma–Siam Railway. Ordered to work to build a bridge, he refused. A Japanese guard reminded him that Jesus Christ was a carpenter who had worked. 'Christ,' replied Wise, 'was not a British officer.'

After 1945 he became a captain in the Paratroop Regiment in Palestine, and then – interrupting a brief career as a rubber planter – he led irregular guerrillas in the Malayan Emergency. After that he turned his hand to journalism. On his first visit to the Australians at the Bien Hoa air base, he descended upon them in the lurid, tiger-striped camouflage combat fatigues of the South Vietnamese marines, a silk scarf at his throat.

'Bloody hell,' snorted one digger to another. 'We'll be okay. We're saved. Tarzan's here.'

'I've done my bit, laddie,' retorted Wise, unfazed. 'Now I'm here to see you do yours.'

It was outside Pleiku that I saw my first corpses. The Americans took us to a village where they had been fired on the day before, and which they had then attacked and burned. About a dozen bodies were still there, blackened and twisted and already beginning to decay. The smell was indescribable.

✧

Also that April, President Nixon ordered the military to plan an invasion of Cambodia, to strike at the Ho Chi Minh trail and to destroy what the Americans called COSVN, or the Central Office for South Vietnam. Many of them imagined COSVN to be a 'Bamboo Pentagon', some sprawling Viet Cong headquarters building hidden somewhere in the Cambodian jungle. Destroying it would allow many more Americans to be withdrawn, it was thought, and hasten the end of the war.

On 25 April, after Nixon and Henry Kissinger had watched the gung-ho movie *Patton*, in which George C. Scott played the eponymous, pistol-packing World War II tank commander, a fired-up Nixon gave the order to go. The ARVN smashed over the border in force on 30 April. The Americans followed with still more force the next day, a Friday. The bombing campaign went into overdrive. Derek and I had been planning a lazy weekend in Saigon. No luck. By that afternoon we were on a chopper heading towards the Parrot's Beak, a salient of Cambodian territory jutting into Vietnam about 65 kilometres north-west of Saigon.

The US Army's 11th Armored Cavalry Regiment was already rolling. They called it the Blackhorse Regiment, its troopers wearing a red-and-white arm patch with a leaping stallion on it. Official motto: *Allons!* Unofficial motto: 'Find the bastards and pile on.' As ever, they made us welcome.

The start point was swarming with tanks and Armored Cavalry Assault Vehicles, or ACAVs, their engines throbbing in a haze of blue diesel smoke. We clambered onto the rear of a big green Sheridan tank in the midst of a column of them and allonsed over the border into the Beak, clinging on for dear life. Again it was exhilarating, the adrenaline flowing. As we crossed the line, the colonel of the regiment was standing there, hoarse from shouting above the roar of the engines and the squeal of the tracks, but still urging his men on. 'Go get 'em!' If you have watched the movie *Apocalypse Now* you will have a sense of the scene.

Further into Cambodia we lurched, jolting down a wide dirt road, past rice fields and dark stretches of rainforest. Wide-eyed villagers came out of their homes and looked up from the fields to watch this mechanised cavalcade of steel thunder by. Some of them waved. We waved back. Every so often the tanks would crunch to a halt for what they called 'reconnaissance by fire' – a military euphemism for shooting the living daylights out of anything and everything that might lie ahead. The shells arced off into the boonies, landing God only knew where.

The major I questioned did not know where either. But it didn't matter. 'It's a declared free fire zone,' he said. 'We can shoot anything in it.'

'Are the local people aware of that? Has anyone told the Cambodians?'

'That I can't say, sir.'

'So you could be killing innocent people?'

'We have our orders, sir.'

It sounded like the Nuremberg defence.

By the second day of this onslaught there were no more waving villagers. There was not a soul to be seen. Perhaps the lucky ones had managed to flee. The squadron we were with was not attacked either. Other Blackhorse units were. As the 11th Cavalry's 2nd Squadron raced on ahead of us, towards the town of Snoul, further into the Parrot's Beak, it was fired on with rocket-propelled grenades. The squadron commander, Lieutenant Colonel Grail Brookshire, ordered his men to destroy Snoul.

For twenty-four hours, the guns of their tanks and wave after wave of air strikes pounded the town to smoking rubble. The next day, when Brookshire – nicknamed 'The Holy Grail' – finally judged it safe to enter the ruins, his men found only seven bodies, four of them Cambodian civilians, including a young girl. If there had been North Vietnamese or Viet Cong troops in the town, they were long gone. Deprived of an enemy, the Americans looted homes and shops, loading liquor, clothing and 'souvenirs' into their tanks. Later, Brookshire would laughingly refer to himself as 'the butcher of Snoul'.[77] He was awarded the US Army's Silver Star 'for gallantry in action', and he retired a brigadier general. 'Cambodia was not a mistake, it was a crime,' wrote the British journalist and author William Shawcross.[78]

We turned and went back into Vietnam on the third day, the soldiers hurling red and yellow smoke grenades in triumph as we crossed the border. Filthy and smelly, we were met in a clearing by a brass band playing stirring martial music – and a welcoming line of 'Donut Dollies', bouncy American college girls who had donned blue Red Cross uniforms to come to Vietnam to raise morale. Yes, they handed out donuts, and hot but undrinkable coffee. And smiles – gleaming white, all-American, Miss Cotton Candy, cheerleader, senior prom smiles. 'Hi, soldier, how you doin'? I'm Lauren, from Mobile, Alabama!'

Across the other side of the field was an open truck full of Viet Cong or NVA prisoners. I couldn't tell which because they had been stripped to their underwear, striped pyjama shorts. They were standing jam-packed. No donuts for them. Some glared back as we filmed them, eyes aflame with defiant hatred. Others just looked scared.

I found a lieutenant seated a little distance from the Donut Dollies, leaning back on his pack, helmet off, nursing a coffee and sucking on a cigarette. He was filthy, his fatigues stained with sweat, his eyes ringed with lines of exhaustion. I introduced myself and asked if he would talk. 'Sure, fire away.' Derek began filming.

'How long are you guys going to be in Cambodia, do you think?'

'Fucked if I know. It's Richard Nixon's war. Why don't you ask him?'

He was a thoughtful and intelligent man in his mid-twenties, an infantry officer troubled by the enormity of invading Cambodia and what it might bring. Nixon had promised a withdrawal from Vietnam, he said, but here they were heading deeper into Indochina. Who knew where it would end?

When we had shot what we needed, and after we stopped filming, he wanted to talk more. He was from Virginia, he told us, a West Point graduate from an army family through and through, with an ancestor who had fought for the Confederacy. But he hated the war he now found himself in. He had been particularly troubled when he'd been ordered to destroy a village early in his tour. After much thought he had come to the conclusion that the war was immoral. Pragmatically, it was also unwinnable for the US.

We made to start filming again. He asked us not to but kept speaking. His dilemma was that he had to command soldiers in combat in a war he did not believe in. They were kids mostly drafted from working-class America, while the families of the rich angled for and got deferments. His little sister had joined the anti-war protest movement at home and he sometimes wished he could be with her.

I thought he might cry, but he squared his shoulders and managed a grin, a shrug. Anyway, it would be over soon, he said. He was 'short' – grunt slang for getting close to the end of your time in 'Nam. Home in two months. We shook hands and parted. I have forgotten his name, but I have always very much hoped it isn't one of the 58,000 engraved on the long, black Vietnam Memorial Wall in Washington, DC.

✧

We went back to Cambodia a week later, but not with the US Army. Mr Pham drove us there in his 1959 Chrysler DeSoto, a rattling yellow-and-white rocket with splendid upswept tail fins, the sort of car that should have had Rock Hudson behind the wheel with an arm around Doris Day. We had used Mr Pham before. There was always a clutch of old American cars and drivers waiting for hire in the square near the Caravelle, and Mr Pham, skinny and helpful, with good English, became our driver when we needed one.

It was Friday, 8 May. Early that morning we headed out of Saigon and north-west along Highway 1, the route to the Cambodian capital, Phnom Penh. It was a risk, to be sure. Sean Flynn and a companion, Dana Stone, had been captured on Route 1 in Cambodia just a month before. Sean, working for *Time* magazine, and Stone, freelancing for the American CBS network, left Saigon riding motorbikes on 6 April, also heading for Phnom Penh. They told friends they'd heard there was a Viet Cong checkpoint on the road and were hoping to get some pictures. It was a brave but foolhardy thing to do. They were never seen again, and their remains have never been found. The best guess is that they were captured at the checkpoint. It's thought they were held captive for more than a year, until they were handed over to the Khmer Rouge, who murdered them.

Derek and I figured, though, that the road would be secure after the invasion, and the MACV media officers assured us it was. We wanted to see what had happened to the countryside and its people.

The highway was busy at first, with the usual chaotic traffic. Mr Pham blasted his way through with horn blaring. But as we approached the Cambodian border, about 60 kilometres from Saigon, the horde began to thin out. There was no frontier checkpoint on either side. We rolled straight into Cambodia on what was now pretty much an empty road with rice fields on either side, and the occasional small hamlet. Sometimes we would pass a lumbering truck or a bus, but not much else, and there were few people. Some of the hamlets appeared to be entirely deserted. The place should have been as busy as Vietnam, with peasants working in the rice, but it was not. It was eerie, with an air of menace, and Mr Pham was beginning to get edgy – not a good sign. 'How much more you want to go?' he kept asking. 'I think we don't go too much further.'

But we did not yet have a story. We needed something more than footage of fields and desolate villages. We decided to give it another fifteen minutes, and then, if nothing happened, we would turn back. That took us to a small village called Prasaut, about 90 kilometres from Saigon, almost halfway to Phnom Penh. The highway cut through the middle of Prasaut, or what was left of it. The place was in ruins, smashed to rubble. Some shops or houses had been battered by heavy artillery, leaving only broken concrete walls or a brick chimney standing. Other buildings had been burned out, their entrails black and ruined. Most had bullet holes and scars. A handful of people picked through the wreckage, watched by a few bored ARVN soldiers with M16 rifles slung over their shoulders. In one house I found burned human bones jumbled together in a heap of broken cooking pots and filthy bedding.

Prasaut had been a village of ethnic Vietnamese. For generations they had coexisted, peacefully enough, with the native Cambodians. But that changed when Cambodia's hereditary ruler, Prince Norodom Sihanouk, was deposed in a military coup in March 1970. The new ruler, General Lon Nol, an American puppet, ordered the expulsion of Vietnamese civilians from the border areas, and – less publicly – encouraged his army to massacre them. An orgy of killing broke out. The Cambodian army shelled Prasaut, and on 10 April its soldiers rounded up about a hundred Vietnamese, half of them women and children, and herded them into a grain store. Then they shot them, in hot-blooded slaughter.

While Derek and Mr Pham got the camera gear out of the car, I wandered across the street to a small, stony clearing between two ruined houses. Then it hit me.

The stench. There was a foul, gassy stink of rotting corpses, coming from what appeared to be a water well about two metres in diameter. I had smelt death's decay before, but never like this. Hand clapped over my nose and mouth, I made myself take a look. The hole was full almost to the brim with a hideous grey-green stew of body parts, badly decomposed but still recognisably human. A child's hand, cut off at the wrist, floated on the surface. I threw up, a heaving, choking, retching, uncontrollable emptying of my guts. Derek threw up too, when I called him over. Tragically, we had our story.

Whose remains were they? It was impossible to say. When the ARVN troops invaded Cambodia that May they discovered the massacre of the Vietnamese there and vowed revenge. Perhaps they executed the remaining Cambodians and threw their dismembered corpses into the well. We asked Mr Pham to question the idling ARVN soldiers for us, but they shook their heads and shrugged, feigning ignorance.

We filmed around the village unhindered, including the well itself, and I did a stand-up, a reporter's piece to camera. It was mid afternoon by then, and Mr Pham was getting anxious. 'We go now, we go now,' he kept saying. We had at least a two-hour drive back to Saigon, and we had to get there before nightfall. In theory, anyway, Highway 1 was safe enough by day, when it was under American and South Vietnamese control, but come the night, the whole equation changed. The VC was known to command large stretches of it.

Mr Pham drove as if the hounds of hell were after us. Derek and I sat in the back, chain-smoking in sombre silence. Just before the border we passed the burned-out skeleton of a car on the edge of the road, a wreck which had not been there when we came through in the morning. How had that happened? As dusk began to fall I found myself wondering if we would round a corner and find a VC checkpoint waiting for us, as Sean and Dana Stone probably had. Or perhaps a rocket-propelled grenade would slam into the DeSoto.

It did not. It was past twilight when we got back. The lights of

Saigon had never looked more welcome. We had a lot to drink that night.

ABC Television ran our story in the seven pm news bulletin the next Monday, 11 May. Only very much later did I discover that the producers had hacked into it. All the footage of that stinking well of death was left on the cutting-room floor, deemed too unpleasant to be seen in Australian homes at dinnertime.

✧

The Americans never found the Bamboo Pentagon. There was no such place, or not as they envisaged it. The Central Office for South Vietnam was in fact a loose and shifting network, highly mobile, widely dispersed through kilometres of tunnels and underground bunkers, many of which the Americans never discovered. It kept its radio transmissions to the bare minimum, often relying on fast motorbikes for communications between its various cells. Most of its people had fled well before the imperialist tanks smashed in.

The invasion, though, did uncover vast Viet Cong and NVA supply dumps, which yielded a huge haul of weapons, literally millions of rounds of ammunition and rockets, and significant stores of food and military equipment. Without doubt those finds disrupted the communist war effort. They bought time. The delusion of Vietnamization could sustain itself a little longer.

But there was a price to pay, in much blood. In the US, anti-war protests erupted across the country, with marches, strikes and demonstrations growing in fury. On Monday, 4 May the protests boiled over into tragedy at Kent State University in Ohio, when National Guardsmen panicked and fired wildly into a crowd of demonstrating students, killing four and wounding nine. Ten days later, two more young protestors were shot by the cops at Jackson State, a black college in Mississippi. The anti-war movement was galvanised, its strength swelling. The protest marches in Washington DC erupted in such violence that Nixon was flown to Camp David for safety. The anti-war movement was stirring in Australia, too.

Cambodia paid a far higher price, in one of the great human disasters of the century. The American invasion rocked the already shaky Lon Nol puppet government in Phnom Penh, and it never regained its balance. The country was plunged into civil war between the government and the newly risen communist Khmer Rouge, supported at first by North Vietnam. In 1975 – Year Zero – the Khmer Rouge seized power and unleashed an insane, Maoist genocide that would render the once peaceful kingdom a blood-drenched killing field. As many as 3 million people were murdered. It was Nixon and Kissinger who sowed the poisoned seeds of that catastrophe, a war crime if ever there was. The Cambodian people reaped the whirlwind.

✧

By the northern summer of 1970 it was time for me to move on. The ABC wanted me to relieve the correspondent in New Delhi.

I was not sorry to leave Vietnam, although I recognised that I had done some growing up there. The profound lesson I had learned was that authority has an infinite capacity to distort and to lie to protect itself from the consequences of its mistakes. The more cosmic the mistake, the more elaborate and persistent the lie. If I am a cynic, Vietnam is why. It came as no surprise to me, none at all, that the second Iraq War of 2003 was launched on a tissue of lies and deceit. Countless millions died in wars that should never have been fought. The man who got it right was General Vo Nguyen Giap, the Defence Minister of North Vietnam, a commander of the NVA and one of the great military and political strategists of the twentieth century. In a speech to political commissars of the army's 316th Division, Giap nailed it in a couple of sentences:

> The enemy will pass slowly from the offensive to the defensive. The blitzkrieg will transform itself into a war of long duration. Thus, the enemy will be caught in a dilemma: he has to drag out the war in order to win it, but does not possess, on the other hand, the psychological and political means to fight a long-drawn-out war.[79]

Giap was actually talking about Vietnam's anti-imperial struggle to overthrow the French in the 1950s, but exactly the same reasoning applied to the Americans twenty years later. When the United States finally left Vietnam, its army was all but broken.

Personally, the tensions of covering the war day by day had taken a toll. It was nothing like the strains faced by soldiers in combat, but it was there nonetheless. If things got heavy, a correspondent could always take the next helicopter out, an option not available to the soldier. But I was tired, and I could use some downtime. I seized the moment.

Almost half a century on, I'm glad I was there. It was a pivotal experience of my life, an awakening to manhood. I have never suffered from any form of post-traumatic stress disorder, although I got Vietnam flashbacks for decades afterwards, and sometimes still do. The sound of a helicopter choppering overhead can do it.

In 1995, to my considerable surprise, a grateful Queen and nation gave me some gongs for it all. I am not entirely sure why, but I am entitled to wear the Vietnam Logistics and Support Medal and the Australian Active Service Medal with a Vietnam clasp on it. I'm quite proud of them, in a funny sort of way, and some years back I wore them once or twice on Anzac Day. But I'm a bit over that now.

11

The *Mona Lisa* was a disappointment

INDIA WAS MAGNIFICENCE AND MISERY. More of the latter than the former. I had seen poverty in South-East Asia, but nothing to match the infinite human tragedy of the blighted masses of the Indian subcontinent. It was sobering, and the more so against the backdrop of the glories of empire, Mughal and British.

The country had been independent since 1947, but the Raj lived on. The ABC house was a white-painted villa of two storeys in the posh Friends' Colony suburb of New Delhi. My bedroom was the size of the Sydney Cricket Ground. Elephants could have sluiced in the bath. Teams of servants glided silently here and there. Those who were permitted to speak called me Sahib. Others just bowed as I passed. Three gardeners seemed to be permanently employed trimming the vast lawn with nail scissors. I still have the guilts about it.

Prime Minister Indira Gandhi, Nehru's daughter, was at the height of her powers in 1970, commanding in the green-carpeted chamber of India's House of Representatives, the *Lok Sabha*. She was campaigning to rid India of the Privy Purse, the millions of rupees that the government showered on the country's former princely rulers in supposed compensation for their lost realms. Maharajahs, Nizams and nawabs fought back. It was a great story to report. Indira eventually won.

I was there for only a few months. In late August I got a telegram out of the blue from Singapore, written in what we called cable-ese. There were just four words. GO LUSAKA SOONEST, it said. HOLLINSHEAD. Always the joker, Peter was mimicking the language of *Scoop*, Evelyn Waugh's classic comedy of a bumbling foreign correspondent in Africa.

This was a surprise. I had a vague idea that Lusaka was somewhere in Africa, but where? And why? A follow-up cable told me I was to cover the Third Conference of Heads of State or Government of Non-Aligned Countries, to begin on 7 September. More puzzlement. My knowledge of the Non-Aligned Movement would have fitted easily on the back of an envelope. I scratched around. Lusaka turned out to be the capital of Zambia, in southern Africa, formerly the British colony of Northern Rhodesia. I flew there via Bombay, Addis Ababa and Nairobi.

Lusaka was dirty, dusty, smelly and ramshackle. In the midst of the squalor, however, there had risen a magnificent hall of marble and glass, specially built for the conference and air-conditioned to an Arctic chill. This was surrounded by sixty-two equally splendid villas for the visiting heads of state and their expansive entourages, who jolted over the rutted roads in fleets of newly imported Mercedes-Benz limousines. Presiding over all was Zambia's president, Kenneth Kaunda, a fighter for independence from the British who had since gone the familiar route of squandering his country's vast mineral wealth, shoving his grasping hands into the till up to the armpits, and fomenting a slavish personality cult.

Kaunda celebrated my arrival by having me arrested and banged up in a police cell. The cops knocked on the door of my hotel room in the late afternoon, demanded my passport and ordered me to go with them. I asked to know why but got no answer. Protest was futile. They escorted me politely enough to a patrol car and carted me off to a police station. Eventually they rounded up sixteen journalists, mostly American or British but all of us white, and all newly arrived for the conference. We were shown into a couple of filthy, dimly lit cells, and left behind bars to stew in the heat for a few hours. There was no explanation. One man, a middle-aged German, collapsed with an apparent stroke. We shouted for help and they came and took him away to hospital. Towards midnight our jailers called us out for questioning, one by one. Were we spies for the South African apartheid regime, they wanted to know.

The questioning was perfunctory, suggesting they weren't all that serious. They were going through the motions, for whatever reason. Probably because they could. I was able to satisfy them by saying, quite truthfully, that I had never been to South Africa. There was no South African visa in my passport. I was returned to the cell.

The next morning it turned out to have been all a terrible mistake. A senior police officer covered in medal ribbons told us there had been an unfortunate misunderstanding. When he had heard of it, President Kaunda himself, the Father of the Nation, had expressed his profound regret and directed that we be freed immediately. Zambia welcomed visitors. Its hospitality was world-famous. As an apology, we would be offered a rare privilege: a private screening of a short documentary film about the life and times of the president, which we would greatly enjoy. We should assemble at the theatre at eleven am.

I was all for failing to appear, but the experienced Africa correspondent for *The Times* of London sensibly urged me to front. 'They'll make life uncomfortable for you if you don't,' he warned.

All smiles, they ticked our names off as we entered. The short documentary ran for about three hours. President Kaunda had directed it himself – one of his many talents. He certainly also starred in it. It turned out he was a crusading freedom fighter, democrat, writer, scientist, engineer, artist, musician, multi-skilled athlete and polymath who had invented everything from hydroelectric power to radio astronomy to a cure for malaria. Beloved by his people, admired and regularly consulted by international leaders who sought his wise counsel, he was Africa's great hope for peace and progress, and a beacon for the world. Our brains fried to scrambled egg, parched and starving, we stumbled out into the twilight and repaired to the hotel bar.

The conference began the next day. It was interesting, but only to see who turned up. The Non-Aligned Movement had kicked off in 1956, founded by Jawaharlal Nehru of India, Sukarno of Indonesia, Josip Broz Tito of Yugoslavia, Gamal Abdel Nasser of Egypt and

Kwame Nkrumah of Ghana; it was intended to be a counterweight to the Western and Soviet power blocs. Tito and Nkrumah were there in Lusaka. So were Suharto, Lee Kuan Yew and Indira Gandhi, but Fidel Castro was a disappointing no-show. My favourite was His Imperial Majesty Emperor Haile Selassie of Ethiopia, fiercely bearded, the self-styled Lion of Judah, who stood about a metre tall in stilt heels. Running him a close second in the exotica stakes was His Beatitude President Archbishop Makarios III of Cyprus, also bearded, black-gowned and sporting an enormous hat. Tito, three times the size of the Lion of Judah, and splendid in a dazzling white suit, seemed to dominate proceedings. The Provisional Revolutionary Government of South Vietnam got a guernsey as an observer. Two rival delegations turned up from Cambodia, one representing Prince Sihanouk, the other sent by Lon Nol. Neither got a seat.

The speeches went on and on and on. And on again, for three days. It was numbingly dull. I dutifully reported back to Australia what I thought might be vaguely newsy, but my heart was not in it. At the end of it they pumped out a lengthy communiqué, pages and pages of lofty principle and unarguably good intentions, lavishly embroidered with ringing declarations about Liberty and the Rights of Man, and the twin evils of colonialism and imperialism. Then they went home, tired but happy. I headed back to Kenya to spend a night at Nairobi's celebrated New Stanley Hotel, oddly pleased that Ernest Hemingway had been there before me.

✧

My time as a foreign correspondent was running out. Five years was the average spell abroad before they called you back home. But Sydney had decided I could have a last fling, partly as a reward for good behaviour, partly to broaden my horizons. The ABC gave me a round-the-world airline ticket, first class, so I could touch base at the offices in London, New York, Washington and Tokyo before heading home. Better still, I could take a month's leave in Europe – at my own expense – before I was due in London.

I flew Lufthansa from Nairobi to Athens. For a week I clambered over the Acropolis and swam in the Aegean at Glyfada Beach, relishing the caress of saltwater after so long away from it. In Rome I stayed in a *pensione* and did the usual tourist stuff, thrilled to walk the streets and gape at the glories. At St Peter's Basilica I wondered vaguely if they had some sort of celestial alarm that might detect the bastard sons of priests so they could be thrown out by the Swiss guards. Turns out they did not.

Unexpectedly, it was Munich that blew me away. At the airport there was a tourist desk where you could use a phone to find a place to stay. I wanted a cheap bed and breakfast, and was floundering with phrase-book German – *Haben Sie ein Zimmer mit Frühstück?* – when an American about my own age stepped in. He spoke the language, he said. His name was Hans. He was a visitor too, just arrived. Maybe we could get a place together. After a couple of rapid-fire phone calls in impressively fluent German, he found two rooms in a comfortable suburban home run by a pink-cheeked *Hausfrau*. Hans' father had been a bomber pilot in the Luftwaffe, he told me, killed in 1945. Hans himself had been born in Munich but after the war his mother had migrated to the US, and they now lived in New York City, where he had just finished a law degree. He had never known his father. This was his first trip back to Germany.

He was a nice guy, good company, and happy for me to tag along while he did the interpreting. We went to the *Oktoberfest*. Affable burghers – portly gents in *Lederhosen*, busty *hausfraus* in dirndls – cheerfully made way for us to join them at the long wooden tables. *Australische! Wilkommen!* This was a few years before swarms of pre-Bogans discovered *Oktoberfest* and transformed the word 'Australian' into a synonym for 'drunken hooligan'. Our hosts tried out their English, but I decided not to take my German for a run. *Bald wird der Führer im Buckingham Palast leben* had passed its use-by date. Together we quaffed great foaming steins of *Löwenbräu* and shovelled down plates of *Wurst mit Senf*. An oom-pah band crashed and thumped on stage, with singing compulsory:

Ein Prosit, ein Prosit,
Der Gemütlichkeit!
Ein Prosit, ein Prosit
Der Gemütlichkeit!

We did the *Bürgerbräukeller*, where Hitler had staged his Beer Hall Putsch in 1923. More oom-pahing, more singing with cheery Bavarians, all very *Gemütlich* – a word with no exact English translation but which means happy-joyful-exuberant. How many of them had been Nazis, I found myself wondering. It was only twenty-five years since the war. Munich had been Hitler's launch pad, his power base. How many of these jolly *Volk* had saluted him through the streets, thrilled to his speeches on the radio, even joined him for that most exalted of the Nazi festivals, the *Alte Kämpfer* (Old Campaigners) gathering in Munich on the anniversary of the putsch each November? How many had been in the SS? There was no knowing.

Then we did Dachau. This was Hans' idea. I had heard of Dachau in those war memoirs I had read as a kid. It was the first concentration camp the Nazis had built, originally for political prisoners, proudly opened by Heinrich Himmler in 1933. But I hadn't known it was near Munich, or that you could visit. Our first problem was how to get there. In Munich's central square, the *Marienplatz*, Hans politely stopped passers-by to ask for directions. As one they fled. Some glared at him. Others barked a rebuke. Some pretended to ignore him. The mere mention of the name was not going down at all well until I suggested that he ask someone about our own age, someone perhaps unburdened by history. That worked. A young girl told us we could take a train from the Munich *Hauptbahnhof* to the village of Dachau, about 16 kilometres away, and from there a bus to the camp itself.

The day was appropriately cold, grey and forbidding, with a light drizzle that turned every so often to sleet. It was like being in a Fritz Lang movie. I huddled in a black leather jacket I had bought. The bus set us down near the main gate, which, like Auschwitz, bore in wrought iron that most cynical and sinister of the Nazi slogans, '*Arbeit Macht Frei*' – Work Brings Freedom. You could feel the horror rising from the ground to clutch at you.

The former SS administration block had been turned into a museum and gallery, with photograph after photograph of the living dead and the very dead, and of their black-uniformed killers, in hideous detail. There were shots of naked corpses, virtual skeletons, piled metres high; there were portraits of small children with sunken eye sockets tortured to death in medical 'experiments'. The SS had kept efficient records. Dachau was not an extermination camp on the industrial scale of Auschwitz II–Birkenau, Majdanek or Sobibor, but more than 40,000 people died there in the twelve years of its existence.

Most were Jewish, but not all. The camp also held common criminals, homosexuals, Gypsies, Poles, Soviet prisoners of war and various political and religious opponents of the Reich – including such luminaries as the Lutheran pastor Martin Niemöller. Murder was common enough, by shooting or lethal injection, but many of those thousands died from typhus, tuberculosis, dysentery, pneumonia or simple starvation. There was one last orgy of mass killing before the US Army liberated the camp in April 1945. On a nearby rail line the Americans found thirty-nine railway cattle trucks piled with more than 2000 bodies.

We walked into the camp in numb silence. A stark memorial sculpture rose above the parade ground, a tableau in black wrought iron of emaciated corpses crucified on barbed wire. Beyond that were the bare timber prisoners' huts, rows and rows of them, with their stacks of pine bunks now scrubbed antiseptically clean. We walked through them almost dazed. Then, in a far corner, we came to the crematorium. Built of rustic red brick and tile, with a backdrop of trees flecked with the last leaves of autumn, it might have been any folksy cottage tucked away in the Bavarian forest. The giveaway was the outsized brick chimney. Inside were three furnaces, red brick again, and each with a steel stretcher-like contraption for trundling the bodies into the flames. Vietnam had hardened me, but not for this.

When we came out into the lowering twilight I could see that Hans was weeping. His shoulders heaved. 'My father was part of this,' he whispered.

'No,' I said. 'He was in the Luftwaffe.'

'But he was part of this machine. He died for this machine, for Hitler . . .'

Hans fell to his knees on the cold earth, sobbing. Little feathers of sleet fluttered down upon us. I knelt with him and held him tightly, murmuring what I hoped were comforting noises. When his tears subsided we walked out the gate, without a backward glance, and caught the bus back to the station.

But the Third Reich had not finished with Hans. We had a half-hour wait for the next train. On the platform there was a little *Bierstube*, a brightly lit cafe with a warming stove, so we took a table and ordered two beers. We had just begun to drink when the door banged open and an old woman, clad all in black, lurched towards us and fell upon Hans. She was wild-eyed and haggard, a Hansel and Gretel witch. Keening and wailing, she clasped him to her breast, babbling in rapid-fire German. All I could understand was the name Jürgen . . . Jürgen. She kept repeating it.

Hans slumped as if he had been shot. I was bewildered. Two men stood up from a corner where they had been drinking. One of them came across and gently detached the crone, propelling her out into the night. The other man sat down and talked to Hans, who was ghostly pale and almost catatonic. It had happened before, quite often, he said. The old woman lived nearby. She came to the cafe almost every day, looking for her son Jürgen, who had been killed on the Russian Front in 1943. She was mad. She had thought Hans was her boy. She thought everyone was her Jürgen. There were so many of them like her. The man was sorry this should happen to foreigners, but we should take no notice. Outside the night was as black as an SS uniform.

Hans and I farewelled each other the next day, exchanging addresses and promising to keep in touch. We never did, of course, but I wish we had.

✧

The *Mona Lisa* was a disappointment. I had expected a canvas at least the size of a bedsheet, but it was smaller than a tea towel. It was also surrounded by Japanese tourists three and four deep, clicking furiously at their Nikons, which made rapt contemplation difficult. Paris herself lifted the spirits after sombre Munich, and – despite the dire warnings I had been given – the people themselves were friendly enough if you had a crack at speaking French first. Mr Slosh's lessons at Barker had not gone entirely to waste. I walked everywhere, the best way to see any city, but especially this one.

By early October I was in London. It felt almost like coming home. There had been so much of the cultural cringe in my school education and my upbringing that central London and the West End were entirely familiar. It was like walking around the Monopoly board: Trafalgar Square, Charing Cross, Pall Mall, Whitehall, Strand . . .

The ABC office then was in Portland Place, a short walk from Oxford Circus and just up the road from the BBC's iconic art-deco headquarters, Broadcasting House. It occupied an entire Georgian terrace house in a long and elegant line of them built in the late eighteenth century by the celebrated Adam brothers, with a mews flat out the back. The ABC had bought the place in the days when London was still regarded as the centre of the known universe, and it was staffed accordingly. At the apex was the 'ABC Representative', an exalted mandarin who acted as an Ambassador Plenipotentiary and Extraordinary to the BBC, to which the colonials still made a deferential obeisance. There were five journalists operating the bureau. I had not met them before, but three would become good friends and colleagues. Richard Palfreyman, Paul Murphy and Paul Lyneham, all about my age, were kind enough to show me the ropes.[80]

Not that there were too many ropes to show. Unlike in South-East Asia, where you had to leave the office and go out looking for news, working as a foreign correspondent in an English-speaking democracy is money for jam. Most of the time the stuff is handed to you on a plate, gift-wrapped. In London the ABC had the rights to use any news broadcast by the BBC; on top of that, you could always nick stuff published in Britain's impressive range of national newspapers. A bit of a rewrite and a polish for an Australian angle, and off to the pub. The country had seen a turn of the wheel, discarding Harold Wilson's Labour government and sending Ted 'Grocer' Heath to Downing Street. Heath's education secretary was a shrill but energetic Margaret Hilda Thatcher. I cannot remember a thing I wrote.

The only downside to this idyll was the bureau chief, Geoffrey Luck, who carried the lofty title of London Editor. Perhaps ten years older than us, he was an officious drone and a crashing bore. Everyone assumed that Sydney had sent him to London to get rid of him. In the admittedly brief time I was there, I don't recall him ever leaving his office to report a story. Perhaps there was the occasional ponderous rehash of a front-page lead from *The Times* or the *Telegraph*, but more often he whiled away the hours nit-picking at the work of his unfortunate underlings. Having run my own bureau in Jakarta, it was galling to have to put up with him, but his career eventually fizzled out. The last I heard, he had retired in well-merited obscurity, scribbling shouty little pieces for the far-right and hugely unread *Quadrant* magazine about wicked left-wing bias at the ABC.

Paul Murphy, a lovely man with a rapier wit, introduced me to a side of British culture I didn't know. He and his wife, Kay, had a flat in Maida Vale. 'Come to dinner and we'll watch this fabulous new BBC television show,' he said. And so I saw *Monty Python's Flying Circus* for the first time. Puzzled at first, I ended up rooted to the Murphys' couch, open-mouthed. The satirical *Private Eye* magazine, which he also showed me, had much the same effect. It was a brave new world of comedy and satire waiting to be explored. I felt like stout Cortez, silent on his peak in Darien.

I was also in love for the first time. Not counting adolescent crushes, that is. Jane Baker was the sister of a British journalist I had known in South-East Asia. Slender as a willow wand, with a waterfall of strawberry-blonde hair and flawless peaches'n'cream skin, she spoke in a velvety upper-class accent that had a captivating hint of West Country burr to it. She laughed a lot, too, and she could look deliciously fabulous in just high-heeled, knee-length boots, a cream trench coat and a careless Burberry scarf. Not that we wore a lot together. After a week I moved out of my hotel in Bloomsbury and into her terrace flat near the antique shops of Camden Passage in Islington, where we lay around naked in the central heating listening to the Rolling Stones, of which I knew a lot, and Beethoven, of whom I knew nothing.

We drank cheap Spanish wine. The Australian wine invasion of Britain had not yet begun. The only Australian stuff you could get at the local off-licence was a sulphurous red that tasted like brake fluid and came in a box uninvitingly labelled Kanga Rouge. Ba-boom. The other Australian invasion, though, was in full swing. Barry Humphries and Clive James had captured a beachhead and were charging up the foothills towards the high peaks of British culture. Richard Neville had transplanted the subversive *Oz* magazine from Sydney and was up to his neck in legal troubles, charged with obscenity and 'conspiracy to corrupt public morals' after publishing the notorious *Schoolkids Oz*, edited by fifth- and sixth-formers in May 1970, and which included, among other atrocities, a cartoon of a naked Rupert Bear with an erection. Streaking ahead of the pack, Germaine Greer published *The Female Eunuch* in October 1970, the month I arrived. Rolf Harris, though, was Britain's favourite Australian, already established as a huge television star. The Harris stereotype was infuriating. You couldn't go into a pub without some oik taking a shot: 'You parked yer kangaroo at the door then, 'ave you, cobber? Yer abos lookin' after 'im, are they?'

Jane was my guide to Swinging London, then at its dazzling peak. She was a script assistant at BBC Television. She knew all the trendy pubs – the packed-to-the-rafters Markham Arms in the King's Road, Chelsea, was a favourite (it's since been turned into a building society) – and she took me window-shopping at the glittering boutiques of Knightsbridge and Kensington High Street. Then we would go to Carnaby Street to buy the same clothes, leather and velvet and bulky knits, for a quarter of the price. An Australian salary went a long way then.

Within about a day of knowing Jane I had acquired a languid London drawl myself, complete with the downward inflexion at the end of a question: 'D'ya know't I mean, Arfer?' It has been both a curse and a blessing of my life that, quite unconsciously, my voice has a chameleon urge to blend with the surroundings. People think I am putting it on but I'm not. I do accents. It just happens. After a week with her I felt I had lived in London forever.

Above all, she was fun and mischievous. We hit Peak Jane one night at Rules, over dinner with Paul Lyneham and his wife, Dorothy. Rules, in Covent Garden, is London's oldest restaurant, founded in 1798. Edward VII regularly dined there with his mistress, Lily Langtry. The place remains a high temple of gilt-and-mirrors Edwardian opulence, its high-class British stodge cuisine served by creepy waiters who might almost have known the king and Lily.

We got giggly drunk. Over champagne and the pudding, Jane impulsively bared her breasts. She sat there looking lovely in the soft half-light, her blonde hair tumbling to her nipples. I leaned over and kissed her. The other diners affected not to notice, as the English always do when suddenly confronted by the unexpected or the downright embarrassing. Not so the maître d'. Within seconds one of the ancient retainers was at the table. 'Your bill, sir,' he said smoothly. Five minutes later we were out in Maiden Lane, laughing and looking for a taxi.

Our parting was passionate. We had been together less than a month but the ABC wanted me in New York. At Heathrow we held each other tightly, misty-eyed. I promised I would return. She vowed she would follow me to the ends of the earth. Even Australia, if need be.

✧

'Your cabin crew has prepared a buffet luncheon for you in the forward section of our aircraft,' said the stewardess. 'We invite you to join us . . .'

We were halfway over the Atlantic, heading west, flying the now extinct Trans World Airlines in a brand new Boeing 747 jumbo jet. The 747-100 had just come into service, and this was the first one I'd been in. In those early days it was so spacious, so un-jam packed, that first-class passengers could stroll around tables laid out with crisp white cloths in the pointy end, forking up the Maine lobster and Virginia ham. Vintage champagne glistened in ice buckets.

Decanted from the plane at Kennedy, I took a cab to the hotel the ABC had booked for me, the Algonquin in midtown Manhattan on West 44th Street, between Fifth and Sixth Avenues. This was the careful choice of Charlie Buttrose, the silver-haired and debonair ABC New York representative (and father of Ita), who had been a journalist himself and who thought I would relish staying in the hotel where Dorothy Parker, Alexander Woollcott, Robert Benchley and other celebrated wits of the *New Yorker* magazine had traded dazzling epigrams over their famous round table lunches in the 1920s. And so I would have if I had actually heard of any of them. My private arts degree had not gone there yet. Charlie urged me to do some fast catch-up, which I did.

The Algonquin was only a couple of blocks from the ABC office, in Rockefeller Center. I walked it every day, sometimes taking a roundabout route to gape at a different lot of skyscrapers. If I did any work in New York I can't remember what it was, but the sightseeing was stupendous. Steam from central heating boilers hissed from vents in the sidewalk. Vendors sold hot roasted chestnuts. The cabbies were surly and rude, as advertised. I did Times Square, the Museum of Modern Art, Macy's and Bloomingdale's. I checked out Tiffany's on Fifth Avenue just in case Audrey Hepburn turned up for breakfast. I zoomed to the top of the Empire State Building. Charlie shouted me and the resident ABC journalist, Terry Brown, a lunch at Toots Shorr restaurant on West 52nd, where we slurped Connecticut Blue Point oysters, downed Bloody Marys and waited – with elaborate nonchalance – for the arrival of Frank Sinatra, Orson Welles, Jackie Gleason, Joe DiMaggio or any other of the joint's celebrity regulars. We were disappointed. Impeccably well connected, Charlie also fixed it for me to meet the legendary journalist and broadcaster Walter Cronkite, and to watch from the studio control room as he delivered the CBS Evening News.

A fortnight later I took the new Metroliner express train from Penn Central Station to Washington, DC, ostensibly to work in the bureau there but in fact for another orgy of sightseeing. After that it was west for a couple of nights at the Fairmont Hotel atop Nob Hill in San Francisco, and a Thanksgiving dinner with a US Air Force captain I had met in Saigon – 'You must try my wife's pumpkin pie.' Then west again across the North Pacific.

✧

Tokyo was hard to like, and in the end I gave up trying. With Christmas coming on, it was freezing – I was colder than I had ever been – and the skies were a constant dismal grey. Even the explosion of lurid neon in the Ginza shopping precinct could not dispel the impression, in my mind anyway, that the entire city was done in a bleak, forbidding monochrome. That included the people. The pavements downtown were thronged with salarymen in identical grey suits, who would halt impassively at traffic lights to be bombarded with commercials blasting from outdoor loudspeakers.

Accustomed to the free-wheeling chaos of South-East Asia, I found Tokyo oppressively, boringly regimented. Across the street from the Foreign Correspondents Club, in downtown Marunouchi, was a glass-walled skyscraper filled with office workers beavering away at their desks. Promptly at one o'clock each afternoon, in obedience to some command, men and women would leap as one from their chairs and hurl themselves into synchronised physical jerks. There was an entire building of hundreds of them, silently jumping and bending in unison. After fifteen minutes of this they would sit down again, simultaneously, and get back to work. It was a frightening sight.

At least there was a house to live in. Again I was doing a relief job, and I moved into the home of the Tokyo correspondent, a two-storey suburban villa with a small back garden. A taxi took me to the office each day and ferried me back in the evenings. The garden was a luxury in jam-packed Tokyo. Today it would be astronomically out of the question.

I quickly realised, though, that the job was beyond me. At the very least, a foreign correspondent in Tokyo requires a thorough working knowledge of economics, business and finance, let alone the more arcane stuff of Japan–Australia trade and investment deals, and I had zilch. I was out of my depth.

All that saved me were two stories that had convulsed all Japan. The first was the flamboyant suicide of the ultra-nationalist novelist, poet and martial arts enthusiast Yukio Mishima, who committed *seppuku* after the failure of a comic-book attempt at a coup d'état at the headquarters of the Japan Self-Defence Force. Crazier still was a tumultuous campaign of violent protest to prevent the building of the new Narita International Airport on farmland outside Tokyo. An unlikely alliance of conservative farmers and left-wing students rampaged across the site every day in their thousands, battling with legions of riot police. It was virtually a civil war. The farmers did not want their land grabbed, and the students claimed the airport was actually going to be an American nuclear base. They chained themselves to trees, barricaded themselves in forts and bunkers, lit enormous bonfires and catapulted rocks and buckets of animal and human faeces at the charging police. Smoke and tear gas shrouded the battlefield. Blood flowed. Thousands were injured, and quite a few were killed over a couple of years. This at least was a story I could comprehend.

My social life was monochrome as well. I had chatted up a Japan Airlines hostess on the flight across the Pacific, and she kindly took me to see the newly released *Tora! Tora! Tora!*, the American-Japanese blockbuster feature about the raid on Pearl Harbor. Good movie, but while filing out of the cinema at the end it was disconcerting to encounter bunches of teenagers from the audience pumping their fists and shouting, 'Banzai!' One of them spat on me. Others hissed. It was not welcoming. 'We won the fucking war,' I spat back, baring my fangs in a crocodile grin.

Swimming saved me, as it has so often in my life. The secretary in the ABC office found me a public swimming pool near the house; being winter, it was not crowded. Living the high life in London and the States had packed some weight on me, and I resolved to lose it. When I finished my first evening of laps I was flabbergasted to whip off my goggles and discover I was being applauded by a ring of five or six swimmers, all male, who were clustered at the edge of the pool.

'Orstraria!' they cried, clapping furiously. 'Kangaroo! Dawn Fraser!' They grinned broadly and gave me the thumbs-up. They shook my hand.

One young bloke about my age spoke some English. They had picked me as an Australian, he said, because I swam like an Australian. And I was wearing speedos, which Americans did not. And of course it was only six years since the 1964 Tokyo Olympics, and everyone remembered the feats of the great Dawn Fraser – not least among them the famous escapade in which she stole a Japanese flag from the palace of the emperor.[81] How honoured they were to have an Orstrarian swim in their pool.

The young bloke was there again the next evening. He had abandoned his trunks and obtained some speedos for the occasion, I noticed, and after a cheery greeting he matched me lap for lap. His name was Hitoshi. He was just finishing university, he said, and hoping for a cadetship at the *Gaimusho*, the Japanese Foreign Office.

He had learned English but had never had the chance to speak it. Would I help him with some conversation? It seemed like a good idea, and it was.

We kept swimming together, and he and his girlfriend – her name eludes me – took me to restaurants and bars and for expeditions on the Ginza. She was beautiful, sweet and demure in Western clothing, but without a word of English. We nodded and smiled at each other. Hitoshi introduced me to the pleasures of the Sento, a local bath house down a little back alley near the pool, where he guided me through the iron etiquette of bathing naked in public.

Snow fell on Christmas Day, the first snow I had ever seen. When I woke that morning, the little white flakes outside my bedroom window startled me at first. Stupidly, I could not work out what was happening until I looked out to find the entire world was white. Hitoshi and his girl came around that afternoon, a Friday, and gave me a present of a shirt they had chosen. We drank beer and played Neil Diamond records. It was touching and I was grateful. They made Tokyo bearable, even delightful at times, but it was never going to be a city I could love, like Jakarta or London. In February I headed south, back to the heat of the tropics.

✧

I wanted one last hurrah in Jakarta before returning to Australia. With a month's leave up my sleeve, I figured I would just bum around, see friends, smoke a little dope and play with the band again.

Ed Blanche had left a few months before, and in a hurry. On a trip to Bali he had been pinged by the cops for a couple of joints they discovered – as if by magic – in his hotel room. It was very likely he had been set up by whoever sold him the stuff. There was no other reason for the police to turn him over so suddenly. The law on drug possession then was not nearly as tough as it is now, but he went through a scary week before a smart lawyer got him off with a fine. His employer, the AP, was unimpressed and he flew out within days.

I had hoped to stay in Ed's apartment but other friends put me up, including Joe Galloway, the UPI correspondent, and I borrowed a car to knock around in. The ABC office, though, was off-limits. My successor there, a twerp named Errol Hodge, made it clear I was not welcome, so I had to renew my friendships with the staff elsewhere.[82]

The band was still going full-tilt, bigger and better than ever, and it was great to get back into it. With some time on my hands I could knock around with them a bit more and we played some good gigs.

In the second week, Jane flew out to join me. We had been writing long and loving letters to each other, and I'd banged on so much about the wonders of Indonesia that she decided she wanted to see it with me. I wanted her too, and she looked as lovely as ever when I met her at the airport. We picked up where we had left off. By day we lazed around the pool at the Hotel Indonesia, she in an eye-wateringly brief bikini made of very small pieces of string. By nights we dined and partied with my friends, both Western and Indonesian, and she came to a couple of the band engagements. The guys thought she was fabulous, and she was.

But slowly the affair began to fall apart. For whatever reasons, the passion we had shared in London was flickering and dying in Jakarta. It was as if we had tried to transplant an English rose to a rice *padi*, and we both came to realise it wasn't working. I was in my element; she felt uncomfortably alien. There were tears and attempts to patch things together, but it didn't happen. It was over and we knew it, with mutual regret. She flew back to London a week later. We never made contact again, but I heard years later she had married happily, with children.

And no, if you're wondering: Jane Baker was not her real name.

✧

Leaving Indonesia was hard, for I knew I would not be back for a while. I was to return to the ABC Sydney newsroom, although I had no idea what job I might be doing. In my madder fantasies I dreamed of staying on, of quitting the ABC and buying a plot of land to become a beach bum in Bali. I still wonder sometimes how that might have turned out.

But sanity prevailed. After a round of farewells, many of them deeply affecting, I caught the Qantas plane for Sydney, arriving home in the winter of 1971.

PART 3

12

Arrogant larrikins and muckrakers

SPLENDID IN MY SINGAPORE tailoring – a hand-made, fitted shirt of crisp white Egyptian cotton, a tropical-weight two-button suit of oyster grey with a slight metallic sheen to it, and bespoke grey loafers (yes, I know, but it was the 1970s) – I turned up at the William Street newsroom on the appointed Monday. This was a mistake, for two reasons. One, I shivered in the cold. Two, I looked like a mug lair, showing off something awful. Which indeed I was. Someone wolf-whistled as I made my grand entrance.

The plan was to send me to Canberra to cover politics in the ABC office in the parliamentary Press Gallery, but I fought it off. After so long away I wanted to be back with my family and my mates and living near a beach, not stuck in the bush capital, and I flat-out refused to go. This caused a problem. Although still only twenty-five, I was now an A-grade journalist – there was only one grade higher, A-plus – and they had trouble slotting me into the system. Cutting the arrogant young fop down a peg or two, they put me on the sub-editors' desk, occasionally as Acting Chief Sub or Foreign Sub, a job of mind-blowing tedium with only a dead end on the horizon. The desk was staffed by people of a ghastly pallor, their shoulders hunched in moth-eaten woolly cardigans, peering at each other with haunted, red-rimmed eyes through the fog of tobacco smoke. I had no desire to become one of them, but there I was. After a few months the ABC decided it would bring in radio news bulletins on the hour, of about seven minutes' duration – just as the vulgar commercial stations had been airing for years – and I was assigned to kick-start them as their first sub-editor. The ennui mounted.

Coming home had been unsettling, and in ways I had not anticipated. My mother was thrilled that I was back, greeting me as if I had returned from a NASA moon landing. For a couple of weeks I slept in my old childhood bed at Chatswood, sharing the room with my now adult younger brother. Peter had begun a successful career in personnel management, as it was called then, but my long absence had seen us drift apart. Coming together again felt strange and a little awkward, almost as if we were meeting for the first time. Nana had become more cantankerous than ever, spending a lot of time gawping at the television she had once derided as a passing fad.

'They're not really worth fighting for,' she said to me one evening as we watched the seven pm news.

'Who aren't?' I asked.

'The fuzzy-wuzzies up where you were.'

'You mean Vietnam?'

'Yes, *them*,' she said, waving a dismissive hand at the screen.

Them was in fact the Royal Fiji Police Band, in blue tunics and white lap-laps, playing on a wharf to welcome a cruise liner to Suva. My heart sank.

I got out as soon as I decently could, sharing a rented house in the bush above Avalon on the northern beaches with a mate I had known since our days in the Cubs. He was a keen yachtie. I plunged back into the surf again. Flush with the cash I had saved overseas, I bought myself a second-hand sports car, a canary-yellow Lotus Elan S2 convertible, which went like a shot dog most of the time and handled beautifully, but occasionally got the sulks and refused to move.

For months I was a fish out of water. My native land seemed oddly alien. The light and the clear blue skies were as beautiful as I remembered, and the air as clean, but where were all the people?

After the teeming crush of Asian cities, Sydney's roads and pavements felt almost empty. I had lost touch with many of my schoolfriends, who had gone their different ways. Those I did meet again would ask politely about my travels, but you could see their eyes glaze over after a few minutes of my answers. And my grandmother was hardly alone in her ignorance of the wider world. Her generation, and my mother's, were bewildered by the pace of the change they felt was being forced upon them, politically and socially. The comfortable verities of the Menzies *ancien régime* had crumbled. The Vietnam War moratorium marches and demonstrations had upset the social order, they thought, and they knew not where this might lead.

Even so, it was ever more clear that Billy McMahon was not going to get us there. Sly and scheming, an inveterate and disloyal liar, McMahon had finagled himself into the prime ministership in March 1971 after John Gorton fell on his sword in a cabinet crisis. Half his ministry despised him. The cabinet turmoil mounted, with ministers, including Gorton, fighting each other tooth and claw. McMahon's public pronouncements were often risible. 'The world has suddenly grown small as it spins furiously down the ringing grooves of change,' he declaimed, in a clunking rework of a line from Tennyson's 'Locksley Hall'. His odd, hobbit-like appearance did him no favours with an increasingly sceptical public. The journalist and satirist Mungo MacCallum skewered him with the line that, when viewed front on, McMahon looked like a Volkswagen with both doors open.

Labor's Gough Whitlam was clearly the coming man. When Whitlam stunned the country with his surprise visit to China in July 1971, where he met Premier Zhou Enlai in Beijing, McMahon spat scorn and derision. There was Labor, truckling with the communist enemy. It was 'instant coffee diplomacy'. In no time at all 'Mr Zhou had Mr Whitlam on the hook, and he played him as a fisherman plays a trout', he jeered. Malcolm Fraser, then the education minister, called Whitlam 'a disgrace to Australia'. Marching in line, the *Sydney Morning Herald* blustered that 'if Mr Whitlam thinks that this wholesale selling out of friends to gain a despot's smile is diplomacy, then Heaven protect this country if he ever directs its foreign policy'.[83]

Just days later McMahon and the Tory establishment, including the *Herald*, were blown to smithereens when it was revealed that Henry Kissinger had also been in Beijing, to set up President Nixon's historic visit. Billy had shot himself in both feet. He became an irrelevant figure of ridicule. Whitlam rode the wave.

More or less apolitical when I had first left Australia in 1966, my engagement with the wider world, and the Vietnam experience in particular, had pushed my politics towards the centre left. I had met Gough briefly in Jakarta and been impressed by his personal vigour and his command of affairs. Now the Tories were crumbling beneath the Whitlam onslaught.

Socially, I was partying hard, both at the rented house above Avalon and with ABC journalists of more or less my own age. My mate Roger Allebone, who had been a cadet when I left, had since carved a swathe through the ABC and Sydney University, where he sailed with distinction through a degree in economics and government, apparently without ever troubling to attend lectures. He knew an extraordinary number of fun and interesting people who had passed me by in my absence, and he rocketed me into their circle, which centred on a grand old stone colonial house he was renting in suburban Cammeray with a fellow student, an up-and-coming young economist named David Hill. The house had a swimming pool. One magic summer's night we partied until dawn, high on pot and dancing stark-naked with the girls. Roger blazed across our skies like a comet, and was much loved.

The partying dulled the boredom of my job. I was drinking hard and dating women, but I eventually gave up cannabis as a bad deal. It was doing nothing for me, and the sole line of cocaine I tried had no effect either, for whatever reason. I decided drugs were a waste of money. All I needed was a way out of the newsroom.

✧

Deliverance came in the unlikely person of Tony Ferguson, the correspondent who had met me at the airport when I first arrived in Singapore. He was fifteen years older than me and married with three sons, but we had become good friends and I had learned a lot at his feet. Tony was a bushie – he had grown up on a dairy farm, and he still wore well-polished R.M. Williams boots – but his laconic countryman's demeanour masked a fine mind. He had made his name as a foreign correspondent with his courageous coverage of the Tet Offensive, achieved at great personal risk. Back in Australia, he escaped the newsroom to become executive producer of ABC Television's *This Day Tonight*, a national current-affairs program broadcast at seven-thirty pm each weekday. He called me in December 1971: would I like to come across?

Would I what? *TDT*, as everyone called it, had fired up a revolution in Australian television journalism. It was still firing it up. From a shaky beginning in April 1967, its eclectic blend of inquiring journalism, satire and bare-faced cheek had captured a vast and influential audience never known before at the ABC, nor again afterwards. *TDT* rated its head off. At its best it was brilliant, incisive. At its worst it could be self-important and smug, and the humour painfully adolescent. But, love it or hate it, everybody who was anybody had to watch it.

Part of its success lay with the presenter, Bill Peach. Another bushie, from Lockhart in the New South Wales Riverina, Bill was one of the best and nicest professionals I have ever worked with. The television camera loved him, as it unaccountably does with some people but never will with others, no matter how they try. The boyish grin and the genial country good humour he radiated on screen were pretty much what you got in person off-camera – no airs and graces. He came across as the bloke next door, always willing to have a beer or lend you his lawnmower – and yet he shone as the ABC's first true television star, a welcome guest in the nation's lounge rooms.

The true drivers of *TDT*, though, were its producers, all of them experienced, creative journalists who had the courage to take risks even if they knew they would occasionally fall flat on their faces. When I joined the show many of the reporters had already become household names: Peter Luck, Richard Carleton, Stuart Littlemore, Paul Murphy, Peter Couchman and the incomparable Caroline Jones were national figures in their own right. They were an elite, ranging in age from their mid-twenties to early thirties. The cameramen and film editors, too, were some of the sharpest in the business. Entering their ranks was like joining the SAS or the Jesuits. Despite my own decent experience as a foreign correspondent, I was spooked, apprehensive.

The news department fought to stop me going. There was a destructive internecine war between the ABC's News and Current Affairs departments, carried to ridiculous heights, and my defection from radio news in William Street over the harbour to the current affairs TV studios at Gore Hill was seen as rank treachery. Keith Fraser, the new Controller of News, hauled me into his office, red-faced with fury, and snarled – like the former Queensland copper he was – that I would never work for the News department again. That was fine by me. And *TDT* was offering a pay rise, an annual salary of $7885. Luxury!

In January 1972 I took over the desk vacated by one of the program's founding reporters, Gerald Stone, who had gone on to higher things. Gerry and I had met in Jakarta a few years before, circling each other warily when he invaded my patch to do some Indonesia stories for *TDT*. We would eventually become close friends, but I was in a degree of awe at taking the slot in the show where he had performed with bravura for five years. I shared a cubicle with another reporter, Tony Joyce, next to the one occupied by Caroline and Stuart. Another new reporter, Peter Manning, had been hired across from the *Bulletin*.

My problem was that I knew bugger-all about making current-affairs television. I could certainly knock off a ninety-second or two-minute news report, complete with pieces to camera. But *TDT* required more. It meant proper filmmaking, with all the skills and arts, for stories that might run from five to fifteen minutes or more. There might be four or five people to be interviewed – the talent, as they were known in the trade. You had to work with a cinematographer and a sound recordist to get the pictures to illustrate the story, and there had to be a coherent beginning, middle and end to the narrative. You write a script which you then handed over to a film editor to knock into final shape, perhaps with sound effects and music. I had never done any of this.

My guide and saviour was Peter Luck, another of the original

TDT reporters. Hired from the *Adelaide Advertiser* in 1967, Peter had known almost nothing of television himself. Pretty much self-taught over five years, he had become a filmmaker of extraordinary creativity. Kindly, he took me in hand and spun me around.

The first story I did under his direction was a nostalgia piece on the fortieth anniversary of the opening of the Sydney Harbour Bridge. Left to my own devices, I would have found some archival footage of the thing being built and opened, shot some new pictures and thrown together a conventional and deeply dull script of the usual when, where, who and how.

It was Peter's idea to dig up Jack Lang. The 'Big Fella', as they called him, had been the firebrand Labor premier of New South Wales when the bridge was finished in 1932, and one of the most controversial political figures of the twentieth century. An Australian nationalist to his boot heels, Lang had infuriated the establishment, from King George V down, by declaring that he – not the British-born state governor – would cut the opening ribbon. On Saturday, 19 March 1932, he had scissors in hand and was about to do the deed when one Francis de Groot, a loony right-wing former cavalry officer, lunged forward on horseback and hacked at the ribbon with a sabre 'in the name of the decent and respectable people of New South Wales'. There was uproar.

Peter persuaded Lang to re-enact the moment. The Big Fella was then ninety-six, hunched and walking at a shuffle, but still a trouper. We arranged for the traffic to be diverted, we put him on the exact spot on the bridge – again with a pair of scissors – and we got him to tell the story and go through the motions. He was magnificent, a political showman to the last. Back in the editing room, Peter intercut the new Lang footage with the grainy newsreel shots of the original opening. I wrote and recorded the script, and we had a compelling piece of *TDT* television. It was a lesson in creativity I never forgot.

Peter and I became at first good colleagues and co-conspirators, then lifelong friends. We discovered in each other a certain ability for comedy and satire, and put it to some use on the show.

✧

Not all was sweetness and light. The Tory ascendancy hated *TDT*. So did the ABC senior management, led by Sir Talbot Duckmanton and his deputy, the right-wing literary critic Dr Clement Semmler. There was a constant moan of complaint from the right – including the editorial writers of the *Sydney Morning Herald* – that *TDT* was a left-wing conspiracy to subvert democracy. Duckmanton and Semmler were inclined to agree. In 1972, with a federal election in the offing, the moaning grew to a howl.

It reached critical mass in a clumsy campaign by the postmaster-general, Sir Alan Hulme, to muzzle the ABC in general and *TDT* in particular. A Liberal Party dullard from Queensland, Hulme was the cabinet minister in charge of broadcasting – both ABC and commercial – and, crucially, of government funding for the ABC. In 1971, in a gross assault upon the ABC's independence, he had demanded specific cuts to the program budgets for *TDT* and *Four Corners*. He didn't get them, but nor did he give up.

Even as the McMahon government was falling apart, he railed endlessly about anti-government bias, and the ABC management, anxious to appease him, issued a new set of 'guidelines' designed to stuff *TDT* into a straitjacket. They were handed down from Broadcast House, the ABC's head office in Sydney's Park Street, which we referred to as Bullshit Castle. There were to be no more stories on 'censorship, dissent, deficiencies of social welfare, etc'. We could no longer run the work of the cartoonist for the *Australian* newspaper, Bruce Petty. There should be no coverage of Anzac Day 'which offered anything but a strictly orthodox view'. Bill Peach was never again to say that any politician had declined to appear, and nor was he to ad lib. Every word he uttered on air had to be scripted and approved by the executive producer. Hulme went further still, demanding the ABC board itself should 'preview controversial items' before they were broadcast. McMahon backed him.

Deviously, Duckmanton tightened the screws still more. Angered by a *TDT* report on the sacking of journalists at the *Sydney Morning Herald* and Radio 2GB, the John Fairfax empire sued for defamation, demanding $200,000 from the ABC and the same, individually, from Bill and Richard Carleton. Against all convention, Duckmanton decreed that the ABC would not defend its two employees. They would be on their own in a legal battle with the Fairfax empire. There were unsubtle threats, too, that their contracts might not be renewed. The suit hung over their heads for most of 1972, until Fairfax quietly dropped it.

The explosion came in August 1972, with a bombshell story alleging incompetence and corruption in the Australian postal service, Hulme's own department. The claims were made by the general secretary of the Postal Union, Jack Baker, who reckoned the taxpayer had been cheated of many millions of dollars. Tony Joyce interviewed him but Bullshit Castle banned the report, decreeing it could not be shown unless the director general of the Post Office, one Fred Lane, was allowed equal time to reply. This was a fix, ostensibly in the name of 'balance' but in fact to skewer the story. Lane well understood this: disgracefully, ABC management had handed him the right of editorial veto. He seized it. He refused to appear not once but five times. The interview therefore stayed banned.

But only for a month. Towards the end of September, the Post Office announced a record profit. Baker, the union leader, repeated his claims of corruption and incompetence, giving more detail. The *TDT* producers again sought to run his interview with Joyce and again offered Lane equal time. Again Lane refused to front.

Everything blew up on Friday, 29 September. The ban was intolerable, a blatant dodge to avoid embarrassing Hulme and his department. The *TDT* producers, Bill himself and most of the reporters held a council of war in the office at Gore Hill late that afternoon, and resolved to defy the management. I was there for this electric, even frightening moment. It was mutiny, but we believed that the public's right to know outweighed the management's clear political bias. With unanimous support, the executive producer, Tony Ferguson, decided to run the Baker interview that night, and then left for home to write his resignation. The duty producer, Tim Bowden, duly put the interview to air. All hell broke loose.

I remember it with stark clarity because I got married the next day.

✧

Kerri Whiting was four years younger than me, a girl from Wagga studying in Sydney to become a medical scientist. Someone brought her to one of the parties at the Avalon house but I drove her home. She had lovely eyes, a beguiling sense of humour and a sparkling laugh. God alone knows what she saw in me: the day we met I was wearing crotch-tight red flares and a white shirt unbuttoned almost to the waist. But she gave me her phone number and I called her at work. 'Can't talk now,' she said. 'I'm up to my neck in uteruses.' We arranged to meet later – I cannot remember how or where – and I found her thrilling to be with. It was not love at first sight, but it headed that way pretty quickly, despite the geographical distance between us. She was sharing a house in inner-city Enmore, a nominal hour's drive from my place on the northern beaches. In the Lotus Elan I could do it in about forty minutes, burning with anticipation. Clumsy as ever, I proposed to her after about three months and then, in a panic, asked her to forget every word I'd said. 'Pretend that didn't happen,' I babbled. She had every reason to think I was mad but she persisted, and eventually took me to Wagga to meet her parents. 'They still think I'm a virgin,' she cautioned me.

She accepted the next proposal. We were an item for about six months before we married. David Hill had tried to wrest her from me at one of Roger Allebone's parties in some rented mansion at Elizabeth Bay, but he graciously conceded defeat. The wedding plans were only slightly disrupted when the Elan caught fire in the week before the great day. On my way to work, the wretched beast once again failed to proceed. I sat at some traffic lights near the office watching flames and thick, oily smoke belching from under the bonnet. Clearly this was not good. The body of the Elan was made of fibreglass, and it began to melt like a Salvador Dalí watch. Frantically, I tried to quell the inferno by beating at it with my suit jacket. I was saved by a bloke from a nearby servo, who ran over with a fire extinguisher.

The wedding was on a sunny Saturday at the suitably picturesque Anglican church of St John's at Ashfield, in Sydney's Inner West. I had pretty much abandoned religion by then but Kerri wanted a church affair, largely for the sake of her parents and public opinion in Wagga. Most of the *TDT* people were invited, and we were gratified to see a flock of newspaper reporters, snappers and TV news crews hovering at the church. Fame at last. In fact, they weren't the slightest bit interested in the happy couple: they wanted to ambush Bill Peach and Tony Ferguson about the *TDT* mutiny.

Deprived of the Elan, we drove away in the new Mrs Carlton's old brown Ford Cortina for brief honeymoon at a pub in the Southern Highlands, unsure if there'd be a program or a job to return to: the shockwaves of the Post Office affair were still spreading. For a while it seemed possible that *TDT* might be sunk, with the mutineers thrown overboard.

✧

In hindsight, it is hardly surprising that the Tories of 1972 believed *TDT* was a subversive attack on all they held holy. These were people not accustomed to being questioned, least of all by the national broadcaster. The Coalition had held power federally since 1949, clinging ever more tightly to the conservatives' born-to-rule mentality even as the voters began to drift away. New South Wales, Victoria, Queensland and Tasmania all had Tory governments. Only Western Australia and South Australia were Labor states.

Right or left, very few politicians at this time understood that the nature of current-affairs television had changed as Australian society had changed. From the beginning, broadcasting had been a deferential medium in which the great and the good were offered a megaphone for their views, largely unquestioned. This was true no longer. The baby boomer generation had come to adulthood radicalised by the Vietnam War, tuned to that archetypal anthem of protest, Bob Dylan's 'The Times They Are a-Changin''. There was an inexorable surge for a new beginning across Australia, and not just political change but economic, sexual, religious and moral. The old orthodoxies were being challenged.

The first baby boomer journalists reflected this and would ask the questions their generation wanted answered, no matter who was in power. Forensic, insistent television reporting and interviewing was, in fact, pioneered in Britain by the likes of David Frost, Sir Robin Day and Brian Walden. As we in Australia followed in their wake, it was an accident of history that the Tories were in the firing line. So far as *TDT* was concerned, Liberal paranoia was deepened by the presence of Mike Willesee, son of the Labor frontbench senator Don Willesee, as the Canberra political interviewer in the program's early years.

Another difficulty for politicians of all stripes was that they had not yet learned the black art of deflecting or ignoring unpalatable questions. There were no spin doctors or media coaches to teach them how to waffle, to fudge or to outright lie. That would come later. Confronted by an interviewer who knew the right questions to ask and would keep putting them until they were answered, all but the most astute politicians of 1972 were rabbits in the headlights. They were aware of this, too, and they hated it.

None loathed it more than the New South Wales Liberal premier, Bob Askin, who had ended a long stretch of Labor governments. Askin contrived to present as an avuncular, no-nonsense man of the people, a facade he had crafted during his years in opposition and which I had fallen for at our early encounters. Privately, he was a foul-mouthed bully who as premier embarked on a lucrative career of corruption.

Askin's first serious run-in with *TDT* was in 1968, after he had boasted to a public luncheon in Sydney of his 'run over the bastards' remark during the Lyndon Johnson visit in 1966. The program the next night threw up one of its most memorable moments, a satirical song to the tune of 'John Brown's Body' lustily performed by a professional actor who was a dead ringer for Askin. Written by one of the program's brighter brains, David Salter, the chorus went:

> Run, run, run the bastards over,
> Run, run, run the bastards over,
> Run, run, run the bastards over,
> As I said to LBJ!

Askin regarded this as gross impertinence and he complained loudly to the ABC management. The final breach came in 1970, after an interview he did with Stuart Littlemore about police violence at

Vietnam War demonstrations in Sydney. Confronted with evidence – including film – which showed that brawling police had removed their service numbers to avoid identification, Askin blustered, ducked and weaved. He looked foolish and devious, and he vowed never to appear on the program again. Nor did he – in person at least. With the stench of corruption beginning to envelop his premiership, he was a worthy target.

By 1973 the stink was acrid. Sydney was rife with illegal gambling clubs, roulette and baccarat joints, openly run by racketeers who were paying big protection money to senior police. Although we didn't know it at the time – or at least could not prove it – Askin was also being paid off, with big money shovelled his way by his two crooked police commissioners, Norman 'the Foreman' Allan and his successor, Fred Hanson. Questioned about the clubs by the media or in parliament, Askin would either assert point-blank that they did not exist, or claim that, if they rose again, the police would swiftly shut them down and arrest and charge their owners. It was a blatant lie. One of the more celebrated joints – the Forbes Club, run by the crook and 'racing identity' Perce Galea – was directly across the road from the ABC's William Street office.

In June 1973 we went for it. In the *TDT* studio, against a backdrop of a blown-up photograph of a surly Askin flanked by grim-faced police chiefs, reporter Peter Manning telephoned the coppers to formally lay a complaint about the Forbes. Up on the roof of the ABC building, with an outside broadcast camera focused on the club's front door, Stuart Littlemore and I banged on about the nefarious deeds done within. Surely the police must now arrive at any minute, we opined archly. They didn't. Nor did the throngs of eager gamblers of whom we spoke; it was only seven-thirty, so all we saw was a truck delivering fruit and vegetables. But the story, and another week of our reports and similar follow-ups in the newspapers, demolished the Askin lie. To his intense fury.

A few weeks later the premier went on the attack. On 23 August he rose in parliament clutching a bulging manila folder, to announce: 'I am going to accuse the people who are running and are behind *TDT* of being extreme radicals and of operating as a subversive unit.

I am going to say that behind their bland and smirky interiors, which they put on for television viewers, I believe that they are making planned attempts to undermine our institutions and to denigrate anything or anybody with a conservative approach or respect for our natural traditions.'[84]

There was a truckload of this claptrap, all delivered with a snarling pomposity. Littlemore had inserted rewritten questions into his Askin interview to make him appear foolish, he claimed. Bill Peach was 'an extreme radical and very arrogant'. And so on: 'trick questions . . . downright dishonesty . . . sneering looks . . . snide innuendo . . . outright lies'. On and on it went. Then the final flourish: 'These arrogant larrikins and muckrakers of *This Day Tonight* – they are arrogant all right, make no mistake – are hard to get at because they are supported by an organization that is financed by public money. They need to be taken down a peg or two and if the Australian Broadcasting Commission has any respect for itself it should get rid of the lot of them and put on a new team of decent, fair-minded Australians who will be completely impartial and not go out acting as scavengers and vultures the way these people do.'[85]

It was a delicious moment for us all, a career highlight I still savour. To his eternal disgrace, Duckmanton eventually ordered *TDT* to back off and leave Askin alone. The defamation laws serving to shield the rich and powerful, as ever, it was only after his death in 1981 that we began to learn something of the scale of his crimes. A former Fairfax editor and journalist, David Hickie, reported in his book *The Prince and the Premier*[86] that Galea had paid Askin $100,000 per year.[87] Askin had also sold knighthoods to business cronies and had been in the pocket of another legendary club-owning criminal, Abe Saffron.[88] After Abe's death, his son Alan Saffron revealed that the cunning old crook had been paying the premier and Commissioner Allan between $5000 and $10,000 per week.

✧

TDT was an exhilarating place to work, a shot of adrenaline almost every day. The entire program unit – producers, reporters, researchers, studio directors and script assistants and secretaries, camera crews and film editors, perhaps forty people in all – was crammed into one floor of the tower building at Gore Hill. We met each morning at nine to toss around ideas for the program that night, a free-for-all to which anyone could contribute, not just the journalists.

The duty producer – they worked twelve hours a day, one week on, one week off – would have the bones of a show sketched out but would willingly scrap them if better ideas came up, which frequently happened. In my day the two principal producers were Don Simmons – the gung-ho former Vietnam correspondent who had stood me up at Saigon Airport in 1966 – and Ken Chown, yet another refugee from the News department and a cadaverous, gangling Englishman who was half-mad and half-genius. As the program deadline approached, with the likelihood of chaos if a story fell over, Ken would stalk the office and corridors, scoffing beer nuts and bawling out the hymn 'Abide with Me'. Puzzlingly, he persuaded himself that I had been to Sydney's posh Newington College, the same GPS school as Duckmanton, a venial sin for which he upbraided me at least once a month.

The production meetings crackled with laughter, the journalists and researchers – egos rampant – regarding it as their duty to one-up each other and entertain everyone else with one-liners. Tony Joyce was the master of that particular art, with a rapier-sharp mind. Yet another Englishman, the same age as me but with an MA from Magdalen College, Oxford, he and his Australian wife, Monica, had settled in Chatswood not far from my childhood home. We became good friends.

Caroline Jones, the only woman reporter and another accomplished wit, had the useful knack of diluting the often volcanic testosterone levels in the room with a raised eyebrow or a gentle rebuke. We called her 'Matron', but if she ever felt oppressed by the overwhelming blokeyness she never showed it. Caro could more than hold her own in any company, both as a genuinely likeable workmate and a professional journalist, and it was evident even then to us posturing alpha males that she was on the threshold of a stellar career.

Paul Murphy skewered pomposity; we practised our Billy McMahon and Gough Whitlam mimicry on each other. Stuart Littlemore would drop the acid-laden depth charges that became his stock in trade as journalist and, later, barrister. The only one to miss out on most of this dazzling display of humour and erudition was Peter Luck, who habitually arrived late for the meeting after whiling away an hour arranging his gleaming locks to their daily state of glossy perfection and then mislaying his car keys or pipe tobacco.

The researchers, too, chimed in. One of them, Tom Molomby, would in later years become a Senior Counsel at the Sydney bar. Peter Collins, then fresh from university, rose in politics to be a Liberal Party leader of the state opposition.

Other reporters came on board after me: the droll and urbane Andrew Olle and the feisty Kerry O'Brien, who had been a reporter on the Sydney *Sun* and rang up on spec one day to ask for a job. He got it, first in the Brisbane *TDT* office. Vincent Smith, who would become another good mate, arrived from the edgy new Fairfax *National Times* weekly newspaper.

You never knew what the day would bring. It could be a breaking news story to be filmed for air that night, which meant rushing around like a hairy goat lining up the facts and the talent, or it might be a longer, deeper report that could take a week or more to shoot and edit. Sometimes there was a Sydney studio interview with some politician or newsy personage, or a comic or satirical idea, which was usually tossed to me, Luck or Murphy – sometimes all three – to brainstorm. In Canberra, Richard Carleton, who had replaced Mike Willesee after his departure to commercial TV, would be throwing up his ideas for interviews. And the interstate producers, principally in Melbourne and Sydney, would be pushing their barrows. If a big news story broke during the day, in Canberra or anywhere else, the whole show might be scrapped and started again from scratch in the afternoon. There were times when panic was never far below the surface, but we came through.

Much of it seems primitive now. Colour television did not arrive in Australia until March 1975. Videotape recording was relatively new, and available only on studio machines the size of refrigerators. Today's digital cameras were still bubbles in the brains of geeks in Tokyo and California. We shot our stuff on 16-millimetre black-and-white Kodak film. In the hands of a skilled cinematographer this produced pictures of beautiful quality, but for a daily current-affairs program it had the huge drawback of having to be processed in a laboratory before an editor could start to cut the story. You 'shot short' or 'cut in the camera', meaning that the absolute minimum of unwanted film ended up on the cutting-room floor. It was a useful discipline. Every unnecessary foot you shot lengthened the processing time and shortened the editing time.

While waiting for the film to get back from the lab down the road, you would bang together a cutting script and a rough voiceover script, sweating for the footage to be delivered to the editor. As the afternoon drew on, the tempo increased, with the clatter of typewriters and strange squawks and bursts of music coming from the nearby edit suites. At *TDT* we had the best editors in the current-affairs business; it was no job for the faint-hearted. Some could bang together a story at warp speed. Others had a more lyrical touch. Many went on to better things. One editor, Richard Francis-Bruce, who joined the ABC at the same time as me, rose to be a three-time Oscar nominee in Hollywood, with *The Shawshank Redemption*, *The Witches of Eastwick*, *Air Force One* and the first Harry Potter movie, *Harry Potter and the Philosopher's Stone*, among his credits. The ABC then was a great training ground.

As air time approached, the tension was palpable. Sometimes we were still cutting, or recording the voiceover, even as Bill opened the show, with only one chance to get it right. When it was done, the editor would sprint along the drab grey corridors to the Telecine department, which ran the projectors, to put the film to air. Hollering like a zombie, mowing down all in his path, he might make it with minutes to spare. Equally manic, the reporter would be racing to the studio control room to let the producer and director know the story was away. Don Simmons would be chain-smoking, pacing like a cat on heat. Ken Chown would be burbling some Methodist hymn. Only the studio director, Andrew Houghton, remained unflappably calm before all the screens and winking lights. A droll, nuggety Scot and former Royal Navy Fleet Air Arm jet fighter pilot, he exuded cool.

'Studio 21, Telecine. Do we have the Carlton story laced up to go?'

'Thirty seconds.'

'I'll need it in fifteen. Floor manager, tell Bill to ad lib till I give you the go.'

Bill would waffle to camera until he got the thumbs-up, and then launch smoothly into the link, the intro.

'Roll Telecine . . .'

'Rolling . . .'

'And take it!'

Somehow, miraculously, it always happened, seamlessly. They were some of the most thrilling moments of my media life.

✧

Socially it was a blast as well. As unlikely as it sounds with these colossal egos in orbit, we largely liked each other. Happily, so did our wives or partners. We partied and dined at each other's homes and went to each other's weddings. Once a year Peter Luck, who had Adelaide connections, would arrange for the Henschke wine dynasty in South Australia to send us a barrel of their signature Hill of Grace shiraz – even then eye-wateringly expensive – which we would bottle and cork over a liquid Sunday afternoon. Bill Peach's Christmas party, lavishly catered in true Australian country style by his wife, Shirley, at their home in Mosman, was the must-do of the calendar. Barbecues were a riot. I have a distinct recollection of a well-lubricated Kerry O'Brien upside down and struggling to extricate himself from a rose bush.

Bill himself had a dressing room in the bowels of the Gore Hill building, known as the green room, which doubled as a reception area if we had a guest in the studio. It had a couch, a mirror, a fridge and not much else. The ABC provided cheap wine for hospitality, which we augmented from our own supplies for refreshments before, during and after the show went to air. Sometimes a guest would linger. Bob Hawke, then the president of both the Australian Council of Trade Unions and the Labor Party, and heavily on the piss, was notorious for it. Hours after the show we would still be there, Hawkie guzzling the stuff down and holding court with defamatory gossip, jokes and anecdote: 'That fucking Gough! I told the prick . . .' You couldn't shift him with a crowbar. Nine o'clock, ten o'clock, eventually he would goad us to go with him to some Kings Cross bar to drink the remains of the night away. One of our waiting wives, exasperated, once told him point-blank to fuck off home to Hazel, but he turned not a silver hair.

Sometimes we would foment our own green room horrors. After a gruelling week, in a fit of depression on a Friday evening, Tony Joyce suddenly picked up an empty wine bottle and hurled it at the wall, smashing it to smithereens. Another journalist in the room, Gordon Bick, did likewise, only his bottle was full. Pent-up tensions and frustrations boiling over, Tony threw a third and then a couple of glasses, shouting at the top of his lungs about the fucking ABC, the fucking program, the fucking producers. Bick, also bellowing, chucked a platter of cheese. There was glass and wine everywhere. It looked like a brawl in the Dodge City Saloon – all it needed was gun smoke.

A studio guest seated in the corner, the fastidious fop Francis James of the Anglican Press, watched in astonishment, ducking the flying shards of glass. 'Is it always like this on Fridays?' he enquired delicately.

Bill stuck his head into the room after the show, took one look and fled. Andrew Olle, Paul Murphy and I tried to restrain Tony, and eventually we shoved him into a taxi and got him home. The next morning, a Saturday, we slipped back in to try to clean up the mess quietly, but too late: it had been discovered.

The sky fell in on Monday morning. Those loutish young puppies at *TDT* had trashed the joint, a point hard to contest. The executive producer of *Four Corners*, Allan Martin, was appointed as a one-man inquisition. We came out with our hands up. Martin, a competent but dour figure, would probably (and quite reasonably) have had the lot of us sacked, but Gordon Bick was one of his own *Four Corners* reporters and a friend. That saved us. Everyone present in the room had a week's pay docked, plus a bill for the not inconsiderable cost of cleaning and repainting, and the outrage was hushed up on pain of death. 'The Great *This Day Tonight* Green Room Atrocity' has never been reported until now. You read it here first.

✧

The game changed with the election of the Whitlam government in December 1972. The Coalition parties, shell-shocked and licking their wounds, were now largely irrelevant. It was Labor in the frame. For the final program of the year, Peter Luck and I did an opening title with the word 'Gough' carved in a towering pile of ancient stones. Thunder crashed, lightning flashed. The most grandiose piece of film music ever written, the theme for the Hollywood biblical epic *King of Kings*, blasted over the top. 'In the beginning there was Gough,' went the sepulchral voiceover. 'And Gough created advisers and aides and press secretaries for his own image, and everything that creepeth on the earth after their kind.' Up came a shot of Leonardo da Vinci's *The Last Supper*, with Whitlam's face superimposed on the Christ figure and the rest of the cabinet as the apostles. The last words were: 'Let us pray.' It worked a treat, although not with the God-botherers, who howled about blasphemy.

Our first big hit on Whitlam Labor, though, came after the bizarre raid on the Australian Security Intelligence Organisation by the attorney-general, Senator Lionel Murphy, in March 1973. Convinced that ASIO was disloyally withholding intelligence on right-wing Croatian terrorism in Australia, Murphy impulsively decided to find it for himself. At eight am on Friday, 16 March, he and a handful of aides barged unannounced into ASIO's Melbourne headquarters and demanded to look at the files. Someone in the Federal Police had tipped off the TV news departments, whose cameras were there. There was uproar. It was startling, unprecedented: the minister in charge of security matters was raiding his own department.

That night Peter and I gave it the full monty. The ABC at the time was running a popular American TV drama, *The FBI*. Airily ignoring copyright, we intercut shots of Murphy and his raid into an episode of dramatic car chases and gun battles.[89] It made him look ridiculous and was the talk of Canberra the next morning. This ramped up the embarrassment for Whitlam, who'd been infuriated by the Murphy stunt. There would be more of the same to come from *TDT*, much more. As the government lurched to its chaotic demise in 1975, it came under more heat than the program ever applied to the preceding Coalition governments, much of it courtesy of Richard Carleton's scorching Canberra interviews.

Doing the satirical stuff was trial and error. We probably had around a 50 per cent success rate. I vaguely recall one effort in which

I cavorted on a yacht in the uniform of a *Waffen-SS* officer; mercifully, time has erased what it was about, but it cannot have been funny. The 1973 wedding of Princess Anne and a cavalry officer, Captain Mark Phillips, prompted a silly and equally forgettable sketch in which David Salter and I dressed in a pantomime horse costume. At the studio doorway the horse collided, full-tilt, with none other than Clem Semmler, one of our bitterest foes. Apoplectic with rage, Dr Semmler extricated himself from the tangled equine embrace, rocketed back to his office and spent the next week firing off ever more furious memos about juvenile antics, demands for an apology, etc. He had a point about the juvenile antics.

TDT was where I cut my teeth writing and performing satire in the media. I had been the class clown at school; now I was discovering the intoxicating pleasure of making a wider audience laugh, and there was a demand for it. This had never been my intention when I entered journalism; I had planned to be an entirely conventional reporter. Almost by accident, my career was heading on a new trajectory.

Funny stuff aside, I am proud of the serious journalism we – all of us – did at *TDT*. Even now, almost half a century later, and even in grainy black and white, much of it stands the test of time. Peter Luck's early stories on Indigenous Australians, made with empathy and passion, and with pictures of great beauty, became beacons along the road to Aboriginal land rights. Less controversial but extremely elegant was his essay on the architect of the Sydney Opera House, Jørn Utzon, shot in both the hot glare of Sydney Harbour and the cool greys of the Baltic. Caroline Jones turned in a scorcher which revealed the Anglican Diocese of Sydney to be a rapacious slum landlord in the inner suburb of Glebe. Richard Carleton took the political interview to new heights.

There are three of my own stories I recall with some satisfaction. In 1972 I scored the first television interview with the author Patrick White. We had heard he was dismayed by controversial plans to build a new sports stadium opposite his home in Martin Road, Centennial Park. 'Might be worth a chat,' said the producer, well knowing that White was a notoriously irascible recluse. By a combination of old-fashioned digging and good luck I managed to find his home phone number.

'Heavens above, goodness me,' he quavered. 'Why would anyone want to hear from a broken-backed old poofter like me?'

They did, though, as he well knew. His partner, Manoly Lascaris, met us at the door of Highbury, their exquisite Federation Villa above the park. Grey and gaunt, but with a gaze like twin machine-gun muzzles, the writer plonked himself into a cane chair. He would have been sixty but he seemed much older and weary with it, dripping acid and aristocratic charm in about equal measure. 'The great god sport!' he spat, with a dismissive grimace. If the project went ahead, he said, he would leave Australia for good. As the film crew was packing up, he asked, rather gingerly, if I'd read any of his books. I hadn't done well with White, but enough to get by. 'Oh, yes,' I said. 'Very much liked *Voss* and *The Tree of Man*.' He seemed pleased, as if my opinion actually mattered.

Further afield, I look back with a nostalgic glow on a report I did on Papua New Guinea's path to oncoming independence. There were no great revelations, but it was invigorating to be filming far from the office, in landscapes and seascapes of tropical beauty. Working as a three-man crew – reporter, cameraman and soundman – we narrowly avoided being ambushed and mugged by *raskols* as we drove on a lonely road outside Port Moresby, and the story took us way out east to the Trobriand Islands, renowned in travellers' tales as the Islands of Love. We had arranged to stay with the son of a local chief, John Kasaipwalova, who had studied in Australia and was then, in his early twenties, an anti-colonial firebrand. (He is now a celebrated poet and novelist.) His people welcomed us. They took us swimming in the limpid blue Solomon Sea, and in an exquisitely beautiful rock pool of cold fresh water hidden deep in a shady cave and filled by a waterfall.

The Trobriands' reputation for relaxed and happily promiscuous sexual mores was well founded. Everyone, men and women, splashed about naked. On our first night in the village we were about to crash asleep when three girls in their teens or early twenties crept into our hut. With not a word of English, by giggling, winking, and gesturing they made it very plain they were available for sex. Newly married,

I politely declined, to my lifelong regret. The crew, though, accepted their hospitable offer. 'It seemed rude not to,' said the cameraman the next morning.

Of the political stuff I did for *TDT*, a double-header during Gough Whitlam's 1974 double-dissolution election stands out. Looking for a different angle, Ken Chown and I decided to profile two young candidates who, we thought, might have a future in federal politics. Paul John Keating, thirty years old and darkly good-looking, already had five years under his belt as the Labor MP for Blaxland. Suave and assured, he was happy to get the exposure on national television, and he handled the attention with aplomb. The Liberal hopeful, making his first run for Canberra in the Sydney suburban seat of Bennelong, was nervous and ill-at-ease, but eager to please. John Howard, a thirty-five-year-old solicitor, owlishly bespectacled and with a row of teeth like a picket fence hit by a truck, was 'not overburdened with charisma', I wrote with lofty assurance. Both men subsequently did indeed do quite well.

✧

In the spring of 1974 I decided to move on. After leaving the ABC, Mike Willesee had set up and fronted *A Current Affair* for the Nine Network, commercial television's first shot at nightly current affairs. More tabloid than *TDT* – and sensibly so for its different audience – it had rated its head off, not least because Willesee had introduced ragingly popular comedy segments with the newly discovered Paul Hogan. Mike himself had become a star, a household name. But in late 1974 he had a spectacular falling-out over money with Sir Frank Packer, and he was snapped up by the rival 0-10 Network, as it was then, to replicate the show there.

My *TDT* friend Vincent Smith had been best man at Mike's first wedding, and he suggested the two of us should go across. The money would be heaps better than the ABC was paying. I had severe stabs of doubt, even fear, about quitting public broadcasting to go commercial, but after ten years at the ABC it seemed like a reasonable jump to make. Kerri agreed. Vincent made a few calls, Mike took us out to a long lunch and we were in. It was exciting. With the Willesee name attached to the show, what could possibly go wrong?

13

'And the Word Was Gough'

IN FACT, WHATEVER COULD go wrong did go wrong.

In spades. With the less than alluring title of *24 Hours*, the show crashed like the wreck of the Old 97, sank like the *Titanic*, exploded like the *Hindenburg*.

It seemed so glamorous to begin with. The 0–10 studios at North Ryde were hip, all chrome and glass, and teeming with gorgeous blonde women. The network had some of the hottest shows on television. The long-running soap opera *Number 96*, set in an apartment block in Sydney's Paddington and spiked with what the tabloid newspapers invariably referred to as steamy sex scenes, boasted a TV world-first gay love affair. Families goggled at winsome tots and precocious teeny-boppers strutting their stuff on *Young Talent Time*, another top-rater.

All well and good, but this was not the sort of audience thirsting for current affairs from Monday to Friday at dinnertime. People who wanted that stuff were already getting it from *TDT* at the ABC and a revamped *A Current Affair* on Nine. They might have switched across if Willesee himself had appeared, but he didn't. For whatever reason, he had decided to take a break off-camera, and spent most of his mornings playing tennis. The show was to be presented by one John Bailey, who had been a popular newsreader at Melbourne's GTV-9 but was largely unknown in Sydney. That, too, might have worked, except that Bailey came down with chronic laryngitis and vanished for weeks on end. The network pleaded with Willesee to go back on air but he declined, so the thing was fronted by the third reporter hired in Sydney, Steve Raymond. That left just Vincent and me on the road to get stories in Sydney, an impossible ask for a thirty-minute nightly show.

The producer, Phil Davis, had been a handy afternoon newspaper journalist and, less happily, a press secretary to Billy McMahon, but he knew bugger-all about television. Whenever a gaping hole appeared in the line-up, which happened almost daily, Davis demanded we plug it with quick and easy 'vox pops', so-called interviews with people in the street in which we asked mindless questions of the weirdest characters we could find. Night after night, in those ever fewer households still watching, there was a parade of drooling loons with one eye in the middle of their forehead or knuckles dragging on the ground as they walked. 'Are there too many heterosexuals on television?' was one question I was instructed to ask. 'Aw, yes,' they grunted. 'Orta be stopped.' I grew to dread it, so much that I have largely blacked *24 Hours* from my mind.

The one plus of the whole experience was meeting perhaps the best cinecamera man I've worked with: Brendan Ward, a master of the art.[90] He hated the show as much as I did. The only decent interview I can recall is one we shot together with Junie Morosi, the mistress of Labor's federal treasurer, Dr Jim Cairns. It was the scandal du jour. Morosi, in her early forties, was attractive and usually described by the media as 'exotic' – code for her being of mixed race. She had no government experience whatsoever, let alone at the lofty apex of Treasury, but Cairns – clearly head over heels – had scandalised first Canberra and then the nation by appointing her as his principal private secretary. The homely Mrs Gwen Cairns remained placidly and loyally in Melbourne. I think I asked Junie if she and Cairns were 'in love', a question she batted away with a Mona Lisa smile and an arched eyebrow.[91]

After about six months of plummeting ratings – it seemed like six years – the network axed the wretched show and put us out of our misery. We were fired not long before Christmas 1974. It had not been a stellar start to my commercial media career. Mike, to his credit, paid out the remainder of my contract, the useful sum of $4000. A prudent young man, married just two years, might have used this windfall as a deposit for a house. I did not. We did not. Kerri had just graduated from university. She had never been overseas and was itching to travel. With a copy of Arthur Frommer's *Europe on Five Dollars a Day* buried in our luggage, we headed for wintry Europe. Economy class this time, for four months. I grew my first beard.

✧

Back in Sydney in the autumn of 1975, I was jobless but not particularly perturbed. Kerri easily found work as a medical technologist at a hospital pathology department and I was confident that something would turn up for me. It did. It was not ideal, but it would do for the time being. The ABC held out a return of sorts to *This Day Tonight*, although under very different conditions. Bill Peach had done his last national *TDT* in 1974, finally quitting after eight years. The management seized the chance to break the show into separate editions for each state. I was offered a relief job for a few months as associate producer of the Queensland program. We needed the money. Reluctantly, I farewelled my wife and headed for Brisbane. The debonair Andrew Olle made me welcome. 'You'll find Queensland is a madhouse,' he warned me.

He was right. The 'Hillbilly Dictator' Joh Bjelke-Petersen, a former peanut farmer, was at the height of his power as Queensland premier, his newly renamed National Party cemented into government by an outrageous gerrymander of the state's country electorates. Of all the politicians I have encountered, Bjelke-Petersen was at once the most pig-ignorant and cynically cunning, a grasping crook – barely literate, bumblingly inarticulate, but most certainly financially numerate – who plundered Queensland and its people and raped their democracy behind a pantomime of hayseed bonhomie. Buttressed by a corrupt and sometimes brutal police force, his palms heavily greased by the usual claque of dodgy 'businessmen' and property developers – the infamous 'White Shoe Brigade' – he ruled supreme. 'Don't you worry about that,' was his invariable rejoinder to any tricky question bowled up at a press conference or in an interview, and for many years it worked a treat. In the nation's most parochial state he successfully portrayed himself as the bulwark against the tide of socialist wickedness flooding north from Canberra. Whitlam famously called him 'a Bible-bashing bastard . . . a paranoid, a bigot and fanatical'. John Howard, at least notionally on the same conservative side of politics, charged: 'He doesn't have a vision for Australia, he has a power lust.'[92]

With the exception of Brisbane's only newspaper, the *Courier Mail*, which was firmly and disgracefully in Bjelke's pocket, the media in general and the ABC in particular were the enemy. 'The greatest thing that could happen to the state and the nation is when we get rid of the media,' he once told the *Australian Financial Review*. 'Then we would live in peace and tranquillity and no one would know anything.'[93]

Interviewing him for television, which I did a couple of times, was a curious experience. Surprisingly, he was invariably courteous and even jocular. Occasionally there would be a flash of fury in his eyes if a question cut too close, but it would vanish in an instant, washed away in the torrent of babble that was his customary way of answering, or deflecting. (Having watched him at close quarters and listened to his ludicrously mangled speech was a boon when I got into the business of radio and television satire a few years down the track.) We suspected at the time that Bjelke-Petersen was corrupt – it was common gossip in Brisbane – but we had no proof of it, not a skerrick, and he was always eager to reach for the defamation laws there, which seemed designed specifically to protect crooks like him.

If Askin in Sydney was a criminal, at least his ministers were not. Many of Bjelke's were. Three of them – and his police commissioner – eventually went to jail, and several more should have, including the premier himself and his oafish sidekick, Russ Hinze, a gross and vulgar mountain of sweaty flesh who was then Minister for Roads and later Minister for Police and for Racing, a gilt-edged invitation for corruption if ever there was.[94] Everyone called him the Colossus of Roads. Hinze backed me into a corner of the *TDT* green room one night, half-pissed, and harangued me on the evils of the federal

Labor government. 'If that cunt Whitlam gets back in at the next election the commos will be running the country in five years,' he blathered. He was stupid enough to believe it. Bjelke and his cronies set out to make sure it did not happen.[95]

Of course, the Whitlam government was doing enough of a job on itself. As 1975 wore on, it was rocked by crisis and scandal, month after month. Some of it was genuine, some of it confected or beaten-up by the opposition and the media, but all of it fomented an air of continuing chaos. Senior ministers were sacked or shifted sideways for a variety of transgressions. The Morosi affair, as it became known, continued to boil away on the tabloid front pages. These crises hit critical mass in June, in a chain reaction which would lead inexorably to Whitlam's downfall.

First, on 28 June, the government was badly mauled at a by-election in the Tasmanian seat of Bass, a vote triggered by the resignation of the former deputy prime minister, Lance Barnard. Bass had been a safe Labor seat since 1954, but a massive swing of 17 per cent swept the Liberal candidate, Kevin Newman, into the House of Representatives. Labor was still digesting that shock when it became apparent that Jim Cairns, as Treasurer, had misled parliament over negotiations for raising a loan overseas. It was an open and shut case, leaving Whitlam no choice but to ask Cairns to resign. When he refused, Whitlam went to the governor-general on 2 July and had him sacked. The news rocked the country and plunged the government and the party into deeper turmoil: the Labor left, always wary of Whitlam, worshipped Cairns as a heroic figure who could do no wrong.

In the midst of this uproar came the funeral of a Queensland Labor senator, Bertie Milliner, who had died of a heart attack on 30 June. This was another milestone on the government's road to ruin. It brought me down as well.

Convention decreed that Milliner should be replaced in the Senate by another Labor figure, a person nominated by the ALP. But Bjelke-Petersen saw an opportunity to cause trouble, and he began to plot. Labor held only twenty-eight of the sixty Senate seats, a minority. As Queensland premier, Bjelke-Petersen had the legal right to decide who should take the vacancy. Trampling convention, he let it be known that he might not accept the Labor nominee and could appoint someone of his own choosing, bringing the government down to twenty-seven Senate seats.

Milliner's funeral in Brisbane was held the day after the Cairns dismissal. Whitlam was there for it, with a slew of other Labor luminaries, including Bill Hayden, the senior Queensland MP, who would shortly take the Treasury portfolio. For the media, it was the first chance to see the prime minister and other ministers in public since Cairns had been punted – and, perhaps, to question them about it.

They behaved abominably. Reporters and camera crews descended on Whitlam and Hayden as they left their cars and entered the chapel. They pushed and jostled. Cameras were thrust in faces and microphones under noses. Some mourners were shoved aside. The PM stalked imperiously through the scrum, his face a mask of cold fury. Hayden, red-faced with anger, snapped at the TV crews to back off. They did not. Some went into the chapel and roamed around filming during the service, blithely unaware of the offence and distress they were causing.

I was there that day to cover the story for *TDT*. At first I had thought of trying to question Whitlam or Hayden myself, if the chance arose. When it was obvious that was not going to happen, I needed a new angle, something different to a straightforward news report. So I decided, instead, to cover the behaviour of the rest of the media, with some thoughts on the politics as well. Staying apart from the scrum, and intruding nowhere, we stood back at a distance and shot wide: the bigger picture.

So the story I put to air that night showed it all: the heaving media melee and the furious reaction of Whitlam, Hayden and other mourners. I scripted some lines about the turmoil within the Labor Party over Cairns, and raised the rumours that Bjelke-Petersen might rort the Senate vacancy. The closing shot of the story showed Milliner's coffin disappearing behind a curtain in the crematorium chapel, with my voiceover saying: 'Rest in peace, Senator Milliner. It is more than your Labor colleagues are doing tonight.'

There was uproar, a storm of protest from politicians and other viewers. The ABC was bombarded with phone calls first, then letters.

My report was 'offensive . . . sick . . . despicable . . . depraved'. Amazingly, because I had shown the disgraceful behaviour of the media, I was blamed for it! I had taken no part in it, and nor had the film crew, but almost everyone assumed we had.

The ABC agreed, and down I went. Without a hearing in person or any chance to explain myself, I was fired and told I would never be employed again. My closest friends and colleagues at *TDT* supported me. Bill Peach would write later that I 'got the bullet for stating the truth'. But it did me no good. I was out on my arse. I took it philosophically enough, pleased at least to be back in Sydney with Kerri.

Four decades later, I think I have been vindicated. Bjelke-Petersen did indeed subvert the Senate by appointing his puppet to the vacancy, an idiot by the name of Albert Patrick Field. When the crisis over supply came up in the Senate that November, Labor did not have the numbers to get its budget through. This led directly to the Whitlam dismissal. I claim a little prescience.

✧

Back in Sydney I went to work for Mike Willesee again, on a weekly one-hour interview show he was doing for the Seven network, imaginatively called *Willesee*. With the largely meaningless title of associate producer, I was lining up his guests and researching them for the interviews. It was boring as batshit but it keep my bank account ticking over, and it was an opportunity to watch Mike's interview technique at close quarters. He was brilliant at it, then and still is a maestro of the art.

The principal trick I learned from him was the pregnant silence. This is a particularly effective device if you are trying to extract information from a hesitant, reluctant or even hostile interviewee. Mike would put a question. When the answer came to an end, instead of diving in with another question he would sit silently, eyes boring into the talent, perhaps with an air of disbelief. Disconcerted, the interviewee might start talking again – sometimes babbling nervously – and would often reveal far more than intended. I filed this away for future reference. It works just as well on radio, where the silence can be even more profound and penetrating.

Sometimes the show was more interesting in the green room afterwards, when the hospitality flowed. I have a cheerful recollection of Margaret Fulton, the delightful cookery queen, savaging a morose and tearful Billy Snedden for his failures as Liberal Party leader. Margaret is apple-pie-and-cream in public but takes no prisoners in private. 'You pathetic dickhead,' she snapped at him.

That winter Peter Luck came to me with an idea. As ever, it was out of left field. We should write a long satire of the Whitlam government, inspired by the *TDT* end-of-year title we had done in 1972 with the word 'Gough' carved in Old Testament stone. It'd be done in mock-biblical language, set to a music score, and sold to a no doubt eager public as an LP record. We scribbled away in fits and starts. The tracks had titles like 'A Star Is Born', 'The Last Prawn Night' and 'Gough Is My Shepherd', which now seem eye-glazingly twee but worked well enough then. We called it *And the Word Was Gough*. Peter found a talented rock musician and composer, Chris Neal, who wrote the music and played it on a synthesiser, the hot new instrument of the era. The M7 record label bought the idea and we did the album cover as we had done the *TDT* sketch, pinching Leonardo's *Last Supper* again, with the heads of Whitlam and his cabinet superimposed on the disciples. After much consideration, we chose Jim Cairns as Judas.

The tricky bit was working out how to end it. That was solved for us on 11 November. Peter called me at home that afternoon. 'Turn on the TV,' he blurted. 'Kerr's just sacked Whitlam.' Perfect. A crucifixion. Gough at Golgotha. Heaven-sent. We did a hasty rewrite, raced into the recording studio and had it out in the record stores about a week later.

We got a few pars in a few newspapers to publicise the thing, but it barely moved until another divine intervention: a public denunciation from that inveterate Sydney God-botherer and serial pest the Reverend Fred Nile, then of the wittily named Festival of Light. Another cleric from Adelaide chimed in: *And the Word Was Gough* was scandalous blasphemy, an outrage, grossly offensive to all decent Christian people, typical of the sort of filth that happened when you had a Labor government in power. It should be banned forthwith.

We could have kissed them. You can't buy publicity like that. In the heat of the election campaign that followed the dismissal, sales took off. Whitlam was actually questioned about it at a press conference, as if he were somehow responsible for the frightfulness. I have felt a little glow of warmth for Fred Nile ever since. But there was no time to count the money. I was up and away on the campaign myself.

✧

Gough stormed on board the plane as if he were about to sack Rome. His face was livid with anger. We, the reptiles of the press on the campaign route, had been sitting there on the tarmac at Adelaide Airport since seven am, waiting for him to appear. The flight was now nearly two hours late.

At the last minute, Gough's advisers had convinced him to accept an invitation to breakfast that morning with bishops and other clerics of the South Australian Council of Churches. These nosy divines, inflated with self-importance, wanted assurances that Labor would not open the floodgates to pornography, indecency and blasphemy. Their concerns had been prompted, in part, by a disgusting, supposedly satirical record produced by two heathen louts from Sydney. Reluctantly, Gough had agreed to go along and hose them down.

The plane was one of the RAAF's VIP aircraft, a BAC-111. The media contingent sat up the back in economy-class seats, separated from the opposition leader and his staff by a partition. Gough entered through the rear door and stalked past us. As he reached the entrance to his compartment, he turned and glared for a long moment, towering over all. 'Why are all Christians cunts?' he boomed. Then he spun on his heel and disappeared. We took off for Alice Springs.

I was on the plane as a reporter for the Nine Network. A few weeks earlier I'd been offered the job by Gerry Stone, then the director of news at Nine and charged with reviving the slumping ratings of the flagship six pm news. It was a good deal, good money, a chance to get back to daily journalism. I would be one of three senior reporters at Nine. The others were Peter Harvey and Jim Waley. Peter and I would cover that 1975 dismissal election campaign, one of us flying with Whitlam, the other with the newly appointed prime minister pro tem, the Liberals' Malcolm Fraser. Halfway through we would swap planes.

The times were febrile, volatile. Labor supporters and many other people had been stunned, then outraged by the dismissal of the Whitlam government, and they seethed with anger. The governor-general, Sir John Kerr – a florid, pompous drunk, and the last man in Australia ever to wear a black silk top hat – was excoriated across the country. Labor's true believers were maintaining the rage, as Whitlam had exhorted them to do in his defiant speech on the steps of Parliament House on the day of his sacking.

The Liberals and other conservatives, though, were exultant. This was a new dawn. Malcolm Fraser's daring political gamble of blocking the Senate vote on supply had been handsomely vindicated by the downfall of the hated socialists. Kerr had acted nobly and bravely, for the good of the nation. Whitlam and all his works would be swept away.

Australia was divided, and fiercely so, far more than I have seen it before or since. Politics was on everyone's lips. The election was another double dissolution, meaning a vote for every seat in the Senate as well as the House of Representatives. It was a campaign of just under a month, with polling day on 13 December. Both leaders drew big crowds as they toured the country. The Labor throngs were throngier and more ardent, reflecting the deep injustice and constitutional travesty of the dismissal. Some of the faithful quite literally struggled to touch Gough on the arm or pat him on the back. Up on the stage, their leader had them in thrall with his familiar, stentorian cadences. Sometimes at the back of the hall those in the know could spot the man who had crafted the words, the master speechwriter and Gough's alter ego, Graham Freudenberg. Rumpled and owlish, Freudy would silently mouth the words between drags on an ever-present cigarette, registering what lines and ideas worked with the crowds and what might be bettered.

Much later, he would write of the delusions which sustained them all:

> The whole truth is that we drew a mantle of unreality around us, some deliberately, others subconsciously, creating a world of

> make-believe. It was only that which allowed us to function and allowed us to keep at bay the effects of the shock of 11 November. But almost all Labor people were infected by the enthusiasm of Labor supporters.[96]

So was the media, at first. Whitlam's policy speech, delivered at Melbourne's Festival Hall on Monday, 24 November, had the fiery passion of a revivalist rally in the American bible belt. There was a thunderous chant of 'We want Gough!' and something close to hysteria as he took the stage. His opening lines were vintage Freudenberg:

> Men and Women of Australia,
> The whole future of Australian democracy is in your hands.
>
> The decision you make on 13 December goes far beyond who shall govern Australia for a few months or a few years. It goes to the heart of how Australia is to be governed into the twenty-first century.
>
> Above all, Australia must be reunited – united about our basic faith in the value of parliamentary democracy, as a means for change, and as a means for good government.
>
> The shame of the past six weeks must be wiped away . . .

In the opening days of the campaign the sheer size of Gough's rallies led me to believe that Labor might prevail, but I was offered a dose of considered wisdom by the Red Fox himself, Alan Reid, the veteran newspaperman who had become Nine's senior political analyst.

'Never trust the crowds,' Reid cautioned in his gravelly growl. 'I learned that from Chifley. He told me that himself.'

At the 1949 election, Ben Chifley, the Labor prime minister, had drawn enormous crowds in support of his plan to nationalise the banks, but it was the nascent Menzies Liberals who won. I took the thought on board.

At one evening rally for Labor, in Sydney's outer Western Suburbs, there was a tap on my shoulder and I turned to see Kerry Packer standing behind me with his formidable lieutenant, David McNicoll. That was a surprise – to see your proprietor slumming it on the road with the peasants. McNicoll and I knew each other. A tall, stately figure with a luxuriant white moustache, he had been a distinguished war correspondent during World War II. Now he was a columnist for the *Bulletin*, spouting political opinions to the right of the Romanovs, but he was still a man of considerable personal charm. He introduced us, explaining that Kerry had come to have a look at the excitement for himself. And for about an hour Kerry stood quietly at the rear of the hall, unrecognised, soaking up the speeches and the atmosphere. Occasionally he would toss me a question: 'Who's that bloke up on stage?' Before he left he asked me who I thought would win. By that time I was pretty sure Labor had lost it, and I told him so. Kerry nodded his agreement, shook my hand again and left.

I had thought I'd be given riding instructions – told the political angles Packer wanted me and Nine to take. To my surprise and his credit, there was not a word of it. At no stage did Kerry instruct anybody on how that 1975 campaign should be covered. The only order I ever got came when he phoned me in Darwin after I'd reported on the news that night wearing an open-necked shirt in the heat. 'Wear a tie on camera, son,' he grunted. 'But you're doing a good job.' That was it.

It was in Darwin that I had my first long and personal talk with Whitlam, by the pool in the hotel where we were all staying. I had already filed my story for the evening news and was sprawled on a towel in the sun after a late-afternoon swim. Gough appeared, unaccompanied, and dropped his enormous frame onto a lounge.

He saw me and beckoned. 'You're Jimmy Carlton's boy, aren't you?' he said.

I was taken aback. At this stage of my life, very few people were aware of my father or mentioned him anymore. How on earth did he know?

'Margaret told me,' he said. 'She knew your father quite well.'

He was pretty well informed himself. Somehow my family had found a niche in that encyclopaedic brain. At the height of this tumultuous election campaign he must have had rather more on his mind, but for half an hour he questioned me about Father Carlton and his marriage to my mother, displaying both an interest and a kindness that at one point had me close to tears. It was like hearing from a favourite uncle.

Then he returned to the present, to the election. 'Who do you think will win?'

I gulped. I dithered. His eyes never left me. Finally, I found the balls to tell him, with every reluctance, that I thought Malcolm Fraser might pull it off.

'And is that what the rest of you think?' he asked, waving a hand at the non-existent Press Gallery.

'I think they do,' I muttered glumly.

'You're probably right,' he said. For a fraction of a second he looked infinitely weary. Then he heaved himself from the sun lounge and was gone. This is the first time I have revealed that conversation.

That encounter was the start of a friendship which grew warmer over the years. I was never one of Gough's intimate inner circle. That rare distinction was for those comrades who had fought alongside him, like Henry V on Crispin's Day. But we held each other in firm regard, although I always felt a tinge of awe in his presence, anxious that I might say something stupid or gauche. Occasionally he would make a phone call or drop me a witty note to say he had enjoyed something I'd written for the *Sydney Morning Herald*. There's a letter I treasure, written in 2000, which begins:

> Dear Mike
> On Saturday on awaking from dreams of Cathy Freeman as a Rhine Maiden, I struggled down to pick up my *Sydney Morning Herald*. As always, I went straight to your article. As always, it made my weekend.
>
> As you know, I am still moved by recollection of your father . . .[97]

We had a few lunches together. Once we encountered each other on the stairs at EJ's, a fashionable watering hole in Sydney's Macquarie Street owned by the vivacious Susie Carleton (ex-wife of Richard) and her friend Eric 'EJ' Walsh, who had been Gough's press secretary. 'Carlton!' he bellowed. 'I enjoy you aurally every morning!' Diners at nearby tables fell about. Mostly we ran into each other at public bashes of one sort or another. Both Gough and Margaret were inveterate first-nighters and reception-goers.

In private, I took to greeting him as 'Choiseul!' – an allusion to the Duc de Choiseul, fired as First Minister of France by Louis XV in 1770. He enjoyed the joke. In return, he would salute me as 'Columnist!' or 'Author!' He had, I think, the most brilliant, cultivated mind I have met, furnished like a Renaissance polymath. His range was extraordinary: he was as much at home with the sages of ancient Athens and Rome as he was with Jeffersonian democracy, British Common Law or the Code Napoléon, Australian novelists, the labyrinthine politics of the ALP, or who was sleeping with whom in the beds of Sydney's Eastern Suburbs *haut monde*. This was a man who, on first meeting Zhou Enlai in Beijing, could ask him – with genuine interest – what he thought had been the lasting effects of the French Revolution. 'It's too early yet to tell,' Zhou memorably replied. Gough's one great lacuna was a lack of interest in the details of economic management, a subject which apparently bored him and which – fatally – he was all too often content to leave to his ministers.

The Whitlam wit was pungent and potent, laced with a sardonic, self-mocking quality which many people took for arrogance. 'I've never said I'm immortal. I do believe in correct language. I'm eternal; I'm not immortal,' he once remarked. Smaller minds thought he actually meant it. Yes, he could be arrogant, like every prime minister I have ever met. It goes with the territory. Crossed or thwarted, he could be spiteful and vitriolic, almost feline. I never experienced one of his temper tantrums but they were said to be thermonuclear. And sometimes he could be devastating. During that 1975 campaign, the Nine Network journalist Sue Smith was assigned to doorstop him as he left a rally at Sydney's Wentworth Hotel. As he swept from the door to his car, she stepped forward, live on air for *A Current Affair*, and nervously introduced herself. Viewers around the nation saw Gough draw himself up to his full height and stare coldly down his nose at her. 'I never speak to strange women who accost me outside hotels,' he snorted.

More often, though, he was gregarious and good-humoured. He enjoyed company, and was always ready to throw back that leonine head in a great guffaw. He also had a sense of the ridiculous, which generally saved him from pomposity. If that failed, as it sometimes did, there was always Margaret to jerk him back to reality when he launched into some long-winded lecture to a captive audience. I recall one lunch at the Chelsea Arts Club in London, of all places, where he harangued about a dozen of us on the more arcane aspects of the Stuart monarchs and the Scottish peerage. 'Do shut up, Gough,' said Margaret, with weary resignation. 'You're boring us all stupid.' The Great Man deflated into meek silence.

Sometimes you could never be sure if he was serious or not. Once, being interviewed on my radio program, he appealed to the audience to help find a piece of music. 'I want it played at my state funeral,' he announced. 'It is the *Marche de la Garde Consulaire à Marengo*.'

'The what?'

'The March of the Consular Guard at Marengo. It is appropriately grand. I gave the sheet music to the army bandmaster at Duntroon, but he lost it.'

It was also mightily obscure but, to my surprise, a clergyman from Sydney's Roseville had the sheet music and a recording, which he sent in. I played it on air the next day. A French brass band crashed and thumped and farted, in a turgid piece of Napoleonic military flatulence that made Chopin's *Funeral March* sound like a giddy polka. Gough was delighted to get it, although it never was played at his funeral. His family thought it was horrible and rejected it out of hand.

For me, and many of my baby boomer generation, Gough Whitlam's initial great triumph was to arouse in us the idea that Australia need not be governed by the Tories for all eternity. It was possible to entertain dreams above and beyond the conservative truisms. Menzies had wielded power for the best part of two decades, astutely playing the sort of politics the burgeoning Australian middle class wished to hear. By the late 1960s his heirs and successors, much smaller men, had blown themselves up. Whitlam was there to articulate the politics of hope and imagination. To borrow the words of the historian Manning Clark, he was an enlarger, not a punisher or a straightener. He was a daring revolutionary, a visionary optimist unswervingly committed to enhancing the quality of Australian life. At first he carried it off magnificently, a typhoon of change.

Certainly his government was fatally flawed, carrying within it the seeds of its own destruction. Hubris reigned. Essentially, Labor had been out of power federally for so long that it retained no corporate memory of *how* to govern, the tedious but essential minutiae of administration day after day, month after month, year upon year. In his own words, Whitlam would 'crash through or crash'. In the end, he crashed. But much of his government's achievements were indeed eternal, from the mundane to the exalted. The Tories since have sought to disparage his legacy, as they would. They ignore the modernisation of family law with no-fault divorce, the move to equal pay for women, the lowering of the voting age to eighteen, the first steps towards Indigenous land title, the opening up of university education, the abandonment of deference to all things British, including the honours system, the cleansing of some of the Cold War sludge in foreign policy, the extension of sewerage to the outer suburbs of Australian cities, the abolition of the death penalty and the building of the National Gallery in Canberra. All these reforms and many more were the fruit of three years of Whitlamism.

One achievement, though, stands supreme and unbreakable. His government's resounding triumph was to create the system of universal health care known first as Medibank and now as Medicare. For that alone Gough Whitlam merits the unstinting gratitude of history. It is one of the abiding joys of my life that I knew him.

✧

Malcolm Fraser in 1975 evoked for me the image of a craggy Scottish laird, flinty and remote, lording it over his tenants in some grim, snow-smothered Highlands stronghold. I have these occasional flights of fantasy, but this one was not entirely removed from reality. He radiated a patrician aloofness, the natural demeanour of Victoria's Western District squattocracy. 'Life is not meant to be easy,' he had famously said in a speech in 1971, a dour epigram that haunted his political career.

One of his nicknames at the time was 'the Crazy Grazier'. Others likened his rough-hewn features to the stone-carved monolith heads of Easter Island. In many ways he was a master politician, an accomplished practitioner of the dark arts, domineering and fiercely ambitious. His ascent through the ranks of the Liberal Party had left not a few bloodied corpses in his wake. He had taken on Gough Whitlam and won.

Yet there was always the feeling that he was ill-at-ease with human contact. The small change of political currency – working a room, shaking hands, slapping backs, downing a beer in a pub, kissing babies – was not his thing. If he had to do it he would, with as much grace as he could muster, but he never looked comfortable. His wife, Tamie, was much better at it. Unlike Whitlam, who enjoyed the company of journalists he trusted, Fraser kept almost all of us at a distance. We were a necessary evil, to be handled with suspicion. Curiously, though, he became close to Richard Carleton, through a shared love of trout fishing in the icy streams of the Brindabella Ranges, outside Canberra. They were an odd couple.

As planned, Peter Harvey and I swapped planes halfway through the campaign. He went with Whitlam and I joined Fraser in Melbourne. I did not know Peter at all well then, although I respected his journalism. Friendship came later. Two weeks before polling day we agreed that Fraser probably had the election in the bag, although by how much we could not tell.

Though I was from the Nine Network and, therefore, supposedly well disposed, I was not particularly welcome in the Liberals' media pack. 'What are you doing here, Hogan?' snarled Fraser's press secretary, David Barnett, when he discovered me on the plane. For some inexplicable reason he had got it into his head that I was not Michael Carlton but Allan Hogan, a reporter on *Four Corners*. Hogan had been refused permission to join the Fraser campaign and yet somehow it seemed the scheming left-wing ABC bastard had inveigled his way on board. Allan and I do look vaguely alike, I suppose – Irish features, curly hair – but we are hardly twins. Barnett would not believe my denials and began to get all shouty, threatening to have me dragged from my seat and arrested. I was enjoying it, and it got madder when he rounded on the rest of the seated media reptiles. 'Is this Mike Carlton or Allan Hogan?' he shouted at them. 'Allan Hogan!' they chorused. Eventually I produced my driver's licence, but Barnett did not forgive me for making him look a dill.

Boredom sets in after a few weeks on an election campaign, for all involved, political staff and the media. You hear the party leader deliver the same speech, the same key phrases, time and again. There will be a small tweak here and there – depending on whether you're in Perth or Townsville, Hobart or Adelaide – but by and large it's the same old stuff, repeated and repeated to the point where you can recite large chunks of it yourself. Malcolm Fraser was nowhere near Whitlam's class as an orator. The policy speech he delivered on 27 November at the old Dallas Brooks Hall in Melbourne was dull and wooden:

> This election results from the dishonesty and incompetence of the Whitlam Labor government.
>
> This election has been caused by the dismissal of two acting prime ministers for deceiving the parliament.
>
> This election has been caused by a prime minister who refused to face the people, who tried to rule without parliament, who defied a fundamental principle of our constitution, and who finally forced the governor-general to dismiss him; the man who took Australia the first significant step on the road to dictatorship.
>
> This election is about the way Labor has been destroying our way of life . . .

I don't think any of the Liberal faithful sought to touch the hem of his garment. There was nothing like the adulation that was showered on Gough. But Fraser was an effective campaigner nonetheless, carried forward by the dogged persistence that had propelled his whole political career. Tamie flew with him on the campaign, and I think he derived strength from her support and counsel.

Towards the end, the campaign boredom became too much. In Hobart, half a dozen of us decided to duck out of Fraser's evening speech to savour the attractions of the Wrest Point Casino. We stumbled into our beds in the wee small hours and woke the next morning, very much the worse for wear, to find that we had missed the Fraser plane. It had left for Melbourne without us. From memory, this vagabond crew of defaulters included John Jost, the debonair political correspondent of the *Age*, and Brian Toohey of the *Australian*

Financial Review. By hook or by crook we managed to talk our way aboard a TAA flight which got us to Melbourne just in time for Fraser's next public appearance, but it was a close-run thing.

Many of the people who disliked, distrusted or despised Fraser in those heady days of the dismissal would come to see much more of the man of principle as we all grew older. In not quite eight years as prime minister, he took in more than 50,000 refugees from the Vietnam War and its aftermath, a policy of decency and compassion. Evidently without a racist bone in his body, he picked up and carried forward much of the Whitlam program on Aboriginal land rights and multiculturalism. As his one-time ally and former treasurer John Howard wrenched the Liberal Party to the hard right, Fraser remained firmly in the centre, one of the last of the Menzian Victorian Liberals. His sometimes outspoken criticism of Howard and his government lost him truckloads of friends and former colleagues, but won him others. In his later years, he was scornful of his successors' unquestioning, grovelling adherence to the American alliance.

As old foes sometimes do when their battles are long done, Whitlam made a rapprochement with the man he had once branded 'Kerr's Cur'. 'Malcolm Fraser has now replaced me as Public Enemy Number One in the demonology of the Australian right wing,' Gough remarked in 1990. 'I must say I am much more relaxed about being supplanted by Malcolm Fraser for a second time than I was the first time.'[98]

Over the years, I interviewed Fraser for radio a few times. It would be wrong to say we had a relationship – we most definitely did not – but I think our attitudes towards each other mellowed. With hindsight, it was a privilege to have encountered him, too.

✧

The election was a bloodbath for Labor. I was on the floor of the National Tally Room that night, watching the results come in from around the country. Everyone there was expecting a Coalition win, but few, if any, had predicted the magnitude of the defeat. It became ever more crushing as new sets of numbers arrived on the big boards. The ALP lost thirty seats in the House of Representatives.

The Coalition finished up with ninety-one seats to Labor's thirty-six and, more important still, control of the Senate with a six-seat majority.

Gough arrived in the tally room to concede defeat, a subdued figure. He spoke of his 'profound regret' at the loss of so many of his colleagues, and he took another swipe at the 'usurpation and abuse of power by the Senate and the governor-general'. I was gutted, for Whitlam himself, and for the end of Labor's grand experiment in progressive politics. Fraser, in turn, spoke of duty, responsibility and humility. Then we all went home to bed.

Back in Sydney, I had more than politics on my mind. Kerri and I had bought a house. After we married we lived first in a cramped, two-bedroom flat at Avalon up on the beaches. Then we moved closer to the city, from the sublime to the ridiculous, renting the bottom half of a shabby Federation mansion at Cremorne, on the northern shore of the harbour. It was full of gloomy Victorian furniture, including a dining table to seat fourteen, and the initial charm wore off fairly quickly.

The house we found was at Willoughby, five minutes' walk from Channel Nine, and on a bus route to the city, which was about fifteen minutes away. For $33,000 we got a two-bedroom Federation cottage of brick walls and slate roof, in good nick, free-standing and with a long back garden. It had a tiny front verandah and a narrow hallway down one side, which opened onto a small lounge room, a smaller dining room and a kitchen barely big enough to boil a jug of water. We loved it. With a deposit of $5000 we made up the price with a $28,000 loan from the ABC Credit Union, a heart-stopping sum which gave us weeks of sleepless nights just thinking about it.

Warming to the magic of home ownership, and assiduously following the latest trends in *House & Garden* magazine, we painted the bedroom ceiling in high-gloss purple, the hallway ceiling a fire engine red, and the ceiling in the lounge a vivid emerald green. The tiles in the kitchen were orange, from memory. Or perhaps a lurid lime green. An elaborate, pale beige macrame hanging thingy – I have no other words for it – displayed a greenish-yellow indoor plant whose tendrils dangled halfway to the floor. This was 1970s haut decor.

Ensconced in this splendour, we held dinner parties offering the latest fad in cuisine, the Swiss fondue. The culinary guru du jour was the infallible Margaret Fulton, cookery editor of the *Australian Women's Weekly*. We – and everybody else – quaffed wine from knobbly cups of hand-thrown pottery. Even today I feel a twinge of guilt at the thought of some much later purchaser having to eradicate the decorative atrocities we inflicted on the place – no easy job. Out of curiosity, as I wrote these lines I did an internet search to see what the house would be worth now: $2.2 million was the startling answer.

No matter. In 1975, about to turn thirty, I had a job and a future in television. Better still, I had a foot on the lower rungs of the Sydney real-estate ladder. Life could only get better, and it did.

14
Thank you, Mr Packer

THE PACKERS DID NOT like spending money on real estate unless they were living in it. They ruled their media empire, Consolidated Press Holdings, from a small building in Park Street near Sydney's Hyde Park, a cramped rabbit warren remarkable only for being utterly unremarkable.

TCN-9, their Sydney television station, was no better. Take away the studios themselves, with their lights, cameras and control rooms, and it could have been a struggling widget factory in Wollongong. The paint was peeling. Plasterboard walls wobbled if you slammed a door. The stairs creaked, the toilets smelt. A lot of the program production was actually done in half a dozen adjacent cottages, crumbling three-bedroom brick bungalows picked up cheap, still with the original cracked linoleum on the floors, cockroaches in the kitchens and rats in the ceilings.

I encountered Sir Frank Packer just once, when I was at *TDT* and assigned to ask him to appear for an interview. This was a long shot, to say the least. Packer had loathed the program since it once reported that he was 'about seventy years old'. The next day his *Daily Telegraph* had splashed in high fury, right across the front page, the news that he was only sixty-four. 'Today Distorted Tonight', shouted the headline. That evening he got a lavishly insincere apology from Bill Peach, and a montage of unflattering photo shots of him cut to the Beatles' song 'When I'm Sixty-Four'.

I'd have had a better chance of getting the pope and the Roman Curia to front at Gore Hill, but I gave it a go. Surprisingly, the numbers for the Packer mansion at Bellevue Hill were in the phone book. The first one didn't answer, so I tried the second, listed as 'Butler's Pantry'. Imagine my surprise when the mogul answered it himself.

He was equally surprised. 'You must be fucking kidding!'

'No, Sir Frank—'

'Bunch of fucking communists. Why would I wanna go on with a bunch of fucking commos?'

'But Sir Frank—'

'You're a pack of lying cunts!'

Click.

Packer Senior ran Nine exactly as he pleased, and fuck you. Old-timers would speak reverently of the day he made a killing with one of his horses at Randwick and ordered the channel to keep replaying the film of the race so he could savour the triumph at home. Bemused viewers that Saturday night found the feature movie interrupted half a dozen times by the duty announcer explaining that 'in response to overwhelming public demand, we bring you once again the running of the fifth race . . .'

Most of his employees saw him as an ogre, capricious and brutal, although it was said he had a sentimental side. Reputedly, he had wept bitter tears when he sold the *Daily Telegraph* to the young Rupert Murdoch in 1972 for $15 million, an offer too good to refuse. But he was a tyrant, not least to his two sons, Clyde and Kerry. He bullied them both. When he died in 1974 the skies over Channel Nine lightened considerably. Clyde, the elder son and heir presumptive, had fallen out with his father and taken himself off to California. The gossips of Sydney had it that Kerry, known to be dyslexic and thought to be stupid, would run the empire into the ground within five years.

Bad call. Shrewd and aggressive, Kerry had a natural feel for the media business, the sort of instinct money cannot buy. Ensconced in Park Street, chain-smoking and guzzling Coca-Cola and Fanta by the litre, he had a very good idea of what people wanted to read in their magazines and watch in their lounge rooms, and he did his best to give it to them. He got it right more often than not. His hulking frame and rough-hewn face, with its full, fleshy lips, made him a formidable figure in any company, and his tycoon tantrums were legendary. I copped one myself when I was at Nine, Kerry shouting down the phone about some story that had offended him. It was genuinely shocking. My spluttering attempt to explain myself made it worse, and when he slammed the phone down after about ten minutes I was skinned and filleted, convinced that my career in journalism was over.

Like most rich and successful business figures, he could also radiate charm when he felt like it. Many years later, when I was working in radio, he heard that I was with my young family and some friends and their kids at Palm Beach, on the sand just below his big pink beach house on Ocean Road. It was a summer Saturday afternoon. He sent down an invitation – a command, really – to come up and watch the cricket on television, and he welcomed us on the front deck with his enormous frame swathed in a voluminous Indonesian sarong and naked from the waist up. It was an imposing sight.

The butler swept up the kids and took them out the back to the jacuzzi, where they were plied with ice-cream. We sprawled on lounges while James Packer, still a teenager, bustled back and forth with beers for us and Coke for his father. Kerry was genial and Ros, his wife, chatted with the women. Most startling of all, Kerry seemed to have a direct line to the Australian dressing room at the Sydney Cricket Ground. Australia was in the field. Every so often he would pick up the phone and snap an order: 'Put McDermott on . . . Give Waugh a few overs . . .' A few minutes later the bowlers would obediently change. When the time came to leave, we whispered to the kids to thank their host. As one, they turned to the butler. 'Thank you, Mr Packer,' they chorused. Kerry snorted a laugh.

Much later again, when I was working in London, Kerri and I were invited to the Packer compound at Wimbledon to watch the 1992 women's final between Steffi Graf and Monica Seles. The tent, in gleaming white, was big enough to house a Russian circus. The luncheon tables shone with silver and crystal, bowls of roses, and ice buckets filled with Krug. Waiters hovered with snowy napkins. The buffet was a kingly spread of lobster and smoked salmon, oysters, cold fowl, rare beef, and every salad, pudding, dessert and cheese known to civilisation. The Duchess of Kent was slumming it nearby in a much smaller tent. The only downside was having to watch the tennis, a game which bores me to sobs.

All up, Kerry Francis Bullmore Packer was a good boss, one of the best I had. He was a hard taskmaster, for sure, but he paid a fair day's wage for a fair day's work, and he knew what he was doing. He returned the loyalty if you gave him yours. Compared to the many knaves, fools, frauds and incompetents I have encountered in the boardrooms and executive suites of commercial radio, he was a paragon of many virtues.

✧

Despite the grot at the TCN studios, it was a fun place to work. Morale was high. The troops were cheerful. The Nine Network was the most profitable in the country, with a slate of high-rating shows right through the day and into evening primetime. Ratings matter to everyone in television, from the toilers in the canteen to the CEO. If the figures are up, then jobs are safe and pay rises are possible. If they are heading south, a studio and a network is plunged into gloom and fear; heads roll with the swift finality of a Politburo purge.

Nine clung to the top with a stable of television's biggest stars. Graham Kennedy, Paul Hogan, Bert 'Moonface' Newton and Don Lane were household names and faces, much loved. Graham had an acrimonious parting with Nine in 1975, but the caravan moved on. Busloads of blue-rinsed grannies arrived at Willoughby each day, buzzing with excitement to queue to watch *The Mike Walsh Show*, live at noon. Walsh, a former radio disc jockey and one of the first talkback radio acts, was a television natural. He, in turn, gave the world Jeanne Little, a blonde comedienne with a voice like a jackhammer and a laugh like a police siren. The show was a well-greased mix of chat, gossip, interviews with visiting Hollywood stars, homely medical advice and music. A lot of people found Walsh difficult to work with, a nit-picking perfectionist, but I liked him. The show was glued together by Nine's in-house band, led by Geoff Harvey, a cheerful Cockney who was the station's much-loved musical director for thirty-eight years, and composer of theme music for its biggest programs.

Of that galaxy of stars, Graham Cyril Kennedy was the brightest, far and away. There has never been a funnier, more talented performer on Australian TV. Small and skinny, with a rubbery face and eyes like two boiled eggs, he could improvise a comedy routine from thin air. Give him a camera and, say, a ping-pong ball, and he would have an audience rolling in the aisles for fifteen minutes with an ad-libbed monologue of wisecracks and double entendres.

Graham and I first crossed paths when – to the surprise of a great many people, including himself – he agreed to front *TDT* for a week while Bill was on leave. He could have commanded Bill's yearly salary for a week's work but he did it for free, flattered to be asked. A fish out of water at the ABC, and with no studio audience to work to, he was a bundle of jitters before his first night, anxiously seeking reassurance in the green room. 'You can do it, Graham, you can do it.' The floor manager practically had to carry him to the studio desk. When the On Air light flashed red he sailed through it with aplomb, nerves forgotten, a bravura performance.

We got on well. He invited me for drinks at his mansion on the harbour at Hunters Hill, and again for lunch. I was mildly surprised and flattered to find that both times it was just the two of us, on a terrace overlooking the water. Graham was gay – although that was a well-kept secret at the time – and I think he enjoyed the company of a young bloke in his late twenties. We talked television gossip and politics – he was articulate, thoughtful and well informed – and I recall him giving me advice on how to further my career: who was an arsehole and who was not, etc. There was a vase of about two dozen perfectly sharpened pencils on the table, and every so often he would pluck one out and use a white foolscap pad to jot down a note of some idea that had occurred to him.

We laughed a lot, yet it struck me that Graham was a lonely figure, imprisoned by the enforced secrecy of his homosexuality and by the fame which meant he could never appear in public, not even at a secluded restaurant, without being besieged by fans and autograph hunters. Long after the lights had gone out and the cheering had stopped, he died a lonely death from pneumonia, nursed by his friends and carers, the actress Noeline Brown and her writer husband, Tony Sattler. Graham Kennedy had paid a high price for his stardom.

And then there was Brian Henderson. I had admired him as a kid at Chatswood, had danced in the teenage audience at *Bandstand*, wide-eyed and starstruck. Hendo was cool, so very cool. Now he was a workmate in the newsroom. I had known platoons of newsreaders at the ABC, ho hum, but I confess I was in a mild state of awe when Gerry Stone introduced us, and was taken aback when Brian actually knew who I was.

Any fool can read television news, and many do: all you need is a more or less symmetrical head and the ability to mouth what's on the autocue without tripping over the words. The trick is to do it well, which very few can. It takes native talent, real application and high maintenance – more so on television than radio – and not many people have that combination. Hendo did. He was the Prince of Newsreaders, a gig he held at Nine for an astonishing forty-six years.

The smartest thing he ever did was to marry his wife, Mardi, maiden name Marie Louise Ozoux. The gossips had a field day when they got hitched in 1966. She was just nineteen, the beautiful daughter of a prominent family on the North Shore. He was thirty-four and a known hell-raiser, knocking around town with his mates, John Laws and the singer Col Joye, drinking hard and pouring his pay packet into the poker machines at the old TV club, the 729. Mardi picked him up, dusted him off, spun him around and masterminded his career, to the extent of choosing his suits, shirts and ties, and regularly critiquing his performance. Hendo had the good sense to go with the flow, and his natural talent kept him afloat. Every on-camera gesture, every smile, every raised eyebrow or slight frown was carefully calculated – not to eclipse the news he was reading, but to enhance the credibility of his presentation. People believed him. For a while *Nine News* ran the slogan 'Brian told me', and it worked because it worked.

After my initial reserve, we became friends. He would arrive in the newsroom in the mid-afternoon, often after a morning of tennis with Col Joye, and get down to the business of pre-reading the stories on the rundown for six pm. Hendo never pretended to be a journalist or a writer, but he knew bad writing when he had to read it, and he could be ruthless in rejecting clumsy or tortured copy. Unlike some newsreaders, who often had not a clue about what they were spouting, Hendo kept abreast of events big and small. If he didn't get some happening or nuance, he would not hesitate to ask. He was a stickler for correct pronunciation, pretty much a lost art these days, and he abhorred clichés.

One slow afternoon in the newsroom we compiled a nonsense news story crammed with every cliché we could think of, and Hendo taped it: 'Thousands wept as heavily armed police, troops and tanks began the heartbreak task of sifting through the flooded wreckage of a shock, mystery blaze which took battling fire-fighters more than three hours to extinguish . . .' The tape should still be somewhere in the bowels at Nine. It was good to be at the lavish farewell dinner Kerry Packer threw for him when he retired in 2002, with his sign-off for the last time: 'And that's the way it is . . .'

It was generally a happy newsroom in 1975, although morale was hit hard by the murder of the Balibo Five in East Timor that October. Five newsmen sent from Australia, two of them from Nine, were killed in cold blood by Indonesian special forces troops advancing on the town of Balibo, where the journalists had based themselves.[99] This was a sobering thought. If I had joined the newsroom a month earlier, it was very likely, with my Indonesian experience, that I would have been on that trip. Yet I think the outcome would have been different. It's sad to write this, but the five were tragically naive and inexperienced, way out of their depth. This was a dirty little war in South-East Asia, in all its infinite complexity. No seasoned war correspondent – white, European – would enter a conflict with the forces of one side, then wait in no-man's land for the other lot to advance, hoping that your non-combatant status and an Australian flag daubed on a wall would protect you. My ability to speak Indonesian might have got me out of trouble, too. This is not to excuse the Indonesian war crime – not at all – but it perhaps puts it in a new light. I also knew Roger East, the Australian freelance journalist shot by an Indonesian firing squad on the docks of Dili a few months later. Roger was a good reporter and a cheerful companion in the pub, but also in the wrong place at the wrong time.

One morning Gerry Stone came to me in the newsroom with a bloke in his early twenties, neatly suited and trailing respectfully behind him, bright-eyed and bushy-tailed. 'This is Malcolm Turnbull,' he said. 'He's here to learn the ropes.' Someone pointed the young hopeful towards a desk and a typewriter and he began to accompany the more senior reporters, me included, on film stories. It was never spelled out, but we had the impression that Malcolm was some sort of protégé of Kerry's, sent over for work experience. Eventually he was permitted to do a spot of reporting without someone holding his hand, but he vanished after a couple of months, as suddenly as he had arrived.

If and when I ran into him over the years he would cheerfully remind me about those happy times 'when we were journalists at Nine', but they are largely a blank to me. He later became a prime minister, I believe, although not a particularly memorable one.

✧

Neville Wran and I were waiting in the wings of some dusty suburban town hall in Sydney, half-listening to a local Labor Party worthy on the stage droning on about the virtues of the working class. It was the autumn of 1976, in the midst of a state election campaign. Neville was making his first run at the New South Wales premiership, avid to end eleven years of Coalition rule in Macquarie Street. This was a big ask. The Whitlam government had been crushed in Canberra less than six months before, and the polls and the pundits were as one: that Labor was still on the nose, in the wilderness, unelectable anywhere.

The orator would not shut up. He was supposed to be introducing Neville, but on and on he went about the dignity of labour, the pride of honest work, the noble aspirations of battling families. The audience was nodding off. The next Labor premier of New South

Wales grew more and more exasperated. He glared at the small knot of people with him, as if it were somehow their fault. Then he saw me and the film crew. We were not filming. 'I'll tell you the only good thing about being in the fucking working class,' he said to me. 'It's getting *out* of it!' It was an intriguing insight into the man and I filed it for future reference.

Eventually the worthy puffed to a halt and plodded through his introduction. Neville had once thought of becoming an actor. He took his cue like a trouper and bounded on stage, beaming and waving. He embraced the bore like a favourite uncle and set to wowing the crowd. It was a textbook demonstration of retail politics. Against all the odds, Labor won that 1976 election by a split hair, fifty seats to the Coalition's forty-eight.

Neville Kenneth Wran QC was an attractive figure, suave and handsome, articulate, cultured and witty. At the age of fifty he had risen a long way from his lowly birth as the eighth and last child of a hardscrabble family in the waterfront suburb of Balmain, soaring to the heights of the Sydney bar. For all the exterior polish of the Phillip Street Queen's Counsel there was a solid core of Balmain within, and he could yarn and swear like a wharfie. He also knew how to charm journalists. In the early years of his ascent to power, recognising that the big Sydney newspapers – most notably the *Sydney Morning Herald* – were irretrievably biased against him and Labor, he turned his attention to television, where, he thought – correctly – he would get fairer coverage. He had two adroit press secretaries, Brian Dale and Peter Barron, both of them former newspapermen, who saw to it that selected television reporters got easy access to their boss for comments on the record and a few beers in the office afterwards. I was one of them. Dale and Barron would kick the relationship along by giving you the occasional exclusive story, one of the tried and true conjuring tricks of media management.

Neville went at the premiership with vigour and imagination, a sea change from the corrupt Askin years and the two Liberal non-entities who had followed. It was a tight ship, probably never bettered in the New South Wales ALP. The party machine in Sussex Street was run by John Ducker, a hard-as-nails Yorkshire-born trade unionist universally known as 'Bruvver'. He was a formidable operator, who ruled the party with Stalinist rigour. Ducker watched the premier's back. Neville himself dominated the parliamentary party with the loyal support of his deputy, Jack Ferguson, a bluff and amiable former bricklayer, and probably the last Labor MP to build his own house with his own hands. Ferguson and Wran were chalk and cheese, but they held each other in enormous affection.

Neville had that skill common to the most successful politicians, of making you believe he'd been waiting eagerly all day to see you. His laugh was infectious. It was flattering to be taken into his confidence, or as much of it as he cared to divulge, for there was also something enigmatic about him. Like dismantling one of those Russian dolls, you would find another layer beneath. And he could be savage to those who crossed him. At a drinks party in his office on the eve of the 1976 vote, he strode towards the *Sydney Morning Herald*'s veteran state political editor, John O'Hara. 'You can get fucked, O'Hara,' he snapped.

On the day his first cabinet took office, he and the ministers-to-be walked together down Macquarie Street to be sworn in at Government House, a pleasant stroll in the sunshine with their families, the cameras clicking and rolling. I managed to get a word with him.

'What's "Buckets" doing in the cabinet?' I asked. 'He'll be a disaster.'

Rex 'Buckets' Jackson, the Member for Heathcote and about to be anointed Minister for Youth and Community Services, was a failed punter, notorious for running up gambling debts all over town.

Neville shrugged. 'Caucus put him there,' he said. 'But he'll be all right. We'll watch him.'

I hate to say 'I told you so.' In 1988 Jackson was sentenced to ten years in prison for corruption. As Corrective Services Minister he had been paying off his debts to the bookies by taking bribes to let criminals out of jail early.

By then Neville had left politics, retiring at the moment of his own choosing in 1986. I liked him a great deal. But we would have a spectacular falling-out.

✧

Sometime in 1976 I left *Nine News* and went to *A Current Affair*, the program that followed at six-thirty pm. This was not then the tabloid, freak-show *ACA* on air today, a circus parade of shonky real-estate agents, fad diets, Kardashians, trashy family vendettas, supermarket rip-offs, drive-by shootings and surgically enhanced supermodels (nothing longer than three minutes). But it was beginning to take some steps in that direction. The executive producer and, for a while, the presenter was yet another of television's endless supply of people named Michael, one Mike Schildberger, of whom I can remember only that Gough Whitlam had taken a dislike to him and invariably referred to him as 'Shitberger'. We put the show together in one of the cockroach-infested cottages.

The pivotal figure was the senior producer, Peter Meakin, a bearded, unkempt garden gnome who appeared much of the time to be weary of the follies of the world. Renowned for his lacerating tongue and for taking no prisoners, he was much feared. We disliked each other on sight, circling warily, poised to strike and kill at the first sign of weakness. He thought I was an effete, North Shore pseudo-socialist and dilettante. I tagged him as a crude vulgarian and irascible Packer stooge. We were both wrong.

Meakin – nobody ever called him Peter – was the son of an Anglican archdeacon, expensively educated in Adelaide, strikingly intelligent, well read and a good cook. He just hid it. I never discovered what his politics were, beyond a medium-level distrust of politicians themselves. Immensely able, with an unerring ability to cut to the heart of the matter, he did not suffer fools gladly. But he was also capable of great kindness to people who needed it, a virtue again well concealed. In short order we grew to like and admire each other, and to lay the foundations for a friendship and respect which endures.

I never worked for a better producer. He had a sure sense of the audience, his golden rule being not to bore them, nor to lecture them, nor to condescend to them. A stellar career at all three commercial networks established his reputation as the country's outstanding television news executive. In a well-ordered world he could have performed miracles as managing director of the ABC, and I often urged him to go for it, but he refused, claiming – probably accurately – that the bureaucracy would drive him mad. Which is not to say he was any shrinking violet. Meakin had the balls to take on Kerry Packer if he thought he needed to.

We did have scorching rows, generally over some story.

'It's too fucking long – take two minutes out of it.'

'Bullshit. If we cut anything, it won't make sense.'

'Crap. We can lose your stupid reporter's piece, for a start.' At this point Meakin would mimic my stand-up to camera, with much lisping, hand-waving and eye-rolling. The film editors, enjoying the stoush, would fall about laughing.

'Fuck off, Meakin. Everyone knows the only reason you're a producer is because you're shit on camera.' More hoots of laughter from the editors. Another ten minutes of this cut and thrust and then, honour satisfied, we would come to some reasonable compromise and life would go on.

One morning he summoned me into his office, rather shyly and ill-at-ease, which was entirely out of character. 'I've got a job for you, mate.'

I expected some story assignment, but no.

'I want you to be my best man at my wedding.'

And so I was.

✧

If Kerry was king at Nine – and there was never a nanosecond of doubt about that – his prime minister, grand vizier and lord high executioner was Sam Chisholm.

New Zealand–born, Sam had famously got a foot on the very bottom rung of the television ladder as a salesman for Johnson's Floor Polish. Hoping to convince Graham Kennedy to plug the stuff on his show, he got down on his hands and knees and polished the star's kitchen floor. It came up brilliantly.

So did Sam. He joined the sales staff at Nine, rocketed skywards and became managing director not long after I went to *A Current Affair*. The media usually described him as a Jimmy Cagney figure, which was reasonably accurate, for he was short and tough and often belligerent. He revelled in the art of the deal, had a mind and a memory like a trap, and radiated more than enough energy to power a small town. It was on his watch that the Nine Network reached the dazzling heights of its glory days in the 1970s and '80s, with a cascade of top-rating shows and a firmament of the biggest stars in the business. God alone knows how he convinced Kerry (he could never have convinced Sir Frank), but Sam recognised that in television you had to spend money to make money, and he went at it with vigour and a showman's flair.

People wanted stars on their television screens. Sam made sure he had them and grew them. He paid them lavishly, massaged their egos and showered their partners with flowers, limousines and vintage champagne. He and Nine's publicity director, the equally ebullient Vicki Jones, could gaily spend tens of thousands of dollars on a single lunch to preview a new program for a few supposedly influential showbiz journalists. The Bollinger and caviar flowed. These were the days when commercial television was a licence to print money, as the old adage had it. 'Winners have parties, losers hold meetings,' Sam was fond of saying.

People who worked off-camera were pretty well looked after too. Sam could not have made even five minutes of television himself and would never have pretended he could, but he valued those who did, aware that the best producers and directors were essential to the operation. And for some reason he seemed to like journalists, which few managers do.

At times he had a curious way of showing it. When I went to Meakin for a pay rise he told me that only Sam could approve it. He arranged a meeting the next morning. I duly turned up in the managing director's office, clad in my best suit, with Meakin at my side, and began to make my case. Sam exploded from his desk, eyes popping.

'Fuck me,' he shouted. 'Why would I want to give you a raise? You! Why are you special?' The tirade went on for about ten minutes, Sam getting louder and more red in the face as he stamped about the room. The impertinence! The greed! The bare-faced cheek! I should be grateful to have a job at all. Did I think Kerry Packer was made of money? The cardboard walls shook. I quailed beneath the onslaught.

Finally he finished. 'Now fuck off out of my office!' He paused and looked skywards, with the heavy sigh of a patient man much put upon. 'Jesus Christ,' he said. 'They'll be coming in the fucking windows next.'

We left. 'I think he actually quite likes you,' Meakin said cheerfully. 'He would have thrown you straight out if he didn't.'

'I'm going to go in those windows,' I said.

'What?'

'I'm going to go in through his fucking window.'

My blood was up. I wanted that pay rise. Sam's office was on the second floor of the studios, overlooking the helicopter landing pad. A narrow ledge ran along the outside of the building beneath his windows, a strip of concrete just big enough to stand on. I would clamber out onto it from the adjoining green room and inch along to his office. Meakin looked at me, eyes widening, and tried to dissuade me. There was no railing. A fall could cripple or kill me.

At thirty you believe you are bulletproof, but still it was terrifying on the ledge. My heart was hammering. I crept along, one foot after the other, not daring to look down. I could see Sam sitting at his desk, back to the window, and I tapped on the glass.

He looked around as if he'd been shot. He sprang from his chair, flung open the window and pulled me inside.

'Pay rise,' I blurted as I collapsed on the floor.

He got down on his knees, laughing uproariously as Meakin entered through the office door. 'All right. You can have your fucking rise,' he chortled. 'How much do you want?' I named a figure. Sam – blessed Sam – added another thousand dollars to it, shook my hand, told me to 'never fucking do that again', and ushered me from the room.

When I resigned from Nine to go to radio he called me to his office again, for a thorough bollocking. 'You ungrateful prick! After all we've done for you. We were gonna make you a star.' He rabbited on for a good ten minutes, eyes boring into mine. I would be a pathetic failure in radio. I must be crazy. Everybody knew that radio itself was fucked, a dying medium. Typical fucking journalist – all ego, no brains. 'And don't think you can come crawling back here, either. Because you'll never work at Nine again.'

Then he paused.

'But good luck, anyway.'

Sam's brusque swagger concealed a good heart. In 2005, when Graham Kennedy was dying, his fortune gone, Noeline Brown and Tony Sattler appealed to Kerry Packer to help with the costs of his nursing care. Gracelessly, inexplicably, Packer refused. Sam and his wife, Sue Ward, quietly sent a cheque for $150,000.

✧

Sue Smith was a beautiful woman, with long brunette hair, a flawless alabaster complexion and eyes like deep, dark pools. If she'd been British, BBC producers would have queued with fat contracts and dripping pens to cast her in a Jane Austen miniseries. But her looks were a cross she had to bear, it being a television rule of thumb that beautiful women had no brains. In fact Sue was extremely smart, and she battled her way up the greasy pole of television journalism at the blokey Nine Network with gritty determination. She reported on the road for *A Current Affair* for a few years, going out in the camera cars and doing the same jobs as the rest of us. Eventually they got her to front the show at the studio desk, making her the first woman to host a national prime-time current-affairs program. Like Caroline Jones, she was a pioneer.

I think that being a single mother drove her on. She had divorced a wealthy grazier and was bringing up their young son, Ben, who was in primary school and to whom she was devoted. That cannot have been easy back in the 1970s, when after-school childcare had barely been heard of and she wasn't getting home until seven-thirty or so. She coped with the help of her mother and sisters.

She also had to fend off men, the legions of trophy hunters who wanted to bed her for the pleasure of boasting about it afterwards. For a few weeks she dated the Sydney celebrity agent and impresario, the late Harry M. Miller, until he assaulted her. She told me about it the next day, still in shock. He had driven her home to Mosman after dinner, drunkenly groping her in the car. When she refused to let him into the house he forced her up against a tree in the dark of the front garden and tried to rip her dress away. She fought back, successfully.

Sue was calm but clearly traumatised by the attack. What should she do about it, she asked me. I was not much help. She could go to the police, but it would be her word against his, I thought. And did she want the hideous publicity and stress of a sensational trial, with all the impact it might have on Ben, who was then about five or six? I am not proud of this – far from it – but the times were different then. The #MeToo movement was decades away. My arguments, well meant, swayed her. Reluctantly, she let it drop. Miller pestered her for weeks afterwards, with persistent telephone calls and deliveries of flowers, which she threw out.

Together Sue and I covered the Granville rail disaster for *ACA*. It was and remains Australia's worst rail accident. On the morning of Tuesday, 18 January 1977, a crowded commuter train from the Blue Mountains came off the rails at speed at Granville, near Parramatta. Tossed like toys, two of the carriages crashed into the supports of a steel and concrete road bridge, bringing it down. Eighty-four people were killed, including an unborn child, either dying instantly beneath the weight of the bridge or later of their injuries. Another 200 or so were injured, some badly.

As the enormity of the tragedy became apparent, *Nine News* and *ACA* geared up for an outside broadcast, no small undertaking with the technology of the time. Vans, cameras, lights and generators were marshalled to the scene, all of them to be deployed where you could see what was happening but without interfering with the rescue.

I had never seen such carnage, not even in Vietnam. The abiding image I have is of a children's train set, smashed by some wilful infant. You could hear the pitiful cries of the trapped and injured, and the roar of oxyacetylene torches trying to cut through to them. Sirens yelped and wailed. Every so often a body would be recovered, or, better, a survivor extracted from the wreckage. This went on all that day and well into the night, beneath burning arc lights. The courage and dedication of the rescuers was extraordinary.

Sue fronted the show at the scene, with me and a couple of other reporters doing the interviews and the pieces to camera. I don't recall that I was traumatised by the death and destruction, although many people there were. Perhaps I had been hardened by Vietnam.

✧

In the winter of 1977 I was phoned by my friend Vincent Smith, who'd been with me at *TDT* and the ill-starred Willesee venture at Ten. He was now working in commercial radio, on air at 2UE with a two-hour show of current affairs and talk that began at noon each weekday. It was rating well, and 2UE's owners, the Lamb family, wanted to extend the format. They wanted to talk to me.

I was taken aback. Radio? *Commercial* radio? It had never crossed my mind. Nine and I were getting on well and I had no particular urge to leave. For all its ups and downs, the Packer Fun Factory, as we called it, was a congenial place to work and my prospects there were bright. Though I had begun my career at ABC Radio, I had done almost nothing in a broadcast studio beyond the voice production lessons they had given us cadets, tedious sessions of reading copy from the newspapers while plum-voiced old soaks taught us to round our vowels.

Vincent was persuasive. The job was fun and the money was good, significantly better than I was making at Nine. On the other hand, it would be a leap into the unknown, at a time when Kerri and I were trying for a first child. I talked it over with her, and we agreed I should at least give them a hearing.

2UE's general manager, Stan Wilmot, asked me to his North Shore home. That at least was familiar territory. Wilmot was a formidable figure, tall and bald, with piercing eyes and an oddly nasal voice struggling to free itself from his adenoids. We sat in his garden to talk. He wanted me to follow Vincent on air for two hours, from two pm until the *Drive* show began at four. The format would be interviews, chat and music from their Top 40 playlist. I recall almost nothing more about the meeting, beyond him swearing me to secrecy. Not a word of his offer must get out, least of all to Channel Nine.

To this day I don't know why they chose me. Nor, really, why I accepted. Flattery and vanity probably had a bit to do with it. 2UE was the glamour radio station in Sydney, top-rating in the crucial breakfast slot with its long-time host Gary O'Callaghan and his talking sparrow. Radio had fascinated me since my teenage years, and now here was a chance to do it. Conveniently, my contract with Nine was coming to an end. I was free to jump. In the back of my mind was a notion, ill-formed, that I should seek a career change every ten years.

I did not want to be doing at forty what I had done at thirty. I was now thirty-one, and the timing seemed right. Odd though it must sound, I was guided by a striking line I had read in one of Arthur Ransome's *Swallows and Amazons* books I had devoured as a child: 'Grab a chance and you won't be sorry for what might have been.' It's a thought that inspires me still.

Wilmot gave me a few days to think it over. Kerri was for it, although cautiously, playing the devil's advocate, sensibly concerned that I could fall flat on my face. Vincent kept pushing me.

So I went for it. Hands trembling as I dialled his number, I called Wilmot back and accepted the money he was offering, which was indeed a healthy advance on my television pay. Stardom!

Working out my notice at Nine, I spent the next couple of weeks tormented by doubt, convinced that I had made a catastrophic career mistake. Sam Chisholm's harangue did not help. On and off, through sleepless nights, I dithered about changing my mind and pulling out. Then I had doubts about my doubts. So I took the line of least resistance and just kept going.

I have been like this after every contract I have signed since, even ones I badly wanted, and for serious seven-figure money. After the nervous tension of the negotiations and the euphoria of clinching the deal comes the let-down. Perverse though it may sound, the bigger the salary involved, the bigger the crunch. Pathetic, I know. Ridiculous. Poor petal, they're throwing money at him. But my post-contract blues can be almost an ache in the pit of the stomach. What have I done? *What the fuck have I done?* Perhaps they've screwed me. Perhaps I've made a disastrous blunder that will end in tears. I have signed on the dotted line and I will now have to live with it for the duration, come hell or high water. It is a melancholy feeling, an intimation of vulnerability. Fortunately, I get over it.

'Wear a suit and tie,' said Vincent. 'The Lambs insist on suits and ties.'

15

Top 40, news, weather and sport

THE FIRST THING I did on my first ever radio program was play a record at the wrong speed. The trauma haunts me to this day. I can still have nightmares about it.

As the two o'clock news and weather ended, the panel operator working with me and watching from the adjoining studio played a station identification jingle – 'The Brighter 2UE, Channel 95!' – followed by a burst of theme music. Then he waved his hand – the cue for me to start talking. The 'On Air' light glowed red.

'Good afternoon. I'm Mike Carlton,' I squeaked. 'It's good to be with you.'

The turntable was spinning. All I had to do was take my finger off the disc and bring up the sound by opening the fader, a sliding switch.

Disaster struck. Too fast. Those long-gone studio turntables, about the diameter of a small car tyre, had three speeds for three different types of vinyl record. I fired this one off at 78 rpm when it should have been at 45. The song was 'Help Is on Its Way', the current hit for Glenn Shorrock and the Little River Band. It sounded like a sack of fighting ferrets. Almost catatonic with shock, hands trembling, I managed to pull the fader down, babble some apology, adjust the speed on the turntable, re-cue the disc, bring up the fader again and get it off at the correct speed. Jesus Christ. Everyone at the station would have been listening to the newbie, not to mention the audience out in the big, wide world. After that, the only way to go was up.

✧

The 2UE studios then were in a low, white box of a building in North Sydney, a significant improvement on the ramshackle cottage I had left behind at Nine. The owners, the famously secretive Lamb family, were not renowned for spending money either, but the place was spacious enough and, unusually for a media operation, as neat and ordered as an army barracks. It was said that Stewart Lamb, the family patriarch and company chairman, knew exactly how many stones there were in the gravel driveway and would complain if any were misplaced.

He and his flock dwelled in hermitic seclusion on the upper reaches of the North Shore, so splendidly isolated that nobody actually knew how many Lambs there were. Stewart would occasionally tear himself away from his daily game of lawn bowls to visit the station, but he contrived to remain invisible. I never once laid eyes on him. Occasionally, though, an edict would come down *ex cathedra* (if that's the right term for a dynasty so dourly Presbyterian). Announcers are to wear ties while broadcasting. The chairman has noticed that desks are becoming untidy. Staff who drink at the Rag and Famish Hotel at lunchtime will not be permitted back in the building. This was a particular blow: the Rag, a short stroll down the street, had a sunny beer garden and did a good counter lunch. 2UE's Keeper of the Gravel Driveway and Chief Tidier-Upper, an officious functionary named Maurie Jacobsen, was sometimes despatched to the pub to catch delinquent staff in any impromptu bacchanalian orgy. Peak edict arrived when Stewart's ears were assailed by the daring innovation of a young woman journalist reading the news during the breakfast show. Women readers have no credibility, came the proclamation. After long deliberation, the problem was solved by putting them on after ten in the morning, when the chairman would be lining up on the bowling green.

There were big photos of the announcers in the foyer, and my beaming mug joined the line-up after a week or so, an exciting moment. I also got my own desk. My first task was to learn to operate a studio control panel, with its daunting array of switches, knobs, dials and little lights and flickering meters. It might have been mission control at Cape Canaveral. They gave me two weeks to get the hang of it and practise before I went on air. The panel operator would play the recorded commercials and the station jingles, and handle some of the fiddly technical bits like crossing to the news and going on and off delay. I would be given the music to play myself, would juggle the scripts for the commercials to be read live, and choose the phone lines for interviews and talkback calls.

Above all, I would have to watch the clock. Time is god in radio, and a malicious, unforgiving god at that. It's done in minutes and seconds; as the hour approaches – or 'the top of the clock', as it's called – you're doing hasty mental arithmetic to make sure you can fit everything in. The 2UE news was immovable because it was syndicated to a network of country radio stations, all of which were expecting to get it on time to the split second. Get the sums wrong and you might have a song crashing into the news bulletin, to the intense and sarcastic fury of everyone at the network, or – a cardinal sin – you might have to drop a commercial or two. With experience the timing becomes second nature, but in the beginning it was scary.

There were some experienced mountaineers to help me. The drivetime announcer was a bloke named Peter Bosley, maybe ten years older than me, and one of those thorough-going all-rounders who had done the long grind of country radio before hitting the big smoke. He knew a studio like the back of his hand, in his sleep. He was also kind enough and patient enough to impart his hard-won knowledge to a blow-in journalist, hovering behind me while I fiddled with the panel, the headphones, the microphones and the four big turntables. 'The Boz', as everyone knew him, was a laid-back, easygoing professional, and I think of him warmly and gratefully.

The hardest trick to master was the delay system, and there was no getting around it. On talkback radio you are required to have it by federal law, to avoid any unexpected frightfulness blasting on to the airwaves. In theory it's simple enough. There's a delay of at least seven seconds between what the announcer or the caller says and what the listener hears. Now it's done in a digital box of tricks, but in earlier days it was just magnetic audio tape, playing on an endless loop. The tape recorded the sound, moved along and then played it to air seven seconds later. If some talkback caller said 'fuck' – or, worse, defamed the state premier as a thieving criminal – you had seven seconds to get rid of it and go live.

You do this by hitting the 'kill button', coloured red and about the size of a matchbox. Easy enough, you would think, but not so. Because it was used only rarely, you had to remember where the bloody thing was on the desk in front of you. Then you would find, invariably, that it was buried beneath a pile of scripts, newspapers, record covers, coffee cups and ashtrays. The seconds tick away. The panel operator also had a kill button, but only as a backup. He usually sat back to enjoy the entertaining spectacle of the announcer panicking.

In all my career, the closest I ever got to losing it was when I was doing a double act, sharing the 2UE morning show with Sue Smith as co-host. It was talkback, taking listener calls, discussing great Australian cricket captains. One clown decided to try it on.

'And we have Fred on the line. Hello, Fred.'

'G'day, Mike, g'day, Sue. I reckon that Ian Chappell was the greatest cricket captain we ever had. He could bat, he could bowl a bit of leg break and he never lost a Test series.'

'Anything else, Fred?' asked Sue.

'Yeah. I'd love to suck his big fat cock.'

Sue recoiled as if she had been smacked in the mouth with a wet fish. We stared at each other in terror. Had he just said what we thought he'd said? Yes, he had. I lunged for the kill button, which was, inevitably, buried. Ever the trouper, Sue decided she should keep talking brightly, as if nothing had happened. 'Thank you so much for your call,' she chirruped.

This was exactly the wrong thing to do. I needed silence. Shaking like a leaf, I found the button and hit it with a nanosecond to spare, just before 'his big fat' got to air.

Yet for all the pitfalls and nasties, I was beginning to enjoy myself. Radio is a seductive medium for its performers, immensely soothing to the ego when you get it right. It pumps you up. And I knew I was getting better with each passing week. There was another reason for happiness, too. Kerri was pregnant. She met me at the station one day to give me the news as I finished work, her eyes afire. We clung to each other in ecstasy. Life was perfect.

The thought of reading commercials troubled me at first. It was so alien – so far removed from my ingrained ABC training – that I shrank from it. George Orwell had famously said that advertising was 'the rattling of a stick inside a swill bucket'. Should a journalist be flogging coffee and car tyres, cornflakes and cat food? It was explained to me, somewhat acidly, that this was the business 2UE was in. That's what paid my salary, and if I didn't like it, etc. I succumbed to that overwhelming logic but I struck a reasonable deal with 2UE, one that I kept to throughout my radio career: I would rattle the swill stick up to a point, but I would not read commercials or endorse products which might conceivably lose money for my listeners or screw them over in any of a hundred ways. So I did no ads for payday loan sharks, fad weight-loss shonks or dodgy car dealers. Years later, when I had more clout in the business, I had it written into my contracts that I could decline to read any commercial or endorse any product that I believed would 'detract from my standing' as an ethical journalist and commentator.

Quite a few times I did just that. In the late 1980s an outfit called Estate Mortgages was one of radio's biggest and noisiest national advertisers. They ran a $6-million campaign at their peak, promising 'mum and dad investors' fabulous returns of 18 per cent and more. Send them your savings and they would make you rich. Instinct and experience told me they were as crook as Rookwood, and so, despite intense pressure from a sales department keen for a slice of those millions, I refused to touch them.

Others did not. Alan Jones read Estate Mortgage commercials with his usual vigorous personal endorsements almost up to the day in 1990 that they crashed in ruins, owing around $170 million to a string of banks. Many of his listeners, pensioners and self-funded retirees, were among thousands of Australians who lost their life savings. The two Estate Mortgage bosses went to jail. 'I was constantly assured there was nothing wrong,' Jones huffed to his audience. 'There's a limit to what you can find out.'[100]

Well, yes. But some in radio are slow learners. Less than a decade later, a similar Queensland-based operation called Storm Financial used high-profile rugby league radio commentators to flog their equally dodgy investments. They too went bust spectacularly, costing more listeners more millions. Sadly, there are plenty of other examples.

✧

There is a pecking order at commercial radio stations. It's determined by the time of your on-air shift, your ratings and the advertising bucks you pull in. Radio's biggest audiences are at breakfast, when the nation is waking up to go about its business. Quite literally, millions of radios are switched on each day for the seven o'clock news, sport, weather and traffic. People time their early mornings to the rhythm and pace of breakfast shows: 'The seven-fifteen sports report – time I was in the shower . . . Eight o'clock, out the front door.' A top-rating breakfast program in any capital city is a goldmine, attracting millions of dollars in advertising revenue. Most of those breakfast listeners are creatures of habit and probably won't touch the dial, staying tuned to the same station all day, or switching it on again when they drive home. This is especially true of talk listeners. Music listeners can be more fickle: if they don't like a song they'll often switch stations. So a successful breakfast presenter is paid truckloads and treated like a god, a rainmaker. Every whim and wish is indulged; mortal sins and star tantrums are forgiven. (Although not forgotten. If the star ever falls from radio heaven, those old crimes can be dragged out and used in evidence.)

The rainmaker when I arrived at 2UE was Gary O'Callaghan, who had been fronting the breakfast show since 1956. 'Uncle Gary', everyone called him. His big break in radio was unique, founded on one of the great upheavals of Australia's Cold War. In 1954, barely out of his teens, still wet behind the ears, he was the only radio reporter at Sydney Airport when the famous Petrov affair exploded into public view. Vladimir Petrov, an intelligence officer at the Soviet embassy in Canberra, had defected. In Sydney, an angry crowd gathered at the airport as Petrov's terrified wife, Evdokia, was hustled on board an airliner by KGB agents determined to get her back to Moscow. By a stroke of luck, Gary was there with a tape recorder. It was big international news. His report – 'The Russian envoys are leading her up the stairs of this Qantas Constellation' – was heard around the world.

By 1977 'The Gary O'Callaghan Breakfast Show' was a rigid format of news, time calls, sport, Top 40 music hits, more time calls, traffic reports, time calls again, and of course the talking sparrow. Gary glued it all together with patter that today sounds teeth-grindingly hokey: 'This is the brighter 2UE, best yet on your radio set, coming to you from the sweetest city in the South Seas, number one from Spain to Balmain, Tokyo to Ultimo . . .'

It was identical every day, unbending. He started at five-thirty am, bidding a cheery good morning to fifty or so regular listeners – service-station attendants, plumbers, cops, hotel maids, the signal station workers at South Head, and all of them named. 'G'day to you, Merv . . .' We used to joke that you could replay Tuesday's program on Wednesday; as long as the weather was the same, nobody would notice. Car accidents were treated with great reverence. So was the arrival of any Qantas flight from overseas. While a song was playing, Gary would be manically eavesdropping on the police, fire, ambulance and air traffic control radios. He'd report what he heard: 'And here comes Qantas flight QF2 flying in from lovely London and sweet Singapore, the big, beautiful Boeing jumbo with Captain Barry Bloggs in the left-hand seat and about to dangle the Dunlops . . .' Gary positively worshipped police officers in general and the Highway Patrol in particular, and they returned the love, giving him rides in their squad cars and calling him with tips and gossip.

Corny though it was, it rated its head off. And it was stiff with commercials, so much so that the couple of Top 40 songs he managed to squeeze into each half-hour were often edited and shortened. Nobody seemed to notice. Gary led the field, with daylight second, although the competition was not as stiff then as it is now. There were only six commercial radio stations in Sydney, all on the AM band.

Commercial FM radio did not appear until 1980. But he was number one in Sydney radio for something like a quarter of a century, an institution.

Curiously, for all his success, Gary made nothing like the money being paid to other stars such as John Laws, Ward Austin or Bob Rogers. He could have held 2UE and the Lambs over a barrel but, for whatever reason, chose not to. He had a far bigger audience than the others, but it was Laws who tooled around town and up to the showpiece country farm in the chauffeured Rolls-Royce, not Gary. He was content with a Holden Statesman, provided by one of his sponsors and updated every two years. It, too, was equipped with a police radio so he could enjoy the after-work thrill of rushing off to rubberneck at a car crash. Less happily, Gary had the habit of listening to 2UE around the clock and snitching to the program manager if he caught one of us lesser mortals stuffing up a time call or playing the wrong bit of tape in a news bulletin. This did not endear him to his workmates.

✧

I began to feel comfortable in the studio as I got the hang of it all, then came to do it instinctively. That meant I could relax and concentrate on what I was actually saying on air. At the same time, I was experimenting with my voice, trying to give it more depth and oomph. If I was going to be in this radio thing for the long haul, best to give it a good shot. Doing a short reporter's piece into a radio or television microphone is one thing; it doesn't require a big voice, although it's a bonus if you have one, as Peter Harvey did at *Nine News*. His was so deep and resonant that they gave him the nickname 'Four Balls'. But spending hours at a studio microphone is something else again, and you have to work on it.

The gold standard was John Laws. 'Golden Tonsils', one of his media nicknames, was well deserved. His warm, rich baritone has never been bettered on Australian radio. Yes, he was born with it, but he polished it over the years, like an antique violin. The technique is difficult to describe. The voice has to come not from the back of your throat or somewhere up in the sinuses, but from deep in the pit of your stomach. You breathe it up, sort of. If you get it right, you can almost feel it happening down there. That gives you tone and timbre. Opera singers know the same sensation.

I listened to John a lot, even before I knew him, and I am happy to acknowledge that I learned a good deal from him. Which is not to say I wanted to imitate him or to sound like him. It just made sense to adapt the master's techniques for my own use. Another pro I learned from was Ken Sparkes, a genial former disc jockey who was Sydney's voiceover king. Ken made a good living recording commercials and doing the on-air promos for Nine and 2UE in a voice almost as rich as John's, with impeccable inflexion and timing. A thirty-second commercial has to run for thirty seconds, not twenty-nine or thirty-one. Ken got it right first try, every time. It sounds simple but not many people can do it.

The next trick was to get light and shade, which is also difficult to describe. It can be a simple matter of raising or lowering your voice at the right moments. Or speaking more slowly and deliberately . . . or more quickly and urgently . . . or learning how and when to pause for a second or two. The well-timed pause can draw your listener towards you, and adds emphasis to what you say next. John was a master of that effect too. You learn to treat the microphone not as a tool but as an instrument to be played.

As I settled in to the afternoon program on 2UE, I began experimenting with what I came to call 'funnies' – little bursts of satire or comedy as a comment on the day's news. Running for a minute or less, they did the same job as a newspaper editorial cartoon, skewering the ridiculous, the outright wrong or the just plain crazy. After a while I came to use them to start the program. I'd had a feel for mimicry and accents since I was a kid. At *TDT* I had often done Billy McMahon's querulous quaver in satirical sketches, and Gough Whitlam's breathy boom. On radio it was open slather. I put in some work to pick up the jerky, hesitant speech of Malcolm Fraser. Bob Hawke's guttural explosions were a gift, as was the hoarse croak that Neville Wran was left with after a bungled throat operation. To my delight, I discovered that 2UE had a huge archive of sound effects on record, relics of the long-gone days of radio drama. You could find anything from a nuclear explosion to a Battle of Britain dogfight to a whistling canary. It was a goldmine. I mixed my own effects, spinning the discs on cue as I read the scripts – another art to learn.

Writing the stuff was fun too. A large part of the trick of mimicking a well-known voice is to capture the patterns of speech and the familiar catchphrases. Bob Hawke, for example, used the phrase 'in respect' a lot, generally following it up with a shotgun blast of multisyllabic verbiage: 'In respect of the underlying assumption of your basic question . . .' Neville Wran's common verbal tic was: 'Let me say just this . . .' Fraser's speech was peppered with 'ums' and 'ahs' and 'look, er . . . you know . . . um . . .'

These funnies were my first steps towards what would eventually be my signature act, *Friday News Review*, a weekly satire on the news. I have kept none of this stuff I did in my first stint at 2UE, and I remember almost nothing of it. One stuck in my head, though, a two-minute song I wrote in early 1978, when Fraser controversially appointed Sir John Kerr as Australia's ambassador to UNESCO in Paris. The idea came to me out of the blue, words set to the music of the can-can (which classical music buffs will know as Jacques Offenbach's spirited 'Galop Infernal' from *Orpheus in the Underworld*). I sang it in Kerr's high-pitched squawk. This was the chorus:

> Oh, I am the former Governor-General of Australia
> Here I am in Paris, what a lovely place to be.
> Thank you, Malcolm Fraser,
> For the cushy job you found for me
> In Paris, France.

It worked a treat. Listeners rang to demand a replay. Whitlam's office asked for a copy. John Conde, a 2UE executive and the son-in-law of Stewart Lamb, came into the studio to tell me it was the funniest thing he had ever heard. For me, this was a milestone. I had the warm, inner glow of realising that I was onto something. Funnies might be worth pursuing.

✧

The patriarch. James Carlton emigrated from Ireland in 1841 and prospered in the colony of New South Wales.

The matriarch. Ellen Carlton bore thirteen children, which might explain that rather haunted face.

Pine Brush, the homestead James and Ellen built at Dungog in the New South Wales Hunter Valley.

Jimmy Carlton, aged nineteen, in London on the way to the Amsterdam Olympics.

On your marks, get set . . .

. . . go!

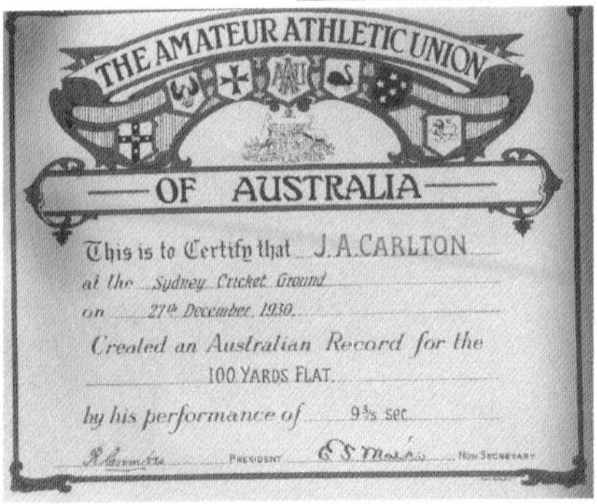
THE AMATEUR ATHLETIC UNION

OF AUSTRALIA

This is to Certify that J.A.CARLTON
at the Sydney Cricket Ground
on 27th December 1930.
Created an Australian Record for the
100 YARDS FLAT.
by his performance of 9 3/5 sec.
President Hon Secretary

The record breaker at the Sydney Cricket Ground, 1930.

Father Jim Carlton celebrates
his first Mass, 24 July 1939.
(Fairfax Images)

Jim and Enid's wedding day, April 1945.

Top left: Backyard television at Chatswood, aged about twelve.

Top right: Patrol Leader Michael Carlton, aged fourteen, a Boy Scout 'clean in thought, word and deed'.

Left: Regimental Sergeant Major of the Barker College Cadet Corps, 1962, aged sixteen. I never drew the sword in anger.

My first offer to join the latte-sipping Green-Left's Long March through Our Institutions.

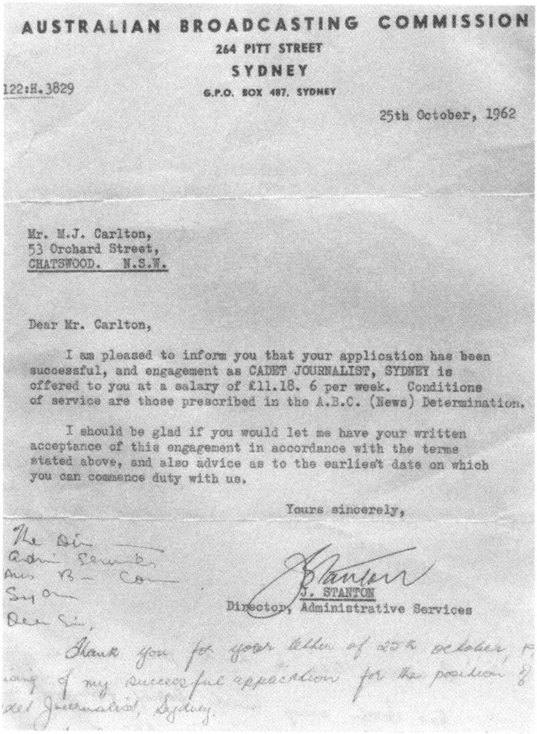

AUSTRALIAN BROADCASTING COMMISSION
264 PITT STREET
SYDNEY
G.P.O. BOX 487, SYDNEY

122:H.3829

25th October, 1962

Mr. M.J. Carlton,
53 Orchard Street,
CHATSWOOD. N.S.W.

Dear Mr. Carlton,

I am pleased to inform you that your application has been successful, and engagement as CADET JOURNALIST, SYDNEY is offered to you at a salary of £11.18. 6 per week. Conditions of service are those prescribed in the A.B.C. (News) Determination.

I should be glad if you would let me have your written acceptance of this engagement in accordance with the terms stated above, and also advice as to the earliest date on which you can commence duty with us.

Yours sincerely,

J. STANTON
Director, Administrative Services

N.S.W. POLICE PRESS, RADIO & TELEVISION
PASS No. 1705

MR. M. J. CARLTON.
Whose Signature and Photograph appear hereunder is an accredited Representative employed on the staff of

AUSTRALIAN BROADCASTING COMMISSION.

EDITOR OR MANAGER

ON PRODUCTION OF THIS PASS THE HOLDER IS AUTHORISED TO ENTER PUBLIC AREAS OR LINES HELD BY POLICE, AND SHOULD BE AFFORDED EVERY REASONABLE ASSISTANCE IN THE DISCHARGE OF HIS DUTIES.

SECRETARY, POLICE DEPARTMENT
7 FEB 1963, 19

PASS NOT TRANSFERABLE

Signature:

In the event of termination of the employment in respect of which this pass is issued, the pass is void and must be returned to Police Headquarters.

First press pass. Useful only for impressing mates at the pub.

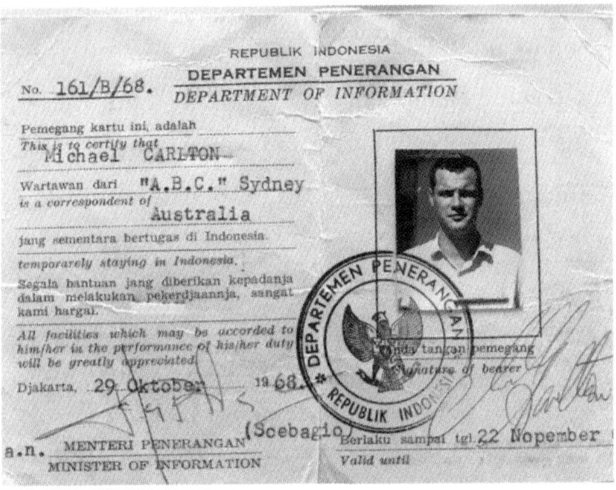

REPUBLIK INDONESIA
DEPARTEMEN PENERANGAN
No. 161/B/68. DEPARTMENT OF INFORMATION

Pemegang kartu ini, adalah
This is to certify that
Michael CARLTON
Wartawan dari "A.B.C." Sydney
is a correspondent of
Australia
jang sementara bertugas di Indonesia.
temporarely staying in Indonesia.
Segala bantuan jang diberikan kepadanja dalam melakukan pekerdjaannja, sangat kami hargai.
All facilities which may be accorded to him/her in the performance of his/her duty will be greatly appreciated.
Djakarta, 29 Oktober 19 68.
(Soebagio)
a.n. MENTERI PENERANGAN
MINISTER OF INFORMATION
Tanda tangan pemegang
Signature of bearer
Berlaku sampai tgl. 22 Nopember
Valid until

Foreign correspondent's press pass for the Soeharto regime in Jakarta.

ABC Bureau Chief Jakarta, 1969. (ABC TV)

1967, with ABC Jakarta journalist Hidayat Djajamihardja, whose talents saved me from foundering without trace.

The foreign correspondent with his mother in Singapore, 1968: her first ever overseas trip.

'Escape', our band in Jakarta. In my Afro period *c.* 1969, with (*from left*) Johan (bass), Bram (lead guitar), Iwan (drums) and Rudi (rhythm guitar).

Probably doing a Rolling Stones cover, with Johan on bass.

The beard is Ed Blanche, Jakarta correspondent for the Associated Press of America and great mate.

Accredited to the Yanks in Vietnam. This gave me the status of a US Army major.

With Derek McKendry, Kiwi-born ABC cameraman and seriously good mate. Wearing stylish US Marine fatigues at a patrol base on the Vietnam-Cambodia border, 1970.

Hitching a ride in a US Army 'Huey' chopper.

With brother Peter and Mum, back home on leave. 'Elbows off the table, Michael.'

This Day Tonight, 1973, with Peter Luck and Bill Peach. (ABC TV)

Kerri Whiting, medical scientist from Wagga Wagga. We married in September 1972.

The kids at home in Turramurra, on Sydney's North Shore. James was about ten, Alex around twelve.

A first shot at commercial TV, with Mike Willesee, 1974.

Early days at 2UE. The cheesy grin conceals my stark terror at contemplating the bewildering studio control panel.

At 2UE, with the beautiful and talented Sue Smith.

The mad whirl of the 1980s, with the Rev. Dr Doug Mulray of 2MMM. I have no idea why we were dressed as bishops. (Newspix)

Above: A newspaper ad with Gibbo at 2GB, about 1980. The copy was gibberish from the ad agency.

Left: Joining the *Sydney Morning Herald* as a columnist, 1984.

With my puppets, conceived by cartoonist Patrick Cook for my *Friday News Review* slot on *Willesee at Seven.*

London calling. And a British Radio Academy award for Best Talk Breakfast Show, 1993.

Our UK home in the 1990s, in the rural depths of the Surrey gin belt. Not too much had changed at East Clandon's Old Post House since this 1907 postcard.

The gorgeous Morag Ramsay and I married in 2006, the year I turned sixty.

Mike and Fitz (pre-bandana) at 2UE, 2006. (Fairfax Images)

The infamous Woolloomooloo lunch with Lawsie.

Lachlan Michael McInnes Carlton joins the world, 22 October 2008.

Lachlan and the E-Type.

Morag and Lachlan at the Sydney Football Stadium, the Wallabies *v* Scotland.

The wave ski at Palm Beach. Board riders call it a 'goat boat'.

My daughter, Alexandra Louise, was born in August 1978. Kerri and I were as deliriously excited as new parents can be. I was present at the birth, at the old Royal Hospital for Women in Paddington. That was unusual then – obstetricians were still wary of permitting fathers into the labour ward, fearing that they would just get in the way or, worse, faint at the sight of the messy bits and drop to the floor. I did neither. I cherish the memory of my wife's courage in grinding her way through the pain, and then of the radiant ecstasy of love that suffused her face when she got to hold the baby. I was in exultant awe of what we had done. The child was beautiful, and still is. On radio that afternoon I announced her birth with the Stevie Wonder song 'Isn't She Lovely'. Parenthood would be a work in progress, especially for me. With no fatherly example to follow, I figured I would have to make it up as I went along. When in doubt we consulted the guru of the day, the American paediatrician Dr Benjamin Spock and his blockbusting bestseller, *Baby and Child Care*. Changing nappies was daunting, less for the contents than the terror of stabbing my wee girl with a safety pin.

✧

Gradually, my ratings began to improve. It was hardly a stratospheric leap, more of a continual nudge upwards, but whatever I was doing was working. Mid-afternoons are a bit of a dead time in radio. People are at work, or out shopping, or picking up the kids from school, and radio is the last thing on their minds. The big audiences begin to switch on again at around four pm, as first the tradies and the schoolteachers begin to drive home, followed by the white-collar workers from five until around seven. But the afternoon shift is expected to pull its weight. I was going okay, and my bosses seemed happy enough.

For commercial radio, ratings are life and death. The ABC likes to pretend to be aloof from the vulgar rat-race, but the figures are followed there just as keenly, a measure of the size of the audiences for its stations and its individual presenters. For commercial stations, though, it's that and more. With high ratings, the salespeople can sell ads – for which they are paid a commission. Life at a top-rating metropolitan station can be relatively easy, with advertisers eager to buy airtime. The money rolls in. Stations at the bottom of the heap have an endless grind to attract sponsors, their balance sheets hovering on the edge of deep pools of red ink, or falling right in.

There are now eight radio ratings surveys a year in Australia's capital cities, with eight sets of results. In my early days it was four, run by a market research company called McNair Anderson. About a thousand diaries were distributed to households in Sydney to capture a cross-section of listeners in working-class, middle-class and wealthy suburbs, areas of younger people and older people and so on. Families were asked to keep a record of the stations they listened to over a week. Then more diaries would go out to other households. That was the theory. It relied on McNair Anderson getting the cross-section right, and on those selected families to keep a conscientious record. By and large, it worked well enough. Sometimes there were glitches. A sudden sharp lurch in a station's figures, either up or down, could well mean a bad diary drop: too many books distributed in the wrong suburbs. Either way, you had to live with it. There was no alternative. McNair Anderson's figures were final. Outside professional sport, few industries and few workers have such an emphatic, public scorecard for their performance. The survey results are seized on by the newspapers, usually with lurid headlines. A win or an improvement brings joy, in floods of relief. A loss or a drop is crushing.

The tension on ratings day was gut-grinding. The air around the radio station would be heavy with both fear and optimism. Some people faked nonchalance. Others were physically sick at the thought of the figures about to arrive, rushing to toilets to throw up. Before the era of internet and email, the results would start to come in at around ten am, always on Tuesdays. Usually there was a gathering in the boardroom. The general manager and his senior salespeople, the program manager, the news and sports directors, most of the on-air presenters, and maybe one or two of the wire benders – the engineers – slumped around the table, slurping coffee, chain-smoking, cracking feeble jokes and picking nervously at a gluey pile of croissants and Danish pastries.

First came the phone call from McNair, always answered by

the general manager. The room would fall silent, everyone intently watching the boss's face.

A smile was good. 'We've picked up two per cent! Still number one!'

The room would erupt, like winning football fans at a grand final.

A frown, a grimace or a sigh was bad. 'We're down two per cent, coming in at number four.'

'Fuck!' A heavy silence would fall, everyone avoiding each other's eyes and returning glumly to their desks.

There was more to come – pages of statistics totally meaningless to the uninitiated, but fodder for the program and sales staff. In the media, you only ever see the headline figures: '3AW is Melbourne's number one station, with a rating of 13 per cent. Ross Stevenson and John Burns are the breakfast kings, on 13.5 per cent.' Those figures are a percentage of the *available* audience – of people actually listening to radio. But there is also a bunch of other stuff grouping listeners by age, by the sessions they listen to and the amount of time they spend listening, by when and how often they turn you on and off, and so on. It is numbingly tedious, but those stats are important for advertisers choosing a station to flog their products. To use 3AW as an example again: its audience is overwhelmingly elderly, above the age of fifty-five. It's worthwhile selling them retirement villages and arthritis remedies, but pointless trying to load them up with jeans and rock concerts.

The end can be swift and merciless. A low-rating presenter, especially one falling behind the rest of the station line-up, will suddenly be switched to the graveyard shift of midnight to dawn – or, more likely, axed altogether. The next head to roll might be the program manager, the executive responsible for the tone and sound of the station. Salespeople who have not been meeting their revenue targets will be hung out to dry. In a full-on bloodbath – with nosediving audiences, sales figures and profits – the general manager will be ordered to turn in the keys to his Mercedes-Benz and leave the building immediately, the contents of his desk to be forwarded later.

This was not always bad. One station manager who had been a particular pain in the arse at 2UE ended up driving a cab; what a pleasure it was a year later when I flagged him down in Macquarie Street. Radio lavishly rewards the successful. It is brutal to the losers. There are few happy farewells.

✧

After a year on the afternoon shift the station added Sunday mornings to my roster: three hours on air from nine am. This meant a six-day working week, but it was worth the extra grind. 2UE had a lot of weekend listeners for music, sport and weather, and this got me into the ears of people who would not have heard me from Monday to Friday.

I added to the mix by replaying the funnies I had done during the week, and I found I was enjoying myself. It was no longer straight journalism – far from it – although I used many of the journalistic skills I had honed over the years. Instead, it was entertainment, in the most direct and intimate medium of all. I found I wanted the approval of an audience. If it wasn't quite the intoxicating smell of the greasepaint and the roar of the crowd, it was heading in that direction, and seductive with it.

A newspaper story or a television program is a collective effort, requiring a lot of people to put it together. In newspapers there is a complex editorial process before one word reaches a reader. In television, even live-to-air, the thing has almost always been planned, researched, scripted and edited before it reaches your lounge room. Almost always, the elements of immediacy or surprise have been drained and filleted. And there is, in those two media, a barrier between the content producer and the consumer. The newspaper reader or television viewer has no meaningful contact with whoever is churning out the stuff. This has broken down to some extent with the arrival of the internet and social media, where anyone can get on a website to fire off a comment on a story or TV show, or just troll away on Twitter, but the barrier is still there.

In radio, you are pretty much naked and on your own. There is no editorial process between your mouth and the microphone. And that's the thrill of it. The danger of it. You are out there, live on the airwaves every day for three hours straight. What you say is what your audience gets, for better or worse. And, love it or hate it, that audience can and will let you know what it is thinking, often within seconds. The telephone switchboard will light up with listeners calling to praise or criticise – and, sometimes, to hurl abuse. This is enormously satisfying if you have done something they like; it can be shattering if you've offended them.

After Sundays came the breakthrough. The station offered me the morning show, weekdays from nine to midday.

This was a big leap. Mornings on radio are a plum gig, regarded as second only to breakfast in importance. Back then the shift was sometimes known as 'housewives', because that was who made up most of the audience, although this has changed as society has changed. Where breakfast radio was and is a sort of broadcast alarm clock, kick-starting the listener's day, morning shows on talk radio are there for companionship. Not counting those in their cars, a breakfast listener probably hears you for only about twelve minutes all up, as he or she moves from bed, to shower, to kitchen and out the door. Morning listeners might well be there for the whole three hours, if not the whole day. And if it's a successful talk show it can be networked around the country, chiefly on rural and regional radio stations, which means another truckload of money for all concerned.

John Laws was the morning giant on 2UW, way out ahead of the pack. UW is no more, but it was then in fierce competition with 2UE. In his late forties, no longer the hip young disc jockey, John was into his second radio incarnation as the social oracle and housewives' sex symbol. Straight out of the nine o'clock news he would kick off with his iconic opening theme, 'El Presidente', a blast of trumpets and crash-bang-thump from Herb Alpert's Tijuana Brass. Augmented with sound effects and a bit of reverb, it hit the decibel scale somewhere between the eruption of Krakatoa and a *corrida de toros* in Fascist Spain. 'Hello, world. This . . .' *long pause* '. . . is John Laws.'

And he was off and away, socking it to his adoring female fans with a unique blend of courtly gallantry – 'Yes, ma'am' – and seductive schmooze – 'Well, that's very kind of you, sweetheart. You're lovely to say that.' Women who behaved themselves – i.e. those who rang Lawsie on air to tell him they loved him – were sent bunches of roses, perfume and autographed books of the impenetrable 'poetry' he was writing by night. 'Oh, John, you're wonderful. You've made my day.' Blokes, less frequently, got bottles of whichever bourbon whiskey John was plugging at the time.

Occasionally a woman would call the show with a tale of tragedy and announce she was on the point of suicide, at which John would swing into action. Ambulances and the police would be summoned, Lawsie would plead and cajole the woman into staying on the phone until help arrived, and the rest of the audience thrilled to the drama of it all. Most of these callers just craved attention and knew how to get it. Shock and schlock – it worked a treat. John had a finely tuned sense of exactly what his audience wanted and he gave it to them with bells on. His show rated its head off and the money rolled in. This was what I was up against.

2UE gave me a bit of extra firepower. They suggested a double act. *A Current Affair* had closed at Nine, and Sue Smith was ready and available to join me in the mornings. The station hired her, hoping that a woman's voice would leaven my blokeyness and add a dimension different to the Laws output. Sue knew nothing about radio and, as many TV people do, assumed it would be a breeze, a stroll in the park compared to the demands of appearing on the box. Just words, no pictures – it had to be easier. In fact, talk radio is infinitely harder than television, requiring intense concentration for hours on end and chewing up material far faster than TV ever does. To her credit, Sue went at it on a fast learning curve.

The station also hired a full-time producer to line up the guests and steer the show. David Lyle was one of the most extraordinary characters I have met in the media. The word 'urbane' was invented for him. Tall, fair-haired, sleepy-eyed and languid, he sailed serenely through life with a detached amusement, as if the human race and all its failings and foibles had been invented for his private entertainment. Nothing disturbed his equilibrium. I saw him angry only rarely, and a terrible spectacle it was. Our careers would intersect several times over the years, before he took himself off to America and scaled the craggy heights of the Murdoch television empire. Scalps on his belt included four years as boss of the National Geographic Channel worldwide.

David was a couple of years younger than me. Unusually for a media junkie, he graduated from Sydney University with a degree in geology, and he did spend some brief time banging rocks with hammers, but it soon palled. At university he had written a few scripts and sketches for *The Mavis Bramston Show*, a hugely popular satirical comedy program aired on the Seven Network in the mid-1960s. *Bramston*, as everyone called it, had a cast of the top comedy actors of the day – June Salter, Barry Creyton, Noeline Brown, Gordon Chater, Ron Frazer, Carol Raye and more – and it did for television comedy what *This Day Tonight* did for current affairs. The experience must have been priceless. Low down the pecking order though he was, David was bitten by the media bug, which meant, almost inevitably, fetching up at the Nine Network. There he worked as a producer on *The Mike Walsh Show*, lining up guests, writing scripts and questions for the star, holding hands, soothing egos. Tiring of television, at least for the while, he came to 2UE.

Time has erased my memory of much of what we did, although a couple of things stand out. There was the last ever media interview with Johnny O'Keefe, the nuggetty, shouty Eastern Suburbs boy who had pretty much started Australian rock'n'roll single-handedly in the late 1950s. Not long after he talked to us, he died of a drug overdose, in October 1978. Johnny was never much of a singer. When you listen back to his records you can hear the bum notes dropping like bricks. But he was an extraordinary showman, a human dynamo in stage suits of leopard print and gold lamé, and a local boy much loved. His ABC television show, *Six O'Clock Rock*, was a rival to Brian Henderson's *Bandstand*, before he moved to Seven for *The Johnny O'Keefe Show* and, later, *Sing, Sing, Sing*. His old-time rock'n'roll antics had passed their use-by date by the 1970s, and at the age of forty-three he succumbed to the usual downward spiral of drugs, alcohol, divorce and depression. He was a nice guy and pioneer of Australian music, and he deserved better.

Clint Eastwood gave us a long interview by phone from his home in Carmel, California. Our most memorable chat was with Muhammad Ali – for me a career highlight. Somehow we found his home phone number in the States. We called it on spec, were astounded when he answered in person, and were more astonished still when he agreed to chat to us in far-off Australia. I recall spending most of the interview not quite believing that we had him on air, but he was laid-back and funny. He had good memories of his 1960 light-heavyweight fight with the Australian Tony Madigan at the Rome Olympics, which he won. I loathe boxing as a sport, but there was no denying Ali's magnetic charisma. We had caught him at home alone, minding his newborn daughter Laila, a task he found challenging. 'I'm the champion of the world,' he chortled. 'But I'm havin' my butt whipped by this lil' baby girl. How 'bout that?'

✧

The Mike and Sue Morning Show rated okay, but no more than that. We were nowhere near overtaking the Lawsie juggernaut. When Sue quit after a year, pleading exhaustion, she was replaced by Geraldine Willesee, another journalist and the rambunctious baby sister of Mike Willesee. Fiercely Irish-Australian, fun to be with but almost perpetually hungover, Geraldine suddenly disappeared with a smooth-talking, visiting fundraiser for Sinn Féin we had interviewed together on the show.

For David and me, the first hint of our demise at 2UE came when we arrived at work one Monday morning to find that we had been given an assistant producer, introduced to us as Stan Zemanek. It was my first encounter with one of the most offensive boors I have known, ever. The 'assistant' line was rubbish. Everyone knew that Zemanek had worked as a producer for John Laws, whose contract at 2UW was coming to an end. His sudden arrival meant that he was there to suss out the territory and lay the groundwork for John to follow.

Squat as a cane toad, smug as a cat with a rat, dumb as a bag of hammers, Zemanek attached himself to the place like some malign fungal growth on a tree. He did no assisting at all. Armoured in ignorance, he spouted his cack-brained opinions on politics, of which he had no experience and still less insight, and his views of humanity in general, to which he seemed only peripherally connected. Occasionally he would let us know where we might have done better. Gloating and smirking, he revelled in our imminent downfall.

After a few weeks of this I was all for taking him outside and beating the shit out of him – no difficult task, I thought – but David, as imperturbable as ever, suggested that a peacemaking lunch might be a better idea. It was not. Over a couple of hours at a little Italian trattoria down the street from 2UE, I got drunk and Zemanek got drunker. Tiring of his bluster, I picked up the remains of a plate of pasta and shoved it in his face. Gobsmacked – literally – he sat there with spaghetti bolognese dripping down his jowls. We swept from the room. Zemanek would later deny this had happened, but it surely did.

David's revenge was a dish served cold. 2UE at this time was opening any mail addressed to its presenters and producers, ostensibly to combat payola. The task was entrusted to a middle-aged secretary named Lalla Morgan, a bossy retainer of the utmost rectitude and loyalty to the Lambs. Imagine her shock when Zemanek's mail began to sprout a selection of gay porn magazines with titles such as *Leather Studs* and *Honcho Hunks*, all graphically illustrated. More kept arriving. *BlueBoys* and *Mandate*, *Cruise* and *Muscle Dudes*. Teeth gritted, Lalla doggedly confiscated them.

After a couple of weeks of this horror, Zemanek was summoned to the office of the general manager, who pushed a handful of the phallic filth towards him across the desk. 'Do you like this sort of stuff, Stan?' he enquired cautiously.

Poor Stan. Naturally enough, he feared the boss was trying to seduce him. He boggled and spluttered. Only years later did I learn of the difficult conversation that had ensued, with much suspicion and distrust on each side, and with the issue never quite resolved. It had cost David a few bucks at a Kings Cross newsagent, but it was worth every cent.

✧

The end came cleanly enough. The harbinger of my doom was an enormous chrome executive chair, extravagantly upholstered in soft black leather, which appeared without notice in the studio one morning, replacing the small and shabby contraption I sat in. The king's throne had arrived. In August 1979 2UE politely dispensed with my services – paying out the few remaining months of my contract, from memory – and I packed my belongings and left the building.

Not unhappily. I had money saved, enough for a five-week holiday in Europe with Kerri. Alex stayed in Wagga with her doting grandparents, on the promise that we would buy her the most beautiful dress in all of Paris. Which indeed we did. We were in London that northern summer listening to the band of the Coldstream Guards at an outdoor concert on the Embankment when Lord Louis Mountbatten was murdered by the IRA. The conductor announced the news in a hushed voice and asked the audience to sing 'God Save the Queen'. It was one of those uniquely British moments: the scarlet tunics and gleaming brass of the band, the muddy Thames in the sunlight, the anthem rising beneath the chestnuts and London plane trees.

I felt an unexpected sense of loss. As an ABC cadet, still a teenager, I had interviewed Mountbatten at Admiralty House in Sydney. I was the only hack there. This cousin of the Queen, Royal Navy Admiral of the Fleet, and last Viceroy of India had invited me to stay for tea in the sunny garden overlooking the naval base across the harbour at Garden Island. I listened wide-eyed to his war stories, of the *Luftwaffe* sinking his destroyer HMS *Kelly* in the Mediterranean in 1941. Mountbatten was genial and hospitable, not at all stuffy, and I was glad to have met him, a brush with history.

Back home in the Australian spring, nervously unemployed, I was hit by the Lucky Stick again. I found there was still a place for me in radio.

16

Mr Carlton, how kind of you to come

THE 1980S WERE A carnival, a grand parade, a masquerade, a theatre of glittering excess. Folly jostled for centre stage with genius. Tragedy and calamity hovered in the wings, awaiting their cue. Crime and corruption ran rampant. Vanities burned in the bonfire. A communications revolution erupted. Bookended at their beginning by the election of Ronald Reagan to the White House and the murder of John Lennon, and at their end by the fall of the Berlin Wall, the debut of *The Simpsons* and the creation of the World Wide Web, these ten years were the most extraordinary of my life. The baby boomers were flying high, to the stars and beyond. So we imagined.

Science and technology triumphed with the wonders of the mobile phone, Microsoft Windows, the first IBM personal computer and the boxy little Apple Macintosh 128k. In 1985, less happily, scientists announced the discovery of the hole in the ozone layer over the Antarctic. A year later, technology failed with the death of seven astronauts in the explosion of the space shuttle *Challenger* and the nuclear catastrophe at Chernobyl. Medical science discovered the acquired immune deficiency syndrome spreading among gay men, haemophiliacs and drug users.

Flag-waving nationalism propelled Britain and Argentina into war over the Falkland Islands and heaped a humiliating defeat on the Soviet Union in Afghanistan. In Moscow, Mikhail Gorbachev let loose the twin genies of *glasnost* and *perestroika* in the last hurrah for Soviet communism. China's paramount leader Deng Xiaoping engineered an economic revolution, while crushing the 1989 political revolution in Tiananmen Square with the slaughter of unknown hundreds or perhaps thousands of protestors. Political and ideological terrorism took on a frightening new aspect with the eruption of 'The Troubles' in Northern Ireland, the IRA bombing of Britain's Conservative Party leadership at the Grand Brighton Hotel in 1984, a spate of airline hijackings and the death of 270 people in the terrorist bombing of Pan Am flight 103 over the Scottish town of Lockerbie four days before Christmas in 1988.

Hubris exploded in Western democracies, including Australia. Conventional wisdom held that the free-market, supply-side, trickle-down economic policies of Reagan and Britain's Margaret Thatcher had routed forever the great evil of socialism, and the only slighter lesser evil of limp-wristed Keynesian policy meddling. Humanity was headed for broad, sunlit uplands. In fact, Reaganomics or Thatchernomics – there was little difference – let greed run riot, under the cloak of economic respectability. At the beginning of the 1980s the richest 10 per cent of the population in OECD countries earned seven times more than the poorest 10 per cent. Now they earn ten times more.[101] The Wall Street crash of October 1987 put only a small dent in this naked triumphalism: two years later, in a spectacular failure of crystal ball-gazing, the American writer Francis Fukuyama wrote his 'End of History' essay – widely admired at the time – trumpeting that the world had achieved 'an unabashed victory of economic and political liberalism . . . the triumph of the West, of the Western *idea*'.[102]

As ever, Australia floated along on these global tides and currents, always the lucky country. Learning from the mistakes of the Whitlam years, the Hawke and Keating governments alternately dragged and cajoled the Australian economy out of the suffocating sloth of Menzies conservatism. There were social advances with the launch of Medicare in 1984 and the decriminalisation of homosexuality in New South Wales that same year, and, later, a royal commission into Aboriginal deaths in custody. Yet crime and corruption flourished on an industrial scale, most notably in the Bjelke-Petersen government and police force of Queensland. In New South Wales the police franchised bank robberies, prostitution and the drug trade to selected criminals, and the notorious Detective Sergeant Roger Rogerson committed a string of murders and shootings, including an alleged attempt on the life of a fellow police officer, drug squad detective Michael Drury.

Corporate Australia wallowed equally in the slime. Alan Bond's 1983 victory in the America's Cup yacht races sent the nation delirious with joy, made him a national hero and rocketed him skywards in his career of corporate thuggery and billion-dollar fraud. Bond was the standard bearer for a slew of Australian boardroom villains, which also included the fugitive media crook Christopher Skase and the criminals of the Perth-based business and political conspiracy known as WA Inc., fostered by the Labor premier, thief and venal liar Brian Burke, and such business cronies as the perjurer and conman Laurie Connell. Massacres had their day, too. In 1984 seven people died in a bikie gunfight in Sydney's west that became known as the Milperra Massacre, while Melbourne had two mass shootings in 1987, in Hoddle Street and Queen Street, with fifteen dead. More deadly still were the Ash Wednesday bushfires that swept Victoria and South Australia in 1983, with the loss of seventy-five lives.

In 1988 Australia revelled in the bicentennial of white settlement. The film industry gathered speed with such box office hits as *Breaker Morant*, *Gallipoli*, *Phar Lap*, and *The Man from Snowy River*. *Crocodile Dundee* made an international star of Paul Hogan, and *BMX Bandits* gave a frizzy-haired sixteen-year-old named Nicole Kidman her first leading role. Mel Gibson gave a bravura performance as the Australian foreign correspondent in *The Year of Living Dangerously*, a story of Indonesia's turbulent 1960s. He spent an afternoon talking to me about how to play the role, and when I saw the film I was amused that he'd adopted my habit of tipping back my typewriter and throwing my feet up on the desk.

Evil Angels came out in 1988. It was the story of the disappearance of baby Azaria Chamberlain and the persecution of her parents, Lindy and Michael, an episode that was by far the biggest circus of all, fascinating the media and the nation for most of the decade, and exposing an ugly streak of religious bigotry and black humour. The Chamberlains were practising Seventh-Day Adventists, a religion little understood. Few people believed their account, that a dingo had taken the child from their tent at a campsite. Everyone had an opinion of their guilt or innocence. Rumours of satanic rituals and infant sacrifice swirled around them. 'The dingo did it!' became a mocking joke, to be chortled over at barbecues when someone burned the sausages. Lindy Chamberlain was found guilty of murder in 1982 and sentenced to life imprisonment. Michael was convicted as an accessory after the fact and handed a suspended sentence.

New evidence emerged in 1986. A piece of Azaria's clothing was found in the remote bush. A dingo *had* done it. Justice finally found the wretched Chamberlains in 1988 and they were declared innocent. The bigots and conspiracy theorists still refused to accept the truth, but decent people recoiled in embarrassment at the horrors that had been heaped upon the family. Despite Meryl Streep's Oscar nomination for her remarkable performance as Lindy Chamberlain, *Evil Angels* took barely $3 million in Australian theatres. The circus had moved on.

✧

In the Australian spring of 1979 I got an offer to join another of Sydney's great commercial radio stations, 2GB. I seized it with relief and was settling in there when a grievous blow knocked me down. My friend Tony Joyce was shot and fatally wounded on assignment in Africa. Paul Murphy, a colleague and mutual mate from *TDT*, rang to tell me. I recall clutching the phone at home with incomprehension, then gut-wrenching horror. We – our families – had been so close. Kerri had hit it off with Tony's wife, Monica, and we had bonded in the way that similar young couples often will: barbecues, dinners, happy talk of work and children and mortgages to come. Daniel Joyce, a beautiful little blond boy and their only child, was just six years old.

Tony had left *TDT* to be a correspondent in the ABC's London bureau. In November 1979 he was in Zambia to report on one of those impenetrably complex and vicious little wars that blow up like African storms. With Derek McKendry, my old cameraman mate from Vietnam, he took a taxi into the bush outside the capital, Lusaka, to film a bridge that had been destroyed by Rhodesian commandos. Zambian soldiers arrested them at gunpoint, shouting that they were spies, and threw them in a police car. Another man, never identified but thought to be a militia officer, pulled his pistol and very deliberately shot Tony in the head. Derek was unharmed. By the time we got the news, Tony was in a hospital in Lusaka, in a coma.

It was some consolation that Derek was there. Experienced, cool-headed and brave, he would have done everything he could to succour and save Tony. But the Zambians were making bastards of themselves, still frothing about 'spies', and Derek was being held in jail. In London, the ABC bureau chief and Tony's boss, Ken Begg, had the wrenching task of giving Monica the news. Then he set about finding a British neurosurgeon willing to fly to Zambia to take charge. Ken moved heaven and earth to get things happening, but the Zambians were obstructive shits, throwing up red tape. Eventually, he and the ABC's London manager, Stuart Revill, flew to Lusaka, where they confronted a senior police officer, the head of the CID. 'An aggressive bastard', in Ken's words, he contemptuously produced a pearl-handled pistol and put it on his desk as they asked for the release of the two. This thug had Derek brought up from the cells, and put forward a ridiculous version of the shooting, a typewritten tissue of lies. Sign and you will be free to go, Derek was told. He refused and was hauled back to the cells. Ken began to wonder if they would ever get them evacuated.

In Australia we pulled out all the stops to urge the foreign minister, Andrew Peacock, to intervene, which he willingly did. It seemed to help. The surgeon arranged for Tony to be flown back to London and St Barts hospital. He never recovered consciousness and died on Sunday, 3 February 1980. Such a loss he was. His waspish, uniquely English wit and his dazzling mind had enlivened us all. I cried as I had never done before.

The Zambians made no attempt to catch the murderer. President Kenneth Kaunda, the tinpot demagogue I had encountered in 1970, had the gall to write to the Australian government to say that Tony had been caught in 'an unfortunate situation'. It seemed unlikely 'that the issue will ever be fully resolved', he smarmed.[103] The Fraser government, anxious to suck up to emergent Black Africa in the Commonwealth, quietly and cynically dropped the matter.

Tony was the first of three good friends and workmates who would die during the decade. A few months later Roger Allebone was killed by an aggressive cancer that began in his brain and spread like a bushfire. Roger had been living in San Francisco with an American girlfriend, Cathy de Paula, and freelancing for Double J, the ABC's youth radio station. In 1979, on a holiday in Mexico with his daughter Zoe, aged seven, he noticed one morning that his left foot was unresponsive. He could barely drag it along. Back in San Francisco, he developed blinding headaches and awoke one morning unable to speak. In hospital they removed two tumours the size of golf balls from his brain – melanoma, they said – and he eventually returned to Sydney. With nowhere to go and no money, he moved in to the little terrace house in Redfern owned by David Hill, who was then working as Neville Wran's economic adviser. David nursed him devotedly. So, too, did Roger's former wife, Lizzie, and his girlfriend, Cathy. Chemotherapy did little but add to his burden. Cannabis helped ease the pain. But in eight months his magnificent triathlete's body became gaunt and broken, 'as light as a feather when I helped him to the toilet', David recalled.[104] Roger died on Thursday, 29 May 1980 at the age of thirty-one. It began to occur to me that we baby boomers were not immortal.

✧

Back to work. Mike Gibson was a lovely bloke. Plump and shortish, with a woofy moustache but going bald on top, he had a perpetual twinkle in his eye and a merry laugh to match. In all my time there has been no sportswriter nor sports broadcaster to beat him.

When 2GB bought the two of us we knew each other only slightly – nodding acquaintances. Gibbo was a couple of years older, a veteran of the sports pages of the Sydney tabloids. He wrote simply and gracefully, with the authentic voice of the good mate you took to the footy, the bloke who would volunteer to get the beers at half-time. Branching out of print, for much of the 1970s he had been half of a popular morning radio show on 2SM, sharing the microphone with a professional jock, George Moore. 2GB, owned by the Fairfax newspaper empire, was bumping along the bottom of the Sydney radio ratings with a mushy format of old pop music which it called 'mellow rock'. Gibson and Carlton were taken on board to revive the station with some journalistic heft.

The man who hired us was Max Suich – pronounced 'Sutch' – head and shoulders the best editor I have worked for. Max was a newspaperman to his fingertips, ink flowing in his veins, steeped in his craft. He had the energy of the Large Hadron Collider. In the closed little world of Sydney journalism, we had bumped into each other at parties when I was an ABC cadet and he was a middle-ranking reporter for Fairfax. He made his name in the 1970s as editor of the *National Times*, a weekly, upmarket tabloid newspaper which specialised in nailing what it fancied to be the high crimes and misdemeanours of the great and good, and dispensing pontifical advice on books, movies, wine and food. Max had a refined nose for news and, better still, that skill required in every editor but displayed by precious few: the ability to direct and inspire his reporters, and to polish the fruits of their labours without erasing their voices. Relentless, he blasted away the fusty conservatism at Fairfax like a Coral Sea cyclone. In 1979 he was posted from the grey-concrete Fairfax headquarters on Broadway – beyond doubt Sydney's ugliest office building – to the 2GB studios in Sussex Street, a block from Chinatown, with instructions to kick-start the place.

By his own cheerful admission, Max knew nothing about radio. He was flying blind. But what he lacked in knowhow he more than made up for in high-voltage enthusiasm and sheer chutzpah. Over a long yum cha lunch he tossed a coin with us to decide which shows Gibbo and I would do, morning or breakfast. I called tails and won. Mike Gibson was lumped with the starts before sparrow's fart, the long, hard slog of three and a half hours of radio Monday to Friday, beginning on air at five-thirty am. I was to do nine am to noon, kicking off in January 1980. Some advertising agency invented a half-arsed slogan for us: we were 'In the Know Radio', we told the world. Listen to us and we would tell you everything you needed for the day. Worse, we shot a cringe-making television commercial with the two of us poncing about in a ghastly soft-shoe vaudeville act, making eyes at each other and the camera as we warbled 'we're in the know'. God knows how we got talked into it. Vanity, I dare say. People fled howling from their lounge rooms when it came on.

Sadly, they didn't flee towards the radio. *The Mike Gibson Breakfast Show* was a class act, with spirited chat and lots of sport, but for some reason it made little or no headway against the competition of Uncle Gary at 2UE and the mordant wit of Clive Robertson at the ABC's 2BL. We had got rid of GB's tiny mellow rock audience but hadn't attracted another one. With a resigned shrug of the shoulders, Gibbo chucked it in after a year and went off to television at Nine, where he carved out a long, stellar career as a sports presenter, much loved.[105]

The hole had to be filled. Everyone looked at me, the last man standing. I squirmed. Both professionally and personally, breakfast is the toughest shift in radio. Professionally because you pretty much carry the station on your back, out there and naked. All else follows, for better or worse. There is no place to hide. Personally, I knew it would mean an earthquake in my home life: in bed by nine pm at the very latest and out of it again at three the next morning. Alex was two years old and we had another child on the way. Kerri and I talked it over and decided, reluctantly, that I should at least give it a shot. There was one plus: the new contract I negotiated with Fairfax was generous. Flinging caution to the winds I rewarded myself by buying a zippy new sports car, a cherry-red Alfa Romeo GTV6. James Charles Carlton was born that August, healthy and handsome, with his arrival announced on the radio.

But what sort of show to do? There was no point reprising the format Gibbo had done. It would have to be new and different, and aimed at the audience demographic most prized by advertisers: listeners carefully defined in two age brackets, from twenty-five to thirty-nine years of age, and forty to fifty-four. At thirty-five myself, with nearly twenty years in the media under my belt, I felt I could take a decent shot at it. David Lyle had joined 2GB as the program manager. We agreed to give it a go.

Max Suich's other hire at the time was a salesman he had lured over from the Fairfax fortress. Nigel Milan was, in the homely old phrase, as flash as a rat with a gold tooth. His suits were sharp. His bow ties were sharper. The son of a Cockney postman and still with a leavening of the East End accent, he was around my age, with an Australian wife, Lindy. I used to fantasise that in Dickensian London he would have been the Artful Dodger, pickpocketing watches for Fagin. But his salesman's schtick was as sharp as his ties, and on a good day he could charm the birds from the trees. Against all the odds he was selling ads that actually pulled in money for the station, and so successfully that he was soon hoiked upwards into the job of 2GB's general manager. Nigel was my new boss.

I liked him. A lot of people found that a little Nigel went a long way, but I enjoyed his breezy self-assurance, his infectious optimism. He was fun to lunch with. He called you 'guv'nor'. Best of all, he had the rare good sense to know where the lines were drawn between the sales department and the people who actually made the programs. This may sound like common sense but it's not. Most general managers of commercial radio stations come up from sales, not programming. When they park their bums in the big leather chair, they believe that programming genius is mystically bestowed upon them. It is not. I long ago lost count of the station general managers I have worked for in Australia and in London, but you could fit in a phone box the ones who actually knew anything about making radio or what an audience wanted. One or two were barking mad but were found out too late. Many were just aggressively stupid. Others muddled through, pretending, faking it, getting by.

Nigel was one of the good ones. 'You do the shows, I'll sell the tickets,' he used to say, and by and large he stuck to that bargain. Tossing ideas around, the three of us – Nigel, David and me – came up with a format we called Newstalk. From memory, the name was Nigel's. There would be no music but lots of news and information, with talkback, in bite-sized chunks, delivered in the most entertaining ways we could devise. In a perfect world we would have road-tested the thing with focus groups and truckloads of audience research statistics, but we didn't have the time or the money. We just went for it, seat of the pants.

News, sports and weather came up every half-hour, for about seven minutes. Regular traffic reports were essential, and we found the perfect bloke to do them: Wayne Hutchings, who was a despatcher with the RSL cab company and a cheerful humorist and family man who knew every road in Sydney. Sport was spruiked by the noisy pair I christened 'the Decibel Duo', Peter Peters and Greg Hartley. Peter, known as Zorba for his Greek ancestry, had played rugby league for Parramatta and Manly and was built like the Acropolis. Greg 'Hollywood' Hartley had recently retired as Sydney's most flamboyant referee, loved and loathed as refs always are. Shouting and arguing with each other – if there wasn't some sort of shock-horror football controversy, they created one – they became the top sports act in Sydney radio. Daily reports from a correspondent in New York, John Raedler, and another in London, Malcolm Stuart, fleshed out the chat.

The rest of it was me, with interviews and editorial opinion. The crucial ingredient was humour and satire, which no one else on radio was doing. At six, seven and eight o'clock I would start the show out of the news with more of the funnies I had experimented with at 2UE: pungent, cartoonish comments on the news of the day, tarted up with impersonations, music and sound effects. At the end of the week I did *Friday News Review* again, a satirical comment on current affairs written as a mock news bulletin, which would normally run for about seven minutes but sometimes – if I was feeling funny – could blow out to ten or eleven.

This became my radio signature but, eventually, a cross I bore with increasing despair. It was bloody hard work, mentally and physically draining. I wrote every word of the scripts, complete with the cues for music and effects, and in the early years I did all the voices myself. It was a golden age for prominent political figures to mimic. As well as Fraser, Hawke and Wran, a bumbling Ronald Reagan and a breathy, dominatrix Margaret Thatcher went into the mix.

The characters all got cartoonish names, which sound arch and laboured today but were fit enough for purpose then. Hawke became 'Prime Minister Bob Hope', Neville Wran was 'Premier Never Wrong', Reagan appeared as 'President Hopalong Cassidy', named for the old movie cowboy of my childhood. Thatcher was 'Gladys Hacksaw'. My favourite character, though, was 'Joh Bonkers-Bananas', my take on the drivelling incoherence of Bjelke-Petersen. To bolt it together I created a 'newsreader', Brian Hambone – a grotesque parody of Hendo at Nine – and a cast of 'reporters', again drawn from the real thing. 'Peter Gravy' sounded very like Peter Harvey. 'George Fungus' was George Negus, the *60 Minutes* reporter and another old mate. 'Martyn Rayne-Coate' appeared as the so-called London reporter with one of those curiously nasal, sing-song BBC deliveries, and 'Chuck Yablonski' did a deep, chocolate baritone American CBS-style drone. The sports send-up at the end featured Rox Messup, a pinch from the top TV rugby league commentator of the day, Rex Mossop, who had won immortal fame by making a citizen's arrest at a nude beach near his Sydney home. 'I don't need the male genitalia rammed down my throat,' he explained to the media.

Writing and recording *FNR* was the killer. I began it on Thursday mornings, after a snatched breakfast when the show finished at nine, and it took around three or four hours, often more, to wrap it up. That meant at least a twelve-hour day which had begun at three in the morning, with another five or six to go before I would be back in bed. Over time I grew accustomed to the hours, but never to like them. As any shift worker will tell you, rising in the wee small hours throws your body clock out of whack. It is like living with permanent jet lag, crushed by the strain of never getting a proper night's sleep. And because you get into the groove of the three am wake-up, it happens to you at weekends too, no matter how ardently you long to snore undisturbed until dawn and beyond. This was the bed I had made for myself. Now I had to lie (awake) in it.

From its uncertain beginnings the show began to smooth itself out, to get into a routine that we could handle with relative ease. My producer, researcher, and personal assistant, who also handled the open line, would arrive in my office at about three-forty-five am, and we'd sit in silence for half an hour while we slurped coffee and flicked through the newspapers. Then we would toss ideas around and put the thing together, slotting in the interviews and talkback segments. Is the premier available today? Maybe we should try for the police commissioner . . . The opposition transport shadow minister wants to come on . . . There's been a fatal house fire in Parramatta . . . A major drug bust in Melbourne. I would dash off one of the comedy skits, hopefully to record it at around five am, and by half-past we were as ready as we'd ever be for the show to start. Most times it worked.

And the audience began to grow. There was no one else doing what we did on Sydney radio. Breakfast television, in the shape of Nine's *Today* show, was still a year away. Our ratings nudged upwards, better each time. The first big news break we got came in March 1981, with John Hinckley Jnr's assassination attempt on Ronald Reagan in Washington, DC. It was perfectly timed for us to report. The shots were fired at Reagan at two-thirty pm Washington time, which was five-thirty am in Sydney on Tuesday, 30 March, smack-bang on target for breakfast radio. John Raedler was onto the story and listeners woke to hear it. It got us noticed, and more people started turning us on. Advertisers began to get interested.

A month or so later, Nigel Milan came to me with a bright idea: would I like to fly to London to cover the wedding of Charles and Diana? Yes, I would.

✧

A vision in pink, shocking pink and then megawatt electric pink, the famous romantic novelist Dame Barbara Cartland reclined on a chaise longue in the drawing room of Camfield Place, her stately home in Hertfordshire, north of London.[106] I thought of a flock of flamingos, cruelly massacred. Surmounted by an explosive blonde wig, her whited face displayed two thick rings of mascara and a pair of enormous black eyelashes, suggesting a raccoon shipwrecked on a coral beach. A ball of doggy white fluff lay across her lap, farting.

'You are welcome to watch Dame Barbara,' whispered the butler, showing me to a gilded fauteuil. 'But please do not speak until she has finished.'

Ignoring my arrival, the Dame was dictating one of her tales to a small brown dormouse of a woman perched on a stool at her feet. I sat in awe.

'The princess felt her bosom heave as Prince Leopold knelt beside her and tenderly took her tiny hand – no, make that *gallantly* took her tiny hand . . .'

I can't claim that was the exact quote but it was along those lines. All her books were along those lines – a prodigious output of more than 700 novels of chaste heroines and their swashbuckling suitors, published in thirty-eight languages with 750 million or so copies sold, she claimed. The dormouse scratched away in shorthand for another five minutes until the author declared herself done for the day and rose from her couch to greet me, clutching the dyspeptic Pekingese. 'Mr Carlton, how *kind* of you to come. And all the way from Orstralia, too!'

Devout royal watchers will recall that Barbara Cartland was Diana's step-grandmother. Her daughter Raine had married Diana's father, Johnnie, the 8th Earl Spencer. This connection, however, was not enough to get Barbara invited to the wedding at St Paul's Cathedral, much to her disgust. It was feared she would upstage both Diana and the Queen, a distinct possibility. Nothing, though, could stop her dispensing prenuptial advice to the British and foreign media, who beat a path to her door in the hope of some juicy indiscretion.

Before I did my interview I was treated to a tour of the drawing room. 'Dear, darling Dickie,' she gushed, hoisting a silver-framed photograph from a table to show me. 'How I loved him!' It was my old friend the late Lord Louis Mountbatten, with whom she had reputedly enjoyed a passionate affair as a pre-war society belle. This might or might not have been true. Dame Barbara, at the grand old age of eighty, could gild a lily like no other. She had famously called off her first engagement, to a Guards officer, after her mother had explained the disgusting facts of procreation. The jilted wretch had threatened to shoot himself with his service revolver in Hyde Park (he didn't).

La Cartland was way too smart to drop a total clanger, but she landed one or two little bomblets for my tape recorder. 'Of course,

Diana is a virgin,' she assured me firmly. 'Despite Charles' best efforts to seduce her.' There was sage advice on what to do when marrying a future king. Diana's first duty would be to produce a male heir, as soon as possible. Then I was invited to stay for tea.

But of course. In an adjoining sitting room she led me to a table piled with flowery Spode china, silver cutlery, plates of little triangular cucumber sandwiches translucently thin, scones with strawberry jam – 'Cook makes it, my own strawberries' – a bowl of clotted cream, chocolate éclairs, a sugary teacake and an enormous chocolate cake. I wolfed it down. So did the dog.

When I eventually tore myself away to drive back to London, she pressed a small blue velvet box into my hand. In it was an acorn on a little chain, dipped in gold. 'It's from that tree over there,' she said, waving a bejewelled claw at an ancient oak across the park. 'It was planted by the queen.'

'Queen Elizabeth?' I said in disbelief. The tree was far too big and old.

Yes,' she said firmly. 'The first one.'

The British establishment sneered at Barbara Cartland as irredeemably vulgar and on the make, which of course she was. But she knew her act, what her public wanted, and she played it unashamedly. I liked her a lot.

For all the fizz and excitement of London *en fête* in summer, it was hard grind covering the wedding of the century, as everyone called it. I worked from a cramped studio somewhere in Holborn, a long way from the crappy tourist hotel we stayed in near Tower Bridge. The time difference meant that to do breakfast in Australia I was broadcasting from eight-thirty pm until midnight, after a long day's work of recording interviews. Sadly, the Queen Mother had knocked me back for a chat, her private secretary explaining, with great regret, that she had never once done a media interview and was not about to start now. But we got lots of colour and movement with vox pops in the streets, a long chat at my first meeting with Clive James in his flat at the Barbican, another terrific interview with the writer and society commentator Jilly Cooper and the actor John Thaw, star of the TV cop drama *The Sweeney* and later *Inspector Morse*.

Another actor, Derek Nimmo, had me for drinks in his elegant townhouse in Kensington. Nimmo is largely forgotten now, but he was hugely popular at the time for his portrayal of upper-class English twits, usually stuttering vicars and the like. It was evidently a profitable gig.

'That looks a bit like a Canaletto,' I said, admiring a large painting of a Venetian canal scene above the fireplace.

He looked abashed. 'It *is* a Canaletto, actually,' he said apologetically.

The night before the wedding was bedlam. All London was out on the town, partying like mad, along with half the tourists of the Western world. The Tube had practically ground to a halt under the strain and cabs were impossible to get. I made it to the studio with just minutes to spare. My sidekick for the occasion was Diana 'Bubbles' Fisher, an Englishwoman with a cut-glass accent who had migrated to Australia and was usually billed as a Sydney socialite, making a buck doing TV panel shows and writing gossip for the women's mags. Well bred, the daughter-in-law of an Archbishop of Canterbury, she was our go-to expert on matters royal. From a distance I had thought Fisher was an annoying poseur, but that proved incorrect. Assigned to cover the evening festivities in Hyde Park, she bravely tramped the 10 kilometres back to the studio on foot, battling the madding crowd, fighting off a drunk who tried to molest her, and delivered her spiel with aplomb. I always admired her for that.

When we finished at midnight we knocked off a bottle of champagne together: Pol Roger, the favourite tipple of Winston Churchill. Stuffed after a week's work, I crashed back at the hotel and slept through the entire wedding, a fact I didn't bother to confess to my audience. By that time I was over the whole thing, but the broadcasts went down a treat. The venture helped cement the perception that 2GB had at long last risen from the radio scrapheap and was seriously back in the game.

✧

The show was not all froth and bubble. We had serious stuff to cover. From the very beginning, the 1980s were years of febrile, often vicious politicking in both New South Wales and Canberra. The Labor government was dominant in Macquarie Street, due in no small part to the premier's considerable political skills and charisma. Wran had seen one Liberal opposition leader turfed from his seat at a state election in 1978, and he managed it again in 1981 in what became known as the second 'Wranslide', which gave Labor sixty-nine seats in the Legislative Assembly against a measly twenty-eight for the Coalition.

But there was trouble on the horizon. Allegations of political and police corruption began to surface, lapping around the foundations of Wran's government like a rising tide. The voters were wearily resigned to the knowledge that corruption flourished in their state, regarding it as an inevitable fact of life, but when Sir Robert Askin died in September 1981 the storm broke. The day before his funeral, the Fairfax *National Times* burst into print with a long feature story headlined: 'Askin: Friend to Organised Crime'. The writer, David Hickie, gave chapter and verse of Askin's criminal conduct, and the bent police commissioners and 'colourful racing identities' who had greased his grasping palm. There was uproar, not at the substance of the allegations, which surprised no one. It was the timing, which was thought to be in regrettable bad taste. His poor widow, they said.

Wran could not be blamed for Askin's crimes, but soon enough he too began to feel the lash of suspicion. With some hopes of cleaning up the cops, he propelled a relatively junior officer, Bill Allen, to the job of Chief Superintendent, Metropolitan Area, a post recognised as a launching pad for future commissioners. Wran had apparently been impressed by Allen's efficiency in cleaning up a notorious tow-truck racket, and had been assured that he was 'pro-Labor'. Seven months later the premier promoted Allen over twenty-two other superintendents to become an assistant commissioner, and not long after that there was another jump, to deputy commissioner.

This was a catastrophic mistake. Allen was bent, and badly. The Australian Federal Police had been watching him, and they had him cold. He had close links with the American mafia, who had given him and his family first-class air tickets and a holiday in Las Vegas. He was hooked in with the local mafia operatives in Australia, had brazenly consorted with Sydney's 'Mr Sin', Abe Saffron, and was eventually found to have bribed junior police officers to lay off his crooked mates. No less a figure than Prime Minister Malcolm Fraser revealed the AFP's information on Allen in a private dinner with Max

Suich, who had returned to the newspaper business as Fairfax's chief editorial director. Fraser knew it would damage Wran politically, and it did. In November 1981 a detailed story by the investigative journalist Marian Wilkinson in the *National Times* blew Allen to pieces.

Wran called a full-dress media conference to manage the scandal but it only made things worse. The cameras clicked and rolled. For the first time in his premiership, the questioning was aggressive. Why had he rocketed Allen up through the ranks? Had he not checked the man's record? Why all the haste? Wran blustered and dodged. I held back, but when the parliamentary press gallery had finished I bowled up some questions of my own. There was anger in his eyes at what he evidently thought was a betrayal. I was just doing my job, but his answers grew more terse and pugnacious until he abruptly ended the conference and stalked from the room. We had done that fatal dance of journalist and politician, in symbiosis. Now it had ended.

After a judicial enquiry, Allen was forced out in disgrace, with a humiliating demotion to the rank of sergeant first class. Foolishly, obstinately, 'Nifty Nev' had backed his man almost to the end, and the voters knew it. His halo was tarnished. And there was more to come, much more.

Sydney has always feasted on scurrilous gossip and rumour. Often this is the figment of colourful imaginations run riot, like the preposterous claims, frequently heard from the Tories, that Gough Whitlam and later Paul Keating were closet gays.[107] People believe what they want to believe, no matter how ludicrous it might be. But sometimes the rumours are true, or at least very close to the truth. They tend to start within a circle of people in the know – politicians, police, lawyers, journalists, business or trade union figures – and they grow with the telling. They radiate through the community like the ripples from a stone dropped in a pond. Generally, the defamation laws keep these tales out of the media, although occasionally they surface under the privilege of parliament. Sometimes, just sometimes, they are brought into the light of day by a judicial enquiry to establish the truth. Or not, as the case may be.

For much of the 1980s, the nation was enthralled by the Costigan Royal Commission, a full-scale enquiry into the Federated Ship

Painters and Dockers Union. Largely centred on the Melbourne waterfront, although with branches in other cities, the Painters and Dockers made the mafia look like your local P&C. In the words of Frank Costigan QC, the Melbourne barrister who headed the commission, the union was involved in 'taxation fraud, social security fraud, ghosting, compensation fraud, theft on a grand scale, extortion, the handling of massive importations of drugs, the shipments of armaments, all manner of violence and murder'.[108]

Nobody was startled by the drugs, violence and murder, but the tax fraud was fascinating. It led directly to the 'bottom of the harbour' scandal, in which literally hundreds of Australian businesses were revealed to have employed complex pea-and-thimble tricks to rort their way out of their tax obligations. Countless hundreds of millions of dollars had simply vanished. With the advice of crooked lawyers and accountants, companies were stripped of their assets and sent to the bottom of the harbour, as the saying had it. For a reasonable fee, members of the Painters and Dockers Union suddenly popped up as shell directors of these stripped entities, beyond the reach of the tax office. This was a federal affair – nothing whatever to do with the Wran Labor government in New South Wales – but it helped stoke the perception among Australians that the big end of town was irretrievably rotten. There would be more to come on that, too, reaching as high as Australia's then richest man, Kerry Packer.

Federally, the Coalition government was beginning to flounder. For all his drive and hauteur, Fraser never looked comfortable in the role of prime minister, perhaps because he understood that he had won it illegitimately. Wran's string of victories had revived Labor's morale after the Whitlam defeat, bringing the party back from the wilderness. The new federal opposition leader, the former treasurer Bill Hayden, was doing his dogged best to place Labor in a credible position to fight the next election, due in 1983. But the rumour mills, spinning as fast as ever, had it that Bob Hawke was readying himself for a shot at the prime ministership. For once they were spot-on. Hawke entered parliament for the Victorian seat of Wills in 1980. He was breathing down Hayden's neck.

I had come to know Hawke better since the *TDT* days. At

A Current Affair I'd filmed him at the opening of a newly refurbished wharfies' pub in Sydney, the famous 'Big House' on the old Hungry Mile at Darling Harbour. Shirt unbuttoned to the waist, drenched in beer, laughing like a drain, Hawkey had cavorted atop the bar, chug-a-lugging schooners and romping with two pneumatically well-bosomed strippers. The wharfies loved him, and he loved them back. A few years later we enjoyed a long afternoon's drinking session in the beer garden of the 2UE pub, the Rag, where he was besieged by well-wishers and autograph hunters. It was amusing to watch. Most politicians can fake it with real people, but Bob genuinely relished the contact, drawing strength and inspiration from it. One of his nicknames, 'the Folk Hero', was bestowed only half in jest.

With the Lodge growing ever nearer, though, he conscientiously reined in his larrikin side. His minders convinced him to abandon the slick, bodgie hairstyle and the flash neckties. On 3 February 1983 Hawke rolled Hayden as Labor's parliamentary leader. By striking coincidence, at that same hour Fraser was at the Lodge to get the governor-general to okay a snap election for 5 March, confident that Hayden could be beaten easily. Returning to his office, he was stunned to find that his opponent would in fact be the vastly more popular Hawke. Labor won in a landslide, picking up twenty-four seats. The stage was set for a Labor revolution, and it would be grounded in the transformation of the economy.

✧

For a lot of the 1980s I was out to lunch. I don't write this with any particular pride of achievement. It just happened that way. I usually put in another three hours' work in the office after the show, and when noon rolled around I was in the mood to kick back. Sometimes it was a working lunch with a politician or some other grandee; more often it was a convivial meeting with mates, mostly journalists.

The favoured haunt was Edna's Table, a restaurant in an old brick and stone warehouse in York Street, a couple of blocks from the studio, run by two of the most open-hearted people I have known. Raymond and Jennice Kersh were brother and sister, children of a waterside worker, born and raised in the gritty streets of waterfront

Pyrmont, long before it was gentrified. 'Dad was the only Jewish wharfie in Australia,' they liked to say. Their mother, Edna – they gave her name to the restaurant – was a Catholic, which was how the kids were brought up. Ray was dyslexic but had taught himself to cook, and brilliantly so. He was experimenting with bush tucker, Australian native foods and ingredients, long before it became trendy. The kitchen was in the centre of the restaurant, in full view, and I loved watching him juggle the pots and pans. Jennice handled the front of house, showing you to your table in killer heels, eye-watering décolletage and about a kilo of extravagant costume jewellery. She had a laugh that could stop traffic.

Between them, the Kershs knew everyone who was anyone in Sydney. The Great and Good and the Big and Bad beat a path to their door for a frenzy of table-hopping. After I began to plug Edna's on air, quite unashamedly, the joint was full every lunchtime. It was trendy, fashionable, the place to see and be seen. Cabinet ministers rubbed shoulders with judges and lawyers, merchant bankers hobnobbed with journalists and economists and TV household names, all grazing and sluicing on a long day's journey into night. Paul Keating's mother, Min, and his sister, Anne, were regulars. Visiting showbiz stars dropped in. The pop of champagne corks punctuated the hubbub. Limousines waited to carry the drunks back to the office or their homes. For the favoured or fortunate few – I take no pride in this either – it was a decade of self-indulgent excess.

There were three riotous red-letter days throughout the year at Edna's. Valentine's Day and Melbourne Cup Day were special, but it was St Patrick's Day, 17 March, which the Catholic Kershs celebrated with mad abandon. Irish dancers, singers, fiddlers and a piper roamed between the tables. Throughout the afternoon and long into the evening the rafters rang with the great Irish ballads and soaring Catholic hymns:

> Hail, glorious St Patrick, dear saint of our Isle,
> On us thy poor children bestow a sweet smile;
> And now thou art high in the mansions above,
> On Erin's green valleys look down in thy love.

The carousing was traditionally led by Their Honours Judge John O'Meally and the late Judge Brian Moroney of the New South Wales District Court, who made up in Irish folkloric enthusiasm what, perhaps, they lacked in vocal ability. More than once we repaired to O'Meally's chambers for a nightcap or three. On one particularly festive evening Moroney rang the Vatican, intent on arguing some doctrinal point with the pope. Regrettably, His Holiness was at his summer palace at Castel Gandolfo and unable to take the call, we were told. Moroney died of cancer, greatly mourned. O'Meally, a jurist of noble aims and deep compassion, ran the New South Wales Dust Diseases Tribunal, bringing succour and financial compensation to the victims of asbestosis and mesothelioma, sometimes taking his court to the bedside of the dying at any hour of the day or night if necessary. No more decent man ever graced the bench.

O'Meally once took me to a grand dinner at the state Parliament House to farewell an outgoing Irish ambassador, James Sharkey. Held in the dining room of the President of the Legislative Council, a likeable Labor stalwart named 'Johnno' Johnson, it was a riotous affair of feasting, drink and song in the Irish manner. Late in the evening I heard that Australia's most odious God-botherer, and a member of the upper house, the Reverend Fred Nile, was on his feet and speaking in a debate. Well oiled, I determined to take him on and lunged for the door of the chamber. It was a close-run thing. My maiden speech to the New South Wales Parliament was only narrowly thwarted when the attorney-general, my friend Terry Sheahan, crash-tackled me to the floor and dragged me back to the dinner table.

Christmas at Edna's was best of all. For lunch and again at dinner, Ray Kersh laid on a yuletide menu of Edwardian extravagance: the full ham, stuffed roast turkey, plum pudding catastrophe and more. His cakes had an almost symphonic grandeur. Carol singers, elves and Santa serenaded the tables, urging you to sing along. On Christmas Eve there was a grand party for the Edna's regulars, eagerly anticipated, with excited kids invited. It was mayhem. The night invariably climaxed with a riotous rendition of 'The Twelve Days of Christmas', with each table assigned a verse to bawl, bellow or holler.

17

Pissed as a parrot

THE RIVALRY WAS WHITE-HOT in Sydney radio in the 1980s. A new station – 2WS – had hit the AM band, with fresh new music programming aimed at the heart of the Western Suburbs. Two bright and shiny new FM stations, 2-Day FM and 2MMM, were beginning to drag audiences away from the AM old stagers. Station executives were at their wits' end dreaming up zany new publicity stunts. At 2GB Nigel Milan had the brainwave of sponsoring a boat in the iconic eighteen-foot skiff sailing races on the harbour, with the Newstalk 873 logo plastered on its mainsail. To launch it, he somehow convinced the Navy to lend us a submarine. I broadcast live from a lavish listeners' breakfast on the beach at Watsons Bay. At the climactic moment, the sub rose from the depths with our boat lashed to the bows.

Another of Nigel's great publicity scams was the 2GB Newstalk Credibility Poll, in which media figures, politicians, actors and other noisemakers in the marketplace were allegedly measured and scored for their supposed public popularity. Some market research company bodgied up a few statistics, and the runners-up and winners were feted at a slap-up lunch at Edna's. The results were solemnly reported in the gossip columns. Almost everybody got stonking drunk. I cherish a memory of Paddy McGuinness, then editor of the *Australian Financial*

Review, bawling ferocious insults at Germaine Greer and copping the same back in full measure.

My task in the breakfast slot was to knock off Clive Robertson at the ABC's 2BL, and then, hopefully, the top-rating Uncle Gary at 2UE. I gradually overtook Clive in the ratings, but Gary was a harder beast to bring down. It occurred to me that satire and humour might be worth a whack, with a send-up of his Sammy the Sparrow character. Sammy was the relentlessly chirpy bird who arrived in Gary's studio by helicopter each morning to crack lame jokes and dispense wholesome, sponsor-flavoured advice to the kiddies before school. 'Make sure Mum buys only Anderson's sausages, girls and boys!' I thought up a character called Victor the Vulture, who also arrived by helicopter sound effect, but invariably suffering a filthy hangover. The helicopter crash-landed in creative new ways, with Victor crawling from the wreckage coughing, spluttering and swearing in a voice like a bucket of gravel hitting a tin roof. 'Jeezes, Uncle Mike, I'm rooted. Out all night, didn't get home till after two. Never been so sick in me life.' Victor made Sammy sound very 1960s, tired and old-fashioned. 'There better not be any bloody kids listening.'

I took it further, allowing the Vulture to whack Sammy on air. 'I passed that bloody Sammy in his chopper on the way 'ere, Uncle Mike. Gave 'im a wave, but the little poof just ignored me.' It was irredeemably crass and vulgar, but it was in tune with the excess of the times, and I began to unstick Gary's audience as well. With each ratings survey, more and more of his listeners were deserting him and coming across.

Like the Vulture, I was drinking hard too. Not every day, but on social occasions I was hurling myself into it like a lemming at a cliff. As the show took off, the invitations began to pile up on my desk. The evil alchemy of public relations lured and seduced me. Invitations to lunches and dinners and wine-tastings fell like autumn leaves. There were VIP tickets to lavishly catered corporate boxes for cricket Tests and football grand finals, and more tickets to movie, opera, concert and theatre first nights, invariably with the riotous after-party to follow.

Until the mid-1960s or so, what passed for Sydney high society had been a closed circle of old-money families whose decorous doings were respectfully reported in the weekend social columns. The Fairfaxes entertained the Horderns, who entertained the Playfairs, who entertained the Whites, who entertained the Foys, who entertained the Dekyveres, the Macarthur-Onslows and the Lloyd Joneses.

Public relations changed all that forever. A coven of corporate PR mavens – they were mostly women – worked out that, for all their money, these A-listers never actually bought anything, nor did they inspire anyone else to do so. They were deadly dull. Newspaper editors thought so too. The solution was to create a new A-list, glittering with the fragile but marketable tinsel of celebrity and glamour. Actors and TV hosts and pop stars, disc jockeys and newspaper columnists and magazine editors, sports greats and medal-winning Olympians, models and fashion designers and society hairdressers, famous authors and a few acceptably non-boring politicians were flung into the mix.

There were two acknowledged queens of the hive, Ladies Sonia McMahon and Susan Renouf, who would go to the opening of a tube of toothpaste as long as there was Krug to drink. Sonia, blonde with rabbity teeth, invariably and understandably left husband Billy at home. Susan, former wife of Andrew Peacock and then the gambling tsar Robert Sangster, once kindly offered me a night in her bed at 'Paradis sur Mer', her fabulous but now demolished harbourside mansion. I politely declined. It would have been intriguing but more trouble than I needed.

With evidently bottomless pits of money to splash around, the mavens battled to outdo each other in grabbing the spotlight for their clients. The next party had to be more extravagant than the last. The acknowledged PR queen was Deeta Colvin, a statuesque redhead of immense charm and steely business brain, who was married to the lawyer Rod McGeoch, the man who kicked off Sydney's bid for the 2000 Olympic Games. The pinnacle of Deeta's triumphs were her Cointreau balls, staged – at what must have been staggering cost – to flog the eponymous French liqueur. The invitations were prized like diamonds. Around a thousand guests were ferried by limousine to a secret outdoor location, different each year. Beneath a vast snowy-white marquee swathed in silks and chiffon and lit by dazzling chandeliers, celebrity chefs and platoons of waiters did their stuff, serving up course after course of five-star delicacies, champagne and enough iced Cointreau to float a supertanker. This bacchanal rocked along until dawn, when the waiting limos carted the reeking survivors home again. The Sunday papers went bananas with the excitement of it all. And, who knows, it might even have sold a few bottles of Cointreau.

For whatever reason, the big French fashion, champagne and luxury goods houses were all battling for a foothold in the Australian market. Largesse showered down. Freebies were flung about. When Kerri and I flew to France on holiday we were entertained for a week by the *Comité Champagne*, the marketing outfit for the great champagne houses. We were put up in a luxury resort hotel near Reims, given private tours of the caves and were wined, lunched and dined by Moët Chandon, Charles Heidsieck and Laurent Perrier.

The *directeur* of Bollinger, Vicomte Arnaud d'Hautefeuille, gave us dinner at his home, an achingly elegant country chateau built for one of Napoleon's ministers. Hospitable and amiable, with flawless English, he uncorked a dozen different vintages, each for a taste. What did I think of the '64 . . . the '78?

I thought they were all very good. 'And what are those strange marks on the floor?' I asked him, indicating some deep gouges in the polished parquet by the dining room fireplace.

'It's where the Germans parked their motorcycles during the war,' he said lightly. 'But they paid for everything they drank.'

Delight and disaster jostled for space in this ever more hectic social life. At the gala opening night of the musical *Cats* at the Theatre Royal, the snappers quite literally pushed and elbowed my wife out of the way so that I could be photographed with Ita Buttrose. More enjoyably, we had drinks backstage with Elton John before a concert in 1984. A vision in shocking pink, frocked and powdered and primped like a high-camp Mozart, in the flesh he was refreshingly normal and un-starlike. We talked about Tony Joyce, who had grown up in the same suburb as Elton, Pinner, in north-west London. Barry Humphries had us to dinner at his flat in the exclusive Astor building in Macquarie Street, and backstage in his dressing room after his shows. Barry might be the most courteous man I have ever met, a solicitous host of almost Edwardian charm and good manners.

The maestro violinist Isaac Stern, beaming like a Jewish cherub, gave me morning tea in his hotel suite. 'I could never play Wagner,' he told me. 'The Nazis stole his music.' Other stars came and went for studio interviews. John Cleese and Michael Palin were gracious and funny. Cleese was so exceedingly polite and eager to please that I wondered if he was sending me up, enjoying some private joke. Perhaps he was. Either way, he knocked my socks off. Mike Love of the Beach Boys was brisk and businesslike. For Dame Edna Everage I wrote and recorded grandiose introductions with trumpet fanfares and a thunderous roll of kettle drums: 'And now, an historic moment in Australian broadcasting . . . as we welcome to the 2GB microphone the Melbourne mother, megastar and millionairess, an inspiration to millions around the globe!' Edna liked them so much she asked me to do them to introduce her live stage shows. Rolf Harris appeared a few times, at the height of his fame. Before he went on he was always brusque, cold and aloof. When the On Air light glowed, though, he was suddenly your best mate. 'Mike, lovely to be with you again!' That act worked for him for a very long time, until his catastrophic unmasking as a predatory paedophile.

The actress and dancer Shirley MacLaine was another stellar encounter. We arranged to meet in the foyer of the Sebel Town House near Kings Cross, a boutique hotel now extinct but then much favoured by visiting glitterati. At the door of her suite she couldn't find her key. 'Fuck it!' she snapped, emptying the entire contents of her handbag onto the corridor carpet. She squatted on her haunches and rifled through the debris. Key found, she ushered me inside, poured me a stiff Scotch and plonked herself on a couch, her gorgeous legs seductively curled around a cushion. I was agape. She was most un-Hollywood. Normally stars of her magnitude were surrounded by platoons of infuriatingly bossy minders who would order you about, but this was just Shirl and me, one on one.

After the formal interview was done I switched off the tape recorder and we kept chatting and drinking. She asked about Australia, about Sydney, about my career. I found her extraordinarily sexy. That famous face, lightly dusted with freckles. Her wide mouth, with its impish grin. The sinuous way she moved her body. I was mesmerised, aroused, my hormones doing handstands. She was having her affair with Andrew Peacock at the time, but she asked what I was doing that evening and suggested I stay for dinner. I chickened out. 'Wife waiting for me at home,' I spluttered. She showed me to the door and gave me a light but very deliberate kiss on the cheek, our bodies brushing together. I floated out into the evening air.

Disaster threatened when the Maori singer Ricky May dared me to join him on stage with his big band to sing duets in the supper club at the old Regent Hotel in George Street. I was silly enough to do it. Ricky, a lovable, gentle mountain of flesh, insisted that I smoke a joint before we went on, which I obediently did, and very good it was too. The pot calmed the nerves and summoned up the blood, just as it had done in Jakarta years earlier, and somehow I got through a brace of Frank Sinatra and Bobby Darin favourites, climaxing with 'Beyond the Sea'. At a front-row table in the audience, the newly elected Liberal MP John Hewson applauded lustily and sent us a bottle of champagne backstage. When Ricky died of a heart attack in 1988 it was standing room only at his funeral at St John's Anglican church in Darlinghurst. It was a conventional service to the end, until a choir converged on the altar from the four corners of the church, singing a haunting Maori lament. The voices soared like angels. I was with a mate, the TV journalist Ray Martin. We stood there together, lost in the simple beauty of the moment, our cheeks wet with tears.

Disaster finally clobbered me in 1983, at the party thrown for the launch of the blockbuster Australian horse movie *Phar Lap*, written by David Williamson and starring Tom Burlinson as the trainer Tommy Woodcock. A cast of hundreds caroused the night away at the newly completed harbourside mansion of the promoter Michael Edgley, a pile of concrete the size of a shopping mall's car park. At around midnight my wife entreated me to leave, pointing out with unarguable accuracy that I was due on air in five hours. Awash with champagne, I refused, so she left without me. I kept drinking, throwing it down. At about four-thirty am it dimly occurred to me that I should perhaps head to the studio, and somehow I hailed a taxi. At five-thirty, airily brushing aside the nervous doubts of my troops, I burst on air.

Honesty seemed to be the best policy. Best to be frank with the audience. 'I have to admit that I'm pissed as a parrot,' I said with laborious clarity and candour. (Listening back to the tape afterwards, it was actually: 'Haveramit, umpishedashaparrt.') With the uncertain help of a few litres of black coffee I blundered through until seven o'clock, when the station executives usually tuned in. They ordered me off the air forthwith and I was suspended without pay for a week.

Years later, the British TV interviewer Michael Parkinson told me he had been listening at the time, on his way to the airport. 'Funniest thing in years,' he said. 'I nearly drove off the road laughing.'

At the time I thought it was funny too. I had no idea it was the first drop of the corrosive acid of celebrity, in all its destructive folly.

✧

Readers who have persevered with this chapter might now be punch-drunk from the name-dropping. Understandably so. But that's the way it was, and it would be silly to conceal it beneath layers of false modesty. Or even genuine modesty. For all the partying and star gazing, I was actually working harder than ever. Kerri was doing most of the child-rearing, a task made more difficult by my unfriendly hours. 'Daddy can't play with you this afternoon, he needs to have a nap.' Truth be known, Daddy was often sleeping off a hangover. I recoil at the memory.

In 1982 Max Suich suggested that I should write a weekly column for the *Sydney Morning Herald*, reviewing TV programs. 'Plenty of jokes,' he insisted.

I did my best. It was a grind watching the stuff, sucking up time when I could have been asleep, but I found that I enjoyed the discipline of writing for print and the pleasure of seeing it on a page – a new avenue of journalism for me. This was the beginning of an association with the *Herald* that lasted, on and off, up and down, for some thirty years.

Adding to the load, I also agreed to do a television version of *Friday News Review*. Terry Willesee, one of Mike Willesee's endless supply of younger brothers, had a half-hour current-affairs show on the Seven network, *Willesee at Seven*. He asked if I was interested.

Yes, I was, but without considering, at first, what an extra burden it would be. On radio you can create the Charge of the Light Brigade, the Mad Hatter's Tea Party or the destruction of the planet with a few sound effects. Television needs the pictures as well. The radio scripts would have to be rewritten for the small screen. Scratching for ideas, I asked the *National Times* cartoonist Patrick Cook if he would draw the characters, to be turned into puppets. Patrick, one of the sharpest, most original minds I have ever met, did it brilliantly. A professional puppeteer made them up in latex rubber and, bingo, away we went. But it meant more long hours at a keyboard, and a tedious drive to the Seven studios to record each episode. I was burning the candle at both ends, running on hype and adrenaline.[109]

The advertising mogul John Singleton hired me to do TV ads for the *Sun-Herald* newspaper, a charade which had me frocked up in a designer dressing-gown in a designer kitchen rented for the shoot. I buttered some toast, munched a boiled egg and waved the newspaper at the camera.

Singo was actually good to do business with. 'Do you want a contract or a handshake?' he asked me. I settled for the latter and he stuck to his word and paid me promptly. I've tried very hard to dislike John Singleton over the years, for all the obvious reasons, but I've failed. He has never done me over, is amiable enough when you run into him at a restaurant, and I figure that anyone who's had to tolerate Alan Jones for so long deserves only sympathy.

More bizarre still, some advertising agency creative genius decided I would be the right person to extol the virtues of the Findus frozen meals made by the Nestlé company. God knows why, but financially it was an offer to good to refuse. That had me perched on a studio stool brandishing a forkful of chicken and vegies with a gluggy white sauce on it, then shoving it in my mouth and smacking my lips in delight. Not that it was the actual Findus product they used in the ad; a chef was installed in a corner off-camera, sauteing far more telegenic morsels of fresh chook, carrot and peas, which were then artistically arrayed on the fork by the props guy. It took about 400 takes to get the thing done to the director's satisfaction. 'That was lovely, Mike, but let's do just one more. Hold the fork a little higher this time, please.' Gritting my teeth and thinking of the cheque, I got on with it, spitting the gunk into a bucket after each take. I have hated making TV commercials ever since. The faffing about is ludicrous. It invariably takes a crew of hundreds to do it: enough directors, writers, script assistants, camera operators, clapper loaders, grips, best boys, gaffers, boom operators, set dressers, standby props and hair and makeup artists to produce a full length Hollywood blockbuster – *Indiana Jones and the Frozen Chicken in Parsley Sauce.* The directors are almost always wankers, carrying on as if they were Steven Spielberg or Ridley Scott for what will be only thirty seconds of airtime. Film industry caterers arrive on the set at dawn to turn out lavish breakfasts, morning snacks, three-course lunches and afternoon teas for the cast and crew, the whole gourmet extravagance billed to the hapless client. It continues to amaze me that advertising agencies get away with it.

I was always ambivalent about the advertising business. Producers of goods and services are entitled to publicise their wares and consumers to be informed of them. A modern market economy could not work without advertising. It kept newspapers and commercial radio and television afloat, and it paid my wages and my bills. But – with a few notable exceptions – the advertising game was all too often a refuge for spivs, poseurs and intellectual pygmies.

✧

The 1982 Falklands War gave me lift-off. Argentina's sudden invasion of Britain's Falkland Islands in the South Atlantic that April stunned the world. At 10 Downing Street, stumbling in the opinion polls, Margaret Thatcher seized the moment to arouse the British lion. On 5 April a hastily assembled taskforce of the Royal Navy sailed south to do battle with the Argentine navy and air force.

Australia had no stake in the war. It was a long way from our shores. There was even a good case that the Falklands – *Las Malvinas* – were actually Argentine territory illegally seized by the British in 1841. But the military dictator General Leopoldo Galtieri was a corrupt and brutal thug, and Australian sympathies were with kith and kin in Britain.

As the British taskforce approached the islands and the fighting began to hot up, Australia began to take notice. We assumed, naturally, that vastly superior Anglo-Saxon pluck and skill would send the upstart Argies packing quick-smart, and this indeed seemed to be happening when a British submarine sank the ancient Argentine cruiser *General Belgrano* on 2 May, with the loss of 323 lives.[110]

That equation changed and the complacency evaporated two days later, when Argentina attacked the destroyer HMS *Sheffield*, with twenty killed. Australians awoke to hear about it on radio. After a long struggle by her crew to keep her afloat, *Sheffield* sank on 10 May. That wasn't supposed to happen, surely. Suddenly we were eager for news of the war, an interest that intensified with the destruction of six more British ships, including another destroyer and two frigates.

The story was perfectly timed for breakfast radio in Australia. Most of the action and the British Ministry of Defence briefings took place while we slept. The news was still fresh when morning alarm clocks went off. At 2GB we were competing against the ABC with our coverage, but we held our own and more. We showed that commercial radio could also be in touch with world events, and more often than not nimbler than the rigidly formulaic ABC breakfast shows. We were gathering speed.

A year later, another contest at sea – if less lethal – fired us up again. In September 1983, in the waters off Newport, Rhode Island, the twelve-metre yacht *Australia II* was carrying the hopes of a nation. The America's Cup, the most famous trophy in world yachting, an ornately decorated ewer crafted from solid sterling silver, had not left American hands since 1851. In this challenge series of seven races, the Australians had won three and the American boat *Liberty* had won three. *Australia II* had to win the final race to unbolt 'the Auld Mug' from its plinth at the New York Yacht Club. On the morning of Tuesday, 27 September 1983, as the race drew towards its close, *Liberty* had the upper hand.[111]

The Australians had done brilliantly to get this far. No other challenger had come so close to victory. The West Australian tycoon Alan Bond, brash and pugnacious, had poured millions into designing and building his boat, with its revolutionary winged keel. Millions more went into mounting the attack, with a handpicked crew of Australia's best sailors. Australians are largely indifferent to yacht racing, a sport for the rich, but we were captivated by this contest. The chance of beating the Yanks fired the nation. National pride and honour were at stake. The races were ideally timed for breakfast radio in Sydney and 2GB had a team there. Our US correspondent John Raedler followed the yachts in a boat, backed up with expert commentary from Jeanine Treharne, a skilled sailor whose husband, Hugh, was the tactician on board *Australia II*.

That morning, millions gathered around their TVs at home. Bob Hawke, prime minister for just six months, was watching at the Royal Perth Yacht Club. Millions more took their radios to work on public transport or listened in their cars. In the 2GB studio I crossed to Raedler and Treharne for regular live updates, hearing them grow more and more despondent at the prospect of defeat. The disappointment and despair around Australia was almost palpable.

In the last leg of the race everything changed. On the run to the finish line, *Australia II*'s skipper, John Bertrand, engaged *Liberty*'s Dennis Conner in a spectacular tacking duel. The breeze favoured Bertrand. Suddenly Raedler was shouting that we might win, we could win. It was electrifying. I never had a more exciting moment in radio. We threw away the log of commercials to be played, abandoned the scheduled news bulletins and let Raedler and Treharne carry it.

In the final minutes *Australia II* forged ahead. 'Stand up, Australia!' Raedler bellowed. It would become one of the classic cries of sports broadcasting. The nation rose to its feet, shouting. As Bertrand crossed the line to win by forty-one seconds, there was an explosion of euphoria, a tsunami of national ecstasy. 'Any boss who sacks a worker for not turning up today is a bum,' gurgled an exultant Hawke to the cameras and microphones. Bond and Bertrand were national heroes.

Our coverage helped to cement the 2GB breakfast show in the hearts of the Sydney audience. Thanks to Raedler and Treharne, we had done it better than anyone. Radio is still the most immediate, the most portable and the most intimate of the mass media, and we had emphatically demonstrated its power and range. The ratings continued to rise, a steady, sustained climb.

To add thrust, the station beefed up its newsroom under the name 'Macquarie News'. This had history, going back to the earliest days of 2GB from 1938. When Max Suich took over 2GB he had unwisely scrapped the Macquarie brand, thinking it was old-fashioned, out of date. Nothing else changed, but truckloads of listeners complained that the news had 'gone off', that the quality had slumped. Macquarie News was hastily resurrected, and a new news director was enticed over from 2UE to kick it along.

Charlie Cox was in his late twenties, raised and schooled in the Sutherland Shire, in Sydney's south. Like most Shire kids he had grown up on a surfboard and messing about in boats. Apart from women, who threw themselves at him in droves, his adult passion was motor racing, first in two Mazda Rotary RX4s in hill climbs and production saloon car events at the old Oran Park and Amaroo Park tracks, where he was a regular winner. With more skill and experience he graduated to a white Brock Holden V8 Commodore, with an engine so hot that it ran on aviation fuel.

We had run into each other briefly when I was at 2UE, where he was reading the news at breakfast. Our new relationship at GB got off to a rocky start early in the piece when I corrected him on the pronunciation of some word, and he – very reasonably – told me over the studio intercom to fuck off. I stormed into his office and we had a fiery row. Our long friendship began there. More than a friendship: although I am twelve years older, Charlie and I are as close as twin brothers, bonded by a shared sense of humour and a similar view of the world and its follies. Over the years our careers have entwined, and we each have a deep understanding of the other. For blokes, I don't think it gets any better. Charlie hit the newsroom running, with energy and skill.

✧

Neil Davis was killed on Monday, 9 September 1985. I heard of it with bruising directness. On holiday in India with my wife, I was idly reading a Reuters teleprinter in the foyer of a hotel in New Delhi. The bells rang for an important story – ting, ting, ting – and the news chattered onto the paper as I watched.

I was transfixed, rigid with shock. Like all Neil's friends, I thought he was immortal. In other times he might have been an Arthurian knight; he would have swum the Bosphorus with Byron, could have flown a Spitfire from Biggin Hill. But the Reuters story was emphatic. He had been shot while covering an attempted military coup in the Thai capital, Bangkok. Later we learned that he and his soundman, Bill Latch, and another Australian journalist, Gary Burns, had been filming rebel soldiers in a tank firing at a government radio station. Bullets and shrapnel were zinging everywhere. Shrapnel killed Neil and Latch, although not instantly. Neil knew he was dying. His last words were, 'Oh . . . shit.' With great courage, Gary Burns stayed with Neil until the shooting stopped and it was safe to drag him away.

I hadn't seen Neil for a couple of years. We had last met in 1981, when we literally bumped into each other in Trafalgar Square while covering the Charles and Diana wedding. He was filming for the American NBC network, I think. 'Got a cigarette, digger?' were his first words, a traditional greeting he offered to all his friends. Neil smoked, but it was his proud boast that he never bought a pack of cigarettes. He cheerfully bummed them, a foible we all indulged. We found a pub for a few beers, reminisced about old times and then went our separate ways.

It was unbelievable, inconceivable that he was dead. After all he had been through in years of war, the dangers he had faced almost daily in Indochina and elsewhere, how absurd that he should be killed in some tinpot coup in Thailand. It was indecent – *unfair* – that he should go that way. Some people who barely knew him suggested he had a death wish, that he deliberately courted danger for some deep psychological reason. I do not think that was true. His biographer and our mutual friend Tim Bowden got it right:

> Davis liked covering stories that required him to display exceptional physical endurance and a cool calculation of the odds in tumultuous actions, to draw on a network of well placed informants and to make perceptive interpretations dependent on a long and sympathetic understanding of other cultures.[112]

Tim also recorded the lines of verse that Neil wrote in the flyleaves of his neatly kept diaries:

> One crowded hour of glorious life
> Is worth an age without a name.[113]

Neil was a kind and generous man. He had mentored me, taught me a lot when I was wet behind the ears. I felt his loss keenly.

✧

Out of the blue, a letter arrived from St Joseph's College, Hunters Hill. It was an invitation from the headmaster, Brother Joseph McMahon. Would I be available to open the annual art exhibition?

I was getting a lot of invitations like this now. Almost every day there were requests for after-dinner speeches, for me to be master of ceremonies at this and that, to officially open something else. Some offered a speaker's fee for the corporate stuff, others with a worthy cause hoped you would do it free. I did a bit of both. The oddest gig I ever accepted was to be a 'judge' for the Fashions in the Field competition at a Randwick spring carnival race meeting, a role for which I was and remain uniquely unqualified. God knows why I did it. Tottering on their $1000 Manolo Blahniks, half a dozen severely blonded matrons of the species usually described as 'of Middle Eastern or Mediterranean appearance' paraded before us in their finery, smiling fiercely. Nonplussed, I followed the lead of a women's magazine fashion editor who knew the ropes. When we chose the winner, the losers scowled at us like the Furies of the *Iliad*.

But St Joseph's, my father's old school? Surely they knew my wicked family history. To the best of my knowledge, Jimmy Carlton was still a non-person there, any trace of him obliterated from the school's records. Why would they invite his bastard son and widow inside their handsome wrought-iron gates? Curious, we accepted the invitation, if only to get a look at the place.

It turned out that the art exhibition was one of the big social events on the St Joseph's calendar. Parents came in droves, dressed to the nines for a gala evening, and the kids' artworks were sold to raise money. I duly fronted on the night, in suit and tie, with a prepared speech of anodyne remarks. I was shown to a seat on stage in a crowded auditorium.

The rest of the evening is a blur. All I remember is that Brother McMahon introduced me with a gracious and moving speech about my father and his time at Joeys. Jimmy Carlton was one of the school's greatest old boys, he said. It came as such a shock, and with such emotional force, that at first I was gobsmacked. Gradually it dawned on me. This was resurrection: the rehabilitation of James Andrew Carlton in the Catholic community which had nurtured him, which he had once loved and served, and by whose sacred rites he was buried. Here was the prodigal son, posthumously welcomed back into the fold. I came close to crying. On stage, before all those parents, students and teachers, I was struggling to keep my composure. My mind was awhirl, my heart racing. I have no idea what I said in reply.

It was 1985. The Sydney writer and scholar-priest Father Ed Campion saw it as a turning point, a sign of a new maturity in the Australian church. 'That night the glory came back to Hunters Hill,' he wrote. 'Here surely was a new, more adult Australian Catholicism.'[114]

I will always be grateful to Joe McMahon for his generosity, and on his watch I kept up a connection with Joeys. My father's football and athletics photographs were returned to the walls. My mother agreed, rather warily, that we could give the school some of his sporting memorabilia to display, and we formally presented it at a student assembly. I was touched by that, too, but Enid was nervous and ill at ease, discombobulated by so much Catholicism in the air. She had not forgotten the nuns who had offered to spirit her first-born child away. I had lunch with the brothers on the teaching staff, and Joe invited me to some rugby games, including that most fiercely contested rivalry, the annual GPS grudge match with the Jesuits of nearby St Ignatius, Riverview. We donated a prize, the Jimmy Carlton Cup, to be awarded each year to the school's best all-round athlete.[115]

Over the years, a few people have sought to portray me as 'anti-Catholic', consumed by old Protestant sectarian hatreds. This is tendentious nonsense. I am an atheist, yes. But for the good and true people of the Roman Catholic faith I have the utmost respect and admiration.

✧

Cloud Valley Farm is as lovely as the name suggests. Its gentle green paddocks rest in the embrace of rain-forested hills in the secluded Yarramalong Valley, about ninety minutes' drive north of Sydney. Black Angus cattle graze on 132 well-fenced hectares watered by the Wyong River. From the front gate a long driveway winds through stands of native eucalypts and sculpted avenues of European deciduous trees to a homestead that is a symphony in honey-coloured sandstone, shaded by wide, pillared verandahs. There are formal gardens bounded by lines of box hedges, tended with care. A paved walk beneath archways of purple wisteria leads to a private outdoor swimming pool and tennis court. There are guests' cottages away from the main house. Hidden behind a shield of trees is a big tin shed, where John Laws kept his collection of vintage Bentleys and Porsches, MGs and Jaguars and motorbikes.

That was Cloud Valley as I first saw it in the mid-1980s. John sold it in 2009, but for years it was a weekend retreat for him and Caroline Laws, his third and final wife, famously known to his listeners as 'the Princess'. We held a joint barbecue there about a year after he came across to 2GB in 1985. 'John and Caroline Laws and Mike and Kerri Carlton invite you . . .' The entire staff of the radio station turned up with partners and kids for a Saturday in the autumn sunshine. Steaks and burgers sizzled. Beer and champagne flowed. There was dancing to an old-style jukebox in the shed. The farmhands gave the kids rides on the bikes and tractors. Kerri and I stayed the night in one of the guest cottages.

This was the apogee of the glory days at 2GB. In a long, hard slog I had beaten both Clive Robertson at 2BL and Gary O'Callaghan at 2UE to have Sydney's top-rating breakfast radio show. At the Fairfaxes' expense, Nigel Milan threw a lavish smorgasbord lunch at the station to celebrate, the tables laden with prawns and oysters, cold chickens, salads and cheeses and desserts. Toasts were drunk and vainglorious speeches made, each more incoherent than the last. John

Laws then was still across the harbour at UE, where his ratings were holding up but the station itself was stumbling. I knew his contract there was coming to an end. Full of champagne that afternoon, and seized with my own importance, I went to my office and called him personally, urging him to join us at GB. John was one of a very few stars in radio who could bring his loyal audience with him, wherever he went. If he came to GB to do the morning program after me at nine am, it would cement the station at the top of the heap.

The call was a leap in the dark, the sort of impulsive thing you do when you are full of champagne and floating on air. John and I knew each other by then, but hardly warmly. Chilly would be a better word. I had occasionally parodied him in *Friday News Review* with send-ups of his poetry, which I knew he resented. If we ran into each other at some restaurant, or at one of those interminably tedious commercial radio industry award nights, we were at best frostily polite. He was the old bull. I was the young steer. We circled each other warily. But he took the call that afternoon, listened to my babbling career advice and said he would consider it.

I returned to the party, took Nigel aside and told him what I had done. He was stunned, although not at the idea of John Laws joining the stable. He and the Fairfax hierarchy had been considering putting that offer to him for a while. It was more that I had made the overture, off my own bat, when they had feared I would be implacably opposed. The last thing they wanted were two feuding stars creating chaos at the station. With that possibility apparently hosed down, the wheels began to turn.

John was bored at 2UE and did not particularly like working for the Lamb family, whom he regarded as stuffy and old-fashioned. There had been one or two awkward scenes when the chairman, Stewart Lamb, found his beloved gravel drive blocked by the Laws Rolls-Royce. The Princess, whom John had married in 1976, was independently wealthy and well connected in the ethereal heights of Eastern Suburbs society, including with some of the Fairfaxes. They would be much more congenial employers.

John had also been doing much the same show for a long while, taking calls from adoring and/or neurotic housewives and their truck-driving husbands, and I suspect he thought it was time to renew the act. One of his strengths over his radio career has been his ability to reinvent himself, a skill which has saved him from the oblivion that awaits so many radio stars unable to change, and he seized the chance. Moving to the 2GB Newstalk format would require him to get into the news and current-affairs business, a radical realignment.

He went at it with a will. My mate Vincent Smith was hired as his new producer, to add journalistic clout. John never wanted nor pretended to be a journalist, but he relished the opportunity to become an influential commentator. There was another incentive too: a contract worth $750,000 a year, with such added frills as eight weeks' leave and two first-class around-the-world airline tickets each summer. On top of that were his national sponsorship deals with the likes of Toyota, Valvoline Motor Oils and sundry others, which pushed his income well into seven figures.

He came on board in the early autumn of 1985, in a blaze of publicity. The King had crossed the water. Newspaper photographers and the TV news cameras shot his grand arrival, and there were obsequious interviews. He got the prime space in the basement car park and an office handsomely redecorated to Caroline's instructions. I watched and learned.

Over a few lunches, the two of us agreed to bury the hatchet. It was in our mutual interest, and we did it. After one lengthy repast at a restaurant in North Sydney, we impulsively pulled a stunt on our former employer. I do not recall whose idea it was but we drove to the 2UE studios and marched in the front door. Watched by the stunned staff, we did a solemn tour of inspection of the entire building, saying not a word, and left again as suddenly as we had come. Then we collapsed with laughter in the waiting Roller. This was a larrikin side to John that I had not seen before, but would grow to enjoy. I think he felt the same about me.

He was fun to be with, a goldmine of gossip and good jokes. I genuinely liked him, and I still do. His conversation sparkled and he enjoyed a laugh. As we got to know each other better he sometimes shed the aura of stardom, which acted like a protective force field to prevent intrusion into his personal life, and he would talk rationally and amiably, at length. He was well read and knowledgeable about politics and world affairs. Politicians cultivated him to get their messages across, at times with truckloads of flattery. 'More than any other prime minister, more than any other government, we've gone out and sought to get the wisdom, the benefit, of John Laws' listeners. Because John Laws' listeners are Australia,' Bob Hawke assured him on air in 1987. Occasionally there were startling lacunae. When Paul Keating famously warned him in an interview that Australia was in danger of becoming 'a third-rate economy . . . a banana republic', it was on the front page of every newspaper. John called me into his office the next day. 'What's a banana republic?' he asked.

So we got along well. We were in the same business, allies in the same cause, shackled to the same demands of ratings and audiences, and we could discuss it as friendly professionals. And I was still a little in awe of him. This was the radio star I had listened to in my teenage years, never once imagining that I would be travelling in the same galaxy.

I also sensed a certain shyness in him, and at times a solitary disposition which hinted at an inner loneliness. He once admitted to me that he had no intimate personal friends, male or female. Caroline was his closest companion. She called him Lawsie, like his listeners. Beneath the carapace of stardom and great wealth was buried the little boy who had been packed off to boarding school by remote, unloving parents, the teenager who had suffered from polio and bad acne. He was a vulnerable and even insecure man, and sometimes it showed. It was there in his drive to possess the trappings of fame – the grand houses, the fleet of cars, the curated works of art, the splendid motor cruiser on the harbour. These possessions reassured him that he had made it, big-time.

And he liked to show them. His mansion in Queen Street, Woollahra, its exterior walls carefully stained to resemble a Venetian *palazzo*, was a virtual museum of Australian art and antiques collected from around the world. Here a Rodin sculpture, there a small Roman marble column dating from before Christ, on the wall a big Brett Whiteley. At my first dinner there I relaxed in a wood-panelled study lined from floor to ceiling with leather-bound books, quaffing the bourbon and Coke he habitually drank as an aperitif. It might have been the library of a minor Medici. I marvelled that such luxury and elegance existed in the media trade.

✧

Not that I was doing too badly. By the mid-1980s we had moved our family up Sydney's North Shore to Turramurra, a suburb invariably described by journalists as 'leafy'. We bought a big two-storey house built in the 1930s for a director of David Jones, a pile of high-gabled, mellow red brick that would have looked entirely in keeping in rural Surrey or Sussex. Giant liquidambar trees lorded it over green lawns, banks of carefully pruned azaleas, and a landscaped swimming pool. The singer Kamahl lived down the road; occasionally we would drop in for one of the truly magnificent curries cooked by his wife, Sahodra. The kids were booked into private schools, Alex at PLC Pymble and James, predictably, at Barker. We had a lovable beagle named Boswell. The garage boasted a midnight-blue Jaguar V12 XJS coupé for me and a silver Range Rover for Kerri, who used it to tow the float for her horse. For weekends we had a getaway cottage in the Blue Mountains, north-west of Sydney, at Mountain Lagoon, a little hamlet off the Bells Line of Road, near the apple orchards of Bilpin. It was a chalet of glass and timber on only a couple of acres, hardly in the class of Cloud Valley Farm, but still an idyllic retreat for long walks and lazy meals before blazing log fires. In autumn the deciduous trees were aflame, and in winter crunchy frost shrouded the grass. Diamond-bright stars shone in the country skies.

I find all this faintly ridiculous now, even embarrassing. It was the North Shore cliché with all the bells and whistles – the well-heeled existence I had sometimes envied in my schoolboy years. I grabbed it with both hands, as if to the manner born. Like most baby-boomer males I had been conditioned from childhood to be the hunter–warrior, bringing the dinosaur steaks back to the waiting womenfolk in the cave each night. My mother was immensely satisfied that I was fulfilling this role and would occasionally tell me so, very proudly. My wife was less enraptured by the domestic bliss. Kerri enjoyed the comforts, to be sure, and was grateful for them, but she had a science degree that she felt was going to waste. Full-time motherhood was all very well, but she worried at times that her brain was atrophying, and she chafed to get back into a laboratory white coat. This was a small warning cloud on the horizon – or would have been if I had seen it. But I was enjoying the rewards for the hard grind of three am starts and the endless pressure for ratings. Like John Laws, I craved the trappings of success.

Then 2GB offered me a new contract. My existing agreement had a year to run, but the station wanted to lock me in for a longer period. The new deal came out of the blue, and it startled me: it was serious big bucks.

But the clincher blew me away. Charlie Cox led me down to 2GB's basement garage. There, in all its glory, sat an E-Type Jaguar sports car, fire-engine red with a black leather interior and gleaming chrome. I had dreamed of owning an E-Type since I first saw one the year I left school, and I recognised this as the 1962 roadster, a 3.8-litre straight six, the classic model once rightly described by Enzo Ferrari, no less, as 'the most beautiful car ever made'. At first I thought Charlie was showing me a new addition to John's fleet, and I made all the right noises. Then he tossed me the keys. Sign the contract, brother, and the car is yours.

I think I stopped breathing for about five minutes. I think I flew around the car park ceiling. Eventually I squeezed into the driver's seat and fired up the engine, blipping the accelerator, exulting in the throaty throb of the twin exhausts. Then I went back upstairs and signed the contract, on the spot.

The bandwagon rolled along, ever noisier and gaudier. For my fortieth birthday, in January 1986, the station threw a gala evening party on board a harbour ferry. Around 200 guests milled about at the Taronga Zoo wharf in the sunset, slurping champagne, waiting for me to arrive. I rode into their midst aboard an elephant hired for the occasion from a circus, clinging on for dear life. The ponderous pachyderm dropped to its knees and I tumbled down its mighty flanks to startled applause. I guess you had to be there ...

PART 4

18
Rupert and me

THE LITTLE WHITE SEAPLANE from Nadi touched down amid plumes of spray and taxied towards the beach. Friendly hands hoisted me and my wife onto a timber jetty.

'Bula!' cried a smiling Fijian, placing garlands of frangipani around our necks. 'Welcome to Turtle Island. My name is Milly. You are a journalist, Mr Carlton?'

'I am, yes.'

'Ah,' said Milly. 'There is another Australian journalist staying here with us: Mr Rupert Murdoch. Maybe you know him?'

My heart sank.

Turtle was one of the first of the small luxury resorts in Fiji, the brainchild of an American advertising man, Richard Evanson, who had fled California for the laid-back life of the South Pacific. On a small, private island in the western Yasawa group a dozen spacious *burés*, or bungalows, were scattered under the palms along a crescent beach of turquoise waters and sand the colour of shredded coconut. You paid a lot of money to holiday in both luxurious comfort and the utmost simplicity, a lazy idyll without television or telephones. There was not even a bar, just deep armchairs on the beach. Pre-dinner drinks and feasts of freshly caught reef fish and lobster were served al fresco at one long, communal guest table beneath the trees. It was there that Rupert and I first met.

He was with his second wife, Anna Torv, and two of their three children, James and Lachlan. There was an iron rule at Turtle that business was not to be discussed in public, but he knew who I was and something of my background, and we shook hands politely, if warily. He was still on his way to global eminence. His Australian newspaper empire was thriving and he was about to ace his Fairfax competitors by snapping up Melbourne's *Herald and Weekly Times* group. In Britain he was battling to destroy the power of the closed-shop printing trade unions, with the encouragement and active help of Margaret Thatcher. His British newspapers – *The Times*, the *Sunday Times*, the *Sun* and the *News of the World* – were being printed on state-of-the-art presses at a new plant he had secretly built at Wapping, in London's Docklands. Thousands of printers had lost their jobs. They formed picket lines that sometimes erupted into violent clashes with the police. In the US he was still on the make as well, with the *New York Post* newspaper and his first foothold in movies and television through the 20th Century Fox corporation. Rupert was running fast.

There were only twenty or so guests on the island, so we were unavoidably thrown together at mealtimes. We obeyed the rules and discussed none of the above, much as I would have liked to question him about it. Nor did he bring it up. To my surprise, he made no attempt to chuck his weight around. I had expected him to come on all Citizen Kane, condescending if he would talk to me at all, but he was amiable company. Pleasant, even. He might have been any business executive on a family vacation. Books, movies, politics and general gossip were okay topics, along with the day's activities. He did make it very plain that he was infatuated with Thatcher. Anna, blonde and elegant, mingled and handed around the canapés. The boys romped on the beach. A couple of times we went fishing together in the little Turtle Island boat, or snorkelling over the reefs.

Those excursions provided a glimpse into the other Rupert. Then in his mid-fifties, he was vigorous, energetic and intensely competitive. The fish he caught had to be bigger than yours. He had to swim further from the boat than you did, or dive deeper into the coral and come up with more shells than you had collected. It was not done offensively, nor was it even calculated, I don't think; it was just the way his brain worked. He wanted to win and he would keep going until he did.

One small cameo was curiously revealing. After one dive he clambered back into the boat proudly clutching a gleaming black shell the size of a small apple. It was beautiful. We all admired it and the two Fijian boatmen told us it was extremely rare to find one.

Rupert beamed. This was a big win. 'What do you think it's worth?' he asked them.

The Fijians looked puzzled.

'If I sold it, what would I get for it?' he persisted.

The men shrugged and laughed, bemused. Clearly such an idea had never occurred to them. Rupert seemed disappointed. Surely everything had a price.

A day or so later he was gone, back to New York, leaving Anna and the boys behind. 'He couldn't stand the isolation anymore,' she explained that evening, rather wistfully. Turtle had only a staticky radio-telephone link to the Fijian mainland, and no connection with the world beyond. Rupert could not rule his empire from afar – could not call his editors or his executives on a whim, as he is so notoriously wont to do – and the lack of contact had agitated him.

I encountered him only once again, at a Christmas party he gave at the Victoria and Albert Museum in London, where we chatted briefly about nothing. That was all. It is one of the happier boasts of my career in journalism that I have taken the Murdoch shilling only once. In 1992 I was hired to write a piece for the *Sunday Times* in London about that horrifying moment when Paul Keating accused Britain of betraying Australia at the fall of Singapore.

There is no denying Murdoch's achievement in creating an international publishing and entertainment colossus from his small beginnings in Adelaide. His success with News Corp in its various guises is unique in the Anglophone world, by most measures a personal and corporate triumph. Its tragedy is the trail of destruction left in his wake on three continents. Journalism itself has been the principal victim, its honourable precepts and practices trampled in the stampede to vulgarity, greed, hypocrisy and arrant dishonesty – and, in the UK, the reckless criminality of the *News of the World* phone-hacking scandal. Fixated upon accruing power, politically amoral, Murdoch has used his newspapers and his television stations not to inform millions of readers and viewers in the public interest but to manipulate politicians and the democratic process for the benefit and profit of his empire. Like most billionaires I have encountered, he instinctively equates wealth with wisdom, a view reinforced by the sycophants clustered around him. Omniscient, imperious, magnificent, he rules unchallenged. The British had very good reason for nicknaming him 'the Sun King'. Another label they gave him – 'the Dirty Digger' – was less flattering but more apt.

It is one of the more ridiculous flourishes of News Corp sophistry that Murdoch editors are independent – that he does not tell them how to think or what to write. The fact is that he does not need to. A few of those editors have been clever and agile, it's true. Kelvin MacKenzie of the *Sun* and Col Allan of the Sydney *Daily Telegraph* and, later, the *New York Post* terrorised their reporters, but they had a hard nose for a story, a rat-like instinct for a tabloid front-page headline, and often the pungent wit to carry it off. (MacKenzie famously fired the *Sun*'s resident astrologer with a letter that began: 'As you will already know . . .') Most, though, have been dull plodders and imitators, frequently with tatty flaws of character – chosen for just those reasons, perhaps. Some in Australia have worked for no other boss, a dismal career. But all have been smart enough to know instinctively what their employer wants, and they doggedly deliver it. When Murdoch publicly supported George W. Bush's disastrous Iraq War in 2003, all 175 of his editors worldwide found themselves in furious agreement. Miraculously, too, they are at one on another bee in the News Corp bonnet, the urge to destroy public broadcasting in Britain and Australia. Rupert does not see why listeners and viewers should get a free service when they could be paying him for it. The jihad against the BBC in Britain and the ABC in Australia is waged like some endless infant tantrum.

The *Australian* newspaper, losing millions each year, exists solely as a megaphone for its master's increasingly eccentric right-wing obsessions, to help him bend Canberra to his will. There are fine journalists working there, some of them my friends, but the paper must be read through the prism of Murdoch's hates and enthusiasms. If it is deemed necessary, the *Australian* and its tabloid stablemates will unleash personal vendetta journalism to destroy their perceived enemies, an onslaught of vicious character assassination. It is often quixotic, done on a whim, because they can. The Fox News cable channel in the US, created by the liar, bully and serial sexual predator Roger Ailes – more character flaws – serves a similar purpose in the American polity.

The trick works a treat. Eager for the Sun King's public benediction, presidents and prime ministers and party leaders of every stripe rush to hurl themselves into his embrace, avid for a quid pro quo. Rupert excels at picking political winners, confident from considerable experience that they will respond with gratitude and favours. Ronald Reagan looked after him handsomely. In 1995 the British Labour leader, Tony Blair, dropped everything to fly around the world to attend a Murdoch corporate séance at Hayman Island on the Barrier Reef. The payoff was the Murdoch papers' fulsome support, which helped sweep Blair to power in the 1997 general election. It is one of the delicious ironies of our time that the bromance collapsed in chaos and loathing in 2013, after Rupert discovered that his third wife, Wendi Deng, had found in the devious and grasping Blair a secret shoulder she could cry on.

And they keep on coming. 'I am very gratified that he thinks I am doing a good job,' said Hillary Clinton when he offered to hold a fundraiser for her Senate campaign in 2006.[116] 'Rupert Murdoch is a great guy who likes me much better as a very successful candidate than he ever did as a very successful developer!' tweeted Donald Trump in January 2017.[117] One of the more depressing sights of Australian democracy is to see our visiting prime ministers – Liberal or Labor – stepping from a limousine outside the Sun King's Manhattan penthouse to perform the obligatory grovel before the throne.

The internet and communications revolution of the twenty-first century has seen a catastrophic collapse in the reach and power of the traditional media. The reasons for this are beyond the scope of this book, but the grim truth is that in almost every case the grand old newspaper mastheads have been hammered hard. Advertisers and readers have fled. Some papers have gone forever; others, much diminished, struggle to cling on. Journalists have never been held in particularly high esteem, but not in all my career have they been so despised as they are now.

Rupert Murdoch bears much of the responsibility. The raw fact is that – as most of us understand – his newspapers and television stations cannot be trusted to provide a fair, responsible report. In the news pages there is all too often a hidden agenda of slant and bias, in fantasies concocted or facts ignored if they conflict with the agenda. The opinion pages of the *Australian* are a farce. So long as they conform to Rupert's broad global view, his far-right bloviators have open slather to indulge their paranoia in the culture wars they have invented, and in which they see themselves as heroic gladiators. The saving grace is that, for all their pomp and circumstance, so few people read them.

✧

As the 1980s wore on, the rising tide of crime and corruption in New South Wales became a flood that threatened to engulf the Wran Labor government. Its dirty waters sluiced through both state and federal parliaments, the police, the media, the judiciary and even the state's favourite sport, rugby league. Month after month the public was buffeted by new scandals. Al Capone's Chicago was a haven of civic tranquillity by comparison.

Much of the muck was raked by a new cohort of investigative journalists. In 1983, at the ABC's *Four Corners*, in an explosive program called *The Big League*, reporter Chris Masters blew the lid on corruption in football. He pointed the finger at the notoriously bent New South Wales chief magistrate, Murray Farquhar, and the NSWRL boss Kevin Humphreys, who had embezzled thousands of dollars. Farquhar had told a junior magistrate that 'the premier has just phoned. Kevin Humphreys is not to be committed.' Sensationally, that raised the possibility that Wran himself might have been involved in an attempt to pervert the course of justice.

There was more to come. The *National Times* journalist Marian Wilkinson nailed the crooked Minister for Corrective Services, Rex Jackson, and then, in another feature story, Farquhar again. More incendiary still were the '*Age* tapes', as they became known, phone taps illegally recorded by the New South Wales police and first published at length in Melbourne's *Age* newspaper. They implicated the former Labor attorney-general and then High Court judge Lionel Murphy in corrupt conduct. Murphy and Wran were the closest of mates.

Nineteen eighty-four was a vintage year. It brought allegations from the Costigan Royal Commission that a business tycoon code-named 'the Goanna' was a tax criminal and drug tsar. An infuriated Kerry Packer thundered into the arena with guns blazing, a young barrister named Malcolm Turnbull at his side, to say it was him they were talking about and to deny every skerrick. He sued Fairfax for defamation, won handsomely and nursed his understandable hatred. That year also gave us the infamous 'Fine Cotton Affair', in which a syndicate of trainers and bookmakers clumsily substituted one dud horse for a much better one at a Brisbane race meeting. The bookmaker Bill Waterhouse, another Wran friend, and his son Robbie were banned from the track for fourteen years. A month later the Comanchero and Bandido bikie gangs fought a gun battle at a pub in Milperra in Sydney's south-west, with seven killed and twenty-eight wounded.

And the New South Wales police themselves were out of control. Early in the evening of Wednesday, 6 June 1984 an honest undercover officer with the Drug Squad, Michael Drury, was shot twice through the kitchen window of his Sydney suburban home, and badly wounded. Rumour had it that the gunman was a notorious hitman, Christopher 'Rent-a-Kill' Flannery, hired by the inevitable Detective Sergeant Roger Rogerson. Flannery himself disappeared without trace in 1985, most likely murdered at the home of the 'colourful racing identity' George Freeman, and his body dumped at sea. Bank robberies were a weekly affair, mostly on payroll Fridays. All this was fodder for my radio program, unending.

Various enquiries and a royal commission began digging. 'Buckets' Jackson and Farquhar eventually went to jail. Wran had been obliged to stand aside from the premiership during the royal commission into the league scandal, but he was found to have done nothing wrong. He had not sought to get the league boss out of trouble. Farquhar had lied. But as the troubles mounted, Wran's association with some of those named, however innocuous, ensured that muck stuck. Sensationally, Lionel Murphy was convicted on one count of perverting the course of justice, but then had that decision overturned on appeal, shortly before he died of cancer. Sometimes Wran acted decisively as the allegations flew about; at other times he ducked and dragged his feet, as if hoping that somehow they might evaporate.

Infuriated by the constant mention of his name during the turmoil, he hit back at a press conference. 'Now I'm thinking of changing my name by deed poll to Marmaduke,' he said in an unusually leaden attempt at humour. 'Because that's a very distinctive name, and if Marmaduke is mentioned in some context then there's a good chance that it might be me.'[118]

I seized on it. In the next *Friday News Review* I changed his name from Premier Never Wrong to Premier Marmaduke, and in a flurry of sketches I satirised the never-ending torrent of corruption. Marmaduke took to appearing amid a rev of car engines, a squeal of tyres and a screech of brakes. 'Are you from the ABC?' he rasped, a line Wran had famously barked at an ABC journalist who'd annoyed him. There was a Minister for Corruption too, who sounded very much like Buckets Jackson.

Wran copped it silently on the chin for a while but eventually decided he'd had enough. Our early friendship long gone, he sued 2GB and me for defamation in the New South Wales Supreme Court. By using the name Marmaduke I was clearly and unmistakably implying that he was corrupt, he complained.

The case went to trial in March 1986. If we lost – if a jury found that we had indeed defamed Wran – we would be up for many hundreds of thousands of dollars in damages. Fairfax would pay my share, but my reputation and my career – that part of me that was a humorist and satirist – would take a hard blow.

✧

Tom Hughes had stage fright. From my seat in the witness box I could see that his hands were shaking slightly as he rose on the first day to begin questioning me. The notes he held were quivering. I was surprised and, better still, encouraged. Thomas Eyre Forrest Hughes QC, a former Liberal federal attorney-general and a titan of the Sydney bar (and, incidentally, Malcolm Turnbull's father-in-law), was nervous.

Hughes was appearing for Neville, a good choice. He was an old campaigner in defamation law, renowned for his skill in the thespian arts of swaying a jury. Nicknamed 'Frosty' for his chilly public demeanour, majestically bewigged and gowned, he looked the part. Our man, Neil McPhee QC, was very different. Small and wiry, with a sailor's weather-beaten face and rolling gait, and the bark of a chain-smoker, he looked as if he had slept in his gown. His wig, which appeared to be moulting, was clapped at a careless angle on the back of his head. Neil was a Victorian. He had sailed his yacht up from Melbourne single-handed and he slept on it in the harbour. Patrick Cook, the great cartoonist, nicknamed him 'the Bosun'. His junior barrister, Steven Rares, would later become a Federal Court judge.

The courtroom was full, standing room only. It was a celebrity show, the talk of the town, covered by a media scrum. There are regular groupies who attend trials the way other people go to football matches, and they had queued to get in, clutching their lunch. Like football fans, they know all the players – judges, barristers, solicitors – and they can give you a well-informed rundown on their style and form. 'That judge is a real bastard. Hang you soon as look at yer.' One little old lady had brought her knitting, which was a touch more Madame Defarge than I would have liked. Neville sat behind his counsel. We opened with a jury of twelve people but when one went down sick we agreed to carry on with eleven. Ten were women, of various ages.

Tom opened the bowling with a couple of medium-pace deliveries. I noticed his hands were no longer shaking. Then he switched to spin.

'Mr Carlton, as a journalist and radio commentator, is it your duty to be truthful at all times?' he asked.

'No,' I said.

That surprised him, as I'd hoped it would. But he turned to the jury with a knowing look and came back again. 'So you are not always truthful?' This in a slightly triumphant tone, with another look at the jury.

'Not always, no.'

The Bosun had ordered me, on pain of death, to keep my answers as short as possible. The last thing he needed was some drivelling radio chatterbox making the defence difficult. I saw him knit his eyebrows. God, where was this going?

Tom fired up again. 'Could you give us an example of where you are *untruthful*, Mr Carlton?' he said evenly.

'Certainly. I might say to my audience that a flock of pink pigs flew past the window. That would be untrue, and they would know it. I joke like that all the time.'

The jury chortled, which again was what I had been hoping for. I needed to impress them. Tom took a deep breath. With an almost imperceptible nod, Neil McPhee at the bar table let me know I had won the exchange.

And so it went. As someone who spent his life asking the questions, I was enjoying answering them for a change. It was an even match. Occasionally a Hughes yorker would beat me. Sometimes I would belt him for four.

After a day of this we encountered each other standing at the men's urinal. I gave him a nod. 'You earn your money, Mr Hughes.'

He nodded back, with the faintest hint of a smile. 'And you earn yours, Mr Carlton.'

The show ran for four days. The judge, John Clarke, was a model of courtesy and fairness. Hughes had to prove that I had exposed Wran to public hatred, contempt or ridicule by branding him as corrupt. McPhee, on the other hand, had to make the jury laugh. If he could get them onside, we stood a chance. He took a punt and asked for examples of my comedy to be played to the court. Hughes strenuously objected but, after much legal blather with the jury absent, the judge let it through. We had chosen the sketches carefully, and for an hour or so we had the eleven good citizens chuckling and chortling. Hughes remained impassive as the sphinx, but there was a faint hint of despair about Neville, who knew crowds and juries as well as any man and could see he was in trouble.

On the final day, McPhee summed up, arguing to the jury that 200 years of Western civilisation, press freedom and the liberty of the individual would collapse in smoking ruins if I was found guilty. Sonorously, and to much rolling of eyeballs from other lawyers in court who had heard it all before, Hughes rolled out his traditional defamation *pièce de résistance*, Iago's stirring lines from Othello:

> Good name in man and woman, dear my lord,
> Is the immediate jewel of their souls.
> Who steals my purse steals trash; 'tis something, nothing;
> 'Twas mine, 'tis his, and has been slave to thousands;
> But he that filches from me my good name
> Robs me of that which not enriches him,
> And makes me poor indeed.

Defo barristers love that one. Invoking Shakespeare makes the show sound posh and learned, and they can be confident that not many jurors will know that Iago was one of the Bard's most sinister villains. After his summing up – and very balanced it was – Justice Clarke sent the jurors away to consider their verdict. They were still out when darkness fell.

This was truly agonising, a heavy, oppressive stasis. Neville and his lawyers and supporters clustered on one side of the small lobby. We huddled at the other, all waiting. The air was blue with cigarette smoke. The hours trudged on. We were within earshot of each other, so not much was said, and then only in whispers, until Neville's press secretary, the very likeable David Hurley, returned to announce that his wife had just given birth to a son. Congratulations all round.

Neville caught my eye. 'At least we've got one fucking result tonight,' he said.

I grinned as best I could. My nerves were shot.

The jury result didn't come until the next day. They were hung. They could not agree. Justice Clarke thanked them and discharged them. In effect, we'd won. Wran had brought the suit but it had failed.

I recall a heady rush of relief, so much that I felt dizzy. I hugged McPhee, Rares and my wife. We went to a lavish victory lunch. Much later, one of the jurors told me they had come down seven my way, four for Wran.

It gave me no pleasure to have beaten him. Despite all that had transpired, I still respected him for the many admirable qualities he possessed. I had neither evidence nor belief that he was corrupt, and I had not meant to imply in my comedy sketches that he was. But I think he'd had enough. A few months later he stunned the New South Wales Labor Party conference and the voters by abruptly announcing his resignation as premier. No one had seen it coming. He quit on 4 July 1986 after ten years in office, a record term for continuous service as premier in the state.[119]

Others, though, believed he was crook. Jim McClelland, a lawyer and former Labor senator for New South Wales, had been one of Wran's closest mates for many years. After politics Wran appointed him chief judge of the Land and Environment Court, which is where they fell out, spectacularly. McClelland knocked back a controversial plan for a sports stadium at Parramatta; Wran flouted his ruling and changed the law to bulldoze it through. The two never spoke again.

McClelland was an attractive character. Invariably known as 'Diamond Jim' – a tribute to his beautifully cut suits, shirts and ties – he radiated humour, charm and intelligence. He hated the nickname. A dazzling raconteur, suave and urbane, he could have been a Parisian boulevardier, although he despised celebrity and might not have handled the gourmet aspects of the gig. Oddly, his favourite meal at lunch was a plebeian plate of sausages and mash, which he would request at even the ritziest restaurants. He had made an international name for himself running a royal commission into Britain's nuclear tests at Maralinga, in South Australia, during which he memorably referred to Margaret Thatcher as 'that silly woman'.

Jim became convinced Wran had gone bent with a secret bank account in either Switzerland or Hong Kong, regularly and handsomely topped up by Sydney crooks, and he would tell you so at any opportunity. I never truly believed him, but he was adamant and earnestly persuasive. His problem was, as a colleague once said, 'that he could see both sides of every question and, what was worse for his friends, argued them both with equal brilliance and vehemence'.[120]

Either way, I enjoyed his company immensely. We were both writing for the *Sydney Morning Herald* at one stage, and ran into each other reasonably frequently. Acidly scathing about friends turned foes, he accused his erstwhile mate and colleague Sir John Kerr of 'behaving like a drunken lout at a country fair'.[121] Malcolm Turnbull was 'a turd', Jim once said. 'He's easy to loathe, he's a shit, he'd devour anyone for breakfast, he's on the make, he's cynical, he's offensively smug. He's a good exploiter of publicity.'

In fairness, Turnbull shot back that he was 'very sorry that many years of excessive consumption of alcohol and professional disappointment have reduced what was once a sharp wit into nothing better than gutter abuse. He's a bitter old man.'[122] Sydney can be like that, and no one more so than the town's lawyers. Jim was not bitter, nor the slightest bit wasted by booze. He died in 1999, reviled by an impressive slate of high-quality enemies but mourned by a far larger legion of admirers.

After a while, mutual friends tried to reconcile Neville and me. David Hill, that good man, had moved from being Wran's in-house economics guru to become chief executive of the New South Wales State Rail Authority, a job he relished. He could play trains. David, too, is an expansive, magnetic character. We are the same age, within months. Born to a dirt-poor single mother in Britain, in 1959 he and two brothers were packed off to Australia as teenage orphans. They endured years of appalling abuse, physical and psychological, mostly at the Fairbridge Farm School at Molong in the central west of New South Wales, a supposedly charitable outfit but run with sadistic cruelty. When he left there and went to Sydney looking for a job in a hardware store, he had never used a telephone or had a bank account. Soaring intelligence and a bursting urge to better himself won him a scholarship to study economics at Sydney University, and he never looked back.

A year or so after the Wran trial, David invited me and some other journalists to lunch in his executive dining room at State Rail near Central Station, a cavern of faded Edwardian splendour. You could have landed a helicopter on the dining table, which boasted, at its centre, an enormous timber tray supporting a sculpted wooden pineapple the size of a shipping buoy. This was impressively and unforgettably forested by toothpicks spiked with cubes of cheese, chunks of pineapple and small pickled onions the colour of traffic lights. Beer and wine flowed in profusion. It was a convivial affair.

As a friend, I stayed on for one or two more drinks after the rest had left. With evening upon us, David suggested that we should 'go and see Neville'. He would pour oil on troubled waters to bring the two of us back together in fraternal camaraderie. This struck me as not a good idea, but Hilly is nothing if not insistently persuasive, and I came around. Indeed, I suggested that we should take the pineapple and its lurid victuals as a peace offering but, exhausted by the exertions of the afternoon, we were unable to lift its mighty bulk. Instead, we grabbed some bottles of Chateau State Rail champagne and armfuls of cheese and crackers and headed off to nearby Woollahra in the State Rail limousine. David had another brainwave on the way: we must come bearing gifts for Jill Wran. At Paddington we found a fruit shop, where I bought the startled proprietor's entire stock of daffodils, buckets of them.

It was dark by the time we unloaded our cargo at the house in Wallis Street. The gates were locked. We buzzed the intercom. The familiar voice answered.

'We've dropped around for a drink,' said David cheerfully, if a little unsteadily. 'Can we come in?'

'Who's with you?'

'Mike Carlton.'

There was a short pause.

'You can come in. But tell Carlton to fuck off.'

✧

In the mid-1980s I was working harder than ever, ground down by the appalling hours and the self-inflicted folly of spreading myself thinly. I still loved doing *Friday News Review* and the audience still clamoured for it, but it was becoming harder to grind it out with fresh jokes. The cast of characters expanded to include Yasser Krakafat, my take on the volatile and controversial Palestinian supremo Yasser Arafat, and a portrayal which, with long hindsight, was shamelessly racist. More successful was Pope Pole, also known as Karol Wojtyła and Pope John Paul II, who spoke enigmatically in couplets lifted from the lyrics of the Paul Simon hit single 'You Can Call Me Al', delivered in a thick Polish accent. Weird, but it worked. My television column was still running in the *Herald* and I had taken on another one, 2000 words or so to fill the back page of the Fairfax *Sun-Herald*, then the country's biggest selling newspaper. Add to that a constant round of personal appearances, lunch and dinner speaking engagements. Aside from the money there were other rewards, of a sort. I won half a dozen or so of the annual commercial radio awards – Best Talk Personality, Best Current Affairs commentator, that sort of thing – for what they were worth. Which was not much.

In truth, I was running on empty. In what should have been spare hours for leisure or family, I was reading newspapers, magazines and catching up with TV news and current-affairs programs. There was unrelenting pressure to stay abreast of events, both important and trivial. Like a newspaper editor, I had to be across whatever was making news or was likely to make news, from a cabinet reshuffle to the latest hit movie, US election, Middle East war or football scandal. It was draining, enervating, making it difficult to concentrate on anything else. Sometimes you could fudge it – as I generally did with any rugby league interview – but there was always the danger of being caught out. Occasionally the prime minister's office would ring: 'He's got a few minutes this morning; he's willing to talk to you in ten.' You don't knock back a prime minister, but it can catch you on the wrong foot, as the media minders well know. Given just ten minutes' notice, it's a scramble to get your head around the current issues and jot down a list of worthwhile questions.

Oddly, it was the audience that helped keep me at least relatively sane. If you ask people to listen to your program, you've got to know pretty much who they are – in the mass at least – and deliver for them. If you do, they respond. And there were some seriously nice people out there. One little old lady, a widowed pensioner (her description, not mine), knitted baby clothes for my kids and never forgot a family birthday. I wish I could remember her name. Others would send gifts of cakes or jam or pickles they had made.

Many more rang or wrote to say what they thought of the show, good or bad, and they could be startlingly frank. Letters had to be answered, each one, which could be another burden. Sometimes they would explain that I was their chief source of information on what was happening in the world, a genuinely humbling thought. I took that seriously, as a responsibility, and I tried to meet those expectations. My ABC training, ingrained, generally impelled me to put both sides of a political fight or some other community brawl. I would take an editorial stance but I felt an obligation to provide a reasonable balance of facts to help those people make their own decisions.

There was abuse, too, from cranks and weirdos, but I learned to shrug it off and not let it get me down. A few times this got serious, with threats of violence or even death, always delivered anonymously but, nonetheless, taken seriously. Once or twice I had armed security guards keeping watch on our home at night.

But I was not alone. For all my radio career I had the help and guidance of producers, researchers, reporters, panel operators and other immensely talented and energetic professionals who made the thing work, mostly very well, and often brilliantly. David Lyle was my first producer, at the head of a long line of them. His future wife, Janne Dennehy, was another early starter at 2GB. Then came Warwick Adderley, a refugee from the ABC's *AM* program, who loyally stuck with me through the turbulent second half of the 1980s.

To bring some sort of system to the joint I had become Michael Carlton Productions, a proprietary limited company employing a staff of my own choice. In effect, the company made the radio programs and sold them to the station. This gave me greater creative control over the show, which I wanted, but added a load of administrative red tape. Much of that was handled by the personal assistant I brought on board, a vivacious and talented young woman named Lisa Joseph. She was the sort of efficiency wizard who could organise anything from cocktails with the Queen to the military invasion of a medium-sized nation, and she took a lot of the weight from my shoulders.

Around this time we hired the first reporter working not for the newsroom but solely for the breakfast program. Mark Llewellyn was another escapee from ABC Radio. In his early twenties, he'd been recommended for the gig by my old *TDT* friend and colleague Paul Murphy. The job was to get out and around Sydney for an on-the-spot cover of whatever we thought would be the big, entertaining or just plain quirky news of the day. Mark was a star player, endlessly good at the job. He had intelligence, judgement, flair and élan. Best of all he had guts and integrity. He went on to commercial television, on an upward curve to land as head of news and current affairs for the Nine Network, under Sam Chisholm. In 2006 he was involved in a famous executive suite brawl with Nine's new boss, the egregious Melbourne media and football panjandrum Eddie McGuire, who foolishly tried to kick him sideways and cut his salary. Undaunted, Mark sailed out the door and off to Channel Seven. McGuire and Nine sued for breach of contract, but Mark won and copped a reputed seven-figure payout. As my on-the-road reporter, he was a big asset.

The competition, though, was hotting up. FM radio had made a shaky start in Sydney but it soon hit top gear, led by one of the great creative brains of the business, Rod Muir, who had been a successful disc jockey himself. With an unmatched combination of marketing savvy and programming genius, Rod launched Triple M into orbit as a mega-trendy rock music station boasting the best young jocks money could buy. The logo he devised, a winged satyr playing a guitar and known in the trade as Dr Dan, has never been bettered. It seemed to be stuck on every second car back window or bumper bar in Sydney. In 1981 he hired a new breakfast jock, Doug Mulray, who went after ratings like a rat up a drainpipe.

Dougie – aka Uncle Doug, Dr Dougie, the Reverend Dr Doug – had made his name at the ABC's hip youth station known first as Double J and then as Triple J. At Triple M, Muir gave him free rein to put together a breakfast show of startling, even shocking creativity. He went off like a small nuclear explosion, smashing the taboos and conventions. The show was out front and loud, sometimes abrasive, smutty and irrepressibly vulgar, but almost always hilarious. The cast of characters he devised – Bogdan the Turnip Boy, a mad middle-European astrologer named Madame Zenda, Hymie Fymie, Jack

Africa, barrel girl Fifi D'Amour and dozens more – took the airwaves and the audience by storm. A lot of talented people went to work with him, both writing and performing, including the young Andrew Denton, who began as a comedy writer but eventually made it on air as Andrew the Wonder Boy from Indoor Cricket. Rod Muir's sister Liz – Miss Lizzie, as Dougie called her – started as a gofer on the program and ended up married to the star.

Eventually, Dougie nudged past me in the ratings to become number one in Sydney breakfast. Understandably, some of my audience went across to him. It was a blow, but I got over it and carried on. Dougie and I became good friends, oddly enough, with a shared passion for Jaguar cars. Our kids were about the same age. Like many people who make a living being outrageously funny for a mass audience, he could be moody and withdrawn in private, lost in thoughts he was unlikely ever to share. People who patronised him or bored him could be flayed alive. Some who worked for him found his iron control difficult to cop. But mostly he was sparkling good company and a compulsively generous host. We spent a fair bit of time together. By coincidence he had bought a country place near ours in the Blue Mountains, its undulating paddocks crowned by a beautiful, low farmhouse built from convict sandstone taken from a colonial building demolished in Sydney's Rocks precinct. Saturday dinners and Sunday lunches together were a riot, although we were always haunted by the thought that, come the Monday, we would both be crawling out of our beds at three am to return to the coalface.

Another figure was also coming into the frame. Alan Jones made his first public mark as a rugby coach. Virtually unknown outside the sport for some years, he became a national name in 1984 when he pulled off the Grand Slam, the remarkable feat of leading the touring Wallabies to victory over England, Ireland, Wales and Scotland.

Away from the rugby field and after an unsuccessful spell of teaching, he had dabbled in the world of politics, always on the conservative side. In 1978 he made two attempts at winning the New South Wales state seat of Earlwood for the Liberals, first at a by-election and then at a general election, losing both times. In the first campaign he stunned an audience of Greek voters by dancing on some suburban town hall stage in Greek national dress, a beguiling costume which included the *fustanella*, the pleated skirt and tights worn by the *Evzones*, the presidential guard in Athens. He looked a treat. For a couple of years he was a minor speechwriter for Malcolm Fraser as prime minister; he claimed – wrongly – to have written Fraser's most famous line, 'Life wasn't meant to be easy.'[123]

When Jones and Canberra tired of each other, he moved back to Sydney as executive director of the New South Wales Employers' Federation, the bosses' lobby group. That job brought him more public notice; he was constantly in the media as the employers' spokesman, a role he relished and handled well enough. I interviewed him several times. In 1985, 2UE took the punt. He had done some football commentary for them. After John Laws moved to 2GB, they hired Jones to replace him. It was a canny move, with a lot of risk attached. But the station's veteran program director, John Brennan, gave Jones intensive coaching in enough of the tricks and techniques of radio to get him by, and he was slotted into the hole Laws had left, the morning program between nine am and midday.

2UE's ratings had fallen off a cliff with Laws gone. Slowly, and at first uncertainly, Jones began to drag them back up. Curious, I listened to him a few times, and was startled by the shrill vehemence, the angry hectoring, the machine gun delivery and the braying laugh. It sounded very odd.

✧

Sir Warwick Oswald Fairfax, grand seigneur of the old and impenetrably convoluted clan of Sydney's Fairfaxes, died in January 1987. I can't remember ever laying eyes on 'Wocka', as he was disrespectfully known, but I was in the congregation of the good and great which overflowed from St Andrew's Anglican Cathedral at his funeral.

It had been ten years since he actually ran the Fairfax empire. The tasks of company chairman had fallen upon the son of his first marriage, James Oswald Fairfax, who went to it as a matter of noblesse oblige. James was fifty-four when Wocka died. I met him only a few times, always formally, in the line of work. Until John Laws arrived at 2GB I was very likely his most highly paid employee, and certainly his most expensive journalist, but that did not mean he wanted to socialise with me. The patrician Fairfaxes moved in another universe, one far removed from mine, on a planet wrapped in privilege and luxury.

For his frequent visits to Britain or Europe, Sir Warwick would have his Rolls-Royce sent ahead from Sydney by sea. His third and final wife, Mary, threw spectacular parties at 'Fairwater', their enormous harbourside estate, with mixed success. At one glittering ball for 1700 people, Imelda Marcos, the wife of the corrupt Philippines president Ferdinand Marcos, made her grand entrance as guest of honour to the strains of that cheerful Scottish tune 'Ho Ro, My Nut Brown Maiden'. An enormous frosted cake appeared, the highlight of the night. Imelda was about to cut it when her security guards, fearing a hidden bomb, seized the thing and hurled it into the harbour.

James was plumpish and bespectacled, with wavy silver hair and expensively tailored suits, which he wore as badly as only the very rich can get away with. He had a quiet, almost diffident air, as if he felt he should not be wasting your time. He was discreetly gay – not exactly closeted, but moving in a refined circle of what the social pages carefully referred to as 'confirmed bachelors'. Retford Park, his magnificent pink-and-white colonial mansion in the highlands south of Sydney, housed his large collection of art, both old and modern, of which he was a discriminating and formidable connoisseur.

He was a generous although often anonymous philanthropist. And he was brave. Taking the chairmanship from his increasingly erratic father had required resolve and courage. There was more. Neville Wran, at the height of his war with the Fairfax newspapers, threatened to humiliate James in public by revealing his homosexuality. In a furious phone call to Max Suich, then the Fairfax chief editorial executive, the premier barked that he would sue the company for defamation and get James in the witness box, where he would be cross-examined about his sexuality and his friends. It would be a sensation, seized upon by the Packers and the Murdochs and blown to the skies. Concerned and apprehensive, Max reported the threat to his chairman. James turned not a hair and told him to carry on as normal; there should be no change to editorial policy, no going soft to mollify Wran.

In the late autumn of 1987, a few months after his father's death,

James came to a formal, well-catered luncheon in the largely unused boardroom at the 2GB studios in Liverpool Street. He brought with him two other Fairfaxes: his distant cousin John Brehmer Fairfax, and his younger half-brother, Warwick Geoffrey Oswald Fairfax.

John Brehmer, usually known as John B., was deputy chairman of the Fairfax board. In his early forties, also quietly spoken and a devotee of fly-fishing, he had trained as a journalist and in marketing. As a substantial, although still very much a minority shareholder in the company, he had oversight of its radio and television interests. I liked him a good deal, and found him easy to talk to. John B. had an ironclad reputation for integrity and straight dealing; like James, he stuck to the corporate policy of not pushing his views on editors, journalists and broadcasters. He once asked me – very hesitantly – to write and record a personal version of *Friday News Review* for a private dinner party he was having, which I happily did.

The third of the trio, Warwick Geoffrey Oswald, was largely an unknown quantity. He was a product of Sir Warwick's third marriage, to Mary Fairfax, and was therefore invariably known as 'Young Warwick'. At twenty-six, he was less than half the age of James, his half-brother. He had just returned from the US with the ink still wet on an MBA from Harvard, and the lunch was part of the program to show him around the company to see how it worked.

I was seated near enough to Young Warwick to make polite small talk as we ate. It was not easy. Small, with a spotty, nerdy face, peering about through large spectacles, he reminded me of a nervous goldfish. He spoke shyly, in short, almost monosyllabic platitudes with a slight American accent. Rumour had it that he had declined to live with his mother at Fairwater, and was sharing a small flat with three or four friends as part of some earnest Christian commune. The rumour was correct.

Everyone at that lunch understood that, one day, many years hence, Young Warwick would inherit the Fairfax chairmanship. The deal had been done for James, the gay half-brother, to eventually leave him his shares. All the young dauphin had to do was to wait patiently and learn the business. Then the throne would be his.

No one at that lunch, least of all James and John B., knew of the ambition that was aflame inside him and about to erupt.

19

In bed with the Fairfaxes

A KNOCK ON THE door interrupted my sunny siesta at the Hopewood Health Centre at Wallacia, in outer Western Sydney. Thinking it might be the housekeeper, I wrapped a towel around my naked loins and opened up.

'Mr Carlton,' said Mary, Lady Fairfax. For it was she, also clad in a fluffy white bathrobe. 'I'm sorry to disturb you. Could we have a talk?' Actually, she said, 'I'm shorry to dishturb you.' For some reason Mary sounded as if she were drunk even when she wasn't.

I was flabbergasted. My jaw dropped. The towel almost did as well. Smiling fiercely, not to be denied, Sir Warwick's widow inserted herself into the room and plonked down onto a chair, like a cockatoo on a fence.

I had come to Hopewood to get off the grog for a few days, eat some sensible food, work out in the gym and, above all, get some regular sleep. So had Mary, a frequent client. Just days before, Young Warwick had stunned the media and business worlds with a multi-billion-dollar takeover bid for the Fairfax empire. When Mary heard I was at the resort, she seized the chance to do some quick PR. Still clad only in the towel, I perched on the bed while she went to work.

'My shun ish a brilliant young man,' she gushed, waving a bejewelled claw. Her eyes gleamed. 'He will shave the company from ruin. I am hoping we can count on your shupport, Mr Carlton.'

Or words to that effect, and there was more of it – a lot more. Incredulous, I listened as she unreeled it. The present Fairfax management – chiefly James, who was technically her stepson – was disastrously incompetent and blind to the disasters that lay ahead. The group general manager, Greg Gardiner, was a bare-faced traitor who was plotting secretly to sell the company to the avaricious West Australian corporate raider Robert Holmes à Court. Or perhaps to the ghastly Packer family. Warwick, on the other hand, had done wonderfully well in his business studies at Harvard. Returning home, he had astutely recognised the evil afoot and had moved decisively to claim his birthright. It would be much appreciated if I could use my influence with Fairfax journalists and in the wider community to back him to the hilt.

My influence? I didn't have any. But this went on for about half an hour. She trowelled on the flattery and dangled plump carrots. I was a widely respected opinion leader; Warwick would reward his loyal supporters. I ummed and aahed. It was like having Lady Macbeth drop in for a chat about the crown of Scotland:

> Come to my woman's breasts
> And take my milk for gall, you murdering ministers,
> Wherever in your sightless substances
> You wait on nature's mischief.

Surreal. At one point I idly considered whipping off the towel to see what might happen, but thought better of it. When Her Ladyship eventually wound up, she regally offered a hand to shake, thanked me profusely for my valuable time, urged me to keep our little talk confidential and sailed serenely from the room.

Still barely believing what I had seen and heard, I went for a swim.

✧

Young Warwick's lunge for John Fairfax and Sons was a catastrophe. As I write this exactly thirty years later, the ramifications of that epic folly are still playing out. Proprietors, directors, chief executives and editors shot in and out of a revolving door that spun ever more crazily.

In this long and winding melodrama, treachery, greed and arrogance jostled with stupidity and incompetence. Fairfax hung by a thread, which has now been broken by the Nine Network takeover, announced in July 2018. After 177 years of publishing history, the Fairfax name is to disappear forever. It can only be a matter of time before the print versions of the *Sydney Morning Herald*, the *Age* and the *Financial Review* vanish as well. It was Warwick who began the great unravelling.

The nuts and bolts are simply explained. Mary Fairfax, erratic and impulsive, fancying herself to possess profound business acumen, was indeed convinced that the company was being snatched from her son. She despised James, not least because he had deposed his father, her husband, as chairman. John B. was not to be trusted either. Nor was Greg Gardiner, who'd had the unmitigated cheek to ask her to pay market value to retain her late husband's company Rolls-Royce. The invaders were circling, she thought, with Holmes à Court to the fore. The Packers and Rupert Murdoch also stood ready to spring. The company was besieged. Gardiner and the traitors within would lower the drawbridge and open the gates. She and Young Warwick would lose everything.

Nineteen eighty-seven was a volatile time for the Australian media. The Hawke government had rejigged the ownership rules and the swamp was awash with easy money and alive with corporate crocodiles. Crooks were rampant. In January that year, Alan Bond bought Kerry Packer's Nine Network and his radio interests for a stunning $1.05 billion, at least twice what it was worth. It was a vanity purchase, a trophy. 'You only get one Alan Bond in your lifetime, and I've had mine,' said Kerry. A month later, Rupert Murdoch put up $2.3 billion to win the takeover war for Melbourne's *Herald and Weekly Times* media group, pushing this newly naturalised American citizen towards owning 70 per cent of Australia's newspapers. Fairfax got some crumbs, paying an absurdly overpriced $365 million for Melbourne's Channel Seven and some regional New South Wales newspapers. In July, Fairfax flogged its TV interests to another crook, Christopher Skase, for $750 million.

A former journalist, PR man and wheeler-dealer had Mary Fairfax's ear. Over dinners at Fairwater Marty Dougherty listened to her fears and encouraged her ambitions. Young Warwick must seize the moment to buy out the other Fairfaxes or be crushed by them. But where would he get the money to make his play? Dougherty pointed them in the direction of Laurie Connell, a figure sometimes described as a 'colourful Perth businessman'. Connell ran Rothwells, an outfit that pandering business journalists would dignify as a 'merchant bank' but which was in fact a lender-of-last-resort operation. If no one else would lend to you, Connell would. He agreed to manage Warwick's bid for a fee of $100 million, of which Dougherty would get 10 per cent. 'Last Chance Laurie' later did a spell in jail for perverting the course of justice in a racetrack scam and died bankrupt with debts of around $400 million.

By late August the ANZ Bank agreed to stump up $1.7 billion. On Sunday, 30 August, Warwick met James and John B. to tell them that, the next morning, he would bid to buy them out. They were shocked to the marrow.

The rest of the world heard the news from none other than John Laws, who had been leaked the story by Dougherty. At nine am on Monday, 31 August, John began his program by revealing that Warwick would bid $7.50 a share for Fairfax, valuing the company at around $2.4 billion. Laurie Connell was 'one of the world's most astute bankers', Laws said. 'If a fellow like Laurie Connell and the Rothwells Bank from Western Australia support a 26 year old, there is plenty of life in the young . . . we will watch that one with interest.'[124]

It was the first that most Fairfax executives had heard of the coup. They too were stunned. That evening, my young reporter, Mark Llewellyn, boldly accosted Warwick outside the Fairfax headquarters on Broadway, tape recorder rolling. He bombarded him with questions about the bid. The would-be corporate king spluttered and dithered and scuttled like a rabbit in the headlights.

The backroom contortions of the next few months are beyond the scope of this book. The battle for control waxed and waned, fiercely.

At one point I came across John B. in the lift at 2GB. 'You should know that the troops are with you and James,' I told him, and shook his hand. It was true. Everyone I knew at Fairfax loathed the idea of Young Warwick running the show, with Dougherty and the odious Connell hovering in the background. John thanked me quietly. His face was ashen and I thought, for a nanosecond, that he was about to break into tears. 'I think we've lost,' he murmured.

Indeed they had, although the great Wall Street crash of 19 October 1987 very nearly derailed everything for Warwick. There was a run on Rothwells, which had to close its doors until it was saved by a $150-million government guarantee, stumped up by yet another of the WA Inc. criminals, the Labor premier Brian Burke. Unnerved, and reasonably so, Mary tried to get her son to call off the bid, but he refused to see her. He pressed on. By 7 December he was the new chairman of Fairfax, with Dougherty and Connell on the board. The next evening there was a long and triumphant victory dinner at Fairwater. It had been the biggest single takeover in Australian corporate history.

✧

Despite the turmoil and my perpetual lack of sleep, I was enjoying myself. The program was humming, with talent coming and going. The veteran Fairfax business journalist Robert Gottliebsen, a witty and knowledgeable character, bowed out and was replaced as a contributor by a newcomer to radio, David Koch. Tentatively at first, Kochie began ending his daily finance report with a joke he'd picked up on his rounds. They were either very funny or crashingly corny, but either way they worked a treat and became a landmark of the show. Now the longtime host of Seven's *Sunrise*, he generously credits me with giving him his break in the electronic media, but if I hadn't someone else would have. From Canberra, the *Herald*'s volatile correspondent Alan Ramsey did political comment when we could jackhammer him out of bed. Ramsey took no prisoners.

In state politics, a former electrician and union chieftain, Barrie Unsworth, had succeeded Neville Wran as premier. Oddly, he took to abusing my researchers while he was waiting on the phone to be interviewed. 'I haven't got all day. Fucking put me through!' he would bellow. One young woman switchboard operator came to me in tears and quivering at the humiliation. I called Unsworth back and told him if he ever did that again he would be permanently banned. He was contrite, and after that we got on okay.

Rather more shaky was my relationship with his minister for Public Works, Laurie Brereton, who was vigorously pushing a pet project for a monorail to run around the western Sydney CBD and Darling Harbour. I thought it was an abomination and joined the very public campaign against it, skewering Laurie regularly in *Friday News Review*. It got a bit tense. Only much later did I come to recognise that Laurie was a creative and vigorous policy thinker, one of the best ministers – state or federal – I have encountered, and a nice guy with it. He, in turn, conceded that the monorail had not been his best idea.

On the other side, the Liberals' Nick Greiner was beginning his ascent to the premiership. He, too, was a quality act. Very gingerly, he asked me privately if I would stop referring to him as 'Kermit the Frog'. When he became premier in 1988 he chose my program to announce he would not be restoring British knighthoods and honours in New South Wales.

Lunch had become almost a religious ritual, and certainly a movable feast. My favourite table companions were usually other journalists. We spoke the same language and relished hurling epigrams, scraps of information and scurrilous gossip back and forth. Sometimes it would be with Max Suich, occasionally the finance writer and editor Maximilian Walsh, or the acerbic Evan Whitton, a former editor of the *National Times* and scourge of the shyster lawyers of Sydney. There was none better at the high art of lunching than the gregarious and rambunctious Peter Smark, a dazzling writer and fine reporter, raconteur and wit. Ten years older than me, portly and rubicund, he was then editor of Sydney's *Sun Herald*, a job he greatly disliked but which had been forced upon him. Often of a Friday, Smark – we used surnames only – would round up and bring with him a fellow toiler in the *Sun Herald* vineyard, Alex Mitchell, or Deborah Light of the *Australian Financial Review*, or another blazing comet of the media galaxy, Robert Haupt, a former Moscow correspondent for the *Herald* and the *Age*. Alex had worked on the vaunted London *Sunday Times* Insight investigative team, and had once edited a Trotskyite newspaper, *Workers Press*. Deborah was one of the best business writers and editors of the day.

'More jokes!' Haupt would cry as the corks popped. With his bulbous nose and an oddly Stalinist moustache he looked like a wayward Marx Brother, but was far funnier. He, too, was a brilliant reporter. Tragically he died of a heart attack in 1996 at the too-youthful age of forty-eight. As I wrote in farewell at the time, 'for him a well-furnished table was a means to an end, and that end was good conversation. Or discourse, as he called it. He relished, above all, the intercourse of intelligent minds and he would toss his thoughts into a gathering like firecrackers.'[125]

Haupt once invited along a gorgeous young blonde, tiny and pert as a sparrow, whose name I did not catch but who chatted knowledgeably and humorously about politics and national affairs. Only as we were leaving did I discover, to my private chagrin, that she was Kylie Minogue. Robert knew an astonishing slate of people. At a dinner at the Savoy in London he brought along the CIA station chief from Moscow. In Sydney he invited me to lunch with the elderly but fascinating Jessica Mitford, the former communist and one of Britain's aristocratic but notorious Mitford sisters.[126] 'Winston Churchill had appalling table manners,' she told us. 'He ate like a pig.'

It was Smark, though, who authored one of the Great Moments. I had never been to a Melbourne Cup. He, Melbourne-born and a boulevardier of the town, insisted on being my guide to its arcane rituals one year. 'Stick close and look confident,' he ordered as we descended upon Flemington's famous Birdcage. I did what I was told. 'Smark of the *Age*!' he proclaimed, talking our way – unticketed and uninvited – into posh marquee after marquee. 'This is my friend and colleague, the distinguished Sydney broadcaster and columnist Mike Carlton.' Gatekeepers and bouncers and PR flacks bowed and scraped. Waiters bustled up. Champagne flowed.

A knowledgeable friend had given me a winning tip for the race and we both trousered a substantial wodge of some bookmaker's dough. After more celebratory drinks it was time to leave.

'By helicopter, I think,' said Smark firmly. 'The trains are uncomfortably crowded.'

'We don't have a helicopter.'

'We shall find one. Follow me.'

We weaved our way unsteadily to a paddock where a dozen choppers were waiting for their owners.

'Which is John Elliott's helicopter?' Smark politely enquired of one of the pilots.

Jesus. The loud and abrasive John 'Pig's Arse' Elliott was then one of the country's storied business titans: filthy rich, on the board of BHP, president of the Carlton Football Club, federal president of the Liberal Party and spoken of as a future Liberal prime minister. We were going to hijack his helicopter?

'Do you know Elliott?' I asked my companion.

'Yes. He's an arsehole. But I'm sure he would *want* to lend us his chopper. If he knew.'

Smiling beatifically, Smark explained to Elliott's pilot that our good mate Mr Elliott had kindly offered us a lift in Mr Elliott's excellent flying machine. In the blink of an eye we were soaring in comfort towards the heliport on the Yarra.

Smark also died far too early, in 2000 aged sixty-three. I treasure one piece of advice he gave to me and, no doubt, to the many young journalists he mentored. 'Never go to a war where the cooking is bad,' he would say, eyes twinkling. Smark and Haupt and a few others had that unquenchable curiosity and proper suspicion of authority that marks the good journalist. Radiating joie de vivre, they laughed a lot, but deep down they cared passionately about the public's right to know. They had no interest in celebrity, only fact. Choice and master spirits of the age, they flowered in that happy era when journalism was a congenial and honourable occupation. How they would have abhorred the dark and reeking battleground of the so-called culture wars that the Murdoch myrmidons wage this century. I miss them so much.

✧

The phone call from Rio de Janeiro came out of the blue. The First Fleet was stranded there, out of money. It needed another $1 million to continue its voyage to Sydney. If that money could not be found, the project would have to be abandoned. Could I help?

It was July 1987. This was the First Fleet re-enactment, a private venture to celebrate Australia's bicentenary, the 200th anniversary of British settlement in 1788. A group of enthusiastic dreamers had put the idea together, led by the Sydney historian Jonathan King, descendant of an original First Fleeter, Lieutenant Philip Gidley King. After years of planning, they'd collected a motley assortment of nine tall ships, windjammers all, and set sail from Portsmouth that May, farewelled by the Queen and enthusiastic crowds ashore and in the Solent. The plan was to sail into Sydney Harbour on that 200th Australia Day, 26 January 1988.

For various reasons, the Hawke federal government and its bicentenary bureaucrats went sour on the deal. The Canberra public servants had made their plans for the celebration, including a regatta on Sydney Harbour, and they didn't want a private venture crashing their party, least of all one they could not control. Behind the scenes, they did their best to sink the re-enactment, or at least to strangle it with red tape. Publicly, the government belittled the idea. Hawke's education minister, the West Australian John Dawkins, sneered that 'the expedition has degenerated into a tasteless and insensitive farce with little educational value and which doesn't deserve any more government funding'.[127]

The Australian people disagreed. There had been a lot of media coverage of the voyage since it left Portsmouth, and Sydneysiders especially loved the idea, in all its romantic idealism. They looked forward eagerly to the historic spectacle it promised. So did I. When the call came from Rio, I rather rashly said I would do what I could to raise the money. We would run a public appeal on my program, urging listeners to contribute. That Monday morning, on air, I gave it all the juice I could muster. I was sure Australians would rally around, and indeed the switchboard lit up with people wanting to contribute.

The new Macquarie Network boss, Bob Johnson, was aghast. After the show he called me into his office. Without asking, off the top of my head, I had committed 2GB and Fairfax to a publicity stunt which might fall flat on its face. I had to admit he had a point.

Media fundraisers, like the telethons that were once in fashion, only ever got about half the money people promised. Listeners or viewers make their pledges, swept up in the hype, but often fail to deliver in the cold hard light of day. Johnson feared, reasonably enough, that this would happen here. I started to get cold feet myself, but we were in too deep. We would just have to push on.

At first to our amazement, then to our delight, the thing took off. Listeners were fired up, many of them indignant and resentful of the bureaucrats trying to chuck a spanner into the works. The station switchboard kept ringing all day, so much that additional operators had to be put on to take the offers. 2GB advertising sponsors began to chip in – all carefully acknowledged on air – and the Westpac Bank agreed to handle the donations. By the afternoon we had decided the radio station would set aside regular programming and run a three-day appeal from the next Friday for as much money as we could drag in. 'Save the Fleet' we called it. Every presenter, every program would back it to the hilt.

Telecom Australia, as it was then called, installed extra phone lines without charge, and the switchboard ran hot for those three days. Pensioners offered a few dollars. Schools chipped in with student contributions. Businesses big and small wrote cheques. I put in a couple of grand myself; so did John Laws. All up, we raised almost $950,000. The bureaucrats and the doubters had been beaten.

Rescued from oblivion, the Re-enactment Fleet sailed from Rio early that August. Its arrival on Australia Day was a triumph beyond even its creators' dreams. The fleet had spent the night in Botany Bay. Before dawn I clambered up a rope ladder and onto the deck of *Our Svanen*, a three-masted wooden barquentine built in Denmark in 1922. She had been with the fleet all the way from Portsmouth. Standing in her bow, wearing the sort of headset microphone used by football callers, I sailed with her north to Port Jackson, broadcasting live all the way.

It was breathtaking. The police and the newspapers estimated that 2.5 million people gathered on the harbour foreshores or on the water. Some had arrived days before to stake out the best vantage spots. The harbour itself was so crammed with craft, from millionaires' yachts to surfboards, that you could have walked across them from the Heads to Circular Quay.

As *Our Svanen* rounded the Heads, perhaps third or fourth in line, the sound of horns and sirens and cheering split the heavens. Waves of noise rolled over us all the way to our anchorage in Farm Cove, by the Botanic Gardens. My family and some friends were waiting there on a yacht we had chartered. Like all Sydney, we spent the day feasting and relishing each unfolding spectacle. It was one of the highlights of my career.

✧

Within months of Young Warwick's takeover of Fairfax he was up to his neck in crocodiles. The details are impossibly convoluted but, in short, he was in deep trouble with loan repayments to his bankers. To help raise urgently needed cash, the eight stations of the Macquarie Radio Network and some other assets of the business were offered to Robert Holmes à Court's Bell Group of companies for an expected $475 million. When that deal fell apart – again for complex reasons – the new Fairfax management began a panicky search for other buyers. In February 1988 a hitherto unknown company named Sonance, chaired by a prominent Queensland businessman, Sir Frank Moore, offered $98 million for the radio stations. It was less than half the value Fairfax had put on the network just six months before, but Warwick and his advisers grabbed it with both hands and the deal was done by April. I was working for new and unknown masters. This was my first real experience of being traded like cattle in the marketplace. It would not be my last.

John Laws had played it much smarter. His contract with 2GB contained a provision which allowed him to leave if the station's ownership ever changed hands. He took one look at the new owners, did not like what he saw and jumped ship back to 2UE, by now owned by Alan Bond, and where Nigel Milan had become the new station manager. At that time I saw it almost as a betrayal, and it touched off a new feud between us. With hindsight I realise it was a sensible commercial and personal decision, one I might have taken myself had I not been shackled by my contract. I had no out clause: if I had simply quit, I could have been sued for millions. I was stuck.

2UE welcomed John back home, with the usual fanfare, and he resumed the nine am to midday slot, not missing a beat. His audience went with him. Alan Jones moved to breakfast to make way.

My new boss was Mark Cassidy, managing director of Sonance. In his late thirties or perhaps early forties, he sported a fake tan, so that you felt at times you were talking to a Chicken McNugget. His suits were flash; his hair was blond. It was a vision only replicated more recently by Donald Trump.

Cassidy had begun as a radio salesman in Brisbane, with the usual gift of the gab. This was the era of Queensland's 'white shoe brigade', the clique of property developers and their ilk who sported that footwear like a club badge. Arrogant and brash, the white shoe mob thought they ruled the world, oozing contempt for anyone and anything south of the Tweed. Many of this lot were behind the 'Joh for Canberra' push, the harebrained campaign to somehow send Bjelke-Petersen south to become Australia's next conservative prime minister.

Cassidy must have had something going for him, if only his quick tongue. His shareholders included the Hong Kong media magnate Sally Aw Sian, the fabulously wealthy heiress to the Tiger Balm fortune, and Harold Mitchell, a savvy Melbourne media buyer who controlled hundreds of millions of dollars in advertising spend. Even Kerry Packer had to be nice to Harold.

From the get-go at our first meeting, Cassidy oozed fake charm. His great desire in life, he told me, had been to own 2GB, the jewel in radio's crown. He was humbled and delighted to be working with a star such as myself. Together we would take the station to even greater heights. Publicly, he pumped out a statement trumpeting that 'the network would be continued and developed. In particular, there was a strong desire on the part of Sonance Ltd to continue, and even expand, the emphasis on talk, news and information in Macquarie.'[128]

This was arrant bullshit. His feet were hardly under the desk before he set to flogging off the joint as fast as he could. Cassidy figured he could make a handsome profit by splitting up the network and selling the stations and other assets individually. Away he went, in the usual orgy of cost-cutting and staff sackings. By the late spring of 1988 only three stations were left – 2GB in Sydney, 4BH in Brisbane and 2WL in regional Wollongong. Even the 2GB building had been sold – to Mary Fairfax, of all people, for $15 million.

Cassidy also utilised the rich reserves of the Macquarie superannuation fund, by causing it to invest the permitted quota of funds in group company assets. It was entirely legal but morally questionable, and eventually the fund was wound up. In the midst of this carnage, Cassidy had the gall to try to sell me and two executives, one of them my mate Charlie Cox, a chunk of shares in Sonance. We decided not to touch the offer with a barge pole. Cassidy purported to be greatly offended by this gross disloyalty.

But the show must go on. There were good people making programs and in the 2GB newsroom, and we kept at it. One of my producers, Gloria Zimmerebner, was a friend from our time together at *A Current Affair* at Nine. Some of the younger ones would become high fliers in the media and elsewhere. A bright young uni student with a beard and below-shoulder dreadlocks turned up to make the coffee and to work the panel and the on-air switchboard. Matt Brown was his name. He is now a distinguished ABC foreign correspondent in the Middle East, one of the best.

John Laws was replaced in the morning by Jane Singleton, who had been a competent and successful ABC broadcaster in Sydney but would sink horribly in the commercial swamp. Earnest and didactic, with a high moral tone, her improving lectures on politics and society sent listeners fleeing in droves.

In the afternoon shift, John Tingle batted on. Older than me, he had been one of my bosses when I was a cadet at ABC Television and we got on well enough, although we were never close. His chief pleasure was shooting things. He had a country property somewhere out west and would regale us with lurid tales of stalking through the scrub with his wife, both stark-naked save their ammunition belts, blazing away at passing fauna. When 2GB eventually fell apart, John constructed a career in politics, getting himself into the NSW Legislative Council as the founder of the right-wing Shooters Party. I guess he needed the dough – he was one of the victims of Cassidy's gouging of the super fund.[129]

And then there was Brian Wilshire, who ran the seven pm to midnight slot Monday to Friday. He was one of the most bizarre characters I have met, wild-eyed and hyperactive. He had been two years ahead of me at Barker College, where I had known him slightly. He was seen as an oddball even then. By the time he made it to radio he was an ardent apostle of the far-right-wing American conspiracy theorist Lyndon LaRouche, with a few twists of his own. LaRouche had begun his public career as a youthful Marxist before lunging to the lunar right. Among his more colourful notions were that international finance is controlled by the Rothschild and Rockefeller families, in league with Henry Kissinger and the American Council on Foreign Relations. The Queen and the Duke of Edinburgh are the kingpins of the international drug trade. There is much more, but you get the picture. To this grab-bag of loopiness Wilshire added the haunting fear that the United Nations was secretly manoeuvring to construct One World Government to rule us all, and that a telephone exchange and data centre in the Sydney suburb of St Leonards was actually the hub of a vast surveillance operation that was keeping watch on every Australian. The country was controlled by a sinister but never fully explained 'they' – as in, 'They are watching our every move.'

Wilshire's listeners, or most of them, lapped it up. A few sane people listen to night-time commercial talk radio, I suppose, but most have better things to do with their lives. The timeslot is the haunt of the aged and the querulous, the lonely and the frightened, the ignorant and the foolish, the bombastic and the tunnel-visioned single-issue fanatics, and the just plain barking mad. There are people who howl at the full moon. Wilshire was a polished broadcaster, and in him they found their leader.

A segment of his show, 'Midnight Matchmaker', was aimed at bringing his listeners together to find companionship and love. They would write or ring with their CVs and their heartfelt longings, and Wilshire would invite other hopefuls to apply. At the station we used to call it 'Find a Fuck'. It rated its head off and genuinely did get like-minded people hooked up. When Wilshire invited this audience to a Midnight Matchmaker Ball, a knees-up at some city hotel ballroom, there was a stampede for tickets. The 2GB executives who went along reported back that they had never seen such a grotesque parade: there were folk whose knuckles dragged on the ground as they walked, or who had one eye smack-bang in the middle of the forehead, or no forehead at all. Some dribbled and drooled. Others just snorted or grunted, or wailed piteously in corners. A few tore their hair or tried to remove their clothes. It was a terrifying tableau but, as the executives assured each other bravely, they all counted towards the ratings.

Wilshire reached peak crackpot with a theory, again imported from the States, that a daily drink of the chemical hydrogen peroxide would ward off HIV and full-blown AIDS. Each night he would urge his disciples to begin the morning as he did, with a hearty glass of the stuff. The authorities – *They* – were wickedly keeping this vital knowledge secret so as not to blow the profits of the international drug companies, Big Pharma, who were raking in billions in research funds to find their own AIDS drugs.

After some months of this, Charlie Cox was surprised to get a letter from the New South Wales Health Department, politely pointing out that Wilshire was quite possibly doing great harm to his listeners. Hydrogen peroxide, when drunk in large amounts, was a dangerous poison. It was also illegal for unqualified broadcasters to provide medical information or to prescribe drugs. Would 2GB please desist? Charlie showed me the letter. 'We're killing the punters,' he said. Wilshire was outraged when Charlie at first asked, then ordered him to stop: the management had joined the villainous global conspiracy to conceal the truth.

I used to have my own fun with him. Sometimes, after dinner with friends, I would call his show, grunting in a broad ocker accent and posing as a red-haired, one-eyed, one-legged, half-crazed Vietnam War veteran. Armed to the teeth, I was ready for the commies and the UN when they came to get us. Wilshire would invariably praise me as a true patriot and an example to all, a heartening response. Whatever: it worked. Though he was later moved to a slot that began at midnight and finished at three-thirty am, Brian Wilshire peddled this mishmash of inane fears and chimerical conspiracies until he retired in 2015.

✧

With the John Laws audience delivered back to 2UE and there for the taking, Alan Jones's ratings on his new breakfast show began to look up. The celebrity huckster Harry M. Miller, released from a three-year jail sentence for fraudulently misappropriating $728,000, was now his agent. Intent on rehabilitating his reputation, Miller began to put together big-money deals for this new client for a cut of 20 per cent. Jones basically copied the format we had pioneered in breakfast at 2GB, almost to the letter, but delivered it in the increasingly strident, prissy, hectoring torrent of verbiage which has become his trademark. As someone later said, Jones broadcast as if he was fleeing a burning building.

Occasionally I would listen to some tapes to see what he was up to. He had found a new bit of theme music, the opening bars of 'Gloria', the 1982 disco hit by Laura Branigan. 'Gloria' would soon become one of his Sydney joke nicknames, hilariously caricatured on Dougie Mulray's breakfast show. The demagoguery grew more insistent and alarmist as Gloria discovered the tricks of pandering to populist prejudice and ignorance. Everything was a crisis, a disgrace, a scandal, an outrage. Only he, Alan Jones, the battlers' champion, the caped crusader, the white knight in shining armour, would stand courageously and fight for the right against wickedness and oppression.

Everything was going gangbusters until, suddenly, it collapsed in a heap. On his summer break at the end of 1988, Jones flew to London to stay in a Mayfair flat owned by a friend, the stockbroker Rene Rivkin. Jetlagged after the flight, he went for a stroll. That morning, Tuesday, 6 December, two plainclothes police officers watched him enter an underground toilet in the cosmopolitan Soho district. When he did not reappear after what the officers thought was a reasonable time, they moved in and arrested him. He was taken to the local nick and charged with 'outraging public decency' and 'committing an indecent act'.

The story caused a sensation – in Australia at first and then in London, when the newspapers there decided to dub Jones a 'future Australian PM'. It must have been devastating, but Jones was not without mates and resources. London friends found him a lawyer renowned for his almost magical ability to extract his clients from the tightest of corners. After weeks of uncertainty and flaming headlines, shortly before Christmas the prosecution declared that the police had no evidence to present. The charges were dropped. Jones was free.

The notoriety and the gossip might have felled a man less armoured in righteous certitude. A lot of people, me included, thought his public career was over, that his conservative audience would turn its back. He was done, finished, kaput. Jones thought otherwise, and 2UE backed him. Harry Miller jerked the PR strings. Drawing on a bottomless well of self-confidence, Jones soldiered on, doggedly proclaiming his innocence. It was a bravura performance. Back on air in January 1989, he found that his listeners, far from shunning him, were rushing to commiserate and proclaim their loyalty. His ratings continued to rise.

It might have been this bruising encounter with the law that propelled him into one of the more ridiculous excesses of his career. In July that year he launched a quixotic campaign to overturn the murder conviction of a millionaire businessman and hotelier from the beachside suburb of Manly, Andrew Kalajzich. It was a prominent case. Kalajzich had been found guilty of murder and conspiracy to murder his wife in 1986, and sentenced to life in prison. For some reason Jones got it into his head that he was innocent. With his customary bombast, flinging both the facts and common sense to the wind, for five years he denounced police officers, politicians, judges and journalists. It was stupid, ignorant and ultimately futile. An eighteen-month inquiry by a retired judge found there was no doubt of Kalajzich's guilt. But to his gullible followers Jones had cemented his reputation as a warrior for justice. Others were less impressed. Stuart Littlemore, at the time the host of ABC Television's *Media Watch*, christened him 'the Parrot'.

✧

By the end of the 1980s Mark Cassidy was doing it tough. He had not found a buyer for 2GB, various banks were hammering him for repayments on business and private loans, and, for a variety of reasons, he had fallen out with most of his fellow Sonance directors, including the influential Harold Mitchell. Charlie Cox had quit in disgust and gone off to Britain to manage two radio stations in London. His replacement, an advertising suit named Harry Ledowsky, was a nice enough bloke but without a clue about running a Newstalk format. The ratings were dropping and advertisers were voting with their feet.

I'd had about enough as well. Cassidy sold 2GB to Harbour Radio, a new company in which he was a major shareholder, and attempted to use that as an excuse to impose swingeing pay cuts on the staff, me included. I told him I would sue for breach of contract. He backed down, but it was a sour, angry encounter. This once happy and successful radio station had become a grim sweatshop where people feared for their jobs, never knowing if each Friday there would be their last.

Deliverance arrived for Cassidy in the unlikely form of the Reverend Dr Gordon Moyes, a minister of the Uniting Church who was well known as the superintendent of the Sydney Wesley Mission. I was partly to blame, I suppose. A few years before, 2GB had been casting around for someone to present what we called 'the God slot' on Sunday evenings. Commercial radio stations were legally required to provide a few hours of so-called religious programming each week. I suggested Moyes simply because his was the first name I thought of. There was never any shortage of priests and parsons wanting to get on air, and he jumped at the chance. Oily, arrogant and disingenuous, he began to fancy himself as a broadcaster par excellence, despite much evidence to the contrary.

Worse, Moyes laboured under the delusion that he was an astute businessman. His Wesley Mission in central Sydney was cashed up, largely on the strength of donations from city businesses. He was certainly a skilled hand at rattling the can to further God's good work – and, as it turned out later, to feather his own nest. Swollen with self-importance, he convinced himself and the elders of his church that he had the talent and knowhow to become a media mogul of the first rank.

Cassidy saw him coming. He trowelled on the flattery. Moyes dug deep. In December 1989 the Wesley Mission paid $3 million for 3 million shares in Harbour Radio, a 15 per cent stake. That valued 2GB at a ludicrous $28 million. It was probably worth less than half that. Cassidy also offered the mission free advertising time to the value of $160,000, which Moyes seized. And he got himself on the board.

I had determined by now that I was getting out, come what may.

My contract was due to finish in the spring of 1990, and then I would be free to go. And go I would, although I had no idea how or where, and didn't much care.

Salvation came for me in the form of Charlie Cox. He called me at home one evening and asked if I would be interested in working in London at the commercial radio station he was managing, LBC.

It was a bolt from the blue. I was stunned. My first reaction was to say no, for all sorts of reasons. I was entirely unknown in Britain: I would have to start a whole new career from square one. And would listeners in London be willing to cop an Australian broadcasting to them? It might be an ignominious failure. Personally, it would mean uprooting my family, not least taking twelve-year-old Alex and ten-year-old James from their schools and their friends. The kids were apprehensive.

Charlie was persuasive and insistent. On the plus side, he was a fine journalist and a shrewd radio manager, with acute good judgement. He would only make the offer if it was going to work for both of us. To my surprise, Kerri was enthusiastic. The two of us had often talked of living in the UK for a while but had never been able to work out how to do it. This was our chance, she said, and she urged me to seize it. Charlie flew me to London to talk and to check out the station. I liked what I saw and heard, and my doubts began to melt. It would be a huge challenge but an exciting opportunity. Back in Sydney, I agreed with Kerri that we would go for it. We began to lay our plans.

Towards the end of 1990, the perma-tanned Cassidy and his electric hair suddenly and surprisingly vanished from the scene. There was no farewell of any sort, which upset no one. He was still on the Harbour Radio board, we were told, but had decided to work in Hong Kong. Gordon Moyes would be the new chairman.

On 24 October, Moyes' shiny Ford LTD nosed into 2GB's basement car park. Impressive transport for a humble parson, I thought. The staff were summoned to meet the great man in the newsroom, where he arrived late enough to demonstrate who was boss. His dark business suit was well cut, and his silk tie perfectly knotted. He rubbed his hands together as if he were washing them, and smiled at us like a shark contemplating a school of fish. Unctuous and arrogant in about equal measure, he instructed us on how to address him.

'My full title is the Reverend Dr Gordon Moyes,' he oozed. 'But you may call me Dr Moyes.'

I had checked all that. His doctorates – three of them! – were from tinpot theological 'colleges' in the US, and all honorary. Academically and theologically, they were not worth the paper they were printed on. Still doing his grey nurse impression, Moyes assured us that, under his stewardship, 2GB would continue with the Newstalk format. 'But let us all remember,' he said, 'that our most important task is to broadcast the good news of Jesus.'

Abandoning my iron self-control, I snorted a laugh.

Moyes glared at me but ploughed on. 'Our first task will be to clean up our workplace,' he told the startled throng.

The newsroom, like most newsrooms, was an untidy warren littered with old newspapers, coffee cups, ashtrays and other detritus of the journalist's trade. The walls were plastered with newspaper clippings, once-funny headlines, photographs and cartoons and the like.

'All this must go,' said Moyes, sweeping an imperious hand like Moses on the Mount. 'A tidy office means tidy minds. Now, let's get to work.' With another glare at me he stalked from the room.

I was out of there two weeks later, packing for London. Moyes stayed on and drove 2GB over a cliff. The ratings went into freefall. A year later, by June 1992, the station had accumulated losses of $34.12 million. The Wesley Mission's investment of millions of dollars was worthless.

My family and I arrived in London a week before Christmas 1990. It was cold and dark, and the city was girding itself for the first Gulf War to expel Saddam Hussein and his Iraqi army from their invasion of neighbouring Kuwait. LBC had rented us a cavernous flat in Queen's Gate, South Kensington, about two blocks away from the Iraqi embassy. The street bristled with barbed-wire barriers and police trucks, and there were SAS snipers on every second roof. Sirens howled day and night.

Contemplating the scrawny Christmas tree we'd hastily bought from a nearby greengrocer, Kerri burst into tears. It was not a promising start.

20

A welcome visitor to England's green and pleasant land

'Wogs begin at Calais,' I said brightly. It was a throwaway line about some European mini-crisis unfolding across the channel. I looked up to see a row of shocked faces staring at me open-mouthed through the studio window. Did he say 'wogs'? Omigod, he *did*.

It was my first day on air in London, and very nearly my last. 'Wog' has been defused in Australia over the years to the point where it can be a term of good-natured affection. Wogs use it themselves, with humour. But not in the UK. There it is still a racist insult, nothing else. The studio phones sizzled with listeners complaining. My producers offered grovelling apologies. The Radio Authority, then Britain's bossy broadcasting 'watchdog', slapped me with an official caution. Typical Australian . . .

It was a huge lesson: I would have to relearn whole chunks of the English language, and quickly. Trousers, not pants. Back garden, not backyard. Constituency, not electorate. Motorway, not freeway. Football, not soccer. Loo, not dunny. There are hundreds more examples and I got better at it with time, although sometimes one would get through. Once I described Prime Minister John Major as 'looking like a shag on a rock'.

'A fuck on a rock?' said my producers.

'No. The metaphor is of a small sea bird, perhaps a cormorant, alone on a stony, sea-girt protuberance, buffeted by fate and circumstance.'

'Means a fuck to us,' they chortled.

I liked them all. They were good and competent blokes, loyal and diligent. John Allen was a placid lad from the Midlands who said things like 'easy peasy' and 'mustn't grumble'. My panel operator, Chris Lowrie, was the right stuff. The senior producer, Peter Kimber, was about my age, a naval officer for a bit before he went into journalism. Plump and florid, he knew his job but did it in a constant state of sweaty nervous exhaustion. Perhaps I caused it. He shouted into telephones. He was one of those Brits who believed foreigners could – and indeed were *obliged* – to understand you if you spoke English loudly and v-e-r-y slowly. He could also drink, as no man I have seen before or since. In the pub after work he would be on his third pint of lager, followed each time by a stiff chaser of Scotch, while I was still finishing my first.

One Friday Peter bade us all farewell for the weekend. On Monday we came to work to find a woman sitting at his desk. Peter, it turned out, had been in the throes of a sex change for months and had finally decided to take the public plunge. 'Please call me Susan,' he said. She had exchanged her Marks & Spencer business shirt and trousers for a Marks & Spencer blouse and skirt, make-up and a somewhat unconvincing wig. It was an arresting sight but, being British – and I had absorbed many of the local ways by then – everyone pretended not to notice and carried on as if nothing had happened. She did too, very bravely.

LBC, originally the London Broadcasting Company, was Britain's first legal commercial radio station, starting up in 1973.[130] By the time I got there it was owned by an Australian businessman and investor, David Haynes, who also ran a string of radio stations in France. The BBC had a chokehold on the UK radio audience then, with four national stations and a slew of smaller local stations. British listening habits died hard. LBC had always struggled to attract an audience and advertisers. Haynes's bold idea was to split the operation into two stations: LBC Newstalk 97.3 on the FM band and London Talkback Radio on AM. Unable to find British commercial radio executives who knew what they were doing in talk formats, he hired Charlie Cox from 2GB.

Charlie arrived in early 1990, like Field Marshal von Bock going through Poland. The place was hugely overstaffed in the BBC manner, although the newsroom was practically moribund. It was run by a coven of gay men, some of them hilariously high camp, others macho, ripped and impressively bronzed even in the depths of a British January. One of the weather presenters had an S&M dungeon in the basement of his suburban home, and was rumoured to give his forecasts while manacled, jock-strapped and leather-harnessed.

Many of the on-air people sounded as if they had one foot in the grave. The much-venerated chief newsreader, Brian Widlake, had begun his career at the Beeb sometime during the reign of George III. His deep, sepulchral voice had won him the nickname 'the Fall of Singapore'. Brian would nip out to the Vineyard, the cramped little wine bar across the road, for a restorative draught between bulletins, rendering himself largely incoherent towards the end of his shift.

Charlie fired and hired with ruthless efficiency, undeniably causing pain but also dragging the place screaming and kicking into the 1990s. Mutinous mutterings about the uncouth Australians wrecking the joint never completely died away, but the smarter people recognised that he was, in fact, their rescuer. It was like stopping and turning the *QE2*, but he set himself to the task. It helped that Charlie could radiate tremendous charm and enthusiasm when he needed to.

The studios were in a new glass office block on Hammersmith Road, in West London. I was there on serious money, with a much-coveted parking space for the silver-grey Jaguar XJ6 that was part of my package. Charlie and I agreed that I would begin on the drive program, from four to seven pm, with the understanding that, if it worked out, I would shift to the breakfast slot, as I had done in Sydney. With my two producers all ears and eager to roll, we nutted out the format: news and current affairs, interviews, finance, sport and traffic reports. And I would have a shot at some comedy spots, scripting and recording funnies as I had done in Sydney. If they worked, I would have a go at a local *Friday News Review*. We began to gather speed.

A lot of the rules were different. British commercial radio – and especially talk radio – was and is far more tightly controlled than its American and Australian counterparts. Presenters are legally required to be 'balanced and impartial', offering no on-air editorial opinion whatsoever, just as at the BBC. In Australia I could rant endlessly about incompetent cabinet ministers or denounce the woeful and the wicked in caustic editorials; in Britain, not so. This took a bit of getting used to, but it had to be done. Nor was I allowed to read commercials on air, which was rather more pleasing. The Radio Authority, which for some very British reason was run entirely by a junta of retired army colonels, watched vigilantly for the slightest breach of the rules, ready to pounce. And to some, my Australian style was novel, even startling. In May 1991 the authority received a pompous complaint that I 'exhibited a frivolous, flippant, often offensive style at odds with the remit of a flagship news and current affairs service'.[131] The complaint was not upheld.

For all that, it was a thrilling, professionally stimulating time to be there and on air. Events rushed in. Margaret Thatcher had pulled the pin just before I arrived, forced out by rebellious cabinet ministers who could no longer stomach her imperious arrogance and batty obsessions. Her successor at 10 Downing Street, John Major, was struggling to impose his authority on a fractious Conservative Party and the country, while battling a recession that would render more than 2 million unemployed. The Labour opposition leader, Neil Kinnock, was on Major's hammer. In January 1991 the Gulf War broke out. In February the Provisional Irish Republican Army dropped homemade mortar bombs into the snow-clad back garden of Number 10 while the cabinet was meeting. A few weeks later they bombed the big rail stations at Paddington and Victoria, killing one person and plunging London into chaos.

Some news stories stayed around, others came and went. IRA terrorism was an ever-present menace while we lived in the UK. Yugoslavia collapsed into murderous conflict between Serbs and Croats. The Soviet Union finally crashed beneath the weight of its folly and incompetence, with the erratic Boris Yeltsin taking charge at the Kremlin. The Warsaw Pact fell apart. In November 1991 the British publisher and corporate crook Robert Maxwell – 'the

Bouncing Czech' – fell off the back of his yacht in the Mediterranean. The lead singer of Queen, Freddie Mercury, died of AIDS. For a broadcast journalist these were great stories to cover, a liberating change from the parish pump drudgery of Australian politics.

Yet they had me on a learning curve as steep as Snowdonia. In short order I had to get my head around culture, society, politics, business, the economy and sport: everything from the geography of London and the British Isles to the names and political leanings of the entire cabinet and the opposition front bench. Westminster was very different to Canberra. The House of Lords and the Australian Senate had almost nothing in common. The House of Commons and the House of Representatives had many similar customs and practices and procedures, but lots that differed significantly. And then there was the nuts-and-bolts stuff. I had to know at least something of the Royal family; British Rail; the National Health Service; the European Parliament; Scottish, Welsh and Irish nationalism; the building of the contentious Cross Channel Tunnel; the cast and plot of *EastEnders*; and the names of mysterious football grounds – Elland Road, Goodison Park, Stamford Bridge and so on. My producers backed me up.

'Who plays at White Hart Lane? Chelsea?' I would bellow down the intercom during a commercial break.

'Spurs.'

I couldn't have made it without them – and another stalwart supporter, the bloke who did the on-air traffic reports in the show, Fred Housego. Freddie was a Cockney, a bespectacled former taxi driver and chirpy as a sparrow. He also had a rapier wit and a kaleidoscopic mind. He had won *Mastermind*, Britain's most famous TV quiz show, and he had 'The Knowledge' – the London cabbie's ability to unerringly navigate to the most obscure lanes or back alleys in the entire metropolis from Hounslow to Barking, Croydon to Cockfosters. Nothing fazed him. 'How very different to the home life of our own dear Queen!' he would exclaim sardonically at news of some political scandal, crime or atrocity.[132] Then back to business: 'On the A3, an accident at Clapham Common with a long tailback heading west towards Battersea . . .' Fred was a gem.

✧

After a few false starts with schools and housing, the family settled in. The kids went first to the American Community School in Surrey, south-west of London, where expatriate Goldman Sachs and IBM executives paid eye-watering fees to shield their children from any contact with the British. The Parent Teacher Association bombarded us with earnest newsletters advising where to find real Oreo cookies, genuine American peanut butter and Halloween pumpkins. This was not a success. Pulling some strings, we managed to get Alex into Bryanston, an even more expensive boarding school in Dorset, which attracted a large dollop of media, theatrical and creative families. The actor Jeremy Irons was one of our fellow class parents. Bryanston offered a sublimely beautiful learning and playing environment, centred upon a grand mansion in the gentle green woods and fields of the West Country, the sort of place I would have killed to go to when I was sixteen. But Alex hated it. She felt foreign and isolated, and missed her Australian friends.

We had more luck with James, when the Royal Grammar School in Guildford, Surrey, agreed to take him. This, too, was an eye-opener for blow-in Australians. Founded in 1509, the school was still headquartered in its original Tudor buildings. The headmaster's study was an ancient library, its oak-panelled walls lined with the illuminated Latin manuscripts of the school's founders, mighty tomes chained to the shelves. Its oldest book had been published in 1409, and there were two early editions of Sir Isaac Newton's *Principia Mathematica*, circa 1687. RGS had a better academic record than Eton. James took to it well and starred in the rugby team; they took to calling him 'Our Wallaby'.

With the kids at school, Kerri was able to work – first part-time as a medical technologist at the Royal Surrey Hospital, after which she did a full-time postgraduate degree in haematology at the University of Westminster.

Home was 'The Old Post House', a four-bedroomed cottage of mellow red brick and timber shingles we rented in the tiny rural village of East Clandon, in the Surrey countryside about 50 kilometres south-west of London. In the nineteenth century the building had been the village shop and post office. Roses and honeysuckle twined up its walls. In the low-ceilinged dining room at the heart of the house there was a Tudor fireplace large enough to roast an ox, supported by a huge, gnarled oak beam. You felt you should be sitting at ease in the pale sunlight of the bay window, cradling a tabby cat, sipping Earl Grey and reading Thomas Hardy. The timbers creaked at night.

East Clandon is listed in the Domesday Book compiled for William the Conqueror, whose tax collectors reckoned its woodlands, buildings and ploughlands – with seven men's plough teams – to be worth a handsome £4. Thatched and half-timbered cottages and farmhouses nestled around the eleventh-century church and graveyard of St Thomas of Canterbury and the seventeenth-century Queen's Head pub. Wildflowers grew in the hedgerows. Grainy sepia photographs taken in the nineteenth century show that little had changed in 150 years. When I brought the E-Type over from Australia, it looked splendid parked in the little laneway beside the house, as if it had come home. Hurling it down the winding country lanes of Surrey was sheer delight.

After their initial British reserve, and when they concluded that the Australians had not come to steal the church silver, start fights in the bar or hold riotous naked orgies, the locals were welcoming, introducing themselves over a crisp gin and tonic in the pub before Sunday lunch. The Queen's Head suffered from the chronic national shortage of ice. Ice – in your drink? They stared at you amazed, as if you'd asked for the band of the Grenadier Guards and an RAF fly-past.

Introductions with the colonials are always an awkward occasion for the English, who like to slot you into their class system but can't easily discern from your Australian accent exactly what your status might be. It bothers them, but they get around it in subtle ways, such as asking where the children are at school. This happened time and again. Our answers were satisfactory. 'Actually, you don't sound much like an Australian at all,' they would sometimes assure me with a cheerful smile, meaning that I didn't talk like Paul Hogan.

We knew we had been accepted when the greying, rather desiccated figure of Commander Ronald 'Busy' Boddie of the Parish Council knocked on the front door. Would we like to help out at the church fete next summer? Perhaps we could run the tombola stall? I had not a clue what a tombola stall might be but we agreed to pitch in. 'I say, awfully good of you,' exclaimed the commander. He had been an engineer in a cruiser in World War II. After a crash course in tombola – it turned out to be something between a raffle and a lucky dip – we carried it off without incident. We had arrived. We were villagers.

In return, East Clandon offered exquisite moments and fragments of its history. At our first Christmas we roasted our turkey outdoors in a charcoal-fired Weber kettle barbecue, to the astonishment of the neighbours. That Christmas Eve we joined them to troop merrily across frosted fields to Hatchlands, an early Georgian mansion built by a successful eighteenth-century admiral – Edward Boscawen, 'Old Dreadnought' – and celebrated for its gorgeous interiors, created by the architect Robert Adam. The National Trust owns it now. In the glow of the music room fire, beneath ceilings encrusted with gilt and plaster anchors, cannon, dolphins, sea-nymphs and Neptune himself, the walls hung with smoke-darkened portraits lit by ensconced candles, we drank mulled wine and sang the hallowed carols of Olde England. It was sublime.

Over time I grew to relish the *Englishness* of England, and the fabric of its past. It could be something as simple as an April walk through a bluebell wood, or the wasps plopping into your beer on a late summer's evening in a pub garden by a mill stream. Once it was the evocative sight and sound of a Battle of Britain–era Spitfire climbing and swooping in the blue at an air show in the Weald of Kent. A friend in the Royal Navy wangled me a visit to the Admiralty boardroom in Whitehall, its elaborate oak carvings, painted wind gauge and long table unchanged since the days of Nelson and St Vincent. On a bleak winter's night in Cambridge we happened upon a rehearsal of the choir of Trinity College. Isaac Newton, in white marble, graced the ante-chapel. Their undergraduate faces pale in the soft glow of little red lamps, the choristers sent their silvery voices soaring to the ceiling.

✧

Englishness was happening to me as well. After a year on air in the drive slot my voice had morphed into an Anglo-Australian hybrid. Brits could still tell I was Australian, but Australians thought I had gone all Pom. It wasn't deliberate; it crept up on me almost by osmosis, the product of my receptive ear for mimicry. And I had to do British accents in the comedy sketches anyway. I could manage Scots and Scouse, West Country, Yorkshire, Welsh, Irish (north and south), upper-class toff and Cockney. The only one that eluded me was Geordie, from north-east England, which I found impossible.

Nineteen ninety-one had gone well. I was grateful for long, on-air interviews with Clive James, who was generous in his welcome, and with Barry Humphries, who did a hilarious Edna again. The audience began coming on board, slowly at first, then with gathering speed. They liked my funnies and my interview style. British radio interviewers tend to be wordy and excessively deferential. 'Minister, could I perhaps put it to you ... There are many people who might think ...' and so on. I bored in with Australian directness. I had an enjoyably sharp clash with that odious Belfast Protestant bully the Reverend Ian Paisley, who angrily cut the interview short. A Tory backbencher, Terry Dicks, the MP for the outer West London constituency of Hayes and Harlington, tried to take me on in a phone interview. Dicks was a truculent runt politically to the right of Attila the Hun; he had once called Nelson Mandela a 'black terrorist' who should have been hanged.

'If you don't like it here in Britain, we can put you on a convict ship back to Orstralia,' he snarled at me.

'Piss off!' I shot back, and cut him off dead.

Such horror had never been heard on British radio before, apparently. This caused a mini-sensation too, but with listeners calling to apologise for Dicks' rudeness. Unamused as ever, the colonels on the Radio Authority slapped me with another reproof.

For 1992, Charlie decided to turbocharge the station. As we had planned, I would swap shifts with the breakfast presenter, Angela Rippon. She did not take this well, seeing the drive slot as a demotion. About my age, with a cultivated cut-glass accent and an annoyingly cheery manner, Rippon was a household name in Britain. She had been one of the BBC's earliest female TV newsreaders, and host of a slew of variety shows. She found it demeaning to work for Australians and made her displeasure plain, but she needed the gig and copped it. We did not get on.

Another of Charlie's picks caused waves. He brought on the young Viscount Althorp – a.k.a. Charles Spencer, little brother of Princess Diana – to do an evening talkback show. I taught him a few tricks of the trade. The Viscount – 'just call me Charles' – wasn't a bad bloke, and he was a quick learner. His show was okay. He told me that Diana listened to me sometimes and had once called me on the open line, disguising her voice.

Charlie's next move was a masterstroke. He pulled off hiring Michael Parkinson for the morning show, nine am to midday. I was thrilled. I had met Michael a few times on his visits to Australia. We'd had drinks and dinner and I'd been a guest on his TV chat show. We got on well. The prospect of working alongside him was inspiring, and so it came to be.

From a standing start, he turned out the best morning radio program I have ever heard, bar none. His genial but probing style was magic, delivered in that Yorkshire baritone as smooth and creamy as a pint of Theakston's Old Peculier. And with Michael what you saw and heard was what you got. Unlike most radio and TV stars, he was the same man off air as he was on. Despite being one of Britain's most famous faces, there was none of the haughty arrogance of stardom. At the wine bar across from the studio, or the Albion pub down the road, he was just another bloke enjoying a drink and talking cricket with his colleagues.

Michael's great career regret was that Don Bradman had never granted him an interview. Privately, he would tell you that he despised British snobbery and privilege. He had been born the son of a coalminer in Barnsley, in Yorkshire's West Riding, and had barely scraped through high school. His generation in the British media, both newspapers and electronic, was dominated by the right sort of people with the right sort of accents, chaps laden with the glittering prizes of Oxbridge and who all knew each other. Against the odds, Michael had broken through the class barrier and scaled the heights by sheer drive, talent and personality. His wife, Mary, was delightful.

Best of all, they liked Australians. Their son, Nick, was then working at a resort hotel near Sydney and they came out often, always in summer so they could also catch the cricket. And Australians liked them. The Parkinsons had a comfortable, sunny house in the village of Bray, in the Thames Valley beyond Windsor, *Wind in the Willows* territory, with a lush green lawn rolling down to the banks of the river. At our first summer barbecue there I was surprised to see a tall Australian red gum growing in the back garden, almost certainly the only eucalypt to be seen on the Thames between Oxford and Gravesend. Michael had brought it back from his travels as a souvenir and a reminder.

'It keeps dropping bark and leaves,' he grumbled. 'What do you do with the bloody things? D'you prune them?'

I advised against it. *The Michael Parkinson Show* on LBC Newstalk ran for two years, until Michael went on to another venture. I loved being there with him.

✧

Nineteen ninety-two was a general election year in Britain. John Major, Thatcher's successor, was seeking a mandate from the electorate to govern in his own right. To cover a British election on the ground from the inside, rather than observing it as a foreign correspondent, was a treat. Suddenly, politicians were clamouring to come to the studio to sell their wares. You had to beat them off with a sharp stick.

After a year on air I was a known quantity. Although I never pulled off an interview or even a meeting with Major, I crossed paths with most of the significant players. Neil Kinnock, the Labour leader, a volatile but likeable Welshman, had me to morning tea in his office at Westminster, where we spoke hardly at all about politics but lots about our mutual passion for rugby. Kinnock came close to winning the election and might well have, but for the feral campaign against him by the Murdoch newspapers. Tony Blair, then a relatively junior frontbencher – all teeth, eager to please and oozing fake sincerity and real ambition in equal measure – was another frequent interview guest. Eternally suspicious of the media, the former peer turned Labour left-winger Tony Benn tape-recorded every interview he did.

On the Tory side, the chancellor of the exchequer, the now rightly forgotten Norman Lamont, was a prissy bore. Far more interesting was Alan Clark, a mad right-winger, Thatcher acolyte, crotchety snob and serial adulterer whose politics were odious but whose breezy contempt for conventional political cant was a hoot. (*The Alan Clark Diaries*, published after he quit parliament, rocked Westminster to the core.) I had a bet on the election result with the leonine Michael Heseltine, one of the cabal of ministers who had unhorsed Thatcher. When I paid him the £10 he won from me on the Conservatives' victory, he wrote a polite note to say he'd framed it and hung it in his loo.

Often the lesser figures were more fun. Over the months I struck up a friendship with another Tory MP, Jerry Hayes, a carousing former barrister who held the seat of Harlow, in Essex, north-east of London. We were about the same age. Jerry was a fountain of salacious Westminster gossip, which he would cheerfully embroider over a bottle of claret or three. One of his favourite yarns was of the Tory grandee Willie Whitelaw, who, at the height of the AIDS scare and much to his consternation, had been deputed to explain anal sex to Margaret Thatcher. It had not gone well.

Jerry and I lunched a bit, sometimes at Wilton's, the venerable fish restaurant in St James's. After one epic feast at the Ritz in Piccadilly he carted me back to the Commons for a drink at Annie's Bar, then a discreet watering hole in the bowels of the Houses of Parliament where journalists and MPs could mix. The rule was that whatever happened in Annie's Bar stayed in Annie's Bar, which was fortunate. As I have little memory of the occasion, I quote from Jerry's own memoir:

> By this time Mike was in full Aussie mode. He was on great form. He fell off a bar stool, thumped a fellow journo and was escorted off the premises. It was a wonderful afternoon.
>
> The next day, the boys thought it might be a good idea to wind him up. So, on House of Commons notepaper, they draw up some mad admonishment from the Speaker for his clear contempt of Parliament which could carry the penalty of imprisonment in the Tower of London. When Mike received it he was petrified.[133]

That is true. When I duly reported to the Commons, fully expecting a public beheading on Tower Green, Jerry and some colleagues waylaid me and fell about in fits of laughter. Gotcha. We had more drinks.

Rather more respectably, on a splendid summer's evening he took me to one of the most spectacular delights of my time in the UK, a formal Beating of the Retreat at Horse Guards off Whitehall, the grandest of all the grand parade grounds of empire. It was the rich panoply of British military grandeur, Shakespeare's 'pride, pomp and circumstance of glorious war'.[134] The Household Division – Guards and Cavalry – stamped and trotted and wheeled in serried ranks of scarlet, gold and gleaming leather, swords and sabres flashing, bands oompahing. There was a royal duke in a cocked hat topped with feathers. We looked down upon this swelling scene from the Old Admiralty Building, on the northern side of the square, sipping champagne and scoffing canapés. I felt like Wellington, Kitchener, Montgomery of Alamein. The Thin Red Line! My quasi-imperial schooldays were marching past before me.

Most marvellous of all, the great room we were in had once been the office of the First Lord of the Admiralty, where Winston Churchill himself had held sway in 1914 and again in 1939. It now belonged to the Northern Ireland office. But with typical British respect for history, it had been meticulously restored as Churchill knew it, down to the vintage telephones on the desk and the vast wall maps showing the disposition of the fleet on the day Britain had declared war on Germany for the second time. For a journalist who had idly dreamed of writing naval history one day, it was pure nectar.

✧

By now I was confident I knew what I was doing. During that 1992 election I scored a scoop interview with Gerry Adams, the turbulent leader of the Northern Ireland separatist political party, Sinn Féin. Adams has always denied it, but he was also almost certainly a senior commander of the Provisional IRA. Thatcher had banned Sinn Féin and the IRA from the airwaves to deprive them of 'the oxygen of publicity', as she called it, and their voices had not been heard in the UK for years, but we found a loophole: Adams was a candidate for the Commons seat of West Belfast and, for that reason, the law permitted a live interview.

He and I went at it bare-knuckled, toe to toe. I am all for a united and independent Ireland, but I despised the IRA's wanton bombing of civilians, and I told him so.[135] My approach was deliberate – to get him riled and off-balance – and it worked. 'Is getting the British Army out of Northern Ireland really worth the murder of innocent men, women and children?' He blew his cool and began to bluster, so I repeated it.

'If that's what it takes,' he snarled.

A phone interview with the Bosnian Serb leader – and later convicted mass murderer – Radovan Karadžić got even more explosive. 'You're a bare-faced liar,' I said to him.

But the stuff I had most fun with was light-hearted and whimsical. British eccentricity was a goldmine. I treasure memories of an interview with one John Gladden, forty-three, of Croydon, a barmy Londoner waging war on his local council for the right to mount a full-sized model of a Spitfire on the roof of his small suburban house. Ordered to court, he turned up in a truck convoy led by a small French tank, a six-metre-tall inflatable model of Winston Churchill and a ten-metre rocket launcher. 'An Englishman's home is his castle,' he cried.

Another delightful crackpot was a winemaker somewhere in Kent who had tried, but sadly failed, to market his product across the channel in France.

'And why weren't you successful?' I asked him kindly.

'My wine doesn't taste very good,' he said glumly.

To circumvent the ban on me giving editorial opinion, we engaged some of Britain's best-known journalists to do it instead. It was borderline legal. Andrew Neil, the craggy, Scottish-born editor of Murdoch's *Sunday Times*, had a daily spot on the show for 'news analysis', as we carefully called it. The *Daily Telegraph*'s political editor, George Jones, had the lowdown on Westminster, and would become a lifelong friend. Peter Preston, then editor of the *Guardian*, was another regular, as was Donald Trelford, editor of the *Observer*.

It was Trelford, a cheerful, pint-sized figure sometimes known as 'Pixie', who scored me an invitation to Buckingham Palace. A lover of cricket, he was a leading light in an obscure society formed to preserve the ancient village greens of England from predatory property developers, to retain these hallowed swards as places where the lord of the manor and the local blacksmith could meet as equals to enjoy the thwack of leather on willow. For some reason he asked me to join, and in time we were bidden to a cocktail reception given by the society's patron, no less than Anne, the Princess Royal.

As we stepped out of the taxi at the palace, Pixie began to get nervous. 'Make sure you bow when you meet her,' he whispered.

'Not me,' I said. 'I'm an Australian republican. No bowing.'

'Oh, Jesus. You've *got* to bow . . .'

'No.'

'When in Rome . . .'

'We're not in Rome.'

I had vaguely expected the palace to be a little shabby, with hints of peeling paint and faded curtains perhaps, all a bit yesteryear. Wrong. It shone, immaculately. A flunkey directed us up the Grand Staircase, a stunning extravagance of marble, gilt and red carpet, and into a high-ceilinged reception room. The walls were stiff with Old Masters. Van Dyck eyeballed Da Vinci, Holbein stared at Caravaggio, Bruegel gazed at Rembrandt. Footmen circulated with drinks and canapés, and high-quality stuff it was – none of your cheap fizz, oily gin, stale crackers or greasy onion dips. There were about thirty of us village green enthusiasts there when Anne arrived and began to mingle, working the room and shaking hands with the aplomb instilled by a lifetime's experience.

When our time came, Trelford bowed like Sir Walter Raleigh.

I did not.

The princess was not the slightest bit fazed. We shook hands. She picked me as Australian from the start and chatted knowledgeably about Shane Warne, Mark Taylor and Michael Slater, who were then taking Britain by storm. And why was I interested in the preservation of village greens? 'Something close to every cricket lover's heart, ma'am,' I assured her stoutly. She smiled and moved on.

'You got away with it,' hissed Pixie, amazed and relieved.

Best not to push royalty too far, though. Diamond Jim McClelland told me once of sitting next to Princess Margaret at a state dinner in Canberra. She was half-pissed and sullenly bored, but Jim felt it his duty to make small talk.

'And how is your sister?' he enquired politely.
'Still Queen,' she snapped.

✧

Above all, I was enjoying myself. By the end of 1992 I had a daily audience of a million people, about five times the size of my Sydney audience at its best. To drag in still more punters to the show, we pumped out some humorous on-air promos I scripted for three of the most popular TV actors of the time: Penelope Keith from *To the Manor Born*, Geoffrey Palmer from *As Time Goes By* and Joanna Lumley, who had just begun to knock them out of the park as Patsy in *Absolutely Fabulous*. La Keith, funny as a wheel, did her poshest *Horse & Hound* accent: 'Australians helped us defeat Hitler,' she intoned grandly. 'You can repay our colonial cousins by tuning in to Mike Carlton on LBC Newstalk.' Joanna, bless her, was indeed absolutely fabulous. When she came to the studio to record her lines, I expected a brisk 'Let's get it done,' but she was sweet and painstaking. I could have drowned in her eyes. '*Do* listen to Mike Carlton,' she breathed. 'He is *such* a darling when you get to know him.' Stupidly, I never kept the recordings.

We had a social reporter on the program, a journalist and former star TV presenter named Lynda Berry, whose job was to gather froth, bubble and a splash of acid, the gossip of London, royal and otherwise. She did it with verve. Lynda was English peaches'n'cream, with forget-me-not eyes, whose highest accolade was to pronounce you a 'good egg'. She spent a lot of time fending off the amorous advances of a figure she referred to, mysteriously, as the Spitting Viscount.

Lynda and her best mate, Sally Bulloch, both about my age, knew everybody who was anybody in town and beyond. They drew me into their circle. Sally – a former child actress, blonde, petite and stunningly elegant – managed the boutique five-star Athenaeum Hotel at 116 Piccadilly, opposite Green Park, where she kept an open house for all comers like some theatrical impresario. Her eyes sparkled, her smile was warm and, great hostess that she was, you felt you'd made her day just by turning up. The glitterati flocked to stay. Steven Spielberg had edited *Raiders of the Lost Ark* in his suite there.

Every so often Sally would call me at work. 'Do drop in for champers this afternoon,' she would trill. 'I want you to meet Sean Connery.' Or: 'Michael Douglas and his wife are in town. And by the way, do you know the Duke of Bedford?' Sally liked Australians too. It was said she had once charmed Russell Crowe into tidying his room, no mean feat. The TV crews from Nine's *60 Minutes* invariably stayed with her in London. Wisely, she did not introduce me to two other close friends, Margaret and Denis Thatcher.

It was from the discreet and hospitable Athenaeum that we sortied forth for Charlie's wedding. I was the best man. We were not in good shape. The previous day Lynda and Sally had taken us for an expansive buck's pre-wedding lunch at the Enterprise, an upmarket pub in Chelsea, where the signature cocktail was a 'Puerto Rican Motherfucker'. I can remember it only vaguely: something to do with a pint of lager, into which the bartender dropped a flaming shot glass of weapons-grade rum. There might have been Cointreau or tequila or something else involved as well, but after six or so the question was academic.

The wedding day found us bleary-eyed and shaking as we tried to dress each other in the sartorial absurdity of white tie and tails hired from Moss Bros. Charlie's bride, an Australian girl from Perth, wanted a traditional English wedding with all the trimmings. Neither of us had ever worn this ridiculous gear before. The waistcoat, and the shirt with its starched, detached collar, involved a bewildering array of tapes, tabs, straps, braces, ribbons, studs and buttons. After an hour or so of fumbling we got it more or less right, we thought, and left for the church, pausing only briefly at the groom's local Thames-side pub for a heart-starter.

It was winter, and St Swithuns Chertsey, fourteenth century, was freezing. Or it would have been, had not Charlie hired an enormous heater to warm the place for the comfort of the Australian visitors. A contraption the size and shape of a Rolls-Royce jet engine was installed in the nave, where it gave off a blast of noise and heat like a 747 on take-off. The vicar, a cranky sod, was aghast. And with fair reason. Not in 600 years had the temperature inside the church risen beyond about twelve degrees. Now it was positively tropical. The timbers creaked alarmingly. Bats expired in the belfry. The organ gave up the ghost: its ancient bits and pieces had expanded in the heat and thrown everything out of whack. When the lady organist struck up the wedding march for the arrival of the bride, it wheezed, farted, squawked and honked with an ear-splitting racket somewhere between a blast of foghorns and a collapsing wooden shed.

My role at the happy nuptials peaked when my shirt collar came unstuck. It might have been the heat as well. With a loud *whang*, a stud popped out, ricocheted across the church and disappeared. One wing of the collar sprang up and lodged itself beneath my ear, resisting all efforts to stuff it back into place again. The vicar couldn't wait to get rid of us.

Sally Bulloch came into an inheritance a few years later and moved to South Africa with a new husband. In 2008 she was found dead in her shower, with bad bruising. The cause was given as accidental death, but many of her friends believe she was murdered.

✧

When Mike Parkinson left LBC, Charlie replaced him on the morning show with another journalist, Richard Littlejohn, who had written a much-read column for Murdoch's *Sun*. Like any newspaper columnist worth the money, he was admired and loathed in about equal measure. Abhorring his political opinions, I was ready to dislike him on sight myself, but he turned out to be a fast learner on radio, an entertaining broadcaster and companionable in the pub. We hit it off.

'I'm having lunch with Peter Cook,' he said to me one day. 'Would you like to come?'

'*The* Peter Cook. As in *Pete and Dud*?'

'The very same.'

Thirty years of journalism had left me by and large inured to celebrities. But I had revered Peter Cook since the 1960s, from the moment I heard the recording of *Beyond the Fringe*, the revolutionary comedy routines he had put together at Cambridge with Dudley Moore, Alan Bennett and Jonathan Miller. I could repeat every word. British comedy had always captivated me: *The Goon Show* and poor, wretched Tony Hancock had been an early inspiration. Cook, the funniest man in Britain, had elevated comedy and satire to a stratospheric plane, with the likes of Barry Humphries, Stephen Fry, Rowan Atkinson, the Goodies and John Cleese and his fellow Pythons drawn along in the slipstream. Privately wealthy, he was the financial godfather to the wickedly subversive *Private Eye* magazine.

We found him at the Queen's Head, a pleasant pub in leafy Brook Green, around the corner from the LBC studios. It was just after midday but he'd already allowed himself a pint or two – to prepare for the rigours of the afternoon, he assured us. He had a couple more with us, and then we walked to a little Italian restaurant in Shepherds Bush Road.

There followed one of the funniest afternoons of my life. I sat spellbound as first the champagne and then the chianti flowed, dazzled by the avalanche of wit, anecdote and invective. Cook told hilarious stories of his 1971 tour of Australia with Dudley Moore, during which, he said, people constantly tried to sell them drugs. 'Most of them were undercover policemen,' he snorted. He dominated the conversation, not in an overbearing way but by sheer force of intellect and personality. Dudley Moore was a cunt, a fucking cunt. Their breakup had been acrimonious. Occasionally he would lunge into character, as the upper-class twit Sir Arthur Streeb-Greebling or the monotonal numbskull E. L. Wisty.

The wine kept coming. Lunchers at other tables gawped. After a lengthy monologue denouncing 'the fucking royal family', he called for paper and pen and scrawled a note which I still have: 'If I ever accept any royal honour or title you may cut me down in a hail of blood and bullets. Signed, Peter Edward Cook. Hampstead, London NW3.'

We lunched on, into the lowering night. As people began to arrive for dinner Cook pelted them with bread rolls. 'Repel boarders!' he bellowed. The restaurateur, until then tolerant to a fault, presented us with an eye-watering bill and nervously but firmly herded us out into the rainy street. Cook urged a nightcap and we found a pub a little way down the road.

The great man led the way and flung open the door with a flourish, to reveal an empty cavern as gloomy as Queen Victoria's mausoleum at Frogmore. A pimpled, lank-haired yoof was glumly polishing glasses behind the bar.

'Potman!' bellowed Cook, in stentorian Streeb-Greebling mode. 'A good evening to you, my good fellow! I bring with me kith and kin from across the oceans, a most welcome Australian visitor to our green and pleasant land. He has travelled far from the Antipodes. Pray, let us show him the best of our English hospitality. We shall rest at ease before your glowing fire . . .'

He looked around for a fire. There wasn't one. The pimpled yoof gaped. Undeterred, Cook galloped on.

'Look sharp, my man. Have your serving wench bring forth a selection of your finest ales, your choicest viands! Lay out the groaning board with the best your hostelry and Olde England have to offer! Call for minstrels, for strolling players! Let there be feasting, merriment and song!'

At that point he dried up. Silence fell. The yoof ceased his glass-polishing and bared his teeth. 'Why don't you fuck off,' he snarled.

'Three pints, please,' I quavered.

Seen through the prism of hindsight, Peter Cook was a tragic figure. He had begun drinking heavily after falling out with Moore in Australia, and the booze gripped him for the rest of his life. He was a helpless alcoholic and near his end by the time we met. He died just two years later, in 1995, at the age of fifty-seven, of internal bleeding brought on by his drinking, and his ashes were buried in an unmarked grave in a churchyard near his Hampstead home. I cherish the memory of our afternoon together.

✧

On a spring evening in May 1993, the grand ballroom of the Grosvenor House Hotel on Park Lane, in Mayfair, was stuffed to the rafters with the cream of Britain's radio talent. The room hummed and table-hopped. It was the night of the Radio Academy Awards, usually known as the Sony awards in honour of their chief sponsor. Most people there were from the BBC, which still dominated the airwaves then, although commercial radio was fast catching up. It was glamorous, black-tie. LBC had a couple of tables for its top presenters, producers and a few executives. Charlie and I were there with our wives.

If you have seen one media awards night then you have seen them all. They go on and on. The famous and not-so-famous came and went on stage to collect their gongs. Around the middle of the evening they got to the category for which I had been nominated: the Gold Award for Best Breakfast Show (Speech-based). I didn't think I had the ghost of a chance. I was a foreigner. My show had been on air for just over a year. The competition was intense: this award was invariably taken out by one BBC station or another, a lay-down misère. The year before it had gone to BBC Radio Four, the venerable national news and current-affairs network, home to such flagship programs as *Today* and *The World at One*.

The presenter on stage doing the honours was Trevor McDonald, a journalist born in Trinidad and who, as the frontman for ITV's *News at Ten*, was one of the best known faces in Britain. He did the customary fumble with the envelope and the usual pause for suspense before announcing the winner. '*The Mike Carlton Morning Report*. LBC Newstalk!'

'Up you go,' said Charlie.

I could barely move. I was gobsmacked. The Gold Award. Best breakfast talk show in the UK, from Land's End to John O'Groats. I have never been so surprised in my life. Not before. Not since. We had beaten the best that British radio could throw against us. Almost in a trance, I stumbled to the stage and collected the trophy.

'Nice to see us colonials get a gong,' whispered Trevor with a grin.

It was a high point of my career. That, and a gold medal I also won that year from the International Radio Festival in New York. With my usual carefree abandon I forgot to take both these trophies with me when I left LBC and returned to Australia, and they have now vanished.

✧

That triumph was followed by disaster. LBC's parent company, Crown Communications, went broke and was put into receivership. David Haynes was in big trouble. It was partly his fault, but by no means all.

The network of pop music radio stations he owned in France, RFM, had been pulled out from under him, a lethal blow. As a foreigner, he was not legally permitted to own radio stations there. To cut a long story short, when his ownership was unmasked he had to get out at a fire-sale price. RFM went for a song and dragged him under. In London, LBC under Charlie's leadership was at last making money after years in the red, but not enough to stave off David's financial collapse. He had to sell us, too.

I was sorry to see him go. He had been a good boss, and loyal too, at those times when I had come under fire from one or two nervous nellies in his boardroom or the blimps at the Radio Authority. He was one of the better men I have worked for, decent and fair. The worry for all of us on the factory floor was who might buy us and what they might do with us. An added concern was that LBC's government licence to broadcast was up for grabs. In Australia, once you have a commercial radio station licence, you pretty much have it for good, unless you commit some unspeakable crime. No one has ever lost one. In Britain it is very different, in radio and television. Every few years the licences are put out to tender, publicly advertised to all comers. If for whatever reason the powers that be aren't satisfied with the job the incumbent is doing, they can choose a new one – and they often do. Just like that.

We learned soon enough who our new owner would be. The news hit us like a punch in the guts. Dame Shirley Porter was the Lord Mayor of Westminster, the city council covering a large slab of West London. Then in her early sixties, Porter was a powerful figure, and stinking rich. She was the daughter of Jacob 'Jack' Cohen, who had founded Britain's giant Tesco supermarket chain, and was an heir to his vast fortune. Dabbling in politics, she had gone into local government and built a reputation as an arch Conservative, out to the right of Margaret Thatcher, no small accomplishment.

She was crooked and hard as nails. Westminster contained some of London's richest districts and some of its poorest. When the Labour-voting peasants almost swamped the Tory gentry and their candidates at a council election, Porter hatched a scheme to get rid of them. She dreamed up a policy innocuously called 'Building Stable

Communities', but which was, in effect, a vicious means of social cleansing. The poor were evicted from their rented council houses in their hundreds and then thousands, and sent packing in misery, sickness and squalor. Their homes were then sold, the assumption – correct, as it turned out – being that the buyers would be likely to vote Tory. It became known as the 'Homes for Votes' scandal, and it was big news. The political deck had been stacked, outrageously.

Down the track, the courts would find the scheme was illegal and Porter was guilty of 'wilful misconduct' and 'disgraceful and improper gerrymandering'. Eventually she was ordered to repay a whopping £43.3 million to the council. Staying one jump ahead of the law, she fled to Israel and skulked there out of reach, in disgrace, shovelling all her assets off to members of her family. After years of tortuous negotiation, she eventually agreed to pay back £12.3 million. In 2002 she was stripped of her title.

Most of this lay in the future. But we knew enough about Homes for Votes to realise what a stinker Dame Shirley was. The law was closing in on her and she had snapped up LBC, intending to use it as a megaphone for her defence.

21

Back home among the gum trees

DÉJÀ VU WENT FOR a gallop around the paddock again. Except that this was no illusion. Shirley Porter appeared before us in the LBC boardroom and spouted much the same blather as I had heard back in Sydney when 2GB had been taken over. 'Talented people . . . unique opportunity . . . great radio . . . challenges ahead . . .' It was a familiar litany. Flanked by her son John and by her *consigliere*, an Old Etonian named Matthew Cartisser, Porter looked like a carrion crow. A few days later, Cartisser drove me to lunch at the River Café in his green Rolls-Royce.

'Have you been in one of these before?' he asked, with the airy condescension that is the special preserve of Etonians.

'Yes,' I said, with the thin smile Australians use when they are being patronised by Etonians. We did not get on.

The thing went further downhill when Charlie Cox pulled the pin. It was becoming abundantly clear that the Porter lot had not a clue about how to run a radio station, and LBC was heading for disaster. Charlie was not about to go down with it. The *Daily Mail* newspaper and media conglomerate DMGT offered him big money to run their string of radio stations in Britain, and away he went. I was stricken to see him go, but it was the right decision for him.

He ascended the heights and is now in the trusted inner circle of advisers to the *Daily Mail*'s proprietor, Viscount Rothermere.

The fatal blow came in September 1993, when the Radio Authority withdrew LBC's licence to broadcast. Another company got the franchise. Nobody knew why. The authority was not required to explain, and it did not. Richard Littlejohn and I assumed there were a couple of reasons: firstly, that Shirley Porter was politically on the nose, and secondly, that we were too. With each month Porter was sinking deeper into the mire of Homes for Votes. And Richard and I had been increasingly bending the rules on editorial comment and opinion, skating on thin ice. Richard had made scathing comments about the various crises and scandals besetting John Major's hapless Tory government, and I had done much the same with some scorching funnies. Now the establishment was hitting back. 'They do not like it up 'em,' Richard told me.

Indeed they did not. The *Guardian* asked me to write a piece about the axing, and with nothing to lose, I went for the Radio Authority and its chairman, Lord Chalfont, one of the retired colonels:

> The noble Lord Chalfont, having helped save the world from the evils of monolithic Communism, has turned his exertions to purifying British broadcasting as Chairman of the Radio Authority.
>
> His moment of triumph came last Friday with a bullet right between the eyes of London's two LBC Talk Stations. Bang. So died after 20 years, Britain's first commercial radio broadcaster.
>
> And the reason why, your Lordship? With that pinguid charm that has made this peer so popular an appointment with his Tory overseers, Chalfont loftily explained to a press conference that the Radio Authority was not obliged to give its reasons . . .
>
> But this is post-Thatcher Nanny-ish Britain and the very word 'Authority' says it all: an affront to free speech . . .
>
> Our jobs have been snatched from us by one of those ridiculous and unaccountable 'quangos' which infest every corner of British public life and multiply like pond amoeba.[136]

This did not go down well. One of the drones on the Radio Authority, a Labour hack named John Grant, hit back. 'I don't see why I should be on the end of a pompous lecture by a middle-aged imported Aussie, overpaid, overbearing and over here,' he wrote.[137]

The LBC switchboard went into meltdown with protests from angry listeners, and there were around 50,000 letters of sympathy and complaint at the decision. To no avail. The axe had fallen.

The BBC offered me a job, which was flattering. The boss of BBC Radio, Liz Forgan, took me to lunch and explained that she was setting up a new network, Radio Five. It would be a full-on competitor to LBC Newstalk. Would I like to come across? She was charm itself and the idea was exciting. Kerri and I considered our options. We were loving life in Britain, but at the same time we were increasingly thinking of home. We were missing that unique Australian environment of space and light. I was yearning to be near a beach again – I had not seen the surf, let alone caught a wave, in more than three years. Kerri was longing for her family back in Wagga. The Beeb would pay me less than half what I had been earning at LBC, which would have meant taking the kids out of their hideously expensive private schools, a disruption we did not want to inflict on them.

A tipping point of sorts came one evening watching television when, for whatever reason, someone came on to sing 'Waltzing Matilda'. James, aged thirteen, was watching with us, and he barely knew the words.

'What's a squatter?' I asked him.

'It's one of those homeless people who moves into a council house and squats there without paying rent.'

'Time to go,' I said to Kerri.

So we made our plans. It would be hard leaving Britain. We'd had visions of the kids doing their A Levels, their secondary school exams, and gliding aloft to Oxford or Cambridge. We had made many friends, both neighbours and in the media, and the farewells would be sad. We were leaving more than Britain, too. We had holidayed in a seventeenth-century Tuscan farmhouse in the hills above Lucca, in a cottage on the Brittany coast, and in a sunny beach resort on Corsica. We had stayed in medieval castles on the Rhine and seen the grey Baltic from Hamlet's Elsinore. Further afield, we had sailed in the Caribbean from the French islands of St Barts and St Martin, and one

Christmas we had flown to Lapland, deep in the snows of the Arctic circle, where the entire world was blue and white and the sun was but a faint glow at midday.

It had been a good time to be an Australian in London. The prejudice and condescension I had encountered back in the 1960s had largely disappeared, washed away by the wave of Australian culture which had swept Britain in the decades since. Clive James, Germaine Greer, Robert Hughes, Barry Humphries, Richard Neville and others had established a beachhead. *Neighbours* and *Home and Away* then splashed ashore to capture millions of viewers. Michael Hutchence and his band INXS rocketed to stardom. *Strictly Ballroom*, the first film by the Australian director Baz Luhrmann, took Britain by storm in 1992. It was almost fashionable to be an Australian, and at times hugely enjoyable. I had been in the crowd at Twickenham, the home of rugby, when Nick Farr-Jones's Wallabies beat England to win the World Cup in 1991. In 1993 I was at Lord's on the opening day of the second Ashes Test to see Mark Taylor and a young Michael Slater knock up a legendary double-century opening partnership. The British were fascinated to learn that they both hailed from Wagga Wagga, a name guaranteed to send the average Brit into fits of laughter.

As if on cue, I got a job offer from Sydney. Radio station 2UW was about to switch from the AM to the FM band. Would I be available for the breakfast show?

2UW was owned by the Albert family, a clan every bit as publicity-shy and secretive as the Lambs at 2UE. The Alberts had made their money in music publishing, branching out into radio as early as 1929. Four generations of them were blessed with a knack for business. They knew their stuff, they invested well and the money kept rolling in. The family seat was Sydney's best-known harbourside mansion, the Spanish mission–style 'Boomerang' at Elizabeth Bay. In the mid-1960s the family company, J. Albert & Son, had signed up a little-known rock group, the Easybeats, to pump out a string of hit records and, after them, no less than AC/DC, the biggest Australian band of all time. Others followed. The Alberts held the Australian rights to overseas artists as varied as George Gershwin, Irving Berlin and the Beach Boys. In 1992 they spent $3 million to fund and produce *Strictly Ballroom*, for a return of around $80 million at the box office.

Working for that kind of outfit seemed like a good idea. I asked Charlie to do the negotiations with the station's program director, Cherie Romaro, and he was able to get me a generous contract. The deal was done.

We had our last Christmas in London as a family. The kids were keen to get home to Australia, but Kerri stayed on for a couple of months with Alex while she finished her Year Ten GCSE exams. I went back to Sydney with James to reclaim our house at Turramurra and to get ready for the new gig in the early autumn of 1994. Over that summer I surfed again, and decided – quite out of the blue – that I might have a crack at writing a novel. Amazingly, it was a comedy about an Australian radio presenter in London, *Off the Air.* There were a few good jokes and it did well enough in Australia, but no British publisher wanted to know about it.

✧

Tony Albert, one of three brothers and a lawyer by trade, was a good boss, a knowing connoisseur of wine, art and antiques, and fun to be with. Almost uniquely in Sydney, he had not an enemy in the world. After I signed my contract, he and his equally likeable wife, Gaish, hosted a Sunday barbecue at their home in Bellevue Hill, with its glorious harbour views. We ate in the cellar, surrounded by vintage wines beyond price, which our host insisted we sample. 'You must try this '55 Château d'Yquem,' Tony cried, hoicking the cork out of about $400 worth of sticky sauternes. Another guest was Angus Young, the lead guitarist of AC/DC. Angus doesn't drink. Tony produced a battered old six-string guitar from somewhere and cajoled him into playing Rolling Stones and Creedence Clearwater Revival songs, which we bellowed long into the night. He didn't seem to mind. Tony died suddenly in 2000, much mourned.

Meeting the Alberts was the upside of my 2UW gig, but that was about it. The rest of it was a disaster, the worst career decision I have ever made. At the beginning, Cherie Romaro had promised me a free hand to put together my own breakfast show. Taking her at her word,

I hired two talented writers and producers. One was Vic Davies, who had been half of Club Veg, a hugely successful comedy double-act on Triple M. The other guy, David Callan, was a talented stand-up comedian. We beavered away at scripts, sketches, comedy characters, oddball humour and satire. The understanding was that we would try it out and polish it on 2UW, then take it across for the breakfast show on the new FM station, MIX 106.5.

Which is where everything fell apart. Without warning, Romaro decided to switch MIX to a music format known as 'adult contemporary'. As always, it was copied from the US. Adult contemporary, sometimes known as 'easy listening', was everything I loathed in pop music: syrupy ballads glued together with lush string arrangements, musical kitsch on Valium. It was aimed squarely at women over twenty-five, the sort of people fascinated by the latest shock-horror from Tom and Nicole, or Michael and Bubbles the Chimp. 'Sydney's *best* mix of the '70s, '80s and today,' said the oily on-air promos.

Actually, the MIX playlist seemed to consist of about ten songs aired on high rotation, half of them by Mariah Carey, who would never sing just one note if she thought six would be better. The other half were by somebody called Michael Bolton, a lugubrious crooner who, on every song, sounded as if he was either painfully constipated or having a nervous breakdown. Or both. The KGB tortured its prisoners by bombarding them with Bolton night and day. It got so bad that Vic, David and I actually wrote comedy sketches sending up the music and the format, which was more than a bit counterproductive but at least helped us retain our sanity. God knows what the audience made of it.

For whatever reason, the Albert family sold MIX and another seven stations in their radio network a year later, in mid-1995. They couldn't stand Mariah Carey and Michael Bolton either. The buyer was APN, Australian Provincial Newspaper Holdings, a media company run by a young Irish-Australian entrepreneur, Cameron O'Reilly. He, in turn, brought in an American partner, a slow-talking Texan whose name I cannot be bothered trying to remember; it was something like Randy P. Sphincter. He turned up in the boardroom one day wearing a white Stetson and gave us his version of the 'Talented people . . . unique opportunity' spiel, with the additional twist of referring to the American radio stations he owned as 'profit centres'.

I was bored to sobs, hating every minute I was on air. Unsurprisingly, the ratings tanked. At the end of 1995 Cameron O'Reilly and I mutually decided to call it quits. He paid me out the remaining three months of my contract and I was a free man again. I have never been so relieved in my life, before or since. It was like getting out of jail.

✧

Andrew Olle died on Tuesday, 12 December 1995. We had known each other for more than twenty years, since our time together at ABC television on *This Day Tonight*. Andrew had stayed with the ABC, becoming ever more prominent. A year younger than me, he rose to host the ABC's flagship current-affairs program, *Four Corners*, for ten years, and presented his own radio program on 2BL. Television audiences loved him, captivated by the sometimes quizzical smile or gently raised eyebrow that were hallmarks of his style. He was cool and urbane. On radio and television his interviews were penetrating but without bluster, an iron fist in a velvet glove. Above all, he was a very fine journalist, accurate and fair, and entirely committed to the people's right to know through independent public broadcasting. At 2BL his daily dissection of Canberra politics with our mutual contemporary and friend Paul Lyneham became essential listening.

Many of us who had worked on *TDT* stayed in touch long after we had gone our separate ways, like old soldiers retired from a regiment. We would see each other infrequently, but the bonds of that shared experience remained strong. There would be the occasional barbecue or dinner at one house or another; our wives got on well and our kids all knew each other. Andrew was inner circle.

The first sign of something wrong came with a plane trip he suddenly took to Melbourne for no apparent reason. Back in Sydney and bewildered, he collapsed with a stroke. At the Royal North Shore Hospital they discovered a massive, cancerous tumour of the brain. His wife, Annette, and his three teenage kids, Nick, Sam and Nina, kept watch, but he never recovered consciousness.

The public interest was extraordinary. There was a clamour for the latest news. (Disgracefully and inexplicably, the ABC bungled the job by reporting his death prematurely.) Peter Luck, Paul Murphy and I took it upon ourselves to shield the Olle family from the persistent but respectful media enquiries.

No journalist ever got a better send-off. ABC audiences are unswervingly loyal to presenters of the first rank who have entertained or informed them, and whose integrity and professionalism they respect, and the suddenness of Andrew's death provoked a wave of national mourning. The New South Wales parliament passed a condolence motion brought by the premier, Bob Carr, and the opposition leader, Peter Collins, who had been ABC journalists themselves. Three days before Christmas the Sydney Town Hall was full for a memorial tribute, with hundreds more gathered outside to listen. The veteran composer Peter Sculthorpe wrote a special arrangement for cello and piano of his 1947 work *Parting*, which was played by Nathan Waks and Kathryn Selby.

Later, when I was at 2BL myself, we came up with the idea of having an annual Andrew Olle Lecture, to be given by a figure prominent in journalism or the media. The ABC took it on board and it has been a fitting memorial ever since. In recent years speakers who never knew Andrew have lauded him as a secular saint, a paragon of all the journalistic virtues, perfect in every way. Modest to a fault, self-deprecating, he would have found this both embarrassing and amusing. But he was one of the choice and master spirits of the age.

✧

The ABC threw me a lifeline in early 1996. They offered me the drivetime slot on 2BL, weekdays from three to six pm. I seized it gratefully. After the inanity of MIX it would be a chance to rescue what was left of my reputation by once again doing talk radio for sentient adults. The dough was the downside: I would be taking a big pay cut. Time to eat humble pie, in large chunks.

After twenty years in the high-rolling world of commercial radio, returning to the ABC felt oddly like going back to school. It was comforting, in a way. The pressure was off. I could detune. They would expect me to turn in decent ratings, which was fair enough, but they were not obsessed with the figures to the mad exclusion of all else. And nor would I have to read ads or put up with commercials on air, although that did have a minus side as well. An ad break in commercial radio generally runs for at least ninety seconds, and sometimes as long as three minutes or more. It can give you time to think, to plan or even to recover from some on-air disaster. At the ABC there would be no such luxury. You're on all the time, with no room for error.

Gone, too, were the days of a private office with a personal assistant taking the calls and guarding the door. 2BL was open-plan, with presenters and producers lumped together at adjoining desks, all beavering away within sight of each other. More humble pie. Gradually I got used to it. A big win was to score my own printer; everyone else had to share one. To my puzzled astonishment, some people did not even have a computer terminal: in 1996 they were still plonking away on ancient electric typewriters. There was one small room where, behind a closed door, you could access something mysteriously referred to as 'the internet'.

The best assets I had were the two producers assigned to hold my hand. Tony Rasmussen, roughly my own age and immensely likeable, was vastly experienced in both radio journalism and the weird and wonderful ways of the ABC. He knew all the ropes, was keen and enthusiastic, and gave wise counsel. His assistant, Morag Ramsay, had been hired only a few weeks before I started. Twenty-one years old, with a brand-new communications degree from Charles Sturt University at Bathurst, west of Sydney, she was new and sensibly apprehensive, but she hit the deck running.

The three of us sat down to plan what sort of drive show we would do. On top of that, I had to do some fast learning in the studio itself, practising how to work the buttons, faders, switches, dials and widgets. If the ABC has a choice between simple and complex, they'll go complex every time. Instead of buying perfectly suitable American or Japanese studio gear cheaply off the shelf, the ABC radio engineers had invented an insanely complicated system of their own called Ouija. When it worked it was terrific, but a lot of the time it didn't, largely because – typically – the ABC had run out of money to finish it properly. Once when I was on air the studio panel actually caught fire, a thin pillar of acrid blue smoke curling up from its electronic bowels. It was a testing moment.

✧

Australia went through seismic change in the 1990s. I had missed a lot of it in London, where Australian news was not reported unless it involved a shark or Kylie Minogue. When I came home I found Paul Keating at the commanding heights of his prime ministership, bent on transforming Australia in the image of his 'big picture'. After his 1993 'true believers' election victory gave him a mandate in his own right, he surged like a champion racehorse in the final straight.

As Bob Hawke's treasurer, Keating had upended the economy and dragged it screaming and kicking from its sclerotic Tory torpor. As prime minister, his reforms continued – a social wage and a national superannuation scheme, Aboriginal land rights, improved diplomatic ties with Asia and, most contentious of all, a vision for an Australian republic. It was exciting, invigorating, but there was one flaw, and it was fatal. Keating was failing to take the Australian people with him.

For all his policy brilliance, he lacked the common touch that had made Hawke such a triumphant election winner. Keating disdained the small change of politics, the walkabouts in shopping malls and the kissing of babies at barbecues. 'Throwing the switch to vaudeville' he called it, and he would do it if he had to, but his heart was never in it. His passions were refined and obscure: collecting clocks and treasures of the French empire. Behind his back, his staff began to call him 'Captain Wacky'. Kim Beazley told me a story of a morning cabinet meeting at which Keating had failed to appear. Sent to look for him, Beazley found him at the Lodge, still in his pyjamas, waving his hands in the air to a Mahler symphony.

For all his idiosyncrasies, Keating was head and shoulders the best prime minister of my lifetime. Driven and visionary, he set Australia up for the twenty-first century. But the pace of change had exhausted the people, and at the election in 1996 they voted for a quieter life under the Liberals' John Howard, who promised them a country 'comfortable and relaxed'.[138] In a landslide to the Coalition, Labor lost thirty-one of its eighty seats. Howard had been written off as a spent force when he lost the Liberal leadership in 1989, but dogged tenacity had brought him storming back, bolstered by the political nous and unswerving ambition of his wife. No one has ever wanted to occupy the Lodge and Kirribilli House more than Janette Howard.

Although I disliked John's politics and would eventually come to despise them, he and I got along reasonably well. He had been kind enough to be a referee for my UK work visa, and I had thanked him for that with a dinner in London. Gone were the car-crash teeth and the geeky specs he had worn when I first met him in 1974. He was invariably polite and even-tempered, and I never heard a swearword pass his lips. We struck up a working professional relationship.

Howard did retail politics well, much better than Keating. One year I introduced him to my son, James, at a rugby Test luncheon. There were far more important people in the room for Howard to talk to, but he took the time to chat and courteously asked my boy about his computer studies at university. A year later, quite by chance, we ran into him again at another Wallaby game. Without missing a beat, Howard remembered James's name and enquired again about the computer degree. He had not been briefed; he just recalled it. A photographic memory is a priceless political asset, and Howard had one.

Political and social change was equally profound in New South Wales. The politics of crime and corruption which had infested Sydney since the days of the Rum Corps were being methodically dismantled by the newly formed Independent Commission Against Corruption. Nick Greiner's Coalition government had set up ICAC with an eye to taking apart their Labor predecessors. In one of life's richer ironies, it blew up in their hands. Greiner became an early victim when ICAC examined some 'jobs for the boys' wheeling and dealing in 1992, and found that he had conducted himself 'contrary to known and recognised standards of honesty and integrity'.[139] The courts eventually overturned that ruling, but Greiner's political career was kaput.

Labor's Bob Carr became premier on 4 April 1995. I was delighted to see it. With a shared background in journalism, we had been friendly for a good while. I was already overseas as a foreign correspondent when he began his career as a young reporter on the ABC's *AM* program in 1969 and had not known him then, but our paths crossed when he became one of Neville Wran's junior ministers. Like his contemporaries Keating and Laurie Brereton, Carr was a new breed of New South Wales Labor politician, well versed in the gymnastics of clambering up the greasy political pole but with aspirations far above the Tammany Hall, ward-heeling fixations of the party elders, whose sole desire was power for the sake of it. Carr had style, wit and erudition, and a pragmatic approach to politics modelled on that of Wran, whom he admired greatly. The hard slog of seven years as opposition leader had ground him down occasionally, not least because he would much have preferred to go to Canberra to indulge his passion for foreign affairs. The ALP's Sussex Street godfathers, however, had decreed otherwise, and pre-selection for the plum federal seat of Kingsford Smith went to Brereton.

I invited Bob to lunch one day at Edna's and found him morose and despairing, convinced he could never win government. His usual midday meal was a lightly grilled lettuce leaf, a couple of organic caraway seeds and a refreshing draught of boiled rainwater, but on this occasion I convinced him to lash out on a steak. He cheered up with the second bottle of red and became quite tipsy, the only time I have ever seen him even slightly taken in drink. Eventually I poured him into a cab.

When he was premier we invited him and his wife, Helena, to stay at Mountain Lagoon, and to join a few of the locals for a barbecue. It was winter in the mountains and what I always thought of as a Banjo Paterson night, cold and frosty with the white stars fairly blazing. Bob hit it off brilliantly with one of the neighbours, Dot Shaw, daughter of an old-time Hunter Valley coalminer and rock-solid unionist. Dot was the epitome of the grey-haired, apple-cheeked granny, but she called a spade a bloody shovel. 'You're not such a bad bastard,' she told him. 'For a right-winger.'

Bob snorted with laughter. 'And now on to Chicago!' he cried, arms raised in triumph, fingers spread in the V-for-victory sign. In the dancing firelight he looked like Bobby Kennedy, and I think he knew it. They were Kennedy's last words before he was shot. Bob enjoyed such arcane political allusion. It was a good night.

Bob repaid the favour by inviting Kerri and me to a private dinner in the premier's office atop the soaring Governor Phillip Tower in Farrer Place, near Macquarie Street. The city far below was a vast, luminous carpet, bisected by the dark of the harbour. Another guest was the critic and writer Robert Hughes, visiting his homeland from New York and talking nostalgically of a Sydney childhood spent messing about in boats.

A ferry crossed the water, a little ship of lights heading from the Quay to Manly. Unbidden, Hughes broke into some lines from Kenneth Slessor's emblematic harbour poem, 'Five Bells':

> Deep and dissolving verticals of light
> Ferry the falls of moonshine down. Five bells
> Coldly rung out in a machine's voice. Night and water
> Pour to one rip of darkness, the Harbour floats
> In the air, the Cross hangs upside-down in water.

He stared out the window, rapt in the vision before him, his craggy features like the head of an emperor on a Roman coin.

'Do you know the whole poem?' I asked him.

He did, and he recited it. A perfect moment.

✧

Tony, Morag and I bolted the show together. It would be newsy, chatty, informative, funny, across the doings of city, state and nation. We lined up ABC journalists around the country to report for a daily segment we called 'Capital Letters'. Newspaper editors and senior journalists talked about the stories of the week and the coverage they had been given. We had a regular slate of up-and-coming politicians to chew the fat in the studio, including Labor's Anthony Albanese and the Liberals' Barry O'Farrell, as well as a very young Gladys Berejiklian. After he became premier, O'Farrell, whom I liked a lot, told me he had cut his media teeth on the show.

The unfailing headline grabber of the era was the torrent of revelations coming from the Wood Royal Commission into the New

South Wales police force, with its motley parade of corrupt coppers squirming in the glare of exposure like grubs under an upturned rock. The striking thing was their endemic stupidity, typified by the likes of Graham 'Chook' Fowler, the boss of detectives at Kings Cross. A lazy and incompetent drunk, Fowler was secretly videotaped trousering a bribe from another corrupt officer turned informer, Trevor Haken. Hilariously, Fowler tried to claim it was not him on screen but a lookalike actor organised by the commission to incriminate him. Attempting to be invalided out of the force on a pension, he staged a fake accident in which he claimed he had injured himself after slipping on a spilled milkshake. He went to jail, along with another six officers. An astounding 284 officers were 'adversely named' in the commission's reports, and hundreds were sacked. But it was not all hilarity and mirth. Twelve people committed suicide rather than face the music. One was a former New South Wales Supreme Court judge, David Yeldham, who had been having sex with men and boys in public toilets while hypocritically posing on the bench as a pillar of Presbyterian piety, the scourge of the criminals who came before him.

The stories that set a journalist's adrenaline running are those that break without warning, sometimes with shocking force. The shooting massacre at Port Arthur in Tasmania in 1996 began on a Sunday, 28 April, but the killer, Martin Bryant, was not captured by the police until the next morning. I was on air that afternoon. The toll of thirty-five dead is incomprehensible, even now. Bryant, aged twenty-eight, with long, blond, wavy hair, looked like any laid-back surfer dude. Listeners rightly want and expect the details of events like that, but reporting and commenting on such an atrocity demands a certain restraint if you don't want to seem a lip-smacking ghoul. It was the same with the story of Ivan Milat, who kidnapped and murdered seven people and buried their corpses in the Belanglo State Forest, south-west of Sydney. In both cases the trials were horrifying. Milat was given seven life sentences in July 1996; Bryant got thirty-five life sentences that November.

Three other stories stand out from my time at 2BL, all of them in 1997, all of them of grief and death. In July eighteen people were killed in a catastrophic landslide at the Thredbo Alpine Village, in southern New South Wales. The sole survivor, Stuart Diver, was rescued from beneath the rubble sixty-five hours later. In August Princess Diana died in that infamous car crash in Paris. In November Michael Hutchence hanged himself in a Double Bay hotel room.

✧

Bill Clinton was working the room like crazy. He moved from table to table, grinning broadly, pumping hands, clapping a friendly arm around the occasional shoulder, listening earnestly, throwing his head back in gusts of laughter. I had never seen anything quite like it. Of Australian politicians, only Bob Hawke could come anywhere near him in the touchy-feely stakes, and then a fairly distant second. I was watching an artist at work.

The invitation had come embossed with the Australian coat of arms: 'Dinner in honour of the Honourable William Jefferson Clinton, President of the United States of America, and Mrs Clinton. Aboard *Aussie One*, Sydney Harbour Cruise, Wednesday November 20, 1996. Dress: smart casual.' Our hosts would be the Honourable John Howard MP, Prime Minister of Australia, and Mrs Howard. It was the hottest ticket in town. Clinton was on an official presidential visit, but there was a lot of socialising.

Aussie One was a big white catamaran with a saloon large enough to seat around 150 people, usually employed carting tourists on sightseeing trips around the harbour. On a cool spring evening we queued to board her at Darling Harbour: cabinet ministers and senior politicians, a few corporate tycoons, sporting names, a handful of selected media hacks. There was a buzz of excited chatter as we passed through metal detectors and got the once-over from both the Australian Federal Police and the US Secret Service. Normally such a high-octane guest list would be the very epitome of cool, blasé even, but not this time. The forty-second president and his wife were hot, and we were agog to see them, like kids on a school excursion.

They came on board with the Howards at the wharf below Admiralty House, Clinton in a dark-blue blazer, pullover and open-necked check shirt. A few steps behind him came a US Navy lieutenant commander in full uniform, neat as a pin but unsmiling, one hand clutching a black leather briefcase. The codes! She was guarding the famous 'football', as it's nicknamed in Washington, containing whatever it is that a president needs to instantly launch thermonuclear war around the globe. Food for thought there.

We glided eastwards down the harbour, sipping champagne before we were called to sit at tables of eight places each. I kept the menu as a souvenir: Wattle seed and Buckwheat Blinis, Tartlet of Atlantic Salmon, Peking Duck Crepes, Rare Beef on Rye, and more for starters. The main course was billed as 'Australian Crayfish Tails, served with prawns, scallops, oysters and cold smoked ocean trout, baby leaves and vegetable salad'. Your choice of a Leeuwin Estate Chardonnay or a Mountadam Cabernet/Sauvignon/Merlot. Howard made a brief speech of welcome, and Clinton replied.

We were into the 'Great Australian Cheeseboard' and somewhere off Taronga Zoo when the president got to his feet unprompted and began to circle the saloon. He came to the nearest table, where I was sitting. 'Hi. Bill Clinton. How you doing?' He extended a hand. I shook it, trying to rise from my seat. As you do. 'Mike Carlton. How are you?'

'I'm fine. Siddown, siddown. Great to meet you. Anything you guys want to ask me? Anything at all.' He grinned. His face was pink and boyish, the hair silver-grey.

It is a stunning thing to realise that you are one-on-one with the Most Powerful Man on the Planet, or the Leader of the Free World, or the Occupant of the Oval Office, or whatever other cliché you want to employ. And he wants to speak to you. A couple of people at the table were literally dumbstruck by this apparition.

Trained to talk under wet cement, I leaped into the breech. I should have asked about his reckless expansion of NATO up to the Russian border, a provocative and unnecessary piece of triumphalism that had cruelled relations between Washington and Moscow. But I thought of that question only as I am writing now, Diderot's *esprit de l'escalier* twenty years too late.

Wanting Bill to love me, I kept it light. 'Mr President, I understand you played rugby at Oxford. Would you tell us about that?'

He gave a big Arkansas guffaw. 'Well, I was no good at it. Didn't know the rules or how to play. But I was big, bigger than most of the guys. So they just pushed me out on the field and said, "Bill, you get on out there and break heads." Which I did. I enjoyed it, but I was no good.'

The table laughed. I remember that conversation pretty much verbatim because that's what I do. It was far as I got. Clinton – my mate Bill – was already gliding smoothly to his next chat, as politicians will. A National Party MP wanted to ask him about beef exports or something. It was a masterclass in the art of the schmooze, and I have never seen anyone better at it. Clinton had the gift of making you feel he'd been waiting all day to meet you, a remarkable facility. For more than an hour he circled around, chatting to everyone in the room.

I went out on deck and had a word to the trim lieutenant commander who held the future of the world in her hands. 'Can I get you a drink?'

She gave me an icy glare, as if she had just been propositioned by Yasser Arafat. 'No, thank you.'

Back inside, Hillary Rodham Clinton was not doing as well as her husband. She looked bored, summoning up a mechanical smile as required, but not engaging. The word was that she and Janette Howard had not exactly hit it off at a women's afternoon tea that day at the Opera House. Hillary had wanted to meet movers and shakers, policy people who shared her interests. Janette had lumbered her with stuffy Liberal matrons. Seated glumly at her table in the *Aussie One* saloon, she looked like the wife who wanted to leave the party but didn't have the car keys.

✧

2BL was a happy enough place to work if you could ignore the cold, dead hand of ABC bureaucracy. Phil Clark's breakfast show was a smooth act. Jenny Brockie, now at SBS, did the first half of the morning shift, followed by Richard Glover, an experienced newspaper journalist who had recently come across from the *Sydney Morning Herald* to have a crack at radio. Richard, not quite forty, was bloody awful when he started; you cringed listening to him. But he learned fast. He took over the drive show when I left and is now probably the best radio broadcaster in Sydney, if not the country.

The fly in the ointment was the management, as it so often is at the ABC. There was a towering pyramid of ABC radio executives with obscure titles and even more obscure functions. I never discovered what half of them did, beyond sending each other memos. Occasionally they would shove in an oar to remind you they existed. Infuriated once when the cranky Ouija system collapsed on me without warning, I bagged it on air. An executive summoned me from on high, sternly explained that I had let the side down and warned that the $5000 increase she'd been planning for my new contract was now in grave jeopardy.

The station manager at 2BL was a hulking, tedious and overbearing apparatchik named Peter Wall. I never worked out what he did all day either. The place was effectively run by his assistant, a cheerful and talented Tasmanian named Melissa Buckley. At lunchtime every Friday, though, Wall would hold a staff meeting to shower us with his wisdom. On one grim occasion he announced that there would be budget cuts, economy measures, belt-tightening, staff cutbacks. There had been a directive from above. Some of the presenters would have to be 'let go'.

'Why is it always the on-air talent that gets the sack to save money at the ABC?' I asked him sweetly. 'Never the managers.'

He looked at me in cold fury. 'Some of us have children at private schools!' he snapped.

Wall liked to summon us to these Friday seances with a little battery-powered megaphone. It amused him to emerge from his office, startle us all with a tinny hee-haw trumpet blast, and then order us to the conference room. I found it insulting to be treated like a Grade Three child. One day when he was away I snuck into his office and pinched the wretched instrument. With my two producers keeping a lookout, I huddled under my desk, dismantled the thing and snipped the wiring. Then I returned it.

The next Friday, Wall appeared before us as usual, to find that his toy had carked it. He thumped and prodded at it, but it remained lifeless. Crestfallen, he returned to his office, where, in the fullness of time, he discovered the cause. Sabotage! Treachery! His search for the culprit rivalled Humphrey Bogart's famous hunt for the strawberry thief in *The Caine Mutiny*. Only now do I confess my guilt.

Wall had me on toast once, though. And it was all my fault. Ouija had failed to proceed yet again. 'I can't get this fucking thing to work!' I snarled to my producers in the control studio. I also snarled it to perhaps a hundred thousand listeners. Carelessly, unprofessionally, I had left my microphone open during a news bulletin. The magic word blasted onto the airwaves.

The newsreader, on air in another studio, paused for a nanosecond on hearing this frightfulness, then carried on magnificently. Morag and Tony watched in horror as the switchboard lit up like a launch failure at Cape Canaveral. There were a few complaints about 'disgraceful filth . . . kiddies listening in the car . . . expect better from the ABC' and so on, but most people seemed to enjoy it. 'Funniest thing he's said all week,' said one.

By and large the ABC audience was a delight to work for. People were intelligent and involved, and when they were critical – which was quite often – it was usually constructive and well meant, and you took it on board. Many listeners were rusted on, it's true. Give or take, the major ABC stations in the capital cities hold around 10 per cent of the available radio audience. They're the people who hate listening to commercials. They would stick with the ABC even if you just read them the telephone book. The challenge is to build on that base. Tony, Morag and I ground away at it, and by the end of our first year together we had propelled the show to be number one in the drive slot, beating our commercial competitors. It was a sweet moment.

Less happy were the outside broadcasts, or OBs, which obsessed Wall and co. The pretext was always that we were getting out 'among the listeners', but it rarely worked that way. We did one in Sydney's Chinatown on a cold winter's evening, with the broadcast van stuck somewhere no one could find it, and no one bothered to try. We could barely be heard over the roar of speeding peak-hour traffic. The OBs at Sydney's Royal Easter Show were the worst. I dreaded them. For ten days or so you were stuck for hours on air behind a glass window, trying to do your stuff while passers-by goggled like goldfish or gave you the two-fingered salute. The brief was to bring all the colour and excitement of the show to our listeners, blah blah. The bush meets the city! The country comes to town! This meant plodding interviews with rustic folk who had made prize-winning jams, knitted prize-winning woolly jumpers or done unusual things with livestock. Worthy beings all, but they tended to be monosyllabic and crashingly dull.

'And how long have you been breeding Angora goats?' I remember asking a tongue-tied, fourteen-year-old hayseed.

'Dunno. Few years,' mumbled the youth.

'And why *Angora* goats,' I enquired brightly.

'Dunno. Me dad's got 'em.'

That was seven minutes of my life I'll never get back. Despair piled on chagrin that year when we were instructed to give out ABC show bags, brightly done up with the familiar logo in blue and white. 'Come and get yours!' we urged the throng. People queued, only to find there was nothing in them, not so much as a Bananas in Pyjamas postcard. The budget hadn't stretched that far. The punters threw them away in disgust.

After so long in the slick commercial racket, I often thought that the ABC's attempts at 'marketing' dropped like bricks. One presenter, Kevin Naughton, asked the ABC Shop if they had any books he could give away as listener prizes. They sent up a small bundle of remaindered junk. One book had the enticing title *Living with AIDS*.

My leaden interview with the reticent young goatherd was topped by a catastrophic encounter with a woman invited into the 2BL studio to tell us about the exciting St Andrew's Day celebrations planned by Sydney's Scottish-Australian community. We can call her Flora MacDonald. She was a high official of the Caledonian Society, or whatever, sent to us as just the person to talk to about haggis eating, caber tossing and assorted highland frolicking. We had a real, live piper in the studio to introduce her with a blast of 'Scotland the Brave'.

'And now, with me in the studio . . .' I began, as the skirl of the pipes died away. 'Flora, what's planned for St Andrew's Day this year?'

She looked at me open-mouthed, her face suddenly white with fear. Not a sound emerged.

This was odd. Perhaps she hadn't heard me. I tried again.

Same result – except that this time she flapped her hands in panic and looked around frantically for a way to escape.

Was she having a heart attack? No. Poor Flora was terrified, almost catatonic with fright. I tried my best to calm her, to encourage her, to soothe her, to coax her, to cajole her, but no deal. She was mute, struck dumb.

Eventually, Morag helped her from the studio, where she recovered a little. 'I'm so sorry,' she spluttered. 'I didn't expect to be talking on the wireless.'

✧

In April 1994 I had begun writing what would become some twenty years of columns for the *Sydney Morning Herald*. It was the idea of the then editor-in-chief, seasoned journalist and former ace crime reporter David Hickie. I would have a whole broadsheet page to myself on Saturdays, the paper's biggest-selling edition, in the News Review section. That would mean about 1200 words, to be split up on three separate topics I could choose from the events of the week.

The *Herald* was enjoying a golden sunset, and I was drawn in by the sheer prestige of a by-lined column in what was then Australia's finest newspaper. I would be in print alongside such giants as David Marr, Alan Ramsey, Ross Gittins, Anne Summers, Adele Horin and Kate McClymont.

David heaped on the flattery, as editors will, and I lapped it up, as journalists do, and extracted a promise that my copy would not be mucked about by sub-editors, or changed without my approval. The paper pretty much stuck to that deal as legions of editors followed Hickie in and back out again through the fatal revolving door of the editor's office. That door should have borne Dante's warning about the Gates of Hell: '*Lasciate ogni speranza, voi ch'entrate*' – Abandon all hope, ye who enter here.

I was cautious at first, even apprehensive. Most of my journalism had been for the spoken word. Churning out words to be read, not heard, is a different craft altogether. Gradually it came to me, but it took time. The trick, I found, was to mix it up, leavening trenchant political and social comment with dollops of satire and humour.

Writing a newspaper column to a deadline can be agony, can be a delight. It is agony when you are uninspired, when you are without a clue where to begin or what to say, when you stare blankly at an empty computer screen with the witching hour drawing closer. The delightful days are when you are smitten by a sparkling idea, with the words tumbling effortlessly onto the page, the thing virtually writing itself. There are many more of the former than the latter.

✧

Towards the end of '97 the earth shifted beneath me. My marriage to Kerri finally came apart, after twenty-five years. There was no sudden catalyst, only the mutual feeling that we had run out of steam, that we should go our separate ways. She had tired of the staid conformity of life on Sydney's North Shore and hankered for some inner-urban sizzle. I was keen to get close to the beach. The break was briefly acrimonious, but we got over that soon enough and parted as civilised adults. We had held it together while James was finishing his Higher School Certificate year, fearing it would be difficult telling the kids, but they were in their late teens, had read all the signs, and had been expecting it to happen.

It was time to leave the ABC, too. It had been a pleasure and a privilege to work those two years at 2BL, with good colleagues and a generous audience, but I wanted to get back to commercial radio money again. The question was: how to do it?

By sheer chance I bumped into John Conde, the chairman and managing director at 2UE. We had known each other for twenty years, from when I first began in radio at 2UE and he was a junior executive there. We lived near each other at Turramurra and we got on well. I saw him at the local BP service station as we were buying petrol. 'Got any jobs?' I asked. I meant it as a joke.

'I think we do,' he said. 'Come and have a talk.'

22

The Parrot and the King

ALAN JONES GAVE ME a cheeky smack on the bum. I was leaning over a desk just inside the door to my office at 2UE, talking to my PA, when I felt a whack on my left buttock and heard a chuckle. Spinning around, I found Jones standing there, grinning like a hobgoblin.

'Very tight,' he chortled gaily. 'Very tight!'

Gobsmacked almost covers it. I was dumbfounded. Jones thought I had a tight bum? And wanted to tell me so? Without another word he gave me a lascivious wink and sailed down the corridor to the lift. I had been at the station only a couple of weeks. This playful amity would not last long.

My arrival at 2UE was not the cause of universal joy. 'I wouldn't piss on the ponce,' Stan Zemanek told his listeners. He was doing the on-air night shift for the usual menagerie of freaks and nutters. 'I hope he never walks into the studio when I'm on air.'[140] Jones was privately aghast at John Conde's decision to take me on for the weekday drive show, but publicly he made at least a half-hearted effort to mend fences. He had constantly bagged me since my return from London, trumpeting that I had been an ignominious failure, that I'd come whimpering home with my tail between my legs. John Laws had done a bit of that too, and was not thrilled either that I had come on board.

Conde urged us to kiss and make up. Jones and I went to dinner at an Italian restaurant in Double Bay; he must have chosen it for the grovel, which was epic, rather than the food, which was horrible. 'I never pay the slightest attention to what people say about me,' he chirruped over the soggy fettuccine. Then he related, chapter and verse, everything I had said about him over the past ten years. Some of it I had forgotten, but a lot of it was quite good, really, and it was pleasing to be reminded. We agreed on an armistice and I fled into the night.

The unfortunate wretch entrusted with keeping the peace and massaging our gigantic on-air egos was John Brennan, 2UE's long-serving program manager. Brenno had been in radio since he began as a dogsbody in Wagga in 1949. In the 1960s he had been a disc jockey and one of the 2SM Good Guys. His cherubic Irish features and cheerful banter concealed a good radio brain and a lifetime's experience.

Miraculously, nobody had a bad word to say about him. In the dog-eat-dog world of commercial radio he was universally liked and respected, no small achievement. But managing Jones, Laws and me – let alone upstart pissants like Zemanek – must have taxed his powers of diplomacy to the limit.

My office was sandwiched between Jones on one side and the Laws suite on the other. Brennan was in and out of them all the time. The first blow-up came within weeks of my start on air. Jones was angered that I had interviewed my friend Alex Mitchell, then the state political correspondent for the *Sun-Herald*. Mitchell had once been unkindly critical of him in the paper, apparently. Jones would never take me head-on, always preferring to sneak in the back way. He went to Brennan and demanded that Mitchell be banned from my program and the station forthwith. Brennan put it to me, rather sheepishly. I replied that I would agree, on one condition: that I would have an equal veto over guests on Jones's program. That ended it. I had Mitchell on again a week later, to hammer home the point. Nothing more was said.

We bumped along until the next crisis, which became notorious when the gossip columnists got wind of it and called it Tissuegate.

Jones went berko when he discovered that someone had nicked a box of his favourite aloe vera tissues from his office desk, plus some cutlery. A mobile phone had also gone missing. There was uproar. The police were called. Ever the drama queen, Jones dictated a lengthy memo to be pinned on the staff noticeboard, proclaiming that he was 'sickened' by this heinous crime and the lack of moral fibre that had led to it.

'There are thieves in the building,' he went on. 'This note is to serve notice that I am in possession of a powder which is invisible on surfaces. However, once touched, it leaves indelible stains for up to five days. So now I'm going to play my game!! It will be left on certain books, pens, phones, staplers, coffee cups etc. Please feel free to steal these from my office at your own risk.'

The place was agog. People chortled behind their hands and sniggered in corridors. Jones's frequent tantrums and his arrogance with junior staff meant he was deeply disliked, and there was much pleasure at his fury. Someone scrawled 'Up yours!' on his memo, and a reply soon appeared, signed 'The Thief'. It read: 'I've been made aware of a magic powder which is being used in a bid to catch me stealing tissues. This note is to serve notice that I am in possession of special gloves which make the powder completely useless.'

Jones and everyone else thought I had written this. Who else would dare such insubordination? It wasn't me and I said so, but no one believed me. The armistice turned distinctly icy. Poor Brenno was at his wit's end. Jones demanded that security cameras be installed in his office. They were hidden in the ceiling, disguised as light fittings. We discovered them only after he had left the station and the office was being renovated for me.

At close quarters Jones was a comical figure. He bustled along the corridors with shoulders hunched, brow creased in a knowing frown, lips pursed like the ABC logo, as someone once remarked. The body language was unmistakable: 'Out of my way. Do not approach me. I am about to address the UN General Assembly, I am translating Machiavelli's *Il Principe* from the Italian, I am plotting the downfall of a police commissioner, I am pondering matters of great pith and moment far beyond the understanding of ordinary mortals like you. Interrupt me at your peril.'

His anger was volcanic, and aimed mostly at his long-suffering female staff. I could hear them through the office wall. 'Stupid, *stupid* girl!' he would screech at some wretched miscreant. At other times, though, there would be a sudden burst of Jones laughter, as raucous and mirthless as a kookaburra's. Young men – panel operators or junior journalists in the newsroom – were bathed in the sunny warmth of Jones's charm, although some found his attentions insufferable; one quietly kept tapes of his tirades in the recording studio. This one was typical, a petulant rant about some advertising copy delivered late:

> Fucking hopeless! Well, it is fucking hopeless. If this is that bloody urgent I should be given it in the morning! I don't see why my life should be turned into a fucking nightmare for the sake of other incompetents. Look, from here on in you can tell them I'm refusing to do something, that I've got my face up against the wall and they want it done immediately. It's absolutely ridiculous! I've got to catch a plane at ten o'clock to raise fucking money for charity and I've got these people here sticking stuff up my nose and my arse. It's just ridiculous![141]

The 2UE staff hated being treated like this but they had to cop it. Jones was a star, the rainmaker. They were underlings, and that was that. The underlings, though, richly enjoyed that fabulous day when Jones appeared on Nine's *Midday Show*, invited there to castigate the celebrity standover man and murderer Mark 'Chopper' Read. A lot of us were watching it on a screen at the station. There was no surprise when Chopper himself popped up on a phone line to the show. Jones went for him, smirking as the studio audience applauded.

Chopper hit back: 'People who throw stones better make sure they don't live in glass houses, Alan.'

'We're not talking about anyone living in glass houses, Chopper.'

'Yeah, well, I never got arrested in a public toilet in London,' retorted the witty old crook.

For a nanosecond there was a shot of Jones's meaty, empurpled face frozen in horror before the equally startled host, Kerri-Anne Kennerley, hastily cut off the interview and threw to a commercial break. The 2UE corridors rang with laughter.

On the plus side, John Laws and I made up. Laws and Jones had loathed each other for years, sniping at each other on air and off. They were rivals for the tinsel crown of King of Radio, which John claimed and Jones sought to seize. The origins of their feud are lost in time, but they ran deep. In 1991, when 2UE moved into its new studios at Greenwich, Jones had sent in his manager, Harry Miller, to check Laws' office with a tape measure to make sure it was no bigger than his. There was surely a turning point when Paul Keating delightfully remarked on Laws' show one day that Jones's program was 'basically middle-of-the-road Fascist'.[142] Laws disdained Jones as an arriviste who had not put in the hard yards of traipsing around country stations to learn the business and build a career, and he had a point. The complete professional, John knew all the bells and whistles of a studio and could work magic with them. Jones would have had trouble turning on the lights; he simply plonked himself down in front of a microphone and talked when he got the cue from his panel operator. In return, he looked down upon Laws as a mere disc jockey.

Out of the blue, John's PA, Jodee Borgo, asked if I would drop into his office for a chat. I was wary. But John shook hands warmly, offered me a seat and took the wind out of my sails by volunteering that he had been foolish in his criticism of me, that he wanted to apologise, and that perhaps we could become friends again. It was magnanimous and welcome. I confessed that I had also gone over the top about him at times, and regretted it. A few days later we went out to a long and liquid dinner, and the friendship was sealed. It remains to this day.

It was good to have an ally at 2UE, at last. John Conde was always supportive, but to have Laws demonstrably on side was a fillip. Unlike Jones, he was largely popular with the 2UE staff and it was valuable to have his seal of approval. And I had terrific producers to back me up: firstly Steve Turner, who came with me from the ABC, and then Steve Burling, who would go on to be a heavy at Channel Nine's *60 Minutes*.

There were times when I felt I needed all the friends I could get. Unsurprisingly, a large chunk of Jones's audience hated me. His right-wing nostrums and loopy obsessions, some of them pursued to hysteria and beyond, were chalk and cheese to the stuff I was doing. There seemed to be a new excess every week.

Perhaps the zaniest was the fantasy Jones had of making Australia's rivers run backwards, away from the coast, to somehow create a vast inland lake for agriculture and limitless prosperity. It was palpable nonsense, both an engineering impossibility and environmental suicide if anyone was ever mad enough to try it, but Jones pushed it for months, shrilly berating anybody who demurred. When I remarked once on air that the idea was a crock, his devotees rang and wrote to complain that I was a fool and an ignoramus who should listen and learn from the master.

This happened a lot. Many of Jones's acolytes thought I was a communist. His schtick was and is an artful appeal to the foolish and the fearful and the frustrated and the failed – the battlers of Struggle Street, as he cleverly calls them, massaging their sense of grievance. His skill is to convince gullible folk, who are predominantly elderly, ignorant and conservative, that the country is going to the dogs, and that only he has the courage to point out this grim truth and the power to get something done about it. He is their champion, their messiah, their sure shield against the malevolent and sinister 'they' conspiring against them in Canberra and wherever else. He has honed this act brilliantly over the years, recklessly shattering other people's lives and careers in the process.

Much of the Jones ire has been stained with his broad streak of misogyny. It crops up time and again, notably in his insensate loathing of Julia Gillard as prime minister. It was displayed typically in his vicious 2001 jihad against a senior New South Wales police officer, Detective Inspector Deborah Wallace, who was battling the drug gangs in the troubled Sydney suburb of Cabramatta. Jones had been captured and conned by a ratbag bunch of self-styled crime experts, some of them failed and disgruntled police officers with axes to grind. Another was a crackpot academic and self-styled criminologist, since discredited. On their behalf he went for Wallace with a pit bull's ferocity. 'Miss Debbie,' he sneeringly called her. With not a shred of evidence he accused her of incompetence, of lying, of corruption, of altering formal police records, of being 'a blindly ambitious and ruthless woman'. It was cruel and hurtful.

Wallace's elderly father had been a Jones fan, and was stunned to hear his daughter traduced. She eventually sued for defamation. Deliciously, her barrister was none other than Stuart Littlemore. 2UE hastily settled the case with a handsome but undisclosed payout.[143] The Parrot's cage is littered with defamation actions, almost all of which he has lost, at great expense to his employers.

Our final breach was thermonuclear. Listening to Jones as I drove to work one morning, I was astounded to hear him waxing lyrical about the afternoon Test cricket coverage on ABC Radio. As ever, it was extravagant gush. 'Brilliant, brilliant radio! Listen to them. Don't miss it! Tune in to 2BL, three o'clock this afternoon!' It was a blatant, provocative encouragement for my audience to desert to the opposition.

To promote a rival radio program at the expense of a colleague has always been taboo. You just don't do it, and I took it as a calculated attack. I'd had enough of Jones by now. Still seething when I got to the studio, I barged into his office unannounced and bawled him out. He denied he had said any such thing and, red-faced and spluttering, he ordered me to go.

'Not until I have called you an unprofessional cunt,' I shouted back. I toyed with the idea of actually hitting him, as John Laws had reputedly done once, but caution prevailed.

He slithered off to dob me in to John Conde, but when the tapes were produced he had to concede he was in the wrong. He wrote me a long and rambling letter of apology that began with a prissy reproof. 'I thought I should write in the light of your extraordinary outburst yesterday,' it began. 'Michael, nothing can condone the kind of language that was used in my office in the presence of women . . .'

The hypocrisy was bottomless. I don't think we ever spoke again.

✧

From its election in 1996 the Howard government had blanketed Australia in a dull managerial greyness. It exemplified the dictum of the writer Donald Horne that 'Australia is a lucky country, run by second-rate people who share its luck'. Visions of social progress and economic reform were scoffed at, supplanted by a cloying, small-minded conservatism of low expectations. The advance of Australia fair could and should be left to the free market, which was never wrong. On cue, with leaden predictability, the free market launched itself into a carnival of greed as if the crash of 1987 had never happened.

Despite his 'comfortable and relaxed' rhetoric, Howard also ignited what the right would come to call the culture wars, a reactionary push by hidebound ideologues to return Australia to the verities of the 1950s. Many of the right-wing spear carriers were Murdoch hacks of derisory journalistic experience, or that emerging species of preposterous twenty-something blowhards from so-called think-tanks, all of them self-aggrandised as policy fellows or visiting scholars or directors of this and that, and all of them pushing the same tired and demonstrably failed neoliberal line that free-market competition is the only possible mechanism for organising human affairs. The language of the culture wars was filched, as ever, from the US, with only minor local adjustments. Evidently incapable of original thought, the spear chuckers seized the sterile clichés of the American Right: 'Virtue signalling . . . identity politics . . . Green–Left elites.' Straight up the Alan Jones alley, playing on the narrow and selfish interests of small-minded populism, it was pervasive and politically effective.

Paul Keating, in his landmark Redfern speech of 1992, had asked Australians to open their hearts to justice and equity for Aboriginal Australians. Howard could speak only of the 'black armband' view of history. There would be no apology to Indigenous people, and still less a treaty with them. On the march to the republic, on equality for women and for gay and lesbian people, on the enrichment of what was already a successful multicultural society, on the rights of Australians to unionise for their protection at work, on the growing menace of climate change, Howard offered only obfuscation and delay or, frequently, outright hostility.

In 1998, after years of industrial peace, he and his bully-boy industrial relations minister, Peter Reith, joined a battle by the stevedoring company Patrick Corporation to crush the Maritime Union of Australia. There were strikes and lockouts on the wharves in Melbourne and Sydney, and scab labour being trained in Dubai.

With the government's active encouragement, Patricks sent in Rottweiler dogs and muscular guards masked in balaclavas, a deliberate provocation to violence. Jones rocketed into daily fits of hysterics, shrilly ordering the New South Wales premier, Bob Carr, and Police Commissioner Peter Ryan to bust union heads and make wholesale arrests on the picket line. Carr and I talked about it privately one afternoon; the premier feared bloodshed or worse.

'Get a band down there,' I said. 'Dancers, comedians, anything to create a diversion.'

Carr took the advice, and within hours the Maritime Union had a rock band playing on the Sydney waterfront to lower the temperature of angry strikers and their families.

At times Howard scaled the heights of absurdity: his daft proposal to insert the word 'mateship' into a preamble to the Constitution was laughed out of court before the preamble itself was knocked back in the referendum of 1999. Even his most ardent partisans found that 'a bit rich', a phrase he often employed himself.

In effect, Howard unleashed the worst of us, the dark side of our national character, as conservative governments almost always do. It's easier that way. You can do it by dog-whistling, by using coded language which is not of itself offensive or inflammatory but which you know will arouse the basest instincts of your supporters. His incessant declarations that a silent majority of decent people were being bullied and cowed by 'political correctness' and were frightened to speak laid the foundations for the rise of Pauline Hanson and the bigotry, racism and sheer stupidity of her One Nation political phenomenon. Only when Howard belatedly realised, to his dismay, that Hanson was actually siphoning off Liberal Party voters did he move against her, expediently seizing most of her policies as his own. His bovver boy, Tony Abbott, set up a secret slush fund to destroy her.

Howard would score a resounding triumph with the 1999 referendum vote against the Republic, his political skills winning hands down over the divided and muddled Republican campaign, nominally headed by Malcolm Turnbull. Adventuring abroad, Howard and his foreign minister, that posturing prat Alexander Downer, were seduced by the flattery of President George W. Bush and the neocons, who would draw Australia into the havoc they unleashed in the Middle East and elsewhere. We are still paying the price of the so-called War on Terror.

Labor's post-war prime minister Ben Chifley had spoken of a 'light on the hill', of 'bringing something better to the people'. Keating talked of seeking 'the golden threads' in society and drawing them out, to be woven into the national fabric. It was a prime task of leadership, he said.

Howard had nothing of that. This was a prime minister whose vision was in the rear-view mirror, a dogmatic Tory yearning for a lost anglo-centric Australia in which everyone knew their place and nothing would change. He found society's black threads and knotted them into his own form of political correctness. Much of the damage Howard wrought could not be undone.

Personally, though, my life was sunny. A single man again, I could remake it as I chose. Living on the North Shore had suited our family well enough while the kids were at school there. But in 1998, with my marriage dissolved and both kids at university, pretty much a free agent, I could move to the place I had dreamed of living since my teenage years: Sydney's Northern Beaches were calling.

And not a moment too soon. One of the locals knocked on the front door at Turramurra one day, an elderly woman from across the street. She was the epitome of the North Shore matron, wife to a retired retail tycoon, a gentlewoman of exemplary pedigree and good manners, pleasant and neighbourly.

'They're coming,' she said, as I invited her in and offered her a chair. 'Mr Carlton, *they are coming!*' There was fear in her eyes.

Who was coming? Russian parachutists with snow on their boots? The stormtroopers of the Galactic Empire? No. Worse.

'The Chinese. They're moving into the street!' she quavered.

And so they were. She thought that somehow I might be able to stop them, but no luck there. A Chinese neurosurgeon and his wife duly moved into a large new house three doors down the road, and sent their two daughters to my daughter's recent school, Pymble Ladies' College. They seemed perfectly well behaved, not evidently running a triad gang or an opium den or a cell of the Peoples'

Liberation Army or anything, but the North Shore was up in arms about this creeping yellow peril. At PLC, girls called Poppy Wong and Winsome Ng were scooping all the academic prizes at speech night, leaving only the cups for hockey, swimming and gymnastics to the Anglo-Celtic lassies. Some parents were seriously pushing the school to nobble these Chinese high achievers in some way, although they could never work out how to do it. A few weeks after my visit from the neighbourly matron, 'CHINKS OUT' was daubed on the fence of another nearby house bought by a Chinese businessman.

The delights of the North Shore had faded. The racism was disgusting. The conservatism was oppressive and endemic, although hardly surprising: there was history. The fascist leadership of the 1930s New Guard had done most of its plotting at a villa just a few blocks from mine. There was also the boredom. Quite simply, almost nothing ever happened on the North Shore. There was hardly a decent restaurant beyond North Sydney. Time to go.

After not too long a search I found an elegant old timber house on what the locals call the Peninsula, that long, green arm of the Northern Beaches with the Tasman Sea on the eastern side and the calm expanse of Pittwater on the other, ending in Palm Beach and Barrenjoey Head. With the surf just minutes away I could indulge a growing passion for riding my Larry Pullen wave ski, as I wrote in a *Herald* column in 2000:

> There is nothing so exhilarating as cornering on a curving green wave, carving a surf ski hard across the wall just ahead of the break, then digging the paddle deep to thunder straight for the beach as the foam crunches down and spits you out like a pip from an orange.
>
> If you get it right, that is. It is also exhilarating, although less fun, to miss the corner and wipe out, surfacing from the whirlpool to find the ski heading fast for the shore 100 metres away . . .
>
> If there's no surf, go for a paddle. It's serious aerobic exercise and balm for the spirit. Happiness is to be alone on the sea in the early morning, with the fish jumping and the sun rising above the great rock of Barrenjoey that guards the entrance to Broken Bay. Way to go.[144]

These days the Pullen wave ski has pretty much been supplanted for me by a long Epic V10 racing ski, which I paddle around the glorious bays and beaches of Pittwater. On a weekday there you can be alone in the world, to think and to dream.

Best of all, and to my intense surprise, I was falling in love again. For a while I could not believe this was happening but eventually I could resist it no longer and I succumbed. Morag Ramsay, who had been one of my producers at 2BL, was twenty-eight years younger than me. That put her just four years older than Alex, and six years older than James, which caused a few surprises. In fact, shock and awe in some quarters: Alex was initially horrified. But Morag was beautiful and talented and intelligent, young and carefree, with a musical voice that sent shivers up my spine. Working with her had been a delight, for, although she was barely out of university, she had a savvy, creative grasp of the media trade well beyond her years. I found myself gazing at her when I thought she was not looking. Surprising as it may seem, our relationship at 2BL was entirely proper, platonic and respectful to a fault. Yet I found she exerted a magnetic attraction, like the moon upon the tides. She felt the same, which brought a few further surprises, not least to her parents. They took it on the chin, well knowing that their only child had a mind of her own. We embarked on a partnership which would continue on to a marriage and a son, and which lovingly endures. The twentieth century was ending well.

✧

In the winter of 1998 I cavorted buck-naked on stage in my one and only appearance in an all-male strip show. As you do. Borrowing an idea from the British comedy hit movie *The Full Monty*, the actor and writer Rachel Ward browbeat, bullied and cajoled twelve blokes to get their gear off at a gala night to raise funds for a children's charity. 'Aussies Without Cossies', she called it. Nudity holds no terrors for me, but I had never been quite this public. 'You can finish up in G-strings,' she promised us sweetly.

We took it very seriously. We being Bryan Brown – Rachel's husband – and his fellow actors Graeme Blundell, Peter Phelps, Hugo Weaving, John Jarratt, Ernie Dingo and Jack Thompson; the rock singers Jimmy Barnes and Angry Anderson; and the odd men out in that lot, journalists George Negus, Bob Ellis and me. Paul Mercurio, fresh from the dancing lead in *Strictly Ballroom*, choreographed some moves to the Joe Cocker song 'You Can Leave Your Hat On' and we rehearsed them for weeks. I usually dance like a cow on rocks but I managed to get most of the steps right. Rachel put the wardrobe together: we would start off in black business suits with shirts, ties and black Stetson cowboy hats. Peeling that off item by item while we kicked and gyrated in a chorus line, we would get down to a pair of star-spangled speedos and, after that – zing! – the G-string. Then the lights would go off while we fled the stage.

Come the night, the main hall of Sydney's Overseas Terminal at Circular Quay was jam-packed with the glitterati Rachel had rounded up, the room awash with champagne, the air sharp with a pleasing whiff of pot. At $200 a throw it was the hottest ticket in town. James Packer turned up. So did Graham Richardson, Andrew Denton, Tom Keneally, Doug Mulray, Kerry O'Brien, Collette Dinnigan and a truckload of other media and movie names.

The lights went down. The music struck up. Fortified by a pre-show drink or three, we sashayed on stage to gales of applause and whoops of laughter. Yee ha! I don't recall any stage fright – just the sudden shock of spotting Nicole Kidman at a front-row table, staring straight at me and laughing her beautiful head off. Bryan Brown is a nice guy, and as sane and normal as an actor is ever likely to be. At his urging, and egged on by Hugo Weaving, we had taken a vote at the dress rehearsal and decided – bugger it – we'd give the folks value for money by going the full monty. We would shuck off the G-strings as well. The actors, used to that sort of thing, took it in their stride. The rest of us were a bit twitchier, but it was too late to back out.

The finish was a triumph. Of sorts. As the cameras flashed we waggled our bare bums at the crowd, and then whipped around for the full-frontal. Ellis, no longer rake-thin, tripped over his feet. Hugo dived into the crowd for a victory lap. The audience erupted, the lights went out and we galloped back to the dressing room, drunk with success. Mission accomplished. A photograph of us standing in line, dicks dangling, was auctioned off on the night. David Leckie, then the boss of the Seven Network, kicked off the bidding at $5000. Eventually it sold to someone – I've forgotten who – for a staggering $31,000. All up, Rachel raised nearly $500,000. Worth every cent.

✧

'Cash for Comment' hit 2UE like one of those fierce Sydney summer storms which whip up from nowhere and flatten the place. It was 1999. The radio station was knocked over like a yacht in a cyclone, on its beam ends, taking water, struggling to stay afloat.

The scandal is well enough known and can be outlined briefly. For years, both John Laws and Alan Jones had been quietly raking in millions of dollars to plug the products or the business interests of corporations big and small. Their paymasters – all secret – included banks, colourful entrepreneurs and such blue-chip names as Optus, Qantas, the publisher HarperCollins, the developer Mirvac and the Sunraysia fruit juice company. 2UE understood vaguely that these payments were happening and turned a blind eye, but had not the foggiest idea of the scale of them.

ABC TV's *Media Watch* blew the scandal wide open when an astute and enquiring researcher, Anne Connolly, noticed that John Laws' regular and vitriolic on-air criticism of the 'bastard banks' had suddenly stopped. It had been replaced by a scripted segment called 'The Whole Story', read by John, in which the banks now miraculously appeared as the kindly benefactors of widows and orphans, small-business battlers and honest farmers down on their luck.

Media Watch had opened a very large can of very smelly worms. Corporate big bucks were raining down in torrents. In 1993 Optus, the new kid on the telecommunications block, had paid Jones $100,000 a year. By 1998, evidently satisfied with what it was getting, Optus had punted that up to $500,000 a year. Walker Corporation, the privately owned property company of the billionaire developer Lang Walker, had Jones on its string for $30,000 a month, for which it was getting lavish plugs for its controversial development proposals around Sydney. On and on it went. *Media Watch* and its killer host, journalist Richard Ackland, went in with forensic skill, uncovering ever more inconvenient truths.

There were two problems here. One was that 2UE had no idea that two of its major stars were creaming these extraordinary amounts of money, which – in theory – the station itself should have been making. They were using 2UE's airtime for their private profit. Second, and rather more tricky, were the official broadcasting codes, which ruled that editorial comment and advertising content had to be kept strictly separate so that ordinary listeners could discern which was which. This clearly was not happening. The rules were being rorted wholesale.

Goaded into action, the industry watchdog, the Australian Broadcasting Authority, ran a full-dress public inquiry, replete with platoons of high-priced Queen's Counsel and headed by none other than the authority's chairman, and yet another lawyer of sorts, Professor David Flint.

At times the inquiry rocketed into high farce. Hordes of journalists and TV crews turned up to report every thrilling twitch and grunt. Flint, a prissy, self-important twerp, was forced to disqualify himself after appearing for an interview on the John Laws show to flog a book he had written, chatting amiably on air to the star he was supposed to be investigating. More hilarious still, it emerged later that Flint had been writing soppy, fan-boy letters to Jones for several months. 'Alan, you have an extraordinary ability of capturing and enunciating the opinions of the majority on so many issues,' he gushed in one epistle. 'This of course annoys those who have a different agenda . . .'

I observed this circus with a mixture of mirth and trepidation. I'd been offered a couple of deals like these over the years, but had touched none of them. As a journalist, I thought they were unethical; I was clean. Laws' defence was relatively straightforward: he was a salesman paid to sell things, and that's what he had done. He could not see what all the fuss was about. His listeners could always tell when he was flogging stuff, he maintained, which was probably true enough. Jones, on the other hand, tried to squirm through the ethical minefield. Golly, sometimes he just hadn't read the contracts, had no idea what he had signed. He left all that stuff to his manager, Harry M. Miller. At other times he would bluster that 'everyone knows Alan Jones's opinions are not for hire'.[145]

The worrying thing was that 2UE itself might go under, and at times that seemed very likely. As punishment, it was conceivable that the ABA might simply order the station to stop broadcasting, which it had the power to do. That meant hundreds of jobs at risk, for salespeople and telephonists, executives and accountants, producers and researchers, engineers and panel operators, and on-air presenters and journalists untainted by the scandal. John Conde, as the company chairman, stood to lose the Lamb family's entire investment of perhaps $100 million. As the inquiry ebbed and flowed, there was real fear in the offices and corridors, and deep anger at those who had brought it on.

Julian Burnside QC, the wily Melbourne barrister and counsel assisting the inquiry, cut Laws and Jones to shreds in the witness box. Jones, in particular, was frequently reduced to spluttering, outraged impotence. As Burnside put it: 'The net effect of the evidence . . . in Mr Jones's part of the case seems to be that he signed without looking, they [sponsors] paid without listening; he spoke without knowing and they heard without complaining. It is simply difficult to accept.'[146]

It was the program director, John Brennan, who loyally fell on his sword and probably saved the station and all those jobs. He took the rap by effectively admitting his own failure: that he should have exercised far greater control over what his stars were doing. In fact, he could no more have stopped the cash for comment loot rolling in than he could have parted the Red Sea, but if anyone was to blame, it was him, he said. On the evening of the day he gave his evidence, I wandered into John Conde's office for a chat. Brenno was slumped in a chair, sobbing his heart out and fast emptying a bottle of Scotch that Conde kept pouring for him. Tears coursed down his normally plump but now haggard cheeks. 'Ruined!' he kept sniffling. 'My entire radio career ruined.' He was inconsolable. It was a terrible sight.

The ABA inquiry found that, between them, 2UE, Jones and Laws had broken the rules ninety-five times. On thirty-one occasions Jones had dishonestly misled his audience by failing to disclose a commercial relationship. On at least nine occasions he had broadcast commercials as news. Laws had sinned on much the same scale.

But after all the fear and loathing, the headlines and the uproar, the penalties were a little more than a slap on the wrist. Jones and Laws would have to disclose their future sponsorships in future, and 2UE was on notice that it would now have to enforce the code rigorously. It had been a close-run thing.

I thought the scandal might finish Jones's career. How naive I was. He had been sliced and diced in the witness box and in the inquiry report, but not in the eyes of his listeners. With an indomitable mix of chutzpah and sheer bullshit, armoured in righteous self-belief, he rose like Lazarus. Just as he had done after the London toilet scandal, he volubly, incessantly protested his innocence, his lily-white purity in all things, and his fans believed every word. It was astounding. His dishonesty and hypocrisy were there for all to see, yet his ratings went from strength to strength. The flocks of politicians who regularly brownnosed him – mostly Tory, but a good few Labor as well – picked up their schmoozing without missing a beat. And poor John Brennan, a devout Catholic, recovered from his misery to write a bizarre letter to the editor of the *Sydney Morning Herald*, singing hosannas to the monster he had created:

> He reminds me of another man some 2000 years ago who had the worst interpretations put upon His kindest actions, yet He went on; who had His words warped, twisted, falsely reported, minimised, yet He went on; was slighted, even laughed to scorn when He gave of His very best, yet He went on. And so will Alan Jones go on . . .[147]

✧

Spirits lifted with the roaring success of the 2000 Olympic Games in Sydney. 2UE had the commercial radio rights and John Conde hired an ocean liner parked at Darling Harbour to entertain sponsors and guests. I'm not sure he made much money out of it, but it was a PR success. Cathy Freeman's hometown gold medal in the 400 metres – especially her lap of honour waving both the Australian and Aboriginal flags – was the most glorious sporting triumph I have seen, impossible to better. The entire nation erupted in joy.

After the highs came the lows. Two thousand and one was a year of tragedy and catastrophe, at home and abroad. The Howard government faced another election, hoping for a third term, yet the polls increasingly pointed to a win for Labor's affable Kim Beazley. Momentous events intervened to shatter Beazley's hopes and to return Howard to the Lodge – or, more accurately, to Kirribilli House in Sydney, where, against all convention, Janette Howard had insisted on living at the taxpayers' expense. On Sunday, 26 August, in the Indian Ocean not far beyond the Australian territory of Christmas Island, the Norwegian container ship MV *Tampa* sailed into Australian political history.

Responding to distress calls, the ship's master, Captain Arne Rinnan, took on board 433 Afghan asylum seekers and five Indonesian crew members from a sinking boat chartered by people smugglers. A diplomatic storm blew up when Rinnan, a fine and humane seaman, entered Australian territorial waters with the intention of unloading his wretched human cargo at the nearest suitable Australian port. Howard seized the moment. In defiance of the international rules and conventions governing both the saving of lives at sea and the treatment of asylum seekers, he proclaimed that these people would never set foot in Australia.

Norway protested forcefully at this breach of international law. Howard responded by sending in the commandos of the SASR, the Special Air Service Regiment, to take control of the *Tampa*. The affair escalated rapidly, with the foreign minister, the egregious Downer, shouting abuse at his Norwegian counterpart during a phone call to Oslo. Military force won out. The refugees were loaded onto the navy transport HMAS *Manoora* and taken to internment camps in Nauru. It was the beginning of the odious 'Pacific Solution', a policy of mounting inhumanity and cruelty visited upon some of the planet's most wretched people.

For Howard it was a triumph, political and personal. He had demonstrated strength and defiant resolve. Beazley and Labor were left hopelessly wedged between humanitarian concern for the *Tampa* refugees and angst about appearing weak on border protection. The opinion polls took a decisive swing Howard's way.

The cards kept falling his way too. He was actually visiting Washington on that shocking, devastating day of Tuesday, 11 September 2001, when Islamist al-Qaeda terrorists hijacked four airliners, two of them slamming into the twin towers of the World Trade Center in New York City. A third aircraft plunged into the Pentagon, and the fourth into a field in Pennsylvania. Two thousand, nine hundred and ninety-six people were killed.

It was late evening in Sydney, and I was at home watching an episode of *The West Wing* on Nine when the horror began. After the initial newsflash Nine switched to broadcast the destruction live, and I sat dumbfounded as the second aircraft smashed into the South Tower. It was surreal, utterly confusing, beyond comprehension, as if the script of *The West Wing* had suddenly taken this monstrous turn. On the spot, Howard, clearly affected, was able to very visibly pledge Australia's support for President George W. Bush and the American people, which was entirely the right and proper thing to do. But in troubled times voters naturally tend to rally around the leader they have, and he benefited from yet another surge in the polls.

October was the month that sealed everything for him, nailed it down. It brought the shameful tissue of lies and scaremongering that became known as the 'Children Overboard' affair. On 6 October, north of Christmas Island, the frigate HMAS *Adelaide* intercepted a rickety refugee boat designated Suspected Illegal Entry Vessel 4, or SIEV 4, which was grossly overloaded with 223 men, women and children. In the ensuing uproar the immigration minister, Philip Ruddock, declared that the refugees had thrown children into the sea to ensure they were rescued by the frigate. Howard seized on this supposed villainy and the media ran it big. 'Overboard: Boat People Throw Children into Ocean', shouted a headline in Melbourne's *Herald Sun*, with a quote from Howard: 'I don't want people like that in Australia. Genuine refugees don't do that . . . they hang on to their children.' He repeated the line to Alan Jones and anyone else who would listen.

It was a blatant lie and it ran for weeks, to the increasing concern of the Navy and the Defence Department, who knew it was untrue. It was the Chief of Navy, Vice Admiral David Shackleton, who blew the whistle. Badgered by reporters at an impromptu footpath press conference in Perth on 8 November, he replied that 'it doesn't appear they were thrown in'.

I had met Shackleton through our shared enthusiasm for naval history, and I liked him a great deal. I knew him to be a straight shooter. The truth was out. By happy coincidence I was interviewing Ruddock live on air that afternoon when the news came through. I went for him, accusing him and the government of lying. Unaware of Shackleton's admission, Ruddock blustered in high dudgeon, but I had him nailed.

Not that it achieved anything. The Children Overboard lie was indelibly cemented in the public mind, and the perceived menace of hordes of refugees heading for Australia was amplified by the sinking of another boat on 19 October, SIEV X, in which 353 men, women and children drowned. All the while Howard was muscling up with George Bush, wrapping himself in khaki and the flag, very publicly despatching Australian troops to the Middle East and to a new war just starting up in Afghanistan. On 28 October, at the Liberals' election campaign launch, his declaration that 'we will decide who comes to this country and the circumstances in which they come' brought the house down and reverberated around the country.

The election on 10 November saw Labor lost at sea, foundering with its lowest primary vote since 1934 and just sixty-five House of Representative seats to the Coalition's eighty-two. Kim Beazley quit the Labor leadership, to be replaced by Simon Crean.

✧

Like flies at a barbecue, buyers had been hovering around 2UE for years. The advertising man John Singleton had been just one of assorted odds and sods and wannabe radio moguls keen to get their hooks into the station. Early in 2001 another of the flies, a Melbourne-based media company, Southern Cross Broadcasting, hit John Conde and the Lamb family with an offer to good to refuse. For slightly north of $90 million, Southern Cross snapped up 2UE and 4BC in Brisbane and a few other bits and pieces as well. It was silly money, but it gave Southern Cross a powerful punch in the commercial radio business. They already owned the successful and profitable 3AW in Melbourne. Now they would have an unbeatable east coast network, plus 6PR in Perth and a small scattering of lesser stations.

By now I was wearily accustomed to being bought and sold. The boss at Southern Cross was Tony Bell, a squat and charmless figure who reminded me irresistibly of a frog. He had the takeover patter down smoothly, though. They all do. 'Synergy' and 'interface' were the business buzzwords of the day and he threw them around like confetti. One Monday we arrived at work to find the ceilings had sprouted gaily coloured, dangling cardboard mobiles announcing that we were a 'Can Do' company, whatever that meant. Piling on the Can Do excitement, Bell had the executive offices repainted an eye-watering shade of lime-yellow, a colour said to keep the toilers in the vineyard awake and working furiously. There was a special company website, too, where you could look up your name, find the tasks assigned to you and read inspiring corporate exhortations to greatness. I looked for my name but the site had never heard of me.

Bell was a rising boardroom star at the time. Southern Cross had been a sleepy little regional media player when he joined in 1993. With a round of acquisitions and the usual chainsaw cost-cutting and sackings he turned the place into a middle-ranking powerhouse, no small achievement. But that was about it. Like so many of his tribe, he laboured under the delusion that he knew all there was to know about creative radio programming, and he set about showering us with the benefits of his wisdom. He held long bullshit sessions for the staff, at which he drew circles on whiteboards and divided them into little segments labelled with impenetrable hieroglyphics. I never discovered what they were supposed to mean or prove, and I don't think anybody else did either.

Alan Jones was the first to crack, and for that I cannot blame him. His contract was up by the end of 2001, less than nine months after Southern Cross had moved in. It was an open secret around 2UE that Jones felt Bell had not treated him with sufficient deference and was looking for a way out. When John Singleton began to scatter birdseed around the cage, the Parrot was more than receptive. Jones had parted ways with Harry M. Miller after Cash for Comment.

Astutely, he asked Sam Chisholm to do the negotiations with Singleton. As always happens, news got out that Jones was about to jump ship and the papers were full of it, despite what was said to be a handsome counter-offer from Bell.

On the morning of Thursday, 7 February 2002, I went to the 2UE executive suite for a chat with the station manager, an inoffensive man named David Bacon. 'Alan will be staying with us,' he assured me cheerfully. 'Tony's got the situation under control.'

'Really?' I said. 'In which case, why are Jones and Singleton having a press conference over at 2GB in an hour's time?'

Bacon reeled as if he had been shot and lunged for the telephone to call Melbourne. Tony did not have the situation under control. Jones was already in Singo's boozy embrace. Jones's biographer, Chris Masters, estimated that, with share options and the like, Singleton had handed Jones as much as $40 million over seven years. Chisholm – who would have known – reportedly described it as Australia's biggest ever deal to sign a radio or television personality.[148]

I was glad to see the back of him. The atmosphere around 2UE lightened; it was like sunshine after a winter storm. But it did not last long.

23

Just like building a Corolla

JOHN SINGLETON WAS GETTING his radio act together. It had not always been that way. He had once briefly mumbled through a program of his own on the old Labor station in Sydney, 2KY; the audience would have had to be drunk to have understood a word he said. He bought into the bottom-feeding oldies' music station 2CH in an unlikely alliance with its owners, the Council of Churches. Then he got tied up with the odious Gordon Moyes as a part owner of the ongoing disaster that was 2GB and the Macquarie Network. Falling out with Moyes, as almost everyone did, Singo gave him the flick and decided to get serious about turning 2GB around.

The key, as he saw it, was rugby league. For years 2UE had held the rights to broadcast premiership games, but when the contract came up for renewal in 1999 Singleton offered what everyone said was stupid money and won. Calling football games on radio counts for very little in these days of the internet, social media and the smartphone, but back then it was a ratings must for a talk station. Even that didn't work for Singleton and 2GB until late 2001, when he lured Ray Hadley across from 2UE to call the games. Then it took off.

Hadley is probably the angriest man I have met, and perpetually so. He boils, he burns. His bulgy eyes are either as cold as ball bearings or aflame with fury. In the seething inner culture of rugby league in Sydney, with its factions and feuds and bare-knuckle hatreds, he wears the nickname 'Bolts', bestowed for what was widely acknowledged to be his uncanny likeness to the hulking TV comedy ghoul Herman Munster. When I rejoined 2UE and met Hadley for the first time, I felt there was acid gnawing at his innards; he was to be handled with caution. Here was a man who woke up each morning to decide who he'd hate today.

We largely kept out of each other's hair. Hadley was undoubtedly good at calling rugby league, with an encyclopaedic knowledge of the game. I was only marginally interested in it, enough to get by on air and leave the details to the experts. If a footy story broke I would defer to his expertise and have him on my program, both of us behaving professionally. There was no sign that he knew much about anything beyond the sport – there still isn't – but we did not trespass on each other's territory. Off air, he was busy terrorising young journalists in the newsroom.

I know of men, senior and successful journalists now, who were reduced to tears by Hadley's threatening rages in their early years at 2UE. He was infamous for it. Kids fresh out of university lived in fear of committing some sin, real or imagined, that would set him off. In fact he had no authority over them whatsoever, but no one seemed willing to rein him in – until the day he more than met his match in a journalist who stood up and took him on.

Mark Piepers, in his late twenties and around 175 centimetres tall, was an overnight newsreader, about as low on the totem pole as you can be. In 2001 Hadley was driving to work when he heard that Piepers had dropped some rugby league results from a news bulletin and replaced them with fresh AFL scores. Infuriated, he berated Piepers on the phone with a torrent of foul abuse, and again when he arrived at the station. Piepers retorted that he would not be spoken to like that. Hadley shot back: 'If you don't fuck off now, I'm going to punch you through that fucking wall.'

Big mistake. Small though he was, Piepers was a martial arts enthusiast, skilled in karate and kung-fu. When he invited Hadley to step outside and settle it, Hadley subsided like a pricked balloon. The encounter became legend around the radio station.

Hadley's aggression blazed into public view in 2013, when he trapped a young production assistant in his 2GB office and savaged him mercilessly for supposedly being slow to upload a podcast. Fearing for his safety, the victim, Richard Palmer, secretly recorded the tirade on his iPhone. Later Palmer had the guts to complain to the 2GB management. It was Hadley's undoing. When the thing got to court, with allegations of 'deliberately inflicting psychological harm' and a charge of false imprisonment, the evidence was ugly. One of Hadley's minders, a man mountain known as Rob 'the Duck' Smith, had barricaded the door. Hadley had ranted and raved, at one stage shouting at Palmer: 'I'll tell you fucking what – and this is not leaving this office – if you repeat it, I'll fucking deny it!'[149] More embarrassing still was an email produced in court, in which the Macquarie Radio Network chairman and Singleton's long-time right-hand man, Russell Tate, referred to Hadley as a 'psychotic bully'.[150] The case was quickly settled for an undisclosed sum of money, and Hadley later delivered what was said to be a tearful apology at a 2GB staff meeting.

When he wasn't kicking down, he was sucking up, most obsequiously to John Laws. Hadley convinced 2UE that he should host the morning slot when John was on leave, and he seized every chance to do it. The on-air gush was sickening, sloshing around waist-deep: never could he match John Laws, of course, but he was honoured and privileged just to sit in the same chair as the Great Man and broadcast to his listeners, the most wonderful people in Australia, blah blah. He, Ray, could only do his humble best, hoping it would be good enough, etc. Assiduously, ambitiously, he mimicked the Laws technique and style, down to the 'stings', as they were known, the little bursts of musical punctuation that John had made his trademark. As Laws would later write, Hadley was 'a copyist at best, and not a terribly good one'.[151]

But it was enough. Hadley carried it across lock, stock and barrel to 2GB, where, fronting the morning program after Jones, Hadley first beat Laws in the ratings in 2003. Then the sycophancy stopped. Uriah Heep disappeared. By 2006, sinking his fangs into the hand that had fed him, Hadley loftily advised Laws to quit radio. 'I don't know whether he's still going around because of ego or power,' he snarled. 'The fact is, John Laws is no longer relevant in the Sydney market. He's not on the radar.'

✧

When the Parrot went to 2GB, he carried a large chunk of his loyal audience with him. In the months that followed, 2UE drove the remainder into his arms with unerring precision. In their wisdom, Tony Bell and his right-hand man at Southern Cross, Graham Mott, quixotically replaced the Parrot with a Melbourne broadcaster utterly unknown in Sydney.

Steve Price arrived at 2UE early in 2002, startling his production team by assuring them he was Australia's finest radio journalist. This surprised a good many other people when it got around, me for one. I had never heard of him. Nor had John Laws. Enquiries revealed he'd been fronting the weekday drive program on 3AW, and with some success. It was Melbourne's top talk show in the timeslot.

But Sydney and Melbourne radio are very different, like the cities themselves. What works in one town almost always bombs if it's tried in the other, particularly in talk radio. As you'd expect in the brash and brazen city on the harbour, Sydney commercial audiences want their talk stars to be shouty, politically populist and right-wing, aggressively in-yer-face. Jones and Hadley personify the breed. Melbourne, more taut and placid, but utterly besotted by every twitch and grunt of AFL football, likes its radio presenters the same way. Politics comes a distant second to the footy.

3AW's accomplished breakfast duo of Ross Stevenson and John Burns have been rating their heads off and creaming the competition for as long as anyone can remember, but they are never quoted as 'commentators' on national affairs, in Melbourne or anywhere else. Nor do they want to be. Neil Mitchell, who follows them on 3AW's top-rating morning shift, is a fine journalist and quality broadcaster entirely in tune with the city he serves so effectively, and he has a substantial national profile too, but compared to Jones or Hadley he is a model of rational restraint. He is vastly better informed and a far superior interviewer to the Sydney duo, but it's oil and water. It is no criticism to say that this Melbourne trio would not make a dent in Sydney, just as Jones and Hadley would die in a ditch if they were networked anywhere south of the Murray.

Price didn't make a dent either, although, to be fair, he gave it his best shot. Backed up by a good team, he worked hard to get his head around what he thought mattered to Sydney. But somehow he still sounded Melbourne and, as they say in politics, the mob will eventually work you out. It didn't help when word got out that he would fly south at weekends to watch an AFL game. But the real killer was his persona, which came across on air as sour and truculent. There was no light touch to Price, only the bludgeon. Apparently devoid of wit or humour, his default position was heavy sarcasm, which has its uses but will get you only so far. Too much of it lands like lead, and Price was heaping it on by the truckload. Some of the troops began to call him 'the Poisoned Dwarf'. John Laws nicknamed him 'the Angry Ant' and began to worry – with good reason – that he was driving breakfast listeners away.

Tony Bell, though, knew best. A Victorian to his bootstraps and chippy with it, he was constantly on alert and ready to take umbrage at the faintest hint of Sydney condescension, real or imagined. Price had been successful in Melbourne; he would therefore also be a success up north. Any suggestion otherwise was merely Sydney being bitchy.

Drawing his circles on his whiteboards and spouting his impenetrable radio nostrums, Bell persisted in this delusion for nearly two years. 2UE's breakfast ratings collapsed, with Jones and ABC 702 (as 2BL became) both streets ahead. Eventually, it occurred to Bell that the Ant, no matter how hard he tried, was not going to change that. 'Regardless of what has happened, Steve is a good broadcaster,' Graham Mott told Melbourne's *Age* newspaper. 'It's just that the Sydney audience has not taken to him because he's not local.'[152]

There was a quick shuffle, with Price moving to drivetime and me slotted into breakfast again. God help me. I had promised myself, and Morag, that I would never do it again: the disturbed, sleepless nights; out of bed in the dark at three am, rain, hail or shine; the constant exhaustion of jet lag; the dislocation of family and social life; the unending pressure to perform. Jones, a self-confessed workaholic and without a family, was far better equipped to handle this punishing regimen than me.

I ducked and dived, twisted and turned to get out from under, but Bell and Mott were insistent, pouring on the usual flattery. They appealed to my loyalty to the station and my colleagues. Cornered, I succumbed, but for the first time in my career I hired a professional agent to cut the deal for me. Sean Anderson, a young lawyer, was just starting out in the talent management business in Sydney, building up a stable of celebrities and wannabes. He had once sent me a letter offering his services and I took him up on it. Sean was astute and personable. Better still, he knew what he was doing and was able to get me an excellent deal.

My typical feeling of sinking dread after signing a new contract returned, though, a crash back to earth. What had I got myself into now? Would I be able to drag back at least some of the audience that Price had driven to 2GB and the ABC? Or had the horse bolted? I was about to find out.

✧

With three election wins under his belt, at the end of 2001 John Howard was master of all he surveyed. In time-honoured Tory tradition he had invoked perils from abroad – boat people, terrorists, militant Islam, Saddam Hussein – and strutted the stage as the prime minister who could be trusted to keep Australians safe. Shrouded in the flag, he, John Winston Howard, stood shoulder to shoulder with George W. Bush and Tony Blair, defiant in the defence of freedom and Western civilisation. The trick worked, as it generally does, most especially if there is a suitable villain such as Saddam to be hauled on stage and reviled. The fawning Murdoch press and the right-wing shock-jocks shouted their approval. Dissent or critical doubt were scorned as weakness, un-Australian, and sometimes as treason. The warmongers were rampant, triumphant. It was the beginning of a decade of catastrophic foreign policy mistakes, which reverberate today.

The external dangers were indeed there. In October 2002 the nation was shocked to the core by the Islamist terror bombings at Kuta in Bali, in which 202 people were killed, eighty-eight of them Australians. Morag was at Kuala Lumpur airport to film a *Four Corners* story in Malaysia when she heard the news. Urgently juggling some flights, by the next morning she was picking her way through the chaos and the corpses at Sanglah Hospital in Denpasar, a profoundly affecting encounter for her.

To be fair, Howard displayed genuine leadership at this time, not least in his attentions to the afflicted families. It was his long-term response that brought on folly and failure. Schmoozed by Bush and his warmongering neocons in Washington, basking in flattery from the super-hawk vice-president Dick Cheney and the defense secretary, Donald Rumsfeld, Howard committed Australia to the disastrous war to overthrow Saddam Hussein in Iraq, and to the unending quagmire that is Afghanistan. Against the mounting evidence, the Australian prime minister was one of the last and most tenacious purveyors of the delusion that Saddam possessed weapons of mass destruction. In his March 2003 speech committing Australian troops to Iraq, he quoted a report in Murdoch's London *Times* newspaper, which had claimed Saddam used 'a human shredding machine' to murder his victims. 'This is the man, this is the apparatus of terror we are dealing with,' Howard intoned grimly.[153] He had no evidence for this, not a crumb. The *Times* story was later debunked as fanciful rubbish, but the lie had been unleashed. Howard never withdrew it.

Rupert Murdoch himself was thirsting for war, publicly and privately urging Bush and Blair to saddle up. 'We can't back down now, where you hand over the whole of the Middle East to Saddam . . . I think Bush is acting very morally, very correctly, and I think he is going to go on with it,' he pontificated in an interview in February 2003. Blair was 'extraordinarily courageous and strong'. Apart from selling newspapers, Murdoch's worldview saw the rationale for war in dollars and cents. 'The greatest thing to come out of this for the world economy . . . would be $20 a barrel for oil. That's bigger than any tax cut in any country,' he blustered.[154] Of course, it has never been anywhere near that figure since. In 2006, when Saddam was executed, oil peaked at $90 a barrel.

With considerable political courage and foresight, the Labor leader, Simon Crean, branded Howard's rush to war as 'unnecessary, reckless and against Australia's national interests'.[155] But by December 2003 he had quit the leadership, to be replaced by Mark Latham, who, at forty-two, was Labor's youngest leader since 1901. Latham had once denounced Howard as an 'arse licker', branded Bush 'the most dangerous and incompetent US President in recent history' and famously scoffed that Australians who followed him were 'a conga-line of suck-holes'.[156] Two days after he became opposition leader, he did some arse-licking himself, bizarrely holding a media conference with a large American flag displayed behind him. 'I believe in the American alliance,' he honked.[157]

Even then Latham struck me as a bit odd. He reminded me of Ray Hadley, a man possessed by a visceral demon. He had the same piercing glare, the same Westie chip on his shoulder, the same aura of suppressed rage. But I was willing to back him, chiefly because Gough Whitlam had once taken me aside at a cocktail party and urged me to. 'He's the next prime minister of Australia, comrade!' Gough was not always the best judge of character. No one, though, could have anticipated that Latham would morph into the lunar right-wing mug lair he became in retirement, living on his parliamentary pension and consorting with a claque of political and media crazies he once would have despised.

In the febrile politics of the war there was not much hope of him winning the Lodge at the 2004 election, although for a while he polled well and was briefly ahead. He diminished his chances in an interview on my program in March that year. I pushed him hard on Labor's policy of getting Australia out of the war, and for a couple of answers he ducked and dived. Homing in, I asked if he would have the troops 'home by Christmas'. It was a shot in the dark but, to my intense surprise, he said he would. I pushed him to repeat it, and he did: a Latham Labor government would have the troops home by Christmas 2004.

It caused a sensation, all over the front pages. Howard and the Murdoch press went for him like dingoes, tearing him to pieces. It was disloyal, treacherous, it would betray the ANZUS alliance. It was Labor at its reckless worst. A couple of months later, Howard stood smirking at a media conference on the White House lawn as Bush – meddling outrageously in Australian politics – said any Australian withdrawal would be 'disastrous', likely 'to embolden the enemy' and 'dispirit those who love freedom'.[158]

Labor's last chance of a win vanished with a handshake. On 8 October, the day before the poll, Latham and Howard encountered each other outside an ABC Radio studio. Latham, very much the bigger man, aggressively jerked Howard towards him and appeared to hold him in a vice-like grip. It was ugly. Television splashed it around the nation that night, and people did not like it. Howard walked it home, picking up five seats to give him eighty-seven against Labor's sixty.

At a dinner years later, Howard privately thanked me for that Latham 'troops home' interview. 'It was very helpful,' he chortled gleefully. I was rueful at the time, much chastened, but I'm not anymore. Like most of us, I shudder to contemplate what Mark Latham might have done as prime minister. It's pleasing to think that, in a small way, I helped Australia dodge that bullet.

✧

Station managers came and went at 2UE, in and out like the little figures on a cuckoo clock, and about as memorable. They would vanish on a Friday afternoon, for reasons never explained, any vestige of them erased with Stalinist efficiency by the next Monday morning. One was Bob Miller, who had been the marketing manager for Toyota Australia and was introduced to us as the creator of the famous 'Oh, what a feeling' leap in the company's TV commercials. In fact that was the brainchild of Toyota's advertising agency in New York, but Miller brought his automotive expertise to the wonderful world of wireless, sublimely transcending the inconvenient truth that he didn't know what he was talking about.

'Doing radio's just like building a Corolla,' he announced at his first appearance before the puzzled staff. 'You start with the chassis, then on go the axles and the wheels . . . then the doors . . . then the handles . . .'

It was a change from Tony Bell's whiteboard circles, but equally fatuous. People looked at each other, eyeballs rolling. After a few weeks Miller retreated behind closed doors and was rarely seen again. His secretary told me he feared his office was bugged, his every word being listened to by Bell and Mott down in Melbourne. He, too, inexplicably disappeared one Friday.

Things were no better at Fairfax and the *Sydney Morning Herald*, where the egg-headed, pixie figure of Professor Fred Hilmer was energetically driving the empire towards the abyss. Hilmer had been a management consultant for the notorious McKinsey company and a Sydney academic, but he had neither run a major public company nor set foot inside a newspaper office before his appointment as Fairfax's chief executive in 1998. It's said he was hired because he was a friend of one of the Fairfax directors, the ubiquitous lawyer–businessman David Gonski. On his arrival, Hilmer dismayed a group of senior Fairfax journalists by telling them he was not an avid reader of newspapers. Kerry Packer summed him up with his customary pithy profanity in evidence he gave to a broadcasting enquiry. 'I wouldn't fucking hire him as a sweeper,' he said. 'For Fairfax to be run by a management consultant is just an act of stupidity. I think it's ridiculous . . . he came from McKinsey and he has never run a business in his life. Now, if that is the right criteria for running a newspaper business then I am a Dutchman.'[159]

Packer's judgement was spot on, as it often was. Hilmer was a disaster. He thought of journalists as 'content providers' and never seemed to get his head around the fact that news did not always happen between nine am and five pm. He could just as well have been making ice-creams or garden furniture. When he took the reins, Fairfax had a virtual monopoly of media classified advertising, the so-called 'rivers of gold'. By turns secretive and tumultuous, and unswervingly confused, in seven years he managed to lose almost all of it, beaten to the punch on the internet by Murdoch and Packer. Young Warwick had started the rot at Fairfax. Hilmer turbo-charged it. For this triumph he was handed a golden parachute of $4.3 million in 2005.

I lost count of the editors-in-chief and editors who were nominally my boss as a *Herald* columnist over some twenty years. Most were as remote as the pope. There were a few I never laid eyes on, quite literally. In all that time I was invited into the *Herald* office just once, and only one editor-in-chief, Peter Fray, ever took me to lunch for a convivial chat about what I was writing and where the paper was going. Other columnists told me they were treated the same way.

Keeping my distance actually suited me, though. There were no riding instructions. They left me alone, which I took as a tacit vote of confidence. At the Murdoch press, the wretched hacks scribble for the approval of the capricious tyrant who butters their bread. I could write what I liked, and I did. The section editors I dealt with were invariably competent and supportive. Each Thursday evening I would email them clean copy – meaning that it did not have to be rejigged, rewritten, punctuated or cut – and on Saturdays there it would be in the paper, word for word, with a crisply written headline and an apt cartoon.

I loved churning it out, both for the intellectual exercise and the voice it gave me nationally, beyond the radio audience. The reader response told me that, most of the time, I was hitting the right marks. On a good week I might receive hundreds of letters and emails, some people simply saying they'd enjoyed the latest effort, others offering constructive criticism or new facts they thought I'd like to know. Sometimes there were thousands of responses. I did my best to reply but was often beaten by the sheer volume. They were a great bunch and loyal to a fault, those *Herald* readers, an asset that Fairfax has now largely squandered through incompetence and neglect.

Some, though, were not entirely lovable. The loonies often scrawled their impenetrable drivel all over the outside of the envelopes as well, sometimes in green or red inks. For a while there, one anonymous imbecile took to carefully clipping my column from the paper and wiping his arse on it; he would then post it to me, smeared with his dried faeces.

✧

Despite the muddled management and the clash of on-air egos, 2UE was mostly a happy place to work. Advertisers who had bought time in my program were loyally sticking with me. Some had been around since the early days at 2GB. Les Schirato, the managing director of the surging Vittoria coffee brand, had begun as a sponsor but became a truly good friend who stuck through thick and thin.

There were bright young journalists in the newsroom, among them a young David Speers, who would become one of the Canberra

Press Gallery's most accomplished television interviewers. The news director, Sandy Aloisi, ran the operation with a light, adroit touch. Her newsreading voice, low and superbly modulated, was one of the best in the business. The two sports experts who survived Hadley's departure – former rugby league internationals Johnny Gibbs and Greg 'Brandy' Alexander – were on top of their game and universally well liked, a refreshing improvement. John Stanley, the afternoon presenter, and George Moore, the weekend host, were easygoing professionals.

Happily, I gathered around me a bunch of bright young people to bolt the show together. They were talented, hard-working, congenial and loyal, and I think of them with fond gratitude and follow their careers to this day. Tom Malone, in his early twenties, was one of those rare journalists blessed with innate ability and an almost uncanny knack for being on the spot when big news broke. If Tommy took a holiday there would inevitably be a tsunami, a cabinet crisis or a sudden small war which he would be perfectly positioned to report. From day one, he was clearly on an upward trajectory. He went on to become executive producer of *60 Minutes*, and then the Nine Network's head of sport.

His successor, Angus Llewellyn, had nothing in common with Tom except talent. In his late twenties, a gifted musician and ocean swimmer, he was loaded with brains and intuitive common sense. Not to mention guts. Once, at a production meeting when I chucked a preposterous wobbly over some trifle, he jerked me back into line. 'This might cost me my job,' he said doggedly. 'But you've just made a complete prick of yourself, and we're not going to put up with it.'

He was right. I slunk out for a smoke, calmed down, came back and apologised. Respect. Angus and I have been firm friends ever since. He and his wife, Anna, are two of the coolest people I know, and I have enjoyed seeing his career as a current-affairs television producer soar at both SBS and the ABC.

Cathy Murray, a vivacious blonde Canadian researcher, worked magic on the telephone, plucking names and numbers from thin air at warp speed. In the studio to push buttons was another twenty-something, Alex Smith, a deft operator whose long hair and beard lent him the air of a medieval Jesus portrait. Alex did dazzling music and sound effects for *Friday News Review*.

To keep me and the show on the rails, I hired a personal assistant, Christine Gallagher. She began pretty much at the bottom of the heap, making the coffee, and answering the office phone and the talkback switchboard. Dogged and determined, but fun with it, she flew the highest of all those kids I like to think of as my alumni, scoring a brilliant postgraduate degree in international relations at Oxford. My early career in journalism had been fostered by older men and women who generously shared their knowledge and experience with me, and pointed me in the right direction. Early on I resolved that I would do the same if it ever became possible, and I am glad to say it happened.

For a while the newly emerging Chaser team did some comedy slots in the show. Charles Firth, Dominic Knight, Chas Licciardello, Julian Morrow, Craig Reucassel and Chris Taylor – an eclectic mix of lawyers and lunatics – were fighting the opening battles of their war on Australia's sacred cows, rather as we had done a generation before at *This Day Tonight*. For what it was worth, I gave them all the encouragement I could.

Doing *Friday News Review* was getting trickier. Try as I might, I could never get my voice around a convincing impression of John Howard. Alexander Downer's petulant, Adelaidey tones were easy enough to mimic, but Howard's oddly querulous and combative persona was beyond my grasp. At which point enter Josh Szeps, yet another twenty-something, and a son of the actor Henri Szeps. Josh had been messing around in the media after university, not sure what he wanted to do with his life. Among other bits and pieces he had briefly been a researcher for Alan Jones. On spec, he sent me a tape of his Howard voice. It was perfect, so eerily accurate that when I played it to a few people they thought it was the real thing. I hired him in a nanosecond, both for *Friday News Review* and a new segment we developed together, *John Howard's Diary*.

As it turned out, Josh could do an even better Downer than me, so he handled that as well. It was a huge fillip. More useful still, he could also write comedy like an angel. We just clicked, recording together in the studio. Often his ad libs were more hilarious than the scripts we had slaved over. When he told me after a year or so that he wanted to move to New York to try his luck in the Big Apple, I was sunk in gloom, until he explained very gently, in words of one syllable, that there was a thing called the internet which could send high-quality audio around the world at no cost. I could email him the scripts. He would record his parts and have them on my desk by the next morning, to be cut together by Alex Smith.

In fact, that was rather more complex than it sounds. His emphases and inflections had to be finely judged to match mine or the thing sounded childishly amateur. Always the perfectionist, though, he hit it out of the park every time. With his surname now changed to the more easily handled 'Zepps', Josh is still in New York, living with his American husband and with some serious television work under his belt.

In September 2006 Morag and I married in a civil ceremony at the Officers' Mess at Sydney's Victoria Barracks. The bride, stunning in cream silk, was given away by her father, Colonel Donald Ramsay. He was kilted in full Scottish highland rig, befitting a much-loved officer and gentleman who had fought with the Black Watch at Monte Cassino in 1944, and with the Australian Army in Malaya. Genial and a fund of jokes and stories, Donald was the ideal father-in-law. My son, James, was the best man. Enid and Peter were there, in a gathering of my dearest. Complete happiness.

✧

Peter FitzSimons joined me on air in 2006. Southern Cross had a successful duo for the breakfast show at 3AW in Melbourne and decided they wanted the same in Sydney. Happily, they told me to pick my own partner. Pete was the obvious choice to me.

We had met at a rugby game not long after I got back from London, hitting it off pretty much from the word go, although he is fifteen years younger than me. We were a little in awe of each other at first, I think. Well over two metres tall, Peter is a commanding figure who looks as if he could run through a brick wall to wrestle a couple of alligators and then take on a bunch of Hell's Angels in unarmed combat before breakfast. He was a Wallaby, with the high distinction of having been sent from the field for supposedly violent play against the New Zealand All Blacks. In fact, the only time I have ever seen him even slightly menacing was during an amusing encounter with one of the *Daily Telegraph*'s right-wing blowhards, Piers Akerman. It was at the annual Andrew Olle dinner in 2002, where – inexplicably – Lachlan Murdoch was the guest speaker. The room was stuffed with his employees. Akerman and I were old foes.

'Come to grovel at the feet of the Young Master?' I enquired politely.

Akerman puffed up in his dinner suit like a penguin inflated with a bicycle pump and began some blustering reply.

Hoping to enliven the evening, I emptied my glass of white wine over his head, much to the pleasure of folk nearby. With the exception, that is, of Akerman's colleague, the *Herald-Sun* bloviator and Melbourne's village idiot Andrew Bolt, who barged in and offered to pick a fight. Hardly were the words out of his mouth when Peter Fitz loomed up silently at his shoulder, towering over him like a cliff. The two Murdoch myrmidons melted away.

When our paths first crossed he was already making his name as a popular sportswriter for the *Herald* and a best-selling author. In turn, he was aware of my record as a journalist and keen to pick my brains about radio and television, at which he was still a novice.

Back then, some people assumed that since Pete had been a rugby forward in the heart of the scrum, he must be all brawn. He bore that cross with amused resignation. He has one of the most searching brains I know, an eclectic mind sucking up knowledge, jokes and anecdotes like a deep-sea dredge. He views the world with a crackling sense of humour, anchored in a passionate disdain for injustice. He cares, and he always acts, with furious energy. Let him out of your sight for a week and you will find he has written another bestselling book, taken up basketball, joined the council of the Australian War Memorial, and become chair of the Australian Republican Movement.

At the time we were together on radio, it fairly could be said that he looked like a very big sack of very big watermelons, 150 kilograms of them. Lunching at his favourite restaurant, Machiavelli in Sydney, we would hoover up enough spaghetti carbonara and scaloppine saltimbocca to feed a small Tuscan village, and think nothing of going the fourth bottle of valpolicella. Until in September 2014 Peter screeched to a halt. Overnight. With iron resolve he gave up sugar, most processed foods, even the grog he loved. Not a drop of alcohol has he touched since, and he has dropped 50 kilos. It was, and is, an astonishing achievement and one which – being Pete – he now insists on the rest of mankind emulating, preaching this virtuous lifestyle with evangelical fervour.

Better still, he comes with his wife, Lisa Wilkinson. At first meeting, they are an unlikely couple. Lisa is beautiful, and radiates elegance. She was a kid from working-class Campbelltown in Sydney's south-west who scraped a job straight out of school to make coffee at *Dolly* magazine and found herself in the editor's chair at the age of twenty-one. Intelligence and talent took her where she is now: arguably one of the most recognised and admired women in the country. The friendship of our families is one of my most precious possessions.

Having Pete across the studio desk lifted the show no end, although it made my life harder to start with. I had to push the buttons and manage the all-crucial timing for the two of us at first, although he got the hang of it quickly enough and became familiar with the microphone. We developed a line in good-natured banter, no doubt helped along by the fact that our views on life were pretty similar. The only time we went head-to-head – hammer and tongs, boots and all – was when a big container ship, the *Pasha Bulker*, ran aground on a beach near Newcastle in 2007. It was a great story with big public interest, live TV coverage, the lot. I was convinced they'd manage to tow the thing free. Pete was adamant they could not, as he explained in his *Herald* column a few years later:

> 'It'll never move,' I was telling Carlton for the hundredth time.
>
> 'It'll never . . .'
>
> Oh, Gawd.
>
> Before my very eyes, the bloody thing started bobbing around. Movement at the station! Movement on the beach! Movement through the water! Within minutes – whooooshka – the *Pasha Bulker* was free, heading out to sea, leaving the airwaves of Sydney

> awash in my stunned declamations and bloody Carlton's roars of laughter.[160]

The listeners loved him. I like to think radio gave him a whole new launch platform but, as always, the lousy hours took their toll. With Lisa doing breakfast television at the same time and three kids to get to school each morning, it was a huge disruption to FitzSimons family life. After two years, at the end of 2007, Pete pulled the pin and went back to being the stay-at-home parent.

✧

Doubling down on the folly of transporting Steve Price from Melbourne to Sydney, Southern Cross replaced him on the 3AW drive show with none other than Stan Zemanek. It was a disaster. Melbourne hated his abrasive ignorance, and other broadcasters at 3AW made it clear that he was bringing them and the station down. The veteran journalist Mark Day, who had done that shift himself on 3AW, told the *Age* that the station was 'traducing a great heritage'. Zemanek was 'a goose who doesn't deserve to be on the air waves'. The *Herald*'s writer on popular culture, David Dale, said the appointment was 'just insane'.[161]

The ratings tanked. After a year Zemanek was back in Sydney, doing the evening shift at 2UE. We rarely saw each other, but our mutual loathing continued. I tended to ignore him, but over the years he had savaged me on air and in the newspapers, at one stage ludicrously demanding that I be 'investigated and sacked' for 'irresponsible journalism'. Mostly, I despised his on-air act. His show was a torrent of crude abuse and right-wing gibberish. Without any research, he merely parroted whatever line the *Daily Telegraph* was taking on any given topic. The broadcaster and writer Phillip Adams thought him 'crass, inarticulate, ill-informed and none too intelligent . . . his brain bore an eerie similarity to a Surprise pea. Prior to immersion.'[162]

Someone once showed me some papers Zemanek had left behind in the studio. His memory being at about goldfish level, he would refer to a typed list of insults and catchphrases before hurling them at listeners he disliked: 'Boofhead . . . imbecile . . . oxygen-thief . . . left-wing loony . . . socialist criminal . . . give yourself an uppercut . . . you're drunk as a skunk . . . poonce . . . dole-bludging layabout . . . wanker . . . bloody poofter.' He condescended to women, calling them 'love' or 'darling'. In fact, some of his talkback callers were fake: Zemanek paid an actor to ring in and spice things up.

The official 2UE line was that cheeky ol' Stan was a lovable, irascible rogue and a 'pussycat' off air. Not so. One of his staff came to me one day in tears, unable to tolerate his bullying any longer. But she needed the job, she said. Could I have a word to the management? I did, but nothing seemed to happen. She quit a few weeks later.

Cancer got him, and he fought it with courage, but he died in July 2007. There was much hullabaloo in the tabloid media, chiefly the gutter-dwelling *Telegraph*. Someone asked me, on air, if I would attend his funeral. Off the top of my head, I shot back that I would only go to check that he was dead. I was not going to join the chorus of hypocrisy. 'I hated him and he hated me,' I said.

The *Telegraph* went berserk, followed by its Murdoch stablemates the *Australian* and Melbourne's *Herald Sun*. With a rival Fairfax columnist in their sights, they went for it for three days. I was despicable, loathsome, embittered, consumed by hatred, trashing the memory of a great, much-loved broadcaster, blah blah. My line that 'I hated him and he hated me' was cut to: 'I hated him.' Warming to the task, the *Telegraph* stationed a photographer outside my house, to pap me bringing in the garbage bins. A couple of commercial TV news programs followed in the wake, pushing the same line.

To my astonishment, in this onslaught of character assassination the Murdoch papers were immeasurably helped by 2UE in the person of the Angry Ant, Steve Price, and by the Southern Cross network manager, Graham Mott. Price, still smarting at his demotion from breakfast, devoted half an hour of his program to savaging my 'bad taste and bad behaviour', and taking carefully selected calls from listeners who agreed. Knowing it would be leaked, Mott put out a memo to 2UE staff describing my conduct as 'disgraceful'. 'Mike has gone too far and his comments are despicable,' he wrote. It was one of 2UE's 'darkest moments'. To hammer home the point, he helpfully repeated most of his memo in an interview with the *Telegraph*, adding extravagantly that 'it's hatred like you see in the Middle East'. My job was on the line. I was living on borrowed time.[163]

Peter Fitz and my staff loyally backed me all the way. So did a lot of other 2UE people who disliked Zemanek and the hypocrisy surrounding his death. Seeking to cool things down, my agent, Sean Anderson, suggested that I should make some sort of apology on air, which I did. Without withdrawing a word I had said, I conceded that my timing had been unfortunately close to Zemanek's funeral.

Even today people occasionally ask if – with hindsight – I would have handled the Zemanek affair any differently. The answer is no.

The lasting effect on me, though, was a growing distaste for radio and the people who managed it. The audience support had been generous and encouraging, but I was becoming tired and bored with being on air, and fed up with having to suffer fools, be they radio executives or the dreary parade of politicians and barrow-pushers to be grilled on the latest shock horror. 'If I have to say just one more time that the transport minister's on the line I think I'll scream,' I told Morag at the time.

More and more I was just going through the motions, sometimes barely holding it together. Eventually, I gave up doing *Friday News Review*. The thing had become repetitive and dull, and when Howard lost the 2007 election to Kevin Rudd, I no longer had him and Lord Downer as targets for satire, a grievous blow. Despite the pleadings of 2UE management to keep it going, I had burned out on the comedy stuff. My heart was no longer in it. After thirty years on air, and now over sixty years of age, I was beginning to look for a light at the end of the radio tunnel – for a way out.

I was not, as it turned out, the only one considering his abdication.

24

You should write naval history

At the very end of the Finger Wharf in Woolloomooloo Bay, the two-storey apartment of John and Caroline Laws has drop-dead views of Sydney Harbour and the city. Warships come and go at the Navy's Fleet Base a stone's throw away. The interior is decorated in a classical European style, suggesting a palazzo in Venice, no expense spared. A garage below holds John's pared-back collection of cars. The actor Russell Crowe is his closest neighbour.

In early June 2007 he invited me for a drink. Unusually, he was despondent, and I recall that he looked weary. The lion in winter, I thought. We sat in his library, knocking back the inevitable bourbon and Coke and talking radio.

'I don't think I can do it anymore,' he told me glumly. 'I just don't think I have it in me. I don't want to go on.'

At first I could not think of a sensible response. He was normally so confident, so effortlessly in command. Now he seemed to be on the ropes. Like everyone, I had always assumed that John Laws was eternal, Methuselah of the microphone, that they would have to carry him out of the studio in a box.

I muttered some platitudes, but eventually put the question to him point-blank. 'Are you going to pull the pin?'

He shrugged with a wry smile. 'I might. We'll see.'

That was all I got from him, and I kept it to myself. On Monday, 25 June, he announced on his program that he was quitting, that he would retire 'in a few months'. The phone lines went nuclear. Flattering tributes showered down. 'We're going to be the poorer for your going,' said John Howard. 'I don't know how the airwaves of Sydney are going to survive without you,' said Kevin Rudd.[164]

Sydney battled along. In truth, 2UE was being beaten in the ratings by 2GB, month after month. The breakfast listeners Alan Jones had taken with him and those pushed in his direction by Steve Price were never coming back. They were now rusted on to 2GB, and they stayed around after nine am to listen to Hadley snarling his way through his Laws facsimile show.

Zemanek had debased the airwaves, but he was small fry compared to the Jones onslaught.

For many people his rubbish was compelling listening. Incendiary rabble-rousing had won the contest, as it so often does. John Laws and I could not and would not match it. At times the 2UE management would plead with me to 'get more right-wing', helpfully pointing me in the direction of ranting editorials or columns in the *Telegraph*, but I ignored them. John and I were caught between the devil and the deep blue sea. As long experience has shown, cities the size of Sydney or Melbourne can support only two successful talk radio stations: one commercial and one ABC. The available audience is simply not large enough to sustain a third. 2GB and ABC 702 held the lead in Sydney. 2UE struggled along in their wake, making barely any money, sometimes none.

John's last day on air at 2UE was Friday, 30 November 2007, a show that was strangely low-key. There was a flood of calls from listeners, more parting tributes from the great and good, and a package of recorded highlights compiled from down the years. He finished with a final version of his signature sign-off: 'I thank you for listening and I hope you can be kind to each other.' The entire station staff lined the corridor outside his studio for a round of applause, which he acknowledged with moist eyes, and then he was into the Rolls-Royce and away. 2UE threw him a farewell banquet lunch that day at Otto, his favourite restaurant near his apartment on the Finger Wharf, where speeches were made and much champagne was drunk towards sunset.

A few weeks later, a few of us enjoyed a smaller private lunch with him and his personal assistant, Jodee Borgo, also at Otto. We were well into it and flying high when a waiter, I think it was, came to our table and told us that Bob Rogers and Derryn Hinch were having lunch together at another restaurant on the wharf. John went to DEFCON 1. Two of his oldest foes! He sprang from his seat and marched towards them. Sensing trouble, I followed. I like Bob Rogers a great deal and I get on fine with Derryn, but John was ready to rip and tear. Their table was outdoors.

'You're a pair of despicable cunts!' John shouted at them.

Bob, always mild-mannered, fell back as if he had been shot. Derryn, combative as ever, returned fire with some choice one-liners of his own. Lunchers at other tables goggled, open-mouthed. I feared John was going to swing a punch, and put a restraining hand on his arm.

He shook it off. 'You're a failed alcoholic!' he bellowed at Derryn.

'And you're a successful one,' Hinch shot back.

There was more, along much the same lines, but eventually I managed to steer John back to our table, where he was cheerfully unrepentant. 'Fucking told 'em,' he grinned triumphantly. We called for another bottle of something. Inevitably, it was all over the newspapers the next day. On balance, I think the four of us enjoyed it a great deal.

'I thought it was wonderful, best lunch I've had in years,' Bob told the *Telegraph*.[165]

Me too. I wouldn't have missed it for quids.

✧

My fascination with Indonesia has never dimmed. In 2007 I accepted a proposal from a TV production company, Essential Media, to make a three-part documentary on the country, to be shown on SBS. It was the idea of Chris Hilton, the Essential Media boss. *A Reporter's Journey* was the title. I took three weeks' leave from radio. With a director, producer and camera crew, I visited some familiar haunts from my days as a correspondent, and travelled to some places I had never been. The idea was to examine the sometimes fraught relationship of our two countries and how this had changed over the years.

Although I had holidayed in Bali often, I had not been back to Jakarta since I left in 1970. It's a peculiar notion I have – that to return to the past is to be disappointed. But the changes were extraordinary. When I lived there the city had just one traffic light and barely any traffic, apart from the teeming hordes of *becak* drivers. Jalan Thamrin, the long boulevard that runs south from Sukarno's National Monument, was lined, then, with crumbling Dutch colonial buildings and the rusting steel skeletons of unfinished skyscrapers. The place stank of poverty and decay. I returned to find a throbbing megalopolis of soaring glass towers ablaze with garish neon, with world-beating traffic jams. An enormous shopping plaza and Hyatt hotel stood on the site of the rank and dingy little press office where I had to submit my copy for army censorship.

More striking than the architecture was the politics. You would have been the laughing stock of any diplomatic cocktail party in the 1960s had you suggested that Indonesia might one day become a democracy. Now, after much agony and for all its flaws, it is arguably the most genuinely democratic republic in South-East Asia. That is no small achievement.

For one film sequence we got the old band back together again. Escape was still going. Johan, the cheeky little bass player, was dead, and two of the other guys had vanished, but Bram Titaley, the lead guitarist, was still around and still playing. We fell on each other like long-lost brothers. I bought him a new guitar and he arranged a gig at a downtown nightclub, where we sang a couple of the old Creedence and Stones songs from back in the day. It felt extraordinarily good, as if I had never left.

My Bahasa Indonesia was holding up, and getting better by the day. It came in handy. Banda Aceh is a provincial capital on the far north-west tip of Indonesia, about three hours' flying time from Jakarta but in every other way a couple of centuries distant. Not a lot of English is spoken there, and its people are the most devoutly Muslim in the country, hardline Islamic conservatives. They tend to regard the infidel with some suspicion, if not outright contempt. Sharia law rules. Alcohol is banned.

As we were filming outside Banda Aceh's beautiful Grand Mosque, getting shots of the worshippers going to Friday prayers, I was approached by a bent and wizened old man wearing the white cap that denotes a Haji, a Mecca pilgrim. He fixed me with a gleaming eye and what I took for a scowl. Trouble here, I thought. He's going to make a scene.

Quite the opposite. He grabbed me warmly by the hand and flashed a gap-toothed smile. '*Kita semua bersaudara*,' he said – we are all brothers.

We had a long chat. Aceh province had been devastated by the catastrophic Boxing Day tsunami of 2004, with entire coastal villages swept away and nearly 200,000 people killed. He wanted to thank the foreigners – the *orang asing* – who had come to the city's aid, and we were the first he had seen.

Being there was moving. Three years later there were still signs of the devastation everywhere. One young man I met, a schoolteacher, was the only survivor of an extended family of thirteen. 'It was the will of Allah,' he told me. I didn't argue the point.

Paul Keating gave me a terrific interview for the program, and so did the long-serving former Indonesian foreign minister, Ali Alatas, and a former president, Gus Dur. To my surprise, we also secured a talk with that nasty little Islamic fascist Abu Bakar Bashir, watched over by a glowering band of young thugs in black T-shirts. Barking mad, Bashir explained that the Bali bombing had been triggered by the CIA from an American submarine. At Kerobokan prison near Denpasar we were allowed to interview poor, wretched Scott Rush, then aged twenty-two and sentenced to death as one of the Bali Nine drug mules. Despite all the denials, I am convinced, to this day, that the Australian Federal Police handed those kids to the Indonesians as a favour, well knowing they could face a firing squad.[166]

A Reporter's Journey went out on SBS in three one-hour episodes early in 2008, well received. I had loved doing the thing, for the intellectual stretch and the sheer delight of getting out of a studio and onto the ground for some old-fashioned reporting. Then it was back to the grind of breakfast radio.

✧

With Peter Fitz gone, I had some new on-air partners to play with. Ken Sutcliffe, then the Nine Network's chief sports commentator, joined me for a bit. So did Ellen Fanning, formerly of ABC Radio and *60 Minutes*. They were both terrific. But eventually we settled for Sandy Aloisi, who was ready for a shot at a full-time show. She, too, was a delight to work with.

But boredom was still gnawing at me. I tried my best to conceal it. I had people working hard for me, loyally and well, and I owed it to them – and to the wider radio station – to keep firing my best shots and earn my pay. At least the federal government was talking to us again. John Howard and his ministers had infinitely preferred appearing on air with Jones, who could be relied on to blow smoke up their backsides. Kevin Rudd's new Labor government had to live with the Parrot, but made little secret of their dislike for him. The tables had turned. Rudd had been a regular with me while in opposition, and he continued as prime minister. Kevin from Queensland was there to help.

Conventional wisdom now has it that Rudd was a petulant autocrat, a neurotic workaholic whose chaotic, impulsive rule drove his staff and his cabinet ministers nuts. If that was true, I was never in a position to see it. Indeed, I confess I rather liked him, and I still do. We got on well, even given that we were both using each other, as journalists and politicians do.

Privately, he occasionally shared his political and policy insights with me, such as they were. I had returned the favour when he was opposition leader, grandly assuring him over a tête-à-tête dinner at an Italian restaurant that he would never become prime minister. 'You're too cerebral and too Queensland,' I told him, with all the lofty authority I could muster. He'd had a bad day, very publicly bungling the names of a couple of Sydney rugby league stars and their club, for which he had been pilloried on talkback radio. 'Sydney won't vote for you if you do that again,' I said. He appeared chastened.

I shudder to think of it now. Mostly he is kind enough not to remind me of that particular piece of smartarsery, but I apologise for it every time I see him.

Julia Gillard was another frequent interview guest as Rudd's deputy and Minister for Almost Everything, as she was in the early days. Mostly she would do it on the phone from Canberra or Melbourne, but she came to the studio twice for a live chat. The first time I met her in the flesh I was so carried away that I flung an arm around her and gave her a friendly peck on the cheek, not something I would usually do to a deputy prime minister. It was impulsive and impertinent, but she took it in her stride, which was handsome of her.

In private, I found her warm and funny, with a delightful lilting laugh. She sparkled. Somehow, though, she could never convey that warmth in her media appearances. She came across as stilted and wooden, uttering every syllable as if she was nervous of putting a foot wrong. She sounded like a newly appointed private-school headmistress at speech night. No amount of media coaching seemed to help. Some people have easy communication skills, and others just don't and never really will. If anything, it got worse when she became prime minister. Eventually the electorate stopped listening to her. But the misogynist attacks upon her were gutter filth, a dark stain on our national life.

Tony Abbott and I were civil to each other, but no more. I despised his reactionary politics and his blatant opportunism, sharing Paul Keating's oft-quoted view that he was the Liberals' 'resident nutter'. Bob Carr always maintained that Abbott was not a Liberal at all but an anachronistic hangover from the ultra-right Catholic politics of B. A. Santamaria's National Civic Council and the DLP. He once asked me to stop calling him 'the Mad Monk' in my *Herald* column. I did for a while, but it was simply too apt to pass up forever.

Intellectually shallow and without coherent policy ambitions, devious and hypocritical, Abbott was, and remains, a destructive force in Australian political life. Even his vaunted 'achievements' in government were essentially negative: stopping the boats, axing the mining tax and scrapping the emissions trading scheme that he and his rebarbative chief of staff, Peta Credlin, deviously portrayed as 'Labor's carbon tax'. Like some stellar black hole, he devoured light.

No doubt it was a political success of sorts to bring down the Rudd and Gillard Labor governments, but to wreck your own prime ministership between elections is a rare and spectacular achievement. It was always all about Tony, but in the end he failed even that ambition.

Other Liberals were easier to deal with. Joe Hockey, a genial figure, pleaded with me to stop writing nice things about him: it was getting him into trouble with his colleagues. Amanda Vanstone's politics were deplorable, but she never backed down from a scrap in an interview and gave as good as she got. She had the rare courage to publicly take on Alan Jones, who called her 'that woman' and kept demanding that she be sacked.

Bob Brown, the Greens' leader, was a genuinely impressive figure. He had the courage of his convictions and the intellectual and moral depth to argue them in a voice of quiet but tenacious reason. I particularly admired him for heckling George W. Bush's speech to the Australian parliament in 2003, a bold act in defiance of the supine grovel all around him. If we ever get to grips with climate change in Australia, history will judge Bob as an ethical visionary. He did even the little things well: most politicians, of all parties, swan about in Commonwealth cars, attended by their minders. Bob turned up to a studio interview with me at 2UE alone and returned to the city by train.

✧

Writing the *Herald* column was helping keep me sane. It was gratifying when people stopped me in the street to say that it was the first thing they read of a Saturday morning, but distressing to watch the paper's consistent decline as the cost-cutting Fairfax management rid itself of some of the best journalists and photographers in the land while pushing the preposterous mantra that 'good journalism' would still flourish at the *Herald*. It was like suggesting you could keep a good hospital going by sacking more doctors and nurses. At times I felt pangs of guilt that I still had a well-paid place while other journalists with kids and mortgages were contemplating a dismal future. Privately, I eased my conscience by never requesting a pay rise – it struck me as indecent to screw for more money when my colleagues had their backs to the wall. These scruples certainly never troubled the upper echelons at Fairfax: money was still sloshing around the executive suite.

My first breach with the paper came in August 2008, when Fairfax journalists in New South Wales and Victoria went on strike to protest yet another round of savage cost-cutting, with the planned loss of 550 jobs. There were picket lines outside the Fairfax building in Sydney. On air that morning I said that I had written my column for the week but would not be filing it. I had been a member of the journalists' union – now the Media, Entertainment and Arts Alliance – since my cadetship at the ABC, and I was not going to betray it. I would not cross the picket lines, either literally or metaphorically. I would not scab.

When I got off air at nine o'clock, there was a phone call from one of the Fairfax editorial grand pooh-bahs, a nonentity whose name I have forgotten but who, like so many of his ilk, had risen without trace or talent. Spluttering with rage, he told me I was sacked forthwith. Not bothering to object, I hung up in his ear.

Pleasingly, there was a torrent of protest from readers, many of whom cancelled their subscriptions. Richard Glover, then doing drive at ABC 702 and also writing for the *Herald*, boldly told the ABC's *Media Watch* that my sacking was outrageous, and that, if necessary, he too would down tools on his day to file. Peter FitzSimons made a private appeal to the new Fairfax chief executive. But I was out, and I stayed out for more than a year, until a new editor-in-chief, Peter Fray, took me back on board.

Being a fine journalist, a vigorous and respected editor with a bold vision for the *Herald*'s future and a good bloke to boot, naturally Fray did not survive the ongoing Fairfax slaughter. He was purged in 2012 in yet another round of bloodletting. Slowly but surely, Granny was cutting her own throat.

✧

For all its professional upheaval, 2008 ended beautifully. On 22 October, Morag gave birth to our son, Lachlan. We barely made it to the hospital on time, well before dawn.

'When's the baby coming?' I asked the midwife as they bundled Morag onto a bed.

'Now!' she said.

And so he did, beating the hastily summoned obstetrician to the punch by about half an hour. I cut the umbilical cord, a procedure newly allowed to fathers since the birth of my first two. There is no more beautiful sight in all the world than a mother clutching a newborn baby to her breast for the first time.

That morning passed in a blur. Lachlan was strong and healthy. A news crew from Channel 7 turned up to film the happy family, including the elderly father at the creaky old age of sixty-two. The weather was foul, a fierce gale driving the rain in horizontal sheets across the hospital car park. My mother was in Brisbane, but Morag's mother, Elizabeth, arrived, ecstatic. Flowers appeared by the truckload.

When Morag had confirmed she was pregnant I was gobsmacked. Logic had told me it was inevitable, but I had not prepared myself for the reality of fatherhood again. My other two children were now adults themselves, heading for their thirties. Alex was the proud mother of my grandson Jack, a beautiful little boy. For a while I was discombobulated, unsure of myself, even selfishly resentful that my life was about to be overturned. I was supposed to be heading for my sunset years. Instead, the laid-back beach existence I had planned would be gone, lost in sleepless nights of vomit and dirty nappies and dribbly noses. Once again there would be all the paraphernalia of babyhood, of cots and strollers and car capsules and regiments of stuffed toys. At this age, could I meet the demands of fatherhood for a third time, of nurturing an infant all over again?

The answer was yes. And joyously so. To my amazement taking care of our new baby brought me intense happiness. And it gets better as he grows older. I am now in my seventies, and to watch him grow up is a privilege and a pleasure beyond all imagination. With Morag working grindingly long hours, I'm the parent who cuts his school lunch, washes his clothes, delivers him to the playground, and takes him to and from swimming lessons, soccer training and cricket practice. I can give Lachlan more attention and dad time than I was ever able to offer my first two kids – about which I feel inevitable pangs of guilt.

✧

Freed from the burden of a weekly deadline for the column, I began to think more seriously of an idea that had been slumbering at the back of my mind for years. All my life I had been reading naval history and stories of sailors and the sea, both fact and fiction. Now, I thought, I might have a go at writing a book myself.

Almost everything naval I had read was British, beginning of course with *The Cruel Sea* back in primary school. That had led me to an enduring fascination with the Royal Navy, which had pretty much ruled the waves since the time of Henry VIII and created the mightiest empire the world would ever know. I was full bottle on the Napoleonic wars at sea: the battles, the strategy and tactics, the fleets and ships, and the men who sailed them. The greatest naval sailor of all, Horatio Nelson, the victor of Trafalgar, is a study in himself, and I went for it.

The son of a humble Norfolk parson, Nelson very deliberately set sail on a course for personal glory, a concept alien to modern ears but which was real, desirable and attainable for a fighting seaman in Georgian Britain. 'My greatest happiness is to serve my gracious King and Country and I am envious only of glory; for if it be a sin to covet glory I am the most offending soul alive,' he wrote to his lover Emma Hamilton.

More books have been written about Nelson than any other Englishman, even Winston Churchill, and I think I have most of them on my bookshelves, standing in a line nearly two metres long. A genius with human flaws, Nelson is a hero of mine. Further along the shelves are the Horatio Hornblower novels of C. S. Forester.

With the two Horatios under my belt I got more modern, moving forward to the great sea fights of the two world wars, especially the Battle of Jutland in 1916 and Britain's life-and-death struggle against Hitler's U-boats in the Battle of the Atlantic from 1939. I was hardly conscious of it, but all the time I was absorbing maritime lore and language and custom and practice, stowing this knowledge away until I might need it on some literary voyage of my own.

My overarching inspiration, though, was the British historical novelist Patrick O'Brian, a colossus of twentieth-century fiction. From 1969 until his death in 2000, O'Brian wrote twenty novels of the life and times of Jack Aubrey, a fighting captain of the Georgian era, and his shipmate Stephen Maturin, a surgeon, scientist and intelligence agent. They are a work of genius, a dazzling amalgam of heroic swashbuckle and learned exposition of the history, society and science of the early-nineteenth-century world. I devoured them more or less as they appeared, then read them all again in chronological order, a task that took a year. If I could just write one-hundredth as well as O'Brian, I told myself . . . but about what?

That was resolved for me by a friend, James Goldrick, an Australian naval officer. We had met when he contacted me about something in the *Herald* column. Lunch followed and we hit it off straightaway. Twelve years younger than me, James is a remarkable combination of sailor and scholar. He is a practical seaman, a studious academic and a much-published naval historian. The son of a naval officer, he joined the Royal Australian Navy as a boy of fifteen in 1974. As a specialist in surface and anti-submarine warfare, over a career of thirty-eight years at sea and ashore, he held some of the Navy's most prestigious and challenging commands, including two tours as captain of the frigate HMAS *Sydney*. In 2002 he commanded the multinational naval taskforce of American, Australian and British ships in the Persian Gulf, which enforced UN sanctions on Iraq. Appropriately, he did two spells as commandant of ADFA, the Australian Defence Force Academy, retiring as a rear admiral in 2012. His major book, *The King's Ships Were at Sea*, is acknowledged as the foremost study of the opening years of World War I.[167] Bristling with honorary degrees and literary awards from here, there and everywhere, James has a global reputation of the first rank. And like almost every naval officer I have ever met, he is a hugely convivial companion as the port is passed around at a mess dinner. I have a cheerful if hazy memory of a particularly splendid feast in *Sydney*'s wardroom.

'You should write about Australian naval history,' he said to me one day.

'But there isn't much of it,' I replied airily.

This was one of the stupidest remarks I have ever made.

James fixed me with a glittering eye, like Samuel Taylor Coleridge's Ancient Mariner. 'I think you'll find there's quite a lot,' he said.

Indeed. The story of the growth of Australian sea power, from its almost comical, Gilbert and Sullivan beginnings in the colonial navies pre-federation, is a rich and fascinating tapestry. Best of all, as I began to look around, I found the field wide open. There were the official naval histories of the two world wars, mighty tomes packed with minute detail, but they were not exactly bedtime reading. Some experts, both professional and amateur, had written valuable histories for the specialist reader. There were edited collections of essays and the like, and very good ones too. A few retired captains and admirals had churned out memoirs of varying quality, often worthy but dull. But very few writers had ventured where I hoped to go, which was to do popular, accessible history that would work for both the professional sailor and the lay reader looking for a rollicking yarn. I'd like it to spank along like Patrick O'Brian, I kept telling myself.

There was one problem: I had never done anything remotely like it. Nor did I know if I could. The *Herald* column each week ran out at about 1200 words. A book, properly done, would be at least 200,000 words and possibly more, a daunting undertaking. I began to get cold feet.

At which point, enter Fitz. 'Of course you can do it!' he breezed. 'Just sit down and start typing. Go for it!'

As ever, he radiated energy, conviction and encouragement. I figured that if he could write and sell books, I could too. To make sure, I also put my doubts to Tom Keneally when I bumped into him at some party. 'Are there any tricks I ought to know about this book-writing business?' I asked.

Tom allowed himself one of his leprechaun chuckles. 'I generally begin at the beginning and keep going until it's finished,' he wheezed.

Casting around for a topic, I settled on HMAS *Perth*, a light cruiser of World War II. I recalled hearing something of her story when I was at school. Now, when I went back to it, I realised what a tale it was. Built in Britain and originally commissioned into the Royal Navy as HMS *Amphion*, she was transferred to the Royal Australian Navy and renamed *Perth* in 1939. She was in the Caribbean on her way to Australia when war was declared. After some uneventful plodding to and fro in Australian waters, she was sent to the Mediterranean at the end of 1940 to fight in the disastrous battles for Greece and Crete. In May 1941, during the evacuation of Crete, she was hit by a bomb, which killed four of her sailors and nine soldiers.

After the fall of Singapore in February 1942, *Perth* narrowly survived a disastrous Allied defeat at the Battle of the Java Sea. The Japanese got her a few days later. In a shattering midnight encounter she and an American cruiser were torpedoed and sunk by an overwhelming enemy force of cruisers and destroyers. Of the 681 souls on board, 353 were killed in the battle, including her legendary captain. All but four of the 328 survivors became prisoners of war, mostly on the infamous Burma–Siam Railway. Only 218 men returned home to Australia at war's end.

It was a story well worth telling. Peter introduced me to his publisher, and over lunch we stitched up a deal. Lunch with my publisher! The phrase had a magic ring to it. I felt like Graham Greene or Hemingway.

As ever, I immediately got that sinking feeling: I was committed, signing my life away with no way out. All I could do was go forward. It would turn out to be one of the happiest decisions of my career.

Slowly at first, but with quickening pace, I began to gather the threads together. There were perhaps twenty or thirty of the ship's survivors still alive and scattered around Australia, all members of the HMAS *Perth* Association, all in their late eighties or early nineties. I set out to contact as many as I could. Some were fit and alert, others were fading away. There were relatives, too: wives, sons and daughters who might have stories to tell, or maybe letters and diaries stored away in long-forgotten boxes in the garage. I hoped they would be willing to talk to me, to allow me to intrude upon their families and their lives. Perhaps the memories might be too painful.

I need not have worried. Without exception, I was received with open-hearted offers of help and hospitality. It was humbling and inspiring. A few books had been written about the ship and her crew before, but not for many years, and not on the scale I was proposing. They were also out of print. People liked the idea of a new one, and were eager for the story to be put before a new generation of readers.

I was about to meet and learn from some truly great Australians, men and women of our finest generation, quietly heroic figures who had endured the Great Depression in childhood and the horrors and fears of war as they came to adulthood.

On the first Thursday of every month, Frank McGovern and Gavin Campbell got together for a few beers and a sandwich lunch at the Bowlers' Club in central Sydney. They had been doing it for more years than they could remember, just staying in touch. Frank had been a twenty-two-year-old able seaman when *Perth* was sunk. Gavin, an officer with the single gold stripe of a sub-lieutenant, had newly turned twenty-one. Each had survived the Japanese atrocities of the railway, even as their mates died or were murdered around them, and had made it back home to rebuild their lives in peacetime.

On the face of it, they were very different young men, in almost every way. Frank – slight and wiry – was a Catholic kid raised in what was then the working-class, inner-Sydney suburb of Paddington. Gavin – tall, lanky and athletic – came from Victoria's Western District, and had been expensively educated at Scotch College in Melbourne before entering the Naval College at Jervis Bay. In the ship – sailor and officer, lower deck and wardroom – they had not known each other. Their mateship, an unbreakable bond, was forged later, in the shared experience of three years of captivity, and the struggle to return to a normal existence after the war.

They welcomed me to one of their Thursday get-togethers. I recall being a little nervous, concerned that if I somehow struck the wrong note they might not want to cooperate, and would clam up. I felt I was on delicate ground. If I was to write this book, I would eventually have to awaken their darkest, most painful memories. I would be probing their souls. What right did I have to do that? None at all, really. Again, my apprehension was unfounded. From that first meeting they opened their minds and their hearts with candour and generosity. And to the delight of the novice author, both men had an extraordinary recall of those times so many years ago. Beyond doubt, they were the bravest men I have met.

Frank's elder brother Vince went down with the ship. Frank himself floated in the Sunda Strait for some hours, until he was hauled on board a Japanese destroyer and eventually packed off to the Changi PoW camp in Singapore. From there he was sent to work on the railway for two years, until in 1944 he and hundreds of other Australian and British prisoners were crammed on board one of what they called the hell ships, to be transported to Japan for slave labour. That ship, the *Rakuyo Maru*, was torpedoed and sunk in the South China Sea by an American submarine. Rescued again by the Japanese navy, Frank then survived the cruelties of imprisonment, hunger and hard labour in the snows of the Japanese winter, only to be badly hurt and very nearly killed in the American fire-bombing of Tokyo. He was still in Japan when the war ended.

Gavin was blown over *Perth*'s side by the fourth and final torpedo, which hit the ship shortly after midnight. Coming to his senses in the water, struggling to inflate his Mae West lifejacket in the dark, he realised that one of his legs was broken. In waves of pain, he scrambled on board a raft, where a sailor bound the leg with make-shift splints of wood from a packing case. Cast ashore on the west coast of Java, Gavin and another sailor, Denny Maher, resolved to walk south, away from the advancing Japanese. Maher fashioned a rough pair of crutches for Gavin from the branches of a tree. For three weeks they trudged along a rough coastal road, Gavin hobbling in agony. Still smeared with stinking fuel oil from the ship, red-raw from sunburn, tormented by mosquitoes, they urged each other on. When they could, they cadged a little food from villagers and drank from puddles. The Japanese eventually found them and they, too, were despatched to the railway, where – by chance – Gavin encountered his elder brother Ian, an army signaller. Gavin was still in Thailand when the war ended. Denny Maher died in the torpedoing of the *Rakuyo Maru*.

I recorded their stories in long conversations over several weeks, our mutual trust growing. There were painful moments, but they surmounted them with courage. Frank broke down just once, at the memory of his dead big brother. The most striking characteristic of each man was humility. They had done extraordinary things and had suffered greatly, but never was there a hint of bragging or chest-thumping heroics. They simply wanted the truth told, as they had known it, and in honour of the memory of their dead shipmates. They spoke matter-of-factly and sometimes with flashes of humour. Frank enjoyed a hearty chuckle. Gavin was wry and laconic. I had expected bitterness, even hatred, for their Japanese tormentors but there was none. They had long recognised the corrosive nature of hate and had surmounted it to find serenity in old age. They gave me their all – including that most priceless gift, their friendship. When Gavin died in 2015 I was honoured beyond measure when his wife, Sue, asked me to deliver the eulogy at his funeral.

As I wrote these words you are reading now, I was struck by an exquisite coincidence. I realised it was 1 October 2017, Frank's ninety-eighth birthday. I rang him at his home in Randwick and found him as cheerful as ever.

'I'm all right, mate. Got a bugger of a cold, though.'

'We need you around for a few more years yet, Frank. I want to have a drink at your one hundredth.'

'I'll be there, mate. I'll be there.'

✧

The Reading Room at the Australian War Memorial in Canberra is in the bowels of the building at the rear, a large, semi-circular space pleasantly lit by sunlight streaming through high windows. There are individual desks to work at, and the silence is complete. You must check your bags before you enter, and no pens are allowed, only pencils. Helpful staff speak in whispers to bring out what you need.

It is a delightful place to work, and not a little awe-inspiring. There you can touch and hold the original letters, postcards, diaries, ships' logs, memoirs and other artefacts of all our wars, the very fabric of history itself meticulously preserved in labelled manila folders. For a historian, it is a powerful thing to recognise that you are reading an original letter written by a sailor at sea for his family half a century ago and more. I love being there.

But the memorial collection is just one of the research resources available. Tentatively, I began to discover the extraordinary possibilities of the internet. Trove, the search engine hosted by the National Library, is an infinite pool of knowledge and information, a recognised world-beater in its field. The digitised newspaper archive alone is a national treasure: it allows you to get at, search and download more than 10 million pages of 700 newspapers published between 1803 and 1954. And all for free. Beyond that, there are museums, archives and resources of naval history around the planet, instantly available to a searching author at the move of a mouse.

As news got around that I was on the job, more and more of *Perth*'s veterans and their families came forward to offer their help. At times it was like striking gold. A Sydney bloke named George Hatfield rang me out of the blue to say he had 'a bit of Dad's stuff stored away', and would I like to see it. I would. It turned out to be the diaries of one of the ship's petty officers, beautifully written in priceless detail. Petty Officer Hatfield had died in the ship on that fateful night, before his son was born. In many of the families I met, the grief of loss was still real and raw. Yet I was never turned away, only welcomed. As I would eventually write in the foreword, this would be 'their story of life and death, love and duty, war and remembrance'.

I had no idea if I was actually up to the job, but I dived in with growing pleasure, like hitting wave after wave at an empty beach on a hot summer's day. Without exaggeration, researching the book on *Perth* changed my life. In my early sixties I had found an exciting new sea to sail. Now all I had to do was cast off, ring down to the engine room for full ahead, and start writing. I took Tom Keneally's advice and began at the beginning.

There was, however, the small matter of the radio show. I had to keep at it. Certainly there was enough news around. In 2009, despite their personal animosity, Kevin Rudd and his treasurer, Wayne Swan, had successfully steered Australia out of the global financial crisis. The year began in catastrophe, though, with the Black Saturday bushfires that swept through much of Victoria and killed 173 people. In Afghanistan, the unwinnable war went on, with the Australian people largely shielded from its contortions. Ironclad media management by the Department of Defence ensured that those few news organisations interested in covering Australia's role in the war were kept on a tight leash, away from the action and any chance of unfavourable stories. It was like Vietnam all over again, only worse. Journalists who did go to cover the Australians found themselves being corralled inside fortified bases or escorted on bus trips by army PR officers. 'Having military personnel trying to sell stories about schools or bridges or hospitals, when the real story is out . . . with the infantry patrols . . . generates major frustrations,' wrote Ian McPhedran, an experienced war correspondent.[168] But most news outfits were not interested. The war did not rate. Commercial TV stations, and often the ABC as well, were idly content to shovel out whatever official footage they were offered.

I almost convinced 2UE to let me go, and I flew down to Canberra for a talk with the chief of the Defence Force, Air Chief Marshal Angus Houston. He was optimistic about the progress of the war, with much talk about sweeping up the Taliban here and al-Qaeda there, and securing this province and that. I like Angus. He is one of the most accomplished defence chiefs we have had, upright and honourable, and a man of great charm with it. He told me once that the worst part of his job was being woken in the morning to hear of another Australian death in action, something he dreaded. He greatly encouraged me in writing the *Perth* book. But in this case he was spinning me the official line, as was his duty.

I could cop it no longer. Politely, I stopped him mid-flight. 'That's exactly what the Russians used to say about Afghanistan, and the British before them,' I suggested. 'Haven't we learned a thing from history?'

He had the grace to look abashed. And in the end I didn't go. 2UE would not cough up the big bucks for an insurance policy. At any rate, no doubt I would have simply been given pep talks from some of the Australian and American military brass, been feted in an officer's mess somewhere and allowed to pose in a fancy flak jacket.

In that winter of 2009 I was beginning to think I wouldn't make it through to Christmas and the end of my contract. Along the way, Fairfax had bought 2UE again and was mismanaging the joint with its customary incompetence. The book was consuming all my professional interest and energies, and at home I was enjoying the delights of a little boy recognising his parents for the first time. The radio program was like an anvil around my neck, dragging me down.

It was beginning to show, too. The new 2UE station manager, Tim McDermott, called me into his office one day. Unusually in that job, McDermott was a no-nonsense straight shooter who actually knew how to run a radio station, even if Fairfax did not. What he had to say quite blew me away.

'Would you like to quit?'

I stared at him, gobsmacked. My contract had three or four months to run.

'It's not working for you, and it's not working for us,' he said.

It was a candid, honest assessment and I didn't quibble. I was pulling in a lot of money; with John Laws gone, I would have been the highest-paid performing monkey in the Fairfax circus. But I was burned-out and not delivering the ratings they needed.

I recall a wave of both relief and excitement washing over me. I was elated. It was the Great Escape from *Stalag Luft III*! Then it was tempered by concern for the people who worked for me and with me, and what might happen to them. I had a duty to try to protect their jobs if I could, and I put that to Tim, who understood. He promised me they would be looked after, and in the end he was as good as his word.

Morag would have supported me in any decision I had taken – or not taken – but she knew the strain I was under better than anyone. Getting out from under daily radio would be wonderful for our life together, for our new family. With three of journalism's Walkley Awards to her name, her career as a producer at *Four Corners* was heading for the heights. She could concentrate on that while I could be the stay-at-home dad – an unaccustomed role, to be sure, but one I could look forward to with relish. She was as excited as I was.

My last show would be a month away. To my astonishment, Brian McCarthy, the Fairfax Chief Executive, agreed to pay out the remaining three months of my contract, but on one condition: that I go back to the *Herald*.

We had a deal.

PART 5

25

People like you started World War II

My last day on air. Friday, 18 September 2009. In the chaos of my study at home there is a disc or a thumb drive with a recording of that final show.

But I don't really want to listen to it again. Or not yet, anyway. Perhaps not ever. For as much as I wanted to get out of radio for a new life, it was gut-wrenching to actually do the deed. I was bringing down the curtain on thirty years of a job I had been privileged to have, had once loved and which had taken me to extraordinary heights.

That morning passed in a blur; my colleagues carried me through it. A slate of VIPs came on air to say farewell, including Kevin Rudd. As always on those occasions, the calls were prearranged by the producers. Prime ministers rarely appear spontaneously. The best, the nicest, the most touching calls were from long-time listeners, some of whom had loyally followed me around for decades. They had supported me often when I had needed it most and I felt more than a pang of guilt at deserting them. Occasionally these days I meet one of them in the street. It is warming when they stop to say hello.

Towards the end of the show I nearly lost it when I looked through the studio window to see my family watching. I had been on radio all Alex and James's lives. For as long as they could remember, that was what Dad did. It was through radio that I had met Morag. She was holding Lachlan. I had not expected to see them, but they were there in support, showing their love. It was almost unbearably poignant.

Somehow I made it through. Alex Smith had compiled a package of some of my best stuff – and some of my worst – and we played that at the end. The pips for nine o'clock came up, the red On Air light went off, and that was it. Done, finis. The 2UE staff lined the corridor outside the studio to applaud me back to my office. I think I got a bit teary then, but that too might be faulty memory. I do remember thinking, in a sudden exciting flash, that I would never need to read the *Daily Telegraph* again, and I never have.

Somewhere along the way there was a lunch and speeches, and Tim McDermott gave me a farewell gift: a gold-and-green Wallaby jersey, signed by the players of 2009, mounted and framed. It has a silver plaque which reads:

Presented to
MIKE CARLTON
In recognition of your outstanding contribution to
RADIO 2UE
January 1998 – September 2009

That frame is one of the few tangible reminders I have of the radio years. Somewhere I have some audiotapes and videotapes, cassettes and compact discs of stuff I did, collected haphazardly. Evanescent, the *Friday News Review* scripts have vanished into cyberspace. The radio awards I won are in a cardboard box in a dusty storeroom.

This is not to turn my back on what I did on air, to reject that past. I am proud of a fair deal of it, not least because it informed and entertained people in two great cities for years, which is a rare opportunity to have had, and a responsibility I did my best to discharge honestly. No one bought my opinions, or my silence. I sought to speak truth to power when I could, full speed ahead and damn the torpedoes, but I was never so foolish or arrogant to believe that I could make or unmake political careers or governments. Occasionally the interviews I did or the stories I covered made lives better in communities or for individuals. At other moments they allowed the voiceless or the poor or the suffering to tell their story.

So often it was exhilarating, exciting. The adrenaline rush of scooping a hot political interview or chasing breaking news was a heady drug, one that gave me wings time and again. And broadcasting – television and radio – had taken me to places and introduced me to people and ideas and knowledge beyond even the wildest imaginings of a teenage boy listening to a transistor radio in his bedroom.

In that, I had the stalwart support of so many creative men and women who carried me along and up. They know who they are, and I hope they know that I am grateful to them. Sometimes it seemed we climbed mountains. But those mountains, now, are A. E. Housman's blue remembered hills, distant in a land of lost content.

✧

Gradually, life began to return to something approaching normal. For as long as I could remember my body clock had woken me at three am, seconds before the alarm went off. It kept doing that for a good while – sometimes it still does – but now I had the sensuous luxury of rolling over and going back to sleep.

More to the point, Morag and I could reshape our lives. She had put her career on hold to have Lachlan. My liberation meant we could swap roles. I would be the parent at home caring for the baby while she returned to the ABC. Cooking was no problem – I fancied my abilities in the kitchen – but the arcane mysteries of the washing machine took some study, a task that remains incomplete. Ironing was and is utterly beyond me.

Juggling my time, I could get back into the water for some recreation and throw myself into writing the *Perth* book – or *Cruiser*, as I had begun to call it. Beginning slowly, I found myself picking up speed and fluency, the words sometimes dashing onto the screen. At other times every sentence could be hard labour, to be jigged and fiddled. Checking and cross-checking the facts was the most time-consuming part, but it had to be done. I was honour-bound to get it right for those whose stories I was telling. Readers of naval history are a knowledgeable, discriminating audience, and they do not suffer error gladly. They politely but insistently let you know where you went wrong, as they have every right to do. I was anxious not to be caught out. In the end, they got me on two small but unarguable points, a fair cop. I had given steam catapults to the Japanese aircraft carriers which raided Pearl Harbor – they were actually a post-war British invention – and I had carelessly put Jamaica south of the equator, not north.

Peter FitzSimons launched *Cruiser* for me, 706 pages in hardback. It arrived in the bookstores in the spring of 2010 and the reviews were good. After a slow start, it took off around the naval community, and I was on the way. Professional sailors, from admirals to able seamen, began to write to say that I had 'got it right', and the word went around the grapevine. All those years of reading naval history and fiction had been worth it.

Most gratifying of all was the unstinting approval of the *Perth* survivors and the families of those who had not made it back. 'Dad never spoke of it much,' they would often tell me. 'We had no idea what he went through.' Other relatives would write to ask if I could find out how grandpa or a much-loved older brother had died, and frequently I was able to tell them. For many the wounds were still raw, but they told me that the book had brought some healing.

With *Cruiser* a success, my publisher wanted another one and asked me to choose a topic. The centenary of World War I was coming up and, with it, Australia's first victory at sea. Over the years there had been a fair bit written about the hunt for the German raider *Emden*, a little cruiser which had played havoc with Allied shipping in the Indian Ocean in 1914. After an epic chase she was caught and destroyed by the Australian cruiser *Sydney*, but the story had not been touched by an Australian author. I grabbed it with both hands. There were no survivors to interview but there were families on both sides, and an absolute goldmine of Australian, German and British books and records and documents to explore. Ever helpful, James Goldrick introduced me to one of his far-flung friends, Henning Bess, a retired rear admiral of the German Navy and the guiding light of *Die Emdenfamilie*, a thriving association of the descendants. Henning was magnificent. Nothing was too much trouble. In turn, occasionally I unearthed facts that he was unaware of.

First Victory came out in 2013, and this time – with the Navy's enthusiastic support – we launched it on the flight deck of the frigate HMAS *Sydney*, the fourth ship to bear the name. Again the book took off. Henning, naturally nervous about the portrayal of his countrymen, was delighted. I had been scrupulously fair, he said.

With two books under my belt, I could now legitimately claim to be a naval historian. Invitations to speak at naval wardroom dinners, and library and bookseller gatherings piled in, to my delight. I was thrilled beyond measure when *First Victory* won the 2014 NSW Premier's Award for Australian History.

Late in years, heading for the age of seventy, I had found a new career. Almost a vocation. It was a heady feeling, like being born again. But my life was about to take a surprising, dismal turn.

✧

In Arabic, *al-Nakbah* means the disaster or the catastrophe. On 15 May each year the people of Palestine commemorate Nakba Day, recalling the war of 1948, in which the new state of Israel drove 720,000 Palestinians from their homes and emptied or destroyed some 400 Arab towns and villages. There are rallies and strikes in the Occupied Territories of Gaza and the West Bank and, more muted, in Israel itself. Sometimes they are peaceable, sometimes they erupt into violence.

On Nakba Day in 2014, in the West Bank north of Jerusalem, there was an angry demonstration outside an Israeli military prison. Rocks were thrown. Two Palestinian boys aged sixteen and seventeen were shot and killed by Israeli forces. The Palestinians hit back. On 12 June three Israeli teenagers hitchhiking home in the West Bank were abducted and murdered in reprisal. A day after their funeral, Israeli settlers kidnapped another Palestinian sixteen-year-old in East Jerusalem and burned him alive in a nearby forest.

The violence spiralled out of control. The 2014 Gaza War had begun. Israel launched artillery barrages and a wave of air strikes upon Gaza, and arrested hundreds of Palestinians. Hamas and other Palestinian military offshoots fired rockets into Israel. On 8 July the government of Prime Minister Benjamin Netanyahu ordered Operation Protective Edge, an assault upon Gaza. As war goes, it was no contest: at the cutting edge of military technology, the Israeli Defence Force swept all before it. Gaza reeled, first beneath air strikes, artillery barrages and naval bombardment, then from a ground invasion of tanks and infantry. Hamas fought back with thousands more rockets and mortar bombardments, fired haphazardly with the express aim of killing Israeli civilians – another war crime.

The atrocities piled up, not least in the deaths of children. On 9 July Israeli missiles killed a family of nine Palestinian youths who had been at home watching football on television. Five days later, another four boys were blown to bits by missiles as they played on a Gaza beach. Western journalists watching nearby reported they had been deliberately targeted. Three separate Israeli attacks on or near schools run by the United Nations killed forty-five people, including seventeen children. Israel alleged these schools had been used by Hamas to fire rockets or were otherwise military targets but produced no evidence, and none was later found. Around 3000 civilians had been sheltering in the third school attacked; at least ten were killed and dozens more wounded, an act described by the UN Secretary-General Ban Ki-moon as a 'moral outrage' and a 'gross violation of international humanitarian law'.[169]

When fifty days of fighting finally lurched to an uneasy ceasefire, much of Gaza was a smouldering ruin. The United Nations estimated that 2251 Palestinians had been killed, including 551 children. Perhaps half a million people had been displaced, about 30 per cent of Gaza's population. Israel had lost 67 IDF personnel, and six civilians.[170] The UN found there had been possible war crimes on both sides, but the bloody calculus of conflict gave a victory of sorts to Israel.

Netanyahu proclaimed the deaths to be the fault of Hamas. 'They want to pile up as many civilian dead as they can,' he said in an interview with the CNN journalist Wolf Blitzer. 'They use telegenically dead Palestinians for their cause. They want the more dead, the better.'[171]

The ABC's Matt Brown reported for *7.30* on the killing of the four boys on the beach, interviewing the bereaved father and an eleven-year-old boy who had been injured by shrapnel but escaped. I watched his *7.30* story shaken to the marrow, choking back tears, achingly conscious of our own little boy peacefully asleep in his bedroom. Sickened, two days later I wrote an angry column for the *Herald*. It ran on Saturday, 26 July under the headline 'Israel's Rank and Rotten Fruit Is Being Called Fascism'. I hit hard from the opening paragraph:

> The images from Gaza are searing, a gallery of death and horror. A dishevelled Palestinian man cries out in agony, his blood-soaked little brother dead in his arms. On a filthy hospital bed a boy of perhaps five or six screams for his father, his head and body lacerated by shrapnel. A teenage girl lies on a torn stretcher, her limbs awry, her face and torso blackened like a burnt steak. Mourners weep over a family of 18 men, women and children laid side by side in bloodied shrouds. Four boys of a fishing family named Bakr, all less than 12 years old, are killed on a beach by rockets from Israeli aircraft.

I also took aim at Hamas:

> Hamas is also trying to kill Israeli civilians, with a barrage of rockets and guerrilla border attacks. It, too, is guilty of terror and grave war crimes. But Israeli citizens and their homes and towns have been effectively shielded by the nation's Iron Dome defence system, and so far only three of its civilians have died in this latest conflict. The Israeli response has been out of all proportion, a monstrous distortion of the much-vaunted right of self defence.
>
> It is a breathtaking irony that these atrocities can be committed by a people with a proud liberal tradition of scholarship and culture, who hold the Warsaw Ghetto and the six million dead of the Holocaust at the centre of their race memory. But this is a new and brutal Israel dominated by the hard line, right-wing Likud Party of Prime Minister Benjamin Netanyahu and his coalition.

With the column was a cartoon drawn by the artist Glen Le Lievre, depicting a Jewish man seated in an armchair marked with a Star of David and operating a TV-style remote control to blow up a Gazan township. It was a pungent spin-off from news photographs – seen worldwide – of Israeli families relaxing with drinks and snacks on a border hillside as they watched Gaza being bombed in the near distance below.

The column, its headline and the cartoon touched off a firestorm.

✧

I had expected a torrent of abusive emails. The Israel lobby in Australia is well organised, hyperactive and loudly vocal. It wields weight and power beyond its size. Anyone working in the media is aware that any criticism of Israel – the slightest hint of it – stirs much of the Jewish community to the wrath of God. But even prepared for that, I had no idea what was about to descend. For more than a week I was engulfed by a tsunami of hatred, bigotry, racism, insult and abuse beyond anything I had ever experienced.

It began with emails, fired off to the Gmail address regularly printed at the bottom of my column for *Herald* readers. The trickle that began early that Saturday morning became a flood over the weekend and beyond.

'Heil Hitler, you ignorant, Jew-hating, anti-Semitic slime,' was one of the first. I was attacked as 'a Hitler lover', 'a Nazi', 'a Palestinian cocksucker', 'a Muslim lover', 'an anti-Semitic motherfucker', 'Palestinian scum' and 'Holocaust denier'. On it rolled, a stream of filth. I lost count of the times I was called a Nazi. 'People like you started World War II,' said one woman. 'You would have gassed my grandmother in Auschwitz,' said another. A nutter named Ziggy, apparently thinking I might be spawn of the SS or similar, helpfully wrote in German: '*Die Nazi-Obst fällt nicht weit vom Stamm.*' The Nazi fruit does not fall far from the tree.

Twitter chimed in. One Alex Ryvchin, the Public Affairs Director of the Executive Council of Australian Jewry and a leading figure of the Israel lobby, berated me with a slew of ever more creative insults. A travel agent from Sydney's Rose Bay announced I was in cahoots with the corrupt New South Wales politician Eddie Obeid. 'Carlton's business is bankrolled by the Obeids,' she tweeted. Others displayed blatant racism. 'We are the Chosen People. Get over it,' was a jaw-dropper. One man wrote: 'Jews make things. Can't remember the last Palestinian invention.' A woman – apparently professional and well educated – thought my supposed religion might somehow be relevant. 'Catholic, much?' she snapped. I did not know whether to laugh or cry at that one.

It became obvious that a lot of the attack was coordinated. Some lines were repeated over and again. 'We gave them Gaza; they gave us rockets,' was a common one. 'Israel takes every care to avoid unnecessary casualties, but Hamas is using children and civilians as human shields,' was another. There were scores of these tweets and emails with identical wording.

Offensive though a lot of this was, it paled against the Twitter ravings of one Sandy Gutman, a small-time Sydney stand-up comic who had attained brief notoriety under the stage name Austen Tayshus and billed himself in his Twitter profile as 'the biggest name in Australian comedy in 30 years'. According to Mr Tayshus I was: 'a disgusting, deranged, anti-Semitic journalist', 'a dickhead racist bigot', 'a Jew hater' and even 'a camel turd'. 'Mike Carlton-Hitler-Mitford aka Puppet Boy is an infortunate [sic] alcoholic jew hating cunt.' 'Mike's Dad was a Catholic priest who taught his autistic son to hate Jews. Holocaust denier.'

Other Tayshus tweets likened me to Goebbels, Göring, and SS mass murderers Reinhard Heydrich and Adolf Eichmann. Another joked lightly that my mother should have been sent to Auschwitz. Unlike the emails, these tweets were there for all to see, but I noticed that none of Tayshus's not-so-many followers tried to shut him up. I blocked him, but people told me he kept at it for months.

A good many Jews did respond politely to me and with reasoned argument. And there were a few brave and often poignant letters from Jews aghast at the horrors of Gaza. This is part of one, from a woman who shall remain anonymous.

> I come from a family with deep Zionist roots. My grandmother smuggled weapons to the Hagganah, my father was presented an award by Menachim Begin for raising money for Israel, and I grew up to work as an educator in one of Sydney's Jewish day schools.[172]

> I thus have all the credentials to be a vociferous 'my country right or wrong' supporter of Israel. I am not. I am ashamed, heart-broken, angry and deeply conflicted. Israel has become a monstrous reflection of everything that Jews have historically feared and hated.

I was also getting support from *Herald* readers. In the week after the column I counted more than 3000 emails of encouragement, including messages from a former prime minister, two former foreign ministers, a former federal treasurer, a former Liberal state premier and a prominent federal Liberal backbencher. There were others from judges and lawyers, academics, Christian clergy, and community, ethnic and business leaders. Muslim community figures were solidly with me. Many Fairfax journalists chimed in as well. Together, they far outnumbered the critics. I began to feel I was not alone.

The emails subsided when my Gmail account was hacked, sending out a torrent of gibberish to all my contacts. There was nothing I could do but close it down.

✧

For the first few days I ignored the abuse, but soon it got to me and it seemed impossible to take it lying down anymore. It wasn't so much the crude obscenity, or the endless, fatuous allusions to the Nazis. The anti-Semitic smear was the one that stung.

I am not the slightest bit anti-Semitic. At the height of the uproar I got a call from my accountant, George Spitzer, a dear, Jewish friend of forty years. As an infant, George had fled with his family from Vienna, one step ahead of the Nazis, to live out the war as refugees in Japanese-controlled Shanghai, of all places. Whatever else they were vile about, the Japanese were not particularly bothered about Jews. The Spitzers came to Australia after 1945, grateful for their deliverance. As my financial adviser, George kept me on the straight and narrow, prudently supervising my investments. His wife, Maya, a bubbly, sparkling Egyptian Jew, was hospitality itself. We lunched together and dined at each other's homes, exchanged Christmas and Hanukkah cards, and watched our children grow. For all his years in Australia, George still had about him an old-world Viennese courtesy.

At his funeral in 2016, the rabbi lauded him as a *Mensch*, a high Yiddish compliment for a man of the utmost decency and integrity.

His call to me was to raise morale.

'Do you think I'm anti-Semitic, George?'

He gave a hoot of laughter. 'Of course not.' Then his voice dropped. 'But, Michael, at synagogue they say you are. And nothing I say will change their minds.'

I should have taken that as a caution but I did not. My patience was exhausted. Provoked, incensed, I hit the keyboard. It's the Irish in me. In emails and tweets a lot of people were told to fuck off. Tayshus was 'a ridiculous turd'. I told the woman who had asked 'Catholic, much?' that she was a vulgar and stupid bigot, which evidently she was. There was a fair bit more in the same vein.

At which point, enter the Israel lobby again. Like Fight Club, the first rule of the Israel lobby is: You do not talk about the Israel lobby. The second rule is: *You do not talk about the Israel lobby!* In high dudgeon piled upon absurdity, the lobby itself denies that it exists. To suggest that it does exist and that it exercises influence is crude and conspiratorial, they say – a sinister attempt to silence the Jewish community by depriving it of its right to speak.

This is arrant nonsense, bordering on paranoia. Nobody, except perhaps a few fringe lunatics, would seek to deprive the Jewish community of its voice. Like any group or community, Jews are entitled to have as many organisations as they like to represent their varied interests, and to lobby for them vigorously. And they do. At the top of a large pile is the Australia/Israel & Jewish Affairs Council, the AIJAC, based in Melbourne. There is also a slate of media outlets, from small magazines and blogs to the *Australian Jewish News*; *J-Wire*, an online newspaper; and the monthly *Australia/Israel Review*.

The lobbying is slick and sophisticated, sometimes subtle and unseen, at other times loud and combative. Huge effort goes into influencing Australian political and public opinion, and media coverage of Israel and the Middle East. Cabinet ministers and editors invariably take the phone calls. The AIJAC is always ready with a free, well-written article to push the current line on the opinion pages. Generous financial donations are slung to the major political parties.

In his entertaining *Diary of a Foreign Minister*, Bob Carr complains at length of the lobby's attempts to browbeat the Gillard government into backing the belligerent Likud hard line in Israel, a situation he thought scandalous and depressing.

The respected Australian journalist John Lyons has explained, in detail, how the AIJAC operates and agitates above and below the wire to advance the policies of the Netanyahu government. Lyons, now a senior ABC editorial executive, is a former editor of the *Sydney Morning Herald* and for six years was the *Australian*'s Middle East correspondent. In his memoir, *Balcony Over Jerusalem*, he writes:

> The longer I was in Israel, the more I realised that key figures in the Australian Jewish community sat on the far right of the Israeli political spectrum. In Israel I was able to have meaningful discussions with key army or intelligence figures about the Palestinian issue. But with many of Australia's Jewish leaders this was just not possible. It was almost as if they felt that, given they were not living in Israel, they needed to take a harder line than many people who were living there.[173]

Lyons details the AIJAC's relentless public and private attempts to discredit him and his reporting, and the work of other Australian correspondents in the Middle East. When all else fails, the lobby hurls the 'anti-Semitic' tag into the ring. You criticise Israel or Netanyahu or the Likud Party: therefore you must hate Jews. You are an anti-Semite. This is a giant leap, as daft as suggesting that to criticise Tony Abbott, say, or to question our defence policies is to hate Australians. But it is a charge almost impossible to rebut, with a dizzying catch-22 dangling from it. We say you are anti-Semitic. You say you are not. But if you disagree with us you *must* be anti-Semitic. Even to suggest that there is an Israel lobby is anti-Semitic.

That's the stick for journalists unwilling to regurgitate the *hasbara* or propaganda pumped out by the Netanyahu government and the Israeli military. There are also juicy carrots for politicians of all sides and pliant journalists willing to be schmoozed. Money is no object. The AIJAC and another group, the NSW Jewish Board of Deputies, run regular 'study tours' to Israel, funded by generous Jewish donors. Selected politicians and hacks are flown business class, put up in five-star hotels, and wined and dined in the best Tel Aviv restaurants while being escorted around showpiece hospitals, kibbutzes and settlements. Lyons writes: 'No editors, journalists or others should take these trips: they grotesquely distort the reality and are dangerous in the sense that they allow people with a very small amount of knowledge to pollute Australian public opinion.'[174]

He is right. They offered me one of these junkets many years ago; I declined it for exactly those reasons. But it is a heroic figure indeed who stands between an Australian journalist and a gravy train. As I write, another eight hacks have returned from one. They were the editor of the *Sydney Morning Herald*, the editor-in-chief of *Huffington Post Australia*, the editor of the *Weekend Australian*'s Inquirer section, the news director of the *Daily Telegraph*, reporters from Channel 7 and Sky Television, and producers from SBS Television and Radio 2GB. Their minder was Vic Alhadeff, from the NSW Board of Deputies.

Alhadeff evidently weaved his magic. At a welcome home reception at Sydney's Australian Jewish Museum in October 2017, the eight brimmed with gratitude. Israel 'captured my heart and my mind', wrote Anna Caldwell of the *Telegraph*. There were 'so many signs of hope ... every day we saw Israelis and Palestinians working side by side – they all wanted peace'.[175] All this discovered in a week. Everyone agreed it had been wonderful. Fancy that. These travelling troupes are sometimes allowed to see Gaza, but only from a distant hill.

Here, then, were the wheels and levers of a powerful media machine aimed right at me. Murdoch's newspapers lined up alongside.

✧

The *Herald* was getting twitchy. There was a snowstorm of letters to the editor from Jewish readers protesting furiously about the column, the headline and the Le Lievre cartoon. The cartoon drew the initial fire; a lot of people assumed I had drawn it, and written the headline as well. There were angry demands for me to be sacked. Dutifully, the editor published some of the more rational letters in the paper. Other people cancelled subscriptions. A number of

Jewish-owned businesses withdrew their advertising, including a big-spending Sydney furniture retailer. On the grapevine, I heard that directors on the Fairfax board were having their arms twisted and their ears bent, not least by the AIJAC. Many were receptive.

On Monday, 4 August the editor-in-chief of the *Herald*, Darren Goodsir, publicly apologised for the cartoon. He also phoned to ask me to apologise to anyone I had offended. Reluctantly, I said I would consider it. The time bomb was ticking.

Unsurprisingly, it exploded in the Murdoch press, led by the *Australian* and the *Daily Telegraph*. I had been on their notorious 'shit list' for years. The *Australian* had managed to get hold of the tweets and a lot of the emails I had sent to my attackers. The tweets were available for all to see, but the emails were not and obviously had been forwarded to the paper in a bunch. By whom? Your guess is as good as mine. The next day they were splashed in a long front-page story. It was heaven on a stick for the Murdochracy. There were two big birds to kill with one stone: the hated Fairfax press in general, and me in particular. Away they went.

'Fairfax Media is under pressure to sack columnist Mike Carlton, who has been ordered to apologise for using anti-Semitic and abusive language towards readers,' it began. On and on it went, a poisonous cocktail of a few facts heavily larded with great globs of bias and invention in the Murdoch gutter tradition. With malicious dishonesty, the paper mentioned not once the torrent of Jewish hatred which had prompted my response. There was not a syllable of the Nazi smear, the 'Hitler's bitch' stuff. The impression given – deliberately – was that I had exploded with rage at polite, reasoned criticism.

I believe the *Telegraph* was even more vile in its attack on me. I never bothered to read what it ran – not then, not since – but I was told it splashed all over the shop as well. Somebody showed me the artwork they had confected. Against the background of a bombed and burning village, my head had been wrapped in a keffiyeh, the chequered Arab scarf, then photo-shopped onto the stooped and evidently fleeing body of a man in burned and tattered clothing. Carlton's a terrorist, geddit?

This was a humungous own goal. Many people were appalled to

recognise the tattered figure in the photograph as a victim of the Boston Marathon bombing of just over a year before. There was an outcry at the lack of taste, grisly even for the *Telegraph*, and the editor had to pull the picture from his website with a grovelling apology to readers, although not to me.

'Sewer journalism,' I told the *Mumbrella* media website when they asked for a comment. Doubling down, the paper stationed a photographer and a reporter at my front gate. The heat was becoming intense. Friends, including Fairfax journalists, rallied around with supportive phone calls and messages. Tom Keneally, bless him, tweeted:

> SMH cartoon racist and to be profoundly regretted; Carlton not. If Carlton's a-Semitic, then I must be too, bec'se I opposed Gaza.

Herald readers also began to send me and the newspaper sympathetic letters and emails, swelling by the day. My wife was a rock, as were my older children. My mate and former ABC colleague Ken Begg made the trip from his home in Canberra to stay with us for a few nights and to give me his wise counsel and strength, a kindness for which I am ever grateful. Other friends and neighbours took Lachlan to and from school to avoid the Murdoch ambush. Deliciously, one of them showered the *Telegraph*'s loitering hack with a stream of colourful advice, sending her retreating in disarray. I was immensely buoyed by strangers who would stop me in the street, pump my hand and urge me to hang in.

It was Fairfax that cracked. Ignominiously. Darren Goodsir, a decent man and a good journalist, was trapped between the devil and the deep blue sea. From the boardroom and the executive suite, his lords and masters were howling for my head on a platter. So was the lobby. They had to be placated, he told me, yet he wanted to keep me writing for the paper. I could see his dilemma, an added distraction he did not need. As the *Herald* slowly imploded, with more and more of its best and brightest journalists 'taking redundancy' – that cloying euphemism – he had to battle to shore up newsroom morale and to keep the show on the road. Nor was his own job safe: notoriously, *Herald* editors had the career prospects of a subaltern on the Somme.

For my part, I was angry that few at the paper seemed at all interested in the filth heaped upon me. Still less was I accorded the courtesy of a face-to-face meeting where I could put my case – a not unreasonable expectation after an association of twenty years, I thought. Our negotiation was by phone and email. Goodsir wanted to suspend me for a cooling-off period of about three weeks until the end of the month, and he pushed me again to apologise to the aggrieved. I reluctantly agreed, with the proviso that I would not grovel to anyone who had called me Hitler's cocksucker and the like. I thought the deal was done.

That evening I got two phone calls. They stunned me. The first was from my brother, Peter, in Brisbane, to tell me that our mother had taken a heavy fall and injured herself badly. Enid, now ninety-two, was living near him in a nursing home, where she had retreated after being comprehensively ripped off at a Sydney 'retirement resort'. She was a fragile shell of the strong, vital woman she had once been, and tortured by senile dementia. Often she could not recognise either of us when we went to visit. Peter explained to me that she was in a coma, barely breathing. The doctors thought it probable she would not live through the night, and had asked, obliquely, if we would consider turning off her life support. What did I think?

After the stress of the day I was almost incapable of thinking. Dimly, through the mists of my mind, I realised that we were talking euthanasia. It was surreal, almost beyond contemplation. My mother was on the edge of death. Would it be a kindness, even an act of love, to hasten it? Or would we simply be making life easier for the hospital by freeing up a bed for the next patient? In principle I support voluntary euthanasia, a peaceful death with dignity, but to be confronted with the reality – and so suddenly – was profoundly disturbing. She had given birth to me, loved me, sacrificed her all to raise me. How could I assent to her death? Peter was equally troubled. We decided to play for time, to wait to see what the morning would bring. Distressed, I explained the call to Morag and we began to make ready for bed.

Minutes later, at around ten pm, the phone rang again. It was Sean Aylmer, Fairfax's editorial director, and therefore Goodsir's boss. I had met him just once, over a coffee a few years before, and had not been impressed. He struck me as diffident, and a far cry from the muscular intellects I had known and admired in *Herald* editors like Max Suich. His record in journalism was mediocre. His chief attribute appearing to be a talent for survival, although in time that failed him and his head rolled too. But he had been amiable enough then, schmoozing me with the assurance that I was one of the *Herald*'s top three best-read columnists. (The others were the brilliant economics writer Ross Gittins and Peter FitzSimons.) He hoped I would keep writing.

This time, though, his voice was cold. 'We've decided to suspend you indefinitely,' he said.

I thought I had misheard him, so he repeated it. Then I assumed that he and Goodsir had their wires crossed. 'Darren told me it would be just three weeks,' I said.

At that point Morag came into the room to see what was happening. As Aylmer kept talking, I clapped a hand over the phone and repeated his words to her.

'We've changed our minds,' he said.

'But we had a deal,' I replied. 'You're reneging?'

'Yes. We are suspending you indefinitely. As of now.'

'Indefinitely!'

Morag's eyes flashed with anger as I relayed this to her. Silently, she drew a finger across her throat. It was the sign that TV studio floor managers make to shut things down in a hurry: stop, finish, end, quit now. Cut.

My fury welled up too. My exhaustion vanished. For that moment I forgot even the possibility of my mother's death. The arrogance, the impertinence of this apparatchik calling late at night to relay this decision was bad enough. But Fairfax had broken its word to me. A rank and cowardly betrayal. Weak-kneed, the company had buckled to the pressure from the lobby and the bullying from the Murdoch press. How they would cheer in Holt Street when they heard they had won. I was not going to cop it anymore.

'You needn't bother suspending me. You can get fucked, Aylmer. I've just quit.'

I slammed the phone down in his ear.

26
Living well

After the initial shock of leaving the *Herald*, I began to feel a curious sense of lightness. Liberation, even. Finally I was out from under the endless pressure to perform. Free, free at last.

There were a few bricks still to drop. Like a junkyard mongrel with a bone, the *Australian* pushed hard to have me charged under the controversial section 18C of the *Racial Discrimination Act*, which makes it an offence to 'offend, insult, humiliate or intimidate another person or a group of people'. The usual claque of News Corpse bloviators duly trooped into line, led by none other than Andrew Bolt, who had a battleaxe to grind. In 2011 Bolt had been found guilty of breaching 18C in two sloppy, rabble-rousing columns containing 'erroneous facts, distortions of the truth and inflammatory and provocative language', as the judge put it.[176] Outraged, he and his cohort of right-wing loonies howled to the heavens about freedom of speech and the evils of censorship, demanding the repeal of 18C forthwith. But not when it came to my turn. 'I fully support this suing of Mike Carlton,' Bolt blathered in his *Herald Sun* blog. 'Why should the *Racial Discrimination Act* be used to silence only conservatives?' The hypocrisy was eye-watering. And ultimately futile. Gerard 'Gollum' Henderson, that hectoring crank from the so-called 'Sydney Institute', contributed a few gobs of bile as well, but to no avail. I had not breached the act and there was no charge laid.

The cheering thing was the reaction of *Herald* readers. After I quit, my inclination had been to come out with guns blazing to denounce Fairfax, but I thought better of it. I was just not interested in the fight anymore. Nor did I wish to precipitate the *Herald*'s decline by offering a few home truths. Journalists still needed jobs there. But readers were furious, firing off angry letters to the editor (none of which got printed) and, more emphatic, cancelling their subscriptions. At one point Fairfax got so panicky that it was offering three months' free subscription if people agreed to stay on. A lot did not.

Some of the anti-Semitic mud stuck to me, as the Israel lobby knew it would. The Goethe Institute in Sydney, the cultural arm of the German embassy, had asked me to give a talk on *First Victory* and Australia and Germany in World War I. A couple of weeks before it was due I got an apologetic phone call: the institute had been warned that if I spoke there would be a Jewish protest demonstration outside their office. They were embarrassed but hoped I would understand that they could not afford that sort of publicity. With much regret, they would have to cancel. I could see their point.

That was pretty much the end of it. And I was glad to be out of the snake pit. I was sixty-eight years old; I had been in the media for fifty-one of those years. A fair innings. Might as well quit with a bang, I thought. Journalism had given me a privileged and happy career: a front-row seat to great events and the chance to closely observe, examine and often meet the players. The highs had far outstripped the lows. There had been travel, fun and excitement, and I had made a good buck, a life never dreamed of by the sixteen-year-old Chatswood boy in his brand-new blue suit who arrived, wide-eyed, at the ABC in 1963.

Not only that, but the game had changed. The larrikin, almost bohemian world of journalism of my early years had long gone, the comity replaced by a cold ethos of brutal rivalries and enmities which I had come to despise. Perhaps this bastardry was inevitable, a reflection of the immense changes in Australian society itself over half a century. I had fought in the culture wars myself, energetically at first, but I had wearied of the pretensions and histrionics. If there ever had been a contest of ideas, there was now only a parade of ideologies, sound and fury signifying nothing. Public trust in politicians and the media had plummeted.

After a few months, when the row subsided, the *Herald* made discreet noises about having me back. Some friends still writing for the paper had been quietly urging the Fairfax hierarchy to take me on again, and Darren Goodsir and I had lunch to talk about it. He was gracious, but vague about how and when I might return. I felt a flicker of interest, but it quickly died. The log of rolled-up newsprint which had once landed on Sydney's front lawns with a heavy thump was a slender reed, and shrinking still as more and more of its best journalists left the building. The Fairfax managing director, Greg 'Plywood' Hywood – another humourless shrinker and sacker – seemed intent on turning the company into a vehicle for flogging real estate, with the newspapers a distraction on the side. Every time another tranche of journalists got the flick, Plywood would repeat the corporate PR bleat about a commitment to quality journalism going forward, blah blah, but the words were hollow. In the end it was he who killed off the Fairfax name altogether, all those years of Australian newspaper history snuffed out like a guttering candle.

These days I will read the work of *Herald* journalists I respect, and some of it is as good as ever. A lot is not. The tragedy is that the paper no longer stands for very much. It has not been required reading for a long time. More often I rely on the ABC, the *Guardian*, the *Crikey* website and the small-circulation but well-written and incisive *Saturday Paper* for my news and opinion fix. The internet and my iPad bring me the great newspapers of the world.

People still stop me in the street to say they cancelled their *Herald* subscriptions after I left. This is both pleasing and humbling, but at bottom it's a sad comment on the decline of a once great newspaper of record. I am sure there will be good years again in journalism, for there are bright young people out there doing, writing, saying and filming interesting things. Their talent will not be suppressed, and the media landscape is changing in ways we are only beginning to comprehend. Aspiring journalists will need to stay true to themselves and resist the lure of prostituting their talents for money and power. If they can, their future is unbounded.

As is the future of our country. The enlargers are winning, not the punishers and straighteners. LGBTQI communities now have the rights so long denied them, and a new generation of feminists is carrying forward the women's revolution. We have yet to deal seriously with climate change and such horrors as the degradation of the Great Barrier Reef, and Indigenous Australians still do not have their rightful place in the sun. But slowly we are moving forward, despite the best efforts of the troglodytes. I would dearly love to be a citizen of the Republic of Australia before I die, but if that is not to happen I am confident my children will see that new dawn of true nationhood.

Living well is the best revenge, said the seventeenth-century priest and poet George Herbert. He was right, although I think he meant a life of quiet piety in the sight of Christ. Not exactly my thing. Living well to me now is the delight of simple things: a tangerine sun rising from the sea over an empty beach; a well-cooked family meal served with love on a scrubbed pine table; feeding the strutting pink galahs on our balcony; Lachlan proudly adding a big new word to his vocabulary, or hitting a six at cricket.

Things I would once have taken for granted, without a second thought, now have the power to move me deeply. Often they involve young people. Sometimes when I watch Lachlan's sturdy little figure disappear through the school gate in the morning, to mingle in a noisy throng of bright-eyed, tanned and happy Australian kids, I get a lump in the throat and my heart bursts at the pure beauty of it. Unless we blow it somehow, Morag and I know he will grow to manhood with the same ethical and moral codes of decency and humanity that animate Alex and James. We have come a long, long way from the innate prejudices of Nana's generation.

Some questions linger. Keeping a promise to my mother, every April I visit my father's grave in a Sydney cemetery. It is the month of their wedding anniversary and his death. I give him a dozen red roses on her behalf and sit beneath the birdsong for a minute or two, wondering what he would have made of me. I am certain James

Andrew Carlton would have loved me, but would he have *liked* me, would he have approved of the life I have led? On the few times that I put these questions to Enid, she was oddly evasive. Yes, he would have been proud of me, but she would never offer anything more. For reasons she would not explain, she stubbornly refused to reveal to me what his politics were, or if his Catholic faith had been strong to his death. In the end I gave up asking. Would I have turned out differently with a father's guidance? It puzzles me still.

Enid lingered until 12 June 2015, dying a few months short of her ninety-third birthday. Perhaps it was the dementia that killed her, perhaps not. Her mind had already long gone. In the end her body gave out, its organs shutting down one by one, the doctors said.

Her last years had been a torment, exacerbated by fleeting flashes of sanity in which she could recognise that 'something's wrong with me' but had no idea what it was. Mostly she was wracked by anxiety and fear. She telephoned me once from Brisbane to complain that my brother had stolen her car and taken it to Russia to go hunting for bears. She held a rambling conversation with him in the tragic delusion that he was our father, her long-dead husband. We had to take the phone away, for she would telephone Peter every half-hour. She was terrified even to move from her bed to the toilet, and had to be carried there and cleaned by a carer at the nursing home, a humiliating debasement for the brave, proud, intelligent and loving single mother who had taken on the world to protect and rear her two boys. Jim's sons.

The last time I kissed her the skin of her cheek was as fragile as a fallen autumn leaf. She lay in her bed pale and unmoving, hardly breathing. I should have cried then but I could not. Overwhelmingly I just wanted the horrors to end for her, without pain. Her death came as a guilty relief.

The funeral was small, in outer-suburban Brisbane. Most of her friends had gone before her, or were too frail to attend. My brother and I, and our wives and kids were there, and a few of Peter's relatives by marriage. True to her word, God and religion got not a look in. Peter and I both spoke – I cannot remember a single word that either of us said – and then those dreadful funeral chapel curtains closed upon her and she was cremated.

Some time later, with my brother's agreement, I scattered her ashes in the Blue Mountains, west of Sydney. She had loved the place all her life, and it seemed appropriate. I was conceived there on her chaotic honeymoon. She had enjoyed taking us to Katoomba in the school holidays, to stay for a few days in a cheap boarding house which we thought to be the pinnacle of luxury because you got sweetcorn on toast for breakfast. On bushwalks we would recoil in mock horror from the gnarled cones of the banksia trees, the villainous 'Banksia Men' of the May Gibbs stories she had read to us. Later, after I bought her another car, she would regularly drive herself to visit an old school friend who lived at Blackheath.

On a cold but sunny winter's day, standing on a jutting ledge of rock in the bush, I sent her drifting away on a light breeze. Nearby, a silvery waterfall splashed down a golden sandstone cliff to the eucalypt forest dark on the floor of the Grose Valley. We are sure Enid would have approved.

✧

Reading and writing naval history has given me more and more pleasure. A part of me is still the little boy devouring *The Cruel Sea* by torchlight. The success of *First Victory* was gratifying. After a pause to breathe, I plunged back in again with a third book, *Flagship*, the story of the heavy cruiser HMAS *Australia* and her sisters *Canberra* and *Shropshire* in the Pacific war on Japan. Again, there were survivors of these ships and battles to talk to, and families with a wealth of letters and diaries. One old bloke, a long-retired lieutenant commander, gave me the only knockback I ever met. 'Never talk to journalists,' he growled. 'You're a bunch of bloody pinkos.' Another sailor, former naval pilot Commander Dick Bourke, more than made up for that, agreeing to speak to me from his bed in a Sydney hospice. I telephoned him first. 'He's very weak. He'll probably only manage about five minutes with you,' said his wife cautiously, but we chatted for about half an hour. She was incredulous when she eventually took the phone back. 'He hasn't spoken like that in years,' she said. In the hospice, through racking coughs and evident pain, he gave me nearly an hour of priceless reminiscence of his wartime days as a young lieutenant. Mrs Bourke and two sons stood listening, solemn and near tears when he finished. I very nearly was too. Dick died before the book came out, but he is in it.

The Royal Australian Navy seems quite used to me by now, from the top down. *Flagship* got a bigger launch than the first two books, at a morning tea on board the new amphibious ship HMAS *Canberra* at the Fleet Base in Sydney. Admirals past and present turned up. In return, I relish the company of sailors, be they still serving or retired as 'the Old and the Bold', as they say. There is a refreshing directness and candour to them, invariably anchored by a quiet pride in their profession.

Few realise that most RAN senior sailors and officers are among the nation's best-educated elite, bristling with postgraduate degrees. Newspaper opinion columnists who bag them, who wouldn't know port from starboard, airily pontificate on defence and naval strategy, or the best buys in submarines. A few defence writers know what they are talking about, or at least have the professional good sense to ask someone who does, but most journalists confidently splash about in ignorance and folly. The average hack has but two narratives for the navy. The good one is lots of grey paint and coloured flags, smart white uniforms, a brass band playing on the wharf, the emotional welcome home for a ship's heroic crew. The bad one is rum, sodomy and the lash: sexual predators, misogynist bullies, and bone-headed admirals squandering countless billions of taxpayer dollars on 'dud ships'. There is no middle ground, just these absolutes. It must be galling if you are commanding what is actually one of the world's most skilled and effective blue-water navies. Perhaps my histories have done a bit to dispel the ignorance. I am more proud of them than of anything else in my career. The supreme compliment remains when sailors tell me that I got it right. Families write movingly to say that for the first time they understand what Dad or Grandpa went through during the war. That means a lot. I like to hope these three books might endure when the rest is forgotten.

✧

In 2015, not long after my mother died, Morag noticed an odd-looking black spot on my back. It was a malignant melanoma, no doubt incubated back in the day when us teenagers would sprawl on the beach and get lobster-red until the skin on our back peeled off in squishy leaflets. A skilled surgeon got the thing before it spread, but it was an intimation of mortality. I resolved then to get fit and to stay fit, to try to prolong my life in the hope, at least, that I will see Lachlan graduate from university and my grandson Jack become the pianist he wants to be. I would be in my eighties.

To mark this solemn resolve I got myself a sailor's tattoo, a handsome anchor in the naval style inked on my left bicep. Morag blinked when she saw it. 'I never thought I'd be married to a tattooed man,' she said.

Late in life I came to know one of the idols of my teenage years, Bernard 'Midget' Farrelly, Australia's first surfing champion. Midget and I agreed that regular immersion in salt water was essential to life itself: when all else fails, catching a few waves, going for a paddle or just swimming laps can set the world right again.

Pittwater, that magic meeting of land, sea and air, lies some 40 kilometres north of Sydney. Geologists call it a drowned valley. Its 18 square kilometres of blue water open onto Broken Bay, between the mighty sandstone crags of West Head and Barrenjoey, then out to the Tasman Sea. Historically, it was home to the Carigal people, a sub-clan of the Guringai tribe, until they were virtually wiped out by the white man's smallpox.

Governor Arthur Phillip found this earthly Elysium in March 1788, two months after dropping anchor in Sydney Cove. Sailing north with a longboat and a cutter and rounding Barrenjoey, he found 'the finest piece of Water I ever saw, and which I honoured with the name of Pitt Water'. It was, he thought, 'of sufficient extent to contain all the Navy of Great Britain'.[177]

White settlement followed, but slowly. For some years it was the haunt of escaped convicts and smugglers. Today the western shore has a few scattered hamlets clinging to the fringe of a national park, the slopes thick with eucalypts and cabbage tree palms and dotted with sandstone caves and oyster-studded rocks as the Carigal would have known it. Wallabies and goannas are there aplenty.

At weekends Pittwater is flecked with boats, from little runabouts to rich men's yachts and cruisers, their wakes foamy white in the blue. I sailed there a bit myself for a while, in a second-hand forty-foot yacht I owned for a few years. On weekdays the water is almost empty, save for a few fishermen and the MV *Ballina*, a stumpy old work boat painted black and buff, which chugs here and there to maintain the buoys in the anchorages. Sometimes I have the place all to myself, the luxury of solitude.

At dawn I might take the ski out for a fast paddle, and perhaps a skinny-dip at one of the little beaches over on the western side, taking care not to tread on the stingrays feeding in the shallows at high tide. In summer the water has a diamond sparkle. When the black nor'easter blows in the late afternoon or the Sydney southerly buster hammers down, the wavelets are lashed to foam. Rainy grey days of fog and mist give Pittwater the aspect of a Scottish loch. At day's end the sun goes down red and gold through the gum trees. The beauty is changing but eternal.

And, after a life on air, it is home. Our house looks down upon it, through the gums and purple jacarandas. I can see it now as I write. Here I will spend my remaining years at peace, with no regrets. I am infinitely happy in the glow of my memories, the strength of my friendships and the love of my family.

Endnotes

1 Sir Walter Scott, *Poetical Works*, vol. II. Baudry's European Library, Paris, 1838, p. 265. The Scots Language Centre in Perth (Scotland) translates this for me as: 'There'll be trouble until that sheriff is boiled and drunk as a brew.'

2 G. H. Kinnear, *History of Glenbervie*, Montrose Publishing, Edinburgh, 1895, p. 21.

3 Enid Carlton, Private Papers, p. 9.

4 Proclamation, Governor Sir George Gipps, 3 March 1840.

5 *Maitland Mercury and Hunter River General Advertiser*, 16 July 1892, p. 5.

6 Ibid., 24 June 1893, p. 4.

7 The school is long gone. The building now houses expensive apartments.

8 Brother Henry coached Joeys' First XV until a leg injury stopped him in 1954, an astonishing record. He died on Christmas Day, 1970.

9 Now largely forgotten, Paavo Nurmi, 'The Flying Finn', won nine Olympic track and field gold medals between 1920 and 1928.

10 *Sunday Sun* (Sydney), 11 December 1927, p. 8.

11 *The Referee* (Sydney), 28 December 1927, p. 15.

12 Gary Lester, *Australians at the Olympics*, Lester-Townsend Publishing, Sydney, 1984, p. 81.

13 *Sporting Globe* (Melbourne), 29 January 1930, p. 4.

14 *Sunday Sun* (Sydney), 6 December 1931, p. 48.

15 *Sydney Morning Herald*, 16 January 1932, p. 11.

16 *Sydney Sun*, 19 January 1932, p. 3.

17 *The Referee* (Sydney), 20 January 1932, p. 3.

18 *Bulletin*, 27 January 1932. Jack Lang was the turbulent New South Wales Labor premier of the Depression era.

19 Letter from Father P. J. FitzPatrick, St Aidan's, Maroubra, 20 January 1932, held in the archives of the Missionaries of the Sacred Heart.

20 Quoted in *Great Australian Athletes* by Robert Solomon, Southwood Press, Marrickville, Sydney 2000, p. 3.

21 Report to the Provincial Council of the Missionaries of the Sacred Heart, 7 January 1935, held in the archives of the Missionaries of the Sacred Heart.

22 'Report Before Priesthood Concerning Brother James Carlton', Sacred Heart Monastery, Croydon, Victoria, 9 May 1939, held in the archives of the Missionaries of the Sacred Heart.

23 *Sporting Globe* (Melbourne), 26 July 1939, p. 19.

24 Enid Carlton, Personal Papers.

25 Ibid.

26 About $2800 in 2018 dollars.

27 Enid Carlton, Personal Papers.

28 Ibid.

29 Ibid.

30 The old Denman Chambers. Miller's colleagues there included the Evatt brothers and a young Gough Whitlam.

31 The Anglican *Book of Common Prayer*, 1928.

32 Don stayed in the US Navy, married an American girl after World War II, fought again in Korea and died in 1962. He is buried in the Golden Gate National Cemetery, south of San Francisco. I saw no point in disturbing the privacy of his descendants for this book.

33 *Daily Telegraph*, 17 August 1945, p. 11.

34 Ibid. (and other newspapers).

35 Report to the Missionaries of the Sacred Heart, 20 August 1945, held in the archives of the Missionaries of the Sacred Heart.

36 Ibid.

37 *Sydney Morning Herald*, 25 July 1949, p. 1.

38 Ross Fitzgerald, *The Peoples' Champion*, University of Queensland Press, St Lucia, 1997, p. 210.

39 *Sydney Morning Herald*, 17 August 1949, p. 2.

40 Rob later became a federal Liberal MP, holding the Tasmanian seat of Denison between 1969 and 1972.

41 Enid Carlton, Personal Papers.

42 In Catholic doctrine the sacrament can be administered within a few hours after death, as it is held that the soul does not leave the body immediately.

43 'Soon the Fuhrer will be living in Buckingham Palace.'

44 Hitler would tell anyone who listened that it was one of his favourite films. He liked the way a handful of white men could control an entire continent.

45 Lord Robert Baden-Powell, *Scouting for Boys*, C. Arthur Pearson, London, 1908. It was a smash hit. My copy is the thirtieth edition, published in 1957.

46 His Melbourne equivalent was Stan 'the Man' Rofe, on 3XY and then 3UZ.

47 *Canberra Times*, 27 January 1962, p. 3.

48 Ibid., 25 May 1962, p. 3.

49 Marcia Hathaway died in the ambulance. There has been no fatal shark attack in the harbour since.

50 The initial cost was $US125 million. This was hugely controversial at the time but was one of the best defence deals we ever did. The last F-111 aircraft was retired in 2010.

51 Glenn A. Baker, *The Beatles Down Under: The 1964 Australia and New Zealand Tour*, Glebe, Wild and Woolley, 1982, p. 102.

52 Indigenous people were given the right to drink in late 1964.

53 *Sun News Pictorial* (Melbourne), 1 November 1965.

54 *Evening News* (London), November 1965.

55 Approximately $21,000 in 2018 dollars.

56 John Farquharson, 'Fitchett, Ian Glynn (Fitch) (1908–1988)', *Australian Dictionary of Biography*, http://adb.anu.edu.au/biography/fitchett-ian-glynn-fitch-12494.

57 Approximately $675 in 2018 dollars.

58 *Hansard*, House of Representatives, 29 April 1965.

59 Quoted in *Vietnam: The Australian War* by Paul Ham (HarperCollins, Sydney, 2007), p. 124.

60 *Hansard*, House of Representatives, 4 May 1965.

61 Always pronounced in the American style, 'Dee Em Zee'.

62 The nickname 'bird colonel' derives from the silver eagle badge of rank. An E-2 was the equivalent of an Australian private.

63 Like many Javanese men, Sukarno had only one name.

64 *Nasionalisme* (Nationalism, which was largely the Armed Forces and secular political parties) *Agama* (religion, mostly but not exclusively Muslim) and *Komunisme* (mostly Moscow-aligned).

65 The Bolivian ambassador to the UN, Fernando Ortiz-Sanz.

66 Sarwo, a baby-faced killer, had personal charm. He eventually fell out with Suharto and was sidelined. His daughter married President Susilo Bambang Yudhoyono.

67 *Tjenderawasih* is the Indonesian name for the New Guinea Bird of Paradise.

68 A heavy hitter, he was later the US ambassador in Canberra during the 1975 Whitlam dismissal. It was said by some that he had encouraged it.

69 Quoted in *Radio Wars: Truth, Propaganda and the Struggle for Radio Australia* by Errol Hodge (Cambridge University Press, Melbourne, 1995), p. 179.

70 Errol Hodge, *Radio Wars*, p. 179.

71 Ibid. (and DFATA 570/3/1), p. 235.

72 Ibid., p. 235.

73 Trish Payne, *War and Words: The Australian Press and the Vietnam War*, Melbourne University Press, Melbourne, 2007, p. 4.

74 Bruce Pigott (aged twenty-three), Michael Birch (twenty-four) and John Cantwell (twenty-nine) were the three Australians. A British journalist, Ron Laramy, also died. Another Australian, Frank Palmos, escaped after playing dead.

75 Named for Captain Jim Kotrc, a popular officer killed in 1969.

76 Ernie was already a member of the Liberal Party. To no surprise, he became a minor Victorian Liberal state MP when he left the army in 1985.

77 William Shawcross, *Sideshow: Kissinger, Nixon and the Destruction of Cambodia*, Simon & Schuster, New York, 1979, p. 150.

78 Ibid., p. 396.

79 Bernard Fall, *The Two Viet-Nams*, Pall Mall Press, London, 1967, p. 113.

80 Palfreyman later became director of communications for the Sydney 2000 Olympic Games. Murphy hosted ABC Radio's *PM* program for many years. The late Paul Lyneham was a big gun in the Canberra parliamentary press gallery, first for the ABC and then for the Nine Network.

81 The claim was that she swam the palace moat and nicked the flag from a palace wall. In fact, she and some others took it from a pole in the avenue outside.

82 A fervent Christian, Hodge apparently tried to convert the Muslims in the office. He made their lives so unpleasant that the staff eventually petitioned for his removal.

83 *Sydney Morning Herald*, 14 July 1971.

84 *Hansard*, NSW Legislative Assembly, 23 August 1973.

85 Ibid.

86 David Hickie, *The Prince and the Premier*, Angus & Robertson, Sydney, 1985.

87 Approximately $1.2 million in 2018 dollars.

88 These included the property developer 'Sir' Paul Strasser, and the transport mogul and mafia associate 'Sir' Peter Abeles. The going

rate was said to be about $30,000, which they paid by 'losing' to Askin at games of bridge.

89 Somehow it's available on YouTube: https://www.youtube.com/watch?v=wT4VcdmKQg0.

90 Brendan went on to *60 Minutes* at Nine, filming some of its most memorable stories. His pictures were never less than exquisite. He later married *60 Minutes* reporter Jana Wendt.

91 Indeed they were 'in love', which Cairns eventually admitted in 2002. Before that, though, Cairns and Morosi had hypocritically and successfully sued journalists and newspapers which had dared to report the fact.

92 *Sydney Morning Herald*, 25 April 2005.

93 Rae Wear, *Johannes Bjelke-Petersen: The Lord's Premier*, University of Queensland Press, St Lucia, 2002, pp. 211–19.

94 Leisha Harvey (former health minister), Don 'Shady' Lane (former transport minister) and Brian Austin (former health minister). Former Commissioner 'Sir' Terry Lewis did ten and a half years for corruption and forgery, and was stripped of his knighthood.

95 Tricky to the last, Hinze escaped a long jail sentence by dying before he could be charged and brought to court.

96 Graham Freudenberg, *A Certain Grandeur*, Macmillan, Melbourne, 1977, p. 405.

97 Whitlam to me, 18 September 2000.

98 *Sydney Morning Herald*, 20 March 2015.

99 Greg Shackleton (aged twenty-nine), Tony Stewart (twenty-one) and Gary Cunningham (twenty-seven) were from Seven in Melbourne. Brian Peters (twenty-four) and Malcolm Rennie (twenty-nine) were from Nine in Sydney.

100 Quoted in *Jonestown* by Chris Masters, Allen & Unwin, Sydney, 2006, p. 216.

101 *Income Equality, Insights*, published by the OECD, 15 December 2015.

102 Francis Fukuyama, 'The End of History?', *The National Interest*, No. 16, Summer 1989, Washington, DC.

103 *Hansard*, Senate, Canberra, 24 September 1981.

104 Email to the author, 19 June 2017.

105 Gibbo's suicide in 2015, after a bout of black depression, stunned his friends and fans.

106 The house had previously been owned by the writer Beatrix Potter, who wrote *The Tale of Peter Rabbit* there.

107 Keating was said to have been spotted dining secretly in Paris with a dark and handsome young man. It turned out to be his son Patrick.

108 Francis Xavier Costigan, *Royal Commission on the Activities of the Federated Ship Painters and Dockers Union, Final Report*, Volume 3, Australian Government Publishing Service, 1984, pp. 119–20.

109 If you are desperate to see one of these performances, you could search Mike Carlton puppets on YouTube.

110 'GOTCHA', said the notorious headline in Rupert Murdoch's London *Sun*.

111 Australian time. It was 26 September in the United States.

112 Tim Bowden, *One Crowded Hour*, Collins, Sydney, 1987, p. 418.

113 The lines are from 'The Call' by Thomas Osbert Mordaunt, a British Army officer and poet writing during the Seven Years War of the eighteenth century.

114 Father Edmund Campion, *Australian Catholics*, Penguin, Melbourne, 1987, p. 247.

115 Brother McMahon later left the Marist Brothers and is now known as Marshall McMahon. He is still a Catholic teacher.

116 *New York Times*, 10 May 2006.

117 @RealDonaldTrump, 9 June 2017.

118 Mike Steketee and Milton Cockburn, *Wran, an Unauthorized Biography*, Allen & Unwin, Sydney, 1986, p. 325.

119 Sir Henry Parkes served longer, but over five separate terms.

120 Former Labor MP Barry Cohen, ABC Radio, *Late Night Live*, 30 October 2000.

121 Conversation with the author.

122 *Good Weekend*, Fairfax, 13 April 1991.

123 Fraser had used it as early as 1971, long before Jones appeared.

124 Quoted in *The Man Who Couldn't Wait* by V. J. Carroll, William Heinemann, Melbourne, 1991, p. 192.

125 *Sydney Morning Herald*, 6 September 1996.

126 Unity Mitford, fanatically devoted to Hitler, tried but failed to commit suicide at the outbreak of World War II. Diana Mitford married the British fascist Oswald Mosley. Deborah Mitford became the Duchess of Devonshire.

127 Quoted in 'The First Fleet and the Re-Enactment First Fleet – Some Historical Parallels and Differences', speech by Richard J. Tanner (one of the Re-enactment organisers), 26 January 2010.

128 *Sydney Morning Herald*, 27 February 1988, p. 33.

129 Also the father of Laura Tingle, the great Canberra political editor for the *Australian Financial Review*.

130 So called 'pirate radio' had been broadcasting since the 1960s, to break the BBC's radio monopoly. The most successful, Radio Caroline, operated from a ship in international waters, out of reach of the British authorities.

131 *Guardian*, 30 September 1992, p. 15.

132 A quote attributed to an elderly lady after watching a late Victorian-era performance of *Antony and Cleopatra*.

133 Jerry Hayes, *An Unexpected MP*, Biteback Publishing, London, 2014, p. 110.

134 *Othello*, act 3, scene 3.

135 Including Australians. In 1990, two Australian tourists, Nick Spanos and Stephen Melrose, were murdered by IRA gunmen in Holland after they had been mistaken for British soldiers.

136 *Guardian*, 6 September 1993.

137 Ibid., 7 September 1993.

138 John Howard on ABC-TV's *Four Corners*, 19 February 1996.

139 Independent Commission Against Corruption, *Report on Investigation into the Metherell Resignation and Appointment*, 19 June 1992, p. 51.

140 Quoted in the *Daily Telegraph*, 17 March 2009.

141 For the full flavour, visit https://www.youtube.com/watch?v=uSFkujgsTmc.

142 Chris Masters, *Jonestown*, p. 285.

143 Wallace, whom I know and admire, went on to a still more illustrious career. As a detective superintendent, she is head of the crack New South Wales Police Gang Squad, in command of 120 officers.

144 *Sydney Morning Herald*, 20 May 2000.

145 Chris Masters, *Jonestown*, p. 384.

146 Ibid., pp. 385–6.

147 Quoted by David Marr, 'Review of *Jonestown*', *The Monthly*, December 2006 – January 2007.

148 Chris Masters, *Jonestown*, p. 419.

149 *Sydney Morning Herald*, 10 March 2013.

150 Ibid., 31 January 2014.

151 John Laws, *Lawsie*, New Holland, Sydney, 2017, p. 239.

152 *Age*, 11 September 2003.

153 Ibid., 20 March 2003.

154 *Guardian* (London), 17 February 2003.

155 *Sydney Morning Herald*, 18 March 2003.

156 Quoted in 'Little America: How John Howard has changed Australia' by Robert Manne, *The Monthly*, March 2006.

157 Ibid.

158 Ibid.

159 Quoted in *Fairfax: The Rise and Fall* by Colleen Ryan, Miegunyah Press, Melbourne, 2013, p. 153.

160 *Sydney Morning Herald*, 24 September 2014.

161 *Age*, 10 March 2002.

162 *Sydney Morning Herald*, 13 July 2007; *Crikey*, 25 July 2007.

163 *Daily Telegraph*, 17 July 2007.

164 *Sydney Morning Herald*, 26 June 2007.

165 *Daily Telegraph*, 6 December 2007.

166 Scott's death sentence was later commuted to life imprisonment.

167 Now extensively revised and reissued as *Before Jutland*, Naval Institute Press, Annapolis, Maryland, 2015.

168 *Media Watch*, ABC TV, 5 October 2009.

169 *Guardian* (London), 4 August 2014.

170 Report of the United Nations Office of the High Commissioner for Human Rights, 23 June 2015.

171 Quoted in the *Times of Israel*, 20 July 2014.

172 Hagganah is an early Jewish/Israeli paramilitary force; Begin was prime minister of Israel from 1977 to 1983.

173 John Lyons, *Balcony Over Jerusalem*, HarperCollins, Sydney, 2017, p. 260.

174 Ibid., p. 288.

175 *Australian Jewish News*, 12 October 2017.

176 Eatock v Bolt [2011] FCA 1103, (2011) 197 FCR 261, Federal Court (Australia).

177 Phillip, letter to Lord Sydney, April 1788.

Acknowledgements

THE HARD PART ABOUT writing this book was trying to recall stuff. I have never kept a diary nor compiled any sort of scrapbook, and I have only rarely bothered to retain copies of the stories, scripts and columns I have churned out over the decades. Often I found that times and dates, names and places, were lost in the mists behind me. I could not have got this memoir together without the generous help of family, friends and former colleagues, who went to a lot of trouble to prod my memory and steer me in the right direction.

My first thanks are to Fr Tony Caruana of my father's Roman Catholic order, the Missionaries of the Sacred Heart in Sydney. I had no idea what reception I would get when I rang one morning a few years ago to see what might be in their files. If anything. Perhaps there would be an impenetrable wall of secrecy, I thought nervously, an abrupt dismissal. It turned out to be the exact opposite. Tony gladly plunged into the archives, unearthed Jim Carlton's file, and had its contents scanned and emailed to me at warp speed that very afternoon. Later he searched for photographs, too. I found this kindness immensely moving and I am very grateful for his generosity.

Peter Carlton, my brother, was the keeper of the family archive, such as it was. Our mother left crumbling boxes of old photo albums, newspaper clippings and assorted bits and pieces such as my first-ever press card, but none of it in any sort of order. These Peter was probably glad to get rid of. But the priceless thing he held was Enid's own typed memoir of her courtship and marriage, not to be opened until after her death. Peter was her keeper in her dying years in Brisbane. This book would have been much diminished without him. Big thanks to Little Brother.

Family members were invaluable, of course. Tony Carlton, a distant cousin, was a mine of information on early family history. My first wife, Kerri Carlton, kindly helped with our twenty-five years together. We remain friends to this day and our adult children, Alexandra and James, chipped in for me as well. With some trepidation, it's fair to say, but I have tried not to embarrass them too much.

My old friend and classmate at Barker College, Christopher Rigney, read the chapters on our school days and recalled a lot I had forgotten. Others who helped are listed here in alphabetical order, and I thank them all: Ken Begg, Tim Bowden, Matt Brown, Fr Ed Campion, Bob Carr, John Conde, Charlie Cox, Bryan Davies, Janne Dennehy, Hidayat and Lilli Djajamihardja, Tim Ferguson, Peter FitzSimons, Christine Gallagher, Johnny Gibbs, Jerry Hayes, David Hill, Caroline Jones, Daniel Joyce, John Laws, Stuart Littlemore, Angus Llewellyn, Mark Llewellyn, Chris Lowrie, Penny Luck, Peter Luck, David Lyle, John Lyons, Tom Malone, Peter Manning, Chris Masters, Frank McGovern, Peter Meakin, Judge John O'Meally, Bill Peach, David Salter, John Stanley, Gerald Stone, Max Suich, Detective Superintendent Deborah Wallace, and Brendan Ward.

Hundreds of people sustained me through my media career, and my private life. There is no room to mention them all here, but they know who they are and many do appear in the book itself. My thanks to them, too.

On Air was not my idea. I had never planned to write a memoir. Honestly, it never occurred to me that anyone might want to read one. But Nikki Christer, the group publishing director at Penguin Random House, gently pushed and cajoled until I promised to sit down at a keyboard again. Her co-conspirator Alison Urquhart was equally insistent and encouraging. They are the publishers every author hopes for but rarely gets. Penguin Random House took on my three books of naval history and now this, an association I cherish. *On Air* is very much the better for the work of Julian Welch, who did the first edit with great skill and infinite attention to detail. The delightful and meticulous Catherine Hill, who had worked on the naval books, again gave this one the final polish, saving me from myself more times than I can count. Any remaining flaws and errors are my own. Photographs have come from here, there and everywhere and, despite some digging, it has not always been possible to discover who holds copyright. I am happy to hear from any copyright owners and to recognise them in subsequent editions.

My final and deepest thanks go to my wife, Morag Ramsay, a better journalist than ever I was, and a wellspring of advice. She and our son, Lachlan, endured my long absences behind a closed study door without complaint. Their love and grace inspired me through the good bits, and sustained me through the bad. And still does.

Index

Index

Index

Index